Lecture Notes in Business Information Processing 537

LNBIP reports state-of-the-art results in areas related to business information systems and industrial application software development – timely, at a high level, and in both printed and electronic form.

The type of material published includes

- Proceedings (published in time for the respective event)
- Postproceedings (consisting of thoroughly revised and/or extended final papers)
- Other edited monographs (such as, for example, project reports or invited volumes)
- Tutorials (coherently integrated collections of lectures given at advanced courses, seminars, schools, etc.)
- Award-winning or exceptional theses

LNBIP is abstracted/indexed in DBLP, EI and Scopus. LNBIP volumes are also submitted for the inclusion in ISI Proceedings.

Monika Kaczmarek-Heß · Kristina Rosenthal ·
Marek Suchánek · Miguel Mira Da Silva ·
Henderik A. Proper · Marianne Schnellmann
Editors

Enterprise Design, Operations, and Computing

EDOC 2024 Workshops

iRESEARCH, MIDas4CS, Doctoral Consortium,
Joint CBI–EDOC Forum and Other Joint CBI-EDOC Events
Vienna, Austria, September 10–13, 2024
Revised Selected Papers

Editors
Monika Kaczmarek-Heß
University of Duisburg-Essen
Essen, Germany

Kristina Rosenthal
Niederrhein University of Applied Sciences
Mönchengladbach, Germany

Marek Suchánek
Czech Technical University in Prague
Prague, Czech Republic

Miguel Mira Da Silva
Universidade de Lisboa
Lisbon, Portugal

Henderik A. Proper
TU Wien
Vienna, Austria

Marianne Schnellmann
TU Wien
Vienna, Austria

ISSN 1865-1348 ISSN 1865-1356 (electronic)
Lecture Notes in Business Information Processing
ISBN 978-3-031-79058-4 ISBN 978-3-031-79059-1 (eBook)
https://doi.org/10.1007/978-3-031-79059-1

This Springer imprint is published by the registered company Springer Nature Switzerland AG
The registered company address is: Gewerbestrasse 11, 6330 Cham, Switzerland

Preface

EDOC 2024 marks the 28th edition of the International Conference on Enterprise Design, Operations, and Computing, continuing its tradition as a prominent forum for researchers and practitioners in the field of Enterprise Computing. This year's conference took place from September 10–13, 2024, in the beautiful city of Vienna, Austria.

A significant highlight of EDOC 2024 was its co-location with the IEEE Conference on Business Informatics (CBI), bringing together two leading conferences in a shared program (which our local colleagues at the TU Wien branded as "BI Week 2024"). This collaboration enabled extensive interaction between the two communities, fostering enriched scientific discussions and a deeper understanding of the evolving landscape of enterprise systems and business informatics. The joint program featured shared keynotes, technical sessions, and social events, providing participants with a unique opportunity to engage with cross-disciplinary insights in an intellectually stimulating environment. In addition to the main tracks of both CBI and EDOC 2024, the joint conference offered a joint forum, a case and reports track, a tools and demos track, journal-first presentations, two tutorials, two mini-Dagstuhl seminars, two workshops, as well as a doctoral consortium.

These proceedings cover contributions from the joint forum, the case and reports track, the tools and demos track, the journal-first presentation, the tutorials, the mini-Dagstuhl seminar on the *foundations of conceptual modelling*, the iRESEARCH and MIDas4CS workshops, as well as the doctoral consortium.

We would like to extend our deepest gratitude to the organizing committees of both EDOC and CBI for their tireless efforts in ensuring the success of this joint event. A special thanks goes to the local organizing team at TU Wien, whose dedication made the smooth execution of the conference and the warm atmosphere possible. We are also grateful to our sponsor, the Mayor of Vienna, for their generous support, which contributed significantly to the success of the event.

Finally, our heartfelt thanks go out to the authors, reviewers, and participants. Your invaluable contributions and engagement made EDOC 2024 a memorable and impactful event. We look forward to the ongoing discussions, collaborations, and innovations that will arise from this year's conference.

October 2024

Monika Kaczmarek-Heß
Kristina Rosenthal
Marek Suchánek
Miguel Mira Da Silva
Henderik A. Proper
Marianne Schnellmann

Organization

General Chairs

Henderik A. Proper	TU Wien, Austria
Miguel Mira da Silva	University of Lisbon, Portugal

Program Committee Chairs

José Borbinha	INESC-ID, IST, Universidade de Lisboa, Portugal
Tiago Prince Sales	University of Twente, The Netherlands

Forum Chairs

Alessandro Gianola	INESC-ID, IST, Universidade de Lisboa, Portugal
Georg Grossmann	University of South Australia, Australia

Workshop Chairs

Monika Kaczmarek-Heß	University of Duisberg-Essen, Germany
Kristina Rosenthal	Niederrhein Univ. of Applied Sciences, Germany
Marek Suchánek	Czech Technical Univ. in Prague, Czech Republic

Tools and Demos Track Chairs

Luiz Olavo Bonino	University of Twente, The Netherlands
Mark Mulder	TEEC2, The Netherlands

Industry and Case Reports Chairs

Pascal Ravesteijn	HU Univ. of Applied Sciences, The Netherlands
Jürgen Jung	Frankfurt University of Applied Sciences, Germany
Andreas Pirkner	Erste Asset Management, Austria

Journal-First Chairs

Asif Gill	UT Sydney, Australia
Sérgio Guerreiro	INESC-ID, IST, Universidade de Lisboa, Portugal

Doctoral Consortium Chairs

Oscar Pastor	Universitat Politècnica de València, Spain
Jolita Ralyté	University of Geneva, Switzerland

Proceedings Chair

Marianne Schnellmann	TU Wien, Austria

EasyChair Meta-Chair

Birgit Hofreiter	TU Wien, Austria

Tutorial Chairs

Dominik Bork	TU Wien, Austria
Simon Hacks	Stockholm University, Sweden

Website, Publicity, and Social Media Chairs

Aleksandar Gavric	TU Wien, Austria
Fabrizio Fornari	Università di Camerino, Italy
Ítalo Oliveira	University of Twente, The Netherlands

Local Organization Chairs

Angela Edlinger	TU Wien, Austria
Monika Malinova Mandelburger	TU Wien, Austria

Steering Committee

Alan Wee-Chung Liew	Griffith University, Australia
Colin Atkinson	University of Mannheim, Germany
Dimka Karastoyanova	University of Groningen, The Netherlands
Georg Grossmann	University of South Australia, Australia
Giancarlo Guizzardi	University of Twente, The Netherlands
Henderik A. Proper	TU Wien, Austria
João Paulo A. Almeida	Federal University of Espírito Santo, Brazil
Marten van Sinderen	University of Twente, The Netherlands
Remco Dijkman	Eindhoven University of Technology, The Netherlands
Selmin Nurcan (Chair)	Paris 1 Panthéon-Sorbonne University, France
Sylvain Hallé	Université du Québec à Chicoutimi, Canada
Zoran Milosevic	Deontik, Australia

Report from the CBI/EDOC Forum Track Chairs

Alessandro Gianola and Georg Grossmann

The BI Week 2024 at Vienna featured for the first time a combined Forum track for both the CBI 2024 and the EDOC 2024 conferences. The CBI/EDOC Forum track was an interactive platform within the CBI/EDOC conferences for presenting and discussing new ideas, novel research reports, and artefacts/tools on the full range of models, methodologies, and engineering technologies employed in Business Informatics and Enterprise Computing. The Forum had the main goal to encourage potential participants to present emerging topics and contentious viewpoints while showcasing innovative systems, tools, and applications, encompassing new and promising research findings, inventive applications, experience reports, as well as proposals for ongoing research in its initial phases. The Forum took place on September 10–12, 2024 at Vienna, Austria, co-located with the BI Week 2024.

The Forum enabled presenters and participants to engage in interaction, discussion, and sharing of ideas. Two types of submissions were considered in the Forum track:

Forum papers that present novel and innovative research in business informatics and enterprise computing that is not necessarily mature or fully evaluated but comprises interesting early results or carries promise for high future impact, possibly presenting novel applications in industrial contexts, or new and innovative research endeavors that are still at an exploratory stage;
Vision papers that have a particular focus on the future of business informatics and enterprise computing or anticipate new challenges and opportunities, possibly describing novel projects that are in an early stage but hold out the strong promise of eventual high impact.

The Forum received 7 submissions from 7 different countries (all in the 'Forum papers' format), covering topics such as security, AI applications, Process Mining, and BPM. Additionally, 9 submissions were invited from the EDOC main research track. These invited papers had already undergone the EDOC single-blind peer review process and were further checked by the PC co-chairs and Forum co-chairs. The topics of these papers ranged from Process Mining and Monitoring to Enterprise, IT and Software Architectures. Each paper of the remaining submissions was carefully reviewed by two PC members from the EDOC main research track. Papers with the highest consensus on novelty and rigor were accepted for presentation at the Forum. Out of the 7 regular submissions, 4 papers were accepted (57% acceptance rate). In total, 13 papers were accepted for the CBI/EDOC 2024 Forum.

We would like to express our gratitude to everyone who contributed to the success of the CBI/EDOC 2024 Forum: the authors, the PC members and Program Co-Chairs of the main conferences, the proceedings chair, and the General Chairs for their invaluable support in coordinating the Forum organization.

October 2024

Report from the Case and Reports Track Chairs

Pascal Ravesteijn, Jürgen Jung, and Andreas Pirkner

The CBI and EDOC research domains take their inspiration from needs and opportunities in practice. It is thus important for the CBI and EDOC conferences to provide a channel to report on interesting cases from practice, even when they are not case studies in the formal sense. Therefore, practitioners and researchers in applied sciences were invited to submit case reports on the CBI and EDOC topics of interest. In order to not focus on results, the structure of those reports was expected to follow the STARRE structure:

1. *Situation*: Motivating the context, risks, opportunities, relevant stakeholders and the reason for initiating the case
2. *Task*: Describing objectives, requirements and restrictions
3. *Approach*: Discussing the method and philosophy that were applied as well as design alternatives
4. *Result*: Presenting and evaluating the outcome of the case
5. *Reflection*: Discussing challenges and limitations together with potential solutions
6. *Evidence* Providing transparency on how results were achieved

Two submissions covering current technological topics were chosen for publication in the proceedings at hand: In *Enhancing Observability: Real-Time Application Health Checks* a hands-on solution to cumbersome log management and application health monitoring practices was outlined reporting on a solution leveraging machine learning capabilities and dynamic visualization tools. The paper titled *Scaling AI adoption in finance: modelling framework and implementation study* was rolled over from the EDOC main track as it has a rather practitioner-oriented focus on the Australian finance industry. The authors experimented with various AI-related technologies and agent-oriented solutions and presented their findings on how multi-agent AI technologies could offer more value for complex business problems like retirement planning.

The cases were presented within two time slots of the BI Week 2024 in Vienna on Tuesday, September 10, 2024. Both sessions had ample time for presentation and discussion (45 mins) as well as networking among the many participants from both academia and practice, confirming the desire for a more regular exchange between teaching and application.

October 2024

Report from the Tools and Demos Track Chairs

Luiz Olavo Bonino and Mark Mulder

The combined CBI and EDOC conference was the second large event organized in Vienna, after PoEM 2023. Both the combined CBI and EDOC conference in 2024 and PoEM 2023 featured a Tools and Demos track.

This year's Tools and Demos track welcomed two industrial participants and three from the scientific community. The level of interest during the sessions was strong, once again suggesting that a similar forum would be well received at future conferences. While the industry participants primarily focused on showcasing how their tools could enhance research, the scientific contributions highlighted advancements in research and the development of specialized tools to support these efforts. Through these sessions, we aimed to foster closer collaboration between science and industry, enabling industry to commercially leverage research outcomes while providing scientists with more effective tools to advance their work.

October 2024

Report from the Journal-First Track Chairs

Asif Gill and Sérgio Guerreiro

This co-location of the CBI and EDOC conferences, as a pilot project, also featured a combined program of journal-first paper presentations.

Journal papers provide academically rigorous and well-developed work, which is usually published in both online and printed formats. While, as such, the work is already accessible to readers, there is little opportunity for readers to discuss the published work and ask follow-up questions to the original authors of the journal article. Thus, in CBI-EDOC, we introduced the Journal-First presentation format with the purpose of bringing mature work to the community for a more *open debate* in order to broaden the discussion beyond experimental-based approaches and encourage other researchers/practitioners to enhance the maturity of their own work. This will also lead to future collaboration with the published authors where research interests are closely aligned. Overall, it contributes to independent and intelligent community dialogue over published work.

This year's "pilot" attracted one submission, allowing us to kick-off this important stream of *open debate* submissions. This pertains to the paper:

Jan A. H. Schoonderbeek and Henderik A. Proper. Toward an ontology for EA modeling and EA model quality. *Software and Systems Modeling*, 23(3):535–558, February 2024. ISSN: 1619-1374 https://doi.org/10.1007/s10270-023-01146-w

In the next years, the ambition is to strengthen the *open debate* aspect of the journal-first submission channel even further.

October 2024

Report from the Tutorials Chairs

Simon Hacks and Dominik Bork

This year's EDOC and CBI shared sessions for tutorials. The tutorials provided foundational knowledge and practical insights into emerging and significant areas of business informatics. The sessions were designed to engage a diverse audience, offering theoretical overviews and hands-on applications. These tutorials bridged the latest research developments and real-world applications, encouraging participants to explore new methodologies and technologies essential to their fields. By combining expertled presentations with interactive discussions, attendees were equipped with actionable knowledge that can be directly applied to their research or professional work.

The first tutorial, titled **FAIR Data Train: A Distributed Data and Services Platform**, focused on the principles of FAIR (Findable, Accessible, Interoperable, and Reusable) data practices in distributed environments. Let by *Luiz Olavo Bonino*, the tutorial introduced the FAIR Data Train, a platform designed to promote data integration and collaboration across various systems and organizations. Participants gained insight into the architecture and functionality of this platform, learned strategies for its implementation, and explored real-world case studies demonstrating its capacity to advance FAIR data practices. This tutorial addressed key challenges in data management, particularly for researchers and practitioners interested in fostering interoperable and reusable data frameworks.

The second tutorial, **Digital Business Ecosystems**, presented by *Jaap Gordijn* and *Roel Wieringa*, explored the concept of digital ecosystems and their role in business innovation. It provided a deep dive into business model design for ecosystems, outlining how companies can create and test value propositions and design value networks. The tutorial highlighted the importance of developing viable business models for digital ecosystems, using examples such as online marketplaces and smart networks. Through exercises and discussions, participants learned how to align business models with enterprise architecture and understood the dynamics of value creation and sustainability within digital ecosystems.

October 2024

Report from the Doctoral Consortium Chairs

Oscar Pastor and Jolita Ralyté

This year marked an important milestone in the sense of the co-location between the CBI and EDOC conferences.

It is a common practice at EDOC conferences to host a Doctoral Consortium aiming to offer a supportive learning opportunity for doctoral students in the early stages of their research to present and discuss their work in progress and to receive feedback and guidance from senior researchers and the audience. We also knew that CBI was aiming to develop such a tradition. Given the firm intention of both CBI and EDOC to co-locate, we expected the Doctoral Consortium to evolve into a joint highlight.

The role of the Doctoral Consortium is to offer opportunities to establish a social network with peers in the field at the EDOC (and CBI) conference, as well as to engage with industry participants.

Since this year, the two conferences were brought together into a single event, called Business Informatics Week 2024, it is only natural that the Doctoral Consortium was also organized as a joint event.

Doctoral students who were midterm in their research activities were invited to submit a paper presenting their work and participate in the dedicated sessions. The topics eligible for Doctoral Consortium submissions were the same as those of the CBI 2024 and EDOC 2024 conferences.

Despite several attempts to attract submissions, we received only one paper. The paper was peer-reviewed by three mentors of the Doctoral Consortium and was unanimously accepted for presentation at the conference and inclusion in the proceedings. We thank the mentors for their efforts in reviewing the paper and providing constructive feedback. We would also like to thank the author for sharing his work with the community. We hope he enjoyed his participation in the conference.

October 2024

Report from the Workshops Chairs

Monika Kaczmarek-Hess, Kristina Rosenthal, and Marek Suchánek

These proceedings include the papers from the workshops at BI Week 2024 in Vienna. The BI Week 2024 connected the CBI and EDOC conferences in a unique setup to bring the two communities together to exchange ideas, identify synergies, build new collaborations, and further promote research in the field of business informatics. In addition to the main scientific program of the co-located conferences, workshops are an essential part of both conferences as they offer the opportunity for in-depth discussions on topics from research and practice.

Workshops

All workshop proposals were reviewed by the Workshops chairs, considering their relevance to BI Week 2024 and their potential to attract an audience. The following two workshops were held at BI Week 2024:

- **Second Workshop on the Modelling and Implementation of Digital Twins for Complex Systems (MIDas4CS 2024).** The concept of Digital Twin is becoming increasingly popular since it was introduced in the scope of Smart Industry (Industry 4.0). A Digital Twin (DT) is a digital representation of a physical twin that is a real-world entity, system, or event. Nowadays, Digital Twins are not limited to industrial applications, but are spreading to other areas as well, such as, for example, in the healthcare domain, in personalized medicine and clinical trials for drug development. This workshop aimed at getting a better understanding of the techniques that can be used to model and implement Digital Twins and their applications in different domains.
- **Second Workshop on Empirical Methodologies for Research in Enterprise Architecture and Service-Oriented Computing (iRESEARCH 2024).** The purpose of this workshop was to initiate a conversation on shaping the cross-fertilization of the disciplines of Enterprise Architecture (EA) and Service-Oriented Computing (SOC) and Empirical Research Methodologies (ERM). The workshop was intended to open up an interdisciplinary debate on the steadily moving frontiers in empirical methodologies in support of EA and SOC research projects, and to expand the network of researchers designing and conducting empirical studies in EA and in the sub-fields of SOC, which in turn will lead to cross-fertilization between these two fields and ERM.

Acknowledgements and Thanks

We would like to thank the workshop organizers for their workshop proposals, adherence to deadlines and their enthusiasm for the workshops as an integral part of BI Week 2024:

- Maya Daneva and Faiza Allah Bukhsh for organizing the workshop on Empirical Methodologies for Research in Enterprise Architecture and Service-oriented Computing (iRESEARCH 2024)
- Pedro Valderas, Fabrizio Fornari, Luís Ferreira Pires, Marten van Sinderen, and João Moreira for organizing the workshop on the Modelling and Implementation of Digital Twins for Complex Systems (MIDas4CS 2024)

In addition, we are grateful to the reviewers for ensuring the quality of the research presented and discussed in the workshops. We further thank all authors of workshop papers for submitting and presenting their research.

Furthermore, our thank goes to the Organizing Committees of CBI & EDOC 2024 for hosting the workshops and for their continuous support.

October 2024

Contents

Joint CBI–EDOC Forum

iRESEARCH – 2nd International Workshop on Empirical Methodologies for Research in Enterprise Architecture and Service-oriented Computing

MIDas4CS – 2nd Workshop on the Modelling and Implementation of Digital Twins for Complex Systems

Joint CBI–EDOC Forum

Enhancing Business Process Models with Ethical Considerations

Beatrice Amico(✉), Carlo Combi, Anna Dalla Vecchia, Sara Migliorini, Barbara Oliboni, and Elisa Quintarelli

Department of Computer Science, University of Verona, Strada Le Grazie, 15, 37035 Verona, Italy
{beatrice.amico,carlo.combi,anna.dallavecchia,sara.migliorini, barbara.oliboni,elisa.quintarelli}@univr.it

Abstract. Fairness has recently emerged as a challenging topic in many areas of computer science, as it is related to algorithms supporting decision-making, experimental research, and information access and processing. As (decision-intensive) business processes are inherently using information to reach their goals, their fairness possibly depends on the kind of information they are allowed to access. In this paper, we deal with this aspect and propose some criteria to consider when conceptually specifying business activities and their related information seamlessly through a recently proposed approach based on the concept of Activity View. More specifically, we distinguish equality and equity as two aspects of fairness and discuss how to enforce them in business process design. Their expression according to the specification of Activity Views is formally proposed and discussed in the paper.

1 Introduction

Ethics in data management has become a challenging topic in recent years [17] since it is essential to ensure the responsible treatment of information. Fairness is becoming of interest in many different computer science research areas: for example, fairness is required (i) when we design decision-support systems, where algorithms have to be fair in their design, (ii) when we perform experimental research, as the derived results have to be explicitly related to some possible bias that could limit their generality, (iii) when data access authorizations have to be granted for a decision-making task, and (iv) when user assignments have to be managed in process-oriented systems where some intertwined activities may create conflicts of interest [2,8,9,15,17].

In this paper, we will focus on the last two aspects of fairness, which are related to the context of process-aware information systems (PAISs). Indeed, information management is required, directly or indirectly, by all organizational activities. PAISs explicitly deal with business processes that use, produce, and manipulate organizational data stored in databases. Business processes, often represented through BPMN (Business Process Model and Notation) [13], and data are intertwined [16], and each of them plays a crucial role in PAISs.

M. Kaczmarek-Heß et al. (Eds.): EDOC 2024 Workshops, LNBIP 537, pp. 3–17, 2025.
https://doi.org/10.1007/978-3-031-79059-1_1

Integrating ethical considerations in business processes is, thus, important to promote trust, fairness, satisfaction, and sustainability and thus to realize the organization's long-term success thanks to a positive reputation. More specifically, in this paper, we will consider the fairness-related concepts of *equality* and *equity* in performing both single tasks and complete (data-intensive) business processes. To this end, a suitable existing methodology proposed in [4,5] will be considered, as it allows the design of BPMN models, together with access to data, in the context of PAISs.

This paper highlights the importance of integrating fairness in PAISs where data-intensive business process models must be suitably designed, considering fairness criteria instead of revealing unfair policies with successive data analysis. The main original contributions of the paper can be summarized as follows.

- We extend a recent formal model for the conceptual design of data-intensive business processes [5] to integrate fairness requirements in process modeling.
- We deal with different aspects of fairness by highlighting its connection to both the considered activity and the data required for the activity. To the best of our knowledge, such an aspect has not been considered in other research contributions.
- We introduce fairness, particularly equity and equality aspects, both for specific activities and for an overall execution path, where fairness may depend on many different intertwined activities.

The structure of the paper is as follows. Section 2 discusses some related research directions. Section 3 provides a motivating example taken from the university domain and discusses some fairness requirements. Section 4 contains the proposal of a new formal model, where activity views are extended to represent different kinds of fairness requirements. In Sect. 5, we discuss how to evaluate some fairness properties of data-intensive business processes, while in Sect. 6, we sketch some concluding remarks.

2 Related Work

This section investigates how fairness has been applied in the literature in different fields, capturing some of the issues and solutions addressed. Although the debate on ethical topics has received growing attention in recent years, especially with the widespread use of machine learning and artificial intelligence techniques in everyday life, there is still a lack of consensus on ethical guidelines [17]. However, a widely accepted factor is that ethical rules depend on the specific circumstances in which they are applied, highlighting their context-sensitive nature.

Regarding the state of the art on ethical issues related to machine learning (ML), in [2], the authors outline different approaches proposed in the literature to enhance fairness in ML, highlighting existing methodologies to avoid possible ethical biases and inequities. They conclude by presenting five dilemmas for future research. It confirms that, although the problem has been explored for years, it is not easy to delineate in a uniform way the concept of fairness [7,12]. The authors in [9] examine the definition of fairness as the absence of discrimination for individuals with the same "merit" and fairness in algorithms as the absence of discrimination. However, they point out three weaknesses of this definition: disparities justified by "merit", the limitation to the algorithm, and the ignoring of the disparities within groups. Furthermore, in [11], the authors survey the presence of bias in various real-world applications and define a taxonomy for the definition of fairness in artificial intelligence (AI) systems. Specifically, they identify two primary sources of unfairness in ML outcomes (i.e., data and algorithms). In [6], the authors discuss how data bias should be managed. From their point of view, it is not always necessary to completely remove the bias. Otherwise, this process may lead to other types of bias. A possible solution could be to provide the users with a tool that allows them to adjust existing biases, enabling them to leverage the benefits of fairness for certain tasks. According to the emerging evidence that ML algorithms can make discriminatory decisions, researchers have been investigating computational techniques that make ML algorithms unbiased and non-discriminatory. Fairness focusing on distributive justice has been a central research topic in computer theory, artificial intelligence, and machine learning. As already highlighted in [6], the authors in [10] propose a procedural justice framework for algorithmic decision-making, which explains algorithmic assumptions and properties displaying inputs and outcomes, allowing interactively adjusting the outcome.

An additional interesting facet of the fairness concept is its relationship with transparency/explanation in AI-assisted decision-making, an issue that numerous studies have emphasized. AI-assisted decision-making that affects individuals brings up essential issues related to transparency and fairness in AI. In [1], the authors extensively analyze this relationship, observing that, according to their experiments, AI explanations increased user trust in AI-informed decision-making, and different explanation types did not show differences in affecting user trust. Furthermore, they explain that AI explanations increased users' perceptions of fairness. Another aspect related to fairness present in literature is the fairness in ranking. In the past few years, research communities have worked a lot on incorporating fairness requirements into algorithmic rankers. They focused on data management, algorithms, information retrieval, and recommender systems. In [18,19], the authors extensively overview the state-of-the-art literature on fair ranking in score-based and supervised learning-based ranking domains. They present a selection of approaches that were developed in several fields.

To the best of our knowledge, the concept of fairness has not been completely investigated in the context of business processes. An initial example of how the concept of fairness can be integrated into the Business Process Modeling Notation (BPMN) [13] is presented in [15]. The authors propose a BPMN-based framework that takes into account different aspects: (i) the design of business processes considering security, data-minimization and fairness requirements; (ii) the encoding of such requirements as reusable, domain-specific pattern; (iii) the checking of alignment between the encoded requirements and annotated

BPMN models based on these patterns; (iv) the detection of conflicts between the specified requirements in the BPMN models based on a catalog of domain-independent anti-patterns. They specify the security requirements, data minimization, and fairness in BPMN models, using existing security annotations from the *SecBPMN2* modeling language and introducing new data minimization and fairness annotations. This extension facilitates the alignment checking of security, data minimization, and fairness requirements with their specifications in BPMN models. The process is automated by extending a graphical query language, *SecBPMN2-Q*, formulating the requirements as reusable procedural patterns that can be matched to BPMN models. Additionally, considering different pairs of requirements in BPMN models, they propose an automated conflict detection technique that uses encoded knowledge about conflicts and potential conflicts between the requirements. They do not explicitly consider the relationship between the activities and the accessed data, and for this reason, in this paper, we try to overcome this limitation.

3 Running Example

This section proposes a running example related to the university domain. In particular, we consider activities associated with managing various student career cases, such as student enrollments, exams, graduation exams, and scholarships. Figure 1 shows a simplified process model related to the considered scenario and represented by using the Business Process Model and Notation (BPMN) [13]. We will give a formal definition of Process Model in Definition 1 of Sect. 4.

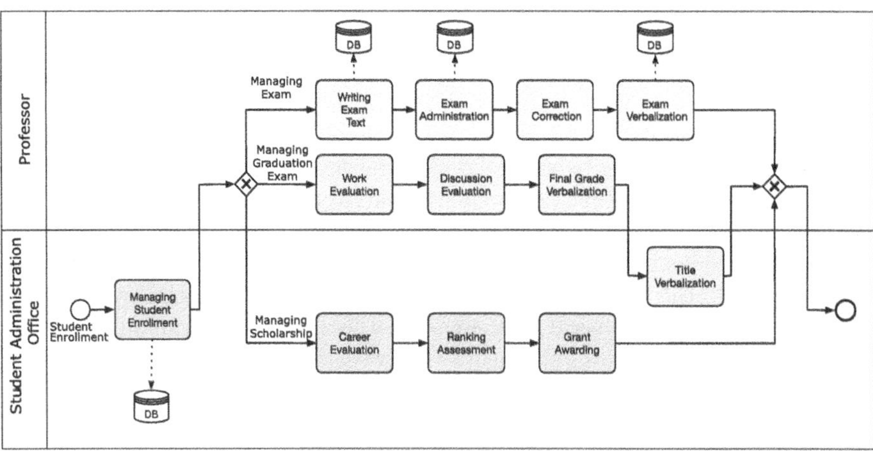

Fig. 1. A simplified business process model representing some activities associated with the management of students' careers. (Color figure online)

In BPMN, a process is defined as a sequence of *activities* and *events*, connected by *sequence flows*, defining their execution order. *Gateways* allow to split the sequence flow into multiple paths and merge them, thus realizing routing. These BPMN elements can be briefly described as follows.

- **Activities** identify work performed within the process. Activities can be either *tasks* (atomic units of work) or *subprocesses* (compound activities). Graphically, tasks are depicted as rectangles with rounded corners and labels specifying their names. An example of *task* in Fig. 1 is "Managing Student Enrollment".
- **Events** represent instantaneous facts that impact the sequencing or timing of process activities. They are depicted as circles, which may contain a marker to diversify the kind of event trigger. *Events* can be *start events*, *intermediate events*, and *end events*. In Fig. 1, the process starts with the "Student Enrollment" *start event* and finishes with an *end event*.
- **Gateways** allow controlling the divergence and convergence of the sequence flow according to data-driven conditions or event occurrence. Graphically, they are represented as diamonds with an internal marker that differentiates their routing behavior. In Fig. 1, the × split gateway represents a data-driven exclusive gateway, i.e., the point in the process where a condition must be evaluated to choose one path out of more. In this example, each path is related to managing a different aspect, such as "Managing Exam", "Managing Graduation Exam", and "Managing Scholarship".

BPMN also provides elements for representing data and participants involved in the process.

- **Data Stores** are visualized as a database symbol and represent data accessed by activities. Some process activities in Fig. 1 are related to a database named "DB" for representing the operations performed on the database.
- **Pools and Lanes** allow the representation of resources (people/roles) involved in the process. The process participants in Fig. 1 are represented through the two lanes "Professor" and "Student Administration Office".

The process in Fig. 1 starts when the student applies for enrollment. The first activity, "Managing Student Enrollment," is carried out by the Student Administration Office and requires access to the "DB" database to insert student information[1]. After the student enrollment, the process presents three exclusive paths, each dedicated to managing a different phase in the student's life cycle. For Managing Exam (yellow path), the professor performs the following activities: "Writing Exam Test", "Exam Administration", "Exam Correction", and "Exam Verbalization". When Writing an Exam Test, the professor needs to access the database to retrieve data about the number of students involved in the examination and the possible special needs of students with disability, if any. During the Exam Administration, the Professor accesses the database to have the list of students with special needs at her disposal, to properly identify the

[1] For sake of simplicity, in the following, we will focus only on the data accessed for the exam management – yellow path.

most suitable exam conditions and duration. Finally, the professor corrects the exam and records the results obtained in the database. Thus, the "Exam correction" activity does not require any access to the data store, while the "Exam Verbalization" activity is connected to the data store to represent the writing operations.

Among the different fairness-related issues, we focus on ensuring an ethical treatment of data accessed while performing activities. More precisely, we need to consider different aspects: (i) the portion of accessed data, (ii) the user who accesses data, and (iii) the ethical dimension to satisfy. Moreover, the ethical treatment of data inside a process model can be evaluated with respect to: a set of activities, such as those belonging to a given path (path evaluation), or all the activities belonging to the whole process (global evaluation). In our process model, for example, data accessed during the "Writing Exam Test" activity can differ according to the considered ethical dimension. When considering *equality*, the professor needs to know only the number of students involved in the examination, while when considering *equity*, the professor also needs to know the possible presence of students with disability, thus acquiring some sensitive information.

To describe in more detail the data accessed by each single activity, we can rely on a recent extension of the BPMN model called Activity View [4,5]. This formalism allows the connection of a conceptual representation of a process model to a portion of a database schema by detailing the operations performed by a process activity on the database. For this purpose, the following section introduces an extension of the Activity View model, which allows the definition of ethical properties in a process model.

4 BPMN and Fairness-Driven Activity View

Starting from the well-known concept of *Activity View* [3], this section formalizes the proposed extension for integrating fairness in process design.

4.1 Describing Process and Data by Means of Activity View

Business process activities need to access and manage data stored in databases. The connection between processes and data is usually handled at the implementation level and is often left implicit at the conceptual level. However, modeling processes and data at the conceptual level supports improving business process models and identifying requirements for data management [4]. For this reason, this paper assumes a formal definition of the process model, as shown below, which combines both control-flow and data-flow aspects and explicitly defines the relationship between the activities and the accessed data.

Definition 1 (Process Model). *A process model m is a tuple $m = \langle N, C, DN, F\rangle$ consisting of:*

- *A finite non-empty set of flow nodes N.*
  The set $N = Ac \cup G \cup E$ of flow nodes consists of the disjoint sets:
  - *Ac set of activities.*
  - *G set of gateways.*
    The set $G = G_s^x \cup G_m^x \cup G_s^a \cup G_m^a$ is partitioned according to the routing behaviour of its nodes into the disjoint sets G_s^x of xor split *nodes, G_m^x of* xor merge *nodes, G_s^a of* and split *nodes, and G_m^a of* and merge *nodes, respectively.*
  - *$E = \{s, e\}$ of start and end events.*
- *A finite non-empty set C of control flow edges.*
  The control flow $C \subseteq N \times N$ connects the elements of N. Given a flow node $n \in N$, $\bullet n \subseteq N$ ($n \bullet \subseteq N$) denotes the set of direct predecessor (successor) nodes of n.
- *A finite set DN of data nodes.*
  $DN = DO \cup DS$ is the set of data nodes, consisting of the disjoint sets DO of data objects, i.e., volatile pieces of information exchanged between activities, and DS of data stores, i.e., persistent data sources such as enterprise databases.
- *A finite set F of data associations.*
  $F \subseteq (DN \times Ac) \cup (Ac \times DN)$ is the data flow that connects data nodes with activities.

The remainder of this paper will concentrate on the subset of the data nodes represented by the data stores DS. In particular, we concentrate on a representation of DS by means of the relational model since it allows us to refer to a set of abstract common operations on data, like projections (π), selections (σ), and joins ($\bowtie$), and write in a compact way the views each activity has to access to.

Definition 2 (Database schema and instance). *A database schema $\mathcal{DS}$ is a set of relation schemata:*

$$\mathcal{DS} = \{R_i(X_i)\}_{i=1}^n = \{R_i(A_{1_i}, A_{2_i}, \ldots, A_{m_i})\}_{i=1}^n$$

where R_i is a relation name and $X_i = (A_{1_i}, A_{2_i}, \ldots, A_{m_i})$ is a list of attributes.

Given a relation schema $R_i(X_i)$, where $X_i = (A_{1_i}, A_{2_i}, \ldots, A_{m_i})$, a relation instance r_i is a set of m_i-tuples $r_i = \{t_1, \ldots, t_{k_i}\}$ each one defined on X. Similarly, the instance $\mathcal{DI}$ of $\mathcal{DS}$ is the set of instances r_i of the relation schemata belonging to $\mathcal{DS}$.

Given two database schemata $\mathcal{DS}_1$ and $\mathcal{DS}_2$, we need to define the concept of containment $\subseteq$ between them to identify the fact that a database schema (or portion of it) extends another one by revealing some additional information. Notice that this notion is particularly useful when database schemata are used to describe different portions of a relational database accessed by a process activity.

Definition 3 (Database schema containment). *Given two database schemata* $\mathcal{DS}_1 = \{R_i(X_i)\}_{i=1}^n$ *and* $\mathcal{DS}_2 = \{P_j(Y_j)\}_{j=1}^m$*, we say that* $\mathcal{DS}_1 \subseteq \mathcal{DS}_2$ *iff* $\forall i \in [1..n]\ \exists j \in [1..m]\ R_i(X_i) \subseteq P_j(Y_j)$*, where* $R_i(X_i) \subseteq P_j(Y_j)$ *means that* $R_i = P_j \wedge X_i \subseteq Y_j$*.*

From this definition, considering the schemata obtained as results of the following two relational algebra expressions, we say that

$$\{\pi_{\mathsf{CourseID,studentID}}(\mathsf{EXAM})\} \subseteq \{\pi_{\mathsf{CourseID,studentID,Date}}(\mathsf{EXAM})\}$$

since in the second schema the relation EXAM is present, with an additional attribute (Date). Another example of containment is

$$\{\pi_{\mathsf{CourseID,studentID,Date}}(\mathsf{EXAM})\} \subseteq$$
$$\{\pi_{\mathsf{CourseID,studentID,Date}}(\mathsf{EXAM}), \pi_{\mathsf{sID,requirement}}(\mathsf{SDISABILITY} \ltimes_{\mathsf{sID=studentID}} \mathsf{EXAM})\}$$

since the relation EXAM is present in both sets with the same schema, and the second set contains an additional relation with respect to the former.

Given the generic notion of the database schema and the containment relation defined on it, we can introduce the concept of *Activity View* [4], which provides a formal representation of the operations performed by a process on a database. In particular, an Activity View describes which database subsets (or portion of the schema) are accessed by a particular process activity and which data operations are performed on them.

Definition 4 (Activity View). *Let* $m = (N, C, DN, F)$ *be a process model and* $\mathcal{DS} = \{R_i(X_i)\}_{i=1}^n$ *a database schema with its instance* $\mathcal{DI}$*, representing a data store* $ds \in DS \subseteq DN$ *inside* m*. An* Activity View $av_{ac} = \{t_1, \ldots, t_m\}$ *of an activity* $ac \in Ac \subseteq N$*, such that* ac *is connected to a data store according to* F*, is a set*[2] *of tuples* $t_1, \ldots, t_m$*, where each tuple* t_k *denotes a particular data access operation performed by* ac *on data in the given database instance* $\mathcal{DI}$*. Formally, each tuple of the Activity View has the form*

$$t_i = \langle Q_i, AccessType_i, AccessTime_i \rangle$$

where:

- $Q_i = \{q_1, \ldots, q_j\} \subseteq \mathcal{DI}$ *is the set of relational algebra expressions specifying the data ac needs to access. In this paper, we will consider only projections and joins, as the main focus is on the attributes accessed by different activities.* $Att(Q_i)$ *is the overall set of attributes appearing in the relational algebra expressions of* Q_i*.*
- $AccessType_i \in \{\text{R, I, D, U}\}$ *defines the type of access to the related information.* R *denotes a* read *of elements of* $\mathcal{DI}$*, whereas* I*,* D*, and* U *denote an* insertion*, a* deletion*, and an* update *operation, respectively.*

[2] We represent data access operations as a set as the same activity can imply the execution of different queries in many possible orders.

- $AccessTime_i \in$ {start, during, end} *denotes when a data operation is performed w.r.t. the activity execution.*

This paper aims to elaborate more on the notion of Activity View to represent and identify different fairness requirements for managing data [8]. More specifically, we concentrate on two main principles "equality" and "equity".

4.2 Introducing Fairness Inside Activity View

The previous section introduces the concept of Activity View to describe how the activities inside a process model access data. In this section, we provide a step forward by discussing how two of the main fairness principles, equality and equity, can be incorporated into a process model for ethical data access and management.

Equality is defined in literature as "the state or quality of being equal". This means providing everyone with the same opportunities. For instance, when you assign offices to two new PhD students and equip them equally, you are practicing equality. However, this does not necessarily mean you are being fair, as this behaviour disregards their individual needs and differences. Consider if one of the students has a physical disability that prevents them from sitting at a desk all day. In this case, their office setup does not meet their specific needs. To this purpose, equity is more appropriate as fairness behaviour in this case.

Equity means "the quality of being fair or impartial". It involves recognizing that people face different circumstances and adjusting to ensure everyone has the same opportunities. Regarding the example above, the benefits of diversity in the workplace are numerous, making fairness and justice essential considerations from the early stages of process design.

As already observed in Sect. 3, equity implies that some sensitive data must be known to understand specific contexts and situations. To suitably deal with sensitive data, we introduce the concept of sensitivity-aware database schema.

Definition 5 (Sensitivity-aware database schema and instance). *A sensitivity-aware database schema $\mathcal{S}$ is a tuple $\langle \mathcal{DS}, \mathcal{SA} \rangle$, where:*

- *$\mathcal{DS}$ is a database schema defined as in Definition 2, namely, a set of relation schemes $\mathcal{DS} = \{R_i(X_i)\}_{i=1}^{n}$, where R_i is a relation name and $X_i = (A_{1_i}, A_{2_i}, \ldots, A_{m_i})$ is a list of attributes;*
- *$\mathcal{SA} \subseteq \bigcup_{i=1}^{n} X_i$ is the set of sensitive attributes inside the database schema.*

We say that a relation schema $R_j(X_j)$ is a sensitive relation schema if at least one attribute of its schema is sensitive, i.e. $X_j \cap \mathcal{SA} \neq \emptyset$.

A sensitive relation instance is an instance of a sensitive relation schema. Similarly, a sensitive database instance $\mathcal{DI}$ of a sensitivity-aware database schema $\mathcal{S}$ is the set of (possibly sensitive) instances r_i of some $R_i \in \mathcal{DS}$.

Table 1 reports a fragment of a relational database related to the university domain where (possibly) sensitive attributes are represented in boldface.

Table 1. A simple Relational Database schema for managing students' careers. Underlined and bold attributes represent primary keys and possibly sensitive information, respectively.

STUDENT(sID, **Surname**, **Name**, **DateOfBirth**, **Gender**, **Citizenship**, **Revenue**, **Working**, ...)
APPLICATION_CANDIDATE(sID, AnonymizedCV)
SDISABILITY(**sID**, **D_code**, **requirement**)
SJOB(**sID**, **type**, **full-time**, **timeslot**, ...)
PROFESSOR(pID, **Surname**, **Name**, **Dateofbirth**, **Gender**, **Citizenship**, **Role**, Sector, ...)
PDISABILITY(**pID**, **D_code**, **requirement**)
HEALTHRECORD(**pID**, **I_code**, **requirement**)
EXAM(CourseID, studentID, Date, Time, Room)
COURSE(CourseID, AYear, pID)
EXAMRECORD(StudID, CourseID, Date, Mark)
CAREERRECORD(StudID, **Avgmark**, **Internship**, ...)
GRADUATION(StudID, **Careermark**, ThesisMark, FinalMark)
...

A process model can realize fairness in different ways. For the purpose of this paper, we concentrate on the fact that each activity can access all and only the information needed to achieve one of the main principles introduced above.

Definition 6 (Fairness-driven Activity View). *Let $m = (N, C, DN, F)$ be a process model and a sensitivity-aware database schema $\mathcal{S} = \langle \mathcal{DS}, \mathcal{SA} \rangle$ with its sensitive instance $\mathcal{DI}$, representing a data store $ds \in DS \subseteq DN$ inside m. Given an activity $ac \in Ac \subseteq N$, the* Fairness-driven Activity View *eav_{ac} of ac is a set composed of at least one of the following activity views:*

- *$av_{ac}^{=} = \{t_1, \ldots, t_m\}$, which denotes the activity view related to ac when the Equality principle need to be implemented,*
- *$av_{ac}^{\doteqdot} = \{t'_1, \ldots, t'_m\}$, which denotes the activity view related to ac when the Equity principle need to be implemented.*

We will denote as $av_{ac}^{=}[\mathcal{S}]$ and $av_{ac}^{\doteqdot}[\mathcal{S}]$ the set $\bigcup_{i \in \{1,\ldots,m\}} Att(Q_i)$, i.e., the schema attributes of $\mathcal{S}$ each tuple of an activity view needs to access, according to the equality- and equity-fairness principles, respectively. Moreover, notations $av_{ac}^{=}[\![\mathcal{S}]\!] = av_{ac}^{=}[\mathcal{S}] \cap \mathcal{SA}$ and $av_{ac}^{\doteqdot}[\![\mathcal{S}]\!] = av_{ac}^{\doteqdot}[\mathcal{S}] \cap \mathcal{SA}$ are introduced to identify the attributes containing sensitive information an activity view needs to access.

Any equality-related activity view $av_{ac}^{=}$ cannot contain sensitive attributes, while an equity-related one $av_{ac}^{\doteqdot}$ needs to have at least one sensitive attribute, which allows the distinction of different cases equity criteria have to consider. More formally, it always holds $av_{ac}^{=}[\![\mathcal{S}]\!] = \emptyset$ and $av_{ac}^{\doteqdot}[\![\mathcal{S}]\!] \neq \emptyset$.

It is essential to highlight that when the process is executed, and a certain activity is associated with more than one activity view because more fairness principles can be implemented for that activity, only one will be selected during the execution, depending on the specific application needs.

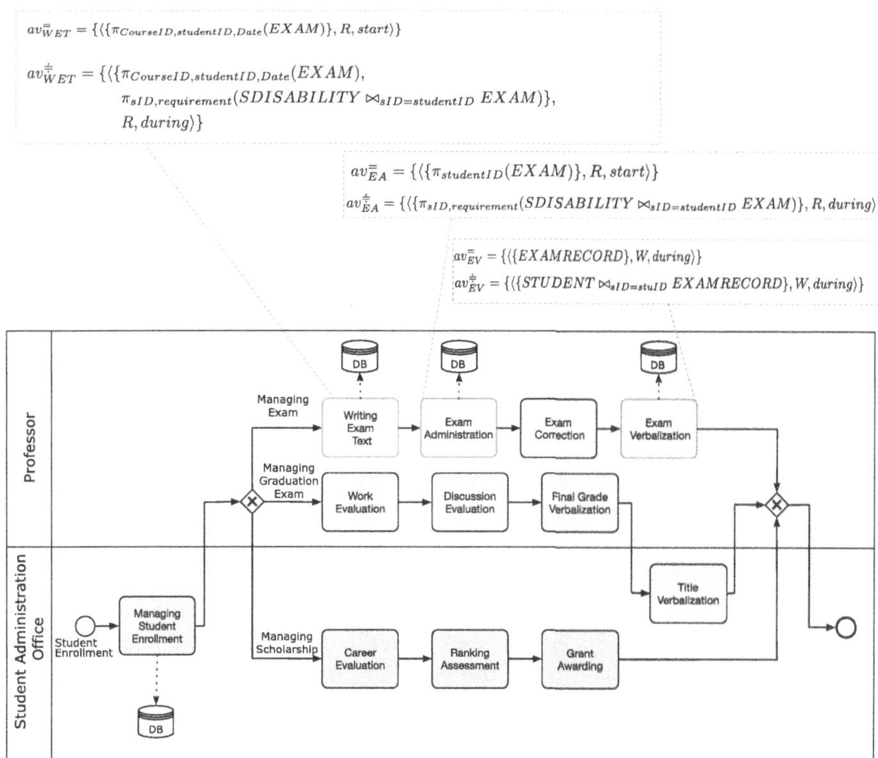

Fig. 2. The business process model for the management of students' careers completed with its Fairness-driven Activity View. (Color figure online)

Referring back to the example introduced in Sect. 3, Fig. 2 enriches the process in Fig. 1 with the Fairness-driven Activity View related to both equality and equity, taking the schema in Table 1 as a reference data store. In particular, let us consider the "Writing Exam Text" (WET) activity; in this case, the professor can need to access two distinct portions of the database schema depending on the fairness principle we want to implement. In the case of equality ($av^{=}_{ac}$), the exam paper will be the same for all the students and thus, it is enough to access information for the exam organization, such as the course and student identifier and the date of the session, to count the number of students who will be present during the exam. Conversely, if the equity principle is taken into consideration ($av^{\div}_{ac}$), the professors need to access some additional and sensitive information about the student, like his/her possible disabilities, to accommodate specific and tailored needs. This kind of information can also be useful during the "Exam Administration" (EA) since also in this case, the special needs of some students need to be carefully considered. The activity "Exam Correction" (EC) does not have any access to the data store since it does not need any additional information. Finally, "Exam Verbalization" (EV) can be performed with respect to both ethical principles. Thus, according to the proposed formalization, stakeholders may specify during the conceptual design of data-intensive process models different fairness-compliant data accesses through *fairness-driven activity views*.

5 Evaluating Fairness Properties

The proposed extension of the Activity View allows the designers to explicitly specify two different fairness features –equality and equity– for an activity with respect to the information it needs to access.

According to the fairness-driven characterization of activity views, we are now able to specify and evaluate some ethical properties at different resolutions, with the scope ranging from a single activity to the entire process.

Starting from the example in Fig. 2, we can easily envision a first property.

Property 1 (Activity Fairness). Given an activity ac, it holds that:

$$av_{ac}^{=}[\mathcal{S}] \subseteq av_{ac}^{\doteqdot}[\mathcal{S}].$$

The rationale under the property is that if an activity can be implemented following more than one fairness principle, then for the equity principle, an activity needs access to a broader set of data, i.e., additional attributes, some of them being sensitive (e.g., presence of disability) or additional relations, with respect to an activity considering the equality principle [14]. For example, in Fig. 2, activity "Writing Exam Test" needs to access only a projection of the EXAM relation when considering equality, and in addition to that, also to a projection of the join of EXAM and SDISABILITY when considering equity.

The notion of fairness can be extended from a single activity to an entire path inside a process model. More precisely, we have to consider, for each path, those activities assigned to the same actor (i.e., in the same lane). While, in principle, for equality, any equality-related activity view may be independent of the other ones, even when related to activities executed by the same actor, specific attention has to be paid to two different aspects:

- how equality-related activity views are related to equity-related ones associated to activities performed by the same actor;
- how equity-related activity views are related to other equity-related activity views for activities performed by the same actor.

As for the first aspect, the following property holds.

Property 2 (Path Equality Fairness). A path of a process model m, given by the sequence of activities inside the same lane, is equality fair if for any activity $a \in Ac$ such that there exists $av_{a}^{=}[\mathcal{S}]$ or a does not access any data store, it holds $\neg\exists b \in \circ\, a\ (av_{b}^{\doteqdot}[\![\mathcal{S}]\!])$, where $\circ\, a$ denotes all the activities preceding a.

The intuition behind this property is that any actor cannot use an equality fairness policy if, in some previous activity, he/she adopted an equity-based approach, as it for sure allowed him/her to know sensitive information, which may influence equality.

As for the second aspect, the following property holds.

Property 3 (Path Equity Fairness). A path of a process model m, given by the sequence of activities inside the same lane, is equity fair if for any activity $a \in Ac$ it holds $av_a^{\div}[\![\mathcal{S}]\!] \subseteq av_b^{\div}[\![\mathcal{S}]\!]$ for all activities b in $a \circ$, where $a \circ$ denotes all the activities following a.

This property states that to ensure equity on a path of a process model, all the successors of activity a, assigned to the same actor executing a, must work on a superset (or the same set) of attributes that activity a accesses. This property enforces that the same actor cannot work on data that, in successive activities, cannot be available if we want to preserve equity.

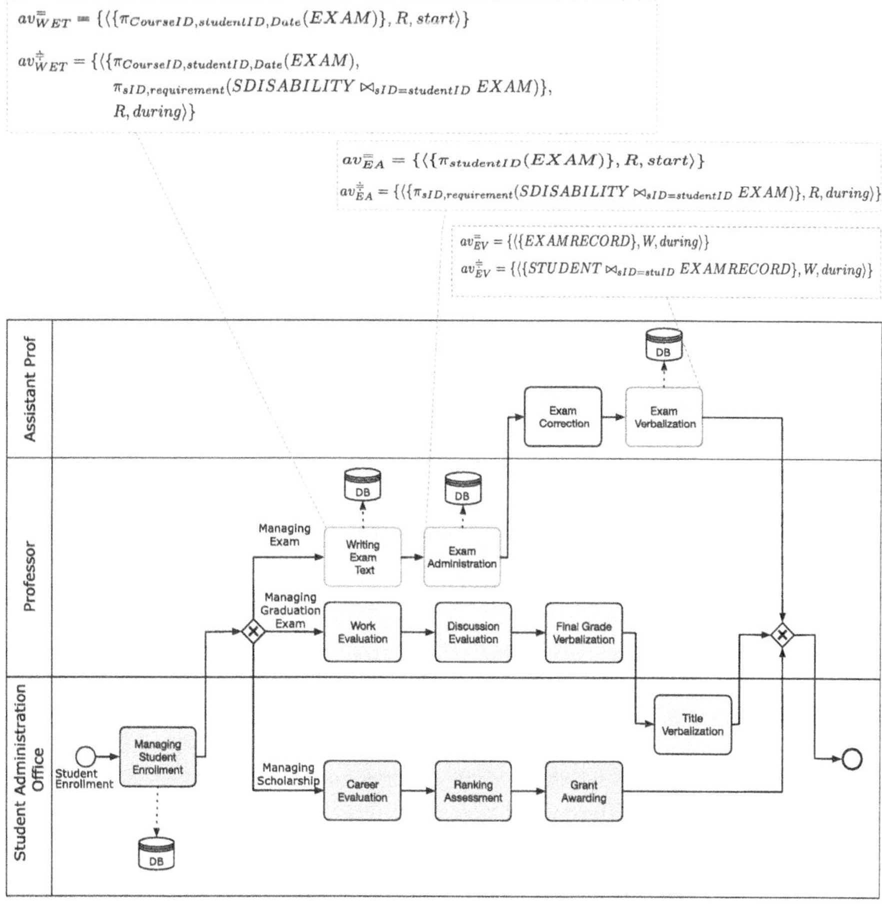

Fig. 3. The re-engineered business process model for the management of students' careers equipped with Fairness-driven Activity Views.

Let us consider again the example in Fig. 2, and in particular, the yellow path representing the activities carried out for managing a university exam. In this case, if the equity principle is implemented for the first two activities, the professor has access to sensitive information regarding the disability of some students. However, these pieces of information cannot be forgotten by the same professor when he/she executes the last two activities related to the exam correction and verbalization. More specifically, during the correction, the professor should not know any information about the student's health status or career. This is represented in the activity view by the fact that the accessed database schema is empty. Therefore, this path cannot be considered entirely fair. For this reason, Fig. 3 proposes a re-engineered version of the process that corrects such an unfair situation. In particular, the solution includes the introduction of a new actor, represented by an additional lane identified by the name "Assistant Professor", which will perform the final two activities requiring a more strict fairness principle. Let us notice that in this case, BPMN lanes are used not only to identify different roles but also to identify different actors covering them.

The property of equity fairness can finally be extended to the entire process model in a straightforward manner.

Property 4 (Process Equity Fairness). A process model m is equity fair if all its possible paths inside the same lane are equity fair.

It follows that when gateways are present in the process model, the fairness of paths needs to be verified on all the possible paths obtained on the base of the gateway semantics.

Let us notice that the concept expressed with respect to a model path can also be true when different instances of the same process model are considered and are under execution over time. The extension from the fairness of process schema to the fairness of the single instances is out of the scope of this paper but can be considered a valid extension point for future work.

6 Conclusions and Future Work

In this paper, we proposed an integrated approach to data and process modeling, which explicitly considers fairness in data and process management. More specifically, we focused on the concepts of equity and equality in the context of PAISs. We considered fairness issues both at the level of single activities and related data, moving up to the overall process model. Moreover, we provided some examples of how different fairness requirements related to data access are also connected to the task-assignment policies for different actors and agents.

As for future work, we plan to study fairness-related issues, together with the characterization of sensitive data, also in the context of more complex role-based activity assignments. In addition, the distinction between individual fairness and group fairness notions can guide the re-engineering of unfair process models.

References

1. Angerschmid, A., Zhou, J., Theuermann, K., Chen, F., Holzinger, A.: Fairness and explanation in AI-informed decision making. Mach. Learn. Knowl. Extr. **4**(2), 556–579 (2022)
2. Caton, S., Haas, C.: Fairness in machine learning: a survey. ACM Comput. Surv. **56**(7), 1–38 (2024)
3. Combi, C., Oliboni, B., Weske, M., Zerbato, F.: Conceptual modeling of inter-dependencies between processes and data. In: ACM Symposium on Applied Computing (SAC), pp. 110–119. ACM (2018)
4. Combi, C., Oliboni, B., Weske, M., Zerbato, F.: Conceptual modeling of processes and data: connecting different perspectives. In: Trujillo, J.C., et al. (eds.) ER 2018. LNCS, vol. 11157, pp. 236–250. Springer, Cham (2018). https://doi.org/10.1007/978-3-030-00847-5_18
5. Combi, C., Oliboni, B., Zerbato, F.: Integrated exploration of data-intensive business processes. IEEE Trans. Serv. Comput. **16**(1), 383–397 (2023)
6. Demartini, G., Roitero, K., Mizzaro, S.: Data bias management. Commun. ACM **67**(1), 28–32 (2023)
7. Hutchinson, B., Mitchell, M.: 50 years of test (un)fairness: lessons for machine learning. In: Proceedings of the Conference on Fairness, Accountability, and Transparency, FAT* 2019, pp. 49–58. Association for Computing Machinery (2019)
8. Jagadish, H.V., Stoyanovich, J., Howe, B.: The many facets of data equity. ACM J. Data Inf. Qual. **14**(4), 27:1–27:21 (2022)
9. Kasy, M., Abebe, R.: Fairness, equality, and power in algorithmic decision-making. In: Proceedings of the 2021 ACM Conference on Fairness, Accountability, and Transparency, pp. 576–586. Association for Computing Machinery (2021)
10. Lee, M.K., Jain, A., Cha, H.J., Ojha, S., Kusbit, D.: Procedural justice in algorithmic fairness: leveraging transparency and outcome control for fair algorithmic mediation. Proc. ACM Hum. Comput. Interact. **3**(CSCW), 182:1–182:26 (2019)
11. Mehrabi, N., Morstatter, F., Saxena, N., Lerman, K., Galstyan, A.: A survey on bias and fairness in machine learning. ACM Comput. Surv. **54**(6), 1–35 (2021)
12. Narayanan, A.: Translation tutorial: 21 fairness definitions and their politics. In: Proceedings of Conference on Fairness, Accountability, and Transparency, vol. 1170, p. 3 (2018)
13. Object Management Group. Business Process Model and Notation (BPMN), v2.0.2 (2014). http://www.omg.org/spec/BPMN/2.0.2/
14. Pujol, D., Machanavajjhala, A.: Equity and privacy: more than just a tradeoff. IEEE Secur. Priv. **19**(6), 93–97 (2021)
15. Ramadan, Q., Strüber, D., Salnitri, M., Jürjens, J., Riediger, V., Staab, S.: A semi-automated BPMN-based framework for detecting conflicts between security, data-minimization, and fairness requirements. Softw. Syst. Model. **19**(5), 1191–1227 (2020). https://doi.org/10.1007/s10270-020-00781-x
16. Reichert, M.: Process and data: two sides of the same coin? In: Meersman, R., et al. (eds.) OTM 2012. LNCS, vol. 7565, pp. 2–19. Springer, Heidelberg (2012). https://doi.org/10.1007/978-3-642-33606-5_2
17. Steen, M.: Ethics as a participatory and iterative process. Commun. ACM **66**(5), 27–29 (2023)
18. Zehlike, M., Yang, K., Stoyanovich, J.: Fairness in ranking, part II: learning-to-rank and recommender systems. ACM Comput. Surv. **55**(6), 1–41 (2022)
19. Zehlike, M., Yang, K., Stoyanovich, J.: Fairness in ranking, part I: score-based ranking. ACM Comput. Surv. **55**(6), 118:1–118:36 (2023)

Am I Allowed to Change an Activity Relationship? - A Metamodel for Behavioral Business Process Redesign

Kerstin Andree(✉) and Luise Pufahl

School of Computation, Information and Technology, Technical University of Munich, 74076 Heilbronn, Germany
{kerstin.andree,luise.pufahl}@tum.de

Abstract. Business processes are constantly changing due to optimization, changes in legislation, or dissatisfaction among participants. Usually, process models are used as the basis for changing process behavior, but the models only provide limited information about possible risks, consequences, and vulnerability of the relationships between activities. Due to the lack of information, changes are implemented too hastily or not at all. In this paper, we elaborate on the relevant information for evaluating behavioral changes in the process. We present concepts and their relationships in a metamodel and show how the application of the metamodel can help to better assess process changes using the travel reimbursement process at a university. Furthermore, we discuss the potential of the proposed metamodel with regard to semi-automated business process redesign support.

Keywords: Business Process Redesign · Activity Relationships · Vulnerabilities · Process Models

1 Introduction

Business processes are subject to a dynamically changing environment which is why the redesign of processes is an important task for organizations performed on a regular basis [18]. Business Process Redesign (BPR) is a core part of Business Process Management (BPM) and provides methods, techniques, and tools for modifying process models [7, Ch.8]. Process models represent business processes by specifying activities and relationships between them [31, Ch.1]. Changing relations in process models, i.e., behavioral BPR, is a difficult and challenging task [2], as each modification needs to be evaluated for its feasibility, associated risks, and consequences to maintain consistency and compliance.

Although several approaches, best practices, and guidance for BPR were introduced in recent years [12], process redesign remains one of the greatest challenges in the BPM community [5]. Since there are only a few solutions for automated BPR [5,9], processes are manually redesigned based on process models. However, these models only depict a subset of all activity dependencies,

M. Kaczmarek-Heß et al. (Eds.): EDOC 2024 Workshops, LNBIP 537, pp. 18–35, 2025.
https://doi.org/10.1007/978-3-031-79059-1_2

making the impacts in terms of risks and consequences of behavioral changes not apparent to users, i.e., process designers. That is why the implementation of BPR is referred to as the *ATAMO* procedure (And Then, A Miracle Happens) [7, Ch.8], stating that redesigning a business process is "more art than science" [19]. To make the implementation of BPR more tangible, Mansar and Reijers [18] introduce a framework to classify and identify best practices. It explains business processes in the context of BPR, providing support for users at a more general level. Risks and consequences of specific model change operations, as well as the question of the vulnerability of relations, are accordingly omitted.

For the redesign of activity relations, Adamo et al. [2] introduce the concept of explanatory rationales to provide background information on the relationship. Based on the origin or motivation of a relationship, users can evaluate if the relationship is violable. However, as an extension to the modeling language Business Process Model and Notation (BPMN), the approach is restricted in its generic applicability. Risks and consequences are not covered. Revoredo [23] also highlights the importance of distinguishing between changeable and non-changeable process parts when repairing business process models. In contrast to [1], Revoredo considers internal and external regulations as non-changeable and neglects risks and consequences associated with a change operation.

We argue for a more detailed assessment of change operations and thus propose a metamodel for the redesign of process behavior, i.e., the modification of activity relationships. It illustrates the interconnection of dependencies between activities, their contextual origins, and the resulting vulnerability, as well as the risks and consequences associated with a change operation. The presented concepts and their relationships are based on insights from various sub-disciplines of BPM, such as risk-aware BPM (R-BPM) [16,21], BPR [19], context-aware BPM [24,26], and compliance checking [10,14]. This metamodel summarizes all the information about business process relations that is necessary to assess and correctly execute behavioral changes without compromising the soundness of the model. It can be used to guide further research on automated knowledge extraction and developing software-supported guidance for users during process redesign. Further application areas of the metamodel, such as process characterizations or enhancing process flexibility, will be briefly discussed in this paper.

The organization of this paper is as follows. Section 2 discusses related work before a motivating example presented in Sect. 3 shows the challenges of behavioral BPR. Section 4 explains important concepts fot the metamodel introduced in Sect. 5. We evaluate our results in Sect. 6 and conclude in Sect. 7.

2 Related Work

Various works have been presented to assist users in performing change operations on process models.

Mansar and Reijers [18] introduce a framework that explains the relationship between the business process and its organizational context, the product or services produced by the process (i.e., the business goal), and the customer. They present best practices and discuss them regarding cost, quality, time, and flexibility. Gross et al. [12] provide an extension of the best practice redesign framework. For each component, the authors specify a set of dimensions and characteristics to further facilitate the exploration of process (re)designs. However, guidance on how to perform a change to a process model is still missing. Thus, our paper fills a gap in BPR: investigating an activity relationship's vulnerability and its risks and consequences when performing a change operation.

Zellner [34] presents a framework to identify business process redesign patterns. Each pattern combines a generic redesign activity, such as "separate", with a general element of business processes, e.g., control flow. Nonetheless, users must assess the application of these patterns in each specific case. The presented metamodel in this paper, however, aims to support BPR based on risks and vulnerabilities, indicating possible changes and their implications.

Weber et al. [29,30] introduce 18 change patterns to support the implementation of process model changes during runtime and design-time. In [29], these patterns are used to examine and compare various approaches and frameworks in the field of process change, focusing on flexibility. Despite the overall overview of changing operations, the patterns lack information about the implications of the change regarding risks and consequential actions to ensure model compliance. In the remainder of this paper, we will use *change operation* as a general term to refer to BPR best practices and change patterns.

Fehrer et al. [9] present an approach for assisted business process redesign consisting of four steps: selecting redesign patterns, identifying suitable process parts, creating alternative models, and evaluating the impact. Depending on the data available, they introduce different types of recommendations. Compared to Fehrer et al., we investigate the behavioral process changes from a contextual point of view by addressing risks and consequences.

Related to BPR is the field of business process repair dealing with changing a given process model according to an event log by identifying mismatches between them to improve conformance while staying close to the original model [8]. Presented techniques are optimized for common metrics, such as fitness and generalization. However, initial approaches do not assess the impact of a change in the process model in terms of associated risks and consequences on different contextual layers. First ideas are presented in Armas Cervantes et al. [4] who include an analysis of the impact of each mismatch pattern based on the frequency of the events involved in the pattern. Thus, the authors can prioritize certain repair operations. Domain knowledge is not integrated so far. In contrast, Revoredo [23] integrates domain knowledge by differentiating between changeable and non-changeable parts of the given process model. However, domain experts make this differentiation manually and do not consider risks and consequences.

3 Motivating Example

This section introduces the check-in process at airports as the running example used in this paper, depicted as a BPMN (Business Process Model and Notation) diagram in Fig. 1. The process example shows the need for classifying activity relationships regarding their vulnerability, including risks and consequences.

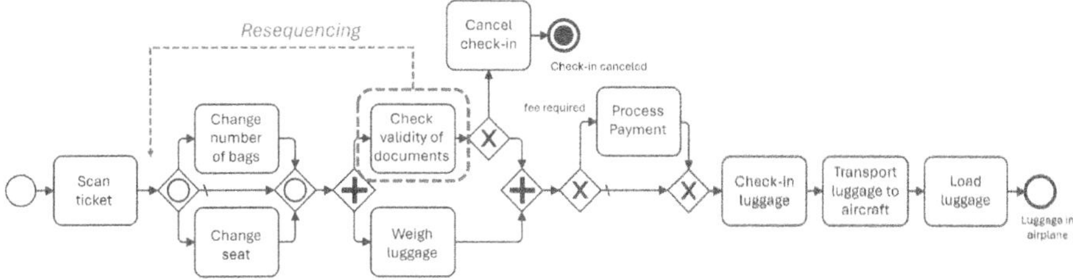

Fig. 1. BPMN process diagram of the check-in process at an airport and a redesign idea marked in red (Color figure online)

The process starts with scanning the booked ticket. Afterward, the passenger can ask for late changes, such as changing the number of bags or changing the seat. Then, the luggage is weighed to check for its weight. In parallel, the airport staff checks the documents of the passenger. If the documents are not valid, the check-in is immediately canceled, and the process terminates. Otherwise, the passenger pays the fees for changes or overweight luggage, if necessary, before the luggage is checked in and transported to the transfer vehicles. Finally, the luggage is put in the airplane and the process terminates.

Imagine redesigning the process to improve its efficiency. We apply the change operation "resequencing" as described in [18] of activity "Check validity of documents" as shown in Fig. 1. We want to move this activity right after scanning the ticket, thus changing the activity execution order to perform the critical check of the documents earlier in the process to avoid unnecessary execution of other tasks in case the documents are invalid. The following questions arise:

- Are we allowed to change the execution sequence?
- What risks are associated with the change operation?
- Which other activity relationships are affected when changing the activity ordering?
- What do we have to do to ensure the consistency of the process model?

Answering these questions by only having the process model is challenging since it only shows the general activity execution order. The last two questions are crucial for automated BPR support since they cover mandatory information about what has to be changed to ensure consistency. Contextual information, e.g., a relationship's origin, is missing when assessing the vulnerability of a relationship. Furthermore, it is unclear which activity relationships are affected when changing the ordering. Besides the relationships represented through the control flow, there are also hidden dependencies implicitly given by transitivity or not represented at all. Consider, for example, the relationship between "Weigh luggage" and "Check-in luggage". Currently, weighing the luggage occurs before check-in, but the fact that the luggage is being weighed does not imply the execution of the check-in task. When we resequence the validity check and the cancellation task to identify false documents earlier, the ordering between "Weigh luggage" and "Check-in luggage" does not change, but now the activities co-occur, i.e., they always happen both or none of them, even though they are still executed in sequence since the activity execution order does not change. Such relationships, particularly the existential dependencies, are not given in a BPMN process diagram but are essential for automated BPR support. Thus, we must understand the risks of a changing operation, which relationships are affected, and how to alter them.

4 Background

To collect relevant concepts that need to be considered when assessing a change operation, we first conducted a literature search to identify BPM disciplines related to behavioral BPR. Based on the forward-backward search approach and the initial idea that contextual information supports users in performing BPR tasks presented in [2], we identified the following relevant BPM disciplines: modeling and activity relationships, compliance checking, risk-aware BPM, and context-aware BPM. For each area, we briefly explain the core concepts used in the metamodel presented in the following section.

Business Process Modeling and Activity Relationships. Business Process Modeling deals with the identification, comprehension, and communication of business processes [31]. Its artifact is the business process model, a (visual) representation of the process. It serves as a blueprint for process instances. Modeling languages, such as BPMN, provide a graphical notation to represent activities and their relationships. Relationships are shown by the control flow through direct linking between activities and gateways. Note that not all activity relationships are given explicitly, which is a common problem in business process representations [27]. Often, such relationships are specified in additional descriptions, process artifacts, e.g., data documents, or domain knowledge. Assuming that a relationship encompasses a set of activity dependencies, Sell et al. [27] emphasize the importance of using a dependency model, e.g., [3,6], to explicitly define those relationships. Moreover, process models have a rather descriptive nature and lack explanatory support for users [13]. Adamo et al. [1,2] address the need for providing contextual information on activity relationships. They introduce ontological constraints, i.e., existential dependencies, dealing with the occurrence of activities rather than their temporal ordering to reveal so-called hidden dependencies, i.e., relationships that are not shown in the process model.

Compliance Checking of Business Process Models. The (re)design of business process models requires checking if the model is free of error and if regulations are met [11]. Compliance checking techniques are applied to answer these questions. We differentiate between *model compliance*, aiming at verifying syntactic and semantic specifications defined by the design properties and *regulatory compliance*, where the business process model compliance is verified towards regulations, e.g., norms. Modeling compliance rules is an opportunity to improve business process models and achieve compliance by design [14]. It highly relates to business process redesign since activity relationships might originate from regulatory compliance rules. Furthermore, it has to be ensured that after a changing operation, the model is compliant with the design properties. Sadiq et al. [25] propose an approach differentiating between business objectives defined by the organization and control objectives capturing regulatory constraints. Based on this approach, Governatori et al. [10] propose a framework to "identify the obligations that will definitely arise in a given process" and which of them are fulfilled or violated. The authors define obligations as regulatory control objectives, i.e., compliance requirements that are mostly specified by external sources, clearly differentiating them from business objectives. Instead of a retrospective checking, the authors address a more proactive way of compliance checking that goes hand in hand with the idea of a preventive approach for business process redesign. Users need to know about violations *before* performing the change operation. The resulting vulnerability, the included risks, and the consequences must be clearly specified.

Risk-Aware Business Process Management. A risk is "the deviation from the expected [...] expressed as [...] potential events [or] consequences" [15, Ch. 3.1] indicating uncertainties and their impact on objectives [28]. Risks are an important phenomenon in BPM and have to be considered when redesigning business processes [21]. Thus, the field of *Risk-Aware BPM* (R-BPM) evolved as the intersection between risk management and BPM [16,28]. R-BPM links process activities to risks and differentiates between *goal risks* threatening the achievement of the business goal, *structural risks* threatening the model's correctness, *data risks* affecting data dependencies or consistency issues, and *organizational risks* threatening compliance rules. Consequences are outcomes of events that can cause further consequences in an escalating manner [15, Ch. 3.6]. Their severity for stakeholders, in combination with the likelihood of a risk occurring, can be used to assess the risk's level of criticality [16]. Consider again the check-in process example at airports. If, for example, the luggage is not weighted, there is a risk that the airplane reaches its maximum capacity and cannot depart due to too much weight. Although this risk has a low probability, its consequences, e.g., delays in airport logistics, lead to severe problems in the process. In this paper, we distinguish between consequences used for defining risks and consequential actions that must be taken to ensure model and regulatory compliance.

Context-Aware Business Process Management. Context is defined as "any information that can be used to characterize the situation of an entity," whereas only context that impacts the control flow, data, and resources is considered relevant [24]. Knowing the internal and external contextual environment of a process is essential to adapt business process behavior. However, business process models are currently designed in isolation, providing prescriptive information about the activity execution order but lacking contextual information [22]. *Context-aware BPM* provides concepts and techniques for context modeling, context learning, and context-aware process operations [22,26]. Different approaches exist to categorize process context. Saidani and Nurcan [26] present four kinds of context, namely location-related context, time-related context, resource-related context, and organization-related context. Rosemann et al. [24] introduce the *onion model*, a context framework differentiating between internal and external context. Whereas the internal layers focus on business objectives, the external layers cover regulatory control objectives for compliance checking [10]. In this paper, we focus on the onion model since it also includes an immediate layer focusing on control flow and central process elements such as data, resources, and applications. Adamo et al. [2] focus on the context of activity relationships, introducing the concept of *explanatory rationales* providing information about the origin and motivation of a relationship. The authors distinguish between norms, goal-related relationships, and the so-called law of nature.

5 Metamodel for Activity Relationship Vulnerability

In general, vulnerability is the quality of being exposed to the possibility of being harmed. In the context of process models, the vulnerability of activity relationships refers to the possibility that this relationship is violated, i.e., changed. It is mainly defined via the origin or motivation of the relationship and includes risks, consequences, and consequential actions. The metamodel in Fig. 2 enhances these concepts given by traditional process models. By analyzing the overlaps between the BPM areas discussed in Sect. 4 we provide an overview of the information that is needed to assess a change operation for a given process model. The linking between the concepts shown in Fig. 2 and the presented BPM disciplines are highlighted in color so that the influence of the BPM topics on the metamodel can be identified. Concepts related to R-BPM are colored in red, compliance-checking concepts are highlighted in yellow, gray concepts originate from context-aware BPM, and blue-colored concepts relate to process modeling and activity relationships. New concepts that we have added are not colored.

In the following, we introduce the metamodel given in Fig. 2 and illustrate the concepts on our running example (Sect. 3).

Process, Activities, and Relationships. A business process consists of a finite set of activities that are executed in a coordinated manner to realize a business goal [31]. Dependencies define relationships that exist between any pair of activities. They can be illustrated in an appropriate dependency model, e.g., using the Web Ontology Language (OWL) [6] or the approach introduced in [3]. In our use case, the process describes the check-in procedure at an airport. It consists of nine activities. Several dependencies exist between them, e.g., checking the validity of documents happens *before* canceling the check-in. Such temporal orderings can be derived from process models. Furthermore, the validity check is *required* for a cancellation, indicating an existential dependency that can be identified via interviews as shown in [1].

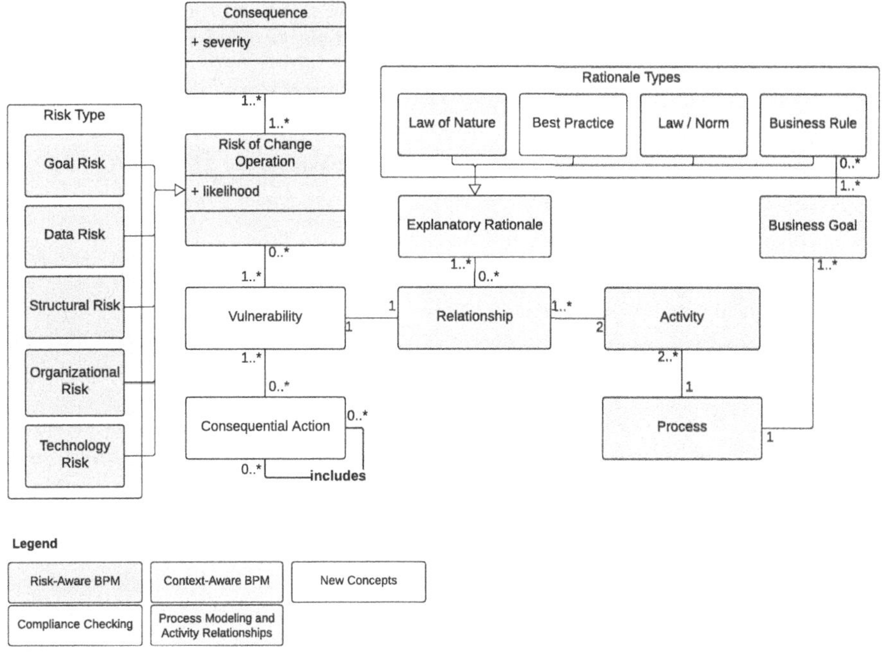

Fig. 2. Metamodel of activity relationships vulnerability for process changes

Explanatory Rationale. Each relationship is further described by explanatory rationales providing contextual information about it, e.g., its origin or motivation [1]. As summarized by the onion model [24], different kinds of context, represented as contextual layers, influence business processes. *Laws and Norms* are usually defined by the external layer. Although laws and norms are different in terms of their consequences, we assign them to the same context layer. For the remainder of this paper, we will use the term *norms* to refer to this category. *Business rules* are defined internally within the organization. Business rules include strategically motivated regulations and relate to the overall goal of the business. *Best practices* are only applied on the immediate layer and are rather a developed way of performing activities based on personal experience than a defined regulation. *Law of nature* as explained in Sect. 4 can originate from all layers. A law of nature cannot be violated without risking a deadlock that cannot be fixed. Please note that multiple explanatory rationales can apply to a given activity relationship. Several relationships of the process example shown in Fig. 1 are motivated by data dependencies, such as the relationship between "Scan ticket" and "Change seat" (cf. Table 1). To change a seat, it must be known which seat was booked before and to which ticket it belongs. Another law of nature, for instance, exists between transporting the luggage to the aircraft and loading it. The luggage must be physically at the aircraft and ready to be picked up by the staff. How it was transported does not matter.

Table 1. Relationships and their vulnerabilities of the check-in process example, non-violable relationships are marked in gray (D: Data Risk, G: Goal Risk, S: Structural Risk, O: Organizational Risk, LoN: Law of Nature)

	Rationale	Violable	Risk
Scan Ticket, Change Seat	LoN/Norm/Goal	no	D/G/S/O
Scan Ticket, Check Validity	Norm/Goal	yes	G/S/O
Scan Ticket, Cancel Check-In	LoN/Goal	no	D/G/S
Change Seat, Weigh Luggage	Norm	yes	S/O
Weigh luggage, Load luggage	Norm	yes	S/O
Check-in luggage, Load luggage	LoN	no	D/G/S

Vulnerability. Based on the explanatory rationale, a vulnerability is assigned to the activity relationship. We differentiate between *violable* and *non-violable* relationships. In contrast to a violable activity relationship, a relationship is classified as non-violable if its origin is a law of nature. For example, luggage loading cannot be performed if there is no luggage physically available for loading. Changing the order of these two activities leads to a deadlock as "Load luggage" never gets enabled. Thus, the relationship is marked as *non-violable* (cf. Table 1). In contrast, weighing the luggage before checking in the luggage is violable because it is logically possible to skip this activity. However, it comes with risks. Please note that we refrain from modeling the vulnerability as an attribute of an activity relationship since a violable relationship may be associated with certain risks and consequential actions.

Risk of Change Operation and Likelihood. Process model changes associated with risks. Risks can affect the achievement of the business goal, the structure of the process model, data, technology, or the organization (cf. Sect. 4). Each risk has a likelihood that helps users assess the severity of violating a relationship. Consider the relationship between "Weigh luggage" and "Load luggage" given in Table 1. Making the luggage weight not mandatory has the risk that the airplane will exceed its maximum weight (organizational risk). Moreover, staff might get hurt because they have to carry weighty luggage (organizational risk).

Consequence and Its Severity. If a risk occurs, consequences follow. If the aircraft has too much weight, it cannot take off, causing delays. Passengers might miss their connecting flight and the airline has to deal with compensation. Consequences vary in severity depending on the stakeholder [16]. For example, if the ticket is not scanned before a passenger changes seats, the passenger's allergies cannot be addressed if specified food preferences do not match the seat. Besides consequences that deal with regulatory or procedural constraints, consequences can also encompass violations in the process model leading to consequential actions.

Consider the resequencing operation again for activity "Check the validity of documents" shown in Fig. 1. Having collected the information from domain experts and structured them according to the metamodel (see Table 1), we can assess a relationship change in terms of vulnerability, risks, and consequences.

Resequencing leads to a change in temporal order between "Scan Ticket" and "Check the validity of documents". As shown in Table 1, we can perform this change operation. However, because the relationship is associated with a structural risk, we know that other activity relationships and dependencies must be changed to ensure model compliance and proper termination. Assuming we resequence both the validity check and the optional cancellation activity, the relationship of "Weigh luggage" and "Load luggage" has to be revisited. As described in Sect. 3, the existential dependency changes. Whenever the luggage is weighted, it is loaded onto the aircraft. According to Table 1 we can perform the change operation since the relationship originates from a norm[1], i.e., it is violable. Changing this dependency leads to structural and organizational risks.

The example shows that risks and vulnerabilities vary depending on the type of the activity dependency. Moreover, it provides an overview of which relations cannot be changed (highlighted in gray). For example, the relationship between "Scan ticket" and "Change seat" can be changed from an existential point of view, but the temporal order cannot be changed due to the law of nature. Changing the ordering would put the process into a deadlock. At this point, no consequential actions can be performed to recover the process from the damage.

Consequential Actions. If a change operation is performed, several consequential actions can be taken to ensure model and regulatory compliance. Consequential actions addressing model compliance can be checked automatically, whereas consequential actions dealing with regulatory compliance require expert knowledge since they rely on contextual information. Note that a consequential action, e.g., changing another relationship, might include further actions.

6 Evaluation in Context

To evaluate the usability and utility of the proposed metamodel, we conduct a single case study to demonstrate how the presented concepts support the assessment of changing a relationship. We consider the travel reimbursement process at the Technical University of Munich and evaluate the introduced metamodel by looking at three observed change operations that are common practices.

We introduce the use case and changing operations before discussing the results.

6.1 The Travel Reimbursement Process and Change Operations

Based on interviews with administration employees, the travel department, and one employee who has already conducted several travels, we documented the travel reimbursement process. The BPMN process diagram is shown in Fig. 3.

[1] Each aircraft has a maximum weight. Moreover, weighing is required to prevent staff health issues.

If employees want to go on a business trip, they must fill out a travel form and attach appropriate documents proving that it is a business trip as defined by law. This request is then signed by the supervisor. The assistant checks the application, scans it, and mails it to the university's travel department. Scanning is necessary because travel requests could get lost when sending them via postal service. The travel department rechecks the application and approves or rejects it. Employees may only go on a business trip if the application has been accepted. After the trip has been completed, employees can apply for reimbursement of travel expenses. The application is voluntary but must be submitted within the first 6 months after the end of the trip. After the assistant scans the request, it is mailed to the travel department, which checks it. The reimbursable costs will be calculated, and the process ends with initiating the bank transfer.

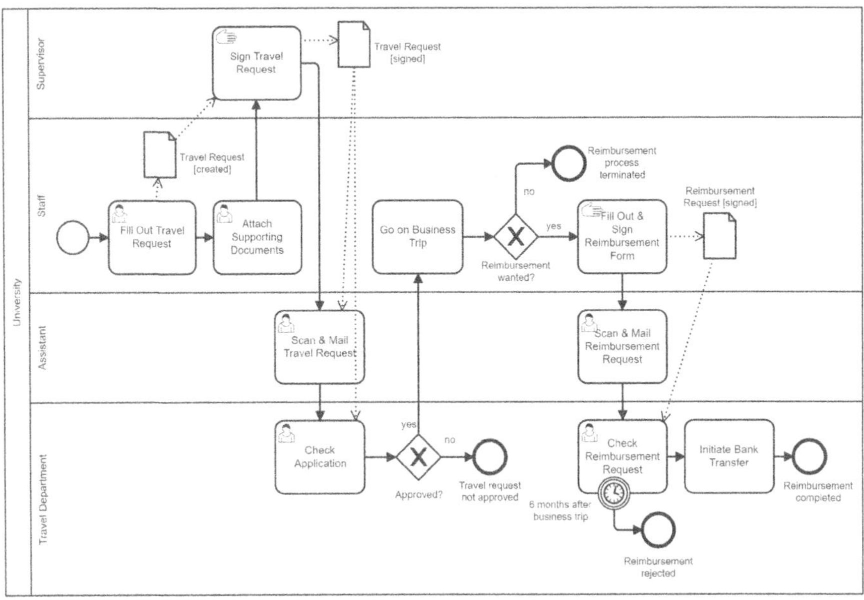

Fig. 3. Travel reimbursement process at universities

The process is primarily determined by the Bavarian Travel Expenses Act[2] and common best practices within the university that have been established over the years. Thus, we identified explanatory rationales by investigating the law and conducting several interviews with the travel department and the administrative assistant. Furthermore, we evaluated each relationship for data dependencies and determined risks, consequences, and severity based on employees' experience.

[2] https://www.lff.bayern.de/themen/reisekosten/reisekosten-allgemeines/ (last access on 18.06.2024).

For this use case, we are examining the following behavioral BPR possibilities:

1) Going on a business trip before the travel request is approved: Parallelize activities “Go on Business Trip”, and the two activities "Scan & Mail Travel Request” and “Check Application” while preserving the ordering between the latter two.
2) Digitalization of the reimbursement process: Remove activity “Scan & Mail Reimbursement Request” because a software program already checks and forwards the request.
3) Initiate bank transfer before travel request submission: Resequence activities “Initiate Bank Transfer” and “Fill out & Sign Travel Reimbursement Form”.

Due to late invitations or long review processes for conference papers, a business trip request may not always be submitted and reviewed in a timely manner before the trip, resulting in employees may travel without approval. This change is achieved by parallelizing the relevant activities.

The abovementioned process was made digital using a software program that automatically checks travel reimbursement requests. Thus, the manual scan and mail activity is not needed anymore, and it was removed.

The third change operation addresses the employees' need to have their travel expenses refunded as quickly as possible. In our single-case study, we evaluate this scenario and discuss if the reordering of activities is feasible in this case.

6.2 Results

In the following, we present the results for each scenario. A summary is given in Table 2. Please note that the contextual information presented in Table 2 was identified explicitly for the change operations described above. Thus, the table only shows those activity relationships mentioned in the scenarios above. Long-term relationships are not considered here. For example, the first scenario describes a parallelization between “Go on Business Trip” and the two activities "Scan & Mail Travel Request” and “Check Application”. Since the ordering between the latter two is preserved, their relationship does not change. Thus, it is not listed in Table 2. Similarly, the relationship between “Fill Out Reimbursement Request” and “Check Reimbursement Request” in the second scenario does not change because the removal of the activity in between does not affect it.

1) Going on a business trip before travel request approval. The ordering between checking the application and going on a business trip is explained via the Travel Expense Act (law). The law clearly defines that going on a business trip without approval is prohibited due to insurance coverage issues. Nevertheless, the explanatory rationale indicates violable relationships, i.e., the parallelization can be performed. It is proven that traveling negatively affects physical health [33]. Typical travel illnesses include gastrointestinal problems like diarrhea, minor injuries, insect bites, or colds[3]. However, more serious illnesses might necessitate

[3] https://www.itilite.com/blog/business-travel-challenges (last access on 01.03.2024).

Table 2. Relationships, vulnerabilities, risks, and consequences of the travel reimbursement process

Relationship	Explanatory Rationale	Violable	Risk (likelihood)	Consequence (severity)
Scenario 1)				
Scan&Mail Travel Request, Go on Business Trip	Business Rule	yes	Organizational (low)	Process delay (low)
Check Application, Go on Business Trip	Norm	yes	Organizational (low)	Costs not covered (high)
Scenario 2)				
Fill Out Reimb. Request, Scan&Mail Reimb. Request	Business Rule	yes	-	-
Scan&Mail Reimb. Request, Check Reimb. Request	Business Rule	yes	-	-
Scenario 3)				
Fill Out Reimb. Request, Initiate Bank Transfer	Law of Nature, Norm	no	Organizational, Goal (high)	Deadlock, Accounting (high)

a hospital stay. Most people rank this risk low. However, the consequences can be severe. If the business trip is not approved, the costs will not be covered by the employer's insurance, and the researcher may potentially be left with expenses. The relationship between scanning and mailing the request and going on a business trip is based on a business rule. There is no technical support for handing in travel requests. Thus, the documents are sent via post. Associated risks are of an organizational nature since mailing the documents after going on a business trip might cause delays in the process, which are considered low in severity.

2) Remove Scanning and Mailing of Documents. The origin of the relationships between filling out the reimbursement request, scanning and mailing it, and finally checking it is based on business rules and best practices. Thus, the relationships are violable. The risk of documents getting lost in the post does not exist anymore because the travel request is now handled via an IT system. Thus, there are no associated risks or consequences with deleting the activity "Scan & Mail Reimbursement Request". From a data perspective, checking the request only depends on the "Fill Out & Sign Reimbursement Form" activity. The scanning and mailing of the request can be omitted. To check a request, it has to be created, i.e., it has to exist, which was done in the previous activity. Such contextual analysis of the explanatory rationales reveals optional process parts, e.g., the activity "Scan & Mail Reimbursement Request". In fact, the digitalization of the process did not violate any non-violable relationships. However, a more detailed analysis would have shown that changing the activity to an optional one is also possible; it does not have to be removed.

3) Initiate the bank transfer before submitting a travel request. Bank transfers require data such as the recipient, the amount of money you want to transfer, the recipient's IBAN, and the BIC. To obtain the data, a request must be made orally via a call or in a written format through a formal document. Thus, we can identify two explanatory rationales: a law of nature due to data dependency and a norm, as the travel expense law requires requesting the reimbursement of travel expenses in written form. Since the relation is based on a law of nature, it is non-violable. The risks include organizational risks; if the request is made orally, the university risks the discovery of an error in accounting, which could lead to serious consequences. Additionally, the goal of reimbursed costs is also at risk, as a different order could lead to a deadlock since the bank transfer cannot be initiated. This risk is very high, and the consequences are also severe. Therefore, this change operation should not be performed.

6.3 Discussion

The evaluation shows that explanatory rationales and vulnerabilities not given by the BPMN process diagram can be identified if the contextual environment is accessible via documentation or stakeholders who can be interviewed. Risks and consequences can also be derived in a feasible manner. This shows the usability of the presented metamodel, i.e., it is feasible to collect the required information.

Nevertheless, the information was collected manually. For more complex business processes, we expect this task of information extraction to be extremely cost-intensive and time-consuming. More structured techniques, e.g., questionnaires and interviews, might help identify relevant contextual information.

In the shown use case, we neglect long-term relationships and consequential actions within the process model. Changing an activity relationship might also violate other relationships not explicitly shown in the process model. An overview of all affected relationships and their adjustment is necessary to ensure consistency and proper termination of the process model. Related work [1–3] already introduces approaches to capture these dependencies and could be used as a foundation for developing an algorithm for detecting consequential actions as stated in the metamodel.

Besides usability, the evaluation also shows the utility of the metamodel. Differentiating between violable and non-violable relationships helps us decide whether relationships are changeable and supports identifying flexibility in processes. Relationships that are not based on a law of nature are changeable and, thus, offer possibilities for flexible process behavior. The overview of risks and consequences helps to assess the implications of a change operation. Furthermore, it helps to understand the overall process and creates awareness of the individual orderings and dependencies. Although the level of detail in defining risks, consequences, and explanatory rationales depends on the available data, the evaluation shows that the concepts presented provide a sufficient overview. All concepts are correct and relevant to the problem of assessing change operations, which proves the feasible validity of the metamodel according to Lindland et al. [17]. Feasible completeness is also achieved since the metamodel would not benefit significantly from adding more concepts.

7 Conclusion and Future Work

Automatized support for business process redesign is still one of the biggest challenges in the BPM community [5]. This paper focuses on behavioral BPR, i.e., the redesign of activity relationships, and presents a metamodel that introduces essential concepts to assess behavioral change in process models. Changing activity relationships in process models is thus examined more profoundly by defining the relationship's vulnerability based on its origin and motivation and by considering the risks and consequences. Thus, the metamodel represents the first step towards automated support for behavioral BPR. After having defined what we need to know, we can extend our research to extracting the required information from domain knowledge. Currently, we are investigating the potential of large language models and questionnaires to compare automized and manual approaches. Furthermore, approaches such as [20,32] present techniques to derive relevant dependencies based on process models and textual descriptions and can serve as a foundation. Future work includes a formalization of change operations on an activity dependency level as introduced in [3] and an automized dependency detection and downwelling[4] adjustment to recover consequential damages to the process model. Having formalized the dependencies between activity relationships and the concrete change operations, we can then work on a semi-automatized tool that integrates the contextual information when guiding users in BPR tasks.

In this paper, we focus on change operations at the type level. However, change operations can also be performed at an instance level. Risks might change in likelihood, and consequences may change in severity. Consider again the example of making the luggage weighing optional. The likelihood that the airplane reaches its maximum weight with one overweight suitcase is lower compared to implementing the change on a model level. Similarly, the risk of a worker getting back problems because of one overweight suitcase is relatively low. In contrast, the likelihood increases if the worker has to load several overweight suitcases in a row. Furthermore, we only looked at assessing change operation at design time. However, contextual information on activity relationships is even more essential for changing a process at runtime to ensure proper termination. Thus, we see great potential in the presented approach to enhance, for example, the so-called change patterns introduced by Weber et al. [30].

In addition to business process redesign at design and runtime, the metamodel also promises enhanced business process repair. Change operations derived from process behavior observed in the event log can be assessed before implementation. Furthermore, we also see a potential use case in characterizing business processes since identifying process flexibility is supported by the metamodel.

---

[4] Downwelling in terms of a cascading effect, i.e., a chain of adjustments needed to recover consequential damages.

References

1. Adamo, G., Borgo, S., Di Francescomarino, C., Ghidini, C., Guarino, N., Sanfilippo, E.M.: Business process activity relationships: is there anything beyond arrows? In: Weske, M., Montali, M., Weber, I., vom Brocke, J. (eds.) BPM 2018. LNBIP, vol. 329, pp. 53–70. Springer, Cham (2018). https://doi.org/10.1007/978-3-319-98651-7_4
2. Adamo, G., Francescomarino, C.D., Ghidini, C., Maggi, F.M.: Beyond arrows in process models: a user study on activity dependences and their rationales. Inf. Syst. **100**, 101762 (2021)
3. Andree, K., Bano, D., Weske, M.: Beyond temporal dependency: an ontology-based approach to modeling causal structures in business processes. In: van der Aa, H., Bork, D., Proper, H.A., Schmidt, R. (eds.) BPMDS 2023, and EMMSAD 2023, Zaragoza, Spain, June 12-13, 2023, Proceedings. LNBIP, vol. 479, pp. 152–166. Springer, Cham (2023)
4. Armas-Cervantes, A., van Beest, N.R.T.P., Rosa, M.L., Dumas, M., García-Bañuelos, L.: Interactive and incremental business process model repair. In: Panetto, H., et al. (eds.) On the Move to Meaningful Internet Systems. OTM 2017 Conferences - Confederated International Conferences: CoopIS, C&TC, and ODBASE 2017, Rhodes, Greece, October 23-27, 2017, Proceedings, Part I. Lecture Notes in Computer Science, vol. 10573, pp. 53–74. Springer, Cham (2017)
5. Beerepoot, I., Ciccio, C.D., Reijers, H.A., et al.: The biggest business process management problems to solve before we die. Comput. Ind. **146**, 103837 (2023)
6. Dean, M., Schreiber, G.: Owl web ontology language reference: W3C recommendation 10 February 2004 (2004)
7. Dumas, M., Rosa, M.L., Mendling, J., Reijers, H.A.: Fundamentals of Business Process Management, 2nd edn. Springer, Heidelberg (2018)
8. Fahland, D., van der Aalst, W.M.P.: Model repair - aligning process models to reality. Inf. Syst. **47**, 220–243 (2015)
9. Fehrer, T., Fischer, D.A., Leemans, S.J.J., Röglinger, M., Wynn, M.T.: An assisted approach to business process redesign. Decis. Support Syst. **156**, 113749 (2022)
10. Governatori, G., Hoffmann, J., Sadiq, S.W., Weber, I.: Detecting regulatory compliance for business process models through semantic annotations. In: Ardagna, D., Mecella, M., Yang, J. (eds.) BPM 2008 International Workshops, Milano, Italy, September 1-4, 2008. Revised Papers. LNBIP, vol. 17, pp. 5–17. Springer, Heidelberg (2008)
11. Groefsema, H., van Beest, N.R.T.P., Governatori, G.: On the use of the conformance and compliance keywords during verification of business processes. In: Ciccio, C.D., Dijkman, R.M., del-Río-Ortega, A., Rinderle-Ma, S. (eds.) BPM 2022 Forum, Münster, Germany, September 11-16, 2022, Proceedings. LNBIP, vol. 458, pp. 21–37. Springer, Cham (2022)
12. Groß, S., Stelzl, K., Grisold, T., Mendling, J., Röglinger, M., vom Brocke, J.: The business process design space for exploring process redesign alternatives. Bus. Process. Manag. J. **27**(8), 25–56 (2021)
13. Guizzardi, G., Guarino, N.: Semantics, ontology and explanation. CoRR abs/2304.11124 (2023)
14. Hashmi, M., Governatori, G., Lam, H.-P., Wynn, M.T.: Are we done with business process compliance: state of the art and challenges ahead. Knowl. Inf. Syst. **57**(1), 79–133 (2018). https://doi.org/10.1007/s10115-017-1142-1

15. Risk management - guidelines. Standard, International Organization for Standardization, Geneva, CH (2018)
16. Lamine, E., Thabet, R., Sienou, A., Bork, D., Fontanili, F., Pingaud, H.: BPRIM: an integrated framework for business process management and risk management. Comput. Ind. **117**, 103199 (2020)
17. Lindland, O.I., Sindre, G., Sølvberg, A.: Understanding quality in conceptual modeling. IEEE Softw. **11**(2), 42–49 (1994)
18. Mansar, S.L., Reijers, H.A.: Best practices in business process redesign: validation of a redesign framework. Comput. Ind. **56**(5), 457–471 (2005)
19. Mansar, S.L., Reijers, H.A.: Best practices in business process redesign: use and impact. Bus. Process. Manag. J. **13**(2), 193–213 (2007)
20. Meyer, A., Weske, M.: Extracting data objects and their states from process models. In: Gasevic, D., Hatala, M., Nezhad, H.R.M., Reichert, M. (eds.) EDOC 2013, Vancouver, BC, Canada, 9–13 September 2013, pp. 27–36. IEEE Computer Society (2013)
21. zur Muehlen, M., Rosemann, M.: Integrating risks in business process models. In: Ljungberg, J., Andersson, M. (eds.) ACIS 2005 Proceedings, Sydney, Australia, 2005, pp. 1606–1615 (2005). http://aisel.aisnet.org/acis2005/50
22. Ploesser, K., Peleg, M., Soffer, P., Rosemann, M., Recker, J.: Learning from context to improve business processes. BPTrends **6**, 1–7 (2009)
23. Revoredo, K.: On the use of domain knowledge for process model repair. Softw. Syst. Model. **22**(4), 1099–1111 (2023)
24. Rosemann, M., Recker, J., Flender, C.: Contextualisation of business processes. Int. J. Bus. Process. Integr. Manag. **3**(1), 47–60 (2008)
25. Sadiq, S., Governatori, G., Namiri, K.: Modeling control objectives for business process compliance. In: Alonso, G., Dadam, P., Rosemann, M. (eds.) BPM 2007. LNCS, vol. 4714, pp. 149–164. Springer, Heidelberg (2007). https://doi.org/10.1007/978-3-540-75183-0_12
26. Saidani, O., Nurcan, S.: Towards context aware business process modelling. In: BPMDS 2007, CAiSE, vol. 7, p. 1 (2007)
27. Sell, C., Winkler, M., Springer, T., Schill, A.: Two dependency modeling approaches for business process adaptation. In: Karagiannis, D., Jin, Z. (eds.) KSEM 2009. LNCS (LNAI), vol. 5914, pp. 418–429. Springer, Heidelberg (2009). https://doi.org/10.1007/978-3-642-10488-6_40
28. Suriadi, S., et al.: Current research in risk-aware business process management - overview, comparison, and gap analysis. Commun. Assoc. Inf. Syst. **34**, 52 (2014)
29. Weber, B., Reichert, M., Rinderle-Ma, S.: Change patterns and change support features - enhancing flexibility in process-aware information systems. Data Knowl. Eng. **66**(3), 438–466 (2008)
30. Weber, B., Rinderle, S., Reichert, M.: Change patterns and change support features in process-aware information systems. In: Krogstie, J., Opdahl, A.L., Sindre, G. (eds.) Advanced Information Systems Engineering, 19th International Conference, CAiSE 2007, Trondheim, Norway, June 11-15, 2007, Proceedings. LNCS, vol. 4495, pp. 574–588. Springer, Heidelberg (2007)
31. Weske, M.: Business Process Management - Concepts, Languages, Architectures, 3rd edn. Springer, Cham (2019)
32. Winter, K., Rinderle-Ma, S.: Detecting constraints and their relations from regulatory documents using NLP techniques. In: Panetto, H., Debruyne, C., Proper, H.A., Ardagna, C.A., Roman, D., Meersman, R. (eds.) On the Move to Meaningful Internet Systems. OTM 2018 Conferences - Confederated International Confer-

ences: CoopIS, C&TC, and ODBASE 2018, Valletta, Malta, October 22-26, 2018, Proceedings, Part I. LNCS, vol. 11229, pp. 261–278. Springer, Cham (2018)

33. Ye, T., Xu, H.: The impact of business travel on travelers' well-being. Ann. Tourism Res. **85**, 103058 (2020). https://www.sciencedirect.com/science/article/pii/S0160738320302024
34. Zellner, G.: Towards a framework for identifying business process redesign patterns. Bus. Process. Manag. J. **19**(4), 600–623 (2013)

Spotting the Weasel at Work: Mining Inappropriate Behavior Patterns in Event Logs

Saimir Bala[1(✉)], Tim Jacobowitz[1], and Jan Mendling[1,2]

[1] Institut für Informatik, Humboldt-Universität zu Berlin, Berlin, Germany
{saimir.bala,tim.jacobowitz,jan.mendling}@hu-berlin.de
[2] Security and Transparency in Processes, Weizenbaum Institute, Berlin, Germany

Abstract. Diverging interests in the workplace may lead to undesirable employee behavior such as taking undue credit, underperforming, shirking responsibilities, and undermining colleagues. This kind of conduct, also referred to as *weasel behavior*, can have significant negative implications for both individuals and the organization as a whole. Therefore, its identification is of crucial importance. Recent work in process science has defined thirteen weasel behavior patterns and proposed the use of process mining related techniques to uncover them from the traces recorded by information systems. However, these definitions have not yet been tested on any event log. This paper aims at closing this gap by providing the design specifications and algorithms necessary to extract weasel behavior from event logs. We evaluate our implementation on the real-world logs provided by the IEEE Task Force on Process Mining and report the extent of weasel behavior present in each dataset. Our results have relevant implications on the application and development of resource-centered process analysis techniques and contribute to better understanding the information present in the widely-used BPI logs.

Keywords: event log · resource analysis · process mining · behavioral process mining

1 Introduction

When stress and conflicts of interest arise in workplace situations, individuals may exhibit inappropriate behavior. This conduct, often labeled as *weasel behavior*, includes activities that are unsanctioned and unrelated to work during work hours. Addressing weasel behavior is crucial for maintaining a productive and healthy workplace, ensuring legal compliance, and protecting employee well-being.

Traditionally, detecting this behavior has been challenging due to individuals' tendencies to conceal it. However, the advent of information systems that support work activities now allows for the recording of traces of these actions, providing

M. Kaczmarek-Heß et al. (Eds.): EDOC 2024 Workshops, LNBIP 537, pp. 36–52, 2025.
https://doi.org/10.1007/978-3-031-79059-1_3

an opportunity to identify undesired patterns. Recent studies [9] have theoretically defined various patterns of weasel behavior, using a Principal-Agent [11] framework to analyze resource interactions in event logs. Thirteen specific patterns have been identified, but these have not yet been implemented as algorithms or tested in real-world event logs.

This paper aims to bridge this gap by providing a specification for these behavior patterns, developing corresponding algorithms, and evaluating them against both synthetic and real-world event logs. The results reveal the distribution of these behaviors in well-known event logs, thereby enhancing our understanding of resource behavior in organizational settings and contributing to the development of resource-centered process analysis techniques.

This paper is structured as follows. Section 2 describes the setting of this work. Section 3 outlines the research methodology devised to translate the weasel-behavior patterns into design patterns for implementation purposes. Section 4 provides the specifications for each design pattern. Section 5 outlines the results of our algorithms on both synthetic and real-world event logs, including a discussion. Section 6 concludes the paper.

2 Literature Review

The scope of this paper is to explore the use of event logs for extracting and analyzing the behavior of resources. Therefore, we consider the literature that takes into account both the resource perspective and the analysis of event logs, at the same time. This section describes previous work, discusses works related to the analysis of behavioral issues and identifies the research gap to address.

Previous Work. This paper follows the research stream started by Leyer et al. [9]. They use Principal-Agent Theory [11] to explain the relationship between resources in an organization. This theory states that there is an imbalance in power held by the principal and in information held by the agent, and their goals. Given that principals cannot fully control the actions of agents, the latter will show opportunistic behavior in to attain their individual goals. The propensity of employees to engage in unsanctioned, non-work related activities during work time has also been referred to as *weasel* behavior. Thanks to the adoption of information systems and the recording of work-related events into system logs, this behaviour can now be uncovered. Leyer et al. [9] have conceptualized this inappropriate behavior into the thirteen patterns provided in Table 1.

Table 1. The thirteen patterns of inappropriate behavior as defined by [9]

Rerouting-related	Performance-related	Social-related
1. Activity Deviation	5. Performance Masking	9. Idling
2. Originator Deviation	6. Performance Blow-out	10. Social Loafing
3. Re-Ordering	7. Overwork Hiding	11. Peer Mobbing
4. Preferential Work Selection	8. Gold Plating	12. Boss Mobbing
		13. Social Borrowing

Related Work. Apart the work of Leyer et al. [9], other related work exists that allows to evaluate resources' behavior. Specifically, in the process mining area, *social network analysis* has been used to examine the interactions and relationships between the resources of a process. Specifically, the work of [2] uses event logs to discover social networks within organizations. Song and van der Aalst [13] developed techniques to automatically extract social networks from event logs of workflow management systems. Moreover, to overcome the complexity of networks discovered in large event logs, Ferreira and Alves [6] focus on discovering communities at varying levels of abstraction. More recent work by Mustroph et al. [12] also considers additional information such as natural language description of the process to identify whether the mined work is deviating from the wanted behavior. Further approaches that inform on resources behavior are the use of standard process mining techniques [1], where the resource information is used as a case identifier. Techniques like the dotted chart [14] are able to pinpoint single events that may point to unwanted behavior.

Moreover, process performance indicators [5] and cycle time analysis [8] can help at pointing out anomalies in resources performance. To aid this kind of analysis, *simulation* [3,10] is a powerful technique that can be used for identifying improper behavior of resources.

Gap. Among the above mentioned approaches, the only work that adopts a theoretical lens to analyze the resource behavior is [9]. While conceptualized and exposed in a structured manner, the thirteen proposed patterns have not yet been implemented. Therefore, we pose the research question *how can we implement such patterns and to what extent can be mined from event logs?*. This paper aims at closing this gap by providing a specification that can be easily implemented as a prototype, an initial implementation and an application on real-world event logs that are commonly used in business process research.

3 Methodology

Next, we present our research approach to achieve the design patterns specifications. We describe the steps undertaken, the data and the framework used to specify the design patterns.

Research Approach. We summarize the steps of our approach in Fig. 1. To start, we consider the behavior patterns conceptualized in [9] as listed in Table 1. Then, we proceed in five steps *i)* analyze pattern description; *ii)* derive requirements for identification; *iii)* derive event log requirements; *iv)* formulate design patterns specification; and *v)* implement and test a pattern detection algorithm.

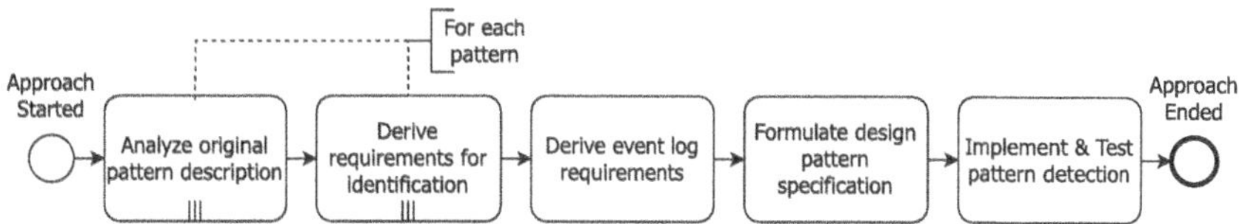

Fig. 1. Steps of the approach to specify and implement the patterns.

Let us describe each step in more detail. In step *i)* we analayze the original description of each pattern guided by the question *what are the inputs required to apply this pattern?*. As a result, we can first classify the patterns whether they can directly be implemented with only the event log or whether they require more contextual information such as a process model. In step *ii)* we consider again each pattern and the information from step *i)* and we identify specific requirements of the input. For example, in order to detect *performance blow-out* the requirement is that the event log contains the attributes `Activity`, `Start` and `Complete Timestamps`, and `Resource`. In step *iii)* we consider the overall knowledge gathered by analyzing each pattern to derive general requirements about the input. This step is guided by the question *can we create one single input with all the required attributes?*. The result of this step is also related to the choice of what specification language used in the next step. In step *iv)* we use a patterns specification language to describe each pattern in a way that it can be easily implemented. In the final step *v)* we implement and test each pattern, according the specification. More specifically, before implementing and testing algorithms in the real data, this step creates synthetic event logs that present the required behavior (by construction). These synthetic event logs are then used to test the correctness of the algorithm in identifying the implemented behavior. The output of this step is further used to analyze the presence of the patterns.

Data, Design Patterns Selection and Specification Format. Next, we describe the kind of data used in this research approach, what design patterns we used for the specification of weasel behavior and their format.

Data. The first three steps of the research approach allow us to grasp an overall understanding of the data requirements for weasel behavior detection. In particular, our approach makes use of two kinds of data: synthetic event logs and real-life event log. Sythetic event logs are generated ad-hoc for each pattern. More specifically, we first create scenarios for each instance of inappropriate behavior. Then we manually create event log traces that directly reflect the scenario, for each pattern. In other words, in the end of our approach, we have 13 synthetic event logs (one per pattern), each affected by the respective inaproppriate behavior.

Design Patterns Selection. Before applying step *iv)*, there is a need for selecting how to transform the conceptualized patterns into a design that can be used for software specification. As the final goal is to implement and test the behavioral patterns in practice, we follow the principles of Design Patterns proposed by Gamma et al. [7]. The main advantage of specifying the thirteen inappropriate behavior types as design patterns is that they can be used to both generally describe the problem in context and as *requirements for algorithm development.*

Specification Format. We keep the original classification of the patterns, but we use a design pattern specification format. Each pattern is described according to the following template, inspired by [7] and adapted to our case. `Pattern Name` conveys the essence of the design pattern, `Intent` gives information on the intent or purpose, `Problem` states the specific problem the pattern addresses, `Solution` gives a details on the solution provided by the pattern, `Required Attributes` lists the attributes required in the event log, `Required Analysis` lists the minimum level of analysis an implementation must provide, `Implementation` explains what are the steps and considerations for implementing the pattern, `Code Examples` provide code snippets or pseudocode to illustrate the implementation, `Sample Applications` describe real-world examples or scenarios where the pattern can be applied, and `Consequences` outlines benefits and potential drawbacks of using the pattern.

4 Design Patterns Specifications

In the following, we provide the specifications for each inappropriate behavior, using the design patterns specification format. For the sake of space, we do not report the implementation, code examples, sample applications and consequences. The implementation and code can be found in [4] whereas applications to real-world event logs and consequences follows in the paper.

Pattern 1. Activity Deviation (Rerouting-related)
`Intent:` This design pattern captures all those activities that are unexpected or undesired by the principal (e.g., the owner of the organization).
`Problem:` The specific problem addressed by this pattern is the conformance of activities to a desired process known by the principal. Specifically, the process model represents the desired work.
`Solution:` The solution provided by this pattern is to perform conformance checking of the activities present in the event log against the given process model. The priority is given to the process model. That is, if an activity is only present in the log, it is considered a deviation.
`Required Attributes:` Activity, Process Model, or a similar data structure containing all expected activities
`Required Analysis:` The activity has to be checked for each event in the log.

The regarded activity then has to be compared with the expected activities specified in the model
`Implementation:` Loop through all activities in the event log. Each considered activity from the event log, should be the next expected activity in the model. If this is not the case, record the deviation. Collect all the deviations for all activities.

Pattern 2. Originator Deviation (Rerouting-related)
`Intent:` The purpose of this pattern is to detect those resources who worked on tasks they were not assigned to.
`Problem:` While it may be desirable that certain resources undertake tasks they were not assigned to, the focus of this pattern is on those cases when certain resources favour doing other tasks instead of their own, as this may give them more credit.
`Solution:` The solution provided by this pattern is to perform conformance checking. Especially, the check should be whether the resources who were assigned certain tasks were also the ones who conducted them.
`Required Attributes:` Activity, Resource, Process Model (or a similar data structure containing the assigned resource for each activity)
`Required Analysis:` Check each activity in the event log to see if it was conducted by the assigned resource. Record any deviations where tasks were completed by non-assigned resources.
`Implementation:` To detect the pattern of Originator Deviation, the assigned resource has to be checked for each event in the log. The resource associated with the regarded event should then be compared to the resource who is expected for the corresponding activity according to the model. If the assignments from log and process model deviate, it is an indicator of the presence of Originator Deviation. Otherwise, it has to be proceeded to the next assignment.

Pattern 3. Re-ordering (Rerouting-related)
`Intent:` The purpose of this pattern is to detect those activities that were performed in an undesired order.
`Problem:` The responsible agent may think that the activities would be better performed in a different order than what is prescribed in the process model.
`Solution:` The solution provided by this pattern is to perform conformance checking. Especially, this pattern should provide discrepancies in terms of sequences of activities performed in the event log versus the model.
`Required Attributes:` Case, Activity, Timestamps, Process Model (Or a similar data structure containing the expected order of activities)
`Required Analysis:` The sequences of activities in the event log, sorted by timestamp must be compared to the expected sequences of activities prescribed in the process model.
`Implementation:` To detect the pattern of re-ordering, it is necessary to check the order in which activities occurred for each case by examining the timestamps. This order then has to be compared to the order prescribed in the process model.

If the order of activities in the regarded case from the log is invalid according to the process model, this is an indicator of the presence of Re-Ordering. Otherwise, it has to be proceeded to the next case.

Pattern 4. Preferential Work Selection (Rerouting-related)
`Intent`: The purpose of this pattern is to detect those resources who choose working on certain tasks disproportionally often.
`Problem`: Agents may chose easier tasks that have a higher pay-off.
`Solution`: The solution must single out all those cases in which work was not performed as assigned (i.e., not in a first-come-first-served (FCFS) fashion).
`Required Attributes`: Case, Activity, (Start and Complete) Timestamps, Resource
`Required Analysis`: Output a list of activities that are chosen on average more often than expected by the resources
`Implementation`: To detect Preferential Work Selection, the frequency of certain activities being chosen by certain resources has to be observed. Average frequencies have to be calculated for each activity on this basis. If the frequency of a resource choosing an activity is significantly greater than the average value for the regarded activity, this is an indicator of the presence of Preferential Work Selection. Otherwise, it has to be proceeded to the next frequency of a resource choosing an activity. Furthermore, it also has to be observed if a resource starts a new activity in a case while still not being finished with work in another case by checking timestamps. If a timestamp reveals that this did indeed happen, this is another indicator of the presence of Preferential Work Selection. Otherwise, it has to be proceeded to the next timestamps.

Pattern 5. Performance Masking (Performance-related)
`Intent`: The purpose of this pattern is to point out agents who try to prevent their performance from being measurable.
`Problem`: An agent could transfer the content of an online work item to finish it offline because the time needed is only measured when the work item is opened online. This way, the actual time needed for the completion of the task can not be measured.
`Solution`: The solution should provide information on how quickly the tasks are performed. Unusually short durations should be collected for further analysis
`Required Attributes`: Case, Activity, (Start and Complete) Timestamps, Resource
`Required Analysis`: Output a list of cases with many events registered in a short time
`Implementation`: To detect the pattern of Performance Masking, cases that have many events registered in a relatively short amount of time have to be observed by counting events in cases and checking timestamps. Activities that occur significantly often in such cases and also have a significantly short duration should then be searched. If the presence of such cases and activities is confirmed, it is an indicator of the presence of Performance Masking. Otherwise, it has to

be proceeded to the next cases with many events in a short time.

Pattern 6. Performance Blow-Out (Performance-related)
`Intent`: The purpose of this pattern is detect agents stretching their work time by pretending they are still working on an activity when they are actually not.
`Problem`: Activities might have working times determined by service-level-agreements, which makes it possible to maximize the time spent on that activity even when the work is already completed. This suggests that the agent might want to gain additional free time.
`Solution`: The solution should provide information on agents who, compared to others, take longer time on performing similar tasks.
`Required Attributes`: Case, Activity, (Start and Complete) Timestamps, Resource
`Required Analysis`: Output all those resources that took different times in performing similar tasks, along with the tasks performed.
`Implementation`: To detect the pattern of Performance Blow-Out, the time different resources need for the same activities has to be inspected by checking timestamps. Those completion times of different resources must then be compared to determine whether they deviate significantly from one another or are approximately in the same range. If the standard deviation of the completion times for an activity is significantly great, this is an indicator of the presence of Performance Blow-Out. Otherwise, it has to be proceeded to the next completion times of an activity. Moreover, the completion times of the same resource for the same activity have to be analyzed. If this duration gets significantly longer over time, this is another indicator of the presence of Performance Blow-Out. Otherwise, it has to be proceeded to the next completion times.

Pattern 7. Overwork Hiding (Performance-related)
`Intent`: The purpose of this pattern is to signal agents performing work outside of their official working times.
`Problem`: Agents are not able to finish their allocated work in the expected time. Since the expected times would usually be set based on the stated skills and experience of an employee, Overwork Hiding might even infer that an agent is less skilled or experienced than stated expected by the principal.
`Solution`: The solution should provide information on agents that perform actions on work items outside of working hours
`Required Attributes`: Activity, Timestamps, Resource, Official working times
`Required Analysis`: Output all the agents that performed work on activities outside working hours
`Implementation`: To detect the pattern of Overwork Hiding, the timestamps have to be investigated for each resource and compared with the working times of the regarded resource. If a timestamp is found that is placed outside of the allocated working times, this is an indicator of the presence of Overwork Hiding. Otherwise, it has to be proceeded to the next timestamp.

Pattern 8. Gold Plating(Performance-related)
`Intent:` The purpose of this pattern is to show circumstances of overwork in which resources weather conduct more work than necessary or perform additional services and tasks
`Problem:` By conducting more work or providing additional services, agents may increase the favour of certain clients or aim for additional performance bonus
`Solution:` Cases with additional duration or cost must be analyzed. Such cases would take longer in certain contexts (e.g., when associated to a specific client)
`Required Attributes:` Activity, Timestamps, Resource, Official working times
`Required Analysis:` Perform variant analysis and point out cases that last significantly longer from others in the same variant group.
`Implementation:` To detect the pattern of Gold Plating, cases categorized by their specific sequence of activities, also called process variants, have to be identified. Next, the average activity duration of each process variant has to be observed. If the average activity duration of a certain process variant is significantly longer than the overall average, this is an indicator of the presence of Gold Plating. Otherwise, it has to be proceeded to the next process variant. Furthermore, it has to be searched for process variants containing significantly rare activities. If a process variant contains an activity that is significantly rare, this is another indicator of the presence of Gold Plating. Otherwise, it has to be proceeded to the next process variant.

Pattern 9. Idling (Social-related)
`Intent:` The purpose of this pattern is to point out agents engaging in non-work related activities during work time instead of working
`Problem:` Agents may perceive work as boring or unfair and use working time for other activities, such as socializing, procrastinating, smoking, etc. Yet, they do not want to be perceived as bad performers.
`Solution:` A solution to this problem would be to assign more stimulating work to resources. Resources that take substantially more time on completing tasks can be extracted from event logs.
`Required Attributes:` Activity, (Start and Complete) Timestamps, Resource
`Required Analysis:` Analyze the actions performed by resources on tasks. Check completion times.
`Implementation:` To detect the pattern of Idling, the timestamps have to be checked to calculate the completion times of each resource for each activity. Based on those completion times, the mean has to be calculated for each activity to be compared with the individual completion times. If there is a completion time value that is significantly greater than the values for other resources conducting the same activity or significantly greater than the values for the same resource conducting other activities, this is an indicator of the presence of Idling. Otherwise, it has to be proceeded to the next completion times. In addition, the timestamps have also be evaluated to detect resources taking possible breaks between two activities. If those breaks are significantly long, this is another indicator of the presence of Idling. Otherwise, it has to be proceeded to the next

timestamp.

Pattern 10. Social Loafing (Social-related)
`Intent:` The purpose of this pattern is to detect when, in the context of group work, an agent avoids, neglects works or free-rides
`Problem:` As group members do not perform team work by shirking work, the whole team productivity is affected
`Solution:` Identify resources that exhibit this pattern and assign them to different groups.
`Required Attributes:` Activity, (Start and Complete) Timestamps, Resource, Classifications of events into group work and individual work
`Required Analysis:` Measure the average completion times of resources in the context of group work
`Implementation:` The completion times must be measure for each resource in the context of groupwork. This performance must then be compared to the completion times of the same resources working alone. If a resource shows a significantly better individual performance while working alone in comparison to working in a group, this is an indicator of the presence of Social Loafing. Otherwise, it has to be proceeded to the next resource.

Pattern 11. Peer Mobbing (Social-related)
`Intent:` The purpose of this pattern is to detect agents or groups of agents who degrade their peers by taking over their work without consent.
`Problem:` Agents steal work items from the entitled resource in order to increase their pay-off, at the same time making the performance of their colleagues look poor.
`Solution:` Resource who exhibit this pattern must be detected and a limit on the items they can take over should be in place.
`Required Attributes:` Activity, Resource
`Required Analysis:` Collect work type that are performed unusually often by certain groups.
`Implementation:` To detect the pattern of Peer Mobbing, it is necessary to analyze the frequency of each activity being performed by each resource. If significantly many resources perform a certain activity significantly more often than a single resource, this is an indicator of the presence of Peer Mobbing. Otherwise, it has to be proceeded to the next resources.

Pattern 12. Boss Mobbing (Social-related)
`Intent:` The purpose of this pattern is to detect agents or groups of agents who repeatedly perform poorly as a team in order to make their boss look bad.
`Problem:` The boss may be too demanding or controlling and a group of agents decides to underperform so that companies goals are not met.
`Solution:` Once these team member are detected, a solution is to assign people to different teams.

`Required Attributes:` Activity, (Start and Complete) Timestamps, Resource, Timestamp when a certain is assigned, Classifications of events into group work and individual work
`Required Analysis:` Collect resource performance before and after the time a boss was assigned.
`Implementation:` To detect this pattern, the average completion times of resources performing in group work, before and after a predefined time, starting when a new boss took over, are analyzed separately. If we observe that resource groups take significantly longer on average after the boss takeover than before, we count this as Boss Mobbing.

Pattern 13. Social borrowing (Social-related)
`Intent:` The purpose of this pattern is to detect agents exploiting other agents by letting them do their work without giving undue credit.
`Problem:` Agents may not be able to perform their work, they may be overloaded or may simply want to increase their performance by offloading work to colleagues.
`Solution:` Agents that exploit other agents must be detected and it should be made sure that they do not work on similar tasks or similar times
`Required Attributes:` Activity, (Start and Complete) Timestamps, Resource, Official working times
`Required Analysis:` Find correlations in performance. Especially, when one resource is present, the performance of another resource is negatively affected.
`Implementation:` To detect this pattern, the average completion times of each resource are calculated, for when each other resource is present at work, and when the same resource is not present. These average times are investigated to check if there is a correlation between the presence at work of a resource and the average completion times of another resource. If a resource performs significantly worse when another resource is present versus when this is absent, that is a hit.

5 Evaluation and Analysis

This section evaluates the feasibility of the design patterns and applies the resulting algorithm to real-world logs, further analyzing and discussing the results.

Evaluation Criteria. We evaluate the applicability of the proposed design patterns by implementing them into a prototype. More specifically we implement each of the thirteen patterns in a dedicated Python script. The scripts are available in the GitHub repository linked in [4]. Our key criterion for evaluation is the effectiveness in translating the design patterns to outcomes. To evaluate this, we proceed in two steps. First, we construct synthetic input in which we represent each weasel behavior, for all the thirteen patterns. We then run our prototype on this synthetic data and improve the implementation until we are able to capture all the behavior. Second, we apply our prototypical implementation on real-world event data made available from the IEEE task force on process mining[1].

The most suitable logs for our analysis were the BPI Challenge 2012 log (BPIC12), BPI Challenge 2017 (BPIC17), both representing a loan application process of a Dutch financial institute, Conformance Checking Challenge 2019 log (CCC19) which represents a medical training process, specifically medical students learning how to install a specific catheter, and the Dutch academic hospital (Hospital) log (only used when a timestamp is not required).

Some patterns require not only an event log, but also a model as an input. In these cases, we create a surrogate by sampling the event log. We make various samples and use them as a reference model. This means that we also repeat the application of the algorithms for each sample and collect the average score.

Analysis of the Results. Next, we analyze the discovered weasel behavior in the real-world event logs. We report the results for each pattern on the event logs where the pattern could be applied. For the sake of space we will only use plots where it is necessary to show comparison. We supply each result with a dedicated analysis, highlighting key information and limitations.

Pattern 1: Activity Deviation. The script implementing the Activity deviation pattern (from expected work) could be applied to BPIC12 (262200 events), BPIC17 (1202267 events), CCC19 (1394 events) and Hospital (150291 events). No activity deviation could be detected in the former three. In the Hospital log, 282 events were flagged as activity deviation, equals to 0.0019%. **Analysis:** A reason for the low occurrence of the activity deviation (as implemented) can be associated to the non-availability of a process model. The sampling technique used 50% of the event log to build a model. Such sample may be too large, and include all the activities that are also present in the log. In this sense, every activity of the log is "expected" in the model.

Pattern 2: Originator Deviation. Originator deviation (i.e., resources who worked on tasks not initially assigned to them) could be applied to BPIC12, BPIC17, CCC19 and Hospital. In this case, while the Hospital log, only showed 1 case of this pattern, CCC19, BPIC17, and BPIC12 presented the highest presence of the pattern, with 13.79, 12.85 and 6.56% of this behavior out of the total possible. The total possible behavior was calculated considering the product of all originators multiplied by all the possible activities. **Analysis:** As in the previous case, given the non-availability of a process model, a sampling technique was used. Because the algorithm samples the log more than once to use the sample as a reference model, it is possible that more instances which present this pattern are detected. This may affect positively the number of hit couples, in case the sampled event log contains too many similar traces to the original.

Pattern 3: Reordering. Re-ordering (i.e., activities performed in an unexpected order) could be applied to BPIC12, BPIC17, CCC19 and Hospital. As

[1] https://www.tf-pm.org/resources/xes-standard/about-xes/event-logs.

the percentage of re-ordering cases is higher than the previous patterns, we display them in Fig. 2. In BPIC12 log, 1213 out of 13087 cases in total are detected (9.27%). In BPIC17 12890 out of the total 31509 (40.91%) and Hospital log 703 out of 1143 total (61.5%) were detected. Finally, in the CCC19 log all the 20 cases got detected (100%). **Analysis:** As in the previous cases, the detection present potentially false positives. This can also be noted by the 100% value score on the CCC19 event log. However, given the non-availability of a reference process model, this is not possible to measure.

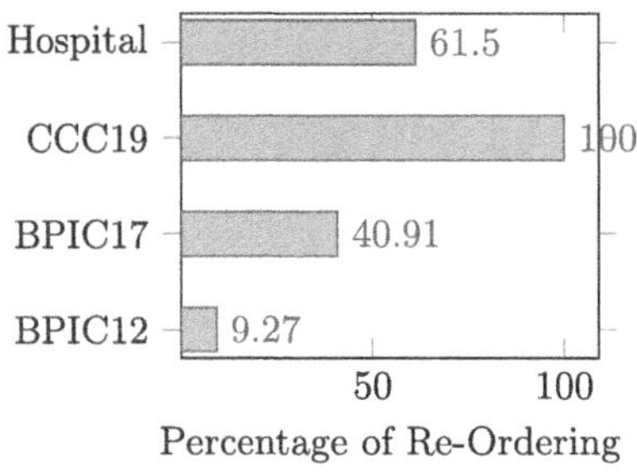

Fig. 2. Re-Ordering percentage in different logs

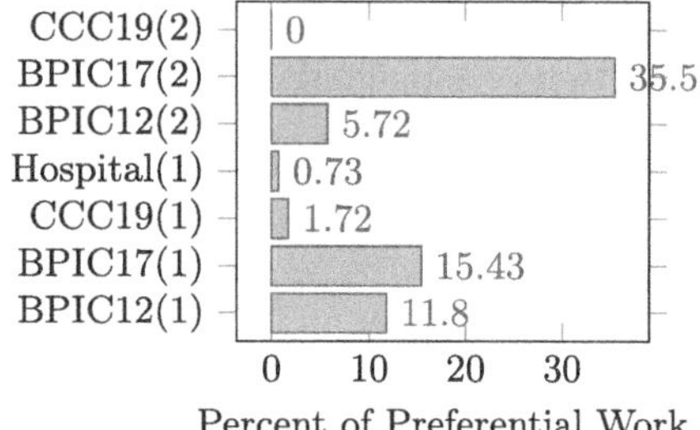

Fig. 3. Preferential Work Selection percentage in different logs

Pattern 4: Preferential Work Selection. This pattern occurs when i) certain activities are chosen more frequently than others by certain resources or ii) when resources start new activities while still working on other ones. We applied both conditions separately to the to BPIC12, BPIC17, CCC19 and Hospital. Condition ii) could not be applied to Hospital as the start timestamp is not available (thus, it is not possible to understand if resources are working in any other task). We report the results in Fig. 3. The number in parentheses expresses which condition was measures. That is, BPIC12(1) means that condition i) was measured. We noticed here that the BPI challenges event logs present the higher occurrence of this pattern. **Analysis:** The values observed in the logs may present false positives or negatives, as the classification of normal frequency depends on a threshold value. Domain experts are required to set this value optimally.

Pattern 5: Performance Masking. Given the requirement on start timestamp, this pattern could not be applied to the Hospital log. In other logs it was detected as follows. BPIC12 is affected as 16583 events over 262200 total (6.32%), BPIC17 as 47608 events out of 1202267 (3.96%), and CCC19 as 37 events over 1394 (2.65%). **Analysis:** The percentages are threshold based. A domain-expert can help setting them more optimal results.

Pattern 6: Performance Blow-Out. We report the results in Fig. 4. The numbers in parentheses denote which condition of Performance Blow-Out the corresponding bar represents: 1 for the first condition (different resources, same activities) and 2 for the second condition (same resources, same activities).

Analysis: No instances of Performance Blow-Out are detected in the CCC19 log. In contrast, the remaining two logs exhibit significant proportions of Performance Blow-Out. The proportion is particularly pronounced in BPIC17, with approximately twice the percentage of signelled instances versus BPIC12, for both conditions of the pattern. These findings reveal that resources perform certain activities slower over time in the two logs.

Pattern 7: Overwork Hiding. This algorithm was applied to BPIC12, BPIC17, CCC19, and Hospital. The detection was as follows 80250 detected events over 262200 for BPIC12 (30.61%), 298728 events over 1202267 total for BPIC17 (24.85%), 1394 over 1394 for CCC19 (100%), and 150291 over 150291 for Hospital (100%). **Analysis:** There are two primary factors that could contribute to false positives and negatives. Firstly, the code assigns default working times of 09:00 to 17:00 to all resources in the four logs due to the absence of predefined working times. This can lead to events registered within the true working hours being falsely detected as Overwork Hiding. However, this issue could also result in false negatives, where events occurring within the default working hours are not flagged despite being outside of the actual working hours for the respective resource. Timezones recorded in the timestamps are a further source of threat.

Pattern 8: Goldplating. We report the deception results of this pattern in Fig. 5. The numbers in parentheses denote which condition of Gold Plating the corresponding bar represents. Conditions are variants with a significantly i) longer duration and ii) rare activities. The highest percentage of hits for both conditions was observed in the BPIC12 log. Specifically, out of 4371 process variants in the BPIC12 log, 927 were found to take significantly longer to complete than others, and 2742 were found to contain a significantly rare activity. In the BPIC17 log, although fewer, still significant proportions of positives were identified, with 2699 and 6447 out of 15930 total process variants. Similarly, in the CCC19 log 1 and 10 out of 20 process variants were detected. **Analysis:** These patterns we always possible to detect in the real-world event logs. The significance threshold was set to 1%. Yet, it was still possible to detect this pattern.

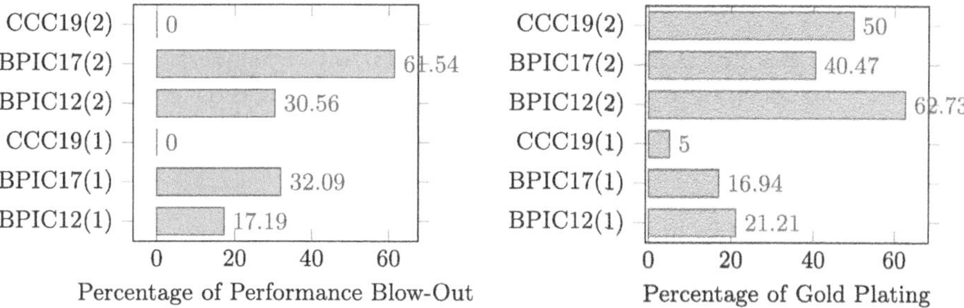

Fig. 4. Performance Blow-Out

Fig. 5. Gold Plating percentage

Pattern 9: Idling. Durations are analyzed for this pattern, so the Hospital log is not considered. Three conditions are calculated: i) count of instances where a resource requires significantly more time for an activity compared to the average resource, ii) resources that require significantly more time for a particular activity compared to their average time for other activities and iii) instances where resources take significantly long breaks without registering any activity. The results are as follows. BPIC12 (i, ii, iii) = (186, 224, 783), BPIC17 (i, ii, iii) = (455, 579, 397), and CCC19 (i, ii, iii) = (0, 0, 0). **Analysis:** No instances of Idling were detected in the CCC19 log for any of the three conditions. The most significant tendency was found in the BPIC12 log, where approximately 31.52% of possible resource/activity combinations were flagged as resources taking long breaks. The proportions of the remaining two conditions in the same log, as well as all three conditions in the BPIC17 log, are between 7% and 15%.

Pattern 10: Social Loafing. This pattern was applied to CCC19, BPIC12, and BPIC2017. No social loafing pattern was detected in the CCC19 log. On the contrary, 42 out of 69 resources in the BPIC12 log and 105 out of 149 resources in the BPIC17 log exhibited such behavior. **Analysis:** Considerable difference was found between BPIC12 and BPIC17 event logs. Respectively, they are affected as much as 68.87% and 70.47%. Possible false positives may be attributed in part to the threshold, as its value determines the extent to which the average completion time of a resource must deviate between group and individual work. It is set to 10 min. Furthermore, the group work detection function also presents potential for false positives and negatives. This function checks for four conditions, which may not 100% accurately identify group work flags for all events, leading to potentially skewed results.

Pattern 11: Peer Mobbing. This pattern was applied to CCC19, BPIC12, BPIC2017, and Hospital. Peer mobbing was only detected in BPIC12, with a 110 instances. **Analysis:** Two threshold values are used in the code for this pattern, which bear potential for causing false positives and negatives again, as the ideal value to use for threshold values always depends on the context and is subjective.

Pattern 12: Boss Mobbing. Among the 13 patterns, Boss Mobbing could not be applied to the real-world data, as there is no information which resources play this role and since when. No realistic assumption could be made about it.

Pattern 13: Social Borrowing. This pattern was applied to CCC19 and BPIC2017. No social borrowing was detected in CCC19. BPIC17 presented 1192 cases of this pattern, equivalent to 5.36%. **Analysis:** A resource may receive multiple flags for a time interval in which it worked slower, especially if there are other resources whose working times align with that interval. This situation can yield false positives. Additionally, the setting of a threshold value to define when the average time difference of the borrowing resource is considered significant, may lead to false positives and negatives.

Table 2. Summary of the percentage of each pattern (P1–13) in event logs.

	P1	P2	P3	P4	P5	P6	P7	P8	P9	P10	P11	P12	P13
BPIC12	0	6.56	61.5	5.72	6.32	30.56	30.61	62.73	31.52	60.87	4	-	-
BPIC17	0	12.85	100	35.51	3.96	61.54	24.85	40.47	10.24	70.47	0	-	5.36
CCC19	0	13.79	40.91	1.72	2.65	0	1	50	0	0	0	-	0
Hospital	0.0019	0.004	9.27	0.73	-	-	1	-	-		0	-	-

Discussion. Table 2 summarizes main results of the detection of the patterns in the real-world event logs. While subject to limitations, this paper presents a first successful implementation of the thirteen behavioral patterns to detect inappropriate behavior at work using event logs. The results indicate varying levels of occurrence and distribution of these patterns across different datasets. While limitations may exist due to assumptions made when applying our algorithms to real-world data, it is still possible to observe a certain degree of presence of inappropriate behavior. This is useful to raise flags for further investigation.

Our results also showcase the challenges associated with detecting these patterns, such as the potential for false positives and negatives due to the subjective nature of threshold values. For instance, the *Performance Blow-Out* pattern's detection relies heavily on comparing completion times of similar tasks across different resources. Variations in these times may not always indicate inappropriate behavior but could be influenced by external factors such as task complexity or resource skill levels. Furthermore, the implementation of these patterns revealed the necessity for contextual information. To avoid misclassification, domain knowledge must be taken into account.

6 Conclusion

In this study, we have developed and implemented a set of thirteen behavioral patterns to detect inappropriate behaviors within organizational event logs, using design patterns to guide our specification. Our results on real-world datasets reveal various significant occurrences of specific patterns that may have potential impacts in the organization.

The implications of our study point towards proactive management and improvement of work conditions within an organization. Future work should focus on refining the behavioral patterns and validate their applicability across various organizational settings.

Acknowledgment. This research was supported by the Einstein Foundation Berlin under grant EPP-2019-524, by the German Federal Ministry of Education and Research under grant 16DII133, and by Deutsche Forschungsgemeinschaft under grants 496119880 (VisualMine) and 531115272 (ProImpact).

References

1. van der Aalst, W.M.P.: Process Mining - Data Science in Action, 2nd edn. Springer, Heidelberg (2016)
2. van der Aalst, W.M.P., Reijers, H.A., Song, M.: Discovering social networks from event logs. Comput. Supported Coop. Work (CSCW) **14**, 549–593 (2005)
3. van der Aalst, W.M.: Process mining and simulation: a match made in heaven! In: SummerSim, pp. 4–1 (2018)
4. Bala, S.: Towards mining inappropriate behaviour at work (2024). https://doi.org/10.5281/zenodo.12656557
5. del-Río-Ortega, A., Resinas, M., Cortés, A.R.: Defining process performance indicators: an ontological approach. In: OTM Conferences (1), pp. 555–572 (2010)
6. Ferreira, D.R., Alves, C.: Discovering user communities in large event logs. In: Business Process Management Workshops (1), pp. 123–134 (2011)
7. Gamma, E., Helm, R., Johnson, R.E., Vlissides, J.M.: Design patterns: abstraction and reuse of object-oriented design (reprint). In: Software Pioneers, pp. 701–717. Springer, Heidelberg (2002)
8. Lashkevich, K., Milani, F., Chapela-Campa, D., Suvorau, I., Dumas, M.: Why am I waiting? Data-driven analysis of waiting times in business processes. In: CAiSE, pp. 174–190 (2023)
9. Leyer, M., ter Hofstede, A.H.M., Syed, R.: Detecting weasels at work: a theory-driven behavioural process mining approach. In: BPM (Forum). Lecture Notes in Business Information Processing, vol. 490, pp. 337–354. Springer, Cham (2023)
10. Martin, N., Depaire, B., Caris, A.: The use of process mining in business process simulation model construction - structuring the field. Bus. Inf. Syst. Eng. **58**(1), 73–87 (2016)
11. Meckling, W.H., Jensen, M.C.: Theory of the firm. Managerial Behavior, Agency Costs and Ownership Structure (1976)
12. Mustroph, H., Winter, K., Rinderle-Ma, S.: Social network mining from natural language text and event logs for compliance deviation detection. In: CoopIS, pp. 347–365 (2023)
13. Song, M., van der Aalst, W.M.P.: Towards comprehensive support for organizational mining. Decis. Support Syst. **46**(1), 300–317 (2008)
14. Song, M., van der Aalst, W.M.: Supporting process mining by showing events at a glance. In: Proceedings of the 17th Annual Workshop on Information Technologies and Systems (WITS), pp. 139–145 (2007)

TrustOps: Continuously Building Trustworthy Software

Eduardo Brito[1(✉)], Fernando Castillo[2], Pille Pullonen-Raudvere[1], and Sebastian Werner[2]

[1] Cybernetica AS, Estonia Mäealuse 2/1, 12618 Tallinn, Estonia
{eduardo.brito,pille.pullonen-raudvere}@cyber.ee
[2] Information Systems Engineering, TU Berlin, Einsteinufer 17, Berlin, Germany
{fc,sw}@ise.tu-berlin.de

Abstract. Software services play a crucial role in daily life, with automated actions determining access to resources and information. Trusting service providers to perform these actions fairly and accurately is essential, yet challenging for users to verify. Even with publicly available codebases, the rapid pace of development and the complexity of modern deployments hinder the understanding and evaluation of service actions, including for experts. Hence, current trust models rely heavily on the assumption that service providers follow best practices and adhere to laws and regulations, which is increasingly impractical and risky, leading to undetected flaws and data leaks.

In this paper, we argue that gathering verifiable evidence during software development and operations is needed for creating a new trust model. Therefore, we present TrustOps, an approach for continuously collecting verifiable evidence in all phases of the software life cycle, relying on and combining already existing tools and trust-enhancing technologies to do so. For this, we introduce the adaptable core principles of TrustOps and provide a roadmap for future research and development.

Keywords: trustworthy software · continuous software engineering · evidence-based life cycle

1 Introduction

Software services pervade many areas of daily life where actions, sometimes automatically, decide how we can access resources, e.g., payment services decide if we are creditworthy enough to buy train tickets, or social media websites decide which news to show us. Users must trust that service providers act fairly and that actions are performed correctly. However, users hardly have the means to evaluate how these services were built or provided to them [10]. Even if publicly available codebases were present, a typical user cannot evaluate them. Magnified by the accelerated pace of modern development practices like DevOps [1], the complexity of these distributed systems, consisting of multiple, independently

M. Kaczmarek-Heß et al. (Eds.): EDOC 2024 Workshops, LNBIP 537, pp. 53–67, 2025.
https://doi.org/10.1007/978-3-031-79059-1_4

developed and configured components, makes independent verification of service delivery even challenging for experts.

Hence, current trust models largely rely on the assumption that service providers follow best practices, adhere to laws and regulations, and that public audit processes will catch issues before they impact users. This reliance on a few large organizations for trust is becoming increasingly impractical and risky, introducing the potential for undetected exploited flaws, unintentional data leaks, or risks due to supply chain attacks, such as the recent XZ vulnerability[1]. Not only must developers employ practices like security tests and well-defined processes, but users should also be able to verify that a service they use was tested and followed all established procedures.

We argue that these challenges necessitate a paradigm shift towards verifiable development and operational processes, where stakeholders can independently verify the integrity and authenticity of such actions. This new approach, which we term TrustOps, aims to address the gaps left by current methodologies, such as DevSecOps [20] and Continuous Compliance [6]. While these approaches incorporate security practices into the development lifecycle, they do not fully address the need for comprehensive, publicly verifiable evidence of the entire service development process. Therefore, we see TrustOps as an addition to these methodologies, focused on ensuring that these practices cannot be bypassed when delivering services. Moreover, we do not attempt to, or assume that risks or flaws can be entirely prevented, but the chain of events that caused a flaw can be followed and discovered early.

TrustOps advocates for implementing or using existing robust, auditable mechanisms that track changes, combine and aggregate development evidence (e.g., change logs, reviews), and collect and provide evidence of test executions and policy actions. The evidence, collected at each stage of the development process, must be independently and automatically verifiable to create an easy-to-consume audit trail. Particularly, in this paper, we:

- Present evidence-based trustworthiness principles that enable the build-up of authentic, attestable, and actionable evidence during the software life cycle.
- Detail the use and application of TrustOps, based on examples and scenarios, along typical DevOps phases.
- Highlight a set of research objectives needed to foster, improve, and adopt TrustOps.

In the remainder of this paper we first present related work in Sect. 2. Then, in Sect. 3, we introduce the main processes of evidence-based trustworthiness, before providing exemplary application scenarios in Sect. 4. Lastly, in Sect. 5, the evidence life cycle is mapped to DevOps, defining the TrustOps approach, with research challenges outlined in Sect. 6, before concluding in Sect. 7.

[1] (CVE-2024-3094) https://nvd.nist.gov/vuln/detail/CVE-2024-3094.

2 Related Work

Trust, as defined by various scholars [9,10,16], is a complex interplay of beliefs, expectations, and reliability. In software systems, trust is the reliance on software's ability to meet specified requirements, even amid uncertainty. It is grounded in the expectation of consistent behavior, despite unpredictable conditions [9,10]. Software trustworthiness involves building confidence in its ability to fulfill intended functions, ensuring reliability, security, and consistency over time [8,9]. The multifaceted nature of trust in software reflects sociological, psychological, philosophical, and computational perspectives [10], making it a socio-technical phenomenon shaped by human perceptions and organizational structures [21].

Adherence to industry standards has been contributing to enhance perceived trust and establish globally recognized quality assurance [6,9]. ISO, IEC, IEEE standards serve as benchmarks for best practices in information security and privacy, aiming, for instance, at protecting Personally Identifiable Information (PII), deploying Privacy Information Management Systems (PIMS), integrating trustworthy elements into software, establishing security for industrial automation and control systems, or standardizing life cycle processes like DevOps and Agile development [11–14].

Additionally, trust mechanisms integrated into mainstream development processes like DevOps have been gaining increasing attention. Various approaches, including DevSecOps, DevPrivOps, and VeriDevOps, have emerged to embed robust security measures, privacy considerations, and trust-building protocols throughout the software life cycle. DevSecOps emphasizes security testing integration at different stages [20], DevPrivOps incorporates privacy engineering [7], while VeriDevOps enhances automation for system protection [5]. Complemented by EU regulations for electronic services, adherence to standards, development methodologies, and compliance protocols are known to enhance trustworthiness, mitigate risks, and build robust stakeholder relationships across the software supply chain [6,9]. These practices will be explored further in this paper, with TrustOps aiming to unify and streamline trust automation, integrated with generalized methodologies like DevOps, across the entire software life cycle.

3 Evidence-Based Trustworthiness

In this section, we first outline the objectives we seek in establishing trustworthy principles in the software life cycle, and then describe the evidence-based process that builds the foundations of TrustOps.

3.1 Objectives

The core objective of TrustOps is to create verifiable development practices, thus enabling all stakeholders in the development and usage process to verify who, when, where, why, or how decisions are made, how changes are rolled out to

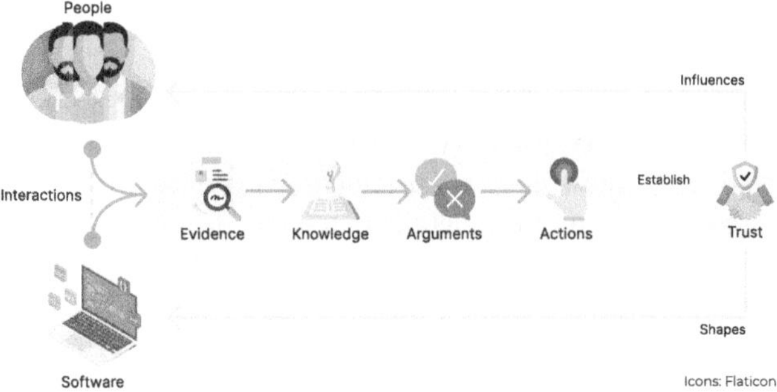

Fig. 1. Trust as a socio-technical phenomenon [21], result of an evidence-based process, that influences people, software, and their interactions [6,19].

users, and how users consume these changes. Ron Ross et al. [19] emphasize the importance of evidence in building trustworthiness. Evidence is, therefore, a fundamental pillar supporting trust and pertains to the availability of verifiable and credible information that vindicates software's claims and behavior [10,19]. This assurance is further fortified by the roles played by authentication and integrity in substantiating the evidence [8,9]. Moreover, while verifiability facilitates systematic scrutiny of trust claims [3], authorization governs access rights [15], and distribution, as articulated by [2], enhances security and reliability guarantees.

Interactions between people and software often exhibit an interplay of these concepts, as illustrated in Fig. 1. This sets possible avenues for the automated trust paradigm that TrustOps aims to establish. Such paradigm is finding its basis in the development of robust electronic and cryptographic mechanisms with ability to establish secure and verifiable interactions [2,3]. Through cryptographic protocols, different trust models may be instantiated, allowing automated verification of software claims, while ensuring that the truth is not easily manipulated or fabricated. The principles outlined in [2], such as the use of secure hardware, consensus mechanisms, or append-only logs, lay the groundwork for constructing distributed-trust systems. As technology advances, other automated trust mechanisms may further enhance the efficiency, security, and reliability of trustworthy software, reducing the reliance on subjective human assessments and further solidifying trust in the digital landscape [3]. TrustOps also aims to provide verifiability without compromising confidentiality and privacy. With recent improvements in practical cryptography [3,4], such as Trusted Execution Environments (TEEs) or Zero-Knowledge Proofs (ZKPs), these so far opposing objectives can be met. TEEs use hardware-based secure computing to process data securely, while ZKPs allow proving the truth of a statement without revealing the actual data. In TrustOps, we highlight that finding a balance between **auditability**, **verifiability** and **confidentiality** is key. Moreover, not every software system requires the full range or full depth of these qualities. Thus, TrustOps should also be flexible in the range of qualities it can add to software development and operation.

3.2 The Life Cycle of Evidence

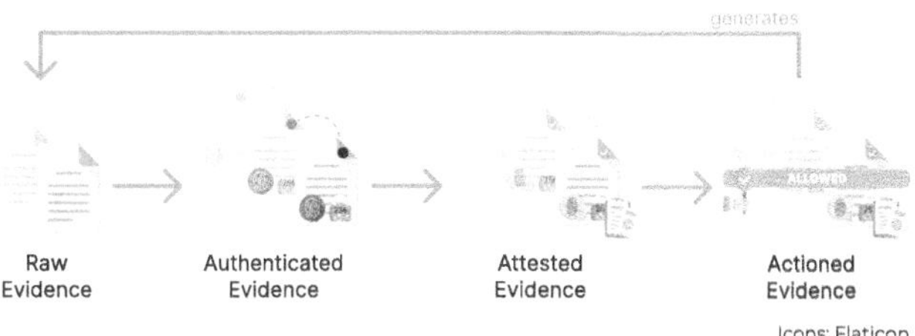

Fig. 2. The continuous life cycle process of enhancing evidence. Interactions with software generate evidence that can be authenticated to produce meaningful knowledge and attest to claims about the software's development or operation, leading to informed actions that can, in turn, produce more evidence.

TrustOps stands on an evidence-based approach that depends on the evolution and enhancement of evidence, as depicted in Fig. 2, for continuously building trustworthiness, throughout the software life cycle.

From Raw to Authenticated Evidence. At the core of TrustOps is the principle of evidence generation, emphasizing the generation of meaningful data and artifacts, throughout the software life cycle. Evidence refers to any information attesting to software events or behavior [19]. For instance, some cases may benefit from tracking code changes and commit metadata, others from storing build logs, deployment details, infrastructure configurations, monitoring data, or end-user feedback. The goal is to gather comprehensive and diverse sets of records, promoting transparency and accountability, to meet eventual auditability and verifiability demands.

Throughout its generation, raw evidence should be enhanced with properties that produce knowledge, such as metadata, or attributes indicating who, when, or where specific events happened. However, a generally trustworthy system should ensure that the generated evidence is not only extensive and meaningful but also genuine. Current approaches establish that such trust should be anchored and validated through identity verification, maintaining the authenticity of critical evidence and processes [9]. Examples, taken from DevSecOps, include authenticating commits and having branch rules verifying contributor identities in version control systems [17].

Integrity, another principle linked to trust, refers to the unicity, consistency, and reliability of data and processes [8]. It ensures that data is unique to any moment and remains unaltered over time, and that related processes intentionally operate with dependability over past knowledge. Accurate, reliable, and tamper-proof information generation is crucial for informed decisions and structural risk mitigation [19]. Both authentication and integrity may rely on cryptographic mechanisms to create unique digital footprints, ensure data consistency, and prevent or, at least, make evident any unauthorized alterations [2]. Digital signatures, proofs of properties, and other mechanisms can be applied to source code, configuration files, documentation, build artifacts, telemetry, and more.

Consequently, this identity-centric approach enables authorization, accountability, and secure evidence distribution, facilitating process automation and the trustworthy generation of new knowledge about software systems [21]. In short, evidence not only forms extensive knowledge, but, through these authentication and integrity mechanisms, can also become genuine and consistently reliable, turning into authenticated evidence that can then be attested.

From Authenticated to Attested Evidence. Following its enhancement, authenticated evidence becomes a valuable asset for informed decision-making, supporting the development process. Authentic evidence can be used to make claims about software properties or events, which can be verified by interested parties, like users or developers, to ensure specific claims are satisfied or establish agreements and coordination over operations [19]. Nevertheless, storing evidence must balance trust demands, privacy considerations, or operational capacity, making evidence collection, enhancement, and management central to TrustOps.

Verifiability refers to stakeholders' ability to independently and succinctly validate evidence, actions, and results, ensuring credibility and trustworthiness through transparent means [3]. Verifiability follows a proof paradigm, where one side convinces the other of the veracity of properties of data or software. Trust begins with authenticating evidence, followed by automated and attestable proofs using technologies like TEEs or ZKPs, to enable, for instance, automated audits, external artifact validation, or reproducible compliance checks [6]. Enabling continuous verifiability allows for automated argumentation and attestation over the trustworthiness of software, enhancing the system's security, reliability, and scalability, and impacting both its objective and perceived trust [4].

Consensus is also crucial for trustworthiness, especially in distributed settings with different stakeholders holding distributed information, resources and responsibilities [2]. Consensus involves stakeholders collectively agreeing on the validity of arguments over software functionality or behavior. The goal is to ensure software systems meet desired trust levels for all parties, by attesting to shared evidence and agreeing on the validity of claims and actions [8,19]. Examples are database replication, distributed ledgers, decentralized key management, or version control systems, which store and act upon shared evidence, enabling its distributed attestation.

From Attested to Actioned Evidence. Once evidence is attested and consensus is reached in distributed settings, informed and automated actions can follow. A typical subsequent action, familiar to the software landscape, is authorization, which involves defining and granting permissions to verified entities, ensuring that only approved actors or processes access specific resources [15]. Code repositories, deployment configurations, or monitoring infrastructure are resources that usually require policy definitions and access control mechanisms. Authorization entails granting permissions based on attested evidence, conceptualizing roles, policies, or attributes [19], and access control mechanisms ensure these permissions are upheld and not circumvented. Following the integration of authenticated and attested evidence, one can, for instance, define the set of actions and access policies for execution environments or roll-out permissions, like ensuring only known, tested, or verified versions of software can be deployed to production. In addition to authorization, further possible actions can be taken upon attested evidence. For accountability, observability, or explainability purposes, attested evidence can also build a chain of verifiable actions that led to or created an observed outcome. Ultimately, such actions feed the continuous cycle by generating more evidence as their output.

To conclude, evolving and enhancing evidence shapes trust, security, and reliability throughout the software life cycle. The outlined evidence-based processes address current trustworthiness challenges and lay the groundwork for adapting to future complexities. The next sections show how these processes can be applied in various scenarios, extending methodologies like DevOps to materialize TrustOps as a continuous set of processes for building trustworthy software.

4 Application Scenarios

In this section, we introduce three scenarios that showcase motivating examples and different possibilities of integrating the evidence-based concepts of TrustOps throughout the life cycle of various types of software.

4.1 Trustworthy Open Software

Open-source tools, libraries, and web repositories inherently promote transparency due to their open nature. Already aligned with a share of TrustOps vision — the source code, collaboration data, contributors and their identities are generally public, roles and rules are publicly assigned, and certain surface metrics are openly scrutinizable. Genuine and trustworthy evidence is, therefore, a widely available byproduct of the public and open collaboration, grounded on the authenticity, integrity, and distributed guarantees provided by modern version control systems. However, some repositories, wielding considerable influence over critical internet systems, deviate from best practices in maintainability and security. Successful projects like the Linux kernel or OpenSSL serve as a positive example, showing transparency and security commitment despite challenges like the Heartbleed vulnerability[2]. Conversely, the EventStream incident in the Node.js ecosystem[3], or the Log4Shell vulnerability in Java[4], highlight the need for stringent measures and community vigilance.

To ease this, maintainers may be required to follow DevSecOps to integrate security practices into every stage of the CI/CD pipeline, promoting early detection and remediation of security issues, continuous monitoring, and compliance

[2] https://heartbleed.com/.

[3] https://blog.npmjs.org/post/180565383195/details-about-the-event-stream-incident.

[4] https://cve.mitre.org/cgi-bin/cvename.cgi?name=CVE-2021-44228.

with security standards [17]. Yet, users have to actually review this open activity to truly benefit from all this public evidence. Hence, a more comprehensive and consequent application of TrustOps may reduce or automate the needed review activity. Further trust enhancements could be integrated, for instance, by pipelining these CI/CD processes within TEEs, with public attestation of the testing and release artifacts, and assurances that all security controls, compliance checks, and vulnerability assessments were properly executed. These trust enhancements and their effects may eventually propagate across the entire software supply chain, as elaborated next. Nevertheless, consideration should be given to finding a balance between heightened trust measures and preserving the collaborative, open, fast-evolving nature of these projects.

4.2 Enhancing Trust in Service Ecosystems

In today's service ecosystems, users can select from a variety of hosted open-sourced services, allowing them to review the code and benefit from public scrutiny unparalleled with close-sourced options. Here, TrustOps can play a critical role in extending this increased trust also into the operation of these open-sourced services. Emerging regulation often necessitate demonstrating adherence to specific requirements, such as the storage and processing of all data of users in the EU within European servers [18]. Applying TrustOps in the operation phase can automate the attestation of such requirements, for example, by collecting and providing attested evidence from the deployment environment for services like MongoDB Atlas, an open-source database service offered by MongoDB.com and other cloud vendors such as Google[5].

Today, each service vendor delineates Service Level Agreements (SLAs) and contractual terms governing data treatment, processors, and hosting locations. However, users inherently rely on trust in these vendors, which may be hard to attest. While the utilization of open-source software may instill confidence, the veracity of vendor implementation remains uncertain. TrustOps mitigates this uncertainty by fostering verifiable evidence of execution. Runtime observation tools, such as tracing mechanisms, container inspection and log aggregation tools, can be instrumented to collect and authenticate evidence, such as what versions are deployed, which servers handle a specific customer request and where data or logs are transferred to. This would turn so far vague statements in privacy policies[6] into records every customer can verify. However, such transparency may create potential conflicts between the provider's need to keep business secrets and the public's need to verify regulatory compliance. To resolve such conflicts, TrustOps advocates for a synthesis of ZKPs or selective disclosure protocols to ensure user-relevant verifiability, without compromising vendors' proprietary information. Striking this balance necessitates advancements in observability tooling and evidence-collection methodologies, as well as a collaborative effort

[5] https://cloud.google.com/mongodb.

[6] "Other optional tools in MongoDB Atlas require customer query log data to transit through our US-based servers." – https://www.mongodb.com/legal/privacy.

between service providers and users and a commitment from service vendors to enhance transparency and verifiability. While this shows how openly developed software can strongly benefit from TrustOps principles in both development and delivery, we also see benefits in internal organization development processes.

4.3 Internal and External Organizational Trust

Particularly concerning software companies with closed-source products and platforms, trustworthiness in the software ecosystem encompasses varying degrees of transparency. As technology advances, it becomes imperative for such entities to explore mechanisms ensuring verifiable trustworthiness, impacting reputation, lawfulness, and potential business development [21]. The establishment of trust may occur both internally and externally, with organizational values and business decisions influencing the boundaries between these domains.

Internally, companies can strive for attestable quality of artifacts and accountability across teams and departments, incorporating elements like verifiable test pipelines, authenticated builds and releases, authorization, or monitoring infrastructure, during development, integration, or deployment. Trustworthiness requirements should be elicited before adopting such TrustOps practices, following a concrete trust and thread modelling approach. Moreover, software companies assess performance using diverse metrics, including pull request and code review statistics, or deployment and quality assessments, serving as potential operational evidence to be transformed into attested trust assurances. Automating attestation of these metrics fastens and strengthens trust in the delivered software and its building teams. However, this requires a judicious approach to prevent compromising other business aspects, for instance, in the spirit of site reliability engineering, with trust budgets instead of error budgets.

Externally, trust in software organizations is shaped by users and stakeholders, influenced by numerous factors, variables, and participants within the software ecosystem [21]. Nevertheless, a shift towards automated and verifiable claims holds the promise of translating abstract notions of trust into concrete data points. Verifiability of software and library versions, certified compliance with standards, and other recurring auditability tasks leading to public and organizational assessments are potential planes of automation and verifiability [5,6,17]. Enabling the publication and verification of authenticated evidence generated during the TrustOps phases has the potential to increase organizational trustworthiness to internal and external stakeholders. Hence, to foster holistic trust in the services delivered, software companies can integrate TrustOps principles and follow the proposed approaches, but stakeholders may also have the agency to demand assurances regarding the incorporation of these practices, ensuring a balance between companies' business interests and everyone's privacy, security, and trust requirements.

5 TrustOps

TrustOps aims to enrich the software life cycle by continuously applying the evidence-based life cycle (Sect. 3) throughout the phases of DevOps. Overall, the aim is to accumulate and combine evidence from prior phases to achieve complex but automated attestation and authorization processes, thus enabling the possibilities sketched in Sect. 4. Similarly to DevOps itself, TrustOps can be applied as needed and can use as many or as few layers of trust-enhancing technologies as required. In the following, we present each of the DevOps Phases [1] and discuss how TrustOps could be applied, exemplified in Fig. 3.

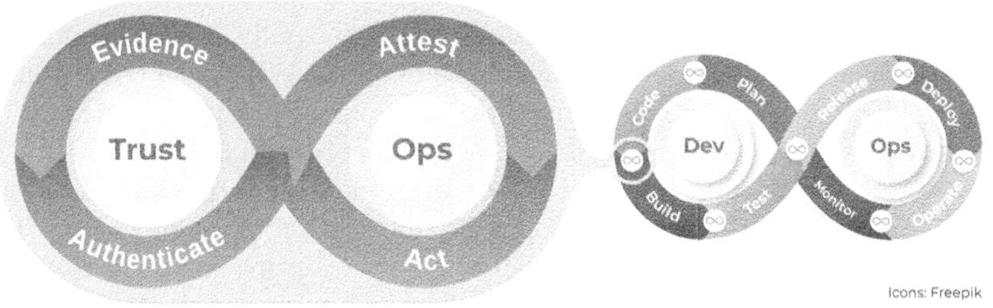

Fig. 3. Overview of the idealized TrustOps life cycle, integrated within DevOps phases.

Plan: During the planning phase, features and changes are typically put into the software development backlog. These proposals are considered evidence in TrustOps and can be captured. The aim is to determine how a change to a software artifact was introduced, starting with the issue or ticket that caused it. Moreover, any policies related to the approval or change management process may be evident as well.

Once evidence is collected, it can be enriched to create authentic planning evidence, for example, by signing the issue or ticket, or providing immutable logs of the decision-making process. This allows the remainder of the development process to be linked to the original issue or ticket and, thus, the cause of a change, even if an issue or ticket is closed or deleted later.

Lastly, authenticated evidence should be attested to be used in conjunction with other planning tools or to authorize or trigger the execution of planned changes, e.g., by checking if a user story meets project standards, is signed by at least one senior developer, or was discussed in a sprint planning meeting.

Code: Coding is the central part of any software project and, thus, also the central source of evidence in TrustOps. At the core of this phase, code may be linked, in a verifiable way, to the developers that introduced the changes.

Moreover, considering the previous phase, we can also link code changes to planned changes, i.e., issues. Depending on the scenario, this may also include the collection of evidence about the development environment, usage of tools (e.g., linters, unit tests), and even the reliance on AI-based code assistants that could introduce intended or unintended changes. Some software tools can already exploit prior attested planning evidence, for instance, by linking and referencing the issues in the commit messages and by authenticating the assigned developers. Similarly, development environments could be augmented to provide evidence of the environment, tools used, and tests run.

This authenticated evidence can then be used to create succinct proofs of correctness, e.g., verifying that a change was linted, tested, corresponds to a planned change, and is signed by the developer. Finally, successfully attesting to these proofs may trigger further phases in the development life cycle.

Build: During the build phase, we follow the automated DevOps principles, which typically rely on CI/CD pipelines for building releasable software artifacts. Evidence represents the input to the build process, including the code and the configuration of the build system. The build process may incorporate or connect the evidence from both the code and planning phases. This ensures that these typically self-contained artifacts remain authentic and attestable, in relation to the evidence from preceding phases and the TrustOps processes as a whole.

One way to produce authenticated builds in this phase would be to run the process inside TEEs, allowing later attestation of non-tampered builds. However, other mechanisms could be similarly valid, depending on the needs of the specific software. Additional attestations could combine and verify the collected evidence of all prior phases to ensure that a build fully complies with standards before pushing the build artifact to the test or release phases.

Test: Some contexts require thoroughly tested software, and the record of these tests should be present when reviewing any released version. Here, similar steps to the build process can be taken, e.g., recording evidence of the test environment and the tests that were actually run, or, if possible, even running tests in TEEs to attest to the test reports and ensure test results were not manipulated.

The aim is, thus, very similar to the build phase, to ensure that a tested build is backed by evidence of the prior phases and that the tests themselves are also backed by authenticated evidence.

Release: Once an artifact is built and tested, it can be released. Here, one of TrustOps' main goals can be seen, as now a released artifact can be backed by a chain of evidence that can be used to verify its authenticity and correctness, ensuring that the release is of claimed quality. Privacy-preserving technologies can also be used, e.g., by utilizing ZKPs, the adherence to specific project polices for testing and reviewing could be proven to the public, without revealing where tests were performed or which person reviewed changes, thus, removing the need to share confidential or private evidence without losing the ability to act on it.

Especially in fully open and public development scenarios, this provides the opportunity to attach evidence to publicly verifiable proofs. These proofs can be checked for compliance, beyond simple hash-based integrity, before they are used as dependencies elsewhere, e.g., to make supply chain attacks more costly.

Deploy: During the deployment phase, artifacts are typically deployed for use. Here, the extent of TrustOps involvement strongly depends on the type of application. In most cases, we assume that both the build artifacts as well as the deployment code are part of the same repository and, thus, are backed by clear lineage on how changes to the deployment were made. However, during this phase, some additional environment information may be needed to turn a deployment template into a concrete and verifiable deployment.

At the minimum, however, we could collect who authorized a deployment and collect a record of what artifact is deployed, including the verification of its correctness and authenticity that was built up in the prior phases. Furthermore, this phase could provide evidence of the deployment environment, e.g., outputs of reproducible deployment mechanisms such as NIX or Docker images and the configuration of the deployment environment. During deployment, the management of the identity of the environment and operators is also a critical component that may require attestation.

Operate: During the operating phase, it is critical to enable reasonable observability to collect authentic evidence. This may include the verification of execution environments and the identification of users. Moreover, this phase will likely produce the highest amount of raw evidence, typically in the form of logs, metrics, or traces. Hence, the evidence collected in this phase is likely to be the most diverse and the most sensitive. Thus, the use of privacy-preserving mechanisms is a key enabler in managing the amount and sensitivity of operational raw evidence. However, developers and operators should make sure that only the necessary evidence is collected, authenticated, and attested. The evidence collected may also be linked to all prior evidence that led to the current state of the software system. Therefore, this phase may require a new category of tooling to support the efficient collection of runtime attestable evidence that goes beyond existing observability solutions.

Monitor: In this last phase, the collected evidence can be used to link and provide verifiability feedback to users or operators, e.g., giving them the means to automatically attest if a software deployment is the same as the one they expect, operating in the way they expect, thus, providing the necessary assurances to trust the running software and its operators.

The evidence collected in this and prior phases can be used to feed the cycle again, as already authenticated input for the planning phase, e.g., utilizing the built chain of evidence as clear information on what interaction caused a fault in the running software that should be fixed.

6 Research and TrustOps Adoption Challenges

This section highlights the main foreseeable challenges of adopting TrustOps, in three categories: evidence management, TrustOps integration and usability.

Evidence collected for TrustOps may contain highly sensitive information or be used for other purposes than TrustOps. Hence, we must consider how to store, manage and use evidence in a privacy-preserving manner while minimizing the overhead of handling it. Different types and life cycle stages of evidence make proposing a standard for evidence management challenging. Different evidence generation and management tools can also cause interoperability issues. Consequently, further work must establish best practices for which evidence to collect and how to manage it.

For TrustOps to be fully integrated into existing practices, it must: a) coexist with applications that do not use or adhere to the proposed method or require particular strategies, and b) establish recommended tools, practices, standards, and guidelines. This necessitates the development of new tools or extensions within existing development or operational environments to effectively support TrustOps across the phases of the software life cycle.

The usability of underlying technologies like ZKPs and TEEs must improve to support the use of TrustOps. This includes improvements tailored for developers and operators to streamline integration processes. Moreover, a thorough threat model analysis and accompanying recommendations are essential for practitioners. These insights should help guide decisions regarding the onboarding of TrustOps. In addition, possible users should be educated regarding the capabilities and shortcomings of verification tools.

7 Conclusion

In this paper, we presented TrustOps, an extension of DevOps that integrates evidence verification and identity management into the software development process. TrustOps aims to build and maintain trust by making software actions transparent, understandable, and verifiable. It adopts an evidence-based approach, focusing on generating, enhancing, and providing authenticated, attested, and actionable evidence at each step of the software life cycle.

We discussed application scenarios demonstrating how TrustOps principles enhance security, transparency, and trust in various contexts, including open-source software, service ecosystems, and organizational development. Key research challenges include evidence management, integration and adoption, and usability and understanding. Through these concepts and challenges, we provide a roadmap for the software engineering, security, and privacy communities, as well as the industry, to advance the TrustOps approach.

Despite the challenges, the potential benefits of TrustOps in enhancing trust, transparency, and accountability make it a promising direction for future research. We already see several emerging projects that offer solutions to cover some aspects of TrustOps[7]. By embracing verifiable development practices and the principles described, TrustOps could improve software development and significantly enhance trust in software systems, across domains and applications.

[7] A continuously updating collection of these resources is available here: https://github.com/trustops/awesome-trustops.

Acknowledgements. Funded by the European Union (TEADAL, 101070186). Views and opinions expressed are, however, those of the author(s) only and do not necessarily reflect those of the European Union. Neither the European Union nor the granting authority can be held responsible for them.

References

1. Bass, L., Weber, I., Zhu, L.: DevOps: A Software Architect's Perspective. Addison-Wesley Professional (2015)
2. Dauterman, E., et al.: Reflections on trusting distributed trust. In: Proceedings of the 21st ACM Workshop on Hot Topics in Networks, pp. 38–45 (2022)
3. Delignat-Lavaud, A., et al.: Why should i trust your code? Queue **21**(4), 94–122 (2023)
4. Eberhardt, J.: Scalable and privacy-preserving off-chain computations. Ph.D. thesis, TU Berlin (2021)
5. Enoiu, E.P., et al.: VeriDevOps software methodology: security verification and validation for DevOps practices. In: Proceedings of the 18th International Conference on Availability, Reliability and Security, pp. 1–9 (2023)
6. Fitzgerald, B., Stol, K.J.: Continuous software engineering: a roadmap and agenda. J. Syst. Softw. **123**, 176–189 (2017)
7. Grünewald, E.: Cloud native privacy engineering through DevPrivOps. In: Friedewald, M., Krenn, S., Schiering, I., Schiffner, S. (eds.) Privacy and Identity 2021. IAICT, vol. 644, pp. 122–141. Springer, Cham (2022). https://doi.org/10.1007/978-3-030-99100-5_10
8. Heiss, J.: Trustworthy data provisioning in blockchain-based decentralized applications. Ph.D. thesis, TU Berlin (2023)
9. Hou, F., Jansen, S.: A systematic literature review on trust in the software ecosystem. Empir. Softw. Eng. **28**(1), 8 (2023)
10. Hühnlein, D., et al.: FutureTrust–future trust services for trustworthy global transactions. In: Challenges in Cybersecurity and Privacy-the European Research Landscape, pp. 285–301. River Publishers (2022)
11. Industrial communication networks - Network and system security. Standard, International Electrotechnical Commission (IEC), Geneva, CH (2009)
12. Security and resilience - Authenticity, integrity and trust for products and documents. Standard, ISO, Geneva, CH (2023)
13. Information technology - Security techniques - Code of practice for protection of personally identifiable information (PII) in public clouds acting as PII processors. Standard, ISO, Geneva, CH (2019)
14. Information technology - DevOps - Building reliable and secure systems including application build, package and deployment. Standard, ISO, Geneva, CH (2022)
15. Manuel, P.: A trust model of cloud computing based on quality of service. Ann. Oper. Res. **233**, 281–292 (2015)
16. Mayer, R.C., et al.: An integrative model of organizational trust. Acad. Manag. Rev. **20**(3), 709–734 (1995)
17. Myrbakken, H., Colomo-Palacios, R.: DevSecOps: a multivocal literature review. In: Mas, A., Mesquida, A., O'Connor, R.V., Rout, T., Dorling, A. (eds.) SPICE 2017. CCIS, vol. 770, pp. 17–29. Springer, Cham (2017). https://doi.org/10.1007/978-3-319-67383-7_2

18. European Parliament and Council of the European Union: General Data Protection Regulation (2018). https://eur-lex.europa.eu/legal-content/EN/TXT/PDF/?uri=CELEX:32016R0679
19. Ross, R., Winstead, M., McEvilley, M.: NIST SP 800-160 Vol. 1 Rev. 1: Engineering Trustworthy Secure Systems (2022)
20. Sánchez-Gordón, M., Colomo-Palacios, R.: Security as culture: a systematic literature review of DevSecOps. In: Proceedings of the IEEE/ACM 42nd International Conference on Software Engineering Workshops, pp. 266–269 (2020)
21. Ting, H.L.J., et al.: On the trust and trust modeling for the future fully-connected digital world: a comprehensive study. IEEE Access **9**, 106743–106783 (2021)

Unraveling the Never-Ending Story of Lifecycles and Vitalizing Processes

Stephan A. Fahrenkrog-Petersen[1,2(✉)], Saimir Bala[2(✉)], Luise Pufahl[3], and Jan Mendling[1,2,4]

[1] Weizenbaum Institute for the Networked Society, Berlin, Germany
[2] Humboldt-Universität zu Berlin, Berlin, Germany
{stephan.fahrenkrog-petersen,saimir.bala,jan.mendling}@hu-berlin.de
[3] Technical University of Munich, Heilbronn, Germany
luise.pufahl@tum.de
[4] Wirtschaftsuniversität Wien, Vienna, Austria

Abstract. Business process management (BPM) has been widely used to discover, model, analyze, and optimize organizational processes. BPM looks at these processes with analysis techniques that assume a clearly defined start and end. However, not all processes adhere to this logic, with the consequence that their behavior cannot be appropriately captured by BPM analysis techniques. This paper addresses this research problem at a conceptual level. More specifically, we introduce the notion of vitalizing business processes that target the lifecycle process of one or more entities. We show the existence of lifecycle processes in many industries and that their appropriate conceptualizations pave the way for the definition of suitable modeling and analysis techniques. This paper provides a set of requirements for their analysis, and a conceptualization of lifecycle and vitalizing processes.

Keywords: Business Process Management · Types of Processes · Process Analysis · Process Models · Lifecycle

1 Introduction

Business process management [8] (BPM) is concerned with the discovery, modeling, analysis and optimization of business processes. These processes structure the different operational tasks within an organization, for instance, the hiring of a new employee or the purchasing of some supplies. BPM provides technological and methodological support for organizations to improve business processes. To this end, a wide range of methods and corresponding tools are available, such as data-driven analysis with the help of process mining [32] or automation of sub-routines by use of robotic process automation [1].

So far, the BPM literature has mainly focused on business processes that are directed towards a desired outcome [8,36], such as having a purchased good available. Van de Ven and Poole refer to these as teleological processes [33]. The

M. Kaczmarek-Heß et al. (Eds.): EDOC 2024 Workshops, LNBIP 537, pp. 68–81, 2025.
https://doi.org/10.1007/978-3-031-79059-1_5

analysis focus of BPM is often to determine the start and end states of a process, as well as the sequence of activities that define the progress from the start to the desired goal [8, Ch.5]. Typically, many cases run in concurrency according to the same process specification. One of our research partners processes 60 million orders per year. Understanding the differences between these cases offers insights that inform process improvement.

Until now, it has gone largely unnoticed that the focus on teleological processes builds on subtle assumptions that hinder the application of BPM techniques to other categories of processes. One important category of such processes are lifecycle processes [33]. An example of a *lifecycle process* is a patient treated in an elderly care facility. This lifecycle process is better described by trying to keep the patient happy and healthy than by a specific end or outcome. To maintain this status stable, different *vitalizing processes* are executed on a regular or irregular basis that are all targeted at the patient as a focal *entity*. While these vitalizing processes could be analyzed using BPM techniques, it has to be kept in mind that each instance influences the state of the entity during its evolution, as captured by relevant *vital signs*. Clearly, it would be inappropriate to compare the effect of the first with the 20th iteration of chemotherapy.

In this paper, we address this research gap by introducing the notions of a *lifecycle process* and corresponding *vitalizing processes*. With these novel categories of processes, we describe processes that are different from typical business processes, such as purchase-to-pay or lead-to-order processes. Instead, these vitalizing processes describe the work performed to prevent an entity from deteriorating or to improve an entity constantly. In this way, vitalizing processes define motors of change for the focal entity and its overarching lifecycle process. Our conceptual contribution provides the basis for the development of novel modeling and analysis techniques that capture the connection between lifecycle and vitalizing processes appropriately.

The remainder of the paper is structured as follows: Sect. 2 conceptualizes lifecycle processes and corresponding vitalizing processes for concrete use cases and relates them to prior BPM research. Section 3 introduces a conceptual model that describes the relationships between lifecycle and vitalizing processes. Section 4 discusses related work and identifies a set of requirements for the integrated analysis of lifecycle and vitalizing processes, as well as relevant analysis techniques from neighboring fields. Finally, Sect. 5 summarizes our work and points to future research.

2 Motivation

This section provides an analysis of lifecycle and corresponding vitalizing processes, and how state-of-the-art BPM techniques are unable to support many analytical questions related to them. First, Sect. 2.1 gives a definition and several examples of lifecycles and vitalizing processes. Next, Sect. 2.2 highlights analytical questions that cannot be answered properly by state-of-the-art BPM techniques.

2.1 What are Lifecycle and Vitalizing Processes

Lifecycle processes are different from classical business processes. Van de Ven and Poole describe business processes as *teleological*, i.e. directed towards a goal, characterized by planning and organizational problem-solving, with an envisioned end state that is reached by purposeful cooperation [33]. In contrast, *lifecycle processes* exhibit organic growth or decay, driven by a pre-configured program or natural rules. Events progress along a sequence of prescribed stages that are often irreversible [33].

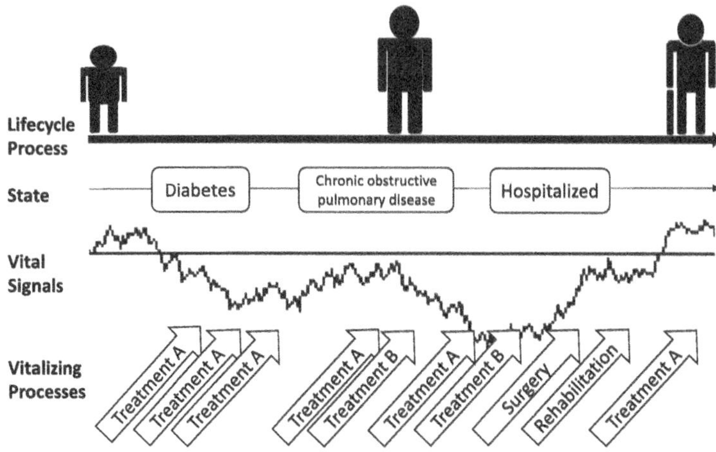

Fig. 1. Lifecycle Processes, Vitalizing Processes, and Life Signs related to a Patient as a Focal Entity.

The essential concepts of lifecycle processes are illustrated in Fig. 1. We define a *lifecycle process* with reference to a focal entity, related events, and vital signs:

Definition 1. *A lifecycle process is the sequence of events and observations of vital signs associated with a focal entity over the entire period or a relevant subperiod of its existence.*

With respect to the lifecycle process of a person, we observe the characteristics described above. This lifecycle process lets us expect some sort of organic growth and later decay, driven by the rules of our natural existence, partially in an irreversible way. However, we are not left to the natural rules of growth and decay alone. Various industries, engineering, and research domains develop processes to keep an entity in a desired condition. Examples of repetitive process structures that stabilize the conditions of an entity are treatment processes to handle the health conditions of a patient, maintenance processes that keep an engine operational, or fertilizing processes that foster the capacity of a field to grow crops. Here, we refer to such processes as vitalizing processes, defined as follows:

Definition 2. *A vitalizing process is a continuous work process that aims to foster or stabilize the condition of at least one entity with a natural tendency to stagnate or deteriorate. Here, the condition of the entity is described through one or more vital signs that provide a proxy for the current state of the entity. Vitalizing processes have the goal of keeping the entity in the desired condition.*

We describe three examples of lifecycle and corresponding vitalizing processes.

1. **Chronic Disease Treatment** is a healthcare process focused on one patient as an *entity* [21]. A patient visit to a medical specialist is one of several *vitalizing processes* to ensure stable health. *Vital signs* like blood sugar level or *events* having contracted pneumonia require actions to be taken.
   The *lifecycle process* is the development of the patient over time. A *practical goal* here is to stabilize the patient's condition. A *modeling goal* is to describe which conditions should be treated with which actions. An *analysis goal* is to understand which actions are most effective for which condition.
2. **Farming** is a process that has been performed by humans since millennia [10]. A field is an *entity* managed to extract a certain crop over an undefined number of seasons. Activities performed by the farmer, such as watering or fertilizing, are *vitalizing processes*, which are motors to ensure optimal conditions for crop growth. The type and amount of actions a farmer performs on the land depend on the state of the soil. *Vital signs* like the level of nitrate, or *events* like a flooding of the field, require certain actions to be taken.
   The *lifecycle process* is the development of the field over time. A *practical goal* in this context is to improve the condition of growing crops on the field. A *modeling goal* is to identify relevant steps and when they should happen in the season, potentially considering environmental conditions. An *analysis goal* is to identify which process steps are most beneficial for future seasons, potentially considering crop order.
3. **Continuous integration** is a process of enhancing the functionality of a software system as an *entity*. Different *vitalizing processes* serve quality assurance, such as testing, issue management, or bug fixing, together with cycles of incremental extensions according to agile principles [4]. *Vital signs* are numbers of fixed bugs or reported issues; *events* like vulnerability reports trigger hotfixes to the software system.
   The *lifecycle process* is the development of the software system over time. A *practical goal* in this context is to add new features to the system. A *modeling goal* is to identify relevant development and quality assurance steps and when they should happen. An *analysis goal* is to assess how certain activities, such as reducing technical debt, lead to changes in the productivity of sprints.

2.2 Challenges for Classical BPM Analysis Techniques

Applying classical BPM analysis techniques for modeling and analyzing the described processes has several issues. A key question for applying many techniques is how to define a case. This comes with commitments to a conceptual window of analysis. In general, the notion of a case can be anchored at the level of the lifecycle process and one specific type of vitalizing process.

First, we can select a specific vitalizing process. Indeed, in the context of chronic disease treatment, this is often one visit to a medical expert [25]. In this way, we can analyze how the specific activities performed during a visit to a medical expert impacts health. This selection, however, abstracts from the medical history of the patient and neglects potential interaction with other vitalizing processes, like a new medication given some visits ago. Second, we can select the overarching lifecycle process. This might be appropriate for chronic cases, since continuous treatment can grant the affected patient a stable life [23] and avoid episodes of exacerbation [35]. In this way, it allows us to consider the whole history of the patient [25]. A challenge is, however, that we have to commit to a specific time window of observation. Also, it might be a challenge to integrate distributed event data from potentially concurrent vitalizing processes in a complexity-controlling way. Third, any commitment to a case notion comes with the challenge of integrating analysis methods that focus on events with time series of vital signs.

The above described challenges lead to the question of which requirements must be considered for capturing and analyzing lifecycle and vitalizing processes. Before we analyze our the requirements we first need a conceptual model that describes lifecycle processes in more details.

3 Modeling Lifecycle and Vitalizing Processes

In this section, we propose a conceptual model for lifecycle processes, vitalizing processes, and their relationships. Figure 2 presents this model as a class diagram. We first discuss the type level, then the instance level. At the type level, we distinguish the entity type and its lifecycle process, potentially multiple motor types and multiple vitalizing processes:

Entity Type. An entity type is a category of entities that share common properties. An entity type has a lifecycle process and several motor types. *Patient* is an entity type.

Lifecycle Process. Each entity type has a lifecycle process that captures its typical evolution. Multiple vitalizing processes can contribute to this evolution. A patient has a typical lifecycle.

Motor Type. Each entity type has several motor types that can stabilize or potentially drive its growth or decay. Motor types represent the rules of nature to which an entity type is subject. Examples are the immune reaction of a patient as a stabilizing motor of the current state, puberty as a progressing motor towards a higher level of capabilities, and diseases as deteriorating motors.

Vitalizing Process. A vitalizing process is an active intervention targeting the lifecycle process of an entity type. A therapy that can serve as a vitalizing process for a patient. Vitalizing processes typically strengthen stabilizing or progressing motor types or work against the effects of deteriorating motors.

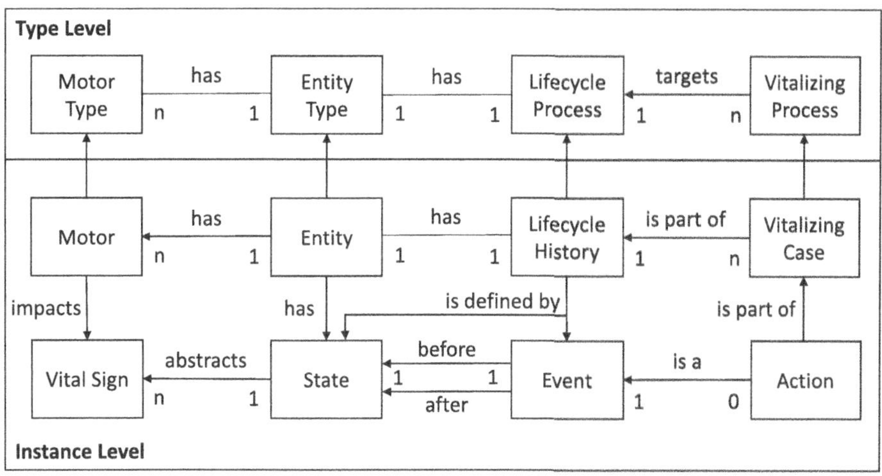

Fig. 2. Conceptual Modeling of Vitalizing Business Processes.

At the instance level, we distinguish instantiations of the concepts at the type level and more fine-granular temporal concepts.

Entity. Each entity instantiates an entity type. It exists in time and space.

Motor. A motor is a natural trend that moves the entity towards a certain state. An entity can have multiple motors. A patient can be infected with COVID-19, which has a (potentially only temporary) deteriorating effect on the patient.

Vital Sign. An entity has vital signs. These are measurements of different types at a given point in time, i.e., a patient has a body temperature value of 38.5° on Christmas Eve.

State. An entity has a state. A state can be defined as an abstraction of vital signs. The patient with the mentioned temperature is in a state of fever.

Lifecycle History. An entity has a lifecycle history. It is defined as the collection of all present and past states and events that relate to the entity. A patient has a lifecycle history of medical records.

Event. Events define the lifecycle history of an entity. They represent state and vital sign changes of the entity itself, as well as relevant state changes in the environment of the entity. A patient becomes infected with Covid-19.

Vitalizing Case. Vitalizing cases are sequences of action that follow the specification of a vitalizing process. A prescription for a fever blocker and its application for a specific patient is a vitalizing case with several regular intakes of pills.

Action. An action is a specific type of event where an actor actively changes some state relevant to the entity's lifecycle. For instance, a medical specialist takes a blood sample from a patient.

4 Analysis of Lifecycle and Vitalizing Processes

This section discusses the requirements for analysis techniques to obtain insights from lifecycle and vitalizing processes. Therefore, Sect. 4.1 assesses related work from BPM research, partly supporting the lifecycle process analysis. Then, we identify a deduced set of requirements from the use cases and related work for the analysis of lifecycle and vitalizing processes in Sect. 4.2 Finally, we discuss how techniques from neighboring research areas might fill gaps and provide an overall discussion on what requirements are supported or not by the previously presented related work in Sect. 4.3.

4.1 Related BPM Analysis Techniques

There are three main streams of BPM research that relate to lifecycle and vitalizing processes: *i)* approaches that address continuous cyclic structures; *ii)* data-centric approaches; and *iii)* time-series related approaches.

In the stream of research that tackles *continuous cyclic processes*, Combi et al. [5] present a proposal for modeling chronic patient treatment with existing BPMN notation elements. The authors highlight the need for a repeating process to stabilize a Chronic Obstructive Pulmonary Disease (COPD) patient and capture it as a loop subprocess. The process can also be interrupted in case of unforeseen needs. Additionally, in case of exacerbation, further activities can be executed in parallel to it. This leads to a complex, multi-level process model. Strutzenberger et al. [30] extend BPMN to model continuous processes, for instance, beer brewing, by regularly adding ingredients to a brewing process. In their work, continuous processes are characterized by a closed loop, having steady inlet and outlet flows as well as temporally stable conditions. This research highlights that activities in continuous processes must be executed for a particular time span to provide high-end quality. For instance, the deterioration of the reactor over time implies lower-quality beer, but the brewing ingredients and steps remain the same. Finally, the issue of repeating process behavior also exists in software engineering when the development process is modelled [20,24]. Overarching methodologies with repeating behavior, such as SCRUM, have been modeled using BPMN [37].

In the stream of *data-centric* approaches, the entity, its associated data and characteristics, and its changing states is in the center of process modeling, analysis and automation [29]. Such approaches provide means to store information on entities structurally as artifacts, objects, or tuples [29]. For example, the artifact-centric approach [18] considers an entity's information model, including the attributes, and an entity's lifecycle describing the order of its allowed states. Nevertheless, data-centric approaches provide no explicit means to represent the repetitive behavior of cases.

In the stream of *time-series-related approaches* in the BPM area, several works exists that combine time-series data and event data or process models. Dunk et al. [9] consider combining process event logs with time-series data. The objective is to use the time series associated with the activities of the process in order to understand better and explain decision points in the process. For process analysis, De Smedt et al. [7] use time series data to capture behavior drift for process mining discovery. Lam et al. [19] focus on modeling business processes using a custom activity model. This allows to identify empirically inefficiencies and ineffective loops that require intervention. Time series are then used to predict the effects of these interventions. Finally, in order to been able to handle time-series data, Fonger et al. [13] propose to use process models to describe time series data. Despite first ideas can be observed, no comprehensive approach exists to relate vital signs, often in the form of time-series data, with the life cycle states of an entity and the events of vitalizing processes.

4.2 Requirement for Analysis Techniques

The data of lifecycle and vitalizing processes exhibits characteristics that are different from classical business processes. Here, we describe requirements that appropriate analysis techniques have to address. The requirements R1 to R5 are retrieved from the issues addressed by related work, and R6 to R7 are derived from the phenomena of an entity discussed in the use cases of the previous section.

R1: Absence of Specific End State. *We observe* that classical business processes are defined with a clear direction towards a desired end [18,36]. Therefore, how to reach efficiently and accurately this end is a pillar for many BPM techniques. The *problem* is that lifecycle processes often do not target one specific desired outcome [30]. Rather, the objective of many vitalizing processes is stabilizing or fostering certain conditions of an entity. For example, in healthcare, the death of a patient is avoided by the medical specialists as a factual end. Accordingly, we *require* techniques for lifecycle processes that are able to analyze processes that lack a particular end state. Techniques for vitalizing processes must be able to analyze how their different runs impact the entity and, additionally, enable a comparison of them.

R2: Recurring Behaviour. *We observe* that classical BPM techniques assume a teleological process from a defined start to a desired end [36]. Often, this idea is already encoded in the name of the business process, as with order-to-cash, procure-to-pay, and lead-to-close processes [8]. Recurring behavior can occur within a process execution and needs special attention in the representation, e.g., the iteration workflow patterns [26]. Recurring behavior is often classified as waste in the process analysis [8]. The *problem* is that vitalizing processes are often enacted repeatedly over the lifecycle of an entity [5]. This is not a matter of waste, but a key feature. Accordingly, we *require* analysis techniques for lifecycle processes that are able to consider recurring behavior. Furthermore, they must be able to incorporate the idea that vitalizing processes might differ, overlap, and depend on each other.

R3: Temporal Regularity of Processes. *We observe* that classical business processes are often expected to be completed as fast as possible [8]. That is why many BPM methods are focused on remaining time [34] or waiting time prediction [27]. The *problem* is that lifecycle processes are often expected to endure as long as possible. A short cycle time is indeed not desired. Vitalizing processes are often naturally scheduled at a specific time [5]. Consider a farming process where the calendar dictates certain activities to be performed. Therefore, the remaining time of a vitalizing process is often known and not a goal for optimization. Accordingly, we *require* techniques for vitalizing processes that are able to consider the temporal regularity of processes beyond cycle time.

R4: Handling Multi-facet Data. *We observe* that event logs can only capture changes of attribute values by representing them as new events [16]. This leads to a *problem* that lifecycle processes of an entity, such as a patient, are characterized by their continuously changing vital signs [9], for instance, to determine if vitalizing actions need to be taken. This might be actively captured, e.g., by a smartwatch with different sensors. We *require* measures to analyze vital signs over time at varying observation interval density. While the action on an entity might be represented in events, the information of vital signs is best represented as time series data [12]. Thus, we *require* techniques for lifecycle and vitalizing processes to handle multi-facet data consisting of different types.

R5: Lifecycle of an Entity. *We observe* that classical BPM techniques focus on the quality of the process output of each process case in isolation [8]. This is a *problem* because vitalizing processes are executed to archive a stabilization or progression of one or multiple entities. The development over the whole lifecycle process is often more relevant than the results of a single execution of a vitalizing process. Therefore, we *require* process analysis techniques for lifecycle processes that capture changes in the entity and the trend of its development.

R6: State of an Entity. *We observe* that classical BPM assumes that each case of a business process has an independent existence. They are executed without reference to each other [26]. This is a *problem* because a vitalizing case needs information about the current state of the entity and the effects of previous vitalizing cases. Thus, a the current state of the entity must be accessible for the vitalizing case. Accordingly, we *require* to be able to specify the relevant states and to track them. The lifecycle process and the vitalizing process must be able to read *vital signs* that serve as a proxy for the current state of the entity.

R7: Motor as Natural Trend of an Entity. *We observe* that classical BPM does not consider the natural trend (i.e., the pre-configured program of natural rules) of an entity or its environment. This is a *problem* because lifecycle processes are naturally driven by motors associated with the entity. A patient might, for instance, have a disease as a deteriorating motor, which sometimes can be stabilized but not always be stopped. Comparing the actual change of the entity with its expected natural trend might give insights into the effectiveness of a vitalizing process. Accordingly, we *require* means to capture the natural trend of an entity, including the expected effects on the vital signs describing that entity.

4.3 Other Related Techniques and Discussion of Coverage

Based on our requirements analysis, we want to discuss how existing areas of research can contribute to the development of new analysis techniques for lifecycle-related processes. We identified three areas of research that provide us with essential components for future analysis techniques: (i) time series analysis, (ii) social sequence analysis, and (iii) mortality analysis.

Time Series Analysis. The research area of time series [11] is concerned with extracting useful information, such as patterns, from time series data. Typical analysis tasks in this area include forecasting time series, clustering similar time series, segmenting a time series, and anomaly detection. However, the most relevant is the area of *motif discovery* [31], identifying frequent unknown patterns with time series. Future techniques for lifecycle-related processes can build on motif discovery and try to link discovered motifs from the vital signs with events or states from the event/state sequences. Furthermore, time series techniques could be applied to vital signs to provide helpful information about the vital signs that could be used to inform actions with vitalizing processes. One specific technique in this context is change point detection. This technique detects the point in time when change occurs [15], making it an integral part of concept drift analysis. Overall, it can be said that existing techniques from time series analysis provide a substantial component for lifecycle-related processes by helping to utilize hidden information from vital signs.

Social Sequence Analysis. Social sequence analysis [2,6] is concerned with tracing social phenomena over time. The input data is typically defined as a sequence of states [14]. Critical design decisions are related to the granularity of the time intervals at which state sequences are captured. Typical analysis tasks for state sequences include describing stochastic patterns, analyzing homogeneity and stationarity, optimal matching, or sequence network construction [6]. Specifically interesting for analyzing the lifecycle process is stationarity analysis. If a sequence is stationary, then the probability to transition from, e.g., state A to B is the same, no matter in which segment it occurs. Understanding such properties might provide indications of recurring behavior, temporal regularity, and the impact of motors on the lifecycle of an entity. Social sequence analysis also offers various techniques for visualizing, sorting, and clustering cohorts of sequences, as well as measures of complexity and turbulence [14]. Overall, techniques from social sequence analysis address the requirements of the lifecycle process well because of their assumption that there is no clear start or end.

Mortality Analysis. Mortality analysis studies the causes of death in populations [22]. This requires various methodologies and approaches to understand mortality rates, life expectancy, and factors influencing death. There are four main types of mortality analysis. First, *descriptive mortality analysis* involves studying death rates, causes of death, and their distribution among different populations, regions, or time periods. Second, *life table analysis* helps analyze mortality rates across different age groups, providing insights into life expectancy and survival probabilities. Third, *cause-specific mortality analysis* examines the causes of death within a population to understand disease burdens and health priorities. Fourth, *f* compares mortality rates across different demographic groups, socio-economic classes, or geographic regions to identify disparities and underlying factors.

Mortality analysis has also seen broader applications such as in finance [3], forest research [17], and even history [28]. Future lifecycle-related techniques can draw inspiration from mortality analysis in multiple ways. The four types of mortality analysis can be applied to the lifecycle history. To this end, events of lifecycle processes will need to be gathered and analyzed. Consequently, vitalizing processes can be redesigned to counter the discovered issues.

Table 1. Overview of requirements for lifecycle-related process analysis techniques and how they are supported by existing techniques. ✓: Is supported; (✓): Is partially supported ✗: Is not supported.

	R1	R2	R3	R4	R5	R6	R7
Combi et al. [5]	✓	✓	✓	✗	✗	✗	✗
Strutzenberger et al. [30]	✓	✓	✓	✗	✗	✗	✗
Hull et al. [18]	✗	✗	✗	✗	✓	✓	✗
Fonger et al. [13]	✗	✗	✓	(✓)	✗	✓	✗
Dunk et al. [9]	✗	✗	✗	✓	✗	✗	✗
Farschi et al. [12]	✓	✓	✗	✓	✗	✗	✗
Time Series Analysis	✓	✓	✗	✗	✓	✓	✓
Social Sequence Analysis	✓	✓	✓	✗	✓	✓	✓
Mortality Analysis	✓	✗	✗	✗	✓	✓	✓

Overall Comparision. In Table 1, we highlight what requirements of lifecycle and vitalizing processes are fulfilled by existing techniques and neighboring research areas. We can observe that most BPM techniques are only focused on specific sub-problems of lifecycle-related business processes. As an example, the idea of repeating behavior, as presented in vitalizing cases, is discussed in several papers [5,30]. Similarly, several papers [9,13] try to integrate time series, as in the form of vital signs, into BPM techniques. In future work, it will be possible to integrate the results from such research into techniques that address lifecycle and vitalizing processes.

Furthermore, we can observe that many requirements for lifecycle and vitalizing processes have been addressed in other research fields such as *time-series*, *social-sequence* and *mortality* analysis (rows 6–8). Notably, these research fields are usually not concerned with the data fusion necessary to address lifecycle and vitalizing business processes. Nonetheless, we can highlight that they support many of the aspects necessary for analysis technique of lifecycle-related processes and therefore can serve as valuable building blocks for novel approaches.

Overall, we can argue that many approaches specialized on specific aspects of lifecycle and vitalizing processes exist. Therefore, we believe that this phenomenon can be addressed by combining existing BPM techniques and knowledge from other areas of research.

5 Conclusion

In this paper, we showed that traditional BPM techniques predominantly address teleological business processes with defined start and end states, e.g., purchase-to-pay processes. This research highlighted the existence of *lifecycle process* of a focal entity, such as a patient, displaying either a natural increase or diminution. They are supported by *vitalizing processes* that foster or stabilize the lifecycle process. We provided a conceptual model with the key ingredients of a lifecycle process and a data model. We discussed the requirements of analysis techniques for lifecycle and vitalizing processes and showed that previous research work only covered parts of them. We have come to the conclusion that many specialized aspects of lifecycle and vitalizing processes are already supported by existing research. This existing research can serve as a foundation for analysis techniques targeted towards lifecycle processes.

This paper is centered on identifying and conceptualizing the problem space without offering direct solutions. We envision this groundwork as a catalyst for a new line of research within BPM. In the future, we plan to develop appropriate analysis techniques for lifecycle and their vitalizing processes and plan to apply them to real-world data. Furthermore, an important next step for the research lies in the collection of data from the lifecycle and vitalizing business processes.

Acknowledgements. This work was supported by the German Federal Ministry of Education and Research (BMBF), grant number 16DII133 (Weizenbaum-Institute). We thank Julian Theis for fruitful discussions about lifecycle processes in industrial settings.

References

1. van der Aalst, W.M., Bichler, M., Heinzl, A.: Robotic process automation (2018)
2. Abbott, A.: Sequence analysis: new methods for old ideas. Ann. Rev. Sociol. **21**(1), 93–113 (1995)
3. Altman, E.I., Suggitt, H.J.: Default rates in the syndicated bank loan market: a mortality analysis. J. Bank. Finance **24**(1), 229–253 (2000)
4. Beck, K., et al.: Manifesto for agile software development (2001)
5. Combi, C., Oliboni, B., Zardini, A., Zerbato, F.: A methodological framework for the integrated design of decision-intensive care pathways-an application to the management of COPD patients. J. Healthc. Inform. Res. **1**, 157–217 (2017)
6. Cornwell, B.: Social Sequence Analysis: Methods and Applications, vol. 37. Cambridge University Press, Cambridge (2015)
7. De Smedt, J., Yeshchenko, A., Polyvyanyy, A., De Weerdt, J., Mendling, J.: Process model forecasting and change exploration using time series analysis of event sequence data. Data Knowl. Eng. **145**, 102145 (2023)

8. Dumas, M., La Rosa, M., Mendling, J., Reijers, A.H.: Fundamentals of Business Process Management, 2nd edn. Springer, Heidelberg (2018)
9. Dunkl, R., Rinderle-Ma, S., Grossmann, W., Fröschl, K.A.: Decision point analysis of time series data in process-aware information systems. In: CAiSE (Forum/Doctoral Consortium). CEUR Workshop Proceedings, vol. 1164, pp. 33–40. CEUR-WS.org (2014)
10. Dupuis, A., Dadouchi, C., Agard, B.: Predicting crop rotations using process mining techniques and Markov principals. Comput. Electron. Agric. **194**, 106686 (2022)
11. Esling, P., Agon, C.: Time-series data mining. ACM Comput. Surv. (CSUR) **45**(1), 1–34 (2012)
12. Farshchi, M., Schneider, J.G., Weber, I., Grundy, J.: Metric selection and anomaly detection for cloud operations using log and metric correlation analysis. J. Syst. Softw. **137**, 531–549 (2018)
13. Fonger, F., Aleknonyte-Resch, M., Koschmider, A.: Mapping time-series data on process patterns to generate synthetic data. In: CAiSE Workshops. Lecture Notes in Business Information Processing, vol. 482, pp. 50–61. Springer (2023)
14. Gabadinho, A., Ritschard, G., Müller, N.S., Studer, M.: Analyzing and visualizing state sequences in R with TraMineR. J. Stat. Softw. **40**, 1–37 (2011)
15. Gama, J., Žliobaitė, I., Bifet, A., Pechenizkiy, M., Bouchachia, A.: A survey on concept drift adaptation. ACM Comput. Surv. (CSUR) **46**(4), 1–37 (2014)
16. Gunther, C.W., Verbeek, H.: XES-standard definition (2014)
17. Hiroshima, T.: Applying age-based mortality analysis to a natural forest stand in Japan. J. For. Res. **19**(4), 379–387 (2014)
18. Hull, R., et al.: Business artifacts with guard-stage-milestone lifecycles: managing artifact interactions with conditions and events. In: 5th ACM International Conference on Distributed Event-Based System, pp. 51–62 (2011)
19. Lam, C.Y., Ip, W.H., Lau, H.C.W.: A business process activity model and performance measurement using a time series ARIMA intervention analysis. Expert Syst. Appl. **36**(3), 6986–6994 (2009)
20. Moyano, C.G., Pufahl, L., Weber, I., Mendling, J.: Uses of business process modeling in agile software development projects. Inf. Softw. Technol. **152**, 107028 (2022)
21. Munoz-Gama, J., et al.: Process mining for healthcare: characteristics and challenges. J. Biomed. Inform. **127**, 103994 (2022)
22. Pan American Health Organization: Basic guidelines for the analysis of mortality. PAHO, Washington, D.C. (2018). https://iris.paho.org/handle/10665.2/34985
23. Pauwels, R.A., Buist, A.S., Calverley, P.M., Jenkins, C.R., Hurd, S.S.: Global strategy for the diagnosis, management, and prevention of chronic obstructive pulmonary disease: NHLBI/WHO global initiative for chronic obstructive lung disease (GOLD) workshop summary. Am. J. Respir. Crit. Care Med. **163**(5), 1256–1276 (2001)
24. Pillat, R.M., Oliveira, T.C., Alencar, P.S.C., Cowan, D.D.: BPMNt: a BPMN extension for specifying software process tailoring. Inf. Softw. Technol. **57**, 95–115 (2015)
25. Remy, S., Pufahl, L., Sachs, J.P., Böttinger, E., Weske, M.: Event log generation in a health system: a case study. In: Business Process Management: 18th International Conference, BPM 2020, Seville, Spain, 13–18 September 2020, Proceedings 18, pp. 505–522. Springer (2020)
26. Russell, N., van Der Aalst, W.M., Ter Hofstede, A.H., Edmond, D.: Workflow resource patterns: identification, representation and tool support. In: Advanced

Information Systems Engineering: 17th International Conference, CAiSE 2005, Porto, Portugal, 13–17 June 2005. Proceedings 17, pp. 216–232. Springer (2005)
27. Senderovich, A., Weidlich, M., Gal, A., Mandelbaum, A.: Queue mining–predicting delays in service processes. In: Advanced Information Systems Engineering: 26th International Conference, CAiSE 2014, Thessaloniki, Greece, 16–20 June 2014. Proceedings 26, pp. 42–57. Springer (2014)
28. Steckel, R.H.: Slave mortality: analysis of evidence from plantation records. Soc. Sci. Hist. **3**(3–4), 86–114 (1979)
29. Steinau, S., Marrella, A., Andrews, K., Leotta, F., Mecella, M., Reichert, M.: DALEC: a framework for the systematic evaluation of data-centric approaches to process management software. Softw. Syst. Model. **18**, 2679–2716 (2019)
30. Strutzenberger, D.V., Mangler, J., Rinderle-Ma, S.: BPMN extensions for modeling continuous processes. In: Intelligent Information Systems: CAiSE Forum 2021, Melbourne, VIC, Australia, 28 June–2 July 2021, pp. 20–28. Springer (2021)
31. Torkamani, S., Lohweg, V.: Survey on time series motif discovery. Wiley Interdisc. Rev. Data Min. Knowl. Discov. **7**(2), e1199 (2017)
32. Van Der Aalst, W.: Process mining: overview and opportunities. ACM Trans. Manag. Inf. Syst. (TMIS) **3**(2), 1–17 (2012)
33. Van de Ven, A.H., Poole, M.S.: Explaining development and change in organizations. Acad. Manag. Rev. **20**(3), 510–540 (1995)
34. Verenich, I., Dumas, M., Rosa, M.L., Maggi, F.M., Teinemaa, I.: Survey and cross-benchmark comparison of remaining time prediction methods in business process monitoring. ACM Trans. Intell. Syst. Technol. (TIST) **10**(4), 1–34 (2019)
35. Wedzicha, J.A., Seemungal, T.A.: COPD exacerbations: defining their cause and prevention. The Lancet **370**(9589), 786–796 (2007)
36. Weske, M.: Business Process Management - Concepts, Languages, Architectures, 3rd edn. Springer, Heidelberg (2019)
37. Zaouali, S., Ghannouchi, S.A.: Proposition of an approach based on BPM to manage agile development processes. In: 2016 Third International Conference on Systems of Collaboration (SysCo), pp. 1–6 (2016)

Ontological Analysis of Advanced Capability Modeling in ArchiMate: A First Step Towards Language Revision

Rodrigo Fernandes Calhau[1,2,3], João Paulo A. Almeida[1], and Giancarlo Guizzardi[3(✉)]

[1] Ontology & Conceptual Modeling Research Group, Federal University of Espírito Santo, Vitoria, Brazil
calhau@ifes.edu.br, jpalmeida@ieee.org
[2] LEDS, Federal Institute of Espírito Santo, Serra, Brazil
[3] Semantics, Cybersecurity & Services, University of Twente, Enschede, The Netherlands
g.guizzardi@utwente.nl

Abstract. In order to support capability management, the field of Enterprise Architecture proposes methods and notations to model enterprises and their capabilities. ArchiMate is one of such notations and includes constructs to support capability mapping and other capability management tasks. However, the notation lacks some fine-grained distinctions that are required to understand intricate phenomena involving capabilities, including capability *interaction* and the *emergence* of capabilities. In this work, we perform an ontological analysis of the language's support for capability modeling based on a well-founded ontology of capabilities aligned with the Unified Foundational Ontology (UFO). Through this ontological analysis, we identify some issues outlining possible improvements for ArchiMate. This is a first step towards language redesign, which may include the proposal of language patterns and/or the revision of language constructs.

Keywords: ArchiMate · ontological analysis · capabilities · emergence

1 Introduction

Enterprises and organizations have been facing challenges with the rapid and unpredictable development of new technologies that impact their operating environments. With these fast changes comes the need for the development of organization-wide capabilities, which emerge from a well-balanced combination of organizational elements.

Given the importance of organizational capabilities, it is no surprise that they have been given attention in disciplines such as capability management and Enterprise Architecture (EA) [6]. In particular, EA aids the capability management process by offering structured visualizations that align strategic goals with IT and business processes, identifying gaps and opportunities for improvement [18]. Notations such as ArchiMate [41] have been widely adopted to support practices such as business and information technology capability planning

M. Kaczmarek-Heß et al. (Eds.): EDOC 2024 Workshops, LNBIP 537, pp. 82–100, 2025.
https://doi.org/10.1007/978-3-031-79059-1_6

and mapping. With this notation, it is possible to construct models to support capability management and visualize important aspects such as capability decomposition and other types of capability relationships [20,42].

Capability modeling faces a series of demanding challenges, especially with regard to how to decompose and compose capabilities, how to trace, relate (or combine), and compare them. Although currently available notations offer resources to represent some aspects of capabilities such as relationships of composition, association, impact, dependence, and realization, they do not fully address the phenomenon of capability emergence. In other words, existing notations may be effective in representing isolated capabilities, but they do not provide a robust framework for dealing with the complexity inherent in modeling capabilities in a broader context.

Some of the limitations of existing notations can be traced to their underlying 'world view'. Making this world view explicit and accounted for is the objective of *ontological analysis*, which has been proposed as a means to evaluate the expressiveness and domain appropriateness of conceptual modeling languages [44]. In this context, ontologies can provide us with reference theories that articulate key domain distinctions; these distinctions are then reflected in modeling constructs, patterns and guidelines.

In this paper, we employ *ontological analysis* as a principled approach to assess capability modeling in ArchiMate. Our starting point is the ontology of capabilities described in [11]. This ontology is based on the Unified Foundational Ontology (UFO) [16] and is represented using the modeling language OntoUML [16]. It takes into account emergence [21,31,34,40] and disposition theories [5,14,29,32] to provide a well-founded conceptualization for capabilities and their relations.

The analysis presented in this paper builds up on our past work which proposes the representation of capability emergence in ArchiMate [9]. It also extends the work of Azevedo et al. [3,4]. Although Azevedo and colleagues also analyzed ArchiMate's support for capabilities using a UFO-based notion of disposition, they did not address detailed capability relationships. We argue that providing a proper account for these relationships is key to guide adequate capability representation in EA models and, consequently, for supporting the use of EA models in capability-based practices. To cite one example, this is needed to account for how organizational capabilities result from the relationships between the capabilities of various business entities (e.g., teams, departments, or other organizational structures).

This paper is further structured as follows: Sect. 2 presents an overview of the literature related to capabilities and the Unified Foundational Ontology and the capability ontology; Sect. 3 presents the ontological analysis based on the capability ontology; Sect. 4 presents preliminary suggestions of enhancement to ArchiMate's capability metamodel and specification which arise out of the ontological analysis; Sect. 5 discusses related work, and Sect. 6 concludes with our final remarks.

2 Background

Capability is generally defined as the "ability to do something" [30], a quality of being capable of achieving specific effects or declared objectives [38]. As noticed in most capability definitions, the meaning of *capability* is closely connected to the meaning of *ability*. Ability is commonly defined as the power to act, or as a kind of dispositional property that allows one to do something (useful or not) [23]. More specifically, the ability concept is defined by [23] as the "power that relates an agent to an action". So, ability is a potentiality (power) related to a bearer and also to an action. What then distinguishes abilities in general from capabilities? A direct reference to value: ability definitions are usually more generic, and not directly related to "desired" results, outcomes, or achievements. They can be "value neutral" with respect to their associated impact. Capabilities, in contrast, are conceived in terms of the usefulness of their outcomes and outputs. For example, in enterprise architecture and systems engineering, capabilities are defined as the "ability to do something useful" [24,25,28]; in information systems as the "ability to achieve a desired effect"; and, in the military field, it is defined as the "ability to achieve a determined military objective" [1]. Thus, a common tenet across these different areas is the reference to a "beneficial" aspect.

2.1 Modeling Capabilities in ArchiMate

ArchiMate is a widely used modeling language for EA. It provides a comprehensive framework for visualizing, analyzing, and communicating architectural blueprints within organizations. The language offers a standardized way to depict, understand, and manage the complexities of enterprise architectures. It serves as a bridge between business and IT domains, enabling stakeholders to align strategic goals with operational realities through a unified visual language [41].

The core of ArchiMate is its metamodel, which categorizes architectural elements into *behavior elements* and *structure elements* [41]. This dichotomy is depicted in the metamodel fragment shown in Fig. 1. Behavior elements capture the dynamic aspects of an enterprise, such as processes, events, interactions, and other behaviors. Structure elements represent the static aspects, including organizational units, actors, roles, and equipment. ArchiMate divides structure elements into *active* structure elements and *passive* structure elements. So, it divides these elements in a way that is analogous to a division present in natural languages, with active structural elements like subjects, behavioral elements (like verbs), and passive structural elements (like objects) [41].

ArchiMate organizes architectural models into distinct *layers*, each representing a different perspective (or viewpoint) of the enterprise architecture. These layers include the *Business Layer*, focusing on organizational services, components, functions, and processes; the *Application Layer*, addressing software applications supporting business functions and services; and the *Technology Layer*, dealing with infrastructure and hardware components. ArchiMate also considers a perspective to represent motivational elements such as goals, drivers, requirements, and so on.

In particular, the *Strategy Layer* focuses on business capabilities and resources [41] (which are shown as specializations of core elements in Fig. 1).

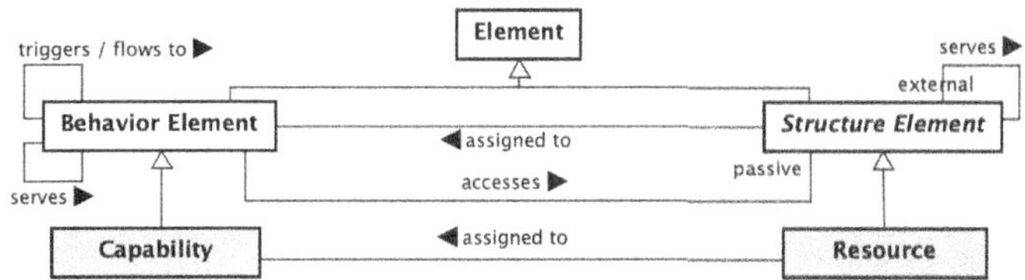

Fig. 1. Fragment of the ArchiMate's Metamodel (adapted from [41])

Capabilities in ArchiMate's metamodel are considered behavior elements (as events and processes) [41], in this case, *strategy behavior elements*. They represent an ability that a Structure Element (organization unit, person, or system) possesses. Figure 2 illustrates an example of a capability model, corresponding to the ArchiSurance case study [19]. In ArchiMate models, they provide a high-level view of the current and desired abilities of an organization. As behavior elements, they can trigger, serve (contribute to), and flow (i.e., exchange matter, energy, or information) to each other (not considered in the figure). In the strategy layer, resources can be *assigned to* capabilities (e.g., the "CRM Automation" resource is assigned to the "Customer Care" capability). They can also be *realized by* other structure or behavior elements (e.g. business actors, business roles, business processes, business function, and so on). For example, the "Customer Care" capability in the example is *realized by* the "Customer Relation" function of the "Customer Service" actor. In this case, this means that these elements can be used to achieve a specific capability. Finally, capabilities can be related to other capabilities through *aggregation* and *composition*. In ArchiMate, "Composition is a whole/part relationship that expresses an existence dependency" [41] while aggregation is supposed to be a parthood realtion that does not imply such a dependence. Whole/part relationships involving capabilities are depicted in Fig. 2 by construct nesting: e.g., the "Marketing" capability encompasses "Marketing Development" and "Campaign Management".

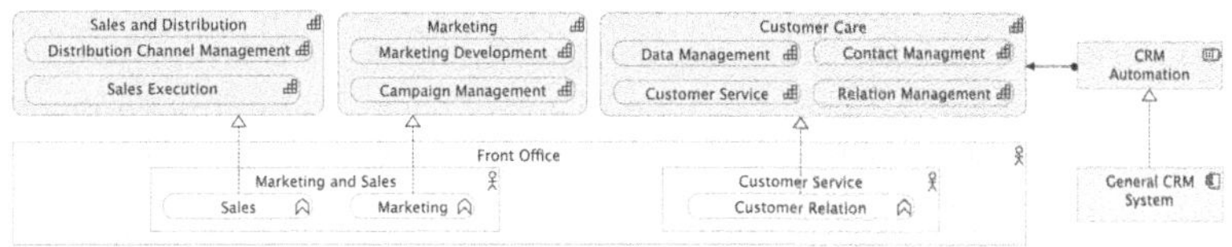

Fig. 2. Example of Capability Modeling in ArchiMate (extracted from [19])

2.2 Ontological Baseline

In order to account for capability-related phenomena more precisely, we employ here a fragment of the UFO foundational ontology [15]. UFO defines a system of domain-independent categories and their ties, which can be used to articulate conceptualizations of phenomena of interest. UFO has been developed based on theories from Formal Ontology, Philosophical Logics, Philosophy of Language, Linguistics, and Cognitive Psychology [16]. The employed fragment captures the first two basic ontological categories: that of the *types* (concepts, universals, e.g., Person, Planet, Music Band) and that of the *individuals* (particular things, e.g., John, Mary, Saturn, The Beatles). Individuals include *concrete individuals* and *abstract individuals. Concrete Individuals* are partitioned into *events* (a.k.a. *perdurants*), *endurants*, and *situations. Events* are *individuals* that occur in time, including processes, activities, actions, and tasks. Events are causally related and can be mereologically atomic or complex. Besides this, events can change, create, or terminate objects, including their aspects [17]. *Endurants* are individuals that persist in time possibly changing qualitatively while retaining their identity (i.e., people, organizations, cars). *Endurants* include *objects* and *aspects.* An *Object* is an endurant that is considered existentially independent from other objects (like John, his car). Objects formed by parts (performing distinct functions) are called *functional complexes.* An *Aspect* is a reified property that *inheres in* an *endurant* (termed its bearer). Inherence is a type of existential dependence relation between aspects and their bearers. Aspects (as full-fledge *endurants*) have a lifecycle of their own and can be created, destroyed, or changed qualitatively in time while maintaining their identity.

Of special interest to us in this work is the UFO notion of *disposition. Dispositions* are *aspects* that can be manifested through the occurrence of *events* (possibly agents' actions, such as Anna's speaking English). In *situations* where *dispositions may manifest,* they are said to be "activated" (e.g., when a magnet is close to some ferrous material, or when Anna is prompted to introduce the topic of a meeting). Again, as endurants, they can themselves bear aspects, and change qualitatively through time [15].

In order to leverage UFO distinctions, we use conceptual modeling language OntoUML [16]. OntoUML is implemented as a UML profile that reflects the foundational distinctions and axiomatization put forth by UFO. Over the years, it has been used to model many core and domain reference ontologies in a variety of complex domains. We use it here to represent the capability ontology proposed in [9,10]), on which we base our analysis (see Fig. 3). As it is addressed, capabilities are considered special types of dispositions. They inhere in a (non-agentive or agentive) *capable object* (including functional complexes as systems). *Capabilities* are manifested through *capability manifestations.* Each capability manifestation is triggered by one or more *capability manifestation context* and brings about a *capability outcome* (both of which are situations). As depicted in this figure, the manifestation of a capability can also employ a *capability input* and produce (or change) a *capability output* (objects with a historical role). Capable objects participate in the capability manifestation with *enabler objects*, a role

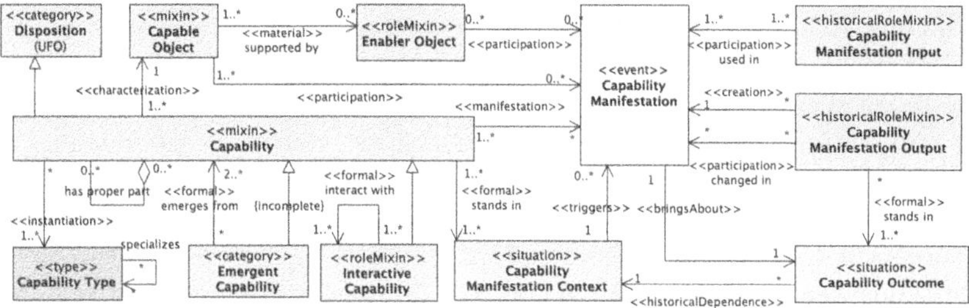

Fig. 3. Fragment of the Disposition and Capability Ontology used in the ontological analysis

that represents objects needed for capable object manifestation (i.e., resources). Capabilities can be *interactive*, when they play a 'role' in certain relations to each other (and other dispositions). The interaction relation, in this case, corresponds to relations that include relations of reciprocity [14,32], enabling [5], and changing [32], among others (not all depicted in the figure). We use the term "interacts with" as an abstract supertype to these relations. *Capabilities* can also be complex or atomic. *Complex capabilities* are those that have other *capabilities* (and dispositions) as proper parts, and *atomic capabilities* are those capabilities that are not complex. *Capabilities* inhere in *objects* (capable objects), which can be atomic objects or functional complexes (including systems). The *capabilities* of capable objects that are complex (functional complexes as systems) can be *emergent capabilities* or *resultant capabilities* [10]. *Resultant capabilities* are those that come "directly" from some *particular dispositions* of components (i.e., component capabilities). They can even be present in system parts in isolation. For example, the capability of a car to play music is a direct result of the capability of the car's stereo to play music. In contrast, *emergent dispositions* are those that, while related to the (interactive) dispositions of system parts, are not present in isolation in the separated parts [8]. For example, the "buoyancy" of a steel ship is not present in an arbitrary piece of its hull in isolation. Finally, capabilities instantiate one or more capability types. As depicted, a capability can specialize another.

3 Ontological Analysis of Capability-Related Elements in ArchiMate

As approached, the phenomena of capability emergence and interaction face challenging issues of capability modeling in EA modeling notations, especially regarding ArchiMate. As a result, these aspects motivate us to employ *ontological analysis* [44] as a principled approach to evaluate and identify ontological deficiencies concerning capability modeling in ArchiMate. This ontological analysis is based on the capability ontology [11] fragment briefly presented above. This principled approach is fundamental to prevent ontological deficiencies such as semantic overload, construct redundancy, construct deficit, and construct excess [44]. *Construct excess* occurs when a notation construct does not align with any ontological concept; *construct overload* happens when a single notation construct can represent several ontological concepts; *construct redundancy* arises when multiple modeling elements can represent a single ontological concept; and *construct deficit* exists when there is no notation construct in the modeling language for a specific ontological concept.

Our approach involves identifying and examining the fundamental capability-related elements and their relationships within ArchiMate's metamodel. We delve into the descriptions and meanings of these elements as specified in ArchiMate's specification, aiming to understand their relevance in enterprise architecture. Then, we compare ArchiMate's capability-related elements with capability ontology concepts, particularly focusing on UFO distinctions. This comparison aims to establish correspondences and clarify how ArchiMate's capability modeling aligns with broader ontological frameworks. Next, we present the ontological analysis and, based on that, we identify some ontological deficiencies in ArchiMate. For each of them, we provide the related context and problems, explaining how this impacts the quality of ArchiMate models.

3.1 Capabilities as Aspects

As presented before, capability is defined in distinct fields as an *ability* of a certain entity (a system, organization, enterprise, person, etc.) to do something and generate some outcome. This ability corresponds to a "power", "propensity", or "potentiality" of the bearer, i.e., a potential to act or behave. Then, when an activating situation happens, the capability manifests itself as an event or behavior. The literature, mainly related to disposition theories, makes a clear distinction between the capability (as a potentiality) and its manifestation (the event). In a similar sense, the definition of capabilities in ArchiMate states that they are abilities owned by organizations, people, or systems. Additionally, as presented in ArchiMate's metamodel, capabilities are categorized as *behavior elements*, similar to events and processes, related to the organization's dynamics (action, events, etc.).

Ontological Analysis of Capability Meaning: For UFO, aspects are intrinsic characteristics of *endurants* (especially objects). Moreover, it takes dispositions to be a subtype of aspects that are manifested in certain situations through events. In addition, according to the capability ontology (and also the ontological analysis performed in [3]), capabilities are dispositions that characterize *capable objects* and are manifested by events called *capability manifestation*. So, according to the ontology, capabilities are not behavior (event) itself; instead, they are aspects (dispositions) inhering in (capable) objects that possibly manifested through events (behavior).

Diagnosis of ArchiMate's Worldview: The notion of capability in ArchiMate is at odds with the understanding of capability as a "potentiality", i.e., a potential behavior, not the behavior itself. Furthermore, the ArchiMate metamodel does not include elements related to "aspect" or "characteristic". In line with [44], this is a case of *construct deficit*, since there is no construct representing capabilities itself (as an aspect) but just their manifestation. As a result, there is no construct to represent capable objects and the inherence relation binding an aspect to its bearer. In summary, ArchiMate's conception of capability as a behavioral element is inadequate because capabilities are aspects of structural elements that manifest themselves as behavior. As a consequence of this ontological deficiency, we have two main *problems*: (i) relations that would usually apply to behavior elements (such as triggers, flow, etc.) should not be applicable to capabilities or overlap with other relations involving capabilities; (ii) ArchiMate has no specific construct to identify the capable object that bears a particular capability. The ArchiMate relation of assignment could in principle be used if one could semantically overload it to represent the relation of inherence.

3.2 Capability Composition and Decomposition

When modeling capabilities in activities such as capability mapping, these are structured hierarchically in order to better support their understanding, as well as of their role in gap analysis [20,36]. For example, in Fig. 2, "Sales and Distribution" is decomposed in "Distribution Channel Management" and "Sales Execution".

Ontological Analysis of Capability Decomposition: There are multiple ways a capability can be related to its parts. Firstly, we can have direct capabilities of an entity that are decomposable into simpler capabilities inhering in the very same entity. Secondly, we can have capability emergence, in which case a capability of the whole emerges from the interaction of more basic capabilities inhering in its parts (e.g., as it happens with capabilities such as resilience, adaptability, innovation, etc.). In this latter case, we must also consider the particular structure relating these parts and affording the interaction between their capabilities. For example, how certain capabilities of a entire organization emerge from the interaction between the capabilities of organizational units, teams, or employees. In other words, in the case of emergence, we have more than just a mereological relation between wholes and parts, but we need to capture the structural unifying relations between the composing capabilities themselves. Finally, we have the case of resultant capabilities, in which a capability inhering in the whole is directly derived from a capability inhering in one of its parts. In summary, according to the reference ontology employed here, capability decomposition can have two distinct meanings: (i) mere mereologically complex capabilities: when a complex capability is just split into simple capabilities independently of the structure of the capable object; and, (ii) emergent and result capabilities: when a capability of a capable object emerges or results from interactive capabilities inhering in its parts.

Diagnosis of ArchiMate's World View: ArchiMate does not identify the bearer of a capability and hence it does not distinguish *capability decomposition* from *capability emergence*. As such, it only allows for the use of the simple mereological relations of aggregation and composition between capabilities. We have then a case here of *construct deficit* [44]. Because of this ontological deficiency, we have the following *problems*: (i) a significant gap between the capabilities modeled at the strategy layer and their implementation in the business, application, and technology layers (since capabilities of the whole are not related to the capabilities of part); (ii) difficulty in understanding (and replicate) patterns and best practices that promote the emergence of desirable capabilities due to not having the phenomenon of emergence in focus.

3.3 Interactions Between Capabilities

Capabilities are not isolated entities since they can be combined, impact, and collaborate with each other. Sometimes, they depend on each other so that can be enacted to satisfy certain goals. For example, in Fig. 2, "Campaign Management" needs the outcomes from "Marketing Development"; the same happens between "Relation Management" and "Contact Management".

In the context of EA, it is important to identify how capabilities impact enterprise elements, especially other capabilities [42,43]. For instance, initiatives to increase the innovation capability in organization can generate unexpected side effects. This, in the end, can harm other capabilities from a global perspective of the organization, as [39] argues about organizational learning. A similar issue happens with technical and social capabilities in organizations as socio-technical systems [2]. Capability interaction is related to capability emergence as previously discussed, as it also involves understanding how capabilities emerge in the whole organization; however, here, we focus not on the hierarchical perspective of capabilities, but with how they relate "horizontally".

ArchiMate allows the representation of dynamic and dependency relationships between capabilities. Capabilities can *serve*, *trigger*, or *flow* to other capabilities. The *serves* relationship is a dependency relationship that indicates a "contribution" from one capability to another. The triggering relationship represents a temporal or "causal precedence" between capabilities. The *flowing* relationship is also dynamic, corresponding to an "exchange" of matter, energy, or information between capabilities. Besides being present in the notation, these relationships are not as commonly used as the hierarchical decomposition in capability models, as evidenced in [19].

Ontological Analysis of Capability Relationships: Analyzing the dynamic relationships (flowing and triggering) from an ontological point of view, we understand that capabilities can interact indirectly through their manifestations: the *flowing relationship* means that capability c_1 manifests through an event e_1, producing output o_1. After this, capability c_2 manifests through event e_2, using output o_1 as input. Thus, it is actually the manifestation e_1 that "flows to" manifestation e_2; in the *triggering relationship*, capability c_1 triggering capability

c_2 means that c_1 manifests through event e_1, generating an outcome o_1. This outcome activates capability c_2, triggering its manifestation through event e_2.

In the case of the *serving relationship*, the term "contribute" - used by ArchiMate to characterize this relation, can have various interpretations. Depending on the interpretation, there can even be an overlap between the serving relationship and other relationships. First, serving could mean that capability c_1 serves capability c_2 if c_1 provides something (matter, information, or energy) to c_2. However, this overlaps with the flowing relationship, where one capability provides something to another. Second, serving could mean "contributing to the manifestation", where c_1 serves c_2 if c_1 contributes to the manifestation of c_2. This interpretation also overlaps with the triggering relationship, as it represents the creation of conditions for the manifestation of another capability. Third, a similar interpretation involves reciprocity. Ontologically speaking, reciprocal capabilities need each other to manifest together (e.g., "Product Purchasing" and "Product Selling"). Here, c_1 serves c_2 if they are reciprocal and contribute to each other's manifestation. Fourth, serving could mean "additionality", i.e., capabilities c_1 and c_2 manifesting through the events e_1 and e_2 that contribute to the same outcome o_1. For example, the capability of software testing contributes to the software coding capability by improving the quality of the software coding output. In the capability ontology, these capabilities are called "additional capabilities". Fifth, serving could mean that c_1 contributes to the development (improvement) of c_2. Ontologically speaking, a capability can change another capability or change the conditions for the latter's manifestations. For instance, the manifestation event e_1 of capability c_1 changes a quality of capability c_2 (a direct change) or change the capability bearer b_1 of c_2 in a way that it changes the possible manifestations of c_2 (e.g., the technological learning capability that makes the development of software development capability possible).

Diagnosis of ArchiMate's Worldview: The conception of capability relations in ArchiMate do not fully consider the nature of capabilities, leading to both cases of *construct overload* and also *construct excess* [44]. This is due to ArchiMate's misguided conception of these relationships purely from the perspective of behavioral elements, as if capabilities were directly comparable to events and processes that have temporal precedence and that can exchange matter, energy, or information. As we have discussed before, capabilities are to be distinguished from their manifestations. Besides this, the ontology also provides further distinction among relationships that can obtain between capabilities (e.g., blocking or disabling) and which are not addressed by ArchiMate, i.e., a case of *construct deficit* [44]. In summary, we conclude that ArchiMate's conception of capability as a behavioral element prevents important ("horizontal" capability) relations from being identified and properly expressed in the language. As a result of these ontological deficiencies, we have trouble: analyzing capability emergence - since these relations are key to explaining that phenomenon; planning and prioritizing capability development - since we cannot properly identify and express enabling and supporting capabilities); identifying negative capability interactions (capabilities that harm others).

3.4 Capabilities and Resources Assignment

Organizations are socio-technical systems that encompass distinct kinds of resources, from people to equipment such as hardware, software, tools, and even the physical environments in which these systems are situated [2,12,27]. The interaction between resources must occur appropriately for the organization to develop its desirable capabilities. However, understanding how resources interact can be an intricate issue given the different natures of these different kinds of resources (especially human and technical ones) [22]. For example, it is common to see in organizations the belief that the acquisition of technical resources (e.g., a new software system) will be sufficient for developing a desired capability. However, in this example, if people do not have the correct skills to properly use such a technology or have a dissonant attitude towards it (e.g., resistance to that technology), such investment will be fruitless [2,13]. So, the acquisition of new resources does not necessarily imply improvements in the people and organization as a whole [2,7,12].

In ArchiMate, resources are structure elements that belong to the strategy layer. According to the specification, resources include *tangible assets* (i.e., physical or financial assets), *intangible assets* (i.e., technological, reputational, or cultural assets), and *human assets* (e.g., skills, knowledge, or know-how). According to the ArchiMate metamodel, resources can be assigned to capabilities. The assignment relationship relates structural elements to behavior elements, indicating the "allocation" of structure elements to a behavior. In the business layer, this relationship is typically used to link business actors to a business role or to a business process they are supposed to perform.

Ontological Analysis of the Resource Assignment to Capabilities: Tangible resources can be considered objects in UFO. In the capability ontology, capabilities are tied to a *capable object* (the bearer of that capability). These capable objects can also be linked to *enabler objects*, which are required for the manifestation of a capability. In ArchiMate, resources are assets owned or controlled by a structural entity, something which is to be expected in this context also for enabler objects. So, we consider resources both as enabler objects, as well as capable objects - since they possess capabilities that interact with the ones from other capable objects. Thus, based on these ontological distinctions, the assignment of a resource to a capability can have two meanings: (i) a resource r_1 is assigned to capability c_1 if it corresponds to a *capable object* characterized by a capability c_2 of same type of c_1 (e.g., the software developer human resource assigned to the software development capability); (ii) a resource r_1 is assigned to capability c_1 if it is an *enabler object* characterized by a capability c_2 needed for the manifestation of capability c_1 (e.g., the laptop equipment assigned to the software development capability).

This understanding aligns with the perspective presented in [3]. There, in order to be assigned to a capability, a (tangible) resources must have dispositions aligned with that capability. However, as the authors note there, this is not necessarily a one-to-one mapping since multiple resources can be assigned to the same capability. Here again, we have two ways of interpreting this assignment relationship: one related to instantiation and the other to emergence. The first case happens when individual resources (objects) o_1, o_2, o_n, characterized by individual capabilities as c_1, c_2, c_n, are assigned to a capability type C. In this case, the capabilities c_1, c_2, c_n are instances of capability type C. An example is the assignment of the resources 'iOS dev. team' and 'Android dev. team' to the software development capability (type): both teams are individuals characterized by their respective individual software development capabilities. The second case happens when resources assigned to a capability c are objects o_1, o_2, ..., o_n characterized by respective capabilities c_1, c_2, ..., c_n. These capabilities interact with each other (i.e., reciprocal, additional, enabling, changing, and so on), and as a result, they are responsible for the emergence of that capability c. For example, the *software development capability* of a company emerges from the combination of various human resources (front-end developer, back-end developer, tester) as well as other tangible resources, e.g., hardware and software resources.

To further deepen this analysis, we can consider the notion of functional complexes from UFO [15] and the distinctions put forth by the system ontology in [10]. In these ontologies, organizations are seen as special types of systems (or functional complexes in UFO) being composed of interconnected functional parts that play functional roles w.r.t. to the whole organization. Thus, an "assignment" of a resource to an organization's capability can be understood as its allocation to a *functional role* in that *organization system* (or subsystem) in order to contribute to the achievement of the referred capability. More generally, the assignment of resources $r_1, \ldots, r_n$ to capability c in organization o_1 is meant to signify that those resources playing the functional roles $f_1, \ldots, f_n$ inside o_1 are necessary *components* of that organization (as a system) needed to achieve that capability. In the example of the "software development capability", behind all distinct human resources assigned to this capability there is a (social) subsystem of the organization – a team – composed of front-end developers, back-end developers, etc., and which collaborates with the "software development capability" achievement. In this case, particularly, the assignment of these human resources to this capability means that they are allocated to a team having that capability.

Diagnosis of ArchiMate's Worldview: ArchiMate lacks a clear semantics for the assignment relationship, and the notation itself does not provide a well-defined meaning for the resource construct. Resources can represent both physical objects (tangible resources) as well as intangible entities like cultural aspects, values, etc. As resources are taken to be structural entities, this implies that intangible assets (such as skill or competences) can also be structural elements, i.e., parts of organizational structure in a way analogous to organizational units. Furthermore, ArchiMate does not allow for explicitly representing that a resource bears a certain capability (a case of construct deficit [44]) but only generically that resources are assigned to capability, without clear guidelines on how these assignments should be made. However, to effectively combine resources in order to achieve a certain capability, it is necessary to understand their nature, their relations, and also their dispositions (including capabilities and vulnerabilities).

We also have again here a case of *construct overload* [44], in which several interpretations can be associated to the assignment relationship: the resource is a capable object that bears that capability; or it is a part of the organization as a capable object; or an enabler object required in capability manifestations (hence also a bearer of capabilities). As a result of these deficiencies, ArchiMate lacks expressivity to proper represent and analyze resources, their interactions, and related capabilities, which also impacts the analysis and representation of capability interaction and emergence.

3.5 Capability Implementation

In the EA context, capability can be approached from a strategic perspective and also from a more operational perspective. In the strategic perspective, capabilities are seen in a more abstract way, independent of their possible implementation. In this case, capability models are more future-driven, focusing on the desired capabilities of the organization. On the other hand, from the operational perspective of capabilities, they are represented as they are in the present, considering the actual stage of the organization. The focus is more on the present and on the "how", not just on the "what". From the operational perspective, understanding how capabilities manifest is important to understand how they work in practice and how to implement them. In this case, one needs to understand not only the manifestation of a focal capability itself but also how the manifestation of how distinct capabilities are linked and also how the results and outcomes of these capability manifestations are related.

Concerning the strategy and operation perspectives, ArchiMate distinguishes between the strategy and other layers business, application, and technological layers). The strategy layer is more abstract and implementation-independent, while the others are more specific, focusing on the present and how the organization is implemented [42]. In ArchiMate, capabilities are represented especially in the strategy layer and are realized by elements in the "lower" layers, such as the business layer. Thus, capabilities represented in the strategy layer are implemented by business functions, business processes, business actors, business roles, and also elements from the application and technology layers. This *realization* relationship indicates that more abstract elements (focused on "what") are realized by more tangible elements ("how"). Thus, an "abstract" capability can be implemented by various elements combined in the business layer, such as business actors, roles, services, processes, events, and so on.

Analysis of Capability Implementation: Capabilities are individuals that instantiate *capability types*, i.e., that are classified by them. As detailed in the ontology, a capability type can specialize others. The ontology allows for considering different levels of abstraction between capabilities. With this distinction in mind, we consider that *strategic capabilities* of an organization are "more abstract" capabilities that focus on the "what" and can be specialized in various ways depending on the "how". *Operational capabilities* are specializations of strategic capabilities that concern a specific way to realize them, making them more concrete and relating them to a specific implementation within the organization. For example, suppose that *software development capability* is a strategic capability for a given organization. In this case, it could be specialized into different operational capabilities such as *web system development* or *mobile app development*, which could further specialize into *iOS app development* and *Android app development*.

Regarding the realization of capabilities by structural elements from "lower" layers (i.e., business, application, and technology), we encounter a situation similar to what we saw with the *assignment relationship* between capabilities and resources. Similarly, we can interpret that structural elements are capable objects characterized by capabilities and which can realize (strategic) capabilities as a consequence. But, the realization of a capability by a structural element can also have distinct meanings, such as: (i) the structural element s that realizes a strategic capability c is a *capable object* characterized by c' - an *operational capability* that specializes c; (ii) the structural element s that realizes a strategic capability c is an "enabler" object necessary for a capable object o to manifest c' - an operational capability that specializes c. If a strategic capability is realized by multiple structural elements, similarly to resource assignment, we have that: the set of structural elements s_1, s_2, ..., s_n are characterized by operational capabilities c_1, c_2, ..., c_n, and that these capabilities, when combined (through interaction relationships), contribute to the emergence of c' - an operational capability that specializes the strategic capability c. On the other hand, if a capability c is realized by a *behavior element* b, this means that: (i) there is a structural element s characterized by the operational capability c', which specializes c and manifests through b; (ii) Or, there is a set of structural elements s_1, s_2, ..., s_n, characterized by operational capabilities c_1, c_2, ..., c_n, which, when combined (through interaction relationships), contribute to the emergence of c' - an operational capability that specializes c and manifests through b.

Diagnosis of ArchiMate's Worldview: ArchiMate does not provide an appropriate representation for the implementation of capabilities. As we saw, structural elements at different levels, such as strategic, business, application, and technology, can also be capable objects characterized by capabilities at different levels. However, ArchiMate does not allow for the representation of the structural elements as bearers of capabilities in any of the layers considered in the notation. This makes it difficult to map strategic-level capabilities to structural elements at other levels, as well as to relate structural elements in a way that combines their capabilities (through interaction relationships) to collectively generate the desired capability at the strategic level. Besides this, the notation only allows for the representation of capabilities in the strategic layer, leaving no construct in the business layer to represent "operational" capabilities. In addition, ArchiMate's *realization relationship* is not precisely defined, being another case of *construct overload* [44] as detailed in the ontological analysis.

Capabilities can be *realized by* both structural and behavioral elements, which can lead to many misunderstandings. There are no guidelines on how to combine these elements in order to implement capabilities. In summary, ArchiMate's capabilities are only considered as"abstract" entities in the strategy layer. Capabilities are not addressed in other layers, in which they are often treated as (but not properly distinguished from) functions. Structural elements in business, application, and technological layers are also capable objects characterized by capabilities, which can also engage in fruitful interactions.

4 Preliminary Suggestions to ArchiMate Enhancement Based on the Ontological Analysis

Based on the ontological analysis we have presented thus far, in this section, we consider some preliminary suggestions to improve the representation of capabilities and their relationships in ArchiMate. These include the suggestion of a few capability-focused viewpoints and the identification of possible revision of language constructs related to capabilities.

Capability-Focused Viewpoints: Regarding capability (de)composition, it would be beneficial to distinguish between complex and emergent capabilities in the hierarchical representation used in capability mapping. Since the strategy view does not allow for the representation of the bearer of capabilities, it would be helpful to represent different levels of organizational granularity. At least three levels could be represented: the organizational level, the organizational unit level (e.g., teams, departments), and the individual level. Capabilities at each level could be then be visually distinguished.

Concerning capability interaction, it would be useful to have guidelines to model capability interaction, focusing on the interaction between capabilities that belong to the same level in the organization. This would help better understand the emergence of capabilities, which arise from their interactions. Additionally, it is important to clarify the semantics of capability relationships, as their current descriptions are generic and similar to other relationships between structural elements, which have a different nature. Specializing the semantics of the *serving* relationship between capabilities is recommended, including all possibilities such as reciprocity, additionality, and change. The serving relationship description would also make clear how it differs from the flowing and triggering relationships. Additionally, the language should provide better guidelines on how to implement capabilities in the resources they are assigned to, ensuring these capabilities are realized by structural elements interconnected in a proper way. A notion such as functional complex (from UFO) is essential in this context.

One way to assist in modeling the aspects mentioned above is through viewpoints, as they can assist modelers by providing perspectives based on the aforementioned aspects. For example, it would be key to have such a support for modeling emergence and interaction between capabilities, as these aspects are closely related to others, such as the assignment of resources and the implementation of capabilities. These viewpoints would offer a clearer way to visualize and manage how capabilities emerge and interact within an organizational structure.

Language Constructs Revision: Regarding the representation of capabilities, a general suggestion is to consider adding an element in the metamodel related to 'aspects' in order to distinguish capabilities from behavioral elements. An option in this case is to refactor the metamodel and possibly introduce a separate notion of "dependent" structural element, and in any case, a relation to establish the active structure element who bears an aspect (capabilities included). In this proposed redefinition, it is also important to specialize the relationships between capabilities based on this new understanding of capability (as an aspect), rather than simply inheriting the meanings of relationships from behavior entities. Additionally, a relationship that can be included in this refactoring is the *characterization relationship*, linking active structure elements (the bearers) to their respective capabilities. Finally, considering these possible changes, it would be valuable to include capabilities in all layers, similar to how ArchiMate handles structural and behavioral elements (e.g., business function, application function, technical function, etc.). In this case, there would be different types of capabilities based on the layer, such as strategy capability, business capability, and application capability, and one could also express that capabilities from higher layers are realized by capabilities from lower layers. An option, in this case, might be to use *business function* elements to represent "operational" capabilities (see Fig. 2). However, this requires some clarification on the interpretation of functions in ArchiMate.

5 Related Work

Other related works that employ Foundational Ontologies in EA modeling include [4,33,35,37]. Azevedo et al. [4] perform an ontological analysis of capability, resource, and competence. The authors discuss especially the definition of capability based on UFO; we adopt and build up on that analysis in the present work. As an application, the authors propose improvements in Enterprise Modeling (using ArchiMate), through a metamodel connecting capabilities and the strategy layer with motivational aspects. Capabilities can be aggregated (with resources) in what the authors call "capability bundles" [3]. The work proposed by Nardi et al. [33] focuses on the ontological analysis and modeling of the Service concept. In a complementary way, [33] states that one dimension of Service Modeling is to represent a manifestation of capabilities. However, although both papers address the subject of capabilities using UFO, they do not delve into this topic since this is not the focus of both papers. Sales et al. [37] proposed improvements in the ArchiMate notation based on an ontological analysis, focusing on the concept of value. In their analysis, they included the concept of capability, given its strong relation to value. According to their interpretation, and as adopted here, capabilities are dispositions with valuable impacts on a value subject. However, fully characterizing is not the main focus of their work. Building on the work in the value domain proposed in Sales et al. [37], Oliveira et al. [35] conduct an ontological analysis of ArchiMate focused on security and propose a redesign of the language. In this security-focused analysis, they considered other types of dispositions, such as vulnerabilities, corresponding to those with undesired effects. Additionally, the authors extend the meaning of capabilities to include *threat capabilities*. Although these related works address capabilities in the context of EA, given their respective foci, none of them all the subtle phenomena related to capability modeling.

6 Final Remarks

In this work, we presented an ontological analysis of ArchiMate based on a well-founded capability ontology. To perform this analysis, we first identified several issues concerning the semantics of the ArchiMate metamodel, especially regarding capability emergence and capability interaction. We also uncovered semantic issues related to the relationship between capabilities and resources, as well as capability implementation. This work may serve as a foundation for proposing language redesign, language patterns, or even language extensions. The issues identified can be a starting point for the proposal of new capability representations. This work not only contributes to enhancing ArchiMate's capability modeling but also impacts capability modeling in general, potentially influencing other EA notations. For example, in future work, we intend to perform a similar ontological analysis of the Unified Architectural Framework [26].

Acknowledgments. This study was financed in part by the Brazilian funding agencies CNPq (443130/2023-0, 313412/2023-5) and FAPES (2021-GL60J, 2022-NGKM5, 1022/2022).

References

1. Antunes, G., Borbinha, J.: Capabilities in systems engineering: an overview. In: Exploring Services Science: 4th International Conference, IESS 2013, Porto, Portugal, 7–8 February 2013. Proceedings 4, pp. 29–42. Springer (2013)
2. Appelbaum, S.H.: Socio-technical systems theory: an intervention strategy for organizational development. Manag. Decis. **35**(6), 452–463 (1997)
3. Azevedo, C.L.B., et al.: An ontology-based well-founded proposal for modeling resources and capabilities in ArchiMate. In: 17th IEEE International EDOC Conference (EDOC 2013), pp. 39–48. IEEE Computer Society Press (2013)
4. Azevedo, C.L.B., Iacob, M., Almeida, J.P.A., van Sinderen, M., Pires, L.F., Guizzardi, G.: Modeling resources and capabilities in enterprise architecture: a well-founded ontology-based proposal for ArchiMate. Inf. Syst. **54**, 235–262 (2015). https://doi.org/10.1016/j.is.2015.04.008
5. Barton, A., et al.: A taxonomy of disposition-parthood. In: Workshop on Foundational Ontology in Joint Ontology Workshops: JOWO 2017, vol. 2050, pp. 1–10. CEUR-WS: Workshop Proceedings (2017)
6. Bernus, P.: Enterprise models for enterprise architecture and ISO9000:2000. Annu. Rev. Control. **27**(2), 211–220 (2003)
7. Bruseberg, A., Lintern, G.: Human factors integration for MODAF: needs and solution approaches. In: INCOSE International Symposium, vol. 17, pp. 1240–1255. Wiley Online Library (2007)

8. Bunge, M.: Treatise on Basic Philosophy. Ontology II: A World of Systems. Springer, Dordrecht (1979)
9. Calhau, R.F., Almeida, J.P.A., Kokkula, S., Guizzardi, G.: Modeling competences in enterprise architecture: from knowledge, skills, and attitudes to organizational capabilities. Softw. Syst. Model. 1–40 (2024)
10. Calhau, R.F., et al.: A system core ontology for capability emergence modeling. In: International Conference on Enterprise Design, Operations, and Computing, pp. 3–20. Springer (2023)
11. Calhau, R.F., Almeida, J.P.A., Guizzardi, G.: A capability reference ontology for the analysis and design of system capabilities. Pre-print. https://purl.org/nemo/paper/creon
12. Cummings, T.G.: Self-regulating work groups: a socio-technical synthesis. Acad. Manag. Rev. **3**(3), 625–634 (1978)
13. Ellen, P.S., Bearden, W.O., Sharma, S.: Resistance to technological innovations: an examination of the role of self-efficacy and performance satisfaction. J. Acad. Mark. Sci. **19**, 297–307 (1991)
14. Galton, A., et al.: Dispositions and the infectious disease ontology. In: Formal Ontology in Information Systems: Proceedings of the Sixth International Conference (FOIS 2010), vol. 209, p. 400. IOS Press (2010)
15. Guizzardi, G., Wagner, G., Almeida, J.P.A., Guizzardi, R.S.S.: Towards ontological foundations for conceptual modeling: the unified foundational ontology (UFO) story. Appl. Ontol. **10**, 259–271 (2015). https://doi.org/10.3233/AO-150157
16. Guizzardi, G.: Ontological Foundations for Structural Conceptual Models. No. 15 in Telematica Inst. Fundamental Research Series, Telematica Inst., Enschede, The Netherlands (2005)
17. Guizzardi, G., et al.: Towards ontological foundations for the conceptual modeling of events. In: Conceptual Modeling, pp. 327–341. Springer, Heidelberg (2013)
18. International Organization for Standardization (ISO): ISO/IEC/IEEE 42020:2019 Software, Systems and Enterprise–Architecture Processes (2019)
19. Jonkers, H., Band, I., Quartel, D., Lankhorst, M.: Archisurance case study (version 3.1). Technical report, The Open Group (2019)
20. Josey, A.: TOGAF® version 9.1-A pocket guide. Van Haren (2016)
21. Juarrero, A.: Dynamics in action: intentional behavior as a complex system. Emergence **2**(2), 24–57 (2000)
22. Kochan, T., Cutcher-Gershenfeld, J.: Integrating social and technical systems: lessons from the auto industry (2008)
23. Maier, J.: Abilities. In: Zalta, E.N., Nodelman, U. (eds.) The Stanford Encyclopedia of Philosophy, Fall 2022 edn. Metaphysics Research Lab, Stanford University (2022)
24. Martin, J., Fairley, D., Lawson, B., Faisandier, A.: Enterprise systems engineering background. In: Guide to the System Engineering Book of Knowledge (SEBoK), version 2.5, pp. 642–650. BKCASE (2021). https://sebokwiki.org/w/images/sebokwiki-farm!w/2/24/SEBoKv2.5.pdf
25. Martin, J., Lawson, B., Faisandier, A.: Enterprise capability management. In: Guide to the System Engineering Book of Knowledge (SEBoK), version 2.5. BKCASE (2021). https://sebokwiki.org/w/images/sebokwiki-farm!w/2/24/SEBoKv2.5.pdf
26. Martin, J.N., O'Neil, D.P.: Enterprise architecture guide for the unified architecture framework (UAF). In: INCOSE International Symposium, vol. 31, pp. 242–263. Wiley Online Library (2021)

27. Mavor, A.S., Pew, R.W. (eds.): Human-System Integration in the System Development Process: A New Look. The National Academies Press (2007)
28. Merrell, E., et al.: Capabilities (2022)
29. Molnar, G., Bradley, N.: Powers: A Study in Metaphysics. Clarendon Press (2003)
30. Morgan, P.: The concept of capacity (draft version). In: Study on Capacity, Change and Performance, pp. 1–19 (2006)
31. Mossio, M., et al.: Emergence, closure and inter-level causation in biological systems. Erkenntnis **78**(S2), 153–178 (2013)
32. Mumford, S., Anjum, R.: Getting Causes from Powers. Oxford University Press (2011)
33. Nardi, J., et al.: A commitment-based reference ontology for services. Inf. Syst. **54**, 263–288 (2015). https://doi.org/10.1016/j.is.2015.01.012
34. O'Connor, T.: Emergent properties. Am. Philos. Q. **31**(2), 91–104 (1994)
35. Oliveira, Í., Sales, T.P., Almeida, J.P.A., Baratella, R., Fumagalli, M., Guizzardi, G.: Ontological analysis and redesign of security modeling in ArchiMate. In: IFIP Working Conference on the Practice of Enterprise Modeling, pp. 82–98. Springer (2022)
36. Open Group: ArchiMate® 3.0. 1 Specification: The Open Group Standard. Van Haren Publishing, Reading (2017)
37. Sales, T.P., Roelens, B., Poels, G., Guizzardi, G., Guarino, N., Mylopoulos, J.: A pattern language for value modeling in ArchiMate. In: Advanced Information Systems Engineering: 31st International Conference, CAiSE 2019, Rome, Italy, 3–7 June 2019, Proceedings 31, pp. 230–245. Springer (2019)
38. Saxena, M.: Capability Management. Global India Publications (2009)
39. Senge, P.M.: The fifth discipline. Measur. Bus. Excellence (1997)
40. Spencer-Smith, R.: Reductionism and emergent properties. In: Proceedings of the Aristotelian Society, pp. 113–129. JSTOR (1995)
41. The Open Group: Archimate 3.2 specification (2023). https://pubs.opengroup.org/architecture/archimate3-doc/
42. The Open Group: TOGAF Business Capabilities Guide V2 (2023). https://pubs.opengroup.org/togaf-standard/business-architecture/business-capabilities.html. Accessed 06 Oct 2023
43. Thorn, S.: Redefining traceability in Enterprise Architecture and implementing the concept with TOGAF 9.1 and/or ArchiMate 2.0 (2013). https://blog.opengroup.org/author/opengroupblog/
44. Weber, R.: Ontological foundations of information systems (1997)

An Enterprise Architecture Approach to Temporary and Permanent Governance Continuum

Bruno Fragoso(✉) and Andre Vasconcelos

INESC-ID, Instituto Superior Técnico, Lisboa, Portugal
bruno.fragoso@tecnico.ulisboa.pt

Abstract. This paper supports the assessment of the alignment of governance structures towards stakeholder's concerns. Considering the characteristics of governance structures and models in project, program and portfolio discipline, and left to the enterprise to handle its integration in the overall enterprise governance, this work contributes to the assessment of temporary governance structures' alignment under an actor-role permanent and temporary evaluation. As contributions from this work we can entail: i) a conceptual map for the temporary and permanent governance roles enrolled in enterprise transformation; ii) a proposal of a viewpoint for stakeholders with the concerns on the identification of permanent and temporary governance transformation roles and serve relations; iii) the views generated from the viewpoint proposal, where the instantiation of the architectural elements allow to add meaning and value to the represented models, adding the required data for the iv) evaluation of alignment of temporary and permanent governance roles against a stakeholder's concern. This last contribution opens the possibility to the stakeholders, either in design phase or in implementation phase, to assess the governance structure alignment adequacy to the expected outcomes of the projects. The demonstration presented, based in a real case study, allows to clarify the opportunities and follow up research in adding other evaluation metrics and taxonomies to the proposed solution.

Keywords: Enterprise Governance · Transformation Governance · Governance Alignment

1 Introduction

The fast pace in the development of technology creates challenges for enterprises to survive, and thrive. One of such challenges is the ability of the enterprise to promote the required transformations from an As Is to a To Be state without occurrences or events that reduce value from the expected benefits.

An enterprise, understood as "any collection of organizations that has a common set of goals and, or a single bottom line" [1] requires to have in place the right instruments that allow to design, plan and implement such transformation within the enterprise, granting alignment between the organizations.

M. Kaczmarek-Heß et al. (Eds.): EDOC 2024 Workshops, LNBIP 537, pp. 101–116, 2025.
https://doi.org/10.1007/978-3-031-79059-1_7

Governance, defined under the scope of this work as "the sum of organizational measures for continuously maintaining unity and integration in the (re-) development and operation of an enterprise (…), concerns enterprise adaptation and renewal: 'changing the mill' [2] organizations, but also in alignment with the 'running the mill' organizations of the enterprise.

These temporary endeavors promote the 'change of the mill' putting the focus on the required transformation, resulting in a gradual change of the enterprise elements' behavior, or the result of a deliberate action [3].

A project, while "a transformation process designed to achieve a goal specified by a to-be state" [4] requires a governance to transform the organization, with a planned finish time, as opposed to governance structure for "running the mill" dealing with daily activities.

It is more and more required for the enterprise to have the agility to change and adapt to new realities (legal, compliance, environment, social or commercial) when a new temporary governing body is created to answer a given need.

As such, there is an empirical need in determine the adequacy of the governing body to deliver the expected value by the stakeholder on a given project. A concern that can be as distinct as to have a project driven on cost and time, or quality and technical expertise.

1.1 Problem Motivation

When approaching the governance concept in the context of enterprises that foster transformation processes for the strategy implementation, we can assume from state of the art that:

- Projects are temporary endeavors, with temporary governance structures [5–9];
- Projects can be conceptualized as an instrument for the Enterprise to achieve its objectives – [10, 11]; or as organizations, relating with other organizations in the same Enterprise – [12–17];
- Projects being either conceptualized as an instrument, or as an organization, have a vast research field on Governance as a key dimension that determines the success of the project (finish on time, on scope, and costs) – [5–8, 13, 14, 18];
- Is up to the Enterprise, more specifically for a formal and permanent governance structure, to integrate and grant unity in the organizational Governance of projects – [8, 19, 20];
- Enterprises tend to have permanent and temporary governance structures that coexist in sharing responsibilities and attributions according to its scope and objectives – [21, 22];
- The higher the maturity enterprises have in handling transformation processes, statistically, have better results – [23–25].

Considering such, it would be expectable to have in place a set of solutions addressing the alignment of temporary governing bodies' governance structures with the enterprise governance and formal authority scheme.

However, it remains evidenced that enterprises still struggle in making the process of strategy implementation as effective and efficient as possible, being the apparent interactions between the permanent governing bodies and temporary governing bodies a critical organizational link, where potential misalignments are most likely to cause a negative impact on the strategy outcome.

In a literature review on project governance and stakeholders [26], its authors concluded that "project management literature lacks from an inclusive framework which defines the roles, relationships and positions of internal and external stakeholders inside and outside of the organization's governance structure" [26]. On the other hand, the existent governance approaches are heavily formal, structural, and management-oriented [27].

So, how can we access and evaluate the alignment between temporary and permanent governance structures against a stakeholder's concern?

To start answering this question, we detail in Sect. 2 the need to validate the existence of a common authority and decisional layered vision of the Enterprise, and any temporary governance structure. By mapping the roles into such decisional layers, it will be possible to place the temporary and permanent roles at a same level in what concerns with their responsibilities and attributions (addressed in Subsect. 2.1). Also the ArchiMate suitability for the identified problem (addressed in Subsect. 2.2). Finally related work on the evaluation and metrics allowed to validate the alignment (addressed in Subsect. 2.3). In Sect. 3 are presented: a conceptual model of the solution (addressed in Subsect. 3.1); a viewpoint and views of the solution (addressed in Subsect. 3.2); and the evaluation and alignment level for the governance structure in place against stakeholder's concern (addressed in Subsect. 3.3).

Finally, Sect. 4 provides a demonstration on the application of the solution to a real case in an enterprise, followed by the Conclusions and Further Work.

2 Related Work

Transformation of the enterprises have different speeds and priorities. The need to steer the enterprise demands accurate and precise information to support decision making. It matters now to understand what to detect. Patterns, rules, procedures, performance indicators or others, to allow, on design phase or during monitoring, to identify potential misalignments in temporary and permanent governance roles.

More than the relation on permanent and temporary governing bodies, the focus is required to be on the permanent governances' roles that share the same actor assigned to a temporary governance role. Following the research in [28], the actor-role, "an entity that is capable of performing behavior, and has the responsibility to perform specific behaviors according to a status", can be assessed on its influence authority from the enterprise permanent governance.

Considering such, the related work on the relevance in addressing a possible governance assessment based on actor-roles' focus in three main requirements:

- The existence of a common authority and decisional level framework for permanent and temporary governing bodies – The authorities and the function level in which a determined temporary role is expected to operate within its temporary governance structure must be at the same level of authorities and functions of the layered enterprise where the project is undergoing. This will allow to have a clear authority line and a common layered vision of the permanent and temporary governances structures - addressed in Subsect. 2.1;

– The validity in using ArchiMate modelling language and framework for the architectural Viewpoint and the associated views – Assuming the adequacy of the metamodel and the scope of the solution of ArchiMate, it matters to understand the viewpoints and views that may already provide a representation of the elements relevant for the scope of his work - addressed in Subsect. 2.2; and
– The evaluation and alignment measures required to assess and validate a temporary governance structure alignment towards a stakeholder concern – the architectural elements resulting from the representation of the set views require assessment metrics in order to determine the alignment level. Those assessment metrics are required to validate the need in assessing the actor-roles in the permanent and temporary governance structures against an expected structure in place by the stakeholder - addressed in Subsect. 2.3.

2.1 Common Authority and Decisional Level Framework

Standards such as ISO 215 series regularly refer to decisional levels in the organization as: Senior Management or Executive Level; Management; and Operations level. In particular in [5] the level of given liberty allows to place the different roles, such as Project Owner, at the executive level of the enterprise. It is visible and understandable the difficulty in imposing a solution that can be adopted to, a less complex organization in decisional levels to a more complex one, being accurate on a decisional level base. Table 1 shows the identified roles or functions normalized into the standard, and classified under a specific decisional level according to [5–7].

Table 1. Roles and Decisional Organizational Levels in ISO 215 series

	Project	Program	Portfolio
Senior Management/ Executive	Steering Committee	Program Governing Body	Portfolio Governing Body
	Project Sponsor	Program Sponsor	-
Management	Project Manager	Program Manager	Portfolio Manager
	Project Management Team	Program Management Team	Portfolio Management Team
Operations	Project Team	-	-

In that direction, the authors in [19] present a reference architecture on projects, programs and portfolios (PPP) governance model. Using ArchiMate, the proposed reference architecture allowed the verification of deviations between different projects, program and portfolio governance models at competences and roles levels.

As we can notice, the authors used the decisional layers presented in PM2 Methodology [29], as seen in the project organization model in Fig. 1.

The PM2 methodology from the European Commission [46], does a strong effort to align classic project management practices to the context of EU funded projects. Such alignment attempt is evidenced with the Project Owner and Project Manager's roles, which appear as part of different sides (Requestor side and Provider side) adapting in this sense to the reality of a project carried on under an outsourcing model.

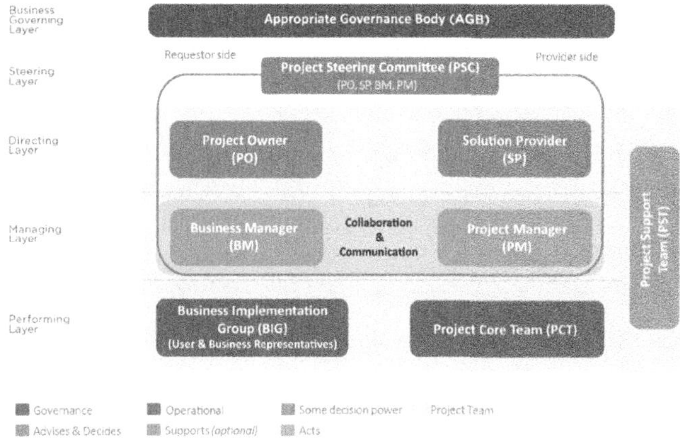

Fig. 1. Project Organization in [29]

Such a proposal on the project organization's layered vision, extrapolated for the overall organization, can provide relevant inputs when applied generally in analyzing the roles defined under a more classical project management approach. A better understanding of the decisional level in a layered vision of the project organization will foster a clearer view of such Governance's scope and the organizational landscapes.

Also, by granting a common decisional layered vision on the actor roles of one or more governing bodies, other elements allow to identify potential misalignments, such as a possible actor assuming a temporary role in a higher or lower decisional level than its permanent role.

For last, the number of roles and respective actors in each decisional layer can have significance, since the higher it is, the higher the risk of losing efficiency and quality in the negotiations and required compromises for decisions.

2.2 ArchiMate's Viewpoint and Views

ArchiMate [30] is the modeling language that has a vast number of resources and tools in the organization's design activities. The standard provides a set of entities and relationships with their corresponding iconography to represent Architecture Descriptions" [30]. This amplitude in the way ArchiMate allows the all organization to be represented under the correct level and aspect, seems to provide a coherent set of elements to assess a governance alignment.

As key attributes for the use of Archimate are: 1) the two main types of elements in the language are structure (nouns) and behavioral (verb) elements, [30]; and ii) it also distinguishes between the model elements and their notation. This last one allows a more varied, stakeholder-oriented viewpoint, framing the notation to the context in place.

In Fig. 2, are referenced the elements under the respective aspects and layers, that are under the scope of the problem to address. The elements by itself allow us to understand the conceptual representation of the problem, locating it in strategy, business and migration & implementation layers. The elements include behavioral, active structure and motivation aspects, alongside one composite element.

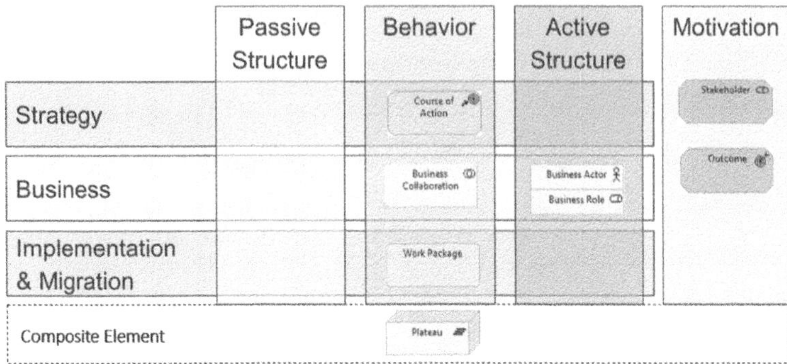

Fig. 2. Aspects, Layers and Elements in the scope of the problem

The viewpoint and related views required for the proposed solution become also a key feature in ArchiMate that expects to provide the necessary tools for the representation and communication necessities for its stakeholders.

Viewpoint and Views

Viewpoints, defined as "a specification of the conventions for constructing and using a view; a pattern or template from which to develop individual views by establishing the purposes and audience for a view and the techniques for its creation and analysis." [1] focus on particular aspects and layers. Such aspects and layers are determined, as seen, by the concerns of a stakeholder.

Looking at Basic Viewpoint classification in ArchiMate specification [30], the closer to the scope of this work is the Organization viewpoint from the Composition Category: "viewpoints that define internal compositions and aggregations of elements".

As, "a viewpoint establishes the purposes and audience for a view and the techniques or methods employed in constructing a view" [1], the purpose expressed in this basic viewpoint falls short in addressing the concerns on designing, deciding and informing on two different organization viewpoints. One regarding the "running the mill" organization, and the other regarding the "changing the mill" organization.

Since by now we can state as required elements, common to organization viewpoint are elements such as: Actor, Role, Business Collaboration or Outcome, the proposal below for a Transformation Governance Viewpoint (Table 2), tries to address the concern on the identification of permanent and temporary governance transformation roles. While maintaining the scope as a multi layer & single aspect of the enterprise.

The views, understood as the "representation of a system from the perspective of a related set of concerns" [1] have its conventions defined by the proposed viewpoint. Containing elements and relationships (concepts) framing the stakeholder's concern.

In conclusion we can note that ArchiMate provides an adequate set of elements to allow an adequate representation of Governance Relationships in a given reality. Due to its language/ notation independence, a better evaluation of the permanent and temporary nature of the governance structures in place is possible by allowing stakeholder-oriented representation.

Table 2. Proposal of Transformation Governance Viewpoint

Transformation Governance Viewpoint	
Stakeholders	Enterprise, Process Architects, Transformation managers, PMO, EPMO
Concerns	Identification of permanent and temporary governance transformation roles and serve relation
Purpose	Designing, deciding, informing
Scope	Multi layer/ Single Aspect

2.3 Evaluation and Alignment Level

[19] evidenced the validity in ArchiMate assessing different frameworks and classifications against a reference architecture for governance roles. This solution allows to better answer to the heterogeneity in complexity, scope, specificities that each transformation process can entail.

Stakeholder's concern becomes in this sense the set of elements that represent his interests. Concern, understood as "an interest of a stakeholder with regards to the architecture description of some system, resulting from the stakeholder's goals, and the present or future role(s) played by the system in relation to these goals" [1].

The stakeholder, restricted to the scope of this work as someone who has approval rights on the suitability of implementation, can determine the adequate governance by at a first stand choosing the focus to be in time and cost, or quality and technical expertise.

A commonly used approach to Project Organization [31, 32] focuses on the collaboration within two roles: i) project manager and ii) functional manager. Temporary and permanent roles respectively. Such organization is based upon two extremes: Project Hierarchy and Functional Hierarchy. If in project hierarchy it is denoted a stronger focus on time and costs control on the project, in functional hierarchy the focus is on quality and technical expertise [31].

As expected, a third category of project organization is the balanced matrix, where the collaboration and negotiation nature required for the project manager and the functional manager roles leads to a higher risk of conflicts and dead end negotiations.

In [32], the author indicates two other types, the Coordinated Matrix, between Functional Hierarchy and Balanced Matrix; and Secondment Matrix, between Balanced Matrix type and Project Hierarchy. Both distribute the authority either to the project manager, or to the functional manager, but with a stronger collaboration link than the extremes (Fig. 3).

If in project hierarchy it is denoted a stronger focus on time and cost control on the project, and in functional hierarchy the focus is on quality and technical expertise [31].

As such, the concern level on Time, Cost, Quality and Technical Expertise seems suitable to determine the alignment between the governance roles in place and their adequacy on the stakeholder concerns. Being possible to present an evaluation on permanent and temporary governance, based in the "matrix continuum" [31], with the purpose to map different characteristics evidenced by the elements in the architecture of the desired transformation action.

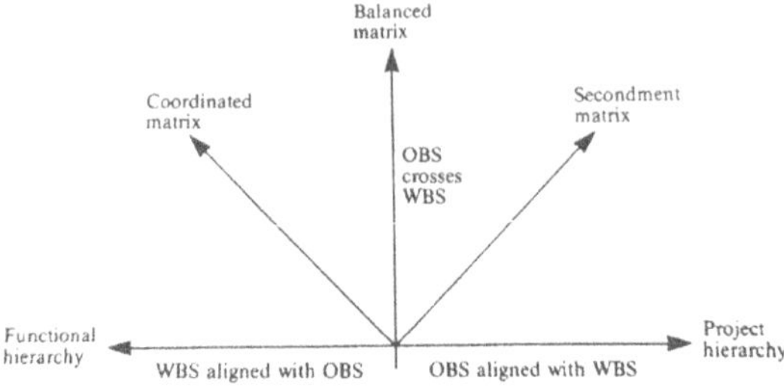

Fig. 3. Range of matrix structures in [32]

Beyond this representation, other approaches such as [33] apply the same matrix but under a Functional or Product influence in the decision making. That represents a different semantic over the governance roles in place, but with the qualities, and disadvantages, of the model.

As visible in the adapted representation of the Matrix Continuum, Fig. 4, we can determine as extremes the functional hierarchy and the project hierarchy for some qualities of the system, but with other sets of qualities being similar in the "middle" of a given governance structure. In fact, each model of governance structure is more suitable than others to other contexts, the awareness of the type of governance structure in place allows a double check on the alignment expected with the stakeholder's concern.

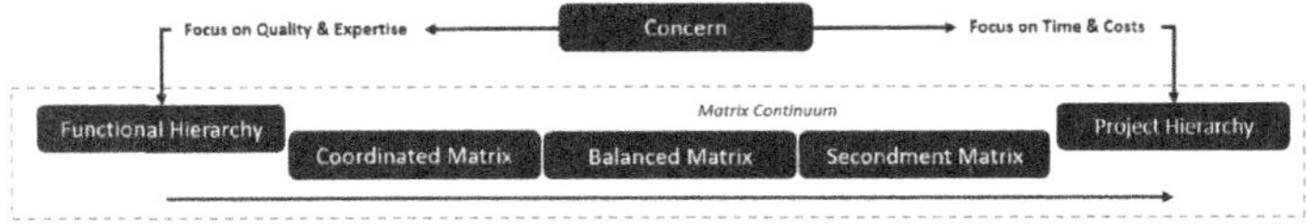

Fig. 4. Matrix Continuum [31, 32], adapted

Bringing to the reality of enterprises and considering the complexity and own hierarchy of the enterprise, and when centered in one same actor a temporary and a permanent role, the efficiency of the governance structure may not be the expected. This is because being a functional manager or a project manager, if in the same actor, misalignment tends to happen.

3 Temporary and Permanent Governance Continuum

Considering the existent models, tools and semantics, we present the solution's conceptual model (addressed in Sect. 3.1), the views and viewpoints (addressed in Sect. 3.2) and how it allows us to promote the measurement and evaluation on the governance alignment (addressed in Sect. 3.3).

3.1 Conceptual Model

The proposed conceptual model in Fig. 5 provides the required concepts to frame the conceptual domain of this work; at the same time that allows a more clear understanding on relations between each concept. If we remove the Permanent Role and the Permanent Transformation Governance roles, the conceptual model can be seen as any other project conceptual model. But, to assess permanent roles, under a permanent transformation governance roles plateau, in the governance continuum of a project, they become key concepts.

The course of action of the temporary plateau regarding governance in place is set to influence the outcome associated with the main stakeholder.

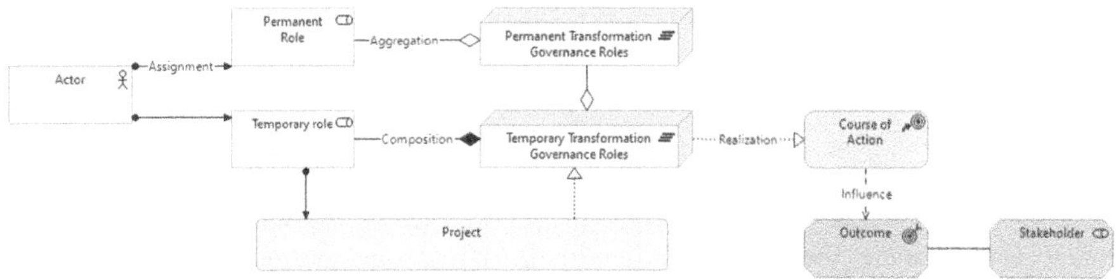

Fig. 5. Conceptual Model of Temporary and Permanent Governance Continuum

The rules associated with the proposed conceptual model are:

1. One actor can have one or more permanent or temporary roles;
2. One role can only have one assignment from one Actor;
3. There are two plateaus for transformation roles, one regarding temporary roles, and a second regarding the permanent roles;
4. Permanent Roles are related with business units from the operations of the enterprise, where the benefits of the transformation are expected to occur;
5. Temporary Roles are related with the governance structure for the temporary endeavor;
6. One actor with a temporary role and no permanent role in the enterprise is considered to be from an external governing body of the scope and benefits of the project;
7. The permanent roles of business areas outside the scope of the transformation are not referenced as permanent roles in an actor with a temporary role;
8. The alignment of temporary and permanent roles can be determined by the adequacy of stakeholder concerns on transformation events (Cost, Time, Quality, Technical Expertise) in place;
9. A concern (represented as outcome) on Time and Costs is in alignment with a temporary roles hierarchy reality of a given transformation event;
10. A concern on Quality and Technical expertise is in alignment with a permanent roles hierarchy model of a given transformation event.

3.2 Views and Viewpoint on Governance Continuum

Building upon Fig. 4 we can see that by applying the solution to the functional hierarchy and project hierarchy, as in Fig. 3, we can set as reference the representations in Fig. 6 and Fig. 7 while the two extreme governance structures expected for a project.

If in Fig. 6 we can evidence that all temporary roles in the project are assigned from actors that also have permanent roles in the enterprise, under the functional scope of the

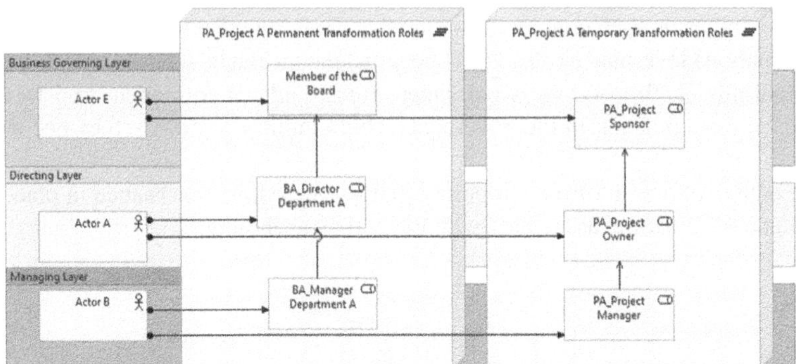

Fig. 6. Functional Hierarchy matrix view on ArchiMate

project. Hence, such view allows us to evidence when a governance structure in place presents the characteristics of a Functional Hierarchy Matrix.

In Fig. 7 we can see a more governance structure closer to the Project Matrix Structure, where Directing and Managing layers are performed by temporary roles.

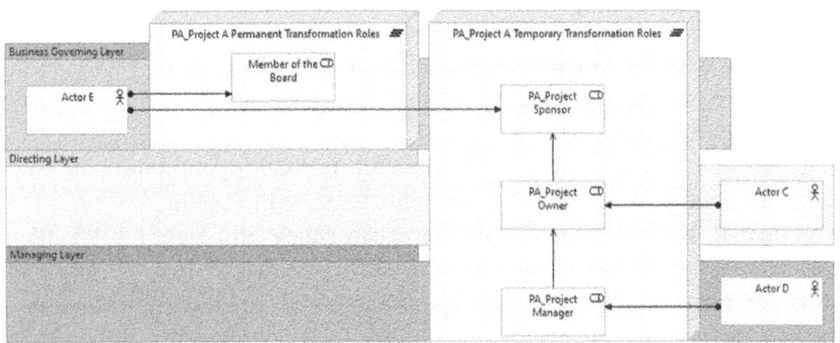

Fig. 7. Project Hierarchy matrix view on ArchiMate

For the two 'opposite' project governance structures we can evidence that, by evaluating the relevance of either permanent roles or temporary roles, we can determine if governance in place is more cost/time, or quality/ expertise oriented, due to the characteristics of the governance structure.

The balanced matrix hierarchy, in Fig. 8, is supposed to be in between the functional and project hierarchy. As said, the risk and the need for collaboration and negotiation in between different roles is a constraint/ risk to address in project implementation.

As set, it becomes clearer the validity in assessing governance alignment between a temporary governing body and the enterprise governing bodies, in a structured and formalized way.

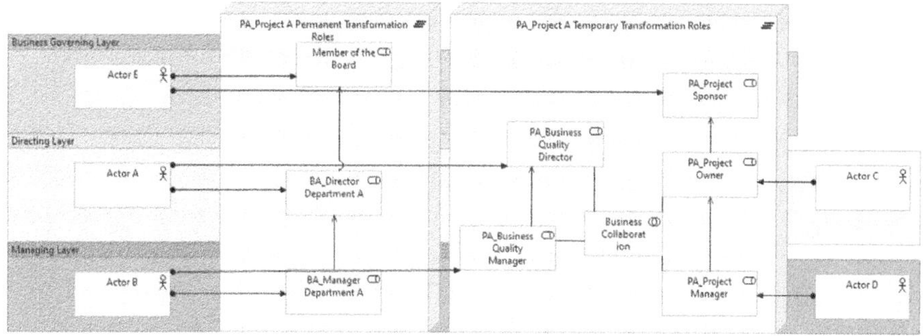

Fig. 8. Balanced Hierarchy Matrix view on ArchiMate

3.3 Evaluation and Alignment Level

The impact that the governance structure in place has in the project outcome, according with the different characteristics of the identified governance structures, is determinant in the value that brings in a project design phase, or ongoing project governance evaluation. By promoting an evaluation, and determining the influence on outcome, we can promote the alignment measure against a stakeholder's concern.

The number of architectural elements and their associated semantics allow to evaluate in a quantifiable way the governance structure in place. As seen in Table 3, the three main governance matrix models are denoted in the ratio of permanent governance roles from the enterprise in the temporary governance structure.

Table 3. Assessment of functional, balanced and project governance structures

Functional Matrix		Actors	Roles	Temp Roles	Perm Roles	% Temp Roles	% Perm Roles
Business Governing Layer		1	2	1	1	50,00%	50,00%
Steering Layer		0	0	0	0	0,00%	0,00%
Directing Layer		1	2	1	1	50,00%	50,00%
Managing Layer		1	2	1	1	50,00%	50,00%
	Total	3	6	3	3	50,00%	50,00%

Balanced Matrix		Actors	Roles	Temp Roles	Perm Roles	% Temp Roles	% Perm Roles
Business Governing Layer		1	2	1	1	50,00%	50,00%
Steering Layer		0	0	0	0	0,00%	0,00%
Directing Layer		2	3	2	1	66,67%	33,33%
Managing Layer		2	3	2	1	66,67%	33,33%
	Total	5	8	5	3	62,50%	37,50%

Project Matrix		Actors	Roles	Temp Roles	Perm Roles	% Temp Roles	% Perm Roles
Business Governing Layer		1	2	1	1	50,00%	50,00%
Steering Layer		0	0	0	0	0,00%	0,00%
Directing Layer		1	1	1	0	100,00%	0,00%
Managing Layer		1	1	1	0	100,00%	0,00%
	Total	3	4	3	1	75,00%	25,00%

As seen in Sect. 2.3, we can now evidence that Project Matrix represents in its structure 100% of temporary roles. However, since that according to standards, a project sponsorship is always represent at the highest level by the enterprise. Considering that, the Project Matrix in Fig. 9 does not have 100% in temporary roles.

On the other hand, in same figure, we can see the Functional Matrix, with 100% of actors with permanent roles assuming temporary governance roles for that project.

Functional Matrix	0%	10%	20%	30%	40%	50%	60%	70%	80%	90%	100%
Permanent roles											
Temporary roles											

Balanced Matrix	0%	10%	20%	30%	40%	50%	60%	70%	80%	90%	100%
Permanent roles											
Temporary roles											

Project Matrix	0%	10%	20%	30%	40%	50%	60%	70%	80%	90%	100%
Permanent roles											
Temporary roles											

Fig. 9. Temporary and Permanent Governance Continuum

Placing the values in a governance continuum between the functional governance matrix and the project governance matrix, we can evidence the shift in governance structure characteristics, such as the more biased information in functional matrix, to full focus on time and cost in the project matrix.

4 Case Study

Based on the proposed solution, we now assess its practical validity under a concrete case that occurred in a Public Company, with a formal PMO, where a concern from the Project Sponsor stop being met, after a change in the actors associated with the roles of a particular project.

The case in question happened in a company, that for anonymity purpose we call Company A. That company had a high maturity level in handling transformation, with a permanent structure with that function, a PMO.

Project A, had as Sponsor a Member of The Board of the company and he made notice to the PMO that there had been a change in the quality of the report of that particular project.

PMO argued that the governance model's recent changes is the only change that could have affected the quality and truth of information on the projects' status.

The mentioned recent organizational change in PMO's enterprise structure had re-allocated the project manager role to an actor that had a role in the business area where its director was also the project owner. The previous project manager was allocated from a pool of resources, managed by the PMO.

Such change, by altering the actor of a temporary role, created the constraint that affected the quality in the expected information from Enterprise PMO reports. To understand the cause, we have to look at the enterprise formal and permanent governance structure of involved actors-roles in two different moments: As Was and As Is.

By mapping the actor-roles under the scope, it was applied the conceptual model presented and the generated lists as are presented in Fig. 10. The same exercise was done for the As Is situation.

ID	Actor ID	Role	Decisional Level (1, 2, 3, 4, 5)	Governance Structure	Temp (0) / Perm (1)	Serves ID
1	Actor E	Member of the Board	1	Board	1	0
2	Actor C	Head of Department	3	Department A	1	1
1	Actor E	Project Sponsor	1	Project A	0	0
2	Actor C	Project Owner	3	Project A	0	1
4	Actor B	Project Manager	4	Project A	0	2

Fig. 10. Map of temporary and permanent actor-roles in Project A - As Was

With that information we can model in ArchiMate the identified actors, roles, decisional levels and governance structures. As we can see in Fig. 11, the generated views make also visually clear on the existent balance between temporary and permanent governance roles. This in what concerns the As Was situation, because regarding As Is, the generated view is the same as we have seen in Fig. 6.

If in Fig. 11 we can see the clear serve line in the temporary transformation roles, in the type of structure identified in Fig. 6, the serve relations becomes in line with what translates the "running the mill", permanent governance. A mirrored serve relation from the permanent governance.

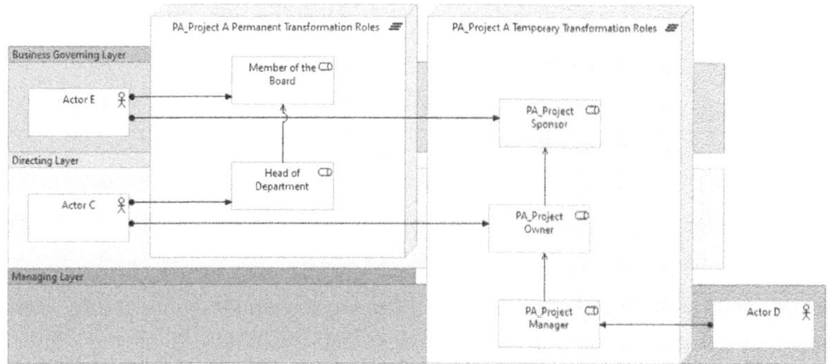

Fig. 11. Case A – governance structure as it was

After 1) mapping Actors under Scope of the project (As Was and As Is) and 2) modelling the different elements under the permanent and temporary plateaus, the structural differences that may have changed the quality in the reporting become visible.

The change in the assignment of the project manager role, changed the balance between temporary and permanent roles, by bringing it to a more functional matrix governance structure, instead of a more balanced one. Not coincidentally, one of the characteristics in governance models based in a more functional matrix is the higher risk of biased information to the stakeholders.

By making clear, through the generated views, the shift in balance between temporary and permanent roles, it allows to better identify in design phase, or implementation phase, the governance structure in place (Figs. 12 and 13).

In conclusion, and as seen in Fig. 14, the change in the temporary role allocation promoted an increase in the permanent role influence on the overall governance of the

	ACTORS	ROLES	TEMP	PERM	% TEMP ROLES	% PERM ROLES
Business Governing Layer	1	2	1	1	50,00%	50,00%
Directing Layer	1	2	1	1	50,00%	50,00%
Managing Layer	1	1	1	0	100,00%	0,00%
Total	1	5	3	2	60,00%	40,00%

Fig. 12. Percentage on temporary and permanent actor-roles in Project A - As Was

	ACTORS	ROLES	TEMP	PERM	TEMP ROL	PERM ROLES
Business Governing Layer	1	2	1	1	50,00%	50,00%
Directing Layer	1	2	1	1	50,00%	50,00%
Managing Layer	1	2	1	1	50,00%	50,00%
Total	3	6	3	3	50,00%	50,00%

Fig. 13. Percentage of temporary and permanent actor-roles in Project A - As Is

project A. By becoming a fully functional governance matrix, it also carried out its cons as a model. In this case the loss of quality in the reporting information.

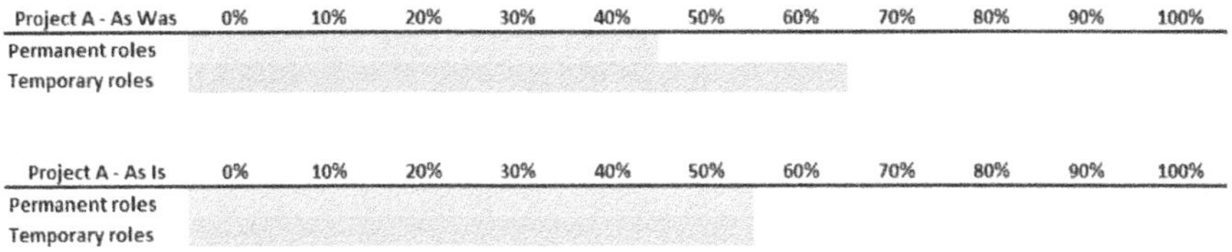

Project A - As Was	0%	10%	20%	30%	40%	50%	60%	70%	80%	90%	100%
Permanent roles											
Temporary roles											

Project A - As Is	0%	10%	20%	30%	40%	50%	60%	70%	80%	90%	100%
Permanent roles											
Temporary roles											

Fig. 14. Project A - Governance Continuum Roles Influence

In what concerns with the proposed solution, we have now evidenced the validity of solution presented in Sect. 3, allowing to assess and evaluate a temporary governance structure, under the enterprise relevant actor-roles, promoting a fine tuning in the impact that some variables have in project outcomes. In this case, temporary and permanent governance roles and a Stakeholder concern.

5 Conclusions and Further Work

The level of knowledge, theoretical or practical, in fields of study in enterprise efficiency and governance is vast and has allowed enterprises to increase their pace in transformations to adapt to new realities, business models, products, or services. The efficiency level required, and increasing, put to enterprises and their workers the pressure for delivery, with quality, under several types of concerns when dealing with transformation.

From this work we can assess the validity in the identified problem: the alignment on temporary and permanent governance roles, towards the stakeholder's concern on Time and Cost Vs. Quality and Expertise (or Functional Vs. Product as [33] put it.

As main contributions from this work we can highlight:

1. A conceptual map for the temporary and permanent governance roles enrolled in enterprise transformation (Fig. 5);
2. A proposal of Viewpoint for ArchiMate, and related views, with the concerns on the Identification of permanent and temporary governance transformation roles and serve relation (Table 2);
3. A method on assessing the governance structure in a project and classify according to governance structures characteristics (Sect. 3 - Temporary and Permanent Governance Continuum).

As for future work, adding other efficiency and control instruments are a way forward in the research. Two directions are being followed: i) the set of rules and elements to measure and represent the influence relationship between permanent and temporary governance roles; and ii) the identification of added rules onto the coherence of the governance structure, from different classifications and models.

Acknowledgements. "This work was supported by national funds through FCT, Fundação para a Ciência e a Tecnologia, under project UIDB/50021/2020 (DOI:10.54499/UIDB/50021/2020) and Project Blockchain.PT – Decentralize Portugal with Blockchain Agenda, (Project no 51, C632734434-00467077), WP 7: Interoperability, Call no 02/C05-i01.01/2022, funded by the Portuguese Recovery and Resilience Program (PPR), The Portuguese Republic and The European Union (EU) under the framework of Next Generation EU Program".

References

1. Lankhorst, M.: Enterprise Architecture at Work. Springer, Heidelberg (2009). https://doi.org/10.1007/978-3-642-01310-2
2. Dietz, J.L.G., et al.: The discipline of enterprise engineering. Int. J. Organ. Des. Eng. **3**, 86 (2013). https://doi.org/10.1504/IJODE.2013.053669
3. Proper, E., Greefhost, D.: Architecture Principles - The Cornerstone of Enterprise Architecture. Springer, Heidelberg (2011). https://doi.org/10.1007/978-3-642-20279-7
4. Tribolet, J., Sousa, P., Caetano, A.: The role of enterprise governance and cartography enterprise engineering. Enterp. Model. Inf. Syst. Archit. J. (EMISA) **9**(1), 38–49 (2014)
5. ISO: ISO 21500:2012 - Guidance on Project Management (2012)
6. ISO: ISO 21503:2017 - Project, programme and portfolio management—Guidance on programme management (2017)
7. ISO: ISO 21504:2015 - Project, programme and portfolio management—Guidance on portfolio management (2015)
8. ISO: ISO 21505:2017 - Project, programme and portfolio management—Guindance on Governance (2017)
9. Steen, J., DeFillippi, R., Sydow, J., Pryke, S., Michelfelder, I.: Projects and networks: understanding resource flows and governance of temporary organizations with quantitative and qualitative research methods. Proj. Manag. J. **49**, 3–17 (2018). https://doi.org/10.1177/875697281804900201
10. PMI: Governance of Portfolios, Programs, and Projects: A Practice Guide. Project Management Institute (2016)
11. Cambridge: Online Cambridge Dictionary. https://dictionary.cambridge.org/dictionary/english/project. Accessed 09 Feb 2019

12. Koskela, L., Howell, G.: The underlying theory of project management is obsolete. In: Frontiers of Project Management Research and Applications, pp. 22–34. Project Management Institute, Seattle, Washington (2002). https://doi.org/10.1109/EMR.2008.4534317
13. Winter, M., Smith, C., Morris, P., Cicmil, S.: Directions for future research in project management: the main findings of a UK government-funded research network **24**, 638–649 (2006). https://doi.org/10.1016/j.ijproman.2006.08.009
14. Winter, M., Smith, C.: Rethinking project management - Final report - EPSRC network 2004–2006, pp. 1–7 (2006)
15. Maylor, H.: Special issue on rethinking project management (EPSRC network 2004–2006). Int. J. Proj. Manag. **24**, 635–637 (2006). https://doi.org/10.1016/j.ijproman.2006.09.013
16. Svejvig, P., Andersen, P.: Rethinking project management: a structured literature review with a critical look at the brave new world. Int. J. Proj. Manag. **33**, 278–290 (2015). https://doi.org/10.1016/j.ijproman.2014.06.004
17. Packendorff, J.: Inquiring into the temporary organization: new directions for project management research. Scand. J. Manag. **11**, 319–333 (1995)
18. Englund, R.L., Graham, R.J.: From experience: linking projects to strategy. J. Prod. Innov. Manag. **16**, 52–64 (1999). https://doi.org/10.1111/1540-5885.1610052
19. Cordeiro, G., Vasconcelos, A., Fragoso, B.: Project, program, portfolio governance model reference architecture in the classic approach to project management. In: Proceedings of the 22nd International Conference on Enterprise Information Systems, pp. 619–630. SCITEPRESS - Science and Technology Publications (2020). https://doi.org/10.5220/0009155706190630
20. PMI: ANSI/PMI 08-004-2008 - Organizational Project Management Maturity Model (OPM3) (2008)
21. Riis, E., Hellström, M.M., Wikström, K.: Governance of projects: generating value by linking projects with their permanent organisation. Int. J. Proj. Manag. **37**, 652–667 (2019). https://doi.org/10.1016/j.ijproman.2019.01.005
22. Musawir, A., Abd-Karim, S.B., Mohd Danuri, M.S.: Project governance: enabling organizational strategy. In: 10th ASEAN Postgraduate Seminar 2016 (2016)
23. Kurek, E.: The value of enterprise architecture on IT projects (2018)
24. PMI: Pulse of Profession 2018 (2018)
25. PMI: Pulse of Profession 2017 (2017)
26. Derakhshan, R., Turner, R., Mancini, M.: Project governance and stakeholders: a literature review. Int. J. Proj. Manag. **37**, 98–116 (2019). https://doi.org/10.1016/j.ijproman.2018.10.007
27. Hoogervorst, J.A.P.: Enterprise governance and enterprise engineering (2009). https://doi.org/10.1007/978-3-540-92671-9
28. Fragoso, B., Vasconcelos, A., Borbinha, J.: On the roles of project, program and portfolio governance. In: Shishkov, B. (ed.) Business Modeling and Software Design, pp. 221–228. Springer, Cham (2019)
29. European Commission, D.: Open PM2: Project Management Methodology. European Commission, DIGIT Centre of Excellence in Project Management (CoEPM^2), Luxembourg (2016). https://doi.org/10.1201/b15518-3
30. The Open Group: ArchiMate 3.2 Specification. The Open Group (2022)
31. Teplitz, C.J.: Making optimal use of the matrix organization. In: Cleland, D.I. (ed.) Field Guide to Project Management, pp. 201–211. International Thomson Publishing Company, New York (1998)
32. Turner, J.R.: The Handbook of Project-Based Management. McGraw-Hill, Berkshire (1999)
33. Kerzner, H.: Project Management - A Systems Approach to Planning, Scheduling, and Controling. Wiley, New York (1998)

On the Alignment of DAO with Socio-political Principles of Decentralised Governance Using TOGAF and ArchiMate

Julien Hue(✉), Irina Rychkova, and Nicolas Herbaut

Centre de Recherche en Informatique, Université Paris 1 Panthéon-Sorbonne, 75013 Paris, France

julien.hue@etu.univ-paris1.fr, {irina.rychkova,nicolas.herbaut}@univ-paris1.fr

Abstract. In this work, we explore the application of Enterprise Architecture (EA) frameworks, specifically TOGAF and ArchiMate, to model the alignment between socio-political artifacts and technological artifacts within Decentralised Autonomous Organisations (DAOs). DAOs are new organisation model that leverages blockchain (BC) technology to implement decentralised governance such as Liquid Democracy (LD) which respect anarchist principles. However, the challenge lies in demonstrating the traceability between socio-political governance processes and the technological artifacts that enables these processes. This paper addresses this gap by applying Design Science Research (DSR) methodology to develop a reference architecture. This Architecture serves as a structured model to analyze and verify the alignment of decentralised governance processes with their technological implementations DAOs. This work contribution is a systematic approach to modelisation and analysis of socio-political structures of decentralised organisations, ensuring they align with the underlying technology supporting them.

Keywords: blockchain · enterprise architecture · enterprise modeling · TOGAF ADM · organisation on Networks · anarchism

1 Introduction

Since Satoshi Nakamoto released the bitcoin whitepaper [40], a new era of decentralised systems began. Initially a peer-to-peer electronic cash system, Blockchain Technologies (BCT) evolved significantly with the Ethereum project [6], introducing Smart Contracts and decentralised Autonomous organisations (DAOs) supporting enterprise use cases. Yet Nakamoto's initial vision, rooted in the cypherpunk movement, aligns with the anarchist idea of a decentralised society.

The anarchist movement, championed by thinkers like Kropotkin [35, 36], Bakunin [4], and Malatesta [37], proposes principles aimed at avoiding exploitation and fostering harmony. However, these principles have never been

M. Kaczmarek-Heß et al. (Eds.): EDOC 2024 Workshops, LNBIP 537, pp. 117–136, 2025.
https://doi.org/10.1007/978-3-031-79059-1_8

implemented at scale. DAOs embedding anarchist principles appeal to activists, technologists, and communities seeking autonomy, offering transparent, secure, and efficient ways to manage organisations without central authority, such as Liquid Democracy (LD), proposed in the early 21st century, combining elements of Direct Democracy and Representative Democracy [10,18,42].

Direct Democracy, central to anarchist principles, faces issues like voter fatigue and scalability. LD addresses these issues by allowing voters to either vote directly or delegate their vote [10,18,42] to others. Thus, LD helps implement anarchist principles in DAOs by reducing hierarchical control and promoting cooperative governance.

To systematically reason about the alignment of DAOs using LD with anarchist principles, we turn to Enterprise Architecture (EA) and Enterprise Modeling (EM) frameworks. Traditionally, EA/EM frameworks demonstrate and analyze the alignment between technology and organisational strategy. They provide tools and methodologies to model enterprises and align business processes with technology. However, little research addresses the alignment between socio-political and technological artifacts in decentralised organisations like DAOs.

In this work, we address the following research problem: *How can socio-political artifacts for decentralised organisations be addressed by Enterprise Modeling?* We use the TOGAF standard[1] to explicitly reason about processes of decentralised organisational governance grounded in anarchism. We specify the business, application, and technology layers of DAOs and LD using ArchiMate. We use Design Science Research Methodology to create an architectural artifact using TOGAF ADM and ArchiMate.

The remainder of this article is organized as follows: In Sect. 2, we discuss the main concepts used in this study and present the related works; in Sect. 3, we present our research methodology and discuss the created artifacts in Sect. 4; in Sect. 5, we empirically evaluate the alignment of our artifact with anarchist society principles and provide recommendations for adapting EA frameworks to decentralisation. In Sect. 6, we provide our conclusions.

2 Background

2.1 Smart Contracts and DAOs

Smart Contracts, first introduced by Nick Szabo in 1994 [51], are protocols for validating the conditions of a legal contract between parties. They execute, control, and document events automatically according to the agreement's terms [33,56]. Embedded within the blockchain, Smart Contracts are immutable and transparent.

DAOs are organisations operating based on rules encoded as Smart Contracts [24,53,54]. They function without human intervention, leveraging blockchain's transparency, immutability, and decentralisation. Key characteristics of DAOs include: *decentralisation:* Operate without centralized authority, distributing

[1] https://www.opengroup.org/togaf.

decision-making power among members. *Autonomy:* Smart Contract code governs operations, executing decisions and transactions automatically. *Transparency:* All transactions are recorded on the blockchain, making them auditable by anyone. *Programmable Governance:* Rules and protocols embedded within the Smart Contract automate governance. *Community-Driven:* Governed by members holding tokens that represent voting power, with decisions made by consensus.

DAOs have various applications, such as decentralised Finance (DeFi), collective ownership, investment funds, charitable organisations, and decentralised governance. They can be categorized into: 1) *Algorithmic DAOs*, which defer entirely to software to structure and coordinate social interactions, and 2) *Participatory DAOs*, which emphasize active community participation in decision-making [54].

This work focuses on Participatory DAOs, specifically decentralised Autonomous Communities where each member has one vote, and decisions require a $\frac{2}{3}$ majority [6]. We plan to use Liquid Democracy as the decision-making process in our system.

2.2 Liquid Democracy

Liquid Democracy combines elements from Direct Democracy and Representative Democracy [10,18,42]. In LD, voters can either vote directly on issues or delegate their vote to a trusted party. This delegation can continue through multiple levels until the vote reaches a well-informed party, a process known as *"Meta-delegation"*. Additionally, voters can recall their vote at any time. Members can choose on which topics to vote directly and which to delegate. *"Issue-based delegation"* allows voters to delegate their vote for a specific topic while voting directly on sub-topics. LD addresses issues in Direct Democracy, such as voter fatigue and uninformed voters, and in Representative Democracy, such as lack of accountability (e.g.: in most Representative Democracy, elected members only handles 1–2 subjects and is incompetent in the others. While voting on a subject the member don't know specifically about he can only vote for a solution he only have vague idea of. Also in this mode, the important is to win the vote and not taking the right decision or being aligned with the social body will) and minority rule (e.g.: in organisation that prefer stability and coherence of choices an entrenched minority can take the power). LD was notably used by the Pirate Party in Germany, but the experiment failed when combined with Representative Democracy [10]. Issues like the concentration of power among a few agents and the emergence of super-voters remain concerns. To address these, proposals include *"Multiple Delegations Options"* (i.e.: helps avoid super-voter by allowing users to specify several potential delegates instead of just one on various criteria), *"Dynamic Redistribution"* (i.e.: system's ability to distribute votes or influence among delegates to maintain a balanced representation to avoid the concentration of votes), and *"Algorithmic Balancing"* (i.e.: using mathematical models and computational techniques to optimize the delegation process) to distribute voting power more equitably [22]. This work explores the use of LD in DAOs to enhance decentralised governance.

2.3 EA Frameworks

Enterprise Architecture is defined as *"the underlying principles, standards, and best practices according to which current and future activities of the enterprise should be conducted"* [47]. According to Fischer [17], EA involves *The Fundamental organisation of a System*, describing system components, their relationships, and their interaction with the environment, and *The Principles Guiding its Design and Evolution*, governing the design, implementation, and development of the architecture, ensuring alignment with business goals. Several EA frameworks and tools are widely acknowledged in the literature [2,29]. The Open Group Architecture Framework (TOGAF) [28] is a comprehensive method and set of tools for developing an enterprise architecture. ArchiMate [29] is a modeling language part of "The Open Group," used to model enterprise architecture. Zachman Framework [55] defines a 6×6 matrix providing a structured approach to defining an enterprise from multiple viewpoints. FEAF (Federal Enterprise Architecture Framework) [26] originates from the US Federal Government. It integrates business and IT aspects of an enterprise. The Gartner Framework [49] Focuses on EA process development and governance.

To explore whether DAOs using LD can achieve an anarchist society organisation, we use TOGAF framework and Archimate modeling language to model and verify our system. Because first TOGAF is a widely adopted and battle tested framework, helps to define the EA from multiple viewpoints, it has a comprehensive and structured methodology to develop EA, ArchiMate bring modeling capabilities that complement very well the TOGAF ADM.

2.4 Related Works

For this section, we conducted a literature review[2] covering 251 articles, to which we added 5 pre-identified relevant articles. After reviewing each, we isolated 19 related works. These were classified into two clusters: 1) EA for socio-political artifacts/E-Government (7 articles), and 2) EA for BC or DAO (12 articles). Each cluster was further subdivided: A) Interoperability and Integration (7 articles), B) Architecture Modeling (9 articles), C) Dynamic EA Planning (1 article),

[2] using this SCOPUS query string: "(TITLE-ABS-KEY("Enterprise Architecture" AND "E-Government" AND "Interoperability") OR TITLE-ABS-KEY("decentralized Autonomous organisation" AND "Blockchain" AND "Governance") OR TITLE-ABS-KEY("Business Process Modelization" AND "Enterprise Architecture") OR TITLE-ABS-KEY("Enterprise Architecture" AND "Digital Ecosystem") OR TITLE-ABS-KEY("Requirements for Enterprise Architecture Frameworks") OR TITLE-ABS-KEY("Validation of Enterprise Architecture Frameworks quality") OR TITLE-ABS-KEY("decentralized Governance" AND "TOGAF" AND "ArchiMate") OR TITLE-ABS-KEY("Liquid Democracy" AND "Anarchist principles" AND "Blockchain") OR (TITLE-ABS-KEY("Enterprise Modeling") OR TITLE-ABS-KEY("Enterprise Architecture") AND TITLE-ABS-KEY("Blockchain" OR "decentralized Autonomous organisation" OR "DAO")))AND PUBYEAR > 2017".

and D) Systemic Design (2 articles). We first present articles related to cluster 1. For sub-category D: [20] modifies TOGAF ADM to include a "Government Strategic Objectives phase", "Security Architecture," and "customized phase.". For sub-category A: [39] develops a structured approach, SGEA, for defining e-government EA scope. [31] proposes a National EA for implementing an e-government interoperability framework in Uganda. [38] explores how EA tools aid in regulation and legislation compliance. [21] examines EA tools in the public sector to achieve business ecosystem maturity. [48] discusses E-Government architecture in Indonesia using TOGAF and Service-Oriented Architecture. For sub-category B: [45] presents a Smart Campus System blueprint using TOGAF ADM, adapting TOGAF for specific domains and modeling socio-political artifacts. Next, we discuss cluster 2, starting with sub-category B: [27] explores BC's potential in enhancing business value creation, particularly in global supply chains, using ArchiMate models. [14] examines how EA approaches, especially ArchiMate, can design BC-based applications. [3] addresses the gap between enterprise engineering modeling methods and blockchain models. [16] proposes Knowledge BC for securely managing and tracking knowledge in organisations. [1] uses EA tools for developing digital twins for dry ports with ArchiMate. [15] discusses integrating BC into enterprise modeling and the mutual support between BC technology and modeling techniques. [30] focuses on structuring and implementing BC in enterprises, emphasizing the necessary layers for a robust BC platform. [34] develops a method for strategic analysis integrating business processes and IT infrastructure, focusing on GoalML, SAML, and ITML. For sub-category C: [12] discusses EA as a strategic tool for aligning business and IT, incorporating case-based reasoning and BC for knowledge storage and sharing. For sub-category A: [50] uses EA tools to address BC interoperability issues, while [41] proposes an architecture integrating BC into Health Information Exchanges (HIEs) to enhance healthcare data management and exchange. Finally, For sub-category D: [7] discusses the systematic design of BC-based applications, integrating business and IT perspectives. Analyzing this literature reveals a gap that our work aims to fill: EA for BC applied to socio-political artifacts/E-Government.

3 Research Methodology

To address our research problem, we employ the Design Science Research Methodology (DSRM) [25,43], which consists of six steps: Problem Identification and Motivation, Objectives for the Solution, Design and Development, Demonstration, Evaluation, and Communication. We merge the Demonstration and Evaluation steps to better address our research questions. *Problem Identification and Motivation.* While DAO provides a set of mechanisms to implement decentralised governance and principles of liquid democracy, there is no evidence on how these organisations form can support other socio-political mechanisms, including principles and governance processes grounded on anarchism. We choose enterprise modeling and enterprise architecture disciplines to address the problem of alignment and traceability of socio-political artefacts in decentralised organisations. This motivates the following research questions: **RQ1:** How can TOGAF and ArchiMate be used to model socio-political artifacts within decentralised organisations? **RQ2:** How TOGAF and ArchiMate should be adapted to address socio-political artefacts in decentralised organisations? **RQ3:** In what ways can LD and DAOs can be used to achieve the organisation of anarchist societies? *Objectives for the Solution.* Establish key objectives: Design an architectural artifact using TOGAF ADM and ArchiMate to model DAOs with LD. Ensure the artifact aligns with anarchist society principles. Validate the artifact's ability to support decentralised governance at scale. Here, we want to ensure that the artifact that we build is aligned with the anarchist society principles. We use the anarchist society principles that we elicit from the literature to design our artifact. *Design and Development.* Develop the artifact using TOGAF ADM and ArchiMate as architectural Framework, and employing modeling languages such as i* 2.0, BPMN and SysML/UML to design the motivation, business, application, and technology layers to assure that the artifact encapsulates the anarchist society principles. *Demonstration and Evaluation.* Demonstrate and evaluate the artifact by applying practical use cases based on anarchist society principles to verify alignment and conduct scenario analysis to demonstrate how to the artifact supports decentralised governance. We use an analytical evaluation as described by Hevner et al. [25] to evaluate the artifact and answer our research questions, more precisely the "Architecture Analysis". *Communication.* We have documented the research process, findings and some recommendations. Then we present the result in this paper.

4 Artifact Design

4.1 Design Principles, Rationale, and Development Approach

In this work, we adopt the TOGAF ADM. It is an iterative process for developing architecture content, transition from the existing (As-Is) to the target (To-Be) architecture and the architecture governance [28].

We focus on the following ADM phases: Preliminary Phase, which describes the preparation and initiation activities required to create an Architecture capability and definition of Architectures Principles; Architecture Vision, which describes the initial phase of an architecture development cycle; Business Architecture, which describes the development of a Business Architecture to support an agreed Architecture Vision; Information Systems Architecture, which describes the development of IS Architectures to support the agreed Architecture Vision; and Technology Architecture, which describe the development of Technology Architectures to support the agreed Architecture Vision.

In the Preliminary Phase, we conduct a literature review of the anarchist literature. We derive the anarchist society principles from the various sources, including the research articles, books and essays. Our results are presented in the Table 1. In our artefact, a strong assumption is present: we believe that participants will follow and commit to these principles. We use these principles in the later phases, to guide the design our artifact.

Table 1. Anarchist Society and Principles

Principles	[36]	[13]	[23]	[35]	[37]	[9]	[46]	[11]	[44]	[4]	[19]
Voluntary Association	✓		✓	✓			✓			✓	✓
Direct Democracy and Consensus Decision-Making		✓	✓		✓			✓	✓	✓	✓
Mutual Aid	✓	✓		✓		✓					✓
decentralisation						✓	✓	✓	✓		✓
Autonomy and Self-Management	✓					✓		✓			✓
Non-Hierarchical organisation		✓			✓		✓				✓
Commons and Communal Resources			✓	✓				✓	✓		✓

4.2 Preliminary Phase

In our study, we consider the organisation grounded on DAO and LD principles for the decision-making process. We model the organisation using Blockchain as the main technological babckbone. Within THIS such organisation, the team of architects that implements TOGAF has to follow the principles of decentralisation and LD. Thus, the TOGAF implementation has to be adopted according to these principles.

We use Dapp and Smart Contracts to implement the LD principles and, in particular, the voting process. We choose NFT as a technological solution to determine the collective ownership of organisations, goods, services etc. We are using the TOGAF ADM from [28] and ArchiMate 3.2 to model our organisation.

4.3 Architecture Vision

In the Architecture Vision phase we use the anarchist society principles from Table 1 to define the vision of the organisation. We present the principles of traditional centralized organisations/societies (As-Is), putting forward the main criticism advanced by the anarchist thinkers, and the principles of the target, decentralised organisations/societies(To-Be), in Table 2. This table illustrates how anarchist thinkers of their time viewed the state of centralized societies, especially the "collusion between capital and the state", which can be understood as "minority rule" as discussed in Sect. 2.2. The term should be contextualized within the specific conditions of that era.

Motivation Layer. In this layer, Table 2 is used to represent the current state of centralized organization with the ArchiMate Motivation "Assessment" concept. We apply the i* modeling language [52] to define actors, goals, tasks, and dependencies. From the literature, we identified three actors: Volunteer, Association, and Delegated. Figure 1 shows a fragment of the goal diagram illustrating a Volunteer's participation in an Association and their dependencies on Federation, LD, Blockchain infrastructure, and Smart contract agents[3]. In i*, an agent

[3] Full goal model available at: https://github.com/edoc2024/paper.

Table 2. As-Is and To-Be Architecture Visions

As-Is traditional Centralized organisation/societies	To-Be decentralised organisations/societies
–Hierarchical and Centralized Power Structures	–decentralised Self-Governance
–Economic Inequality and Exploitation	–Collective, consensus and decentralised Decision-Making
–Competition over Cooperation	–Voluntary Association and Mutual Aid
–Lack of Autonomy	–Direct Action and Self-Management: This involves self-management practices where individuals and collectives take initiative and responsibility for managing tasks and projects
–"State and Capitalist Collusion" or Minority Rule	–Autonomy and Independence
–Resistance to Change and Innovation (the capitalist mode of production resists changes that threaten existing power structures or profit margins, even if such changes could benefit society as a whole)	–Restorative Justice
–Environmental Exploitation	–Equitable Resource Distribution
	–Continuous Learning and Adaptation

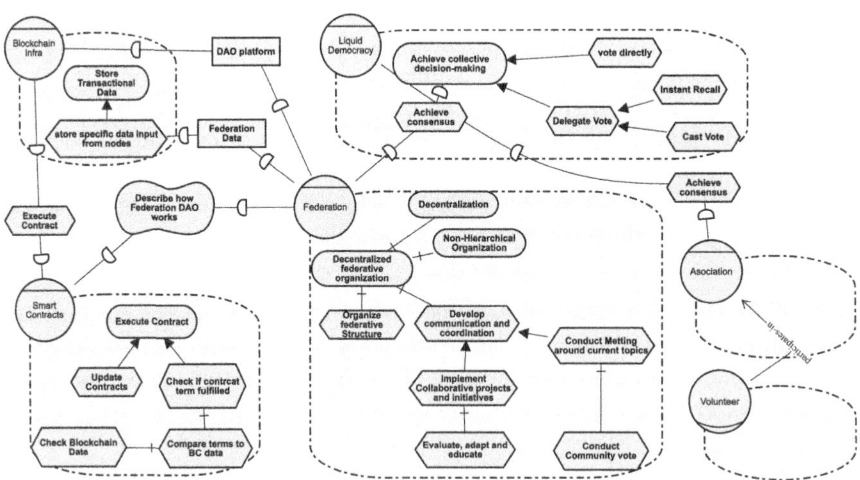

Fig. 1. Goal Diagram of the Architecture Vision

is "an actor with concrete, physical manifestations, such as a human individual, organization, or department" [8]. Goals derive from principles in Table 1. Several agents can share the same goal. Tasks associated with goal realization are based on anarchist literature analysis from the preliminary phase. Goals and tasks for Blockchain and Smart Contract agents are specified following [52]. Dependencies between agents' goals/tasks are also added, e.g., Federation and Association depend on Liquid Democracy for consensus, and Federation depends on Blockchain for enabling the DAO and data storage. Smart Contracts depend on Blockchain for execution. Using Fig. 1 and principles from Table 2 and Table 1, we define the ArchiMate motivation layer[4]. ArchiMate Drivers link Assessments, Goals, Requirements, and Principles to stakeholders, isolating five drivers: 1) Community Need, 2) Social Expectation, 3) Organizational Culture, 4) Technology Advancements, and 5) Regulations. We use the literature analysis to further refines the motivation layer, including items not expressible in the i* diagram, such as the requirement for "Sustainable Practices."

4.4 Business Architecture

The Business Architecture phase defines the organisation's business processes. We use BPMN to model the business processes. The main business processes are: 1) The unified process for voluntary association, mutual aid and self-management, 2) The Decision-Making Process using LD, 3) The Equitable Resource Distribution Process. In this paper we present the process diagrams for Unified Process for Voluntary Association, Mutual Aid and Self-Management[5].

Unified Process for Voluntary Association, Mutual Aid and Self-Management

We define process activities and constraints using [4,9,11,13,19,23,35,36,46]. The Run Federation process diagram shows how members organize within federations, which are networks of autonomous groups based on mutual aid, voluntary association, and non-hierarchical organization (see [44]). Members establish goals, principles, structure, and coordination, operating by consensus and creating associations to meet needs. We describe how to run and manage associations following anarchist principles in the Collaborative and Initiatives Project Process and Conduct Association Operations. Associations are voluntary, cooperative groups pursuing common goals. We outline the global lifecycle of associations and the strategies for managing them. We define three main forms of association, each with its own processes: Run Community Engagement Project for addressing issues like education and healing; Run Awareness and Advocacy Project for promoting ideas; and Run Economic Project for providing goods and services. These processes facilitate organizing society without central authority, adhering to anarchist principles.

---

[4] Complete motivation layer diagram available at: https://github.com/edoc2024/paper.

[5] Extra BPMN diagrams: https://github.com/edoc2024/paper/tree/main/BPMN.

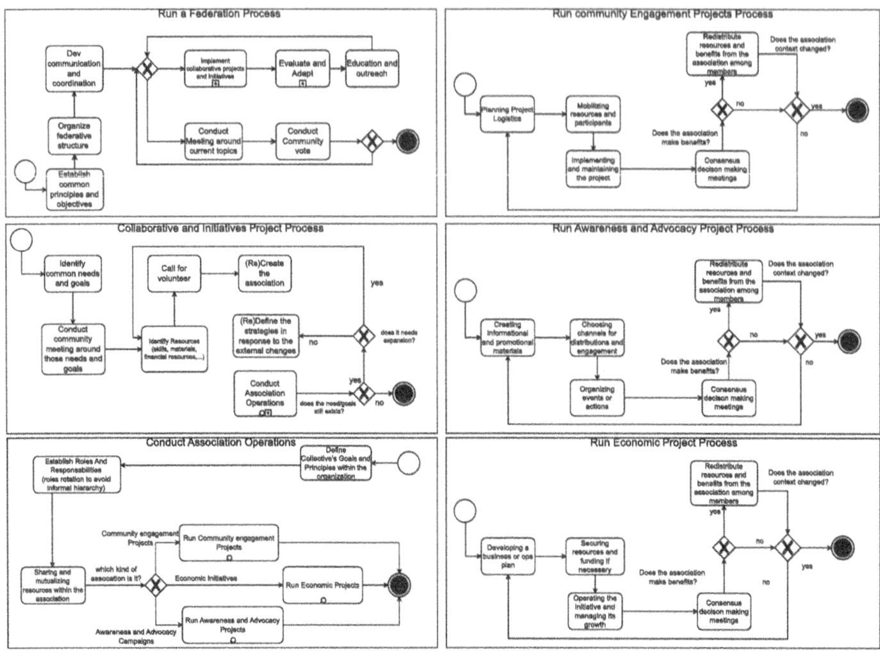

Fig. 2. BPMN of the Unified Process for Voluntary Association, Mutual Aid and Self-Management

Business Architecture Layer

We integrate all the business processes (including those not present in this paper) into the Business Architecture Layer in ArchiMate[6]. The Unified Process for Voluntary Association, Mutual Aid, and Self-Management is the organisation's core. It uses the LD process for decisions at both the federation and association levels. The Equitable Resource Distribution Process ensures fair resource distribution, from raw materials to dwellings, at both levels. For this paper, we present only a simplified version of the Unified Process for Voluntary Association, Mutual Aid, and Self-Management (see Fig. 3). We can observe that the Run Federation Process achieves the decentralised Federation organisation Business Service. The Voluntary Association, Mutual Aid, and Self-Management Business Services are realized by the Collaborative and Initiatives Project Process, which embeds all of the other subprocesses described in Fig. 2.

4.5 Application and Technology Architecture Layer

To design the Application and Technological Layer we use a detailed sysML Block Definition Diagram. As shown in Fig. 4, we make some technology choices due to the need to study LD in DAO. To enable DAO, blockchain is used in the

[6] The complete business layer can be found here: https://github.com/edoc2024/paper.

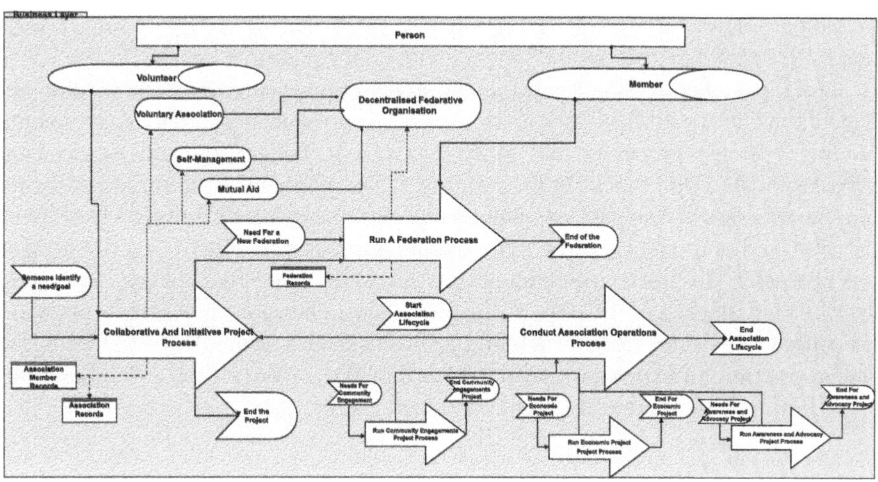

Fig. 3. Simplified ArchiMate Model of the unified process for voluntary association, mutual aid and self-Management

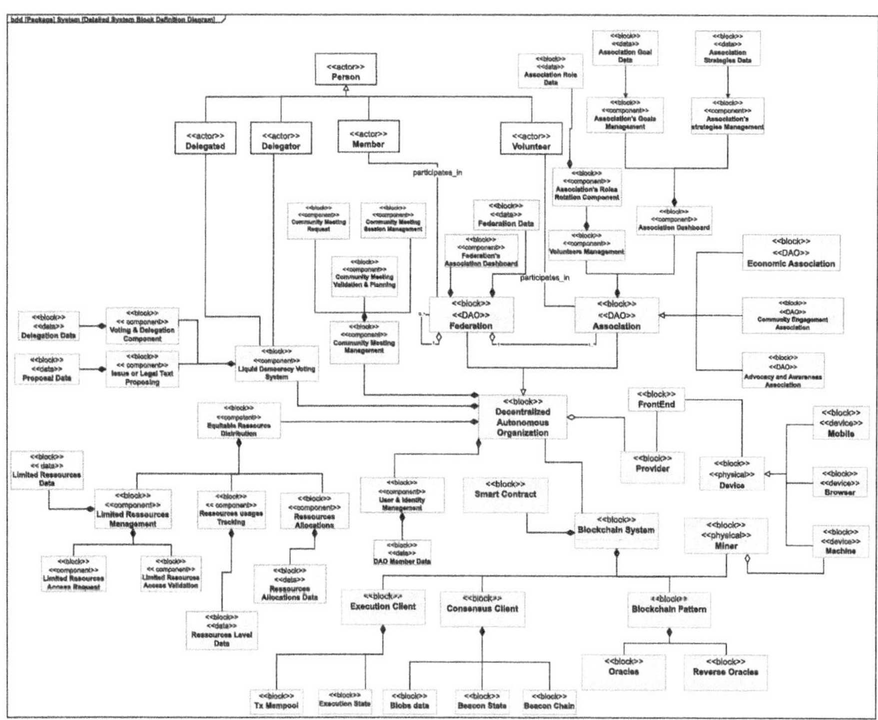

Fig. 4. Detailed Block Definition Diagram of the system

Technology Layer. The blockchain must support Turing-complete smart contracts. To construct this model, we use the goal diagram (see Fig. 1). In white are actors identified during the anarchist and LD literature analysis. In blue are elements in the ArchiMate Application Layer, representing software components enabling business processes and motivation goals. Federation and Association derive from the DAO block, built with the LD component, Community Meeting component, User & Identity Management component, and Equitable Resources Distribution component. These components support previously described business processes. In green are elements in the ArchiMate Technology Layer. We describe the Blockchain System to provide comprehension, including execution and consensus clients, and blockchain patterns like Oracle and Reverse Oracle for user interaction and smart contract triggering. We implemented a simplification of the BDD of the system in ArchiMate (see Fig. 5).

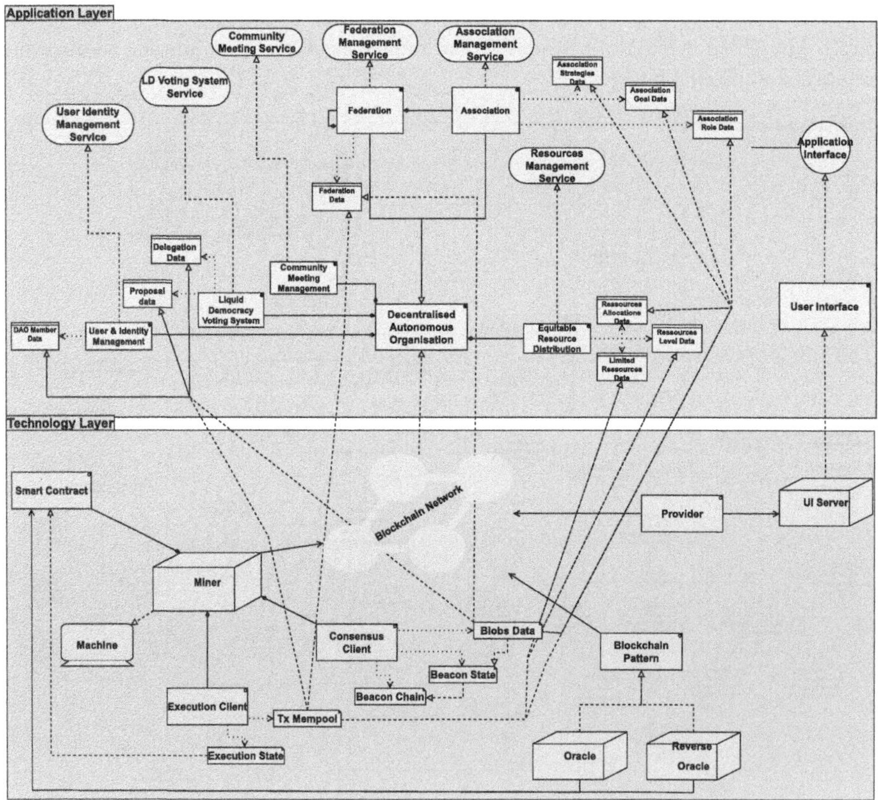

Fig. 5. Simplified ArchiMate Model of Application & Technology Layers

5 Evaluation

5.1 Evaluation Strategy

Here, we are assessing how well the designed architectural artifact aligns with the anarchist society principles, goals and principles. Here is our evaluation objectives: 1) Validate the alignment (i.e.: make sure that every elements from the motivation layer is linked to elements from the business, application and technology layer. And that the layer business is supported/realized by the application layer and that the application layer is supported/realized by the technology layer [29]) of the architectural artifact with anarchist society principles, 2) Asses the effectiveness of the artifact in supporting decentralised governance using DAOs and LD.

This evaluation is conducted using the ArchiMate enterprise model and according to the analytical methods described in [25]. Therefore we will follow these steps: 1) Map principles to architecture elements, we are using ArchiMate viewpoint to be able to highlight the alignment, then we ensure that each principles, goals and requirements are supported by the architectural artifact 2) Scenario based analysis, here we develop hypothetical scenarios to test how the architecture handles specific challenges To do so, we will use the motivation layer[7] that describes all of our requirements, principles goals.

5.2 Evaluation Criteria and Measures

Goals and Principles Alignment and Traceability
Using the ArchiMate viewpoint of the requirements realization[8], we can see that all of the business, application and Technology layers are used to support the motivation layer. We sum up these alignments in the Tables 3 and 4. To better understand them we recommend first to look at Fig. 6.

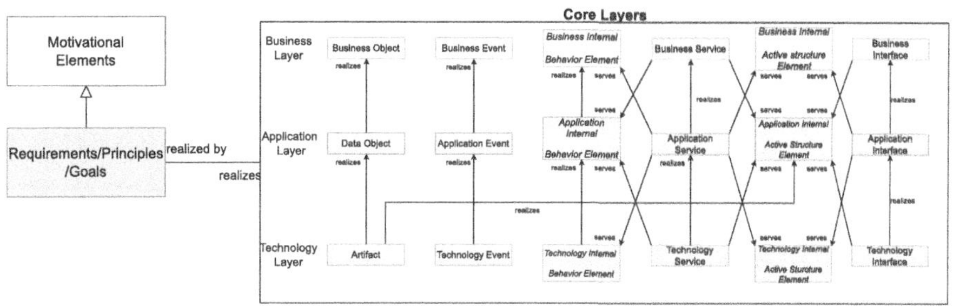

Fig. 6. ArchiMate & TOGAF layers alignment

[7] The motivation layer can be found here: https://github.com/edoc2024/paper.
[8] The complete view can be found here: https://github.com/edoc2024/paper/.

Table 3. Goals alignment and Traceability

Goals	Business Layer	Application Layer	Technology Layer
Non-Hierarchical organisation	"decentralised Federative organisation", "Mutual Aid", "Voluntary Association", "Self-Management" and "Run a Federation Process" and all the subprocesses	"Community Meeting Service", "Federation Management Service", "Resources Management Service", "Liquid Democracy Voting System" and all of the application supporting these services	"Blockchain Network" and all the elements supporting the network
decentralisation	"decentralised Federative organisation" and "Run a Federation Process" and all the subprocesses	"Community Meeting Service", "Federation Management Service", "Resources Management Service", "Liquid Democracy Voting System" and all of the application supporting these services	"Blockchain Network" and all the elements supporting the network
Equitable Resource Distribution	"Resource Sharing" business service and the "Equitable Resource Distribution Process"	"Resources Management Service" and all the application supporting this service	"Blockchain Network" and all the elements supporting the network
Mutual Aid	"Mutual Aid" business service and the "Collaborative and Initiatives Project Process" and all the subprocesses of this process	"Federation Management Service", "Association Management Service" and "Resources Management Service" and all the application components supporting these services	"Blockchain Network" and all the elements supporting the network
Autonomy & Self-Management	"Self-Management" business service and the "Collaborative and Initiatives Project Process" and all of the subprocesses of this process	"Association Management Service", "Community Meeting Service", "Liquid Democracy Voting system" and all of the applications supporting these services	"Blockchain Network" and all the elements supporting the network
Voluntary Association	"Voluntary Association" business service and the "Collaborative and Initiatives Project Process" and all of the subprocesses of this process	"Association Management Service" and all of the applications and services supporting it	"Blockchain Network" and all the elements supporting the network

Table 4. Motivation Layer Requirements alignment and Traceability

Requirements	Business Layer	Application Layer	Technology Layer
Transparent Governance and Conflict Resolution Mechanism	"Achieve Consensus" service and the "Consensus decision making through Liquid Democracy" process	"Liquid Democracy Voting System", "User Identity Management Service", "Community Meeting Service"	"Blockchain Network" and all the elements supporting the network
Community Engagement and Collaborative Projects	"Collaborative and Initiatives Project Process"	"Community Meeting Service", "Federation Management Service", "Resources Management Service", "Liquid Democracy Voting System" and all of the application supporting these services	"Blockchain Network" and all the elements supporting the network
Equal Access to Resources	"Resource Sharing" business service and the "Equitable Resource Distribution Process"	"Resources Management Service" and all the application supporting this service	"Blockchain Network" and all the elements supporting the network

In the Table 4, we merge "Transparent Governance" and "Conflict Resolution Mechanism" because they rely on the same Business, Application and Technological elements. Same thing for "Community Engagement" and "Collaborative Projects". Finally only the "Sustainable Practice" is not covered directly by the architectural artifact but this requirements apply to how individuals are behaving in the system and how they decide to respond to members' needs, so this principle will be used when association are created to ensure sustainable practices. Finally the Principle "decentralised organisation" is applied to all of the system as well as "Liquid Democracy" principle.

Scenario Based Analysis
We examine five scenarios involving our architectural artifact: 1) Federation Management of Member Needs, 2) Deciding the Direction for an Association, 3) Resource Sharing Among a Federation, 4) Conflict Resolution Between Associations, and 5) Emergency Response and Resource Reallocation. 1) In the first scenario, a member submits a need request. The federation analyzes it, drafts a proposal, and uses the Liquid Democracy process for consensus. If approved, a new association is formed to address the need, with roles assigned. Outcomes include effective need fulfillment and a transparent, inclusive process following anarchist principles. This scenario involve the following principles: "voluntary association" [4,19,23,35,36,46] and "direct democracy and consensus decision-making" [4,11,13,19,23,37,44]. 2) In the second scenario, if an association needs a change in direction, feedback is gathered. The LD system aids in building consensus, refining goals, and developing an action plan. Roles and responsibilities are assigned, and progress is monitored and adjusted as needed. Outcomes are clear strategic direction and adherence to anarchist principles. This scenario involve the following principles: "direct democracy and consensus decision-making" [4,11,13,19,23,37,44] and "autonomy and self-management" [9,11,19,36]. 3) In the third scenario, resource requests are evaluated within the federation. Resources are categorized, and limited resources are allocated based on priority. Outcomes are effective resource use and fulfillment of members' needs. This scenario involve the following principles: "commons and communal resources" [11,19,23,35,44] and "Mutual Aid" [9,13,19,35,36]. 4) In the fourth scenario, conflict reports are discussed in a federation meeting. A resolution proposal is submitted to the LD process. If approved, the resolution is implemented, and the outcome is reviewed in the next meeting. Outcomes include fair conflict resolution and process transparency. This scenario involve the following principles: "direct democracy and consensus decision-making" [4,11,13,19,23,37,44] and "Non-Hierarchical Organisation" [13,19,37,46]. 5) In the fifth scenario, an emergency prompts a rapid assessment and reallocation of resources. The LD system prioritizes emergency needs, reallocating resources from non-essential projects. Outcomes are efficient emergency response and improved system resilience. This scenario involve the following principles: "decentralisation" [9,11,19,44,46] and "autonomy and self-management" [9,11,19,36]. These scenarios demonstrate that our architectural artifact supports anarchist society principles, effectively handling challenges in a decentralised organisation.

5.3 Discussion

The key findings are as follows: **RQ1:** TOGAF ADM and ArchiMate effectively model socio-political artifacts for decentralized organizations. By structuring the model with the Motivation Layer (covering goals, requirements, and principles) and supporting it with the Business, Application, and Technology layers, we could visualize and manage alignment with anarchist society principles. The final steps of TOGAF ADM (*Opportunities and Solutions*, *Migration Planning*, *Implementation Governance*, and *Architecture Change Management*) were not implemented as they are meant for bringing the architecture into the real world, while our focus was on constructing the architecture and verifying its alignment. However, these steps can be carried out using this reference architecture. **RQ2:** We found minor areas for improvement in ArchiMate, but not in TOGAF ADM. For example, translating the Technology layer from Fig. 4 into ArchiMate required compromises like making the miner central in the technology layer rather than the blockchain system. These issues are mainly syntactic, not semiotic. Overall, modeling decentralized organizations is feasible with ArchiMate and TOGAF ADM in their current forms. **RQ3:** Our evaluation shows that the architectural artifact aligns with anarchist society principles, indicating that DAOs using LD can support an anarchist society (see Sect. 5.2). We also developed a model for LD decision-making, but due to space constraints, it is not included here[9]. Anarchist literature underpinned the artifact's development, with elements in the Motivation Layer (Sect. 4.3) representing principles and goals from the literature. Business processes enable the creation of federations and associations using LD-based decision-making and equitable resource sharing, operationalizing preferences while adhering to anarchist principles (see Sect. 4.4). These processes are supported by DAOs and decentralized applications, powered by blockchain and smart contracts, as detailed in Sect. 4.5.

6 Conclusion and Future Work

This paper provides a foundational model for integrating DAOs and LD with anarchist society principles, but further exploration is needed. **Empirical Validation:** Our theoretical model needs real-world validation. We plan to implement and observe the system and individual behaviors in this new socio-political context. The goal will be one to document the instantiation of such an artefact and then conduct an Ethnography on the organization to be able to empirically validate the anarchist principles and this artefact already theoretically validated. **COMSOC instead of LD:** Computational Social Choice [5] can be another way to make decisions within DAOs. We believe that applying the same kind of research we conducted on DAOs using COMSOC is very interesting. **Enhanced Modeling Techniques:** We identified new modeling languages and techniques, such as the DECENT framework by [32], to enhance our model. **Blockchain Patterns**: We identified blockchain patterns to enhance the technology layer such as the "Oracle" or "Reverse Oracle" to let the real world interact with the blockchain and enables Smart Contracts. During the implementation of our artefact we might faced issues (e.g.: Token management to determine collective ownership). Therefore We will conduct a systematic literature review to identify

[9] These models can be found at: https://github.com/edoc2024/paper.

all relevant patterns to cover all of our use cases. This work could not be included in this paper.

In this research, we investigate *How can socio-political artifacts for decentralised organisations be addressed by Enterprise Modeling?*, focusing on how DAOs and LD can model anarchist societies. We designed an architectural artifact using TOGAF ADM and ArchiMate for this purpose. Our main contribution is the reference architecture presented in this paper and where a more detailed version is available here https://github.com/edoc2024/paper.

References

1. Antunes, J., Barata, J., da Cunha, P.R., Estima, J., Tavares, J.: A reference architecture for dry port digital twins: preliminary assessment using ArchiMate. In: Araújo, J., de la Vara, J.L., Santos, M.Y., Assar, S. (eds.) RCIS 2024. LNBIP, vol. 513, pp. 131–145. Springer, Cham (2024). https://doi.org/10.1007/978-3-031-59465-6_9
2. Anwar, M.J., Gill, A.Q.: A review of the seven modelling approaches for digital ecosystem architecture. In: 2019 IEEE 21st Conference on Business Informatics (CBI), vol. 1, pp. 94–103. IEEE (2019)
3. Babkin, E., Komleva, N.: Model-driven liaison of organization modeling approaches and blockchain platforms. In: Aveiro, D., Guizzardi, G., Borbinha, J. (eds.) EEWC 2019, LNBIP, vol. 374, pp. 167–186. Springer, Cham (2020). https://doi.org/10.1007/978-3-030-37933-9_11
4. Bakunin, M.: Principles and Organization of the International Revolutionary Society, March 1866. https://theanarchistlibrary.org. https://theanarchistlibrary.org/library/mikhail-bakunin-principles-and-organization-of-the-international-revolutionary-society
5. Brandt, F., Conitzer, V., Endriss, U., Lang, J., Procaccia, A.D.: Introduction to computational social choice. In: Handbook of Computational Social Choice, pp. 1–29 (2016)
6. Buterin, V.: Ethereum white paper. GitHub Repository **1**, 22–23 (2013). https://github.com/ethereum/wiki/wiki/White-Paper
7. Curty, S., Fill, H.G.: Exploring the systematic design of blockchain-based applications using integrated modeling standards. In: PoEM Workshops (2022)
8. Dalpiaz, F., Franch, X., Horkoff, J.: iStar 2.0 language guide. arXiv preprint arXiv:1605.07767 (2016)
9. De Santillán, D.A.: After the revolution. LibCom.org (1937). http://libcom.org/book/export/html/33181. Accessed 4 Sept 2011. Accessed 22 June 2024
10. Deseriis, M.: Is liquid democracy compatible with representative democracy? Insights from the experience of the pirate party Germany. Partecipazione e Conflitto **15**(2), 466–481 (2022)
11. Dolgoff, S. (ed.): The Anarchist Collectives: Workers' Self-Management in the Spanish Revolution, 1936–1939. Black Rose Books Ltd. (1974)
12. Ettahiri, I., Doumi, K.: Dynamic enterprise architecture planning using case-based reasoning and blockchain. Proc. Comput. Sci. **204**, 714–721 (2022)
13. Fabbri, L.: The anarchist organization, 15 June 1907. https://theanarchistlibrary.org. Accessed 22 June 2024

14. Fill, H.G.: Towards the comparison of blockchain-based applications using enterprise modeling
15. Fill, H.G., Fettke, P., Rinderle-Ma, S.: Catchword: blockchains and enterprise modeling. Enterp. Model. Inf. Syst. Archit. **15** (2020)
16. Fill, H.G., Härer, F.: Knowledge blockchains: applying blockchain technologies to enterprise modeling (2018)
17. Fischer, C., Winter, R., Aier, S.: What is an enterprise architecture principle? Towards a consolidated definition. In: Computer and Information Science 2010. SCI, vol. 317, pp. 193–205. Springer, Heidelberg (2010). https://doi.org/10.1007/978-3-642-15405-8_16
18. Ford, B.A.: Delegative democracy. Technical report (2002)
19. Franks, B., Jun, N., Williams, L. (eds.): Anarchism: A Conceptual Approach. Routledge (2018)
20. Gebayew, C., Arman, A.A.: Modify TOGAF ADM for government enterprise architecture: case study in Ethiopia. In: 2019 IEEE 5th International Conference on Wireless and Telematics (ICWT), pp. 1–6. IEEE (2019)
21. Ghezzi, R., Kolehmainen, T., Setälä, M., Mikkonen, T.: Enterprise architecture as an enabler for a government business ecosystem: experiences from Finland. In: Chbeir, R., Benslimane, D., Zervakis, M., Manolopoulos, Y., Ngyuen, N.T., Tekli, J. (eds.) MEDES 2023. CCIS, vol. 2022, pp. 219–233. Springer, Cham (2023). https://doi.org/10.1007/978-3-031-51643-6_16
22. Gölz, P., Kahng, A., Mackenzie, S., Procaccia, A.D.: The fluid mechanics of liquid democracy. ACM Trans. Econ. Comput. **9**(4), 1–39 (2021)
23. Guérin, D.: Anarchism: From Theory to Practice, vol. 175. NYU Press (1970)
24. Hassan, S., De Filippi, P.: Decentralized autonomous organization. Internet Policy Rev. **10**(2), 1–10 (2021). https://doi.org/10.14763/2021.2.1556
25. Hevner, A.R., March, S.T., Park, J., Ram, S.: Design science in information systems research. MIS Q. **28**(1), 75–105 (2004)
26. White House: FEA consolidated reference model document version 2.3. Technical report, Executive Office of the President of the United States (2007)
27. Jiang, S., Ræder, T.B.: Experience on using ArchiMate models for modelling blockchain-enhanced value chains. In: Proceedings of the 26th International Conference on Evaluation and Assessment in Software Engineering, pp. 375–382 (2022)
28. Josey, A.: TOGAF® Version 9.1-A Pocket Guide. Van Haren (2016)
29. Josey, A.: ArchiMate® 3.0.1-A Pocket Guide. Van Haren (2017)
30. Kaczmarczyk, A., Sitarska-Buba, M.: Enterprise architecture of the blockchain platform. J. Internet e-Bus. Stud. **2020** (2020)
31. Kanagwa, B., Nakatumba-Nabende, J., Mugwanya, R., Kahiigi, E.K., Ngabirano, S.: Towards an interoperability e-government framework for Uganda. In: Odumuyiwa, V., Adegboyega, O., Uwadia, C. (eds.) AFRICOMM 2017. LNICST, vol. 250, pp. 16–28. Springer, Cham (2018). https://doi.org/10.1007/978-3-319-98827-6_2
32. Kaya, F.: Decentralized governance design: a model-based approach. Phd dissertation, Vrije Universiteit Amsterdam, The Netherlands (2024)
33. Khan, S.N., Loukil, F., Ghedira-Guegan, C., Benkhelifa, E., Bani-Hani, A.: Blockchain smart contracts: applications, challenges, and future trends. Peer-to-Peer Netw. Appl. **14**, 2901–2925 (2021)
34. de Kinderen, S., Kaczmarek-Heß, M., Ma, Q., Razo-Zapata, I.: A modeling method in support of strategic analysis in the realm of enterprise modeling: on the example of blockchain-based initiatives for the electricity sector. Enterp. Model. Inf. Syst. Archit. (EMISAJ) **16**(2), 1–36 (2021)

35. Kropotkin, P.A.: Kropotkin: 'The Conquest of Bread' and Other Writings. Cambridge University Press (1995)
36. Kropotkin, P.A.: Fields, Factories and Workshops: Or Industry Combined With Agriculture. Forgotten Books (2019)
37. Malatesta, E.: Anarchism and organization (1897). https://theanarchistlibrary.org. Accessed 22 June 2024
38. Molnár, B., Báldy, P., Menyhard-Balázs, K.: Architectures of contemporary information systems and legal/regulatory environment
39. Nakakawa, A., Namagembe, F., Proper, E.H.A.: Dimensions for scoping e-government enterprise architecture development efforts. In: Panetto, H., Debruyne, C., Proper, H., Ardagna, C., Roman, D., Meersman, R. (eds.) OTM 2018. LNPSE, vol. 11229, pp. 661–679. Springer, Cham (2018). https://doi.org/10.1007/978-3-030-02610-3_37
40. Nakamoto, S., Bitcoin, A.: A peer-to-peer electronic cash system. Bitcoin **4**(2), 15 (2008). https://bitcoin.org/bitcoin.pdf
41. Osei-Tutu, K., Hasavari, S., Song, Y.T.: Blockchain-based enterprise architecture for comprehensive healthcare information exchange (HIE) data management. In: 2020 International Conference on Computational Science and Computational Intelligence (CSCI), pp. 767–775. IEEE (2020)
42. Paulin, A.: An overview of ten years of liquid democracy research. In: The 21st Annual International Conference on Digital Government Research, pp. 116–121 (2020)
43. Peffers, K., Tuunanen, T., Rothenberger, M.A., Chatterjee, S.: A design science research methodology for information systems research. J. Manag. Inf. Syst. **24**(3), 45–77 (2007)
44. Proudhon, P.J.: The Principle of Federation (1979). Translated by Richard Vernon
45. Rerung, R.R., Wahvuni, A., Susrini, I.: Blueprint of smart campus system using TOGAF ADM. In: 2020 6th International Conference on Computing Engineering and Design (ICCED), pp. 1–5. IEEE (2020)
46. Rocker, R.: Anarchy and organisation, January 2003. https://theanarchistlibrary.org. https://theanarchistlibrary.org/library/rudolf-rocker-anarchy-and-organisation
47. Schekkerman, J.: How to Survive in the Jungle of Enterprise Architecture Frameworks: Creating or Choosing an Enterprise Architecture Framework. Trafford Publishing (2004)
48. Setiawan, A., Yulianto, E.: E-government interoperability and integration architecture modeling using TOGAF framework based on service oriented architecture. Asian J. Technol. Manag. **11**(1), 26–45 (2018)
49. Smith, M., Apfel, A.L., Mitchell, R.: The Gartner business value model: a framework for measuring business performance. Technical report, Gartner (2006)
50. Sotto-Mayor, S., Belchior, R., Correia, M., Vasconcelos, A.: An enterprise architecture approach to semantic blockchain interoperability
51. Szabo, N.: Smart contracts: building blocks for digital markets. EXTROPY: J. Transhumanist Thought **18**(2), 28 (1996)
52. Vingerhoets, A.S., Heng, S., Wautelet, Y.: Using i* and UML for blockchain oriented software engineering: strengths, weaknesses, lacks and complementarity. Complex Syst. Inform. Model. Q. **26**, 26–45 (2021)
53. Wang, S., Ding, W., Li, J., Yuan, Y., Ouyang, L., Wang, F.Y.: Decentralized autonomous organizations: concept, model, and applications. IEEE Trans. Comput. Soc. Syst. **6**(5), 870–878 (2019)

54. Wright, A.: The rise of decentralized autonomous organizations: opportunities and challenges. Stanford J. Blockchain Law Policy **4**, 1 (2020)
55. Zachman, J.A.: The Zachman framework for enterprise architecture. Primer for Enterprise Engineering and Manufacturing (2003). [si]: Zachman International
56. Zheng, Z., et al.: An overview on smart contracts: challenges, advances and platforms. Future Gener. Comput. Syst. **105**, 475–491 (2020)

Introducing Variables to Data Objects in BPMN

Maximilian König[✉], Tom Lichtenstein, Anjo Seidel, and Mathias Weske

Hasso Plattner Institute, University of Potsdam, Potsdam, Germany
{maximilian.koenig,tom.lichtenstein,anjo.seidel,mathias.weske}@hpi.de

Abstract. The management of data is crucial in today's organizations, making it necessary to specify exactly how data is created, accessed, and manipulated during business process enactment. Given the importance of data, it comes as a surprise that approaches like BPMN only provide limited support for modeling data and how it is read and written. In particular, they cannot represent multiple data objects of the same type, and they lack concise semantics for multi-instance data objects. Against this background, this paper proposes an extension to BPMN process models by introducing variable identifiers to distinguish individual data objects of the same class in a given process. The behavior is detailed using translational semantics to Colored Petri nets, and a set of verification mechanisms is presented that allow for a more precise analysis of data objects in business processes.

Keywords: BPMN · Data in Processes · Translational Semantics · Colored Petri Nets · Variables

1 Introduction

Helping organizations to maintain an overview of the complex processes driving their value creation is an important aspect of business process management. For that purpose, a variety of methodologies is provided to support the entire lifecycle of business processes, from design and analysis to configuration, enactment, and evaluation [35]. While control flow has been the main focus of process modeling languages, recent endeavors emphasize data objects that are manipulated through process activities. This can also be seen in object-centricity as a novel paradigm [1,3,15], in which business processes are considered from the perspective of data objects rather than process instances.

In industry and academia, BPMN process diagrams [25] are a widely used activity-centric modeling language [12]. However, its support for data is limited [24]. While version 2.0 introduced concepts to approach that deficiency, capturing the processing of multiple objects of the same class in a single process is not well-supported. The current specification also does not allow for the unique identification of two objects of the same class in the same process. For example, one might want to single out the best paper and the runner-up from the collection of accepted papers at a conference. Unfortunately, BPMN does not allow

M. Kaczmarek-Heß et al. (Eds.): EDOC 2024 Workshops, LNBIP 537, pp. 137–154, 2025.
https://doi.org/10.1007/978-3-031-79059-1_9

us to independently refer to two data objects of class 'paper' in one process instance. Additionally, concise semantics that allow for verification and precise enactment only have been introduced for control flow [8,10] and simple types of data interactions [5,28,30]. Complex constructs involving collections of data objects and the unique identification of different objects of the same class, on the other hand, have not been addressed sufficiently.

To approach these issues, we propose a simple, but very relevant extension to BPMN to include variable identifiers for data objects as motivated in [19]. Therewith, different objects of the same class can be defined and individually accessed in a given process instance. The extension is underpinned with a concise execution semantics, and verification properties to detect potentially erroneous behavior are discussed.

This paper is structured as follows: Sect. 2 introduces foundational knowledge on BPMN and Colored Petri nets, based on which Sect. 3 motivates the paper's contribution. In Sect. 4 we then informally describe the proposed extension to BPMN before Sect. 5 formally specifies the behavior using Colored Petri nets as formalism. Afterward, we show how the formalism can be used for verification and compliance checking in Sect. 6. Section 7 provides an overview of other works in the field, followed by Sect. 8 discussing the results of this work and Sect. 9 outlining future research opportunities and concluding the paper.

2 Foundations

This section presents the key concepts our approach utilizes. We provide an overview of BPMN's data representation capabilities and introduce Colored Petri nets.

2.1 Data in BPMN

BPMN provides a widely used standardized modeling language for business processes with an emphasis on control flow [25]. Activities, i.e., units of work performed in the context of the process, and events, i.e., instantaneous, process-relevant occurrences, can be ordered using control flow structures such as gateways which allow the representation of decisions and concurrency. To address the increasing significance of data in processes, version 2.0 of the standard introduced concepts to describe relevant data and its interaction with the control flow. *Data object nodes* (document shapes in Fig. 1) visualize the interaction of activities and events with certain types of data. Specifically, each node specifies a label, and a state denoted in square brackets. Following other works, we interpret the labels as data classes defining the structure of the objects belonging to them [17,24,29]. Data states induce conditions on the expected data an object contains. BPMN does not provide a notation to define either data classes or data states in more detail.

The availability of data objects can be a precondition for activity instances' enablement which is indicated by a read operation, i.e., a data object node having an arc toward the activity. Otherwise, if the arc points toward the data object node, a write operation is performed. Two kinds of write operations must be distinguished. If an object is written without being read, this constitutes the creation of a new object. If an object of the same class is also read by the activity, that object is updated to the state specified in the outgoing data object node. For example, activity 'Review paper' in a BPMN process diagram in Fig. 1 requires a 'Paper' in state 'submitted' for enablement. After terminating, the activity writes that object in state 'reviewed'.

According to the BPMN specification, a data object node always refers to the same data object per process instance [25, p. 206]. Therewith, *blind writes* as known from database terminology may occur. Given an activity creating a new object. If an object of the same class has previously been created, the existing object's content will be blindly overwritten because we cannot distinguish the objects on a model level.

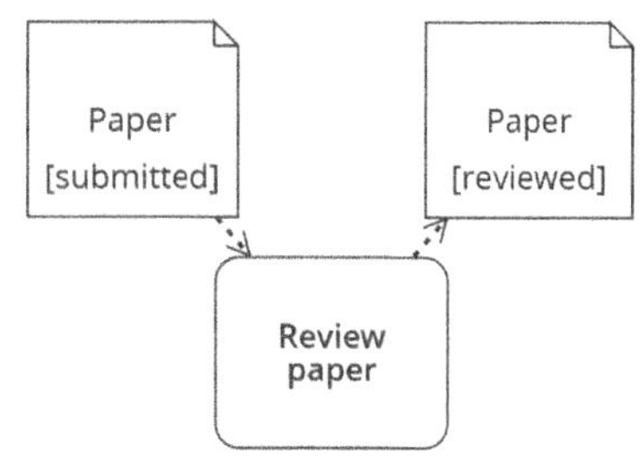

Fig. 1. Data object read and written by an activity

To reference a collection of data objects of the same class in the same state, but not the objects within that collection individually, a data object node may be annotated with the multi-instance marker III. In that case, all objects in the specified state are accessed. If such an object collection is read by an activity, it must contain at least one object to enable the activity.

For BPMN activities, a set of markers exists to indicate that multiple instances will be executed sequentially (≡ or ↻) or concurrently (III). For the loop marker, the number of instances can be specified using text annotations. For the others, a data object collection node in the precondition specifies that the activity will be executed once for each element in that collection. If there is no data precondition, the number of instances is undefined.

2.2 Colored Petri Nets

Petri nets [27] are a formal modeling language initially introduced to describe concurrent behavior. They are bipartite graphs consisting of transitions and places connected by arcs. The state of a net is represented by the distribution of tokens over all its places, called a marking. State changes occur upon the execution of a transition. A transition can fire, if all places in its preset, i.e., the set of places with an arc toward that transition, hold at least one token. Upon execution, a token is consumed from every place in its preset, and a token is produced in every place of its postset, i.e., the set of places with an arc from the transition toward them.

Colored Petri nets (CPNs) are an extension of traditional Petri nets introducing *colorsets*, i.e., data types, for tokens [18]. Therewith, tokens can be distinguished, enabling the representation of multiple different objects in the same net. In addition, tokens may hold concrete data values based on which the behavior of the net can be further specified.

Arc expressions bind token values to variables and specify the values of newly created tokens. Transition guards determine under which conditions a transition is enabled based on the values of tokens it would consume. For example, Fig. 2 shows a small example CPN. The place *counter* of type *INT* holds one token with value *5*. Before transition *Increment* can fire, the value of a token is bound to *c* and the guard checks whether $c < 10$ holds. In case the guard evaluates to true, a token with value $c + 1$ is returned.

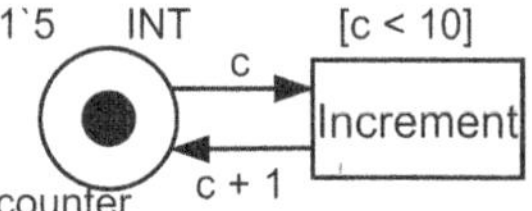

Fig. 2. Example of a counter implemented as Colored Petri net.

3 Problem Statement

Although BPMN provides basic data modeling capabilities, it has limited support for modeling multiple data objects of the same class within a process. Based on the semantics of the standard, we identified three main limitations in this regard. This section outlines and illustrates these limitations using the examples shown in Fig. 3.

Distinguishing Data Objects. As described in Sect. 2.1, data object nodes of the same class always refer to the same data object upon their first assignment. Consequently, several data objects of the same class cannot be referenced separately within a process and therefore cannot be distinguished from one another. In the example shown in the Fig. 3 (a), the activities 'SBP' and 'SRP' both write to data object nodes of the 'Paper' class with the intention of referencing the best and runner-up best paper separately for later use. However, according to the BPMN standard, both activities are writing to the same data object, resulting in the second activity overwriting the data written by the first activity. Given the current semantics, the intended behavior cannot be modeled for objects of the same class.

Delineating Create and Update Operations. Figure 3 (a) indicates a second problem. Following current BPMN semantics, it is unclear whether activities 'SBP' and 'SRP' should perform create or update operations. They could update an object of the input collection, as intended in this particular example. However, the same notation might be used to depict that, given the collection, a new object of the same class is to be created.

Distinguishing Data Object Collections. Similar to individual data objects, BPMN does not support distinguishing between collections of the same class. In addition, objects referenced by a collection node must have the same state.

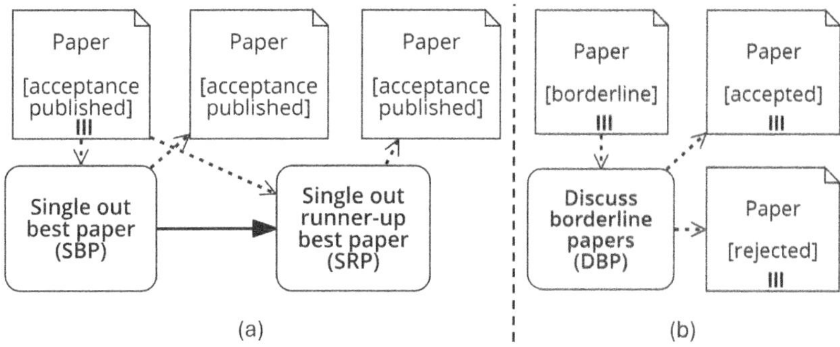

Fig. 3. BPMN process model excerpts visualizing deficiencies in data handling.

These restrictions imply that collections cannot be split or merged during process execution, as discussed in [20]. In the example illustrated in Fig. 3 (b), the 'DBP' activity writes to two collections of papers in different states. While the intended behavior is to split the collection of 'borderline' papers into 'accepted' and 'rejected', the semantics require the activity to write to only one of the collections during execution. Similarly, merging multiple collections of the same class into a single collection is not supported.

In summary, the data semantics of BPMN restrict the handling of multiple data objects of the same class within processes. These limitations, as illustrated by the examples in Fig. 3, can complicate the accurate modeling of data flow in business processes.

4 Handling Data Object Nodes with Variables

To address the limitations of the current data semantics of BPMN outlined in Sect. 3, we extend BPMN data object nodes with variables. A variable serves as an identifier denoted on the data object node that is assigned to a concrete object at runtime. If the variable is reused on another node in the model, the same object can be referenced again. Therewith, we can lift the assumption that every node of the same class refers to the same object, allowing for independent processing of multiple objects of the same class in one process.

In the following, we will informally describe the notation and intended behavior for create, read, and update operations on objects alongside the extended paper review process example depicted in Fig. 4, before Sect. 4 provides a formalization.

Variables are specified in the labels of data object nodes as prefixes to the data class, separated by a colon. For example, 'P:Paper' indicates that variable 'P' references a certain set of objects of the class 'Paper' at runtime. As a convention, variables starting with uppercase letters are used to identify data object collections, e.g., 'P:Paper', while those starting with lowercase letters refer to single objects, e.g., 'bp:Paper'. In the example, that allows us to identify the best paper 'bp:Paper' singled out from the collection of accepted papers

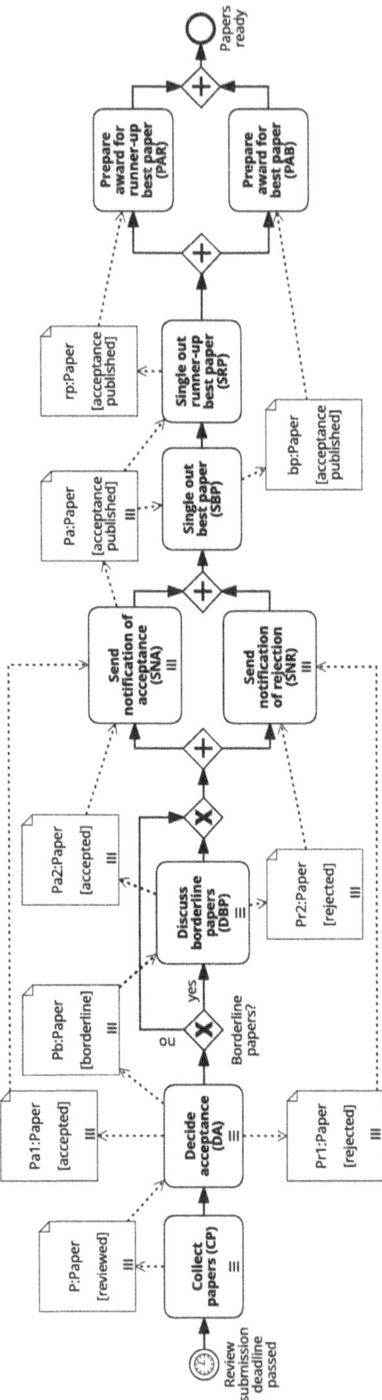

Fig. 4. BPMN process model of a paper reviewing process using data objects with variables.

'Pa:Paper' and reuse it later to prepare the award for the respective winner. At the same time, we can assign the runner-up best paper to 'rp:Paper' without overwriting the previous reference. Similarly, we can now split and merge collections. For example, deciding on the reviewed papers' acceptance ('DA') results in three collections of accepted ('Pa1'), rejected ('Pr1'), and borderline ('Pb') papers, showing that variables can effectively address the shortcomings detailed in Sect. 3. Note that, regarding reusability, data object nodes with the same variable can be used multiple times within one BPMN process model.

Create. The semantics of create operations in BPMN originally depended on the existence of an object of the same class, making it a blind write if an object exists already. With our approach, we modify the semantics in a way that create operations always create a new object. In addition, created objects are assigned to the variable denoted in the respective node for future reference. This may also include the reassignment of a variable, if it was previously assigned to another object. The same concept applies to collections, where all created objects are assigned to the same variable. In Fig. 4, this happens for the collection 'P:Paper' created by activity 'Collect papers'.

Read. Reading a data object from a variable requires (1) that there is an object assigned to the variable through a previous write operation and (2) that the referenced object is in the state specified in the data object node in the model. If that is not the case, the reading activity is not enabled, i.e., cannot be executed.

Reading an object collection assigned to a variable follows a similar pattern. Instead of one object, all referenced objects of the specified class in the required state are accessed. For activity enablement, at least one object adhering to these criteria must exist. If an activity reads multiple collections of the same class assigned to different variables, they are merged before activity execution. It is sufficient if the union of these collections contains at least one element for enablement. This is visualized in Fig. 4 for activity 'Send notification of acceptance', where collections 'Pa1:Paper' and 'Pa2:Paper' are both accessed.

Update. Updating a data object requires that the object is read and written by the same activity. In that case, the object is assigned to the variable specified in the outgoing data object node. If the target variable is the same as the source variable, the assignment remains the same. However, an object might also be assigned to a new variable. Therewith, multiple variables can reference the same object. That also holds if a state change occurs. For example, activity 'Send notification of acceptance' accesses two collections 'Pa1' and 'Pa2' and assigns their union to collection 'Pa'. After that, 'Pa1' and 'Pa2' still refer to the same objects as before and could be reused later on in the model. By allowing different variables to reference the same objects, we address the third issue presented in Sect. 3. Single objects can now be selected from a collection. For example, 'Single out best paper' now copies a reference to one of the incoming objects to the variable 'bp' for future use.

Another benefit of variables in the context of updating collections is that they can now be split and merged. For example, 'Discuss borderline papers' takes the collection of reviewed papers 'P' and returns two collections of accepted and rejected papers, which constitutes the desired behavior described in Sect. 3. The decision on each individual object is made at runtime. As discussed in [20], this may result in empty collections. With this behavior, we extend our previous approach in [20], where a first semantics for splitting and merging collections is presented. However, the prior mapping distinguishes collection data objects only via disjoint states. Extending on that, the novel mapping also allows referencing the same object with different variables, i.e., from different process perspectives.

Next, Sect. 5 proposes a translation of BPMN process diagrams with variables to colored Petri nets, providing a concise execution semantics of the described behavior.

5 Formal Execution Semantics

The proposed notational extension allows for the specification of additional behavior in BPMN process models. To formally describe that behavior, this section introduces a formal semantics for the introduced concepts by translating them to CPNs.

Assumptions. To focus on the formalization of the new concepts and avoid unnecessary complexity, we make several assumptions: (1) Data object collections must contain at least one element to fulfill an activity's data precondition. An exception is multiple collections of the same class being read in one activity. In that case, their union is required to contain at least one element. With this assumption, we avoid multi-instance activities being executed zero times, which would lead to potentially inconsistent process states. (2) Every data object node in the BPMN refers to a variable. If none is specified in the model, they implicitly refer to a class-specific default variable.

Colorsets. For the translation to colored Petri nets, we first define the data types, i.e., colorsets, for our places and tokens. As primitive units, we will use *int* for integer values, *unit* for tokens without a specific value, and *string*. Colorsets consisting of sets of another colorset are denoted as $Set < colorset >$. Based thereon, we define $Object : ID \times State$ for data objects consisting of an ID of type *int* and a *state* of type *string*. Any additional attributes of objects are abstracted from in the course of this paper. Control flow tokens will be of type $CF : unit$ since we do not need any specific data to be transported by them.

Places. The first step of the translational semantics is to create a set of places. For each data class in the data model, we create a single place of type $Set < Object >$ and an initial token of value [ ] (cf. Fig. 5 (a)). As a general rule, the set of all objects of one class is always represented by exactly one token in exactly one place, similar to a table in a database. That token can then be queried in transition guards to access specific objects. Every variable introduced for data objects is also mapped to a place. If the variable references a single object, that place is of type ID with an initial token 0 (cf. Fig. 5 (b)), if it references a collection of objects the type is $Set < ID >$ with [ ] as initial marking (cf. Fig. 5 (c)). To generate new object IDs, we will use a unique *counter* place of type *int* with an initial token of value 1 (cf. Fig. 5 (d)). Whenever a new object is created, that token's value serves as its ID and gets incremented by one. The initial value ensures that uninitialized variables can be recognized by holding a token of value 0 or [ ].

In general, a control flow arc in BPMN corresponds to one place of type CF without an initial marking in the CPN (cf. Fig. 5 (e)). Additional rules considering gateways are discussed by Dijkman et al. [10]. Since the translation of the control flow is not the focus of this work, we will utilize their mapping rules for gateways.

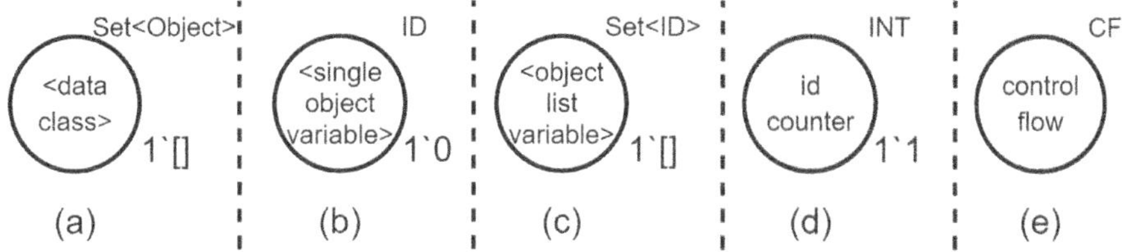

Fig. 5. Created places for the translational semantics to CPNs. The top left denotes a place's colorset, its name is in the center, and the initial marking is specified on the bottom right in the format $< \#tokens >$ \` $< value >$. Mapped concepts are (a) all objects belonging to one data class, (b) variables referencing a single data object, (c) variables referencing a collection of objects, (d) the counter to provide unique objects IDs, and (e) control flow arcs.

Single-Instance Data Access. Following [10], we map single-instance tasks to a single transition each. The transition is connected to the places representing preceding and succeeding control flow arcs. Additionally, we connect the transition bidirectionally to the places of all data classes on which the respective task performs a read operation.

Creating an object in a specific state s requires the token holding all objects of the respective class O and the token of the id counter place c. In the arc expression returning O, a new object is added with id c and state s: $O \cup \{(c, s)\}$. In addition, $c + 1$ is returned to the ID counter place. If a variable is explicitly specified in the BPMN model, the transition also overwrites the token in the variable's place to hold the id of the newly created object. Exemplarily, this is shown in Fig. 6 with activity 'Export Paper'.

Reading an object of class C in a state s is implemented through a guard expression querying the collection of objects of the class stored in a token O. The query includes the required state as well as the id, as specified in the respective

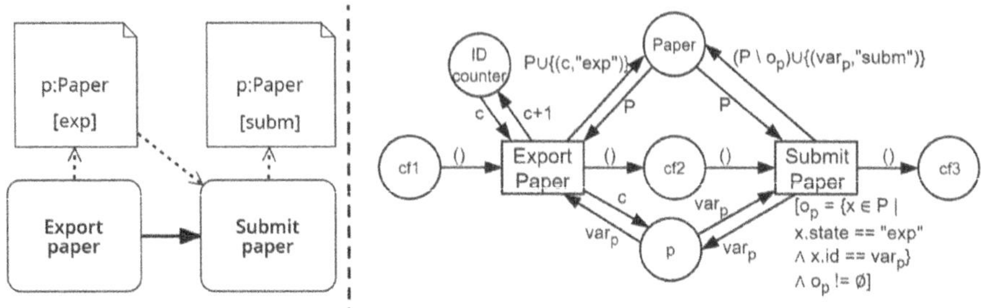

Fig. 6. CPN translation of basic data access operations. *Export Paper* creates a *Paper* in state *exp* by incrementing the *ID counter*, adding a new object to the place holding all *Papers*, and assigning the object's ID to the variable *p*. *Submit Paper* queries the collection of all papers *P* for the object in state *exp* with the ID stored in *p*. If such an object exists, its state is updated to *subm* in *P*.

variable v. The result is assigned to an arc variable. If the arc variable is empty, the guard does not evaluate to true. Generally, the guard looks as follows: $[o_{C[s]} = \{x \in O \mid x.state == s \wedge x.id = var_v\} \wedge o_{C[s]} \neq \emptyset]$. In Fig. 6, this is visualized for activity 'Submit Paper'. In the example, variable p is used to uniquely identify the paper object. After reading the paper object, 'Submit Paper' also performs a state transition. To capture that, we extend the arc expression that returns the token holding all papers P. We remove the outdated element stored in the variable o_p and add the updated element consisting of the ID stored in the variable and the new state as specified in the model: $(P \setminus \{o_p\}) \cup \{(var_p, `subm')\}$.

Multi-instance Data Access. Working with sets of objects of the same class requires some adaptations to the previously introduced mappings, but the general concepts remain identical.

The creation of a collection iterates the behavior for creating a single object. Hence, multiple transitions are required to represent that behavior, namely a starting transition, a terminating transition, and a transition repeatedly creating new objects. A *running* place holds the control flow token, and the creating transition adds elements to a temporary collection of objects. If at least one object has been created, the terminating transition can fire, adding the temporary collection to the token holding all objects of the respective class. The set of IDs of the created objects is added to the referencing variable's place. An example is shown in Fig. 7 for activity 'Collect papers' from the example process in Fig. 4.

Reading a data object collection retrieves all objects of the specified class in the required state referenced by the assigned variable. Hence, instead of filtering for the object with a specific ID as shown in Fig. 6, we select all objects with an ID matching those stored in the variable's place. If there is no suitable object, the guard evaluates to false. An example can be found in Fig. 8, where transition 'Begin Discuss Borderline Papers' accesses all papers of collection 'Pb' in state 'borderline'. If multiple collections are read, the guard comprises the conjunction of the expressions for each collection. As per assumption (2), if multiple

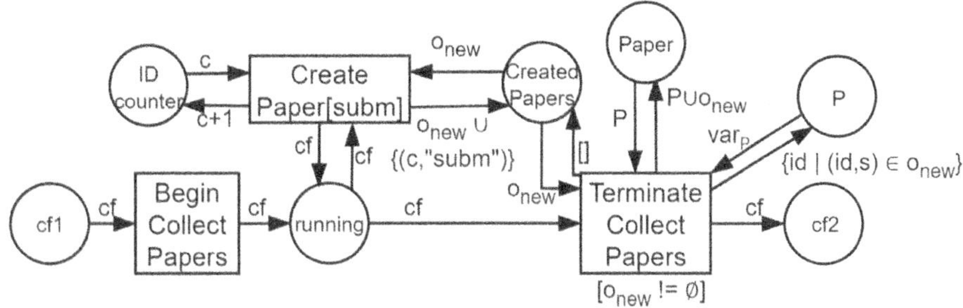

Fig. 7. CPN representation of creating a data object collection.

collections of the same class are read, the union of all collections must contain at least one element, rather than requiring each collection to be non-empty.

State transitions for collections of objects build upon the mapping for reading collections. To transition read objects to a new state, an arc expression is added to the arc toward the place storing the objects. Essentially, all entries for read objects $O_{C[s]}$ of a class C in state s are replaced with entries for the same objects in the new state: $(C \setminus O_{C[s]}) \cup \{(id, \text{'}newState\text{'}) \mid id \in var_X\}$ where C represents all objects of class C and X refers to the read and written variable. If transitioned objects are assigned to a new variable, the transition writes the collection of their IDs to that variable's place. If multiple output collections may be created from one collection, multiple transitions are required. An initial transition reads the required objects and temporarily stores their IDs, while removing them from the place holding all objects of that class to avoid concurrent access. Afterward, transitions for each target state can update the state of one ID at a time. Finally, a terminating transition takes all temporary objects and assigns them to their variables, and returns the objects to the place of their class. An example can be found in Fig. 8, where the transition 'Discuss Borderline Papers' reads all borderline papers and transitions all objects to either accepted or rejected, effectively splitting the collection and assigning the resulting subcollections to new variables 'Pa2' and 'Pr2'.

With the presented translational semantics, we concisely define the intended behavior of variables for data objects, effectively extending BPMN's data modeling capabilities to handle multiple objects of the same class. The full application of the mapping to the examples in Fig. 6 and Fig. 4 can be found on GitHub[1]. To view and execute the CPNs, an installation of CPN Tools[2] is required.

6 Analysis

In this section, the formal semantics of Sect. 5 is used for compliance checking and verification. For that purpose, we use BPMN-Q, a BPMN-based visual query

[1] https://github.com/bptlab/bpmn-data-object-variables.

[2] https://cpntools.org/.

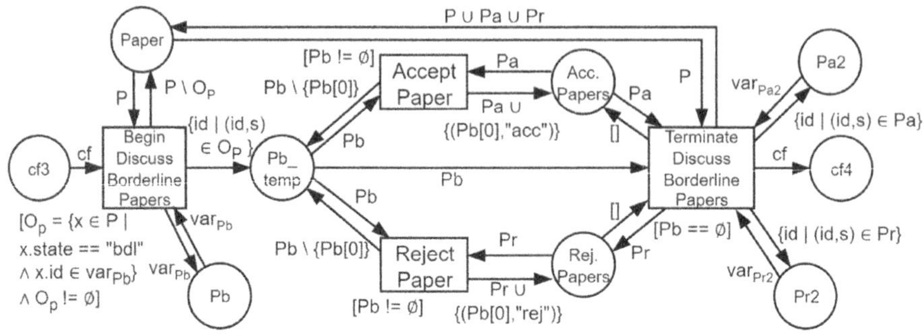

Fig. 8. CPN representation of splitting a collection into two collections with different states.

language for business processes [4]. It provides an easy-to-understand approach to specify conditions for model verification and compliance checking. While the initial version of the language exclusively considered control flow constructs, an extension presented in [7] introduces data objects and their states to it.

An exemplary query can be found in Fig. 9. It represents the constraint that *there must be a paper whose acceptance has been published before the award for the best paper can be prepared.* '@A' represents a *variable activity*, indicating that there must be any activity fulfilling the required condition. The arrow with the // marker means that we look for a path from its source to its target, and the data condition implies that an object matching the node must be written by the respective activity. Next to *precedes* relations, BPMN-Q also supports *leads to* relations as shown in Fig. 10.

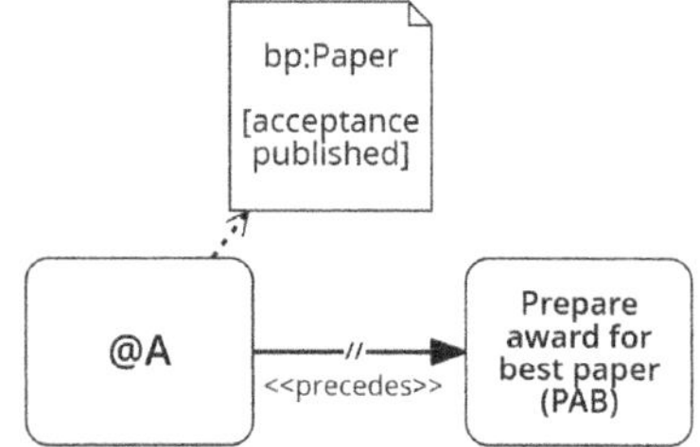

Fig. 9. BPMN-Q query using a data object node with variables.

As our approach integrates the declaration of variables into the labels of data object nodes, it can be seamlessly integrated with the BPMN-Q notation. Instead of requiring an unspecified object of a certain class in a state, queries may include objects assigned to certain variables. For example, the query visualized in Fig. 9 specifies that the paper in state 'acceptance published' must be assigned to the variable 'bp', i.e., the one being the result of 'Single out best paper' in Fig. 4.

Further, using BPMN-Q allows detecting erroneous behavior. For example, ensuring that a variable is assigned before being accessed (cf. Fig. 10 (a)) or that a collection of rejected papers must be written by activity 'Decide acceptance' before the notification of rejection can be sent (cf. Fig. 10 (b)). Notably, the second query is not fulfilled in our example in Fig. 4, since all papers might be accepted or borderline, resulting in an empty collection that does not fulfill this query. Therewith, we can identify situations where empty collections may result in deadlocks. As a solution, the parallel gateway could be replaced with an inclusive gateway and conditions requiring the collections of accepted and rejected papers to be non-empty before the respective path gets enabled.

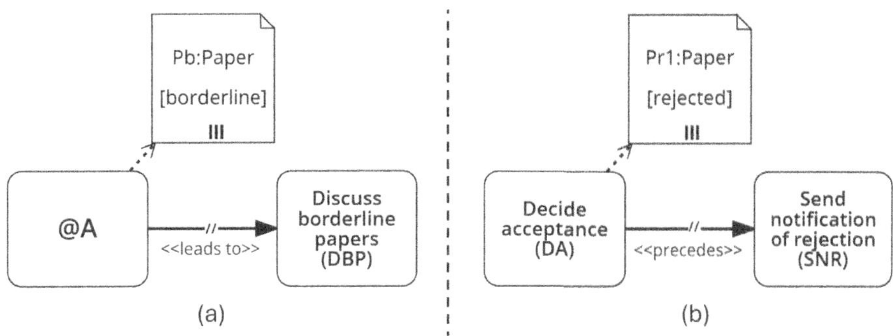

Fig. 10. BPMN-Q queries checking (a) whether borderline papers will always be discussed if collection 'Pb' is written to state 'borderline' and (b) if activity 'Decide acceptance' writes a collection of rejected papers 'Pr1' before notifications of rejection are sent.

To evaluate BPMN-Q queries, Past Linear Temporal Logic (PLTL) [22] statements are derived from each query [6]. For example, the PLTL query for Fig. 9 is: $G(ready(PAB) \rightarrow O(state(bp : Paper, acceptancepublished)))$ where *ready* is the function returning whether activity 'PAB' is control flow enabled in a marking, *state* determines whether an object is in the specified state, and G (always) and O (once) are PLTL operators as introduced in [22]. To check the query for a given process model, the model is translated into a Petri net and its state space is generated [6]. In our case, this is done by applying the translational semantics from Sect. 5 and computing the state space in CPN Tools. Based on the state space, the PLTL queries can then be evaluated. The state space for Fig. 4 can be found in the respective CPN file in the GitHub repository.

As stated in [6], a finite state space is required for such evaluations. However, the translational semantics presented in this paper innately result in nets with infinite state spaces if an activity creates a data object collection, exemplified in Fig. 7. To circumvent that, we introduce a guard to the creating transition ('Create Paper[subm]') in the example), checking that the collection of newly created objects ('o_{new}') has at most as many elements as there are variables defined for that data class in the BPMN model. If all variables defined for this data class depend on the created collection, this measure ensures that the state space includes a state where each of them is assigned to at least one object.

7 Related Work

A number of BPMN extensions to improve data representation exist in related work. Meyer et al. extend BPMN with foreign key relationships between objects and a mapping to SQL queries for read and write operations on data objects [24]. A similar approach is proposed by Combi et al., assigning an SQL statement specifying the data abstracted from by a data object [9]. Haarmann et al. address the issue of data objects shared by multiple processes [16], including a translational semantics to colored Petri nets. However, neither approach considers data object collections. Ghilardi et al. present delta-BPMN, combining an SQL-based data specification language with BPMN instead of a visual representation through data nodes [14]. That greatly increases the modeling complexity and required domain knowledge, which is why we stick to the abstract representation of BPMN with data object nodes and data states. In a previous work, we introduced an approach to cover collection creation, splitting, and merging [20], which we extend with this work. There, only data object collections were considered, with the state serving as an additional identifier besides an object's class. That comes with a number of deficiencies that were addressed in this paper: On the one hand, referencing single objects from collections is not defined with this approach. On the other hand, multiple collections in the same state, as shown in Fig. 4, are not supported. Hence, an object can always be referenced by one data object node.

To address the intersection of process control flow and data, object- and data-centric process modeling approaches have been introduced. An overview of existing approaches along with a framework to compare them is presented by Steinau et al. [31]. Instead of focusing on control flow, many of these approaches, e.g., PhilharmonicFlows [21], fragment-based case management [17] or object-centric behavioral constraints [2], employ a data-first approach, focusing on the object lifecycles more than control flow dependencies between activities. However, these approaches are not yet adopted in organizations. BPMN, on the other hand, is an already established language in industry in academia [12], which is why we focused on extending it regarding its data modeling capabilities.

Formalizing BPMN execution semantics is not a novel topic. Target formalisms include, but are not limited to, process algebras (e.g., CSP, π-calculus) [8,36], graph rewrite rules [11], WS-BPEL [25,26], and Petri net-based languages [5,10,20,23,28,30]. However, most of these approaches do not consider the data dimension at all. Stackelberg et al. include data objects in their translational semantics to Petri nets, but disregard data states and explicitly enforce the single instance assumption introduced by the standard [30]. Similarly, Awad et al. also implement that assumption while considering data states, but exclude data object collections from their mapping [5]. Choosing CPNs as target language, Ramadan et al. present another formalization including complex control flow constructs such as subprocesses and boundary events [28]. However, they do not go into detail regarding data object collections.

Our approach builds on BPMN-Q for data flow analysis in processes. In the context of compliance checking on processes with data, Voglhofer et al. provide an overview of contemporary literature [34]. A language-independent categorization of data anomalies has been presented by Sun et al. [32], which was adapted to BPMN by Stackelberg et al. [30]. Other approaches extend Petri nets with data operations and define data flow error detection mechanisms for them [33, 37]. Neither of these approaches, however, supports our extension out-of-the-box.

8 Discussion

The proposed approach does not consider all data modeling capabilities BPMN provides. For example, input and output sets as well as *input output specifications* describing the relations between them are not covered. Their inclusion would further increase the expressiveness of the extension, for example, by allowing to model explicitly that the resulting collections might be empty after splitting. Further, the semantics of BPMN multi-instance activities interacting with multiple data object collections remain underspecified. If several object collections of different data classes are read by a multi-instance activity, the activity could be executed once for each element of each collection. At the same time, objects could be correlated, meaning that one activity instance processes one or multiple related objects of either collection. For example, the latter would be desirable if the decision on a paper's acceptance in Fig. 4 also depended on the reviews for each paper.

Besides colored Petri nets, other formalisms were considered to define the semantics of the presented extension. While traditional Petri nets lack token differentiation, recent works propose new Petri net-based languages tailored to object-centric processes, namely object-centric Petri nets (OCPNs) [3], object-centric Petri nets with identifiers (OPIDs) [15], and synchronous proclets [13]. All of these approaches include the capability to model single objects and object collections. However, only OPIDs explicitly define identifiers for objects, and only synchronous proclets define the use of labels as variables that can be reused for synchronizing objects. In comparison, our approach allows for variables in the model and explicit object identifiers in model instances. Further, OCPNs and OPIDs cannot ensure that all objects with certain properties must be processed by a transition, which is required for BPMN semantics as discussed in Sect. 2.

BPMN-Q cannot evaluate queries on infinite state spaces [6]. The introduction of variables to BPMN data objects introduces additional constructs that may result in infinite behavior due to the added object identities. For example, the cyclic reassignment of variables to newly created objects leads to unboundedly many different states. Even though this might be desired behavior, it currently cannot be analyzed by our approach.

9 Conclusion

In this paper, we describe an approach to extend BPMN to capture complex data behavior involving different objects of the same class. For that purpose, we introduce the concept of variables to BPMN data object nodes to differentiate individual objects and object collections within one process instance. The described behavior is underpinned with a translational semantics to colored Petri nets. To analyze models incorporating variables on data object nodes, we propose to build on the visual query language BPMN-Q for verification and compliance checks. The BPMN-Q queries can be applied to a formal representation of the process model derived from the translational semantics.

The presented approach currently requires a manual translation of process models to CPNs, which is tedious and error-prone. Hence, tool support is desirable and will be approached in future work. Additional research regarding the incorporation of additional BPMN data concepts such as input and output sets should be conducted. At the same time, to improve the usability of the approach in general, a set of guidelines would help to draw attention to, for example, the explicit handling of potentially empty collections.

References

1. van der Aalst, W.M.P.: Object-centric process mining: Dealing with divergence and convergence in event data. In: Ölveczky, P.C., Salaün, G. (eds.) SEFM 2019. LNTCS, vol. 11724, pp. 3–25. Springer, Cham (2019). https://doi.org/10.1007/978-3-030-30446-1_1
2. van der Aalst, W.M.P., Artale, A., Montali, M., Tritini, S.: Object-centric behavioral constraints: integrating data and declarative process modelling. In: Artale, A., Glimm, B., Kontchakov, R. (eds.) Proceedings of the 30th International Workshop on Description Logics, Montpellier, France, 18–21 July 2017. CEUR Workshop Proceedings, vol. 1879. CEUR-WS.org (2017). https://ceur-ws.org/Vol-1879/paper51.pdf
3. van der Aalst, W.M.P., Berti, A.: Discovering object-centric Petri nets. Fundam. Informaticae **175**(1–4), 1–40 (2020)
4. Awad, A.: BPMN-Q: a language to query business processes. In: Reichert, M., Strecker, S., Turowski, K. (eds.) EMISA 2007. LNI, vol. P-119, pp. 115–128. GI (2007). https://dl.gi.de/handle/20.500.12116/22195
5. Awad, A., Decker, G., Lohmann, N.: Diagnosing and repairing data anomalies in process models. In: Rinderle-Ma, S., Sadiq, S., Leymann, F. (eds.) BPM 2009. LNBIP, vol. 43, pp. 5–16. Springer, Heidelberg (2009). https://doi.org/10.1007/978-3-642-12186-9_2
6. Awad, A., Decker, G., Weske, M.: Efficient compliance checking using BPMN-Q and temporal logic. In: Dumas, M., Reichert, M., Shan, M.C. (eds.) BPM 2008. LNISA, vol. 5240, pp. 326–341. Springer, Heidelberg (2008). https://doi.org/10.1007/978-3-540-85758-7_24
7. Awad, A., Weidlich, M., Weske, M.: Specification, verification and explanation of violation for data aware compliance rules. In: Baresi, L., Chi, C., Suzuki, J. (eds.) ServiceWave 2009, ICSOC 2009. LNPSE, vol. 5900, pp. 500–515. Springer, Heidelberg (2009). https://doi.org/10.1007/978-3-642-10383-4_37
8. Boussetoua, R., Bennoui, H., Chaoui, A., Khalfaoui, K., Kerkouche, E.: An automatic approach to transform BPMN models to Pi-Calculus. In: AICCSA 2015, pp. 1–8. IEEE Computer Society (2015). https://doi.org/10.1109/AICCSA.2015.7507176

9. Combi, C., Oliboni, B., Weske, M., Zerbato, F.: Conceptual modeling of interdependencies between processes and data. In: SAC 2018, pp. 110–119. ACM (2018). https://doi.org/10.1145/3167132.3167141
10. Dijkman, R.M., Dumas, M., Ouyang, C.: Semantics and analysis of business process models in BPMN. Inf. Softw. Technol. **50**(12), 1281–1294 (2008). https://doi.org/10.1016/j.infsof.2008.02.006
11. Dijkman, R.M., Van Gorp, P.: BPMN 2.0 execution semantics formalized as graph rewrite rules. In: Mendling, J., Weidlich, M., Weske, M. (eds.) BPMN 2010. LNBIP, vol. 67, pp. 16–30. Springer, Heidelberg (2010). https://doi.org/10.1007/978-3-642-16298-5_4
12. Dumas, M., Pfahl, D.: Modeling software processes using BPMN: when and when not? In: Kuhrmann, M., Münch, J., Richardson, I., Rausch, A., Zhang, H. (eds.) Managing Software Process Evolution, pp. 165–183. Springer, Cham (2016). https://doi.org/10.1007/978-3-319-31545-4_9
13. Fahland, D.: Describing behavior of processes with many-to-many interactions. In: Donatelli, S., Haar, S. (eds.) PETRI NETS 2019. LNTCS, vol. 11522, pp. 3–24. Springer, Cham (2019). https://doi.org/10.1007/978-3-030-21571-2_1
14. Ghilardi, S., Gianola, A., Montali, M., Rivkin, A.: Delta-BPMN: a concrete language and verifier for data-aware BPMN. In: Polyvyanyy, A., Wynn, M.T., Van Looy, A., Reichert, M. (eds.) BPM 2021. LNISA, vol. 12875, pp. 179–196. Springer, Cham (2021). https://doi.org/10.1007/978-3-030-85469-0_13
15. Gianola, A., Montali, M., Winkler, S.: Object-centric conformance alignments with synchronization. In: Guizzardi, G., Santoro, F., Mouratidis, H., Soffer, P. (eds.) CAiSE 2024. LNCS, vol. 14663, pp. 3–19. Springer, Cham (2024). https://doi.org/10.1007/978-3-031-61057-8_1
16. Haarmann, S., Weske, M.: Cross-case data objects in business processes: semantics and analysis. In: Fahland, D., Ghidini, C., Becker, J., Dumas, M. (eds.) BPM 2020. LNBIP, vol. 392, pp. 3–17. Springer, Cham (2020). https://doi.org/10.1007/978-3-030-58638-6_1
17. Hewelt, M., Weske, M.: A hybrid approach for flexible case modeling and execution. In: La Rosa, M., Loos, P., Pastor, O. (eds.) BPM 2016. LNBIP, vol. 260, pp. 38–54. Springer, Cham (2016). https://doi.org/10.1007/978-3-319-45468-9_3
18. Jensen, K., Kristensen, L.M., Wells, L.: Coloured petri nets and CPN tools for modelling and validation of concurrent systems. Int. J. Softw. Tools Technol. Transf. **9**(3–4), 213–254 (2007). https://doi.org/10.1007/s10009-007-0038-x
19. König, M., Lichtenstein, T., Seidel, A., Weske, M.: Data objects with variables in BPMN. In: del Río Ortega, A., et al. (eds.) BPM 2024, OBJECTS Workshop. CEUR Workshop Proceedings, vol. 3758. CEUR-WS.org (2024). https://ceur-ws.org/Vol-3758/paper-29.pdf
20. König, M., Weske, M.: Multi-instance data behavior in BPMN. In: Fonseca, C.M., et al. (eds.) ER Forum. CEUR Workshop Proceedings, vol. 3618. CEUR-WS.org (2023). https://ceur-ws.org/Vol-3618/forum_paper_4.pdf
21. Künzle, V., Reichert, M.: PHILharmonicFlows: towards a framework for object-aware process management. J. Softw. Maint. Res. Pract. **23**(4), 205–244 (2011). https://doi.org/10.1002/smr.524
22. Laroussinie, F., Schnoebelen, P.: A hierarchy of temporal logics with past. Theor. Comput. Sci. **148**(2), 303–324 (1995). https://doi.org/10.1016/0304-3975(95)00035-U
23. Meghzili, S., Chaoui, A., Strecker, M., Kerkouche, E.: An approach for the transformation and verification of BPMN models to colored petri nets models. Int. J. Softw. Innov. **8**(1), 17–49 (2020). https://doi.org/10.4018/IJSI.2020010102

24. Meyer, A., Pufahl, L., Fahland, D., Weske, M.: Modeling and enacting complex data dependencies in business processes. In: Daniel, F., Wang, J., Weber, B. (eds.) BPM 2013. LNISA, vol. 8094, pp. 171–186. Springer, Heidelberg (2013). https://doi.org/10.1007/978-3-642-40176-3_14
25. OMG: Business Process Model and Notation (BPMN), Version 2.0.2. Technical report, Object Management Group (2014). https://www.omg.org/spec/BPMN/2.0.2
26. Ouyang, C., Dumas, M., ter Hofstede, A.H.M., van der Aalst, W.M.P.: From BPMN process models to BPEL web services. In: ICWS 2006, pp. 285–292. IEEE Computer Society (2006). https://doi.org/10.1109/ICWS.2006.67
27. Petri, C.A.: Kommunikation mit Automaten. PhD Thesis, Institut für instrumentelle Mathematik, Bonn (1962)
28. Ramadan, M., Elmongui, H.G., Hassan, R.: BPMN formalisation using coloured petri nets. In: Proceedings of the 2nd GSTF Annual International Conference on Software Engineering & Applications (SEA 2011), pp. 83–90 (2011)
29. Snoeck, M.: Enterprise Information Systems Engineering - The MERODE Approach. The Enterprise Engineering Series, Springer, Cham (2014). https://doi.org/10.1007/978-3-319-10145-3
30. von Stackelberg, S., Putze, S., Mülle, J., Böhm, K.: Detecting data-flow errors in BPMN 2.0. Open J. Inf. Syst. (OJIS) **1**(2), 1–19 (2014)
31. Steinau, S., Marrella, A., Andrews, K., Leotta, F., Mecella, M., Reichert, M.: DALEC: a framework for the systematic evaluation of data-centric approaches to process management software. Softw. Syst. Model. **18**(4) (2019)
32. Sun, S.X., Zhao, J.L., Nunamaker, J.F., Sheng, O.R.L.: Formulating the data-flow perspective for business process management. Inf. Syst. Res. **17**(4), 374–391 (2006). https://doi.org/10.1287/isre.1060.0105
33. Trčka, N., van der Aalst, W.M.P., Sidorova, N.: Data-flow anti-patterns: discovering data-flow errors in workflows. In: van Eck, P., Gordijn, J., Wieringa, R.J. (eds.) CAiSE 2009. LNISA, vol. 5565, pp. 425–439. Springer, Heidelberg (2009). https://doi.org/10.1007/978-3-642-02144-2_34
34. Voglhofer, T., Rinderle-Ma, S.: Collection and elicitation of business process compliance patterns with focus on data aspects. Bus. Inf. Syst. Eng. **62**(4), 361–377 (2020). https://doi.org/10.1007/s12599-019-00594-3
35. Weske, M.: Business Process Management - Concepts, Languages, Architectures, Third Edition. Springer, Heidelberg (2019). https://doi.org/10.1007/978-3-662-59432-2
36. Wong, P.Y.H., Gibbons, J.: Formalisations and applications of BPMN. Sci. Comput. Program. **76**(8), 633–650 (2011). https://doi.org/10.1016/j.scico.2009.09.010
37. Xiang, D., Liu, G., Yan, C., Jiang, C.: Detecting data-flow errors based on petri nets with data operations. IEEE CAA J. Autom. Sinica **5**(1), 251–260 (2018). https://doi.org/10.1109/JAS.2017.7510766

Conceptualizing Change Activities in Process Mining

Steven Knoblich(✉), Lukas Pfahlsberger, and Jan Mendling

Humboldt-Universität zu Berlin, Rudower Chaussee 25, 12489 Berlin-Adlershof, Germany
{steven.knoblich,lukas.pfahlsberger,jan.mendling}@hu-berlin.de

Abstract. In an increasingly dynamic world, business processes must be able to respond to frequently occurring and random changes during their execution. Consequently, this means that the process models must be able to handle this complexity and enable process analysts to derive the right conclusions quickly. However, current approaches in the field of process mining do not distinguish between process activities associated with *change* and those with *routine*. This condition leads to more complicated, overloaded, and sometimes misguided process visualizations that make it difficult for analysts to evaluate them. In this paper, we address the research problem by conceptualizing a new type of process activity that we call *change activity* which we base on causal knowledge. We thereby extend the *causal process mining* approach with another important aspect for handling random occurrences of events. We evaluated our findings through a survey of process mining experts from research and practice. Our results indicate that a dedicated visualization of *change activities* reduces the complexity of process visualizations. In addition, unimportant information is hidden and important information is highlighted so that analysts can make better assessments.

Keywords: Change Activities · Causal Process Mining · Visual Analytics

1 Introduction

In today's rapidly evolving business environment, the ability of business processes to adapt to unexpected and frequent changes is crucial for organizational success. *Classic* process mining approaches neglect to explicitly designate such *out-of-the-ordinary* changes and treat them as such. In most cases, *changes* are treated the same as *routine* tasks which are on the happy path of the process. This lack of differentiation and explicit visualization poses challenges for process analysts since they are confronted with complex, cluttered, and sometimes misleading visualizations (e.g., so-called spaghetti models) [1,2].

Business process professionals can benefit greatly from analyses and visualizations that go beyond simple directly-follows representations and enrich models

M. Kaczmarek-Heß et al. (Eds.): EDOC 2024 Workshops, LNBIP 537, pp. 155–168, 2025.
https://doi.org/10.1007/978-3-031-79059-1_10

with insights on *changes* [3,4]. On the one hand, it can help to reduce the time and cost for the process model analysis, but also for the training and onboarding of new analysts. On the other hand, it can increase the quality of the analysis due to a more precise detection of *real* problem root causes, decrease wrong and misleading statements but also increase the flexibility during the analysis by switching the focus on different undesired changes and their impact. Despite the stated merits, the literature has only dealt with the subject in a rudimentary way. For example, they investigated robust process discovery [5] or probabilistic approaches to event-case correlation trying to connect events to the same case with the challenge of including *change* behaviour [6]. Moreover, Lu et al. [3, p. 1] detect contextual activity and claim that it "can affect the performance of any process discovery algorithm". We thus pose the following research question:

How can process mining approaches be conceptually enhanced to effectively differentiate change activities from routine activities in business processes?

In this paper, we address this research question by conceptualizing and visualizing a new type of process activity, called the *change activity*. This activity differentiates from what we call a *routine activity* which has, per definition, one or more causal relationships with other *routine activities*. We build our concept on the basis of the *causal process mining* approach by Waibel et al. [7]. We further evaluate our concept conducting an online survey with business process management professionals.

The remainder of this paper is structured as follows. Section 2 presents the research background against which we position our work. Section 3 presents our concept for change activities by drafting general assumptions and proposing a visual representation. Section 4 presents our evaluation design, data collection procedure, and results. Section 5 gives the conclusion of our paper.

2 Background

In this section, we present the background of our research. First, we illustrate the problem. Then we summarize research on change and random occurrences by contextual factors in business process management. Finally, we describe causal process mining as a foundation for our solution.

2.1 Problem Statement

Business processes are typically not executed in isolation. Rather, they are embedded in specific contexts that can trigger *changes* at unexpected times that affect the outcome of the process. *Changes* in processes are one of the most significant factors for the increased complexity in process visualizations. As a theoretical thought experiment, imagine a process with 20 successive process activities which are executed in a row as one process variant. By adding a single change activity, which can theoretically take place after each of these 20 activities, the number of variants in the process model grows rapidly. In fact, this results in a binary decision (add or not add) after each of the 20 activities independently, potentially leading to $2^{20} = 1,048,576$ process variants:

This complexity triggers numerous problems that affect the time, quality, and costs of process analysis in the context of business process management.

The consequences of a lack of differentiation between *routine activities* and *change activities* leads to the following problems. First, the exponential increase in the number of process variants leads to significantly longer times required for process analysis and the training of new process analysts. Each additional variant introduces a new branch of potential actions and outcomes, which complicates the understanding and documentation of the process. Analysts must consider and evaluate each possible variant to determine whether the behavior is desired or undesired, which can be exceedingly time-consuming.

Second, quality can suffer when process complexity becomes unmanageable. Analysts might overlook certain process variants or fail to identify critical issues or causal relationships, leading to suboptimal process improvements. Moreover, the intricate nature of complex processes can make it challenging to maintain consistent quality across all variants. The risk of errors and inconsistencies increases, which can degrade the overall quality of process outcomes.

Third, with increased complexity comes higher costs. The time required to analyze numerous process variants directly translates to increased labor costs. Additionally, complex processes may require a higher skill level and cognitive capabilities from analysts, adding to the overall expense for senior experts. Businesses must also consider the costs associated with potential errors or inefficiencies that arise from inadequate process understanding and management.

2.2 Change and Context in Business Processes

Prior research on context and change of business processes has proposed techniques for modeling and mining. Van der Aalst and Dustdar [8] mention four types of *contexts*: Case context, process context, social context, and external context. The case context includes properties directly related to individual process instances, such as customer type or order size. The process context involves the interactions and competition among multiple instances of the same process, such as resource availability and workload. The social context refers to human and organizational factors, including social networks and individual performance variations. The external context encompasses broader environmental factors, such as weather, economic conditions, and regulatory changes that influence process handling [8].

Lu et al. [3, p. 108] use the term *context activities* indicating that these process activities do not follow a causal order. They attribute this to the fact that it is not the control-flow that influences its execution, but rather random external factors. It is often unclear whether such context activities should be regarded as noise or as part of the control flow. In practice, this results in the generation of the so-called spaghetti or flower models, which are often too complex for analysts to comprehend [3].

Guo et al. [9] develop an algorithm to detect what they call *invisible tasks* that are difficult to determine and sort relate to a *routine* process. Viewed from a similar angle, Goedertier et al. [5] stress that process analysis must deal with challenges such as expressiveness, noise, incomplete data, and the inclusion of prior knowledge. They propose the inclusion of so-called *artificial negative events* to better contrast the ordinary from the extraordinary.

Di Ciccio and Montali [10] introduce the concept of *declarative process mining*, which focuses on behavioral rules and uses the DECLARE language and graphical notations. Building on this work, van Dongen et al. [11] developed a mixed paradigm approach to conformance checking that combines the strengths of procedural and declarative representations. The authors applied their solution to real-world event logs, using a common software to visualize their result, but focusing on other aspects such as execution time or fitness.

None of this previous work has provided a specific classification of different activities such as *change* or *routine activities*.

2.3 Causal Process Knowledge in Process Mining

Process mining is a data-driven technique that involves extracting insights from event data to analyze and improve business processes. It combines principles from computational intelligence, data mining, and process management to visualize, monitor, and optimize business processes within an organization [12]. By revealing discrepancies between intended and actual processes, process mining facilitates better decision making and process optimization [13].

Causal process mining is an approach described by Waibel et al. [7]. It is different from classic process mining in that it takes causal knowledge into account. More specifically, it transforms relational data structures based on the causal template into a causal event graph that internalizes the complex interrelationships between data objects that trigger other objects based on *causation*. Figure 1 illustrates the differences between both approaches.

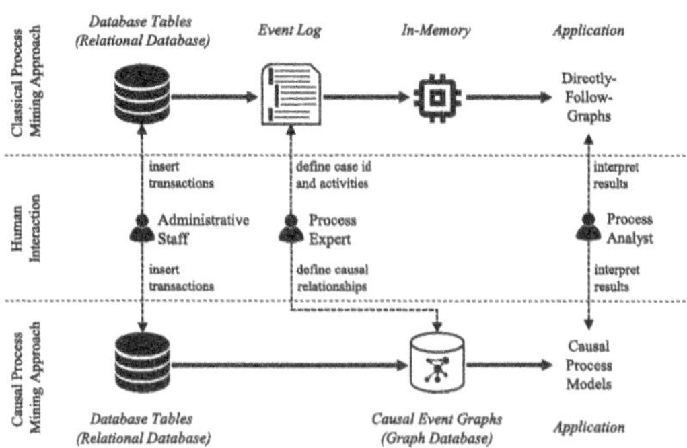

Fig. 1. Difference between *classic* process mining approaches and causal process mining [7].

As a foundational figure in the philosophy of causation, Hume [14] asserted that all knowledge is derived from experience and hinges on the associations between perceived events. Building on this concept, Waldmann [15] explored knowledge-based causal induction, emphasizing causal directionality as the crucial element in interpreting statistical correlations.

Regarding causal knowledge in business processes, experts with extensive domain-specific experience are invaluable for process improvement. Their experience equips them with an accurate understanding of the causal relationships between individual activities within business processes. For instance, a process owner of an order-to-cash process intuitively understands that a customer order will eventually result in an invoice being created. In contrast, it is evident to the process owner that an invoice followed by a customer order would contradict the causal logic of the process [7].

Translating these concepts to process mining algorithms is mostly missing in research [7,16]. An experiment by Rembert et al. [16], which incorporated prior knowledge, shows that this approach enhances robustness against noise, thereby reducing the likelihood of measurement and ordering errors, especially in processes with a high degree of infrequent behavior. In a related study, Diamantini et al. [17] show that domain knowledge repairs event logs and generates more accurate models for complex and highly variable processes. A template developed by Waibel et al. [7] supports the integration of causal sequences to discover the structure of processes, especially of control flows. This creates simpler process models, with less self-loops and spurious arcs, compared to the classic approach.

Based on this, Pfahlsberger et al. [18] present multi-perspective path semantics based on causal knowledge differentiating between *desired* and *undesired* behavior. We describe three of these path semantics here and use them for conceptualizing the representation of change activities and their causal relationships.

- Conformance path:
  The conformance path merges desired and observed behaviors in a process. It represents the expected flow based on the analyst's hypothesis and actual behavior from data. Any deviation is seen as unexpected. Visually, it is shown as a gray angular arrow to subtly indicate the desired behavior.
- Hypothetical path:
  The hypothetical path represents unobserved yet desired behavior, based on causal process knowledge. It implies alternative paths exist, allowing parallel activities or arbitrary follow-up choices. Visually, it is depicted as a gray dashed arrow with a filled arrowhead, indicating indefinite nonconforming behavior.
- Prohibited path:
  The prohibited path represents undesired but observed behavior, where the process violates against causal process knowledge. Visually, it is shown as a solid red arrow with a curvilinear course, contrasting with the allowed shortcut path, indicating undesirable behavior.

This previous work by Pfahlsberger et al. [18] focused on path semantics. A conceptual approach for different types of activities, especially change activities, is missing.

3 Conceptualizing Change Activities in Process Mining

In this section, we conceptualize the term *change activity* by formulating general assumptions and designing a visual representation. In this regard, we build on the fundamental concept of *causal process mining* developed by Waibel et al. [7]. Our proposed approach further extends the visual components for multi-perspective path semantics by Pfahlsberger et al. [18].

We define the term *change* in the context of a business process as a principally undesired event that cannot be clearly sequenced within a chain of process activities, as its execution time can occur randomly during execution. For instance, a *change* in an order-to-cash process can be an adaptation of a price for a specific item. Alternatively, during the execution of a purchase-to-pay process, a *change* could manifest itself in the form of adapted supplier terms. What is defined as *change activity* as part of the process mining analysis, always depends on the context and must be specified by a process domain expert in the causal event graphs before. With reference to the previous example, a price change may be part of the standard process in one company, hence not be considered as a *change activity* because it is desired. On the other hand, in another company, such an event clearly qualifies as a *change activity* since its occurrence is undesired.

3.1 Assumptions About Change Activities

In this section, we formulate four central assumptions to delineate the concept of *change activities.* We are placing our focus on the analysis and visual representation of such *change activities* in regard to its impact on the structural effects of the process execution. By structural effects, we mean the triggering of unwanted process patterns such as *rework*, *correction*, *disarray*, or *negligence*, as conceptualized in the approaches of Pfahlsberger et al. [18]. On the one hand, we define a *neutral impact* on the process as a nonmeasurable influence on unwanted process patterns. On the other hand, we define a *negative impact* as a subsequent triggering of such an undesired process pattern.

- Change activities are only relevant for the analysis if they have a negative impact on the process[1]. It is therefore necessary to identify the earliest possible point in the process at which a change has a negative impact. As a consequences, the change also has a negative impact on any subsequent activity.

[1] In this case, negative impact primarily refers to structural effects with regard to rework, correction, disarray, or negligence [18]. For example, changing the delivery address after a parcel has been sent to a customer has negative consequences for the customer experience.

- Change activities that have a neutral impact on the process[2], do not have to be analyzed and visualized in relation to the exact point in time at which they were performed. The quantity of their occurrences should be displayed aggregated at the last point in the process, from when a negative impact could be expected.
- Change activities can not be directly triggered by a specific preceding process activity, meaning that the analysis and visualization of incoming paths serves is not necessary. If there is a causal relationship with another preceding process activity, it can not be considered a change activity.
- Change activities can not be directly triggered by another change activity of an identical or different type. This means that it is assumed that there is no causal relationship between the temporal sequence of multiple change activities.

3.2 Visualizing Change Activities

In order to make the assumptions made previously visually accessible to process analysts, we conceptualize four different visual constellations all illustrated in Table 1. The constellations are divided into two categories. First, with or without negative change activities, and with or without neutral change activities. Each pattern is visually depicted for easy recognition of an underlying behavior. We also exemplify the patterns from the perspective of a simple process.

The changes are represented by different visual elements, such as solid lines for observed and dashed lines for unobserved/ hypothetical change. Rectangular black lines for accepted behavior and curved red lines for unaccepted observed behavior, indicating the nature of the change. The diagram represents all possible combinations in four quadrants:

- The top-left quadrant shows the scenario without neutral and without negative change activities. The hypothetical path from the change activity to last activity where the change has a neutral impact is represented.
- The top-right quadrant shows the scenario without neutral change but with negative change activity. The prohibited path links the change activity to the following routine activity.
- The bottom-left quadrant shows the scenario with neutral change activity and without negative change activity. The conformance path from the change activity to last activity where the change has a neutral impact is represented.
- The bottom-right quadrant shows the scenario with both neutral and negative change activity. The conformance path and the prohibited path are represented.

These patterns and the different visual representations of *routine* and *change activities* help to understand the different impacts and implications of changes

[2] In this case, neutral impact primarily refers to no structural effects with regard to rework, correction, disarray, or negligence [18]. For example, if a delivery address is changed before a delivery is sent to a customer.

within a process instance, providing a clear visual representation of the combinations and their potential consequences. In addition, the lack of a link to the *change activity* reduces the complexity of the visualization. Finally, it helps analysts improve root cause analysis for process inefficiencies.

Table 1. Overview of visual components for representing different change constellations

Overview change constellations	Without negative change activities	With negative change activities
Without neutral change activities	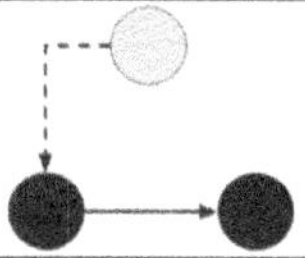	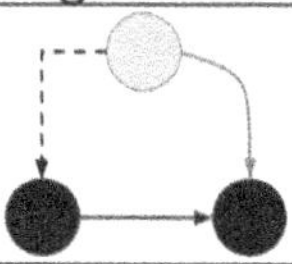
With neutral change activities	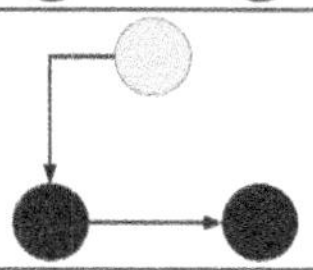	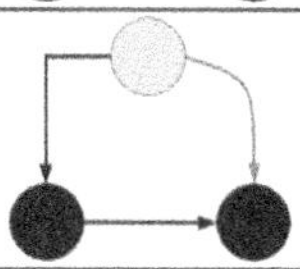

Legend: & Routine Activity, & Change Activity,
& Hypothetical path, & Conformance path, & Prohibited path

4 Research Method

In this section we describe the research method used for the evaluation, including the survey tasks. This is followed by a description of the data collection and the results. This section concludes with an acknowledgement of the limitations.

4.1 Evaluation Case Setting

To evaluate our concept, we drafted a fictitious case of a food ordering process with 87 orders executed. We chose this case because it is easy to understand and both experienced and unexperienced participants are familiar with such a setting. The overall process contains six *routine activities*, namely, *Answer Call*, *Receive Order*, *Request Delivery Address*, *Prepare Order*, *Deliver Order*, and *Receive Payment* as well as one *change activity*, namely, *Update Ordered Quantity*. The process always starts with the activity *Answer Call* and is sequentially followed by the remaining five routine activities. Every process instance is terminated with *Receive Payment*. During the execution of the process sequence, the *change activity Update Ordered Quantity* was randomly triggered 13 times. We visualized the process in two variants. Figure 2 shows a visual representation of a classic process mining approach. Figure 3 depicts the same process visualized with the extended *causal* process mining approach.

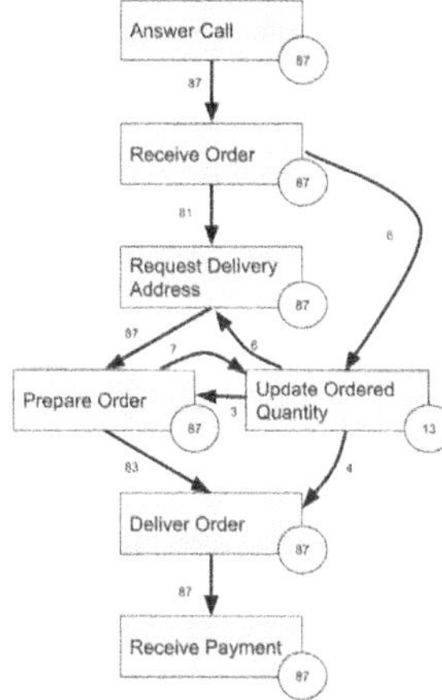

Fig. 2. Visualization of a directly-follows graph from *classic* process mining

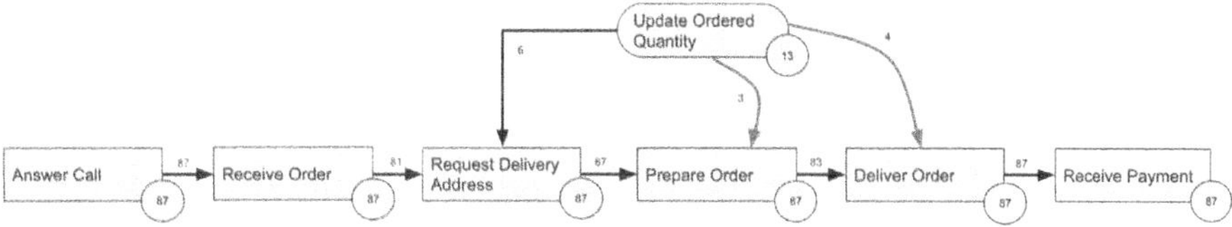

Fig. 3. Visualization of a causal event graph from *causal* process mining

4.2 Survey Tasks

To evaluate the performance effect of our concepts, we designed an online survey. The objective of the survey was to test the understanding of visualizations of the *classic* process mining approach (based on directly-follows graphs) in comparison with the *causal* process mining approach (based on causal event graphs with our extended elements for change activities). Both approaches differ visually through different path semantics, coloring, and activity symbols. We presented all participants with a visual representation of both approaches that both cover the same fictional case:

- The *classic* process mining approach (based on directly-follows graphs): Each node in the graph represents an activity, while the directed edges between nodes indicate the immediate succession of activities based on event logs [12].
- The *causal* process mining approach (based on causal event graphs): Each node in the graph represents an activity, while the gray directed edges between nodes indicate causal relations and the rounded red relations indicate temporal violations [7].

In the survey, we asked participants to solve the following two tasks:

Task 1: What is the change activity in this processes?
Task 2: How many undesired executions of the change activity happened in the process?

Answer options were randomized to mitigate order effects. Two primary metrics were recorded. First, the number of correct responses for identifying change activities and counting undesired executions. Second, the time taken by participants to complete each question. The data collected was analyzed to compare the effectiveness of the *classic* and *causal* approaches. Specifically, we assessed the accuracy of participants' responses as well as the efficiency required to answer each question. These metrics are critical for validating our new visualization technique and addressing the research question.

The visualizations of the *classic* approach served as the control condition, maintaining the current visualization logic without specific highlights or causal assessments. The experimental condition employed our proposed visualization, which incorporated specific highlights for change activities and visual assessments of causal relationships. The purpose of this comparison was to determine whether the new visualization improved the participants' ability to accurately and quickly identify change activities and/or their undesired executions.

4.3 Data Collection

Participants were recruited from a diverse pool of individuals to ensure a comprehensive analysis. Recruitment efforts were carried out through various channels, including direct email contact with two groups from business and research sectors at Humboldt University of Berlin, as well as two LinkedIn posts by the paper's authors. These posts were widely shared on the platform. This multifaceted approach resulted in 27 completed questionnaires. Prior to administering the main survey, participants' experience with business process management and their professional background were collected to contextualize the findings. The online survey was conducted anonymously for a one-week period from Monday, June 24, 2024, to Sunday, June 30, 2024. The majority of responses were received within the first three days, and the final response recorded on June 28, 2024.

The survey was send out via mass emailing to contacts from the authors' network. Additionally, it was shared on social channels such as *LinkedIn* and *X*. A total of 57 people visited the survey page. 37 of them started filling out the survey, of which 27 completed the survey to the end. One participant did not answer the second question regarding the directly-follows graph visualization. Among the participants, 19 had a background in business and eight assigned themselves to the academic field. One of the participants did not identify with either an academic or a business background. In terms of experience in business process management domain, ten participants reported having one to three years of experience, 11 had three to seven years, and five participants had more than seven years of experience. The descriptive statistics are depicted in Fig. 4.

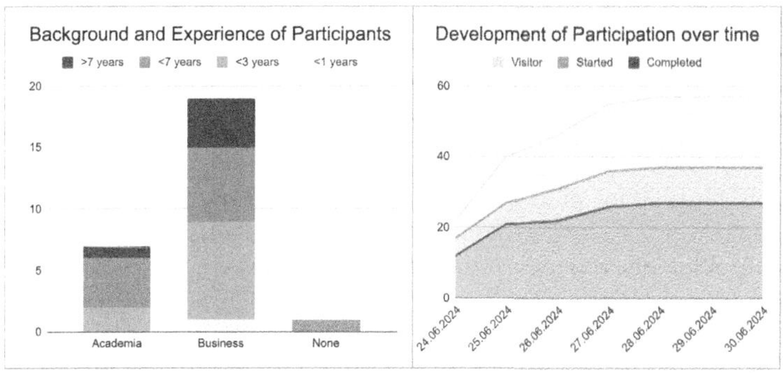

Fig. 4. Development of participants and their background.

4.4 Results

The study yielded several noteworthy findings. First, participants using the causal event graph generally required more time to interpret the visualizations compared to those using directly-follows graphs. This indicates that causal event graphs might be more complex or less intuitive than directly-follows graphs for the participants. Academics were more familiar with the visualizations than business professionals, responding significantly faster than the latter. This finding underscores the need for clearer process mining visualizations in practical applications, as business professionals may require more time and effort to interpret the same data. For the directly-follows graph, the median response time was 50 s, whereas for the causal event graph, it was 61 s. When broken down by background, the median response time for participants with a business background was consistently 85 s across both types of graphs.

Second, the variability in response times was greater among business professionals compared to academics. This suggests differing levels of knowledge between the two groups and highlights a clearer understanding of process visualizations in the academic domain, particularly among those using directly-follows graphs.

Third, the level of experience did not have a strong significant impact on the participants' response times. However, there was a slight trend indicating that individuals with more than three years of experience exhibited less fluctuation in their response times, with most responding within 100 s. The data suggests that less experienced participants had more difficulty interpreting the causal event graphs. Of the three participants who took more than 200 s to respond, two had less than three years of business process management experience.

Fourth, when answering Question 1, participants were able to identify the sought-after *change activity* in the fictional example at almost the same speed, likely due to the straightforward nature of the activity label. Notably, there was only one incorrect response from a participant with a business background and one to three years of business process management experience for the directly-follows graph. This uniformity suggests that some tasks in process mining may be universally intuitive regardless of the visualization used.

Lastly, a clear pattern emerged in the responses to Question 2. The directly-follows graph seemed to prompt participants to respond very quickly; however, their interpretations were significantly less accurate than those using the causal event graph. Only 3 out of 27 participants answered correctly with the directly-follows graph, whereas 16 participants provided correct answers with the causal event graph. This discrepancy indicates the importance of selecting the appropriate visualization method to ensure both efficiency and accuracy in process mining tasks.

In summary, while directly-follows graphs may facilitate quicker responses, the accuracy of interpretations is higher with causal event graphs. This finding highlights the trade-off between speed and accuracy in the interpretation of process mining visualizations and suggests that different contexts may require different approaches to visualization. Consequently, our research suggests that enhancing process mining approaches with more intuitive and clear visualizations of *changes* can effectively improve their differentiation from *routine activities.* This differentiation increases the quality of the process analysis and improves decision-making (Fig. 5).

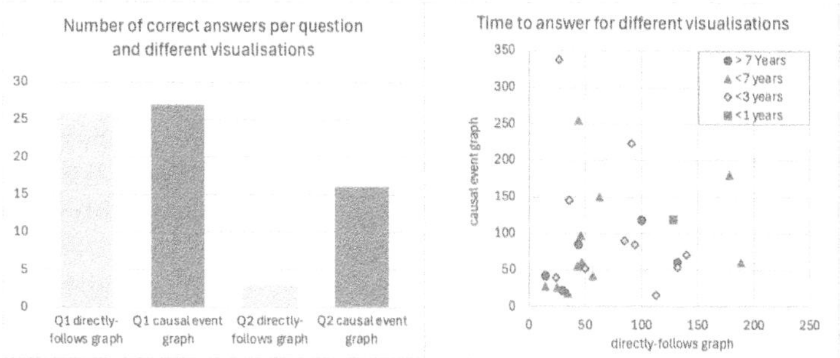

Fig. 5. Results from survey.

4.5 Limitations

We acknowledge the following three limitations. First, our survey compared the classic with the causal process approach, including the conceptualization for change activities. It is important to note that previous research has already demonstrated a positive impact of the causal approach on process discovery and interpretation [7,18], so the effect of our extension needs to be seen in this context. Moreover, the causal representation in our study was supported by color-coding, which may have influenced the results. Future research should also consider the effect of the orientation of process discovery visualizations, as this factor could significantly affect user comprehension and interaction. Second, the sample size is limited and the demographics of the study participants were not fully balanced. Variables such as user experience levels and their professional or educational background were not uniformly distributed. Future studies should aim to include a larger, more diverse and representative sample to better generalize the findings and apply more rigorous techniques. Third, the fictitious case used in our study was relatively simple, consisting of only seven activities and up to eight connections. Although this simplicity helped control for confounding variables, it may not accurately reflect the complexity of real-world process discovery scenarios. We anticipate that more complex data sets and visualizations could amplify the observed effects and provide a more comprehensive understanding of the relative benefits of our concept, by mitigating biases at the same time.

5 Conclusion

In this paper, we conceptualize a new *type* of process activity – the *change activity* – that helps analysts to better differentiate between *change* and *routine* activities. We thus address a still existing research problem that classic process mining approaches often lead to complex and misleading visualizations, such as Spaghetti models. Our aim is to encourage future research to confront persistent representational bias in process mining, which often skews the true nature of the underlying process [2]. Our paper contributes in two ways. First, we propose general assumptions for change activities and then outline a visual representation based on the *causal process mining* approach. Second, we evaluate our concepts based on a fictitious case of a food delivery service with an online survey of process experts from practice and science. Our results indicate that process analysts can benefit significantly from a differentiation between *change* and *routine* activities by pointing out root causes of the problem related to changes during the process execution more accurately compared with *classic* process mining representations. Nonetheless, at least according to our survey, they need slightly more time for this. In fact, by incorporating a more context-aware visualization in regard to changes, analysts can reduce cost associated with process model analysis and enhance the overall quality of their analysis.

Acknowledgements. This work was supported by the Einstein Foundation Berlin [grant number EPP-2019-524, 2022].

References

1. Van der Aalst, W.M.P.: Process mining: discovering and improving Spaghetti and Lasagna processes. In: 2011 IEEE Symposium on Computational Intelligence and Data Mining (CIDM), pp. 1–7. IEEE (2011)
2. van der Aalst, W., Buijs, J., van Dongen, B.: Towards improving the representational bias of process mining. In: Aberer, K., Damiani, E., Dillon, T. (eds.) SIMPDA 2011. LNBIP, vol. 116, pp. 39–54. Springer, Heidelberg (2012). https://doi.org/10.1007/978-3-642-34044-4_3

3. Lu, Y., Chen, Q., Poon, S.K.: Detecting context activities in event logs. In: Augusto, A., Gill, A., Bork, D., Nurcan, S., Reinhartz-Berger, I., Schmidt, R. (eds.) BPMDS 2022, EMMSAD 2022. LNBIP, vol. 450, pp. 108–122. Springer, Cham (2022). https://doi.org/10.1007/978-3-031-07475-2_8
4. Knoblich, S., Mendling, J., Jambor, H.: Review of visual encodings in common process mining tools. In: 1st Visual Process Analytics Workshop, vol. 1 (2024)
5. Goedertier, S., Martens, D., Vanthienen, J., Baesens, B.: Robust process discovery with artificial negative events. J. Mach. Learn. Res. **10**, 1305–1340 (2009)
6. Bayomie, D., Di Ciccio, C., La Rosa, M., Mendling, J.: A probabilistic approach to event-case correlation for process mining. In: Laender, A., Pernici, B., Lim, E.P., de Oliveira, J. (eds.) ER 2017. LNISA, vol. 11788, pp. 136–152. Springer, Cham (2019). https://doi.org/10.1007/978-3-030-33223-5_12
7. Waibel, P., Pfahlsberger, L., Revoredo, K., Mendling, J.: Causal Process Mining from Relational Databases with Domain Knowledge. CoRR, abs/2202.08314 (2022). https://arxiv.org/abs/2202.08314
8. Van der Aalst, W.M.P., Dustdar, S.: Process mining put into context. IEEE Internet Comput. **16**(1), 82–86 (2012)
9. Guo, Q., Wen, L., Wang, J., Yan, Z., Yu, P.S.: Mining invisible tasks in non-free-choice constructs. In: Motahari-Nezhad, H., Recker, J., Weidlich, M. (eds.) BPM 2016. LNISA, vol. 9253, pp. 109–125. Springer, Cham (2015). https://doi.org/10.1007/978-3-319-23063-4_7
10. Di Ciccio, C., Montali, M.: Declarative process specifications: reasoning, discovery, monitoring. In: van der Aalst, W.M.P., Carmona, J. (eds.) Process Mining Handbook. LNBIP, vol. 448, pp. 108–154. Springer, Cham (2022). https://doi.org/10.1007/978-3-031-08848-3_4
11. van Dongen, B.F., De Smedt, J., Di Ciccio, C., Mendling, J.: Conformance checking of mixed-paradigm process models. Preprint Submitted to Information Systems, pp. 1–65. arXiv:2011.11551v1 [cs.FL] (2020)
12. Van der Aalst, W.M.P., Weijters, A.J.M.M.: Process mining. In: Dumas, M., van der Aalst, W., ter Hofstede, A.H.M. (eds.) Process-Aware Information Systems: Bridging People and Software Through Process Technology, pp. 235–254. Wiley, Hoboken (2005)
13. Van der Aalst, W.M.P.: Process mining: overview and opportunities. ACM Trans. Manag. Inf. Syst. **99**(99), 16 (2012). https://doi.org/10.1145/0000000.0000000. Article 99
14. Hume, D.: An Enquiry Concerning Human Understanding, 2nd edn. Hackett Publishing Company, Indianapolis (1977). Original Work Published 1748
15. Waldmann, M.R.: Knowledge-based causal induction. In: Psychology of Learning and Motivation, vol. 34, pp. 47–88. Elsevier (1996)
16. Rembert, A.J., Omokpo, A., Mazzoleni, P., Goodwin, R.T.: Process discovery using prior knowledge. In: Basu, S., Pautasso, C., Zhang, L., Fu, X. (eds.) ICSOC 2013. LNCS, vol. 8274, pp. 328–342. Springer, Heidelberg (2013). https://doi.org/10.1007/978-3-642-45005-1_23
17. Diamantini, C., Genga, L., Potena, D., van der Aalst, W.M.P.: Building instance graphs for highly variable processes. Expert Syst. Appl. **59**, 101–118 (2016)
18. Pfahlsberger, L., Rubensson, C., Knoblich, S., Vidgof, M., Mendling, J.: Multi-perspective path semantics in process mining based on causal process knowledge. In: Companion Proceedings of the 16th IFIP WG 8.1 Working Conference on the Practice of Enterprise Modeling (2023)

Enhancing API Labelling with BERT and GPT: An Exploratory Study

Gabriel Morais[1(✉)], Edwin Lemelin[1,2], Mehdi Adda[1], and Dominik Bork[1,3]

[1] Université du Québec á Rimouski, Lévis, QC G6V 1L8, Canada
{gabrielglauber.morais,edwin.lemelin,mehdi_adda}@uqar.ca

[2] Université Laval, Québec, QC G1V 0A6, Canada

[3] Business Informatics Group, TU Wien, Vienna, Austria
dominik.bork@tuwien.ac.at

Abstract. Application Programming Interfaces (APIs) enable interaction, integration, and interoperability among applications and services, contributing to their adoption and proliferation. However, discovering APIs has relied on manual, time-consuming, costly processes that jeopardize their reuse potential and accentuate the need for effective API retrieval mechanisms. Leveraging the OpenAPI Specification as a basis, this paper presents an exploratory study that combines BERT and GPT machine learning models to propose a novel API classifier. Our investigation explored the *zero-shot learning* capabilities of GPT-4 and GPT-3.5 using relevant terms extracted from API descriptions using BERT. The evaluation of our approach on two datasets comprising 940 API descriptions sourced from public repositories yielded an F1-score of 100% in the small dataset (17 APIs) and 39.1% in the large dataset (923 APIs). These results surpass state-of-the-art on the small dataset with an impressive 29-point improvement. The large dataset showed GPT can suggest labels not in the provided list. Manual analysis revealed that GPT's suggested labels fit the API intent better in 18 out of 20 cases, highlighting its potential for unknown classes and mismatch detection. This emphasizes the need to improve dataset quality and availability for API research. Our findings show the potential of automated API retrieval and open avenues for future research.

Keywords: API classification · OpenAPI Specification · GPT · BERT

1 Introduction

API descriptions are essential in software engineering as they serve as documentation [7], enabling developers to understand and interact with them effectively [21]. Acting as a contract between different components, they ensure seamless integration and rapid development. In this context, the OpenAPI Specification (OAS) [15] standard provides a machine-readable format for describing RESTful APIs, allowing automation capabilities, e.g., code generation [7].

Getting a general understanding of an API is the most critical task when mining API for use in specific contexts [7,21]. In most cases, this task is executed manually [10], and the number of APIs to explore could impede its completion.

M. Kaczmarek-Heß et al. (Eds.): EDOC 2024 Workshops, LNBIP 537, pp. 169–182, 2025.
https://doi.org/10.1007/978-3-031-79059-1_11

The first step toward an effective retrieval mechanism is organizing and classifying data. Automatic text classification is a long-standing research field [18], and recent advances in machine learning, e.g., large language models (LLM), have opened up new avenues to increase the accuracy of automated text classification approaches [4].

Automatically processing OpenAPI documents (OADs) could enhance API discovery and cope with time-consuming manual exploration. Nevertheless, OADs are specific textual documents that combine structured data with a blend of general and technical lexicons. Previous works have explored using OADs and natural language processing (NPL) techniques to improve API discovery [23,33,35]. However, the potential of labelling APIs from OADs using current state-of-the-art LLM algorithms is a significant area yet to be fully explored, with the potential to make a substantial impact in the field.

In this exploratory study, we present preliminary results of applying GPT-4 and GPT-3.5 in combination with KeyBERT to label OADs. The explored approach used KeyBERT to extract relevant words from OADs, which were then passed to GPT through a prompt to find the corresponding label of the document. We relied on KeyBERT to help us enhance prompt engineering, cope with prompting payload restrictions, and limit costs related to OpenAI API consumption.

We experimented with a small labelled dataset comprising 17 OADs used in Microservices research [3]. Our approach achieved an F1-score of 100 in this dataset, an improvement of 29 points from previous works [23]. Encouraged by these results, we assessed the approach's generalizability using a dataset of 923 OADs from the APIs.Guru repository [2] and achieved an F1-score of 39.1.

The experiments further revealed that data cleaning is not required, as words extracted by KeyBERT could be used as-is. Similarly, a manual analysis of labelling mismatches showed that 18 out of the 20 analyzed mismatches were caused by inappropriate labels on the *apisguru* dataset, unveiling the need for accurate datasets to support machine-learning approaches in API labelling research, and new application perspectives, e.g., applying GPT to mislabelling detection. All the artifacts used and produced during our experiments and evaluation are available at this paper's code companion [24].

The remainder of this paper is organized as follows. Section 2 provides the essential background to understand the proposed approach. Section 3 introduces our approach. Section 4 presents the results obtained. These results are discussed in Sect. 5, along with the impacts of our study. Finally, Sects. 6 and 7 provide the future research agenda and concluding remarks, respectively.

2 Background

This section introduces concepts that support readers' understanding of the proposed approach. First, we present the OpenAPI Specification applied to API descriptions Sect. 2.1. Then, we provide a high-level description of the Transformer machine learning architecture Sect. 2.2, providing basic knowledge to understand how BERT and GPT models work.

2.1 OpenAPI Specification

The OpenAPI Specification (OAS) [15], formerly known as Swagger Specification, is a formal specification defining a standard to describe, document, and communicate RESTful APIs. OAS-based API descriptions are formalized hierarchically using a key-value approach, where the keys are the OAS parameters, ensuring consistency throughout different OAS-based API descriptions [30]. These descriptions are typically serialized in YAML Ain't Markup Language (YAML) or JavaScript Object Notation (JSON), which makes them machine-readable.

OAS includes general information about the API, such as its paths, operations, input and outputs, and security details. The values associated with OAS keys can be in any language and follow any standard. Often, they are represented as natural language terms using programming languages' conventions [7]. Listing 1 shows an excerpt of an API described using OAS in YAML.

While the OpenAPI Specification provides various benefits, its effectiveness depends on the accuracy and diligence of the individuals creating the API descriptions [13]. Human errors, oversight, or lack of attention to detail during the API documentation process can result in inaccurate or incomplete descriptions, leading to discrepancies between the documented API and its actual implementation. This risk of unreliability is not limited to using OAS for API descriptions but seems inherent to API documentation [37].

```yaml
openapi: 3.0.1
info:
  title: Checkout API
  version: v1
paths:
  "/api/v1/Checkout":
    get:
      tags:
      - Checkout
      parameters:
      - name: userName
        in: query
        schema:
          type: string
          nullable: true
      responses:
        '200':
```

Listing 1. EShopOnContainers Checkout API's OAD

```
swagger
api
apis
json
yaml
apisguru
openapi
$ref
ref
jsonschemadialect
servers
paths
webhooks
components
security
tags
...
```

Listing 2. Ignored terms

2.2 Transformers-Based ML Models

Transformer is a deep learning architecture built on the attention mechanism and comprising two main layers: *Encoders*, which create a representation of the input data, and *decoders*, which generate the output sequence step by step [38]. These components enable the Transformer architecture to handle sequence-to-sequence tasks, such as machine translation, text classification, and generation.

Transformer *encoders* and *decoders* are almost similar; both have a self-attention mechanism and a feed-forward network. However, decoders have an additional sub-layer that applies self-attention to encoders' outputs. The self-attention mechanism captures long-distance context without a sequential dependency, allowing each position in the sequence to attend to other positions, capturing long-range dependencies [25]. This additional self-attention mechanism copes with *decoders* limitation of accessing only previous positions. Sequence ordering is captured through a positional embedding, which is added to the input embeddings in the encoder and decoder stacks to provide information about the sequence's relative or absolute tokens' position. Mainly, encoders are helpful for text classification tasks, while decoders are helpful for text generation tasks.

Generative Pre-trained Transformer (GPT) [31] is a state-of-the-art deep learning model for NLP tasks built upon *decoders*. It is trained in two steps, first by unsupervised generative pre-training of a language model using a massive amount of unlabelled text data, then by a supervised discriminative fine-tuning of the pre-trained model on specific downstream tasks. During fine-tuning, the model adapts its learned representations to suit the task at hand, enabling it to improve performance on various NLP benchmarks.

GPT-3 is a significant improvement of the GPT series that introduced a 175 billion parameters model, 100 times bigger than its predecessor (GPT-2). GPT-3 relies on the model size to learn more from diversified sources, resulting in models that can achieve various tasks without task-specific training, starting the era of large language models (LLMs) [16]. GPT-3 allows users to bypass the supervised fine-tuning of the pre-trained model by directly providing instructions during inference, such as a task description and output examples [6]. This approach is called *in-context learning*. It dramatically reduces fine-tuning efforts without losing the model's accuracy. GPT-4 is the last evolution of the GPT series, comprising 170 trillion parameters and supporting text and image inputs [1]. OpenAI made GPT-3 and GPT-4 available through an API, allowing developers and businesses to access and utilize the models' capabilities on a broader scale, contributing to their popularity and hype.

Bidirectional Encoder Representations from Transformers (BERT) is an NLP model composed of 340 million parameters and trained on an extensive dataset of 3.3 billion words [9]. It is considered a state-of-the-art technique in various NLP tasks [22]. It employs a multi-layer Transformer-Encoder architecture with self-attention mechanisms and feed-forward neural networks, following a two-step process of pre-training and fine-tuning. The pre-training process relies on a masked language modelling task, where specific tokens are randomly masked. The model then recovers these masked tokens by considering the

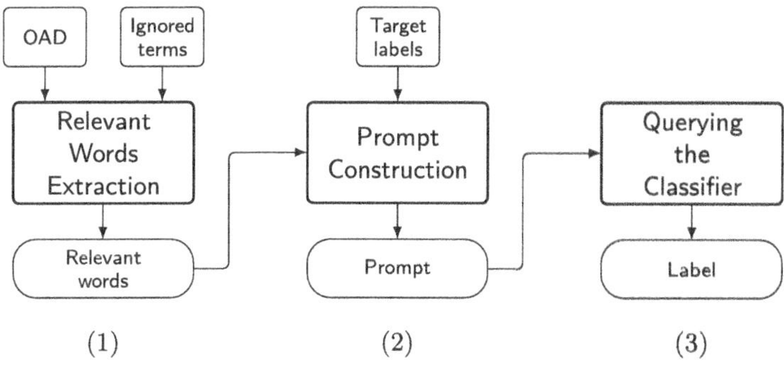

Fig. 1. Overview of our BERT and GPT-based API Labelling Approach

encoding vectors from a bidirectional Transformer, allowing it to understand the context from both the left and right sides. The fine-tuning process is achieved by training with reduced resources and smaller datasets to optimize its performance for specific tasks. BERT comes in different sizes and has variants called the BERT family [22].

In summary, each model has strengths and limitations. The choice of the model depends on the problem, use case, and the available data. Recently, the combination of GPT and BERT has mutually improved their abilities to solve question-answering tasks [17]. This work inspired our approach.

3 Approach

Our approach, as depicted in Fig. 1, offers a comprehensive solution for API classification. Given an OpenAPI document (OAD), a list of terms to be ignored, and a list of target labels, our approach proceeds through a series of systematic steps to achieve classification. First, we extract a specific number of relevant words from the API description while excluding OAS terms and English stopwords from the provided exclusion list (1). Next, we build a classification prompt using the extracted relevant words and a list of target labels (2). Finally, the classifier is queried using the generated prompt, assigning the OAD to its corresponding label (3).

3.1 Relevant Words Extraction

To extract relevant words from an OpenAPI Document, it initially needs to be parsed from YAML or JSON and converted into a single string of lowercase words. Then, unique words within the text that are not in the list of terms to ignore are counted. This list comprises common English stop words and OAS key names (see Listing 2). For recall, API documents formalized using the OpenAPI standard follow a key-value approach, with keys defined within the specification, leading to the recurrence of these terms (keys) in OADs.

```
system : "You will receive keywords extracted from OpenAPI documents.
Your task is to classify the document into one of the following
categories: {target_labels}.
Respond only with the category name."
user : "{relevant_words}"
```

Listing 3. GPT Prompt Template

As an illustrative example, by ignoring these words, the OAD excerpt from Listing 1 contains nine unique words: `cancel`, `eshoponcontainers`, `header`, `info`, `ordering`, `orders`, `requestid`, `service`, and `v1`. The number of relevant words to extract is determined as 20% of the total count of unique terms in the document, following Pareto's principle [34], also known as the 80/20 rule, which states that roughly 80% of the effects come from 20% of the causes. Thus, we considered that 20% of the OAD content is enough to characterize it.

Keywords are retrieved using KeyBERT [11], a Python package that leverages BERT word embeddings. It extracts terms or sentences that are most similar to the document based on cosine similarity. Using KeyBERT, we provide the number of words to extract and the list of terms to exclude, as shown in Listing 2. This ensures that the keywords obtained are significant. Once the process is finished, these words are compiled into an enumeration for use in the prompt.

3.2 Prompt Construction

The large language model prompt used to classify OADs is constructed by combining the relevant words extracted with KeyBERT and user-defined target labels. The prompt comprises two parts: `system` and `user`. The motive for this segmentation is explained in the following Subsection. We use basic string concatenation techniques to incorporate the user's input in this configurable prompt. Listing 3 presents the template used in our approach. The characters in black are fixed, while those in orange and magenta correspond to the variable names of target labels and relevant words, respectively. This template has proven to work best in our testing.

3.3 Querying the Classifier

Both the `system` and `user` segments of the prompt are sent to GPT using OpenAI's API and its chat completion endpoint. The `system` message conveys high-level information or context to guide the model's behaviour. In contrast, the `user` part contains the direct inputs from the users, representing prompts they want the model to respond to [28]. Thus, the GPT API is queried using this prompt, and the response is trimmed and converted to lowercase. Only the first label is selected if the response includes an enumeration of labels. Listing 4 shows the query employed to classify the EShopOnContainers OAD file, depicted in Listing 1. In this classification example, the `assistant`'s response is accurate.

```
system : "You will receive keywords extracted from OpenAPI documents.
Your task is to classify the document into one of the following
categories: audit, rooting, cart, frontend, order, catalog, user,
currency, location, emailcontact, marketing, payment, product,
recommendation, shipping.
Respond only with the category name."
user : "checkoutordercommand,int32,checkout,info"
assistant : "order"
```

Listing 4. EShopOnContainers Checkout API Prompt

3.4 Experiment Settings

Datasets – In this study, we exploited two datasets used in previous works [23]. The first dataset, named *eshopping*, is an extension of the one used by Morais et al. [23]. It comprises 17 API documents describing four microservices-based systems from the e-shopping domain proposed by Assunçao et al. [3]: *EshopOnContainers*, *Eshop-netcore*, *Shopping Cart*, and *Socksshop*. These API documents were originally unlabelled but could be matched to functional classes identified by Mendonça et al. [20]. They extracted 14 features (*Frontend, User, Payment, Catalog, Cart, Order, Product, EmailContact, Shipping, Marketing, Recommendation, Audit, Currency, and Location*) from six e-shopping microservices architectures (cf. [3]). We used these features as the target labels in our controlled experiments.

The second dataset, *apisguru*, comprises data extracted from APIs.Guru [2], a repository of public API documentation containing 3826[1] API documents formalized using the OpenAPI standard, 2117 defined using OAS version 2.0, and 1709 defined using version 3.0. APIs.Guru allows adding a particular parameter to API documents, the *apisguru-categories* tag, allowing contributors to manually specify a tag related to the functionality or domain of the described API, such as *financial*, *media*, or *entertainment*. Although this parameter is not mandatory, we noted that 96% (3658) of the API documents in this repository were associated with at least one tag.

We identified 31 categories that we used as labels to which the API documents should be classified. To enhance the automatic analysis of classification results, we excluded OADs having multiple tags (579 OADs). Furthermore, a random exploration of the dataset revealed significant imbalances among certain categories. For instance, the category *cloud* contained 2157 documents, accounting for 56% of the entire dataset. Furthermore, the *cloud* label seemed more related to the API provider industry rather than to the actual functionality delivered by the API described in the OAD. Thus, we decided to exclude APIs tagged as *cloud* to maintain the reliability of our experiment. The final dataset consisted

[1] As of May 2024. This number excludes documents we were unable to open due to various parsing errors.

Table 1. Summary of the Experiment's Settings.

Datasets	KeyBERT	GPT
eshopping(17 OADs, 15 labels)	`msmarco-distilbert-cos-v5`	`gpt-3.5-turbo`
apisguru(923 OADs, 31 labels)		`gpt-4-turbo`

Table 2. Results of the experiments.

Model	Dataset	$Precision_M$	$Recall_M$	$F1 - Score_M$
`gpt-3.5-turbo`	*eshopping*	100.00	100.00	100.00
	apisguru	47.28	38.62	38.58
`gpt-4-turbo`	*eshopping*	100.00	100.00	100.00
	apisguru	47.75	40.71	39.12

of 923 OADs. We relied on this dataset to evaluate the generalizability of our approach.
Tools – All experiments were performed on a Google Colaboratory [5] Notebook using the free plan with the following specifications: Intel Xeon CPU 2.20 GHz, Tesla T4 GPU, and 13 GB of RAM. Datasets management was handled with Pandas [19], while NumPy [12] and Scikit-Learn [29] were used for metrics calculation. The extraction of relevant words was performed using KeyBERT and the pre-trained sentence transformer model `msmarco-distilbert-cos-v5` [14,32]. The models used for classifying OADs were `gpt-3.5-turbo` [26] and `gpt-4-turbo` [27] for both the small and large datasets. Table 1 summarizes the experiment settings.

4 Results

In this section, we present the results of our experiments from the *eshopping* dataset, which consists of 17 OADs and 15 labels, as well as the applicability results from the *apisguru* dataset, which comprises 923 OADs and 31 labels. We tested each dataset with GPT-3.5 and GPT-4 in order to assess the model's respective capabilities in the same API classification task. To evaluate the performance of our classification method, we used macro precision ($Precision_M$), recall ($Recall_M$), and F1-score ($F1\text{–}Score_M$) metrics [36], ensuring that each class of our imbalanced datasets contributed equally to the overall results. All the compiled data can be found in Table 2. The findings provide valuable insights into the effectiveness of the proposed approach and shed light on the impact of various factors on API classification accuracy.

4.1 Overall Results

Our approach exhibited better performance than those obtained by Morais et al. [23] in a similar dataset (16 OADs); our *eshopping-dataset* was an extension of theirs. Indeed, our approach achieved a 100% F1-Score, whereas they obtained 71%.

Finding 1. The BERT-GPT API Classifier outperformed previous works by 29 points.

During prompt construction, we observed that the words extracted by KeyBERT comprised composed terms, such as *orderingapi*, *ordernumber*, and *orderitems*. We reproduced the experiment of Morais et al. [23] and found out that their approach could not handle such terms. Thus, we found that GPT was able to handle complex terms (not respecting syntactic rules) without data preprocessing. The same extends to acronyms. This finding could explain the precision improvement achieved by our approach.

Finding 2. The approach avoids the need for complex data preprocessing and is able to adapt to lexicon diversity and word structure in OADs.

Results also indicate that in our BERT-GPT classification method, the performance improvement from GPT-3.5 to GPT-4 is minimal, with both models achieving an F1-score of 100 on the *eshopping* dataset and approximately 39 on the *apisguru* dataset. Indeed, accounting for the variability and randomness in LLMs behaviour [8], the observed difference between the two versions of GPT is not significant enough to conclude that GPT-4 outperforms GPT-3.5.

Finding 3. Using GPT-4 negligibly improved the approach's performance.

4.2 Evaluation of Generalizability

We evaluated the generalizability of our approach using a more extensive and diverse dataset, the *apisguru* dataset, including 923 OADs from various sources and domains, providing an extended range of scenarios for evaluation. Indeed, the dataset's diversity, encompassing domains such as Finance, Education, Entertainment, and more, allowed us to examine how well the approach generalizes across different application domains. This enabled us to assess the approach's performance in the face of variable data, providing valuable information on its practicality in real-world settings.

The experiment yielded key insights. We observed that the BERT-GPT classifier performance had substantially declined, dropping from an F1-score of 100 to around 39 for both GPT-3.5 and GPT-4. By manually analyzing 20 random labelling mismatches, we discovered that 18 of them were caused by inappropriate labels on the *apisguru* dataset. We also observed that GPT proposed additional labels not in the provided list, which, in most cases, were more accurate than those associated with OADs in the source dataset.

Table 3 shows a sample of the analyzed mismatches. In the first row, the *player*, *sportdata*, *mbl* and *nfldata* keywords point to the sports label, thus specifying the original entertainment label. In the second row, the *zipcode*, *area* and *getzipinfo* keywords clearly point to a location functionality, not a developer tool. In the third row, the *proxy* and *vnp* keywords point to a security feature, not a location one. The same is observed in the fourth and fifth rows where *charity*, and *marketing*, *advertise*, *ads* and *promotionsale* keywords point respectively to charity and marketing labels, not to e-commerce.

These observations suggest that the classifier's performance might not be indicative of its actual potential due to the dataset's labelling inaccuracies.

> **Finding 4.** GPT provided additional labels from those provided by the user, opening opportunities to handle APIs belonging to unknown classes or improving the precision in classifying APIs.

Table 3. Sample of analyzed mismatches.

Keywords	Labels		
	APIGuru	*GPT-3.5*	*GPT-4*
rotoballerarticlesbyplayer,rotoballerarticlesbyplayerid,playerinfo, rotoballer,**mlb**,**sportsdata**,**player**,players,**nfldata**,entries, rotoballerarticles,playerid,profile_image,apikeyheader,info	entertainment	sport_data	sport_data
zipcode,zip,interzoid,**getzipinfo**,providername,code,info,detailed, getzipcodeinfo,profile_image,developer_tools.www, areasquaremiles,city,information,	developer_tools	location	location
ip2proxy,ip2location,**proxies**,proxy,profile_image,px2,px1,ip,px9, proxytype,**vpn**,px10,server,isproxy,providername,px11,lookup,ipv4	location	security	security
api_**charity**,**charity**_org,commerce_charity_v1_oas3,api_auth,array, api_scope,charity_org_id,charityorg,www,charityorgid,charityorgs, ebay_gb,**charity**,website,ebay_us,charitysearchresponse,org,com, providername,clientcredentials,ebay,charitable,support,link,users, marketplace,supported,application,profile_image,twitter,assistance, basepath,help,imageurl,search,user,servicename,implementation, page,html,access,errorid,10,subdomain,individual,accessing,server, ecommerce,developers,header,helps,associated	ecommerce	charity	charity
api_**marketing**,**marketing**,sell_marketing_v1_oas3,promote,**advertise**, promotes,promoting,ebay_it,item_promotion,ebay_au,promotions, promotional,**promotionsale**,**ads**,ebay,ebay_us,marketplaceid,selling, ebay_fr,ebay_de,ebay_gb,bulk_update_**ads**_bid_by_listing_id, promotion_name,promotiondetail,supportedmarketplaces,sales promotion_type,create_**ads**_by_inventory_reference,teasers,attract, bulk_create_**ads**_by_listing_id,promotionreportdetail,marketplace, bulk_update_**ads**_bid_by_inventory_reference,advertised, bulk_create_**ads**_by_inventory_reference,ebay_es,sells, listing_quantity_sold,**advertising**_eligibility,**promotion**, get_**ads**_by_inventory_reference,promoted,**promotion**type, bulk_update_**ads**_status_by_listing_id,**promotion**typeenum, ad_campaign,promotionid,active_seller_count,marketplace_id	ecommerce	marketing	marketing

5 Discussion

The findings of our study hold several implications for API classification. First, our experiment shows the potential of the combined BERT-base and GPT-based classifier in accurately labelling API descriptions. The approach demonstrated high accuracy rates on a controlled dataset, and the evaluation of its generalizability offered promising prospects for its application to solve practical problems.

Second, the experiments demonstrated GPT's capacity to handle acronyms, abbreviations and composed terms without complex data preprocessing. Indeed, GPT directly processed the terms extracted from API descriptions, which allowed it to effortlessly adapt to the diverse terminologies and structures in the OADs.

Third, findings demonstrated the limited performance increase between GPT-4 and GPT-3.5 (+0.54 for the F1-Score). However, one must consider additional aspects when choosing between using one or the other, e.g., model utilization costs. GPT-4 was 20 times more expensive than GPT-3.5 at the time of our experiments. Therefore, the marginal performance gain of GPT-4 must be carefully considered in light of its increased costs.

Fourth, findings demonstrated the approach's capability to suggest alternative labels when judged more representative of the API intent, which dropped the approach accuracy on the *apisguru* dataset. Further research, particularly time-consuming manual evaluation, is required to dive deeper and provide conclusive answers to the extent to which the quality in the *apisguru* dataset causes the performance drop—which is what we currently can only hypothesize based on our random sample tests. Nevertheless, GPT suggestions of alternative labels open exciting research opportunities to explore applying the proposed approach to identifying unknown labels, detecting mislabelling, and improving the precision in existing API classification approaches.

Finally, the experiments were conducted with a limited sample of API documents, and their characteristics may only partially represent how OADs are created. We relied on specific ML pre-trained models, introducing limitations inherent to these models. Additionally, the effectiveness of the classification may be influenced by the prompt used to query the classifier. The lack of transparency in how GPT arrives at its decisions, also known as the "black-box" nature, makes it challenging to interpret the specific factors or features that heavily influence the classification outcomes [8,22].

Consequently, our ability to validate and explain individual classifications may be restricted. Without a comprehensive understanding of GPT's decision-making process, we cannot ascertain the precise reasons behind its classifications. We could rely on prompt instructions to unveil the rationale behind each labelling. However, it would require a manual, time-consuming analysis of each explanation, which is out of the scope of this exploratory study. This lack of explainability of GPT choices may introduce an element of uncertainty and limit the extent to which we can fully trust and interpret these experiments' results.

Despite employing a quantitative approach, the exploratory nature of our study allowed for some level of subjectivity in data interpretation. The use of automated algorithms and data processing techniques aimed to reduce bias; however, the potential for subjective decisions in data handling and analysis remains a limitation to consider when interpreting the results.

6 Future Plans

This exploratory study unveiled various challenges and perspectives toward applying LLM for API labelling using OpenAPI documents. A critical root challenge in this context is the creation of a larger curated dataset that allows researchers to evaluate the performance of LLM-based approaches in this task comprehensively. Therefore, we are building a process and tool to support the creation of such a dataset. Besides, using a proprietary LLM model imposes usage limitations induced by costs, and accessing these models through an API restricts the size of the prompts due to payload limitations. To cope with these challenges, we are currently exploring using open-source LLMs (e.g., LLAMA3, Gemma 2, Mistral, and Mixtral) deployed locally, working with the hypothesis that doing so could simplify the approach by avoiding the need to restrain the data sent to the LLM model, i.e., eliminating the use of KeyBERT to limit the amount of sent data. Similarly, we are collaborating with an industry partner to collect evidence of the effectiveness of such an approach in solving practical problems related to API mining and understanding.

7 Conclusion

This exploratory study suggested and experimented with a practical solution for efficient and accurate API classification based on state-of-the-art LLM models. The simplicity of data handling contributes to the approach's overall effectiveness. By bypassing the need for extensive data preprocessing, our approach achieved a remarkable enhancement in efficiency and simplicity in implementing an API classifier.

Eventually, we would like to stress that our approach pointed us to the inadequate or imprecise classification of openly available datasets. On the one hand, this is a severe threat to all research performed with these datasets; on the other hand, random sample manual investigation led us to the conclusion that the classification proposed by our approach could be more adequate and precise. We thus see a further use case of our approach in revising existing API classifications and also see a call to action for the community to clean and improve the available datasets.

Acknowledgments. We acknowledge the support of the Natural Sciences and Engineering Research Council of Canada (NSERC), 06351.

References

1. Achiam, J., et al.: GPT-4 technical report. arXiv preprint arXiv:2303.08774 (2023)
2. APIs.Guru: APIs.Guru APIs repository (2021). https://github.com/APIs-gurul
3. Assunção, W.K., Krüger, J., Mendonça, W.D.: Variability management meets microservices: six challenges of re-engineering microservice-based webshops. In: Proceedings of the SPLC (A), pp. 22.1–22.6 (2020)
4. Balkus, S.V., Yan, D.: Improving short text classification with augmented data using GPT-3. Nat. Lang. Eng. 1–30 (2022)
5. Bisong, E., Bisong, E.: Google colaboratory. In: Building Machine Learning and Deep Learning Models on Google Cloud Platform: A Comprehensive Guide for Beginners, pp. 59–64. Apress, Berkeley (2019). https://doi.org/10.1007/978-1-4842-4470-8_7
6. Brown, T., et al.: Language models are few-shot learners. Adv. Neural. Inf. Process. Syst. **33**, 1877–1901 (2020)
7. Casas, S., Cruz, D., Vidal, G., Constanzo, M.: Uses and applications of the OpenAPI/Swagger specification: a systematic mapping of the literature. In: 2021 40th International Conference of the Chilean Computer Science Society (SCCC), pp. 1–8. IEEE (2021)
8. Chen, L., Zaharia, M., Zou, J.: How is ChatGPT's behavior changing over time? arXiv preprint arXiv:2307.09009 (2023)
9. Devlin, J., Chang, M.W., Lee, K., Toutanova, K.: BERT: pre-training of deep bidirectional transformers for language understanding. arXiv preprint arXiv:1810.04805 (2018)
10. González-Mora, C., Barros, C., Garrigós, I., Zubcoff, J., Lloret, E., Mazón, J.-N.: Applying natural language processing techniques to generate open data web APIs documentation. In: Bielikova, M., Mikkonen, T., Pautasso, C. (eds.) ICWE 2020. LNCS, vol. 12128, pp. 416–432. Springer, Cham (2020). https://doi.org/10.1007/978-3-030-50578-3_28
11. Grootendorst, M.: KeyBERT: minimal keyword extraction with BERT (2020). https://doi.org/10.5281/zenodo.4461265
12. Harris, C.R., et al.: Array programming with NumPy. Nature **585**(7825), 357–362 (2020)
13. Hosono, M., Washizaki, H., Fukazawa, Y., Honda, K.: An empirical study on the reliability of the web API document. In: 2018 25th Asia-Pacific Software Engineering Conference (APSEC), pp. 715–716. IEEE (2018)
14. HuggingFace: msmarco-distilbert-cos-v5. https://huggingface.co/sentence-transformers/msmarco-distilbert-cos-v5
15. OpenAPI Initiative: OpenAPI Specification v3.1.0. https://spec.openapis.org/oas/latest.html (2021)
16. Kalyan, K.S.: A survey of GPT-3 family large language models including ChatGPT and GPT-4. Nat. Lang. Process. J. 100048 (2023)
17. Klein, T., Nabi, M.: Learning to answer by learning to ask: getting the best of GPT-2 and BERT worlds. arXiv e-prints pp. arXiv–1911 (2019)
18. Korde, V., Mahender, C.N.: Text classification and classifiers: a survey. Int. J. Artif. Intell. Appl. **3**(2), 85 (2012)
19. McKinney, W., et al.: pandas: a foundational Python library for data analysis and statistics. Python High Perform. Sci. Comput. **14**(9), 1–9 (2011)
20. Mendonça, W.D., Assunção, W.K., Estanislau, L.V., Vergilio, S.R., Garcia, A.: Towards a microservices-based product line with multi-objective evolutionary algorithms. In: 2020 IEEE Congress on Evolutionary Computation, pp. 1–8 (2020)

21. Meng, M., Steinhardt, S., Schubert, A.: Application programming interface documentation: what do software developers want? J. Tech. Writ. Commun. **48**(3), 295–330 (2018)
22. Minaee, S., Kalchbrenner, N., Cambria, E., Nikzad, N., Chenaghlu, M., Gao, J.: Deep learning–based text classification: a comprehensive review. ACM Comput. Surv. **54**(3) (2021). https://doi.org/10.1145/3439726
23. Morais, G., Adda, M., Hadder, H., Bork, D.: x2OMSAC-an ontology population framework for the ontology of microservices architecture concepts. In: Rocha, A., Adeli, H., Dzemyda, G., Moreira, F., Colla, V. (eds.) WorldCIST 2023. LNNS, vol. 800, pp. 263–274. Springer, Cham (2023). https://doi.org/10.1007/978-3-031-45645-9_25
24. Morais, G., Lemelin, E., Bork, D., Adda, M.: Companion source code repository (2024). https://github.com/UQAR-TUW/enhancing-api-labelling-bert-gpt
25. Norvig, P., Russell, S.: Artificial Intelligence: A Modern Approach, vol. 1, pp. 1239–1269. Pearson, Harlow (2021)
26. OpenAI: GPT-3.5-Turbo. https://platform.openai.com/docs/models/gpt-3-5-turbo
27. OpenAI: GPT-4-Turbo. https://platform.openai.com/docs/models/gpt-4-turbo-and-gpt-4
28. OpenAI: OpenAPI-Python. https://github.com/openai/openai-python
29. Pedregosa, F., et al.: Scikit-learn: machine learning in Python. J. Mach. Learn. Res. **12**, 2825–2830 (2011)
30. Alexandre Peixoto de Queirós, R., Simões, A., Pinto, M.: Code Generation, Analysis Tools, and Testing for Quality. Advances in Computer and Electrical Engineering (2327-039X). IGI Global (2019). https://books.google.ca/books?id=Ieh_DwAAQBAJ
31. Radford, A., Narasimhan, K., Salimans, T., Sutskever, I., et al.: Improving language understanding by generative pre-training (2018)
32. Reimers, N., Gurevych, I.: Sentence-BERT: sentence embeddings using Siamese BERT-networks. In: Proceedings of the 2019 Conference on Empirical Methods in Natural Language Processing. Association for Computational Linguistics, November 2019. http://arxiv.org/abs/1908.10084
33. da Rocha Araujo, L., Rodríguez, G., Vidal, S., Marcos, C., dos Santos, R.P.: Empirical analysis on OpenAPI topic exploration and discovery to support the developer community. Comput. Inform. **40**(6), 1345–1369 (2021)
34. Sanders, R.: The Pareto principle: its use and abuse. J. Serv. Mark. **1**(2), 37–40 (1987)
35. Serbout, S., Pautasso, C., Zdun, U., Zimmermann, O.: From OpenAPI fragments to API pattern primitives and design smells. In: 26th European Conference on Pattern Languages of Programs, pp. 1–35 (2021)
36. Sokolova, M., Lapalme, G.: A systematic analysis of performance measures for classification tasks. Inf. Process. Manag. **45**(4), 427–437 (2009)
37. Uddin, G., Robillard, M.P.: How API documentation fails. IEEE Softw. **32**(4), 68–75 (2015)
38. Vaswani, A., et al.: Attention is all you need. Adv. Neural Inf. Process. Syst. **30** (2017)

A Conceptual Framework for Resource Analysis in Process Mining

Christoffer Rubensson[1,4(✉)], Luise Pufahl[2,4], and Jan Mendling[1,3,4]

[1] Humboldt-Universität zu Berlin, Berlin, Germany
{christoffer.rubensson,jan.mendling}@hu-berlin.de
[2] Technische Universität München, Heilbronn, Germany
luise.pufahl@tum.de
[3] Wirtschaftsuniversität Wien, Vienna, Austria
[4] Weizenbaum Institute, Berlin, Germany

Abstract. Resource analysis is an emerging branch in process mining that aims to understand behavioral and structural aspects of resources in business processes. A problem of current resource analysis is its fragmentation. The spectrum of corresponding process mining techniques is diverse but scattered, with contributions often focusing on one or the other specific aspects. An overarching framework that could organize resource analysis, tie it to theoretical foundations, and, in turn, inform the development of new analytical methods is missing. In this work, we address this research problem by conducting a systematic literature review to organize the scattered landscape of the state-of-the-art resource analysis methods in process mining. Our work is guided by the question of what resource-related organizational and behavioral patterns can be analyzed with current methods. We classify the methods according to two aspects: what type of phenomenon was analyzed and what design principles were utilized in the development. Our findings highlight that most resource analysis methods in process mining are data-driven, developed to solve a specific business problem, or loosely based on resource analysis concepts from other disciplines. Some good examples of techniques defined for theoretical questions give directions for future research.

Keywords: Process mining · Resource analysis · Systematic literature review

1 Introduction

The effective management of resources is a key concern of Business Process Management (BPM) [23]. Organizations rely on a multitude of business processes to deliver products and services to their customers. Activities within a business process are performed by various resources, such as human labor, machinery, and software services [23, p. 96]. Given that these resources are valuable, often expensive, and limited in availability [6], optimizing their occupation is essential for the success and efficiency of business processes. With the growing availability of process execution data, behavioral and structural aspects of resources in business processes [2] can be analyzed with the help of *process mining* techniques. Process mining is a family of techniques that rely

M. Kaczmarek-Heß et al. (Eds.): EDOC 2024 Workshops, LNBIP 537, pp. 183–202, 2025.
https://doi.org/10.1007/978-3-031-79059-1_12

on a so-called *event log*, including structurally the events that happen in the execution of a business process, and help to shed transparency into the real-world process enactment. Compared to traditional methods in resource analysis such as labor-intensive and time-consuming interviews and observations, process mining techniques have proven effective for studying resources based on event data [23].

The portfolio of resource analysis methods has expanded in recent years with a diverse spectrum of techniques being proposed [13]. The diversity of resource analysis techniques is a positive sign of research progress that yet provides challenges. Many of the new techniques have been developed for specific analysis questions, often inspired by available event data in a bottom-up fashion. This poses the problem of a fragmented and scattered research landscape of resource analysis. Nevertheless, some efforts have been made to review techniques for resource analysis.

A first comprehensive study on using and representing (primarily human) resources in existing process execution systems was given by Russel et al. [47], who studied how resources are integrated into workflow systems. Their work provides a resource metamodel and a collection of patterns to create, pull, push, and detour tasks to resources, however, without considering resource analysis based on execution data. Cabanillas et al. [13] examine research on resource handling in process- and resource-oriented systems, providing a framework with a selection of representative studies. The representative studies are categorized into *resource assignment* (defining resource requirements for process activities at design time), *resource allocation* (assigning specific resources to tasks during runtime), and *resource analysis* (evaluating process execution with a focus on resources). Exhaustive or systematic literature studies are provided for resource assignment, such as Oyang et al. [42], and resource allocation, such as Arias et al. [7] and Pufahl et al. [46]. However, a systematic review of the field of resource analysis is still missing.[1] By looking at existing works, different resource analysis types are supported, such as the collaboration between resources [30] or work prioritization patterns by resources [53]. So far, there is no structured overview of the analysis concepts for identifying existing solutions, understanding the relation between the concepts, and stimulating future research.

This paper addresses this research problem by conducting a systematic literature review (SLR) to organize the scattered landscape of the state-of-the-art resource analysis in process mining. Our primary focus is on the following research goals: (1) *structuring the analysis concepts for resources in business processes*; and (2) *identifying the design approaches of the works.*

By following these research goals, we lay the foundation for a conceptual framework of resource analysis in process mining. We identified 29 studies that addressed 27 different resource analysis concepts, which could be categorized into task-, relation-,

[1] During the publication phase of this article, Martin and Beerepoot [38] published a similar study on resource analysis. However, we differ in two fundamental ways. First, [38] focus on resource analysis use cases, whereas we investigate behavioral constructs. Second, [38] have adopted a broader understanding of *resource analysis*, as they also examine adjacent resource-related areas, such as resource assignment and resource-aware process model discovery. Our study is, in contrast, more focused on the analytical aspect. Because of these slight differences in perspective, our findings complement each other.

and actor-oriented concept types as either directly or indirectly observable phenomena. Moreover, we divided the literature based on their primary design approach. To this end, our framework highlights the need to advance resource analysis in process mining by applying existing theoretical constructs.

The rest of the paper is structured as follows. Section 2 discusses the importance of *resources* in related scientific disciplines. Section 3 describes our research method. Section 4 presents the results from the SLR, which are subsequently discussed in Sect. 5. Our work is concluded in Sects. 5 and 6.

2 The Notion of a Resource

The term *resource analysis* requires some clarifications. To this end, we provide a brief background on the multifaceted nature of resource analysis, tracing its origins in organization science, management, and BPM. This context supports the understanding of the results of the literature review.

In organization science and management, resources are often viewed as any physical or non-physical capital or assets a business may utilize to achieve a competitive advantage (e.g., [8]). Yet, a precise definition and its role in resource analysis depend on the theoretical discourse. The *VRIO* framework evaluates the internal resources of a firm based on their strategic value to achieve a sustained competitive advantage [8]. More recent work emphasizes the social aspects of inter-organizational collaboration and discusses how sharing of resources can lead to strategic advantages (e.g., [29]). Social network analysis [50] is closely related to these discussions and has found use in computer science.

BPM, in turn, is a collection of techniques and concepts to improve the operational performance of organizations by managing their processes throughout their lifecycle [23]. Here, resources are referred to as both human and non-human actors of activities in a process [23, p. 96]. The main focus has been on the process activities and their control flow, for which the resource perspective has played a secondary role. However, several research works have explicitly addressed this gap in the last decade. On the one hand, the modeling of resources has been targeted to support the definition and visual representation of certain resource needs of the process activities, for example, by extending process models with advanced role-based access control rules [52] or the graphical modeling language RAlph specifying advanced resource selection constraints [14]. Further, a general understanding of resource characteristics and attributes was developed [42]. On the other hand, the allocation of resources to tasks, where the best fitting resource for performing an activity is selected, has been researched for process automation solutions. To support this, different allocation patterns (e.g., [47]), allocation techniques (for an overview see [46]), and systems (e.g. [32]) have been created. Certain techniques also use insights from resource analysis, such as the measurement of team effectiveness for team assignment [37].

With the rise of process mining as a sub-domain of BPM, the support of analyzing resources in business processes and their behavior using event logs [2] has emerged. There are two main directions in this context: *organizational mining* and *resource behavior mining*. Organizational mining considers the relational or social structures

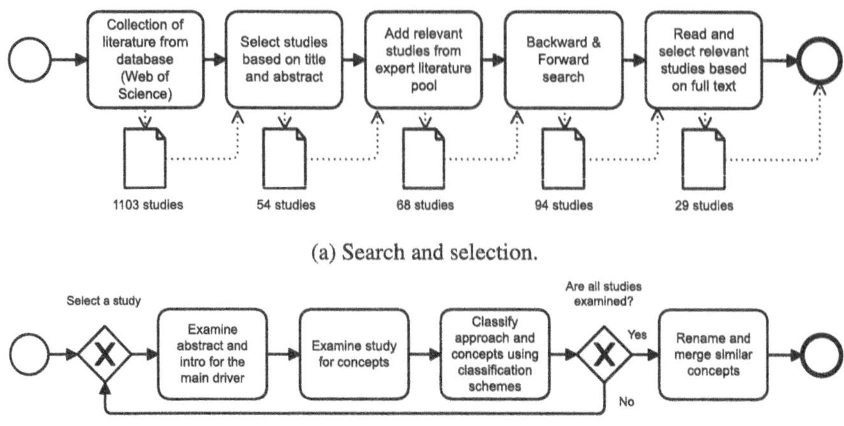

(a) Search and selection.

(b) Extraction and classification.

Fig. 1. Literature review procedure.

of organizations, where social network analysis concepts [50] are commonly applied to investigate, for instance, social interactions (e.g., [3]), team discovery (e.g., [48]) or role mining (e.g., [12]). On the other hand, resource behavior mining studies the behavioral patterns of resource units, meaning *how* resources execute work. These concepts are predominantly quantitative representations of concepts from social science, organizational science, or BPM, such as the measurement of resource collaboration [30,36,44,57,62] or batching behavior [40,45].

3 Research Method

This section describes the SLR methodology we adapted from Kitchenham [35]. This specific methodology was explicitly developed to suit the needs of computer science. It provides support for a descriptive review with a clear scoping and qualitative analysis [43], which meets the objective of our research.

Figure 1 outlines the SLR process in this work, which we describe in the subsequent sections. Section 3.1 formulates the research objectives. Section 3.2 describes the literature search and selection procedure. Section 3.3 illustrates the extraction and classification procedure.

3.1 Research Objectives

This review aims to structure state-of-the-art resource analysis methods in process mining. We approach this objective by formulating the following research questions:

RQ1 What type of resource-related organizational and behavioral patterns can be analyzed using current process mining resource analysis methods?

RQ2 What design approaches were used in the literature to create the resource analysis methods?

The first research question (RQ1) aims to provide an overview of current resource analysis methods and to what extent process mining can capture various resource-related phenomena. RQ1 also identifies gaps for future research. The second research question (RQ2) concerns the premises on which a method was grounded. Specifically, it investigates to what extent a method was rooted in an existing theory, a hypothetical construct or idea, a business problem, or if it was technique-oriented.

3.2 Literature Search and Selection

We structured the literature extraction process in five distinct steps, as depicted in Fig. 1a. First, in *step 1*, we utilized a keyword search using the *Web of Science database*, using the following query of keywords: *TS=("Process Mining" OR "Business Process") AND TS=(resource$ OR staff OR personnel OR employee$ OR workforce) AND TS=(analysis OR analytics OR metric$ OR measurement$ OR indicator$ OR behavio$ r OR performance) AND LA=(English)*. The term "TS" indicates the search to include title, abstract, author keywords, and *keywords plus*[2]; and the term "LA" indicates the language of the study. The search was first done in November 2022 and included papers published within the years 1994 and 2022. The search was then extended in February 2024 to further include the years 2023 and 2024. We want to note that the two searches were executed based on different institutional subscriptions, which may lead to different outcomes for the same query.[3] Furthermore, we used only one database to keep the article within scope. Nonetheless, the Web of Science is one of the largest multidisciplinary databases (cf., [16, p. 3]). Step 1 resulted in 1,103 studies.

The literature selection (steps 2, 4–5) was guided by the following inclusion (IN) and exclusion (EX) criteria:

IN1 The study proposes at least one novel process mining *technique*[4] for extracting and analyzing a behavioral or organizational pattern in event logs from a resource perspective.

EX1 The study can be replaced by an extended or complete publication.
EX2 The study solely proposes an event log preparation technique.

[2] Index terms from *Web of science*, please see: https://webofscience.help.clarivate.com/en-us/Content/wos-core-collection/wos-full-record.htm (accessed: 2024-09-18).

[3] https://support.clarivate.com/ScientificandAcademicResearch/s/article/Web-of-Science-Search-in-All-Databases-refined-by-an-individual-database-may-return-more-results-than-the-same-search-in-that-individual-database?language=en_US (accessed: 2024-09-18).

[4] We define a *technique* according to the classification framework of information systems development methodologies by Iivari et al. [33] as a "well-defined sequence of elementary operations that more or less guarantee the achievement of certain outcomes if executed correctly" [33, p. 186]. In other words, a technique could be a simple function, a metric, an algorithm, or similar. A technique is to be differentiated from higher abstraction levels development methodologies starting with *methodologies*, continuing with *approaches*, and after that *paradigms* on the highest level [33, p. 186]. In the context of resource analysis, examples of techniques are the *handover of work* metrics by Aalst et al. [3] and the *competence* measure by Huang et al. [30, pp. 6461-6462]. We use the terms *technique* and *method* interchangeably in this article.

EX3 The study focuses on another perspective, such as control flow.
EX4 The study proposes primarily a simulation model or a resource allocation mechanism.
EX5 The study proposes an approach that requires additional input, such as survey-based data or declarative models.

In *step 2*, we analyzed the title and the abstract of each study from the resulting 1,103 studies from the keyword search. We used the inclusion and exclusion criteria above as a guidance to select potentially relevant studies. Step 2 resulted in 54 studies.

In *step 3*, we then added 14 relevant studies from our existing expert pool. The expert pool is a collection of articles gathered from multiple research projects concerning resource-related topics in BPM and process mining we and colleagues have participated in for more than a decade. This step was necessary because most relevant articles are hard to find through a keyword search. The essential vocabulary to distinguish different resource-related directions in process mining and BPM (cf., resource allocation, and resource analysis) has yet to be established. Note that, compared to previous steps, we did not explicitly apply the inclusion and exclusion criteria. The reason for this was to include these studies in the backward and forward search, because of their high thematic relevancy. Nevertheless, the inclusion and exclusion criteria were still applied to these papers in the final selection step. Step 3 resulted in 68 studies.

In *step 4*, based on the 68 studies from the previous step, we conducted a backward and a forward search using the Web of Science and Scopus[5]. Step 4 resulted in 94 studies.

Finally, in *step 5*, we read all the resulting 94 studies from the previous step based on their full text and then selected relevant studies using the inclusion and exclusion criteria from above. The complete literature search yielded 29 relevant studies.

The entire literature search and selection procedure was designed by all three authors and conducted by two. The studies used as input for the final step (step 5) were discussed by all three authors before final selection.

3.3 Data Extraction and Classification

In the classification process, we wanted to investigate the *main* driver for developing the respective approaches and *what* type of concepts[6] they can analyze. A challenge with classifying the different approaches is the lack of consistency in definitions and a shared vocabulary in the broader context. A single concept can often have various names, or multiple concepts can be hidden under one term. In addition, ideas borrowed from other disciplines may only have a tenuous connection to their original definition. To find commonality, we developed two classification schemes (Fig. 2). We describe these schemes below before explaining their application in this work.

[5] https://scopus.com (accessed: 2024-09-18).

[6] We refer to a *concept* as a resource-related behavioral pattern that an author aims to measure, directly or indirectly, using some technique. In the literature, other termonologies are often used and sometimes interchangeably, such as *notion*, *construct*, or *perspective*.

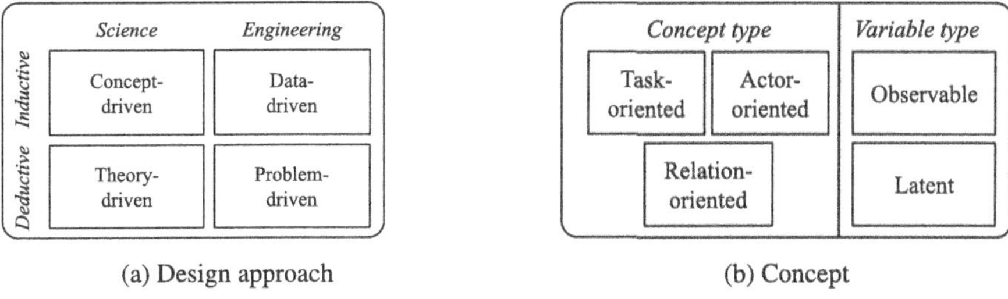

(a) Design approach (b) Concept

Fig. 2. Classification schemes.

The first scheme (Fig. 2a) was inspired by the differentiation of descriptive and prescriptive knowledge in design science research [27]. We developed four classes depending on the type of inference (deductive or inductive) and research focus (science or engineering):

- *Data-driven approaches*: are created to explore the technical possibilities of extracting insights from a data set.
- *Problem-driven approaches*: are created as a direct solution to a business problem.
- *Concept-driven approaches*: are based on an existing resource-related concept.
- *Theory-driven approaches*: are based on a resource-related theory or theoretical framework.

The primary motivation for science-oriented approaches is to create, expand upon, or investigate theoretical constructs. On the other hand, engineering-oriented approaches take on a more practical perspective, i.e., to better understand or solve a problem. Moreover, inductively motivated approaches focus on particular phenomena or observations, while deductively motivated approaches utilize a more generalized phenomenon, such as a theory or a prevalent problem.

The second scheme (Fig. 2b) comprises two dimensions to classify the concepts that the approaches address. The first one defines three types of concepts, as inspired by theories on socio-technical systems (e.g., [11]):

- *Task-oriented concepts*: Patterns that emphasize how work is executed rather than the resources that execute them.
- *Relation-oriented concepts*: Patterns that emphasize relational, organization-structural, or transactional aspects of work.
- *Actor-oriented concepts*: Patterns that emphasize the resources and their attributes rather than the work they execute.

The other dimension divides concepts depending on their variable type (see Fig. 2b):

- *Observable*: The concept is directly measurable.
- *Latent*: The concept is only in-directly measurable.

The extraction and classification procedure, in which we applied the classification schemes above, is illustrated in Fig. 1b (p. 4) and described in the following. For each study, we first read the abstract and the introduction to identify the *main* driver for their work. Second, we identified the resource analysis concepts by analyzing the full text of the study. Third, we applied our classification schemes (Fig. 2) to classify both the main driver of the approach and the identified concepts. We additionally indicated whether a concept is *primary*, i.e., a prominent contribution of work, or *supporting*, i.e., integrated into the primary solution to enhance it.

After analyzing all studies, we finally grouped similar concepts under one terminology to enhance clarity and understandability. We also deliberately excluded concepts related to similarity measurements, often named as *importance*, *relatedness*, *similarity*, *distance*, and *dependency* measures, as they are primarily statistical techniques integrated into different types of resource analysis methods. Furthermore, we have not considered the concept of *resource profiles*, as it is a collection of diverse measures rather than a specific technique.

4 Results

This section describes the result of the SLR. Section 4.1 provides some metadata of the resulting 29 studies. Section 4.2 discusses the concepts identified in the literature. Section 4.3 closes by discussing the design approaches used in development.

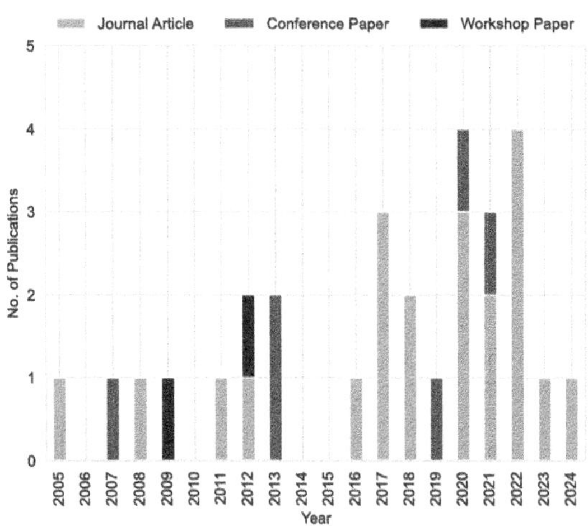

Fig. 3. Overview of relevant studies according to publication year and type.

4.1 Overview of Selected Studies

The SLR resulted in a selection of 29 relevant studies. As illustrated in Fig. 3, there has been an overall slight increase in studies since 2005. Most of the studies identified in this SLR were published in journals (21 studies), followed by conferences (six studies) and workshops (two studies). Moreover, the journals that published more than two studies according to our observation are *Decision Support Systems* (four studies), *IEEE Access* (two studies), and *ACM Transactions on Management Information Systems* (two studies). In contrast, the most common venues among the conference and workshop studies were *Business Process Management* (two studies) and *Business Process Management Workshop* (two studies).

4.2 Resource Analysis Concepts

In this section, we approach the first research question (RQ1): *What type of resource-related organizational and behavioral patterns can be analyzed using current process mining resource analysis methods?* We identified 27 resource analysis concepts from the 29 studies, all classified into one of three concept types (task-, relation-, or actor-oriented) and according to variable type (observable or latent). Table 1 illustrates the result of this classification. Figure 4 extends Table 1 with a graphical overview of the total number of primary and supporting concepts according to concept and variable type. We elaborate on this result in the following subsections.

Table 1. Concept-matrix (*•: Primary concept; ○: Supporting concept*).

Concept type	Task													Relation										Actor				
Variable Type	*Observable*						*Latent*							*Observable*					*Latent*					*Latent*				
Concepts	Execution Type	Execution Costs	Execution Frequency	Execution Time	Exeuction Quality	Multitasking	Avaliability	Batch Processing	Performance	Prioritization	Productivity	Utilization	Workload	Delegation	Exclusiveness	Handover	Joint work	Subcontracting	Collaboration	Entity Discovery	Network Discovery	Participation	Work Distribution	Adaptability	Capability/Skills	Competence	Preference	
No. primary (•)	***1***	***1***	**-**	***2***	***1***	***3***	***4***	***2***	***3***	***1***	***2***	***1***	***2***	***1***	***1***	***4***	***1***	***2***	***5***	***13***	***7***	***2***	***1***	***1***	***1***	***1***	***3***	
References / *No. support (○)*	*9*	*1*	*8*	*9*	*2*	*2*	-	-	-	-	-	-	*5*	*3*	*1*	*10*	*5*	*3*	-	*2*	*5*	*1*	-	-	*2*	-	-	**Design Approaches**
[3] van der Aalst et al. (2005)														•/○		•/○	•/○	•/○			•							Data-driven
[34] Jin et al. (2007)	○																			•		○						Problem-driven
[51] Song & van der Aalst (2008)																○	○	○		•/○	•							Data-driven
[41] Nakatumba & van der Aalst (2009)				•/○					•				•/○															Theory-driven
[61] Yingbo et al. (2011)						•																						Concept-driven
[26] Ferreira & Alves (2012)																	○			•	○							Data-driven
[30] Huang et al. (2012)		○					•						○						•							•	•	Concept-driven
[12] Burattin et al. (2013)																•/○				•								Concept-driven
[36] Kumar et al. (2013)																○			•									Problem-driven
[62] Zhao et al. (2016)		•		•	•											○			•					•				Data-driven
[40] Martin et al. (2017)				○				•																				Concept-driven
[44] Pika et al. (2017)	○		○	○	○	○			•		•	•	○	○			○		•						•		•	Problem-driven
[53] Suriadi et al. (2017)										•																		Data-driven
[5] Appice (2018)																	○			•	•/○							Data-driven
[58] Ye et al. (2018)	○																			•	•/○							Data-driven
[10] Bidar et al. (2019)	○												○	○		○									○		•	Concept-driven
[19] Delcoucq et al. (2020)			○																	•								Data-driven
[39] Martin et al. (2020)				○			•																					Problem-driven
[54] Tan et al. (2020)																○				•	•/○							Problem-driven
[55] Utama et al. (2020)				○			•																					Data-driven
[20] Deokar & Tao (2021)															•/○	•/○		•/○		•								Data-driven
[24] Estrada-Torres et al. (2021)				○		•	•																					Data-driven
[57] Yang et al. (2021)	○		○	○	○				•		•		•			○			•			•	•					Problem-driven
[31] Hulzen et al. (2022)	○			○		•/○														•								Problem-driven
[45] Pika et al. (2022)	○		○					•																				Concept-driven
[56] Yang et al. (2022)	•/○		○																	•/○		•						Data-driven
[59] Yeon et al. (2022)			○																	•	•/○							Problem-driven
[18] Delcoucq et al. (2023)			○																	•								Data-driven
[21] Diamantini et al. (2024)	○		○	○									○			•/○					•				○			Data-driven

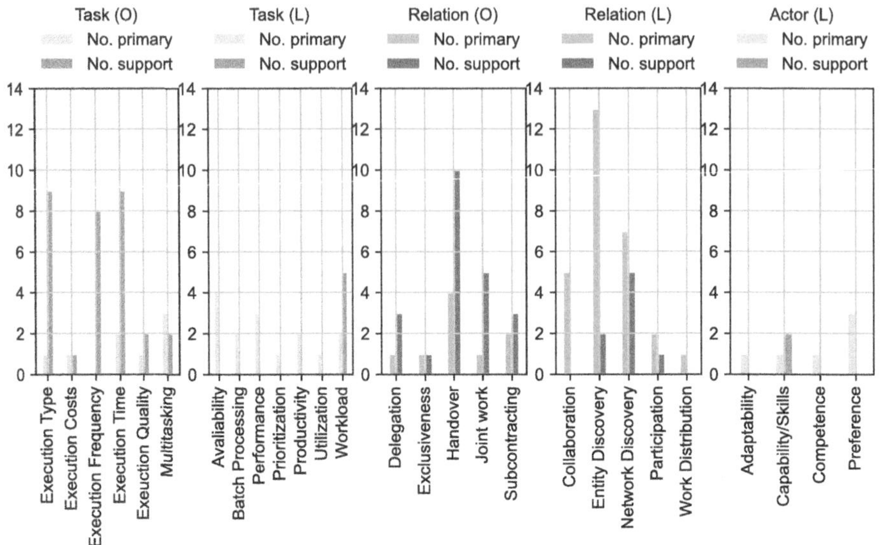

Fig. 4. Overview of the number of primary and supporting concepts according to concept type and variable type (O = observable variable, L = latent variable).

Task-Oriented Concepts. The task-oriented concepts focus on the work rather than the resources utilized for it. More specifically, these concepts aim to answer *how* or *how well* work is executed. In this category, we identify 13 concepts, six of which are directly observable and seven of which are latent.

Observable: Task-oriented concepts that are directly observable are various metrics to count or measure work-related properties in the log. *Execution type*[7] comprises various metrics and concepts that measure the amount of work executed by a resource unit related to a specific type of execution, such as the indicator "distinct activities" by Pika et al. [44], which counts how many activities of a certain type was executed by a resource [44, p. 1:9]. *Execution costs* measures the cost of work [30,62]. *Execution frequency* measures activity frequency, yet independent of activity type or property, such as the indicators "activity completions" by Pika et al. [44, p. 1:9] or "amount-related productivity" by Yang et al. [57, p.352]. *Execution time* comprises metrics measuring various time aspects, such as "processing speeds" according to Nakatumba & van der Aalst [41, p. 8] or other notions of execution durations (e.g., [21,24]). *Execution quality* refers to any property that measures the quality of work, often related to the quality of the execution itself [57,62] or customer satisfaction [44]. Lastly, *multitasking* measures a resource's simultaneous engagement in multiple or parallel activities [24,31,44,61].

[7] All concepts starting with the term *execution* are umbrella terms for multiple metrics with or without specific concept names. An example is Pika et al. [44], who propose multiple *execution frequency* metrics to measure the concept *utilization*, such as the indicators "activity completions" and "number of case completions" to count the instance involvement of a resource on an activity and case level respectively [44, p. 1:9].

Latent: Task-oriented concepts that are indirectly observable combine or extend behavior indicators to provide a deeper analysis of the work executed. *Availability* measures when a resource is available for work and includes concepts such as *shift work* [55] and timetabling [24]. *Batch processing* investigates how resource units organize their work in batches [40,45]. *Performance*[8] comprises methods and indicators measuring how well work is executed in terms of *efficiency* [41,44,57]. On the other hand, *productivity* comprises methods and indicators to measure how well a resource unit performs in terms of *effectiveness*, i.e., outcome- and goal-oriented [44,57]. *Prioritization* investigates how resource units order the execution of tasks [53]. *Utilization* comprises descriptive measures of what a resource unit is *actually* doing [44, p. 1:8]. Finally, *workload* measures the work done by or assigned to a resource unit within a time period (e.g., [30,41,44,57]).

Figure 4 shows that the most common primary task-oriented concepts are *multitasking* (3 studies), *availability* (4 studies), and *performance* (3 studies). The most commonly supporting concepts are *execution type* (9 studies), *execution frequency* (8 studies) and *execution time* (9 studies). Most supporting concepts are observable rather than latent, which is to be expected. An exception is the concept *workload*. The reason for this is likely that the concept is well-established in the process mining literature. *Execution frequency* is another outlier, as it is only observable as a supporting concept.

Relation-Oriented Concepts. The relation-oriented concepts focus on relational patterns between entities in the data, such as resource-activity or resource-resource patterns. These concepts concern the socio-structural aspects of work, such as how work is transferred between resources or how resources are related to one another. We identified ten concepts in total in this category; five are directly observable, and the other five are latent.

Observable: The observable relation-oriented concepts are often metrics that measure task transferals and executions between multiple resources. *Delegation*[9] comprises metrics that count how many tasks, within their lifecycle, were transferred from one resource to another for further processing [3, p. 560], often requiring event log properties about activity transitions such as *assign*, *reassign*, or *schedule* [1]. *Handover*[10] metrics measure how often work is directly or indirectly transferred from one resource unit to another after task completion (e.g., [3,21]). *Exclusiveness*, on the other hand, is an "anti-handover" measure, as it measures how often work was *not* transferred between resources [20, p. 759]. *Joint work*[11] measures how often the same type of work was executed by different research units, either on an activity level or a case level [3, p. 560]. *Subcontracting* measures the work executed "in-between" resource units [3, p. 560].

[8] *Performance* and *productivity* are often used interchangeably in the literature. Yet, we aimed to separate these concepts.

[9] *Delegation* is often referred to as *reassignment* (e.g., [3]) or *previous owner* [10, p. 414] in the literature.

[10] *Handover* is an umbrella term for different handover relation concepts, such as *handover of work* [3,21,51,54,57], *handover of roles* [12], or simply *hand-offs* [36] or *handovers* [10]. Some work are less explicit (e.g., Zhao et al. refers to "transfer [of] work-items" [62, p. 309]).

[11] *Joint work* refers to metrics based on "joint activities" or "joint cases" (cf., [3, p. 560]).

Latent: The latent relation-oriented concepts can be divided into two streams of concepts. The first stream of concepts aims to discover and analyze organizational models: *Entity discovery*[12] comprises methods that identify new resource entities such as roles [12,34,54,58,59], groups and teams [18–20,31,51,56], or communities [5,26,58], and *network discovery* utilizes techniques from social network analysis to create and analyze social networks of resource units (e.g., [51,58,59]). The other stream of concepts considers work-related aspects but is viewed from a social perspective: *Collaboration*[13] assesses how well resources communicate or work with other resources (e.g., [30,36,44]). *Participation* measures a resource unit's involvement in work compared to other resources, such as the indicator "attendance" [57, p. 350] and "group member contribution" [56, p. 8]. *Work distribution* examines how work is distributed among multiple resources within an organizational unit [57, p. 350].

The most common primary relation-oriented concepts (see Fig. 4) are *entity discovery* (13 studies), *network discovery* (7 studies), and *collaboration* (5 studies). The most common supporting concepts are *handover* (10 studies), *network discovery* (5 studies), and *joint work* (5 studies). *Handover* and *joint work* are often used for *entity* and *network discovery*. Moreover, both concepts, *entity* and *network discovery*, are often used complementarily. An example is creating social networks to discover communities [5,58] or create social networks based on already discovered resource units [51].

Actor-Oriented Concepts. The actor-oriented concepts focus on resources and their ability to pursue work. These concepts examine resource attributes with the aim of better understanding how to best employ them in work, with little emphasis on the work itself. We identified four concepts in total in this category, all latent. *Adaptability* concerns a resource unit's time to adjust to new tasks [62, p. 310]. *Capability* relates to the type of work a resource unit is able to perform, such as *skills* [21,44] or *experience* [10, p. 414]. It is the only actor-related concept that is also used as a supporting concept (cf., [10,21]). *Competence* measures how well a unit can perform a particular task [30, p. 6458]. Finally, *preference* estimates the type of work or work behavior a resource may prefer to execute over another [10,30,44]; or a resource unit's *preference* in working with another resource [10, p. 408].

Compared to the other concept types, *task* and *relation*, there is a lack of actor-oriented concepts. Among the four actor-oriented concepts, *preference* is the most prevalent. Note that the approaches proposed for this concept have varying degrees of complexity, ranging from simple metrics [30,44] to machine learning methods [10].

4.3 Design Approaches

In this section, we approach the second research question (RQ2): *What design approaches were used in the literature to create the resource analysis methods?* Table 1 depicts the result from classifying each approach in one of four design approach types based on their primary driver for development (see Fig. 2a). We elaborate on this next.

[12] *Entity discovery* is an umbrella term. The methods in this category are commonly named after the type of entity they discover.

[13] *Collaboration* includes the concepts *cooperation* and *compatibility*, as they are often used interchangeably in the process mining literature (cf., [36,57]).

Data-Driven Approaches. Data-driven approaches explore the technical possibilities for extracting valuable insights from event logs. These investigate *what* insights can be retrieved, often by applying an existing technique, with minor emphasis on a specific problem or analytical phenomenon. We identified 14 studies in this category, making out nearly most of the publications. There is no clear tendency toward any stream of resource analysis or theme in the literature in this category. However, two possible outliers are [21,62], as they are the only authors within this category that include an actor-oriented concept in their approaches.

Problem-Driven Approaches. Problem-driven approaches start with a specific business problem for which no sufficient solution exists in process mining. We identified eight studies within this category. The authors in this category address the need for solutions to obtain objective insights about resources to improve managerial decision-making. There are three noticeable thematical tendencies in the literature. Three studies focus on creating resource profiles either as frameworks for combining various resource analysis metrics [44,57] or with the aim to find profile similarities [31]. Four studies use resource analysis to provide decision support for resource assignment or allocation mechanisms [34,36,39,59]. The last study focuses on discovering possible information flow between organizations [54].

Furthermore, there is a difference in the type of actor as a focal point of the problem. On the one hand, [31,44] analyze resources at a micro-level, i.e., single-unit resources such as employees or single machines. On the other hand, [31,34,36,54,57,59] address resource analysis at a meso-level, i.e., resources within a larger community comprising groups or roles. [54] explicitly examines actors as part of cross-organizational processes, thus setting them slightly apart from [31,34,36,57,59], as they concern smaller resource unit constellations.

Concept-Driven Approaches. Concept-driven approaches implement or extend previous concepts in resource analysis from any relevant academic field. We identified six studies in this category. Focusing only on the proposed primary concepts, the most common ones in this category concern how work is organized, such as through multitasking or batch processing. Another common concept is *preference*. Huang et al. [30] propose multiple primary concepts, *preference* included, whereas Bidar et al. [10] explicitly advance the notion of *preference* using supporting concepts and machine learning.

Most concept-driven approaches expand on concepts from process and organizational science. Only Huang et al. [30] explores concepts explicitly from the social sciences, i.e., *preference*, *availability*, *competence*, and *cooperation* [30, pp. 6458-6459]. This is, to some extent, also true for [12] because of the utilization of social network analysis.

Theory-Driven Approaches. Theory-driven approaches utilize an existing theory as a basis for a resource analysis method. We identified only one study in this category. Nakatumba & van der Aalst [41] translate the socio-psychological framework of stress-performance relation, also known as the *Yerkes-Dodson Law of Arousal and Perfor-*

mance[14], into a process mining setting. This is achieved by applying the supporting concept *execution time* (processing speed) and *workload* to a linear regression model. As the Yerkes-Dodson law dictates the impact of mental arousals, such as stress and emotional pressure, on human performance, [41] assumed that the processing speed depends on the workload.

5 Discussion

The result of our SLR provides an overview of the concepts in resource analysis that can be measured using process mining techniques. Based on this, in Sect. 5.1, we want to highlight some opportunities for future research. In Sect. 5.2, we discuss some of the limitations of our work.

5.1 Future Research

We have identified five directions for future work, which we discuss in the subsequent paragraphs.

Enhance Existing Concepts Through Variation. As most concepts are abstract ideas of resource behavior, each provides an opportunity for future work through modification and variation. As implied in Table 1, it is already a common practice to leverage existing approaches by adapting the underlying mechanisms, e.g., changing metrics or using other techniques. Good examples are works that propose some *entity discovery* method. Burattin et al. [12] create roles by defining a version of handoffs called *handover of roles*. In contrast, Ye et al. [58] identify multi-role resources based on weighted community networks using social network analysis. Moreover, the concept of *preference* is another example. Huang et al. [30] base this notion on the activity type a resource has bid on within a time frame [30, p. 6460]. Pika et al. [44] view the concept as a category of multiple resource behavior indicators, such as *multitasking* [44, p. 1:10]. Bidar et al. [10] utilize machine learning methods to leverage the concept. All in all, every concept and associated techniques can be further modified and expanded upon, hence is an opportunity for further development in the future.

Leverage Actor-Oriented Concepts. The most covered concept types are task-oriented and relation-oriented, whereas only a few authors have proposed an actor-oriented concept. A logical reason is that event data represents work-related states and transitions, and actor-oriented concepts concern a resource's innate ambition or ability to work. The latter is hard to measure with event data. Nevertheless, the authors

[14] In a strict sense, the Yerkes-Dodson law is not a theory but an empirical phenomenon in psychology (cf., [22]) based on the original findings by Yerkes and Dodson [60]. Nonetheless, the phenomenon is well-studied and has a long history in the psychological literature, often characterized as a U-curve-shaped model (cf., [22]). Hence, we have treated the law as a theory for our purposes.

within this category have shown that it is indeed possible to create process mining techniques that can measure more abstract behavioral patterns not explicitly provided by the data. An example of this is to measure the strength of *collaboration* between resources (e.g., [30,36,57]), collaboration, which is a rather complex social phenomenon. Whereas task-oriented and relation-oriented concepts tend to describe the actual work, actor-oriented concepts with associated techniques could provide a deeper understanding of the reasons behind behavioral patterns. Correspondingly, the outcomes from such methods can be used in other areas, such as process enhancement, simulations, and resource allocation, to facilitate a sense of realism in the analysis.

Utilize Theories and Concepts. There is a noticeable gap between theory-driven and concept-driven approaches. Resource analysis is a broad multidisciplinary topic, and other academic fields, such as organizational science or social sciences, have a rich theoretical basis from which future work could profit. The process mining literature already benefits from theories and concepts outside its domain to some extent. In organizational mining, many approaches borrow concepts from social network analysis (e.g., [3,5,26]). In resource behavior mining, Huang et al. [30] explicitly borrowed the concepts *preference*, *availability*, *competence*, and *cooperation* from social sciences. Moreover, Nakatumba & van der Aalst [41] based their approach on the Yerkes-Dodson Law, a social-psychological phenomenon. Nevertheless, only a few pieces of literature are *explicitly* theory- and concept-driven. We believe that future work could benefit from making explicit use of existing theories and constructs from other academic disciplines, such as the social sciences, to create new concepts or refine existing ones.

Apply Techniques to Behavioral Studies. Process mining techniques can be applied as methodologies in behavioral studies [28]. The medical domain has shown a special interest in this regard (e.g., [4,17,25]), as process mining provides simple and objective means to study complex behaviors in event data. Our work supports future authors with an overview of the different aspects of resource analysis and their corresponding literature. In addition, most authors reviewed in this work have also implemented their approaches in easy-to-apply process mining tools such as *ProM*[15] or *PM4Py*[16], making their contributions more accessible for both academic and practical purposes.

Establish the Resource Definition. A last remark can be said about the *resource* definition itself and how it may impact how to develop techniques and interpret their output for different data sets. Most approaches define a resource in broad terms, such as *any* human executing tasks in a process or even any performer, regardless of whether human or not. However, the resource type may significantly impact the interpretation of the result or even the validity of a technique. To give a simple example, the performance measure of a machine writing e-mails is not the same as the same measure of that of a human for the same task. Machines execute such tasks in near-zero time,

[15] https://promtools.org (accessed: 2024-09-18).

[16] https://processintelligence.solutions (accessed: 2024-09-18).

whereas humans require minutes, hours, and days. Similarly, for concepts like *collaboration*, where at least two resources are involved, there is a critical distinction to make when the concept concerns only humans, as when they concern human-machine interactions or that of only machines. Even on a fine-granular level, where resource types may be slightly different, such as the distinction between a doctor and a nurse, may have a significant influence on how we should develop techniques and interpret their results. Defining such nuances and creating techniques accordingly is an exciting future research direction in resource analysis.

5.2 Limitations

The first limitation of our work regards the selection procedure. We collected the literature from a single database using rather restrictive search criteria focusing on studies presenting process mining techniques with similar requirements. The reason for this was to stay within the scope of this work but also to simplify classification, yet this came at the cost of important work on resource analysis (e.g., from BPM and Role mining [9,15,48,49]). We tried to mitigate this limitation through a backward and forward search and by including additional studies using expert knowledge. The second limitation relates to the extraction and classification procedure of concepts. As many concepts are abstract behavioral constructs not sufficiently defined in the literature, the classification procedure is a difficult task prone to subjectivity. Correspondingly, some similar techniques refer to different concepts, further challenging the classification process. To mitigate these problems, we discussed the classification within our research team and adapted the terminologies or created umbrella terms.

6 Conclusion

In this work, we conducted an SLR to identify resource analysis concepts in process mining and their primary driver for development. We found 27 resource analysis concepts in 29 studies, which can be classified as task-oriented, relation-oriented, or actor-oriented concept types. They can also be discriminated in observable or latent variable types. Furthermore, four design approaches distinguish the approaches: data-driven, problem-driven, concept-driven, and theory-driven. Most concepts are data- and problem-driven. Only one author developed a theory-driven approach. Future work can create new approaches by advancing existing ones, e.g., changing the underlying technological foundation or creating new resource analysis tools grounded in theories from other disciplines.

Acknowledgements. The research of the authors was supported by the Einstein Foundation Berlin under grant EPP-2019-524, by the German Federal Ministry of Education and Research under grant 16DII133, and by Deutsche Forschungsgemeinschaft under grant 496119880.

Disclosure of Interests. The authors have no competing interests to declare that are relevant to the content of this article.

References

1. IEEE standard for eXtensible Event Stream (XES) for achieving interoperability in event logs and event streams. IEEE STD 1849-2016, pp. 1–50 (2016). https://doi.org/10.1109/IEEESTD.2016.7740858
2. van der Aalst, W.M.P.: Process Mining - Data Science in Action, 2 edn. Springer (2016). https://doi.org/10.1007/978-3-662-49851-4
3. van der Aalst, W.M.P., Reijers, H.A., Song, M.: Discovering social networks from event logs. Comput. Support. Cooperative Work. **14**(6), 549–593 (2005). https://doi.org/10.1007/S10606-005-9005-9
4. Alvarez, C., et al.: Discovering role interaction models in the emergency room using process mining. J. Biomed. Informatics **78**, 60–77 (2018). https://doi.org/10.1016/J.JBI.2017.12.015
5. Appice, A.: Towards mining the organizational structure of a dynamic event scenario. J. Intell. Inf. Syst. **50**(1), 165–193 (2018). https://doi.org/10.1007/S10844-017-0451-X
6. Arias, M., Munoz-Gama, J., Sepúlveda, M., Miranda, J.C.: Human resource allocation or recommendation based on multi-factor criteria in on-demand and batch scenarios. Eur. J. Ind. Eng. **12**(3), 364–404 (2018). https://doi.org/10.1504/ejie.2018.092009
7. Arias, M., Saavedra, R., Marques, M.R., Munoz-Gama, J., Sepúlveda, M.: Human resource allocation in business process management and process mining: a systematic mapping study. Manag. Decis. **56**(2), 376–405 (2018). https://doi.org/10.1108/md-05-2017-0476
8. Barney, J.B.: Firm resources and sustained competitive advantage. Advances in Strategic Management, vol. 17, pp. 203–227. Emerald (MCB UP) (2000). https://doi.org/10.1016/s0742-3322(00)17018-4
9. Baumgrass, A., Strembeck, M.: Bridging the gap between role mining and role engineering via migration guides. Inf. Secur. Tech. Rep. **17**(4), 148–172 (2013). https://doi.org/10.1016/j.istr.2013.03.003
10. Bidar, R., ter Hofstede, A., Sindhgatta, R., Ouyang, C.: Preference-based resource and task allocation in business process automation. In: Panetto, H., Debruyne, C., Hepp, M., Lewis, D., Ardagna, C.A., Meersman, R. (eds.) OTM 2019. LNCS, vol. 11877, pp. 404–421. Springer, Cham (2019). https://doi.org/10.1007/978-3-030-33246-4_26
11. Bostrom, R.P., Heinen, J.S.: MIS problems and failures: a socio-technical perspective. Part I: the causes. MIS Q. **1**(3), 17–32 (1977). https://doi.org/10.2307/248710
12. Burattin, A., Sperduti, A., Veluscek, M.: Business models enhancement through discovery of roles. In: IEEE Symposium on Computational Intelligence and Data Mining, CIDM 2013, Singapore, 16–19 April 2013, pp. 103–110. IEEE (2013). https://doi.org/10.1109/CIDM.2013.6597224
13. Cabanillas, C.: Process- and resource-aware information systems. In: Matthes, F., Mendling, J., Rinderle-Ma, S. (eds.) 20th IEEE International Enterprise Distributed Object Computing Conference, EDOC 2016, Vienna, Austria, 5–9 September 2016, pp. 1–10. IEEE Computer Society (2016). https://doi.org/10.1109/EDOC.2016.7579383
14. Cabanillas, C., Knuplesch, D., Resinas, M., Reichert, M., Mendling, J., Ruiz-Cortés, A.: RALph: a graphical notation for resource assignments in business processes. In: Zdravkovic, J., Kirikova, M., Johannesson, P. (eds.) CAiSE 2015. LNCS, vol. 9097, pp. 53–68. Springer, Cham (2015). https://doi.org/10.1007/978-3-319-19069-3_4
15. Cabanillas, C., Resinas, M., del-Río-Ortega, A., Ruiz-Cortés, A.: Specification and automated design-time analysis of the business process human resource perspective. Inf. Syst. **52**, 55–82 (2015). https://doi.org/10.1016/J.IS.2015.03.002
16. Carrera-Rivera, A., Ochoa, W., Larrinaga, F., Lasa, G.: How-to conduct a systematic literature review: a quick guide for computer science research. MethodsX **9**, 101895 (2022). https://doi.org/10.1016/j.mex.2022.101895

17. Conca, T., et al.: Multidisciplinary collaboration in the treatment of patients with type 2 diabetes in primary care: analysis using process mining. J. Med. Internet Res. **20**(4), e127 (2018). https://doi.org/10.2196/jmir.8884
18. Delcoucq, L., Dupiereux-Fettweis, T., Lecron, F., Fortemps, P.: Resource and activity clustering based on a hierarchical cell formation algorithm. Appl. Intell. **53**(1), 532–541 (2023). https://doi.org/10.1007/S10489-022-03457-9
19. Delcoucq, L., Lecron, F., Fortemps, P., van der Aalst, W.M.P.: Resource-centric process mining: clustering using local process models. In: Hung, C., Cerný, T., Shin, D., Bechini, A. (eds.) SAC 2020: The 35th ACM/SIGAPP Symposium on Applied Computing, online event, [Brno, Czech Republic], March 30 - April 3, 2020, pp. 45–52. ACM (2020). https://doi.org/10.1145/3341105.3373864
20. Deokar, A.V., Tao, J.: OrgMiner: a framework for discovering user-related process intelligence from event logs. Inf. Syst. Front. **23**(3), 753–772 (2021). https://doi.org/10.1007/S10796-020-09990-7
21. Diamantini, C., Pisacane, O., Potena, D., Storti, E.: Combining an LNS-based approach and organizational mining for the resource replacement problem. Comput. Oper. Res. **161**, 106446 (2024). https://doi.org/10.1016/J.COR.2023.106446
22. Diamond, D.M., Campbell, A.M., Park, C.R., Halonen, J., Zoladz, P.R.: The temporal dynamics model of emotional memory processing: a synthesis on the neurobiological basis of stress-induced amnesia, flashbulb and traumatic memories, and the Yerkes-Dodson Law. Neural Plast. **2007**(60803), 1–33 (2007). https://doi.org/10.1155/2007/60803
23. Dumas, M., Rosa, M.L., Mendling, J., Reijers, H.A.: Fundamentals of Business Process Management, 2 edn. Springer (2018). https://doi.org/10.1007/978-3-662-56509-4
24. Estrada-Torres, B., Camargo, M., Dumas, M., García-Bañuelos, L., Mahdy, I., Yerokhin, M.: Discovering business process simulation models in the presence of multitasking and availability constraints. Data Knowl. Eng. **134**, 101897 (2021). https://doi.org/10.1016/J.DATAK.2021.101897
25. Fernández-Llatas, C., Benedí, J., García-Gómez, J.M., Traver, V.: Process mining for individualized behavior modeling using wireless tracking in nursing homes. Sensors **13**(11), 15434–15451 (2013). https://doi.org/10.3390/S131115434
26. Ferreira, D.R., Alves, C.: Discovering user communities in large event logs. In: Daniel, F., Barkaoui, K., Dustdar, S. (eds.) BPM 2011. LNBIP, vol. 99, pp. 123–134. Springer, Heidelberg (2012). https://doi.org/10.1007/978-3-642-28108-2_11
27. Gregor, S., Hevner, A.R.: Positioning and presenting design science research for maximum impact. MIS Q. **37**(2), 337–355 (2013). https://doi.org/10.25300/MISQ/2013/37.2.01
28. Grisold, T., Wurm, B., Mendling, J., vom Brocke, J.: Using process mining to support theorizing about change in organizations. In: 53rd Hawaii International Conference on System Sciences, HICSS 2020, Maui, Hawaii, USA, 7–10 January 2020, pp. 1–10 (2020)
29. Hardy, C., Phillips, N., Lawrence, T.B.: Resources, knowledge and influence: the organizational effects of interorganizational collaboration*. J. Manag. Stud. **40**(2), 321–347 (2003). https://doi.org/10.1111/1467-6486.00342
30. Huang, Z., Lu, X., Duan, H.: Resource behavior measure and application in business process management. Expert Syst. Appl. **39**(7), 6458–6468 (2012). https://doi.org/10.1016/J.ESWA.2011.12.061
31. van Hulzen, G.A.W.M., Li, C., Martin, N., van Zelst, S.J., Depaire, B.: Mining context-aware resource profiles in the presence of multitasking. Artif. Intell. Med. **134**, 102434 (2022). https://doi.org/10.1016/J.ARTMED.2022.102434
32. Ihde, S., Pufahl, L., Völker, M., Goel, A., Weske, M.: A framework for modeling and executing task-specific resource allocations in business processes. Computing **104**(11), 2405–2429 (2022). https://doi.org/10.1007/S00607-022-01093-2

33. Iivari, J., Hirschheim, R., Klein, H.K.: A dynamic framework for classifying information systems development methodologies and approaches. J. Manag. Inf. Syst. **17**(3), 179–218 (2000). https://doi.org/10.1080/07421222.2000.11045656
34. Jin, T., Wang, J., Wen, L.: Organizational modeling from event logs. In: Grid and Cooperative Computing, Sixth International Conference on Grid and Cooperative Computing, GCC 2007, 16–18 August 2007, Urumchi, Xinjiang, China, Proceedings, pp. 670–675. IEEE Computer Society (2007). https://doi.org/10.1109/GCC.2007.93
35. Kitchenham, B.: Procedures for performing systematic reviews. Technical Report TR/SE-0401, Keele University, Keele, UK (2004)
36. Kumar, A., Dijkman, R., Song, M.: Optimal resource assignment in workflows for maximizing cooperation. In: Daniel, F., Wang, J., Weber, B. (eds.) BPM 2013. LNCS, vol. 8094, pp. 235–250. Springer, Heidelberg (2013). https://doi.org/10.1007/978-3-642-40176-3_20
37. Liu, R., Kumar, A., Lee, J.: Multi-level team assignment in social business processes: an algorithm and simulation study. Inf. Syst. Front. **24**, 1949–1969 (2022). https://doi.org/10.1007/S10796-021-10211-Y
38. Martin, N., Beerepoot, I.: Unveiling use cases for human resource mining: a framework of past and future research. Bus. Inf. Syst. Eng. (2024). https://doi.org/10.1007/s12599-024-00894-3
39. Martin, N., Depaire, B., Caris, A., Schepers, D.: Retrieving the resource availability calendars of a process from an event log. Inf. Syst. **88**, 101463 (2020). https://doi.org/10.1016/J.IS.2019.101463
40. Martin, N., Swennen, M., Depaire, B., Jans, M., Caris, A., Vanhoof, K.: Retrieving batch organisation of work insights from event logs. Decis. Support Syst. **100**, 119–128 (2017). https://doi.org/10.1016/J.DSS.2017.02.012
41. Nakatumba, J., van der Aalst, W.M.P.: Analyzing resource behavior using process mining. In: Rinderle-Ma, S., Sadiq, S., Leymann, F. (eds.) BPM 2009. LNBIP, vol. 43, pp. 69–80. Springer, Heidelberg (2010). https://doi.org/10.1007/978-3-642-12186-9_8
42. Ouyang, C., Wynn, M.T., Fidge, C.J., ter Hofstede, A.H.M., Kuhr, J.: Modelling complex resource requirements in business process management systems. In: Australasian Conference on Information Systems, ACIS 2010, Brisbane, Australia, 1–3 December 2010 (2010)
43. Paré, G., Trudel, M., Jaana, M., Kitsiou, S.: Synthesizing information systems knowledge: a typology of literature reviews. Inf. Manag. **52**(2), 183–199 (2015). https://doi.org/10.1016/J.IM.2014.08.008
44. Pika, A., Leyer, M., Wynn, M.T., Fidge, C.J., ter Hofstede, A.H.M., van der Aalst, W.M.P.: Mining resource profiles from event logs. ACM Trans. Manag. Inf. Syst. **8**(1), 1:1–1:30 (2017). https://doi.org/10.1145/3041218
45. Pika, A., Ouyang, C., ter Hofstede, A.H.M.: Configurable batch-processing discovery from event logs. ACM Trans. Manag. Inf. Syst. **13**(3), 28:1–28:25 (2022). https://doi.org/10.1145/3490394
46. Pufahl, L., Ihde, S., Stiehle, F., Weske, M., Weber, I.: Automatic resource allocation in business processes: a systematic literature survey. CoRR abs/2107.07264 (2021). https://doi.org/10.48550/arXiv.2107.07264
47. Russell, N., van der Aalst, W.M.P., ter Hofstede, A.H.M., Edmond, D.: Workflow resource patterns: identification, representation and tool support. In: Pastor, O., Falcão e Cunha, J. (eds.) CAiSE 2005. LNCS, vol. 3520, pp. 216–232. Springer, Heidelberg (2005). https://doi.org/10.1007/11431855_16
48. Schönig, S., Cabanillas, C., Ciccio, C.D., Jablonski, S., Mendling, J.: Mining team compositions for collaborative work in business processes. Softw. Syst. Model. **17**(2), 675–693 (2018). https://doi.org/10.1007/S10270-016-0567-4

49. Schönig, S., Cabanillas, C., Jablonski, S., Mendling, J.: A framework for efficiently mining the organisational perspective of business processes. Decis. Support Syst. **89**, 87–97 (2016). https://doi.org/10.1016/J.DSS.2016.06.012
50. Scott, J.: What is social network analysis? Bloomsbury Acad. (2012). https://doi.org/10.5040/9781849668187
51. Song, M., van der Aalst, W.M.P.: Towards comprehensive support for organizational mining. Decis. Support Syst. **46**(1), 300–317 (2008). https://doi.org/10.1016/J.DSS.2008.07.002
52. Strembeck, M., Mendling, J.: Modeling process-related RBAC models with extended UML activity models. Inf. Softw. Technol. **53**(5), 456–483 (2011). https://doi.org/10.1016/J.INFSOF.2010.11.015
53. Suriadi, S., Wynn, M.T., Xu, J., van der Aalst, W.M.P., ter Hofstede, A.H.M.: Discovering work prioritisation patterns from event logs. Decis. Support Syst. **100**, 77–92 (2017). https://doi.org/10.1016/J.DSS.2017.02.002
54. Tan, W., Zhao, L., Xu, L., Huang, L., Xie, N.: Method towards discovering potential opportunity information during cross-organisational business processes using role identification analysis within complex social network. Enterp. Inf. Syst. **14**(4), 436–462 (2020). https://doi.org/10.1080/17517575.2018.1562106
55. Utama, N.I., Sutrisnowati, R.A., Kamal, I.M., Bae, H., Park, Y.J.: Mining shift work operation from event logs. Appl. Sci. **10**(20), 7202 (2020). https://doi.org/10.3390/app10207202
56. Yang, J., Ouyang, C., van der Aalst, W.M.P., ter Hofstede, A.H.M., Yu, Y.: OrdinoR: a framework for discovering, evaluating, and analyzing organizational models using event logs. Decis. Support Syst. **158**, 113771 (2022). https://doi.org/10.1016/J.DSS.2022.113771
57. Yang, J., Ouyang, C., ter Hofstede, A.H.M., van der Aalst, W.M.P., Leyer, M.: Seeing the forest for the trees: group-oriented workforce analytics. In: Polyvyanyy, A., Wynn, M.T., Van Looy, A., Reichert, M. (eds.) BPM 2021. LNCS, vol. 12875, pp. 345–362. Springer, Cham (2021). https://doi.org/10.1007/978-3-030-85469-0_22
58. Ye, J., Li, Z., Yi, K., Al-Ahmari, A.: Mining resource community and resource role network from event logs. IEEE Access **6**, 77685–77694 (2018). https://doi.org/10.1109/ACCESS.2018.2883774
59. Yeon, M., Lee, Y., Pham, D., Kim, K.P.: Experimental verification on human-centric network-based resource allocation approaches for process-aware information systems. IEEE Access **10**, 23342–23354 (2022). https://doi.org/10.1109/ACCESS.2022.3152778
60. Yerkes, R.M., Dodson, J.D.: The relation of strength of stimulus to rapidity of habit-formation. J. Comp. Neurol. Psychol. **18**(5), 459–482 (1908). https://doi.org/10.1002/cne.920180503
61. Yingbo, L., Li, Z., Jianmin, W.: Mining workflow event log to facilitate parallel work item sharing among human resources. Int. J. Comput. Integr. Manuf. **24**(9), 864–877 (2011). https://doi.org/10.1080/0951192X.2011.579168
62. Zhao, W., Liu, H., Dai, W., Ma, J.: An entropy-based clustering ensemble method to support resource allocation in business process management. Knowl. Inf. Syst. **48**(2), 305–330 (2016). https://doi.org/10.1007/S10115-015-0879-7

Revision of a Smart Factory Software Architecture from Monolith to Microservices

Ronny Seiger[1(✉)] and Lukas Malburg[2,3]

[1] Institute of Computer Science, University of St. Gallen, 9000 St. Gallen, Switzerland
ronny.seiger@unisg.ch
[2] Artificial Intelligence and Intelligent Information Systems, University of Trier, 54296 Trier, Germany
malburgl@uni-trier.de
[3] German Research Center for Artificial Intelligence (DFKI), Branch University of Trier, Behringstraße 21, 54296 Trier, Germany
lukas.malburg@dfki.de
https://ics.unisg.ch/ , https://www.wi2.uni-trier.de

Abstract. Software architecture plays an important role in the development of modern, complex software systems as it influences a system's quality attributes and ability to grow with future demand. Designing the software architecture of cyber-physical systems (CPS) becomes even more challenging due to their capability of directly influencing the physical world and thus introducing new non-functional requirements related to fault-tolerance, safety, and resource scarcity. Existing research focuses on systems engineering to achieve the vertical integration of CPS with an organization's information systems and processes, but not on software architecture to horizontally extend existing systems with new CPS. In this report we describe the process of revising an existing monolithic software architecture for a smart factory towards a microservices-based architecture to meet these new requirements and prepare the factory to be extended with new CPS. For the revision of the existing architecture, we provide an analysis of its code base before and after changes, a description of the refactoring process, and discuss relevant new non-functional requirements and architecture options. We elaborate on the architectural decisions favoring microservices and analyze the new architecture regarding improved quality attributes to evaluate the system.

Keywords: Cyber-physical Systems · Software Architecture · Internet of Things · Microservices · Industry 4.0

1 Introduction

The architecture of a complex software system has a significant influence on its quality attributes and on the feasibility of extending it with new components and

M. Kaczmarek-Heß et al. (Eds.): EDOC 2024 Workshops, LNBIP 537, pp. 203–220, 2025.
https://doi.org/10.1007/978-3-031-79059-1_13

functionality in the future [7]. Decisions related to software architecture have a strong impact on the software system and are challenging to revise later [30], which is why they are based on extensive trade-off discussions by software architects [26]. Software architecture has also become of increasing importance when developing systems that influence and are influenced by the physical world–Cyber-physical Systems (CPS) [16]. Typical systems engineering approaches discuss the *vertical* integration of compounds of sensors and actuators forming CPS (e.g., production machines) with a company's information systems (e.g., based on the ANSI/ISA-95 pyramid [25]). However, these CPS become increasingly complex and the *horizontal* integration of CPS [42] requires deeper investigation of software architectural aspects. Here, CPS might introduce novel non-functional requirements (NFRs), e.g., related to safety, energy consumption, connectivity, or constraint resources, which are usually not considered when deciding about software architectures in purely digital software systems [30]. On the other hand, common NFRs, e.g., related to performance and elasticity, might not be relevant in CPS as computing resources are constraint. Nevertheless, the CPS software architecture should enable all components to flexibly interact with each other while fulfilling functional and non-functional requirements.

In this paper, we report our experience with revising the software architecture of a model factory as a typical CPS. Starting from a monolithic software system controlling the factory that has originally been developed as a proof-of-concept prototype with focus on vertical integration [21,22,34], we present an analysis of its architecture and code base [6], our experience working with it, and new non-functional requirements. Then, we will discuss breaking down the monolithic architecture into a microservices-based architecture to address the new NFRs. For these changes we elaborate on the architectural decision forces and decisions related to the architectural styles and service sizes, including their implementation, communication, and orchestration. These developments are driven by requirements from Industry 4.0 [11] with the goal of achieving more flexible production scenarios that exhibit high fault-tolerance, extensibility, and maintainability while also considering resource constraints and safety [25].

The paper is structured as follows: We elaborate on experiences with the existing smart factory architecture and problems we have identified in Sect. 2. Here we also identify new requirements as objectives of a solution in a first design science cycle [28] to improve the operation of the smart factory system. In Sect. 3 we build and develop a revised version of the software architecture as the main artifact to serve as basis for an extension of the CPS. We evaluate and demonstrate this solution in Sect. 4. Section 5 presents related work. Section 6 concludes the paper and shows potential future work.

2 Existing Smart Factory Software Architecture

2.1 Software and Hardware Components

We use a smart factory model with components provided by Fischertechnik as basic hardware platform for our Business Process Management (BPM) related research [20–22,34]. The smart factory simulates a production line that consists of 6 production stations, each representing a different capability that can be executed in a production process (e.g., burning, milling, or transportation). A production station is managed by an embedded controller that executes low-level commands to control connected sensors and actuators. These commands are sent from a self-developed, monolithic control software running on a dedicated computer. The software architecture of this software system is technically layered with *one* Web Service (cf. Fig. 1) exposing the capabilities of all production stations as REST resources [21,22,34]. The encapsulation of the low-level commands as high-level capabilities that view each production station as an entity is achieved via an object-oriented Domain Model (cf. Fig. 1) following domain-driven design [4]. As depicted in Fig. 1, we use a Workflow Management System (WfMS) as an orchestrator of the production that facilitates the modeling of processes in BPMN 2.0 [27], their automation, adaptation [20], and mining [34].

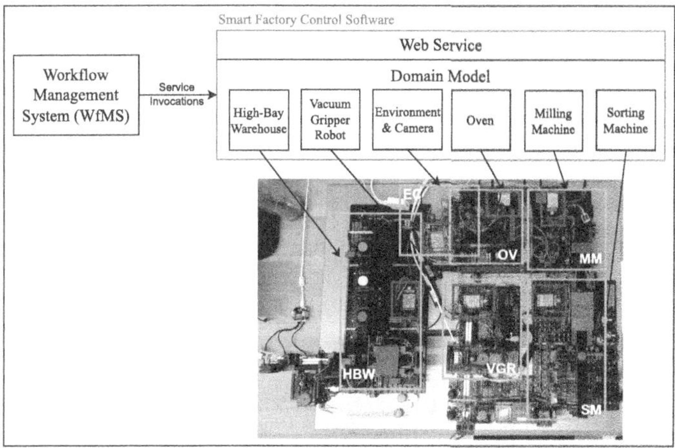

Fig. 1. Original architecture of smart factory control software.

2.2 Architectural Decisions

The decisions regarding the design and implementation of the smart factory control system have mostly been driven by functional requirements to control the production line for BPM-based research, and focused on the vertical integration of all hardware components from sensors to services [25] in a proof-of-concept prototype. The goal was to encapsulate the sensors and actuators belonging to the production stations at a reasonable level of abstraction and to provide service-based access to this high-level functionality [34]. NFRs related to agility, elasticity, or scalability did not play an essential role as the operation of the smart factory is limited by the physical resources (i.e., sensors, actuators, materials) available to execute requests and activities in the production processes [21,34]. A detailed description of the existing software system and driving functional requirements can be found in [34] and [21]. We decided to base the initial implementation of the smart factory control system on a **monolithic** service-based architecture for the following reasons (NFRs) [30]:

- *Costs of Prototype*: To serve as basis for several research projects [22], we aimed to have a quick and relatively low-cost proof-of-concept implementation of the smart factory control system. Priorities here were not on the software architecture, but on the prototypical implementation to have a basis for advanced research on flexible and adaptive processes in CPS [19,20].
- *Simplicity*: We aimed for a rather simple solution to achieve a quick implementation of the factory control system that is relatively easy to maintain.
- *Functionality*: The functionality of the individual stations is not too complex. Each station usually offers 1 to 3 different types of capabilities [21,34].
- *Configurability and Deployability*: The control software should be easy to configure, to deploy, and to run on a standard desktop computer.

2.3 Experience and New Requirements

We informally collected anecdotal experience from three research groups working with the monolithic implementation of the smart factory control system. All agree that the low operational costs and easy deployability of the monolithic architecture lead to a positive experience when using the software system to control the smart factory. In normal operation mode, a high degree of fulfillment of the *functional* requirements related to the production stations can be observed. However, over time all groups identified new NFRs related to *fault-tolerance*, *recoverability*, and *extensibility* [32] that are not fulfilled by the system. Moreover, all groups experienced an increased complexity of debugging and maintaining the software system, in particular during experimental evaluations [19,20,34]. New requirements originated from the interactions of the system with the physical world and the rather unreliable hardware/software components of the smart factory model, which often lead to exceptions, unexpected behavior, and network disconnects of its embedded controllers [20]. Furthermore, the smart factory control system is intended to serve as basis for our BPM-related research [13,22], which entails extending its functionality and features to fulfill new requirements from the implementation of research prototypes on a regular basis. Here, the software system does not perform well either. The non-functional characteristics that became more prominent include:

- *Fault-tolerance:* The operations of the smart factory are frequently interrupted by unexpected events at the physical production stations or by errors within the embedded controllers (e.g., loss of network connection) and software. These errors regularly lead to the entire system not working properly anymore and thus, to reduced availability and need for human interventions.
- *Recoverability:* Although errors typically relate to only one production station or one hardware component, the entire control system has to be stopped and restarted to recover from the errors, which leads to unnecessary downtimes for all stations. Recoverability of the system is low.
- *Extensibility and Maintainability:* The smart factory will be extended with additional CPS (robots) to simulate more complex production scenarios [32]. However, the extensibility of the existing software system is rather low as

adding new devices and functionality requires many changes in the existing code base. This symptom also leads to low *maintainability* of the software system as fixing errors, modifying code, and adding new features often result in performing many changes that may also break the system [12,23].

These insights motivate us to investigate the following two research questions:

RQ1 What are reasons for a CPS software system to show symptoms of poor fault-tolerance, recoverability, extensibility and maintainability?
RQ2 How does the architecture of a CPS software system need to be designed to address these non-functional requirements?

2.4 Code Analysis of the CPS Software System

In Sect. 2.3 we already provided indications to answer RQ1 related to the smart factory's hardware. Learning factories offer a suitable, low-cost playground for CPS and BPM research as discussed in [22]. However, the hardware components are less reliable than in real production settings, and the hardware-software controllers (PLCs) do not implement any safety or fault-tolerance mechanisms. Thus, issues related to hardware have to be addressed by the software system controlling the smart factory. To further investigate RQ1, we performed a static code analysis of the Python-based code base of the existing factory control system[1] using Sonargraph Architect[2]. Our main focus here was on code entanglement, dependency cycles, large files/classes, complexity, and code duplication, as issues in any one of these may lead to the symptoms described in Sect. 2.3 [2].

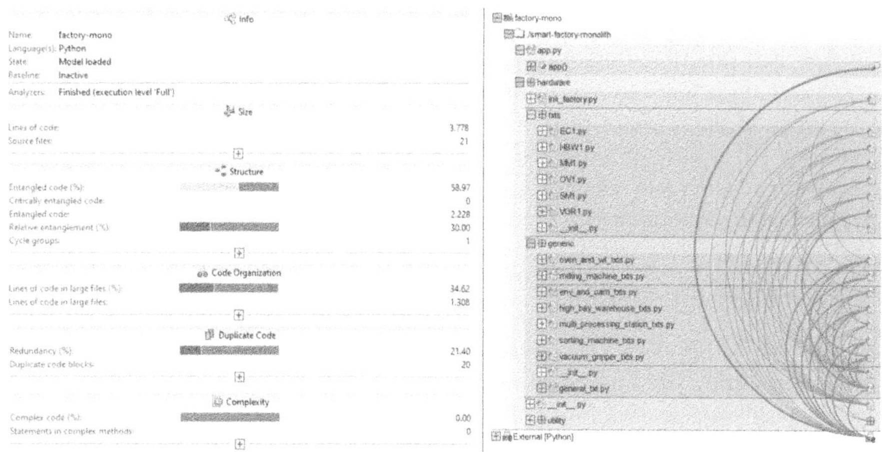

Fig. 2. Code analysis of existing smart factory control software.

1 https://github.com/ics-unisg/smart-factory-monolith.
2 https://www.hello2morrow.com/products/sonargraph/architect9.

A summary of the analysis results is shown in Fig. 2 (left); a simplified dependency graph comprising all Python files organized in packages in Fig. 2 (right). Even though the complexity of individual classes, methods, and code fragments is low, a relatively high percentage of code is entangled, indicating a rather rigid software design [23] and technical debt resulting from the quick prototype implementations, which lead to a high effort in maintainability and low extensibility. The same holds for the identified code redundancy indicating issues in the object-oriented design. However, almost no cyclic dependencies exist, which is a good sign of clean architecture. The main issue influencing fault-tolerance and recoverability is related to the implementation of the web service on top of the domain model (cf. Fig. 1) and the single class initializing the entire functionality of the domain model (file: `init_factory.py`). While the rest of the domain is already structured into individual, functionally cohesive modules per production station, the web service (file: `app.py`) contains all REST end points and logic to call the methods of all classes in the domain model. This one file with >1.3k lines of code (LoC) and the initializer class make the software system a monolith–violating the single-responsibility principle [23], among others–and impose the rather poor performance regarding fault-tolerance and recoverability on it [30]. As indicated in Sect. 2.3, an issue with the hardware of one production station (e.g., loss of network connection to a controller) requires a restart of the entire software system to recover from the error. With these insights, we can confirm in response to RQ1 that a monolithic architecture and the identified issues (smells) in the code base lead to a decrease of fault-tolerance, recoverability, extensibility and maintainability, also for software systems controlling CPS [7,36].

3 Revision of the Smart Factory Architecture

The new non-functional characteristics discussed in Sect. 2.3 became the driving forces influencing the operation of the existing software system. To prevent the accumulation of more technical debt and architecture erosion with future extensions [7], and to improve the fulfillment of the new NFRs (cf. RQ2), we decided to redesign and refactor the software system. Thereby, the fulfillment of the functional requirements (cf. Sect. 2.1) should not be affected.

3.1 Architecture Options

The new NFRs (cf. Sect. 2.3) motivated the revision of the monolithic software system controlling the smart factory. Based on these new driving forces we evaluated typical software architectural styles summarized by Richards and Ford in [30] regarding their suitability. In addition to the NFRs, the authors discuss the type of partitioning of an architectural style–technical partitioning or domain partitioning–and the number of possible standalone software components (*Architectural Quanta)* the specific style might lead to (one or many) [30].

With maintainability, fault-tolerance, and extensibility being among the main driving forces, we decided that the main strategy of revising the architecture and implementation is to focus on *decoupling* of components. Thus, we discarded all options that involve monolithic styles resulting in only one architectural quantum (e.g., layered architecture, modular monoliths, microkernel architectures, and service-oriented architectures) as these are likely to not improve fault-tolerance and availability [30]. The software system controlling the production stations of the factory does not require a sophisticated database infrastructure or shared access to data from the stations [3]. For this reason, we discarded the options of service-based and space-based architectures as non-monolithic architectural styles. Finally, we decided that a **microservices** architecture is the best fit regarding fault-tolerance and extensibility as driving forces addressing RQ2 [30].

3.2 Architecture Decisions and Implementation

As discussed, we found the best trade-offs in a *microservices architecture* [30]. While keeping the functionality intact, the main question regarding the redesign concerns the *integrators* and *disintegrators* that determine the size of one microservice, i.e., *how* the monolith should be split up. Typical integrators and disintegrators in digital services include different levels of: 1) performance and throughput, 2) code volatility, 3) data security, and 4) transactional boundaries in specific parts of a software system [30]. If parts of a system show similar characteristics regarding one or more of these aspects, then they might be put together (integrated) in one service. If they exhibit different characteristics, then these parts are likely to be disintegrated into different services. However, the aforementioned four aspects do not apply in the given CPS setting. In addition to the new NFRs (cf. Sect. 2.3), we determined the following aspects to influence the decisions about the size of a microservice in the smart factory:

- *Functionality*: Despite the low amount of functionality associated with each production station (cf. Sect. 2.1), the one web service controlling the factory depicted in Fig. 1 implements in total 15+ resources that expose the high-level functionality of all stations [34]. As stated in Sect. 2.4, this is a sign of low functional cohesion [23]. We see a need for smaller web services.
- *Physical setup*: The physical layout and configuration of the production line naturally groups all sensors and actuators belonging to one production station (or production cell). These sensors and actuators are wired to the embedded controllers on a per-production-station basis (cf. Fig. 1), i.e., one embedded controller is responsible for one production station.

Service Sizes: The physical setup as a novel aspect influencing architectural decisions in CPS became the main force to decide about the service granularities. The physical grouping of components related to one embedded controller and thus to one production station–one responsibility–is a natural disintegrator and fits well to the size of one microservice [3]. In addition, we often encounter issues in the factory's operation on the level of individual controllers, which supports this service granularity as it isolates failures on the level of a production

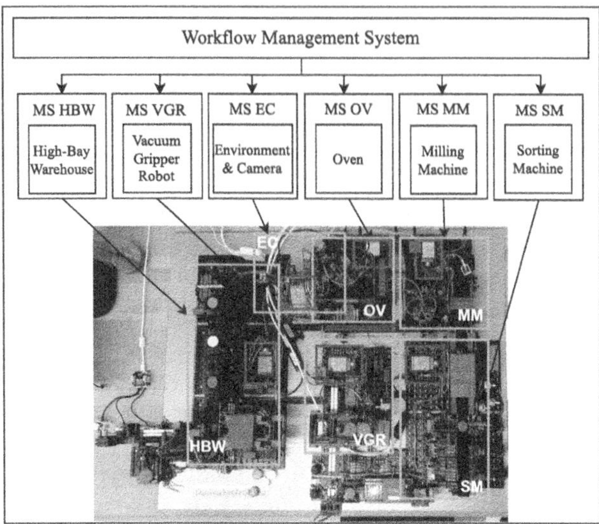

Fig. 3. Revised microservices (MS)-based architecture of the smart factory system.

station. The decision of having *one microservice per production station* partitions the architecture related to the domain functionality and capabilities of individual production stations, i.e., we will have a bounded context per station (subdomain [3]) and thus a higher functional cohesion per service [4].

Refactoring: The implementation of this new architectural style based on the results from the static code analysis of the original system [6] was straightforward as the domain core of the existing monolithic system was already structured based on the different production stations (cf. Sect. 2.4). With the original source code and additional metadata (e.g., architectural diagrams) available, we were able to follow the decomposition process described in [6]. In the object-oriented domain model, there was one class per type and instance of a production station [21,34], which contained the low-level logic to control the station's sensors and actuators via the respective embedded controller. The monolithic web service on top of the domain core also grouped the resources based on the production stations [21,34]. Therefore, it was relatively easy to refactor the monolith and to extract the relevant logic and service implementations into individual microservices. The main refactoring that needed to be done was splitting up the web service (file: `app.py`) and factory initializer class (file: `init_factory.py`) based on the individual production stations. As we were not using a sophisticated database infrastructure to persist data, decomposing the software system into microservices was straightforward [3]. Fig. 3 shows the resulting new architecture. The interactions of the microservices as part of the production processes are still orchestrated by one WfMS [34]. In our setup, all 6 microservices are deployed to and running in a container-based Docker environment on a desktop computer, which is connected to the embedded controllers via Ethernet.

3.3 Code Analysis of the Microservices-Based System

Similar to the code analysis for the existing system described in Sect. 2.4, we analyzed the code base[3] of the revised, microservices-based smart factory control system using Sonargraph, considering code entanglement, dependency cycles, large files/classes, complexity, and code duplication.

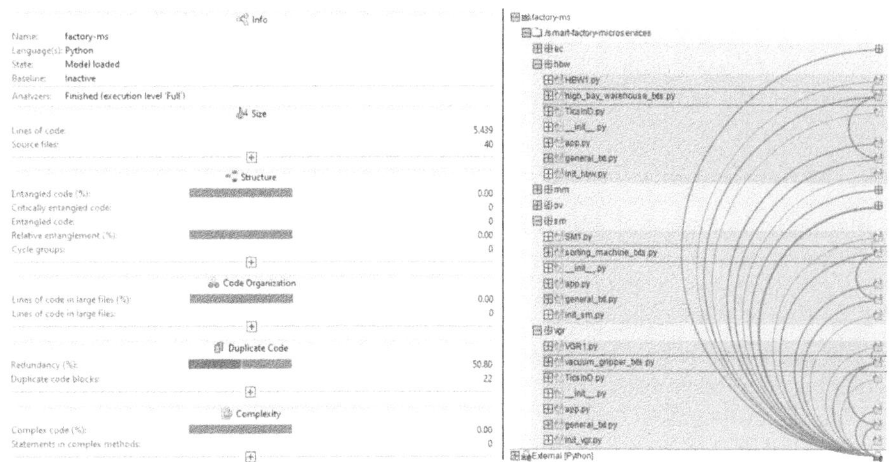

Fig. 4. Code analysis of revised smart factory control software.

A summary of the analysis results can be seen in Fig. 4 (left). A simplified dependency graph showing all microservices in dedicated modules and exemplary Python files is depicted in Fig. 4 (right). Here we see that the code has been reorganized from a more object-oriented structure into domain-partitioned modules (e.g., hbw, sm, vgr, etc.) each representing a microservice for one production station. The redesign and refactoring show a major improvement and reduction regarding code entanglement and code in large files. We achieved this through decomposition, reorganizing the code, and splitting up the web service implementation into the individual microservices. However, we also observe an increase in code redundancy, which is often encountered when migrating from an object-oriented monolith to microservices [5]. In our implementation, each production station has common functionality and attributes implemented in a base class that is then specialized by the production station. When migrating to microservices, we decided to replicate this base class for each microservice, which led to an increase of the code base by 44 % and duplicated code by 20 %. Several strategies exist to deal with shared code (e.g., shared libraries, shared services, sidecar pattern [5]). In our revised implementation, we decided to use code replication as we do not expect many future changes to the base class [5].

[3] https://github.com/ics-unisg/smart-factory-microservices.

4 Evaluation and Discussion

By investigating RQ1 based on the analysis of the original code base and architecture in Sect. 2.4, we identified various issues in the design and code of the monolithic system that led to a poor performance when fulfilling the new NFRs fault-tolerance, recoverability, extensibility, and maintainability discussed in Sect. 2.3. In this section we evaluate the effects of the revised, microservices-based architecture on these NFRs based on a qualitative discussion to answer RQ2. These discussions partially refer to the results of analyzing both versions of the software system using Sonargraph. The detailed metrics are contained in the repositories provided for the monolith and microservices-based implementation.

4.1 Maintainability

Maintainability improved due to the microservices being less complex regarding their functionality and implementation [15]. A stricter adherence to the single responsibility principle led to smaller microservices with individual sizes between 871 and 2175 LoC (compared to a total of 3778 LoC for the monolith) and cleaner implementations with higher functional cohesion, less coupling, and less dependencies. The average component dependency ACD [2] decreased from 3.71 to 1.55; the propagation cost metric according to MacCormack et al. [2] strongly decreased from 17.69 to 3.88; and the cumulative structural debt index for the system decreased from 11 to 0 [2]–all indications of a cleaner implementation and improved structure [23]. Thus, we can assume that the individual microservices are easier to maintain and to debug [2]. Bugs can be more easily located and associated with a specific microservice as there is higher functional cohesion and less source code inside one service [12]. However, in Sect. 3.3 we have also identified an increase in code redundancy due to a common base class being reused in all microservices, which increased the Average Complexity (based on McCabe's cyclomatic complexity) [2] of the entire system from 1.36 to 1.59. In general, replicated code leads to an increase in maintainability of a software system as all changes at one location need to be tracked and consistently changed across all copies, often requiring code versioning [5]. In our implementation, we assume the implementation of the base class to be stable and barely changing–circumstances where replicated code is acceptable in a microservices context [5].

4.2 Fault-Tolerance and Recoverability

The NFRs *fault-tolerance* and *recoverability* became the most important driving forces when working with the smart factory system. Among many sources, Richards and Ford attribute an improved fault-tolerance and recoverability to a microservice-based architecture compared to monolithic approaches [30]. We can confirm this observation in our CPS context as decomposing the monolithic architecture into per-production-station microservices increased fault-tolerance and recoverability. By focusing on the decoupling of components, we were able to confine potential errors to the scope of a production station. Hence, hardware errors (e.g., related to the connectivity of a production station's controller) do not affect other stations or services. We can easily resolve issues at the granularity of a production station and recover the failed component by restarting the corresponding controller and microservice to restore normal operations. The application of techniques from fault-tolerant programming may further improve the system's tolerance against software errors. Our focus was on addressing hardware-related issues as primary source for interruptions of the smart factory.

The deployment and operation of the now 6 microservices has become more complex. However, the platform used for running the containerized microservices greatly reduces this complexity as all containers can be started at once and redeployed and restarted individually to recover from errors [8], without adding significant overhead to the computer's resource consumption [37]. So far, our experience working with the revised software system, especially for experimental settings, confirms an increased fault-tolerance, better recoverability, and thus a higher overall availability of the production system. Nevertheless, a higher number of involved (micro)services also means an increase of network communication among the services, which may result in higher latency and communication issues [1]. These aspects do not play a significant role in our setup with all services running in the same local, container-based environment. A more systematic analysis of the software system's availability, ability to recover from errors, and need for human interventions remains subject to future work.

4.3 Extensibility

One of the main goals of this work was to prepare the smart factory software system for an extension with additional CPS. As acknowledged in literature [30], a microservice-based architecture exhibits a better extensibility than a monolithic system, which motivated us to revise the existing software architecture. The results of analyzing the revised implementation (cf. Sects. 3.3 and 4.1) show a decrease in dependencies, coupling, and code entanglement, which are indications of improved extensibility. Adding new microservices to the software system is facilitated due to the lower coupling and no shared code and dependencies between services. A new Fischertechnik-based production station of known type can be added non-invasively to the production line by simply instantiating a second container for the respective microservice with a slightly different configuration (e.g., IP address). A new production station of unknown type can be added based on a new microservice where the common base class is reused and extended with the machine specific implementation. We have successfully extended the implementation and instantiated the containers for a different smart factory configuration with multiple instances of Fischertechnik-based machines [21].

To further demonstrate the extensibility, we added four robots–two mobile robots of type TurtleBot 4 Pro and two robotic grippers arms of type Dobot Magician–to the existing CPS (cf. Fig. 5). As the microservices-based style of the CPS dictates the software architecture, it has been straightforward to integrate the control systems for the robots into the overall CPS, also in a (micro)service-based manner with dedicated services for each robot. Putting these systems

Fig. 5. Extended smart manufacturing setup with new CPS.

together with one or more of the existing microservices of the smart factory would have led to a more monolithic approach negatively impacting the quality attributes. The two robotic gripper arms have been integrated in a service-based manner, sharing a common instance of ROS2 [18] to control both robots and expose their capabilities via web services. The shared ROS2 instance is suitable because of the close physical proximity of both robots and the need to save resources on the available computer running the ROS2 instance. The two mobile robots are regarded as standalone microservices, which are each controlled by a dedicated ROS2 instance on a Raspberry Pi 4. The main driver for having one microservice per robot was to enable both robots to operate autonomously from any other software service and thus not to rely on a constant network connection [33]. Adding the robots in this (micro)service-based way did not require any modifications to the existing microservices-based software system controlling the smart factory, and it allows us to orchestrate all services of all components uniformly based on REST using a WfMS. In our setup, additional communication among all services is facilitated by using a messaging and stream processing system [34]. Table 1 summarizes all decision forces and decisions we took when revising the smart factory system and adding the robots to the CPS.

4.4 Research Questions and Limitations

With answering RQ1 in Sect. 2.4, we identified in our case study the monolithic style and issues in the software design and code base related to code entanglement, high coupling and low cohesion, as the main reasons for the existing CPS software system to perform rather poorly regarding the NFRs fault-tolerance, recoverability, extensibility, and maintainability [36]. The results of discussing these NFRs after revising the existing monolithic software system to a microservices-based architecture indicate an improvement of all these NFRs. Thus, as an answer to RQ2, we suggest to focus on decoupling monolithic CPS control systems towards more individual standalone components, prefer-

Table 1. Summary of architectural decisions in the extended CPS.

CPS	Architectural Style	ServiceSize	Decision Forces
Smart Factory	Microservices	1 production station	Physical setup, fault-tolerance, extensibility, functionality
Robotic Gripper Arms	Service-based	1 robot	Physical setup, computing resources, fault-tolerance
Mobile Service Robots	Microservices	1 robot	Autonomy, energy consumption, connectivity, fault-tolerance

ably *microservices* the size of a production station or production cell, to improve fault-tolerance, recoverability, extensibility, and maintainability.

As a limitation we acknowledge that we work with a small-scale learning factory [22], which does not have any hard real-time and safety constraints, and which allows us to interface with the embedded controllers using high-level programming languages from desktop computers. Assuming that these kinds of open interfaces and full control of the hardware exist in a real industrial production environment might not be completely realistic, but with machine interfaces becoming more accessible and standardized (e.g., based on the *Asset Administration Shell* [32]) we can observe a trend towards more openness and interoperability in the future. The learning factories serve as bridges between completely simulated, virtual environments and real-life production settings. They can be used to educate shop floor personnel and to conduct sophisticated low-cost and low-effort research of CPS and BPM in more realistic settings [22]. Therefore, we deem the insights of this work to be also relevant more generally in CPS as existing CPS software systems are usually structured in a more monolithic way and also exhibit typical software design flaws and code smells [36], which negatively impact the quality attributes of the software systems. We hypothesize that our proposal of moving towards more decoupled service-based architectures, where the physical setup of the individual CPS components has a strong influence on the service granularities, can be generally applied to improve non-functional characteristics of distributed CPS. Moreover, we observe an increasing number of research groups using a variant of the learning factory as basis for their research in BPM, CPS/IoT, software engineering, and automation. The insights and artifacts presented in this experience report might facilitate their setup of the factory based on our proposed microservices-based software architecture.

5 Related Work

Literature surveys on using microservices-based software architectures in the context of IoT can be found in [35] and [29]. In [35] the authors discuss about NFRs relevant in IoT and they provide pointers to different approaches that discuss solutions to fulfill these NFRs.

In [15] the authors highlight the flexibility and versatility of using microservices to implement small features bounded within processes in IoT, in contrast to heavy weight inflexible monoliths. A microservice architecture for the industrial IoT (IIoT) is presented by Dobaj et al. in [3]. The authors discuss different types of design patterns for IIoT and relevant decision forces such as dependability, performance, and flexibility. Based on these, a layered microservices-based architecture and the application of the design patterns to address the IIoT-related NFRs is presented. Among others, the aspects of decomposition into subdomains and shared data access in the microservices architecture are discussed, which are well aligned with the decisions and discussions we have presented in our approach. The design of a microservice architecture for a smart city IoT platform that organizes the microservices around business capabilities, similar to the production stations representing the capabilities of the smart factory, is presented in [14]. Deciding about the granularity of individual microservices based on business capabilities is also a common strategy in purely digital, non-CPS systems as pointed out by the authors in [8] discussing their move from monoliths to microservices. NFRs around architectures for IIoT are discussed in [39]. Besides high availability, extensibility, and interoperability, which are discussed in our work, too, the authors emphasize real-time operations and cyber-security as critical aspects in IIoT. We agree that these are highly relevant in real-world deployments, but we found them less significant for the smart factory model used in our laboratory environment. We skipped these non-functional aspects due to their complexity and refer to the discussions in [39].

A literature study on the migration of monoliths to microservices is presented in [1]. In addition, the authors provide a case study on how to benchmark the migration by comparing the performance and consumption of computing resources of the system before and after migration. This study can be very helpful for our future work to conduct a more quantitative analysis of our proposed revision of the existing CPS software architecture. The aspect of migrating existing software architectures in CPS towards microservices is discussed in [17] and [31]. Sarkar et al. showcase their migration of a complex monolith controlling an industry automation system to containerized microservices [31]. Among others, they are faced with strong couplings between components, which increases the difficulty of breaking down the monolith. Liu et al. present migration strategies that consider economic factors to reduce downtimes and costs when moving an active production line to microservices [17], which is only partially relevant in our laboratory environment. In [24], the authors discuss the migration of a software system for autonomous UAV-based infrastructure inspection from monolith to microservices. They nicely show the benefits of microservices for scalable data processing in their work, which will become relevant for our smart factory once we put a stronger focus on processing of the data emitted from the factory.

Several works discuss the design of specific IoT architectures in smart production [10,38,41], which also address the aspect of integrating different types of robots based on ROS [38]. All approaches follow service-based architectures that feature messaging systems for loosely coupled interactions, similar to our proposed architecture. Furthermore, various works discuss the use of workflow engines, as we do, to orchestrate processes [38] and (micro)services [40].

From the discussion of related work we can conclude that we identified and addressed NFRs with high relevance for IIoT and CPS in our work. The methodological approach, decision forces, and architectural decisions we took when breaking down the smart factory monolith into microservices and extending it with robots are well aligned with existing literature. Moreover, we can confirm that containerization of microservices, messaging systems for communication, and WfMS for orchestration of processes are suitable means for creating flexible and extensible software architectures that promote high fault-tolerance, autonomy, and loose coupling in complex software systems controlling CPS.

6 Summary and Future Work

In this work we discussed the case of revising an existing monolithic software architecture for a smart factory control system towards a microservices-based architecture. The original design and implementation of the monolith was driven by functional requirements and the goal to have a quick, low-cost implementation of a prototype to serve as basis for more advanced research. However, the experience from working with this prototype led to the emergence of new non-functional requirements (NFRs) related to fault-tolerance, recoverability, maintainability and extensibility, which became the main driving forces to decompose the monolith into microservices as it did not fulfill these new NFRs sufficiently. We analyzed the monolith and its code base to identify the reasons for not fulfilling these new NFRs. A discussion of architectural options and ways to mitigate identified flaws in the software design and code base led us to focus on decoupling of the monolithic system's components and breaking the system down into microservices. The physical grouping of sensors and actuators belonging to one production station that is managed by one embedded controller became a natural fit to dictate the size of one microservice representing the station's business capabilities. An analysis of the new system's design and code base showed improvements regarding maintainability, coupling, and cohesion of components. The characteristics of the new microservices-based architecture confirm an improved fault-tolerance, recoverability, and extensibility, which we demonstrated by non-invasively adding new robots controlled by (micro)services to the existing CPS software architecture. All microservices are orchestrated by a workflow management system enabling advanced research on BPM and IoT [9].

In future work we plan to adapt the implementation of the individual microservices to be compatible with the asset administration shell to improve extensibility and interoperability with other systems [32]. Furthermore, we will conduct a more systematic quantitative evaluation of the CPS where we will compare different architectural decisions and their impact on NFRs and resource consumption. In this context, we plan to develop a formal model based on [26] and a case base of experiences regarding architectural decisions in CPS to document their impact on NFRs and provide guidance to software architects.

References

1. Bjørndal, N., et al.: Migration from monolith to microservices: benchmarking a case study. Technical report (2020)
2. Ciceri, C., et al.: Software Architecture Metrics. O'Reilly Media, Inc. (2022)
3. Dobaj, J., Iber, J., Krisper, M., Kreiner, C.: A microservice architecture for the industrial internet-of-things. In: Proceedings of the 23rd European Conference on Pattern Languages of Programs, pp. 1–15 (2018)
4. Evans, E.: Domain-Driven Design: Tackling Complexity in the Heart of Software. Addison-Wesley Professional (2004)
5. Ford, N., Richards, M., Sadalage, P., Dehghani, Z.: Software Architecture: The Hard Parts. O'Reilly Media, Inc. (2021)
6. Fritzsch, J., Bogner, J., Zimmermann, A., Wagner, S.: From monolith to microservices: a classification of refactoring approaches. In: Software Engineering Aspects of Continuous Development and New Paradigms of Software Production and Deployment: First International Workshop, DEVOPS 2018, Chateau de Villebrumier, France, 5–6 March 2018, Revised Selected Papers 1, pp. 128–141. Springer, Cham (2019)
7. Furrer, F.J.: Future-Proof Software-systems. Springer (2019)
8. Gouigoux, J.P., Tamzalit, D.: From monolith to microservices: Lessons learned on an industrial migration to a web oriented architecture. In: 2017 IEEE International Conference on Software Architecture Workshops (ICSAW), pp. 62–65 (2017)
9. Janiesch, C., et al.: The internet of things meets business process management: a manifesto. IEEE Syst. Man Cybern. Mag. **6**(4), 34–44 (2020)
10. Jepsen, S.C., Worm, T.: Designing and evaluating interoperable industry 4.0 middleware software architecture: reconfiguration of robotic system. In: European Conference on Software Architecture, pp. 205–220. Springer (2023)
11. Kagermann, H., Wahlster, W.: Ten years of industrie 4.0. Sci **4**(3), 26 (2022)
12. Kalske, M., Mäkitalo, N., Mikkonen, T.: Challenges when moving from monolith to microservice architecture. In: Current Trends in Web Engineering: ICWE 2017 International Workshops, Liquid Multi-Device Software and EnWoT, practi-O-web, NLPIT, SoWeMine, Rome, Italy, 5–8 June 2017, Revised Selected Papers 17, pp. 32–47. Springer (2018)
13. Kirikkayis, Y., Gallik, F., Seiger, R., Reichert, M.: Integrating IoT-driven events into business processes. In: International Conference on Advanced Information Systems Engineering, pp. 86–94. Springer (2023)
14. Krylovskiy, A., Jahn, M., Patti, E.: Designing a smart city internet of things platform with microservice architecture. In: 2015 3rd International Conference on Future Internet of Things and Cloud, pp. 25–30. IEEE (2015)
15. Lai, C., Boi, F., Buschettu, A., Caboni, R.: IoT and microservice architecture for multimobility in a smart city. In: 2019 7th International Conference on Future Internet of Things and Cloud (FiCloud), pp. 238–242. IEEE (2019)
16. Lee, E.A.: Cyber physical systems: design challenges. In: 2008 11th IEEE International Symposium on Object and Component-Oriented Real-Time Distributed Computing (ISORC), pp. 363–369. IEEE (2008)
17. Liu, Y., Yang, B., Ren, X., Liu, Q., Liu, S., Guan, X.: E2MS: an efficient and economical microservice migration strategy for smart manufacturing. IEEE Trans. Serv. Comput. (2024)
18. Macenski, S., Foote, T., Gerkey, B., Lalancette, C., Woodall, W.: Robot operating system 2: design, architecture, and uses in the wild. Sci. Robot. **7**(66), eabm6074 (2022)

19. Malburg, L., Brand, F., Bergmann, R.: Adaptive management of cyber-physical workflows by means of case-based reasoning and automated planning. In: 26th EDOC Workshops. LNBIP, vol. 466, pp. 79–95. Springer (2023)
20. Malburg, L., Hoffmann, M., Bergmann, R.: Applying MAPE-K control loops for adaptive workflow management in smart factories. J. Intell. Inf. Syst. 1–29 (2023)
21. Malburg, L., Klein, P., Bergmann, R.: Semantic web services for AI-research with physical factory simulation models in industry 4.0. In: International Conference on Innovative Intelligent Industrial Production and Logistics, pp. 32–43. ScitePress (2020)
22. Malburg, L., Seiger, R., Bergmann, R., Weber, B.: Using physical factory simulation models for business process management research. In: Del Río Ortega, A., Leopold, H., Santoro, F.M. (eds.) BPM 2020. LNBIP, vol. 397, pp. 95–107. Springer, Cham (2020). https://doi.org/10.1007/978-3-030-66498-5_8
23. Martin, R.C.: Clean Architecture. Prentice Hall (2017)
24. Matlekovic, L., Schneider-Kamp, P.: From monolith to microservices: software architecture for autonomous UAV infrastructure inspection. arXiv preprint arXiv:2204.02342 (2022)
25. Monostori, L.: Cyber-physical production systems: roots, expectations and R&D challenges. Procedia Cirp **17**, 9–13 (2014)
26. Nowak, M., Pautasso, C.: Team situational awareness and architectural decision making with the software architecture warehouse. In: European Conference on Software Architecture, pp. 146–161. Springer (2013)
27. Object Management Group: BPMN 2.0 specification (2011). https://www.omg.org/spec/BPMN/2.0/
28. Peffers, K., Tuunanen, T., Rothenberger, M.A., Chatterjee, S.: A design science research methodology for information systems research. J. Manag. Inf. Syst. **24**(3), 45–77 (2007)
29. Razzaq, A.: A systematic review on software architectures for IoT systems and future direction to the adoption of microservices architecture. SN Comput. Sci. **1**(6), 350 (2020)
30. Richards, M., Ford, N.: Fundamentals of software architecture: an engineering approach. O'Reilly Media (2020)
31. Sarkar, S., Vashi, G., Abdulla, P.: Towards transforming an industrial automation system from monolithic to microservices. In: 23rd International Conference on Emerging Technologies and Factory Automation (ETFA), vol. 1, pp. 1256–1259. IEEE (2018)
32. Schnicke, F., Kuhn, T., Antonino, P.O.: Enabling industry 4.0 service-oriented architecture through digital twins. In: Muccini, H., et al. (eds.) ECSA 2020. CCIS, vol. 1269, pp. 490–503. Springer, Cham (2020). https://doi.org/10.1007/978-3-030-59155-7_35
33. Seiger, R., Herrmann, S., Aßmann, U.: Self-healing for distributed workflows in the internet of things. In: 2017 IEEE International Conference on Software Architecture Workshops (ICSAW), pp. 72–79. IEEE (2017)
34. Seiger, R., Malburg, L., Weber, B., Bergmann, R.: Integrating process management and event processing in smart factories: a systems architecture and use cases. J. Manuf. Syst. **63**, 575–592 (2022)
35. Siddiqui, H., Khendek, F., Toeroe, M.: Microservices based architectures for IoT systems-state-of-the-art review. Internet Things 100854 (2023)
36. Sonnleithner, L., Oberlehner, M., Kutsia, E., Zoitl, A., Bácsi, S.: Do you smell it too? Towards bad smells in IEC 61499 applications. In: 2021 26th IEEE Inter-

national Conference on Emerging Technologies and Factory Automation (ETFA), pp. 1–4. IEEE (2021)
37. Sun, X., Liang, Y., Huang, H.: Design and implementation of internet of things platform based on microservice and lightweight container. In: 2020 IEEE 9th Joint International Information Technology and Artificial Intelligence Conference (ITAIC), vol. 9, pp. 1353–1357. IEEE (2020)
38. Traganos, K., Grefen, P., Vanderfeesten, I., Erasmus, J., Boultadakis, G., Bouklis, P.: The horse framework: a reference architecture for cyber-physical systems in hybrid smart manufacturing. J. Manuf. Syst. **61**, 461–494 (2021)
39. Urbina, M., Acosta, T., Lázaro, J., Astarloa, A., Bidarte, U.: Smart sensor: SOC architecture for the industrial internet of things. IEEE Internet Things J. **6**(4), 6567–6577 (2019)
40. Valderas, P., Torres, V., Serral, E.: Modelling and executing IoT-enhanced business processes through BPMN and microservices. J. Syst. Softw. **184**, 111139 (2022)
41. Xia, C., Zhang, Y., Wang, L., Coleman, S., Liu, Y.: Microservice-based cloud robotics system for intelligent space. Robot. Auton. Syst. **110**, 139–150 (2018)
42. Zuehlke, D.: Smartfactory-towards a factory-of-things. Annu. Rev. Control. **34**(1), 129–138 (2010)

Scaling AI Adoption in Finance: Modelling Framework and Implementation Study

Thomas Sepanosian[1(✉)], Zoran Milosevic[2], and Andrew Blair[3]

[1] University of Twente, Enschede, The Netherlands
t.sepanosian@student.utwente.nl
[2] Deontik, Brisbane, Australia
zoran@deontik.com
[3] Westpac, Sydney, Australia
andrew.blair@westpac.com.au

Abstract. There is an increasing potential for using AI applications in finance, ranging from simpler Generative AI applications to more complex, agent oriented solutions. This paper reports on our experience in applying early AI solutions in an Australian fintech landscape. We first present a framework developed to support industry experts and practitioners in adopting AI solutions in a scaleable manner, to ensure the adoption of fit-for-purpose AI systems. We then focus on a longer term research dimension, which addresses more complex business problems for which the emerging multi-agent AI technologies may offer more value. We experimented with these technologies, including their integration with more mature approaches such as RAG. Our proof of concept for retirement planning application, highlights benefits and directions for LLM-powered AI agents, and also identifies limitations of current technologies. Specifically, deploying multi-agent technologies on low-powered infrastructure presents challenges. These limitations can hinder the implementation of solutions that require reliable reasoning and collaboration. Our proof of concept highlights both the potential of multi-agent technologies, and the limitations that need to be addressed.

Keywords: LLM powered agents · Multi-agent AI · RAG · Fintech

1 Introduction

The financial services industry is undergoing a radical transformation fueled by Artificial Intelligence (AI). From fraud detection to algorithmic trading, AI is automating tasks, improving efficiency, and generating valuable insights. For example, David Walker, the Chief Technology Officer at Westpac, one of Australia's leading banks, predicts that these advancements will help revolutionize the banking industry [8]. His insights highlight the potential for AI to provide personalized interactions and recommendations through context-aware systems, potentially enhancing engagement with both customers and employees.

M. Kaczmarek-Heß et al. (Eds.): EDOC 2024 Workshops, LNBIP 537, pp. 221–236, 2025.
https://doi.org/10.1007/978-3-031-79059-1_14

This paper addresses the need for practical AI applications in finance, specifically wealth management tools like retirement planning. We aimed to understand the value of current AI capabilities while accommodating future developments.

There are two key contributions of this paper. The first is an industry-focused framework designed to support Australian financial services professionals in adopting AI solutions in a scalable manner. Starting from simpler, more mature AI technologies and evolving into complex systems capable of addressing advanced business challenges, this framework empowers industry experts and practitioners, such as risk managers, data scientists, and solution and enterprise architects to make informed decisions throughout the AI adoption process. It addresses key considerations such as consumer value proposition and regulatory compliance, ensuring the selection of fit-for-purpose AI systems.

Our second contribution delves into a longer-term research dimension, exploring the possibilities of emerging multi-agent AI systems, demonstrating their potential to deliver more efficient solutions for existing use cases and tackling more complex financial challenges. In particular, we utilized a multi-agent orchestration framework, crewAI [13], wherein agents are powered by Large Language Models (LLMs) and capable of utilizing techniques such as Retrieval-Augmented Generation (RAG), to develop a proof-of-concept retirement planning assistance application. This exploration not only highlighted the significant benefits of LLM-powered agents, such as improved productivity and personalization, but also revealed limitations related to explainability, consistency, biases and computational demands.

The remainder of this paper is organized as follows: Sect. 2 presents related work. This is followed by providing the description of the problem of scaleable adoption of AI within a finance organisation and a framework we developed to facilitate this, Sect. 3. Section 4 describes in detail our proof of concept implementation for a retirement application, utilizing the crewAI multi-agent orchestration framework. Section 5 discusses lessons learnt in developing this proof-of-concept. Finally, Sect. 6 concludes the paper and outlines future directions.

2 Related Work

There are a number of technological, regulatory and commercial efforts that influenced our work, which enabled us to developed a more focused solution approach while reflecting the specific business case and business environment we have addressed.

Our use case required specific access to relevant retirement information, consumer specific information, and regulatory information, such as relevant retirement policies, as a way of enhancing the semantic context and functionality of the LLMs powering the agents. We initially identified RAG to augment the LLMs' capability and provide contextually relevant and accurate information. By integrating RAG, LLMs harness the power of not only their pre-trained data, but also dynamically retrieved information, helping prevent hallucinations [10]. This comes with the added benefit of not having to retrain a model when new information becomes available. A more advanced, Agentic RAG extends these capabilities further by enabling LLMs to adjust retrieval strategies based on the evolving context and goals within a conversation. By integrating Agentic RAG, these agents move beyond static information retrieval to a more proactive, agent-driven approach [23].

The term 'agentic' above reflects the ability of agents to exhibit their agency, in terms of their autonomy of decision making. These advanced AI-driven programs, designed to independently pursue defined goals, have the potential of helping industries including healthcare, finance and more [9]. With the emergence of LLMs such as OpenAI's GPT series and Meta's open-source Llama models, LLM powered agents specifically have become more prominent. These are agents where the core controller is an LLM, instead of classical techniques such as rule-based systems. Using an LLM enables the agent to have memory, the ability to plan to achieve its goals, and the ability to use tools, as opposed to merely performing an action [25]. The process of constructing autonomous AI agents involves the consideration of which architectures to use, to achieve optimal results [24].

Pivotal advancements in this area include Microsoft's AutoGen, which provides a framework wherein customizable agents can converse with each other, offering the opportunity for multi-agent LLM application development [26]. They propose that multi-agent conversations are feasible due to the abilities of LLMs to respond to feedback, handle a wide range of tasks, and to perform well on complex tasks by simplifying them into simple subtasks. Another recently emerged framework is crewAI [13]. Built on top of LangChain, the crewAI framework provides the capability of defining agents, tasks, and tools to rapidly compose a crew of agents which fulfill given tasks autonomously.

The increased interest in adopting AI within fintech organisations has also led to new regulatory efforts in Australia. The Australian Banking Association (ABA) has proposed several recommendations to the Australian government for integrating AI in the banking industry [1]. These include building upon existing sector-specific practices and maintaining legislative neutrality to ensure that AI-driven and human-made decisions adhere to the same regulatory standards. Furthermore, King & Wood Mallesons, a leading international law firm, acknowledges Australia's adoption of AI and its regulation, and highlights the importance of transparency, security, and associated risks when employing AI [16].

There are also some commercial providers that have recently starting offering Generative and Conversational AI solutions for the Fintech industries. Such solutions range from intelligent digital assistants, contact center support and generative AI, which were specifically developed for finance industry, based on curated financial knowledge sources [15,22].

Despite these advancements, challenges remain in the scalability and integration of LLM applications within several industries, such as the financial industry. This study aims to address these gaps by proposing a novel modeling framework and conducting an implementation study. Our approach seeks to enhance both the scalability and efficacy of AI in financial environments, thereby overcoming existing limitations and harnessing the full potential of autonomous agents.

3 Background and Problem

Scaling AI adoption within financial organizations presents significant hurdles. Implementing AI ethically and responsibly is paramount due to the potential for biased outcomes and reputational risks. Additionally, the multifaceted nature of financial challenges necessitates a diverse toolkit of AI techniques, from traditional statistical models to advanced deep learning. Finally, successfully integrating AI across an organization requires a strategic approach that builds upon foundational applications, such as automating routine tasks, before progressing to more complex endeavors like personalized financial advice.

To this end, we developed a comprehensive framework to guide financial institutions in their AI journey. The framework categorizes AI applications into distinct problem areas, so that organizations can tailor their AI strategies accordingly. This framework encompasses intelligent information retrieval, content generation, data analysis, decision support, and task automation. Progressing from foundational to advanced AI capabilities is crucial. For instance, intelligent information retrieval using techniques like natural language processing can support basic customer queries. Building upon this, content generation with AI can create tailored financial reports. More complex data analysis tasks, such as fraud detection, require sophisticated machine learning models and data science methodologies. As AI applications become more intricate, techniques like RAG can enhance system performance by incorporating relevant information.

To address complex, multifaceted financial problems, multi-agent systems and expert systems can be employed, while conversation AI can facilitate human-machine interaction. By strategically combining these techniques, financial institutions can develop sophisticated AI solutions that drive business value and improve customer experiences.

Figure 1 presents a spectrum of AI problem complexities, ranging from simple to more complex. Each level demands different AI techniques and capabilities. For instance, automating routine tasks requires relatively straightforward AI applications, while developing sophisticated AI-powered advisors, such as those for retirement planning, necessitates advanced techniques like RAG, knowledge graphs, and potentially multi-agent systems

4 Implementation Study

This section described how we used a specific multi-agent AI solution, crewAI [13] to implement functionality common to many retirement planning applications typically used by finance organisations in Australia. We also demonstrate the progression of using RAG tools as part of this multi-agent framework.

4.1 Use Case: Retirement Planning Support

The retirement planning industry is multifaceted, encompassing regulatory policies, industry trends, retirement product offers and individual customer circumstances. Effective retirement advice relies on understanding these elements.

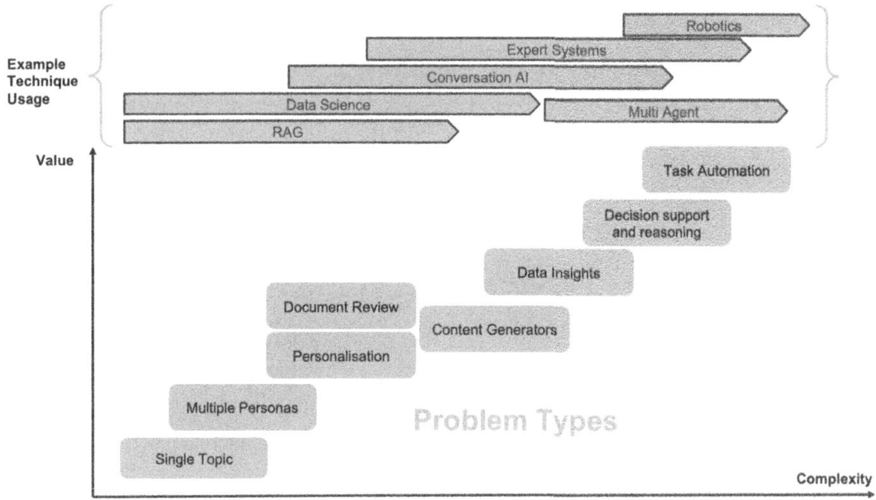

Fig. 1. AI adoption framework

Therefore, an organization's customer support staff are typically required to understand the following domains of knowledge:

- **Retirement Policy Knowledge:** This includes legislative aspects such as the maximum contributions permissible by age, and specific regulations such as the Superannuation Industry Act [2].
- **Retirement Industry Knowledge:** This encompasses knowledge regarding the current state of the industry, such as average performances of investments, and how much people need to save to live comfortably.
- **Customer Specific Knowledge:** Providing advice to customers requires careful consideration of their situation. This includes general information, such as their current investment choices, their savings situation, and how much they are being charged, but could also extend further, such as their personal risk tolerances.

Equipped with this comprehensive knowledge, support staff can address common customer inquiries, such as:

- *Can I increase my contributions by x amount per year?*
- *How is my retirements saving investments performing compared to others?*
- *Am I on track for retirement?*

However, ensuring consistent and effective utilization of these knowledge domains can be challenging due to continuously evolving regulations and industry trends. Furthermore, personalizing advice requires a thorough understanding of the customer and their situation, which could be time-consuming and error-prone. We explored the potential of applying AI for this case, specifically through a multi-agent system, powered by LLMs.

4.2 Implementation

We employed crewAI, a multi-agent orchestration framework designed to manage a team of specialized LLM-based agents that have the ability to delegate tasks, and utilize tools to solve complex problems collaboratively. We created four agents, three of which are related to the associated domains previously mentioned. The fourth agent is responsible for quality assurance. These agents, with their assigned tasks, tools and grouping in multiple crew compositions, support activities associated with retirement planning. A visual overview of the implementation is provided in Fig. 2. In the following sections, we discuss how we have used crewAI [12] to achieve this[1].

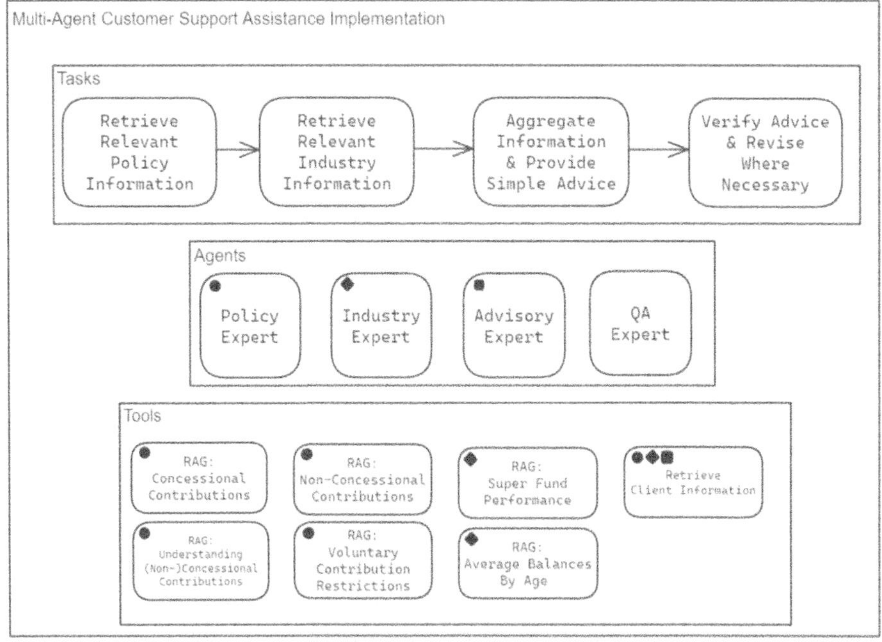

Fig. 2. Overview of the implementation in crewAI - Showcasing the `Tasks` and `Agents`, including the `Tools` available them, as indicated by distinctly shaped icons

Agents. In the crewAI framework, agents are autonomous units which perform tasks, make decisions and communicate with other agents. Each agent is defined by a specific `role`, which captures its function in a structure called `crew`. The agent's expected behavior, including decision making, are specified using a LLM.

[1] Implementation available at GitHub: https://github.com/Thomas-mp4/Multi-Agent-Retirement-Planning.

More specifically, each agent has a `goal`, and `backstory`, which serve as a way to provide further context to the agent, such that it can potentially exhibit more desirable behavior [27]. For this case study, we defined four agents:

- **Retirement Policy Expert**: Specializes in retirement policies and regulations, ensuring that relevant policy information is accurately provided in response to the client's inquiry.
- **Retirement Industry Expert**: Expert in industry data and trends, with the responsibility to highlight relevant information in the context of the client's inquiry.
- **Advisory Expert**: Primarily responsible for aggregating information received from the experts, and delivering clear and concise advice tailored to the client's needs.
- **QA Expert**: Acts as a final fact-checker, reviewing the proposed advice for inconsistencies or errors, and assigning tasks to the appropriate expert if any discrepancies are found.

The first three agents are based on the aforementioned knowledge domains and do not have the ability to delegate tasks themselves. The fourth agent, the quality assurance agent, focuses on the validity of the advice, and delegates tasks accordingly as it deems fit to achieve this, based on its defined identity. However, this final check is limited by the capabilities of the LLM that powers the agent, and the definition it has been assigned within the framework, and should thus not be considered equivalent to a thorough review.

An example definition of an agent is provided in Fig. 3. We experimented with several LLM providers to power the agents including Ollama [18], and Groq [11], utilizing Meta's llama models. However, due to compatibility issues and rate limiting issues, the final iteration utilizes OpenAI's GPT-4o [19] instead, to power the agents.

Tasks. Tasks in crewAI are assignments that agents must complete. Each task requires a `description`, an `expected_output` and, if the crew is running sequentially, a pre-assigned `agent` responsible for fulfilling the task. In case the crew runs hierarchically, a managing agent, either declared explicitly, or implicitly by the crewAI framework, becomes responsible for assigning tasks to agents. In our application, we employed a sequential process, where we only allow the QA agent to delegate tasks, such that revisions can be made where necessary in collaboration with other agents. Additionally, we enable the crew to utilize a memory system, implemented in the crewAI framework, such that coherence over a sequence of actions is maintained for all agents. We defined four tasks, each corresponding to an agent for our system:

- **Policy Task:** Retrieves relevant policy information, such as applicable contribution caps
- **Industry Task:** Retrieves relevant industry information, such as average balances

```
advisory_agent = Agent(
    role="Advisory␣Expert",
    goal=("Understand␣the␣client's␣inquiry,␣and␣based␣on␣the␣information␣
        gathered␣by␣colleagues,␣"
         "provide␣the␣best␣retirement␣advice␣in␣a␣simple␣manner␣"
         "that␣is␣easy␣for␣the␣client␣to␣understand."),
    backstory=("With␣a␣background␣in␣client␣advisory␣services,␣"
               "you␣specialize␣in␣understanding␣client␣inquiries␣and␣synthesizing␣
                   complex␣information␣into␣clear,␣"
               "actionable␣advice.␣"
               "Your␣communication␣skills␣ensure␣clients␣feel␣confident␣in␣their␣
                   financial␣decisions."
               "Make␣sure␣to␣provide␣full␣complete␣answers,␣and␣make␣no␣
                   assumptions."),
    tools=[retrieve_client_information],
    allow_delegation=False
)
```

Fig. 3. Example of the Advisory Expert Agent (Python)

- **Advisory Task:** Aggregates information from the results of the previous tasks, and provide simple advice
- **Quality Review Task:** Reviews the information provided by the other agents, and ensure they are correct and meet the client's needs.

Figure 4 provides an example of task definition. The formatted string literals refer to a hypothetical client's full name and the query they have provided to customer support. By inserting this information into the task description, it allows the designated agent to be aware of the necessary context, and helps keep agents' behavior relevant to the client and their query.

Tools. Tools can help agents fulfill their tasks effectively. The crewAI framework offers a toolkit with ready-to-use tools [14] such as RAG. Note that the crewAI framework is built on top of LangChain [7], and thus LangChain tools are fully compatible. Additionally, if no existing tools satisfy the application's requirements, custom tools can be implemented as well. Importantly however, the usage of tools by an agent is only possible when the LLM powering the agent is capable of function calling [17].

In our application we used tools to facilitate obtaining relevant and up-to-date information by the policy expert and the industry expert agents. We selected a collection of openly available articles and webpages, and converted them into plain text representations, in order to utilize crewAI Toolkit's `TXTSearchTool`, which employs RAG. These include information about the following, where notably the policy related information is based on articles from the Australian Taxation Office [3–6], primarily concerning contribution policies:

```
advisory_task = Task(
    description=(f'Understand␣the␣client\'s␣inquiry,␣and␣based␣on␣the␣
        information␣gathered␣by␣'
                f'the␣policy␣and␣industry␣experts,␣provide␣the␣best␣retirement␣
                    advice␣in␣a␣simple␣manner␣'
                f'that␣is␣easy␣for␣the␣client␣to␣understand.'
                f'The␣client\'s␣request:␣{query}'
                f'The␣client\'s␣name:␣{client}'
                f'Consider␣which␣tools␣you␣actually␣need,␣and␣also␣consider␣
                    whether␣this␣task␣is␣necessary␣given␣the␣client\'s␣request.'),
    expected_output="A␣clear␣and␣concise␣retirement␣advice␣report␣that␣
        addresses␣the␣client's␣inquiry"
                  "␣and␣integrates␣insights␣from␣policy␣and␣market␣analysis.",
    agent=advisory_agent
)
```

Fig. 4. Example of the Advisory Task (Python)

- (Non-)Concessional contribution caps
- (Non-)Concessional contribution information
- Voluntary contribution information
- Industry average performance return
- Average super balances by age

Additionally, we defined a custom tool to retrieve client information, given their full name. In our proof-of concept, this function merely returns the contents of a text file corresponding to the given full name, but in a deployed environment, this could be implemented as a call to a retirement application or its underlying database. The agents adapt to the utilization of custom tools by inspecting its Python docstring, and by inspecting thrown runtime exceptions, if applicable. For instance, if an agent attempts to retrieve a client's information using the custom client retrieval tool without proper formatting of the parameter, a `FileNotFoundError` would be thrown specifying the appropriate format, which allows the agent to adapt accordingly, akin to how a developer would handle such an exception.

4.3 Results

To test this system, we employed a fictional client John Doe, who's query is as follows: *"Am I on track for retirement?"*. John Doe is aged 55, is male, has a current balance of \$530,000 AUD, has made \$20,000 AUD of contributions for the current year, and experienced a performance return of 6% and 7% in 2022–2023, and 2021–2022, respectively.

The application produced a report with several interesting sections. One key section includes the comparison between the client's performance to the industry average, depicted in Fig. 5. By using RAG and a text representations of a web articles that also incorporate tables, the agents were able to gather accurate and relevant information. Additionally, the agents compared the client's age and balance to industry statistics, and revealed that the client's investments were performing well, as can be seen in Fig. 6. Beyond these comparisons, the report discusses relevant policies and recent adjustments, such as changes to (non-)concessional contribution caps, provides recommendations to the client, and includes projections and calculations, providing the client with a comprehensive report, autonomously.

Based on industry data from ..., the performance of super funds over various periods is as follows:
1 Year:
Growth (61 – 80% growth assets): 9.9%
3 Years
Growth (61 – 80% growth assets): 5.9% per year
5 Years:
Growth (61 – 80% growth assets): 7.3% per year
10 Years:
Growth (61 – 80% growth assets): 7.0% per year
John's portfolio return of 6% for 2022–2023 and 7% for 2021–2022 is within the range of industry averages, showing that his investments are performing competitively

Fig. 5. crewAI Retirement Planning Output Excerpt - Industry Comparison

According to industry data, the average superannuation balances for men and women by age are as follows:
Age 55–59:
Men: $316,457
Women: $236,530
John's current balance of $530,000 AUD is significantly higher than the average balance for his age group, indicating that he is in a strong financial position compared to his peers.

Fig. 6. crewAI Retirement Planning Output Excerpt - Balance Comparison

In order to generate this report, the crew executed all tasks sequentially, using tools where necessary, until the chain reached the quality assurance expert. Upon inspection, the QA expert deemed it appropriate to verify the policy related recommendations, and thus delegated this task to the policy expert. Using the tools available to them, the policy expert cross-referenced the report it was given with its own information, and verified the information was correct. After receiving the response from the policy expert, the QA expert decided that that no further verification is necessary, and that its task had thus been fulfilled, finally providing the report as the crew's output. This workflow is depicted in Fig. 7. It is important to note that this workflow, and the output of this crew are non deterministic. That is to say, even with the crew's agents and tasks being defined in a specific way, results slightly differ from each run. This can be attributed to the nature of LLMs, such as, the temperature of an LLM. The temperature of an LLM determines how creative the model becomes, that is to say, the chance of the model selecting a less or more probable next token. A higher temperature value, above 1.0, will result in more randomness, whereas a lower temperature, below 1.0, will be more deterministic. It is however important to note that even at a temperature of 0.0, the system will still be non-deterministic, as this is inherent to LLMs [20].

Running the crew without any adjustments to the codebase results into different behavior and different results. It approximately takes 4 min for a crew to fulfill all its tasks, with the crew taking longer when agents decide to utilize their tools more extensively, such as making additional RAG calls, or when the QA agent delegates additional tasks.

5 Discussion

This section captures some observations from our experiments, some of which have influenced our thinking about future work.

5.1 Responsibility

Explainability and Transparency. As we expected, LLMs, such as those employed in the proof-of-concept to power agents, produce outputs that are less deterministic and more difficult to explain compared to traditional machine learning models, such as decision trees. For example, we noted instances where the same agents, with the same configuration would make different assumptions regarding the client's retirement contribution (non-concessional vs concessional). This unpredictability highlights the need for maintaining transparency about how data is processed, and how the system reaches its conclusion. It is also important to consider the implications of this lack of explainability in relation to regulations.

Additionally, it is important to be aware of any biases present in the employed LLMs due to its computational power. Even if RAG is utilized with correct data, the LLM is still capable of misinterpreting or misrepresenting the data, potentially resulting into negative outcomes. Potential ways to mitigate these problems include auditing the decision-making process of agents, such as the interactions it makes with tools to deduct an answer, and encouraging agents to clarify their reasoning themselves, such as by adding the sources it utilized when providing an answer. This would be especially valueable in scenarios such as depicted in Fig. 7, where the QA expert deemed it necessary to ask for verification of specific information in the final report. Furthermore, verifying the task outputs

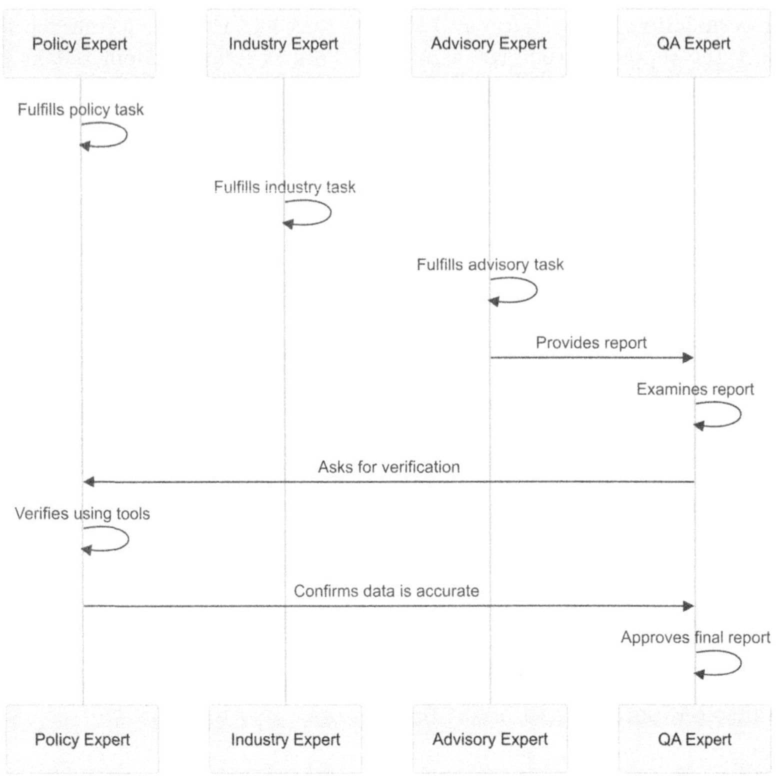

Fig. 7. crewAI Retirement Planning Output - Simplified Visualized Workflow

per agent minimizes the chances of false information being passed to other agents and accepted as truth, which given that the system runs sequentially, would cause a ripple effect.

Security. Utilizing LLMs to power a multi-agent system that assists with retirement planning also involves handling sensitive personal and financial information, which introduces specific security challenges. We encountered that lower-capacity models, such as llama-8b, may inadvertently expose parts of the crew's internal mechanisms, such as the Python Docstring of tools. This could potentially leak sensitive information, or expose vulnerabilities which could be exploited by malicious actors. Furthermore, incorporating external technologies or services, such as utilizing the OpenAI API to utilize LLMs, or augmenting the system using web scraping tools, introduces risks associated with external data breaches and unauthorized access.

It is possible to run crewAI completely locally, but this does come with the corresponding computational costs, especially considering that smaller LLMs do not perform as well as models that require larger inference budgets. Thus, it is important to make an appropriate assessment of security risks involved when designing multi-agent applications in order to make a balanced decision.

5.2 Scalability

Preprocessing of Data. Handling complex data types, such as documents containing tables, web pages containing images, or markup content requires preprocessing which adds additional overhead. The use of RAG also includes obtaining embeddings. It is essential that agents that handle different types of data are capable of accurately parsing the various mediums they are presented in. Failure to do so could potentially lead to misinterpretation of information, causing undesirable behavior.

Architecture Design. One of the inherent challenges in designing systems such as the one we described in this paper is striking the balance between constructing a system effective at solving the known problems, while also maintaining enough flexibility to address unforeseen problems. This becomes increasingly important the more the system scales, as changes become more difficult and costly to implement ad-hoc. In order to overcome this challenge, it could be beneficial to apply the separation of concerns principle, especially considering this is also potentially beneficial to the behavior of the agents themselves.

Furthermore, optimizations of performance are also necessary in order to scale to increasingly complex tasks. The more tasks are involved, the more likely it is more agents will be necessary to successfully fulfill them. If agents do not make proper use of their memory, or ineffectively share information, they could make redundant calls, which consequently has a negative effect on performance, and thus also on sustainability. For instance, we observed that agents tend to exhaust all the tools available to them to acquire as much context to fulfill their tasks, without taking into consideration whether they require these tools. We also encountered an increase of redundant calls when employing an hierarchical approach as opposed to a sequential approach. The managing agent in the hierarchical approach tends to repeats its task delegations, despite them being fulfilled before. Moreover, the stability of the frameworks utilized to create multi-agent systems have a significant impact on performance. We experienced attempts of executing the system, where it failed mid-way due to errors, or where agents got caught in a loop, trying to perform the same action with seemingly no apparent reason. As this is an emerging and rapidly developing field, with new frameworks and features being frequently released, it is important to consider these risks.

In summary, the lessons learned from these experiments should serve as input in designing new architectures for other solutions, to avoid making inadequate design and implementation choices, which can be difficult to correct.

6 Conclusions and Future Work

This paper was an attempt to bridge practical and research issues associated with the adoption of LLM-based and emerging AI technologies in financial organisations. Motivated by one specific problem, i.e. providing AI support for a retirement planning application to help customer centre staff deliver better customer service and more efficient processing of many document sources, we decided to experiment with simpler, RAG solutions, in part, to better understand the emerging multi-agent AI techniques. In fact, we managed to establish links between the two, by letting agents make use of RAG itself. The results were quite encouraging, as for example agents provided insights similar to a human expert. On the other hand, the path to reaching this level of development had many challenges, associated with both the native LLM issues such as its stochastic nature, but also the maturity of the multi-agent solution chosen.

We believe that experiments such as this, can also help the workforce within a financial organisation to develop their own understanding of the maturity of AI based solutions, and better prepare them for liaising with technology experts, specialist solution providers and AI platforms vendors, in selecting and procuring the most cost-effective solutions. The scalability of adoption is thus capturing what technologies are best fit-for-purpose and how to move from proof-of-concept to production stage of AI adoption, and continuously applying lessons learned to adapt to higher complexity problems.

There are several directions for our future work, inspired by lessons learned so far and other use cases. One of them is exploring the value of knowledge graphs as a way of integrating them for LLM solutions. We would also like to explore the potential of a distributed multi-agent system, wherein the system can compose of agents hosted in several environments, instead of a single environment. This could allow for better performance, as well as redundancy within the system, which adds to the system's overall resilience.

Furthermore, the topic of consistency and quality of agent output is a valueable avenue for future work. Currently, our system employs fairly generic definitions for agents and tasks, which provides more flexibility, enabling the system to handle a wide variety of client inquiries. However, this flexibility can lead to variability in the results, which might impact the reliability and predictability of the system's output. By refining and specifying the definitions of agents and tasks, particularly aligning more closely with a specific topic in context of retirement planning advice, the system could potentially produce more consistent and high-quality results. This increased specificity might reduce the system's ability to handle a wider range of inquiries, but it could lead to more predictable and desirable behavior. Experimentation with this trade-off between flexibility and consistency is a valueable future work avenue in order to determine what is most appropriate. The use of several LLM models, instead of utilizing the same model for each agent instance could have an impact on this as well.

Additionally, the consistency and adherence of agents to their assigned tasks and roles, while complying with clearly defined guardrails, should be further explored. For instance, it would be desirable for developers to have fine grained control over the permission levels of agents, such that it is certain they handle data conform to a set of defined business or legal rules, despite being powered by a stochastic LLM. This is particularly of essence when handling sensitive data that could impact client privacy. One potential approach to achieve this is through reinforcement learning, enabling agents to adjust their behaviors based on human feedback, utilizing the agents' reflection capabilities [21] or involving humans as ultimate decision maker and enforcer. Utilizing a scalable test environment, where agent outputs can be evaluated for quality and variability across separate runs on the same client inquiry, could prove useful in these endeavors.

Acknowledgements. We would like to express our gratitude to the anonymous reviewers for their valuable feedback and constructive comments. Their insights contributed to the improvement of this paper during the revision process.

Disclosure of Interests. The authors declare no competing interests relevant to the content of this article.

References

1. Australian Banking Association: Positioning Australia as a Leader in Digital Economy Regulation - Automated Decision Making and AI Regulation (2022). https://www.ausbanking.org.au/submission/automated-decision-making-and-ai-regulation/. Accessed 07 July 2024
2. Australian Government: Superannuation Industry (Supervision) Act 1993 (1993). https://www.legislation.gov.au/C2004A04633/latest/text
3. Australian Taxation Office: Understanding concessional and non-concessional contributions (2023). https://www.ato.gov.au/individuals-and-families/super-for-individuals-and-families/super/growing-and-keeping-track-of-your-super/caps-limits-and-tax-on-super-contributions/understanding-concessional-and-non-concessional-contributions. Accessed 07 July 2024
4. Australian Taxation Office: Concessional contributions cap (2024). https://www.ato.gov.au/individuals-and-families/super-for-individuals-and-families/super/growing-and-keeping-track-of-your-super/caps-limits-and-tax-on-super-contributions/concessional-contributions-cap. Accessed 07 July 2024
5. Australian Taxation Office: Non-concessional contributions cap (2024). https://www.ato.gov.au/individuals-and-families/super-for-individuals-and-families/super/growing-and-keeping-track-of-your-super/caps-limits-and-tax-on-super-contributions/non-concessional-contributions-cap. Accessed 23 June 2024
6. Australian Taxation Office: Restrictions on non-voluntary contributions (2024). https://www.ato.gov.au/individuals-and-families/super-for-individuals-and-families/super/growing-and-keeping-track-of-your-super/caps-limits-and-tax-on-super-contributions/restrictions-on-voluntary-contributions. Accessed 23 June 2024
7. Chase, H.: LangChain (2022). https://github.com/langchain-ai/langchain
8. David, W.: David Walker's tech trends to watch in 2024 (2024). https://www.westpac.com.au/news/in-depth/2024/02/david-walkers-tech-trends-to-watch-in-2024/. Accessed 07 July 2024
9. Dodig-Crnkovic, G., Burgin, M.: A systematic approach to autonomous agents. Philosophies **9**(2), 44 (2024). https://doi.org/10.3390/philosophies9020044
10. Gao, Y., et al.: Retrieval-Augmented Generation for Large Language Models: A Survey (2024). http://arxiv.org/abs/2312.10997

11. Groq: Fast AI inference (2024). https://groq.com/. Accessed 07 July 2024
12. João, M.: CrewAI documentation. https://docs.crewai.com/. Accessed 05 July 2024
13. João, M.: CrewAI (2024). https://github.com/joaomdmoura/crewAI
14. João, M.: CrewAI tools (2024). https://github.com/joaomdmoura/crewai-tools
15. Kasisto: Conversational AI solutions for banking and finance. https://kasisto.com/. Accessed 07 July 2024
16. King & Wood Mallesons: Australian government interim response on the regulation of AI: inching towards safe and responsible AI (2024). https://www.kwm.com/au/en/home.html. Accessed 07 July 2024
17. Mistral AI: Function calling (2024). https://docs.mistral.ai/capabilities/function_calling/. Accessed 07 July 2024
18. Ollama: Ollama (2024). https://github.com/ollama/ollama
19. OpenAI: OpenAI API platform (2024). https://openai.com/api/. Accessed 07 July 2024
20. Ouyang, S., Zhang, J.M., Harman, M., Wang, M.: LLM is Like a Box of Chocolates: The Non-determinism of ChatGPT in Code Generation (2023)
21. Park, J.S., O'Brien, J.C., Cai, C.J., Morris, M.R., Liang, P., Bernstein, M.S.: Generative Agents: Interactive Simulacra of Human Behavior (2023). https://doi.org/10.48550/arXiv.2304.03442
22. Posh.AI: Ai built for banking. https://www.posh.ai/. Accessed 07 July 2024
23. Takyar, A.: Agentic RAG: What it is, its types, applications and implementation (2024). https://www.leewayhertz.com/agentic-rag/
24. Wang, L., et al.: A survey on large language model based autonomous agents. Front. Comput. Sci. **18**(6), 186345 (2024). https://doi.org/10.1007/s11704-024-40231-1
25. Weng, L.: LLM Powered Autonomous Agents (2023). https://lilianweng.github.io/posts/2023-06-23-agent/. Accessed 07 July 2024
26. Wu, Q., et al.: AutoGen: Enabling Next-Gen LLM Applications via Multi-Agent Conversation Framework (2023)
27. Xu, B., et al.: ExpertPrompting: Instructing Large Language Models to be Distinguished Experts (2023)

Joint CBI–EDOC Case Reports Track

Enhancing Observability: Real-Time Application Health Checks

Tim Eichhorn[1(✉)], João Luiz Rebelo Moreira[1], Luís Ferreira Pires[1], and Lucas Meertens[1,2]

[1] University of Twente, Drienerlolaan 5, 7522 NB Enschede, The Netherlands
t.s.eichhorn@student.utwente.nl
[2] CAPE Groep, Transportcentrum 16, 7547 RW Enschede, The Netherlands
https://www.utwente.nl/

Abstract. Log management and application health monitoring practices are cumbersome and often still require significant human intervention to prevent inaccurate data and information. Existing technologies like Elasticsearch and Grafana offer opportunities to automate and improve these practices. This paper reports on a design solution aimed at enhancing log categorization, anomaly detection, and real-time application health reporting for CAPE Groep's service application. The proposed solution leverages Elasticsearch's Machine Learning capabilities and Grafana's dynamic visualization tools, alongside a newly developed dashboard named Horus, to centralize log data and automate monitoring processes. Preliminary results indicate that the proposed solution significantly improves the accuracy and timeliness of health reports, reduces manual intervention, and provides comprehensive real-time insights into application performance. This paper outlines the requirements, architectural design, and phased implementation plan, demonstrating the potential to streamline operations, enhance service delivery, and support future more stringent scalability requirements.

Keywords: Observability · Application monitoring · Log Management · Log Analytics · Elasticsearch · Dashboard

1 The Situation

This paper explores the enhancement of log management and real-time application health monitoring for CAPE Groep's service application, leveraging Elasticsearch's machine learning capabilities, Grafana's visualization tools and the development of a custom dashboard, that we called Horus. This section introduces application health monitoring through log management and provides an overview of CAPE Groep and the CAPE Service Point (CSP) application, detailing the current challenges and proposed solutions to improve log management and application health reporting.

M. Kaczmarek-Heß et al. (Eds.): EDOC 2024 Workshops, LNBIP 537, pp. 239–263, 2025.
https://doi.org/10.1007/978-3-031-79059-1_15

1.1 Application Health Monitoring

Application health monitoring is critical in modern software development and operations, providing essential insights into the behaviour of systems in production [4]. Effective monitoring allows for the detection and diagnosis of undesired behaviours, contributing significantly to system reliability and operational efficiency. Central to this monitoring is log management and analysis, which involves collecting, processing, and analyzing log data generated by applications and their runtime environments [4].

Log data records events about the internal state of a system, and plays a pivotal role in understanding system behaviour, diagnosing issues, and improving overall reliability. As highlighted in [4], monitoring complex systems and deriving actionable insights from log data is a challenging task, requiring sophisticated tools and techniques. Despite the availability of advanced log management solutions, such as the Elastic stack, challenges remain in effectively leveraging these technologies to extract meaningful insights. Current log analysis processes are often time-consuming, error-prone, and lack real-time data insights, underscoring the need for fully automated solutions. Furthermore, the importance of data visualisation for complex data, such as application health metrics, has been repeatedly highlighted in literature [26]. However, the adoption of Machine Learning and advanced log analysis methods, and real-time visualisation offer promising avenues to enhance the efficiency and effectiveness of log management practices. By automating the categorization, analysis, and visualisation of log data, organizations can improve their ability to monitor application health, detect anomalies, and respond proactively to potential issues.

1.2 CAPE Service Point

CAPE Groep[1] is an IT consultancy firm specialized in developing applications and integrations for organizations in the transport and logistics, supply chain, smart construction, and agrifood sectors. They leverage low-code technology, specifically Mendix[2] and eMagiz[3], to quickly create effective solutions with flexibility for future needs. Next to development and consultant services, CAPE Groep also offers application monitoring and support services. These services include, but are not limited to, monitoring the status and health of applications, providing insights into causes of issues and problems, and managing customer contact through tickets.

To provide these support services, CAPE Groep has developed the CAPE Service Point (CSP) application that is used by customers in a customer's specific environment and by various CAPE Groep employees. Originally the system was created as a ticketing system for the support department of CAPE Groep, however, it has evolved into a system that provides multiple functionalities and services. For the support department to provide the highest quality of services to

[1] https://capegroep.nl/.
[2] https://www.mendix.com/.
[3] https://emagiz.com/.

both clients and employees, automation and optimization of the many processes within CSP is essential. Furthermore, automation and optimization provide scalability, allowing CAPE Groep to work towards taking a more proactive role in predicting and solving issues before they affect customers. However, although the system has many automated components, there is room for improvement.

1.3 Log Management and Analytics

In the current setup, CSP collects log files daily using direct API integrations provided by Mendix. At the same time applications send log entries in real-time to a database leveraging Elastic's Elasticsearch, which is an open-source, highly scalable, and distributed real-time RESTful search and analytics engine [12]. These logs are transmitted using a custom LogTransporter module publicly available [5]. Initially, logs were to be centralized in Elastic, however, due to the perceived inability for categorization, logs are also collected by CSP for this purpose. Log categorization refers to the process of grouping similar log entries to prevent data from being cluttered by a single repeating error message. This results in large volumes of redundant data that not only consume storage space but also complicate data management processes. Apart from redundancy, currently Elasticsearch effectively aggregates logs from various applications but is not extended with functionality to categorize or analyze these logs meaningfully. The current setup only allows for alerting on the total count of log messages, which is not a very informative performance indicator [4,7]. This limitation results in a significant underutilization of Elasticsearch's capabilities, particularly its powerful data processing and analysis tools which could provide insightful analytics and real-time reporting.

Health Check Reports. One of the services CAPE Groep performs is regular health checks of applications, including reports for customer review. These health check reports are crucial for maintaining transparency for clients about performance and status of their applications. However, the current implementation for generating these health checks is notably inefficient and often produces undesirable results, requiring manual intervention.

In the current setup, a daily scheduled event within CSP collects all log files of each managed Mendix application individually using the Deploy API [20]. CSP then compares log entries line by line to combine individual log lines into categories if they are similar. This is computationally intensive as log files contain between 4 million and 20 million entries. Therefore, the process only runs during the night and even rejects log files with a size larger than 15MB to prevent CSP from crashing due to CPU and memory issues. Given that large log files are often an indicator of problems [4], potentially excluding this valuable information is not only undesirable but also partially defeats the purpose of log collection and categorization.

Furthermore, the reports generated based on these data often provide incomplete information on issues that occurred. In this scenario, manual intervention is

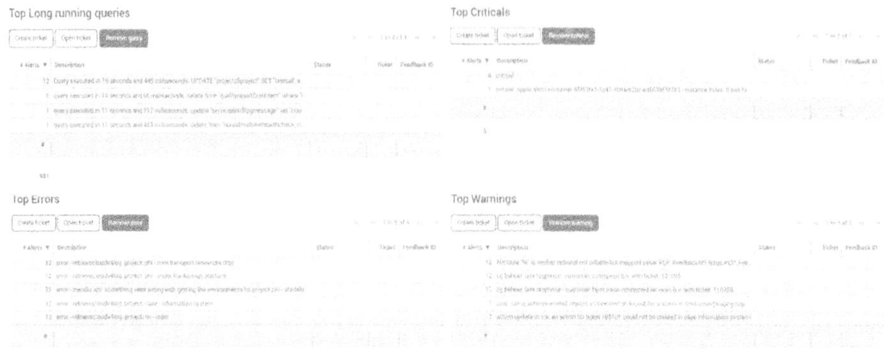

Fig. 1. The log analysis data in a health check report

required by the support staff, who manually download the log files from Mendix, convert them to categories using a Python script that runs locally on a personal computer and then generate the health check report based on these data instead of the CSP database. This process is both time-consuming and error-prone because a support member has to spot missing data in the automatically generated health check report, before being aware of the need to import log files manually. Figure 1 shows example of how log data is presented in the health check report.

Dashboard. Besides the health check reports, the current dashboard available in CSP provides functionality for monitoring alerts and managing tickets. This system enables support staff to receive and respond to notifications regarding various application issues, and to track the status and resolution of tickets. However, to gain comprehensive insights into application health additional steps are necessary, as the existing CSP interface lacks an advanced analytical overview that combines this information with application health metrics, such as log data. Consequently, staff often need to access multiple systems such as Grafana and Mendix separately to gain a comprehensive view. In this scenario, Grafana is used for real-time data visualization and general monitoring dashboards, while Mendix displays application-specific metrics. Consolidating this information into a single overview should provide users with a single source of information related to application health displayed on a dashboard.

1.4 Challenges and Opportunities

The internal consultants at CAPE Groep face challenges in monitoring their IT landscape effectively because they need to simultaneously view data from multiple sources, which is time-consuming and error-prone. This fragmented approach hinders efficient workflow and comprehensive system health assessment, requiring a more integrated and streamlined solution within CSP. Furthermore, the current system lacks accurate real-time data, diminishing the value of the health reports, highlighting the need for improved log management and analytics as well as a comprehensive, real-time dashboard to improve operational efficiency and decision-making. Additionally, shifting the log collection and analysis to a separate dedicated system allows CAPE Groep to extend their observability services beyond Mendix applications, and potentially support other projects.

The current state of log management and reporting in CSP highlights a significant gap between the capabilities of the utilized technologies and their application within the observability infrastructure. The reliance on manual processes for critical functions such as application health reporting and the underutilization of Elasticsearch for data analysis represent key opportunities for improvement. By leveraging the advanced features of Elasticsearch for log categorization and employing automated tools for data analysis and reporting, CSP can significantly improve its operational efficiency, reduce costs, and enhance service delivery to clients. This project aimed to exploit these areas of improvement.

2 The Task

2.1 Goals

The primary task of the project was to enhance the CSP system and CAPE Groep's observability infrastructure by designing and implementing improvements to its log collection and analytics capabilities, focusing specifically on overcoming the challenges related to partial matching and grouping of log messages. Furthermore, we also enhanced the presentation and visualisation of the improved data and insights for both internal consultants and in the future customers through the development of a new customized dashboard, which we called Horus.

The project was conducted within the constraints of a Master's student internship period, totalling 14 weeks. Although budget details were not specifically outlined at the start of the project, the inherent nature of an internship project implies limited availability of both time and funding. Furthermore, one of the goals was to reduce the needed computational resources for log analysis, therefore the added costs from the solution should not exceed the saved costs.

Furthermore, the initial requirements of the project were:

- The proposed solution had to seamlessly integrate with CSP and the broader observability infrastructure of CAPE Groep.
- The solution had to be scalable to handle increasing volumes of log data efficiently. Performance efficiency was essential to ensure that the log analysis process did not negatively impact the overall system performance.
- CAPE Groep expressed a preference for the solution to be built with technologies already applied in their IT landscape, therefore reducing the need for new major investments and training employees.
- The new dashboard should provide a comprehensive overview of the metrics and information related to the application's health status while also supporting a landscape overview.

2.2 Stakeholders

The key stakeholders related to this project include the Support team lead, the CSP product owner, and various consultants who utilize CSP. The Support team lead was the company-assigned supervisor for the project. This role involved participation in regularly scheduled progress meetings and feedback sessions, and overall guidance. The CSP product owner was responsible for overseeing the development and enhancements of the CSP modules. The product owner was consistently available to guide the project, approve key decisions, provide suggestions, and ensure alignment with the CSP goals and purpose. Finally, various consultants were contacted during the project. To provide valuable input for understanding the broader use cases and integration requirements of the system. Furthermore, they provided direct feedback on the layout and functions of the Horus dashboard. The consultants were intermittently available but participated in focused interviews and feedback sessions.

3 The Approach

The approach applied in this project consisted of a structured process aimed at addressing the identified challenges and meeting the set objectives. The methodology was primarily iterative and incremental, leveraging principles from Agile development to ensure flexibility and responsiveness to evolving requirements and potential solutions. Additionally, a user-centred design philosophy was adopted, focusing on enhancing the user experience and addressing the specific pain points identified during stakeholder interviews. This approach facilitated continuous improvement through iterative cycles of development, feedback, and refinement ensuring that the solution remained aligned with user needs and organizational goals.

3.1 Project Steps

The first step of the project was an analysis and review of the current observability infrastructure at CAPE Groep as well as the internal workings and architecture of the CSP system. In this step, we also performed stakeholder interviews to gather detailed requirements and gain insights into the pain points of the current implementations within CSP. We focused on the support team and internal consultants as they are the main actors who interact with both the CSP system and the observability infrastructure.

After that, we performed a literature review on both Elasticsearch and other existing state-of-the-art Machine-Learning techniques for log analysis. Based on the results of this review, further investigation and research were conducted to identify the benefits of implementing the Elastic Common Schema (ECS), which defines a common set of fields to be used when storing event data, such as logs [10], and capturing the requirements for this.

The next step was the development of a proof-of-concept to explore the feasibility of using Elasticsearch for log categorization and analysis given the determined requirements. This involved setting up a test environment, configuring Elasticsearch, and setting up and validating log parsing and categorization functionalities.

After validating the quality and feasibility of the proposed solution, the new log categorization setup was integrated with CSP, ensuring compatibility and minimal disruption to ongoing operations. Furthermore, various dashboards were developed leveraging Grafana's visualisation capabilities on the newly available data and insights. Next, feedback was collected from the stakeholders on the proof-of-concept and initial implementation, identifying areas for improvement.

Due to the large scope and limited time, a decision was made to focus on showing the feasibility and quality of the solution design rather than fully implementing it and deploying it to the production environment. We also developed a migration and implementation plan that describes various migration strategies and their associated benefits and downsides.

Finally, the Horus dashboard was also interactively developed. Design ideas and decisions were continuously discussed with both the CSP product owner and consultants to ensure requirements satisfaction and a user layout that provides a streamlined user experience. After the validation, the first version of this dashboard has been deployed to the production environment and is currently being used by the staff, confirming the success of the project.

3.2 Solution Design Requirements

Requirements were gathered from a comprehensive analysis of CSP's current challenges, the capabilities of Elasticsearch, and the business processes supported by the current log collection and aggregation infrastructure. Following the CSP analysis, and a discussion with the product owner, the main requirements and objectives of this solution design have been:

- *Improved log categorization (RQ1):* the proposed solution should improve the ability to analyse individual log messages and combine them into coherent categories, ultimately improving the accuracy and relevance of the generated health check reports. This should support CAPE Groep's analysis of common issues and trends across their IT landscape.
- *Enhanced anomaly detection (RQ2):* building upon the enhanced log analysis and categorization, the solution should provide improved automated anomaly detection capabilities, preferably with customised alerting options.
- *Insightful dashboarding and reporting (RQ3):* by providing dynamic insights into top recurring log entries and operational anomalies, the dashboard should enable proactive management and optimization of CAPE Groep's IT operations. Furthermore, it should replace the current implementation for health check report generation.

3.3 Technical Requirements

Apart from the solution design requirements, the technical foundation of the proposed solution should also adhere to the following constraints, amongst others:

- *Scalability and performance:* the solution should scale efficiently with CAPE Groep's growth and be able to handle the increasing volume and velocity of log data.
- *Integration compatibility:* the solution is seamlessly integrated with the existing CSP and CAPE Groep's observability infrastructure, requiring minimal changes to the current operational workflows.
- *Data ingestion and processing:* the solution should support log data ingestion from at least Mendix applications. Furthermore, the log ingestion and processing is preferred to be a single solution to ensure the overall observability architecture does not become too complex.
- *API integrations:* the solution has to offer API endpoints to facilitate integration with both CSP and the other applications in CAPE Groep's IT landscape, allowing for automated retrieval and transmission of logs, alerts, and reports.
- *Security:* all log-related data should be handled in a both fast and secure manner, ensuring that all data and information within the solution adhere to relevant security standards and privacy regulations while minimizing the performance overhead.

This solution design should set the foundation for a robust observability framework that leverages advanced data processing and analysis techniques to enhance operational intelligence and efficiency.

4 The Results

This section presents the findings from our study on enhancing log management and real-time application health monitoring. The results encompass three key areas: the insights gathered from our literature review on Machine Learning techniques for log analysis, the capabilities of Elasticsearch in our context, and the detailed design of the proposed solution. Together, these findings offer a robust framework for improving log categorization, anomaly detection, and real-time health reporting.

4.1 Machine Learning in Log Analysis

In the ever-evolving landscape of computing, the volume and complexity of logs generated by systems and applications have escalated dramatically due to the scale of distributed systems [1]. This section delves into various state-of-the-art methodologies currently found in the literature on log analysis, leveraging machine learning and advanced computational techniques to extract meaningful insights from vast datasets of log entries. Furthermore, at the end of the chapter, a discussion on whether these methodologies are suitable for the current problem is presented.

The analysis of logs, especially in large-scale IT infrastructures, has transitioned from simple pattern matching to more complex machine learning models that predict, classify, and help in the proactive maintenance of systems [1]. The problem with the Log-based Anomaly Detection (LAD) problem consists of detecting anomalies from execution logs that record both abnormal and normal system behaviour [1]. In the current literature, there are many different streams of ideas towards optimizing log anomaly detection such as using Natural Language Processing [2,17,31], Word2Vec [18,28,29] and Deep Learning [21,31,34]

Natural Language Processing (NLP), techniques are increasingly utilized in the analysis of log data to automate error handling, pattern recognition, and predictive maintenance within complex systems [2,17]. The integration of NLP with log analysis leverages the textual nature of log data, applying various linguistic models to interpret, categorize, and analyze data in a way that mimics human reading and comprehension [2]. This enables the extraction of valuable information from log files as if they were regular text documents. Leveraging modern NLP techniques to analyze the grammatical structure and context of log events, features and patterns can be extracted and then processed by standard machine learning algorithms for anomaly detection [2].

Furthermore, using NLP techniques makes log mining for anomaly detection more efficient, automated, and scalable overall reducing the need for manual intervention in log analysis processes. One of these modern NLP techniques is word embedding, specifically Google's Word2Vec algorithm [22], this algorithm can be applied to map words in log files to high-dimensional vector representations. These representations can then be used as a feature space for training classifies to detect anomalies in log data [28,29].

Word2Vec, as stated previously Word2Vec techniques provide powerful tools for feature extraction from text data, which is instrumental in analyzing and interpreting large volumes of logs. Developed by Tomas Mikolov and his team at Google, Word2Vec models capture semantic relationships between words by learning to predict a word from its neighbours in a sentence, or vice versa [22]. It employs a shallow neural network architecture with one of two model frameworks: Continuous Bag of Words (CBOW) or Skip-Gram [22]. Both of these models use a similar approach, however they differ in the direction of the prediction objective. CBOW predicts a word based on its context words and Skip-Gram predicts context words from a target word [21].

The paper by Wang et al. [29] introduce LogUAD, a Word2Vec-based log unsupervised anomaly detection method designed to address challenges in analyzing system logs in large-scale distributed systems. The authors discuss the challenges in analyzing logs in large-scale distributed systems due to log instability, the increasing volume of logs, computational costs and lack of labelled data for supervised methods [29]. LogUAD is proposed as a solution to these challenges, showing promising results when compared to existing methods [29]. Another example is that of the Log2Vec framework presented in [21]. This framework extends the traditional Word2Vec model by incorporating domain-specific semantics that significantly enhances the effectiveness of log analysis [29]. This is done by embedding the out-of-vocabulary (OOV)[4] words at runtime and extracting semantic information from the logs, which is crucial for tasks such as anomaly detection and system monitoring [4].

Although all of these start-of-art methods and machine learning models look very promising, there is a major downside, as most of these are not fully developed and tested in practice. Most have been tested against commonly used Log datasets for research and comparisons, however, most of the models have not been implemented in a real-life scenario. Furthermore, most of the papers discussed do not provide the model or steps for recreation, therefore the time needed to fully develop and test a setup leveraging these advanced machine learning concepts will not be feasible in the limited time available for the assignment.

4.2 Elasticsearch Capabilities for the Project

Elasticsearch is a widely used open-source, highly scalable, and distributed real-time RESTful search and analytics engine designed for horizontal scalability, reliability, and easy management. One of the most common use cases for Elasticsearch is for logging [30], which is also used for monitoring applications in real-time and analyzing large datasets on the fly [32]. This is because Elasticsearch leverages the robust, full-text search capabilities of Apache Lucene [3], a popular search engine Java library, making it an adequate choice for applications requiring complex search features across large volumes of data. Lucene indexes a document through inverted index [3], which is a data structure that tracks which documents contain certain values, allowing efficient document search [12].

Elasticsearch Text Categorisation is a built-in component that uses machine learning (ML) for categorizing text documents or sentences into predefined categories. It examines the content and meaning of the text and then assigns the most suitable label through text labelling. In particular, the Elasticsearch categorization anomaly detection ML job aims at automatically categorizing similar text values together [8]. This feature enables the analysis of large volumes of machine-written text like log messages, being a suitable candidate for our scenario. The model is trained on the incoming log data and learns the normal values and patterns of a category over time. This allows the detection of anomalous behaviour based on the number of occurrences or based on the rarity of a message. The categorization job uses an unsupervised ML model, so it does not require predetermined categories or prelabeled training data. Instead, it automatically identifies patterns and similarities in the provided log data. The main

[4] Out-of-vocabulary (OOV) words refer to words that appear in a text but were not included in the training set vocabulary when a language model or a word embedding system, like Word2Vec, was initially trained.

downside of the ML job is that it only returns anomalies. Although it categorizes log messages in a desired manner, it will not return all categories, only the anomalous ones. This is useful for anomaly detection, however, it is insufficient given the fact that we also want to provide insight to the end users into, for example, the top 10 most occurring errors of a specific period.

Categorize Text Search Function is another built-in feature, introduced in Elasticsearch version 7.16, for text aggregation categorization [6]. This is a multi-bucket aggregation that groups semi-structured text into distinct categories based on textual similarity [9]. Similar to the anomaly detection job this process involves analyzing the text with a tokenizer, which breaks down the text into tokens. Once the text is analyzed, the tokens are clustered together with a modified version of the DRAIN algorithm [14]. The DRAIN algorithm is an online log parsing method that can parse logs in a streaming and timely manner. To accelerate the parsing process, DRAIN builds a token tree and considers earlier tokens as more important. Elastic has modified the algorithm slightly to allow for earlier merging of tokens in the provided text when building categories [27]. The difference between this function and the ML job is that this is done once when the search request is sent to Elasticsearch. Therefore it is not well suited to use for constant anomaly detection, however, this feature is particularly useful for creating overviews of top log messages occurring in applications, allowing system administrators to quickly identify and address frequent or critical issues.

Elastic Common Standard (ECS) is an open-source specification published and maintained by Elastic [10], which defines a set of common fields to be used when storing event data in Elasticsearch, such as logs and metrics. Transitioning current Elastic indices to adhere to ECS can bring significant benefits to the current log monitoring and analysis setup [4,33]. However, like any significant system update, this transition also comes with potential downsides and costs [33]. Among the main benefits, we highlight that log data and its formats are one of the most important parts of a system observability or analysis input setup [4]. However, they often offer many possibilities of different formats, often custom-defined, which makes interpreting the fields a big challenge. This is a common challenge associated with using data from multiple heterogeneous data sources [16], and a common language for all log events can address this problem [4].

Implications. Although Elasticsearch does not offer one built-in solution that satisfies all of our requirements, it does offer solutions that can be combined with each other to realise the desired situation. In order to leverage the full functionality and benefits of Elasticsearch we further developed the current logging infrastructure to a more mature state by not only addressing the analytical processes but also the overall data format and structure. In a landscape with many different applications and systems, the struggle and need for interoperability and scalability is ever-increasing [11]. A standardized logging schema like

ECS makes it easier to manage and scale the logging infrastructure, enabling seamless communication among different systems [33]. Establishing and documenting a single vocabulary to describe the various field names of data reduces the chance for ambiguity and confusion. This also directly improves data analysis by making analysis and querying data more straightforward [16]. The same principle applies to alerting, standardizing streamlines the creation of alerting rules because the structure and meaning of logs are predictable and consistent. Combined these result in a reduced learning curve, minimized chances of errors, more accurate alerts, and faster incident response times.

Apart from general standardisation benefits, ECS has a few specific benefits in comparison to other standards. First of all, ECS is not only a standard for log formats. Implementing ECS simplifies the analysis of disparate data sources, supporting a wide range of use cases, including application performance, security, and other metrics from all types of sources [10]. Defining a common set of fields and objects to ingest data into Elasticsearch enables cross-source analysis of diverse data. As a result, cross-source correlations become implicit with every search, but if necessary you can still filter down to specific data sources.

Secondly, implementing ECS unlocks and unifies all modes of analysis currently available in the Elastic Stack. This includes search, drill-down and pivoting, data visualization, machine learning-based anomaly detection, and alerting [23]. Alongside this, it provides the ability to easily adopt analytics content directly from other parties that use ECS, whether Elastic, a partner, or an open-source project within the environment without modifications. Furthermore, fully adopting ECS allows users to search with the power of both structured and unstructured query parameters [10]. Overall, by implementing ECS we leverage the full power of both the ever-growing Elastic stack and all other projects built upon this community-driven standard.

Nevertheless, we also have to be aware that adopting ECS involves certain downsides, potential pitfalls and costs that are both general to any system's migration and ECS. First of all, transitioning to ECS from the current custom schema can be a resource-intensive process, requiring development effort and adjustments to existing data pipelines and log transmitting modules. Next to this, changing the current naming conventions necessitates investment in both training and documentation updates. Additionally, during the migration process, CAPE Groep and its customers might face temporary reductions in logging and monitoring efficiency, which could (in)directly affect operational capabilities.

Furthermore, as always with the implementation of standards there is the risk of over-standardization, where the schema might not support all custom use cases without significant customization, potentially leading to data being fitted into unsuitable fields or losing granularity in data [11]. ECS allows for customisation, and while this does offer flexibility it could undermine some of the benefits of adopting a standardized schema by introducing inconsistencies and complicating data analysis. Furthermore, relying heavily on ECS's new releases means that regular updates to logging practices are required to align with the new versions of the schema, resulting in ongoing maintenance costs and efforts.

Finally, there is also a risk for the potential of increased storage costs, as ECS encourages the inclusion of extensive contextual information alongside each event, which could lead to larger indices in Elasticsearch. Without proper monitoring and management of these indices to optimize performance and size it could increase costs. However, given that the number of stored fields for the current format is 9 fields and compliance with ECS requires 10 fields the risk should be minimal.

Overall, the choice to fully adopt ECS in the logging setup is not merely a technical upgrade but also a strategic move towards a more integrated, scalable, and efficient observability architecture. Apart from optimizing the current process, it paves the way for future innovations in the overall monitoring and analysis capabilities.

Grafana is an open-source platform renowned for its powerful capabilities in querying, visualizing, alerting, and exploring metrics, logs, and traces, regardless of where they are stored [13]. It serves as a valuable tool for creating insightful graphs and visualizations from time-series data, enhancing the observability and operational intelligence of IT environments. Grafana's flexible plugin framework supports integration with various data sources, making it a versatile choice for data analytics [15].

Next to this, in a log observability infrastructure, Grafana can be seamlessly integrated with Elasticsearch to enhance monitoring and analysis capabilities. Elasticsearch efficiently handles storage and querying of large volumes of log data, while Grafana provides the user interface to visualize and explore this data. Together, they offer a comprehensive solution for monitoring applications. Furthermore, in comparison with Elastic's visualisation component, Kibana, it offers more suitable pricing models for CAPE Groep's needs. Due to these reasons, CAPE Groep has opted to use Grafana for all its time-based data visualization needs.

4.3 Proposed Architecture of Observability Infrastructure

Figure 2 shows an excerpt of the high-level architectural overview of the observability infrastructure, showing only the relevant components to ensure readability and understanding. As we agreed before, the direct connection between Mendix applications and CSP made little sense given the structure of the rest of the setup. This connection represented the daily collection of log files for aggregation, categorization and finally reporting. Furthermore, the current setup already focused on leveraging Elastic as a central processing and storage environment. Therefore it was logical to focus on further centralizing this flow of data. The changes in the architecture are shown using a red cross for the removal of the integration and a green plus for the addition of categorised log anomaly detection.

Reduced Complexity and Resource Requirements. Figure 2 shows that CSP relied on a direct integration, with nightly API calls to Mendix for log collection, which are inefficient and should be removed as we discussed in Sect. 1. The new architectural scenario removes the connection between the Mendix applications and CSP, as indicated in 2, simplifying the overall monitoring infrastructure. By centralizing log data, CSP makes multiple direct integrations unnecessary reducing the complexity of the application. Moreover, with centralization computational tasks previously handled within CSP can be removed, thereby freeing up resources that can be redirected to improve application performance, and user experience, and enable future innovations.

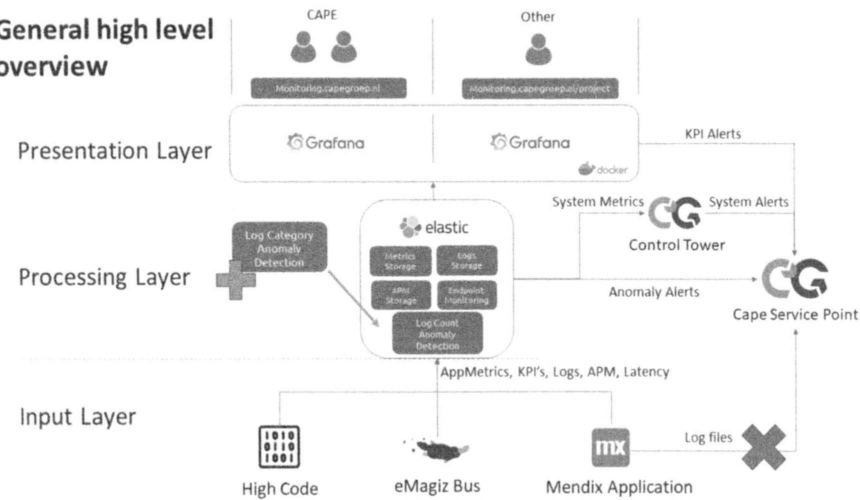

Fig. 2. Changes to the observability infrastructure architectural high-level overview

Centralisation of Log and Metrics Data. The proposed solution also centralises all log and metrics data in Elasticsearch. This approach offers several advantages, such as simplified data management and improved correlation capabilities. By consolidating all logs and metrics into a single system, CAPE Groep can manage its observability data more effectively, reducing the complexity and overhead associated with handling multiple data sources, providing performance and scalability. Furthermore, storing data related to different components of applications allows for cross-functional and domain analysis by allowing different types of data from various sources to be correlated and analysed together. This is particularly useful for gaining comprehensive insights across various operational domains within CAPE Groep, and has the potential to even be further extended in the future, for example with security data.

Standardisation to ECS. To fully leverage the benefits of centralizing logs, metrics, and other data, the data format should be standardised inside the company. Adopting ECS will facilitate this by providing a consistent framework for data formatting across all domains. Leveraging this standardisation, administrators and users can perform searches, analyses, and correlations across diverse data sets. Furthermore, standardizing ensures that as new types of data are incorporated into the system, which in turn can be easily integrated and analysed without significant modifications to the existing infrastructure.

Grafana. In addition to changes to Elasticsearch, we integrated advanced visualization capabilities in Grafana to further improve CAPE Groep's observability infrastructure. Grafana has been employed to effectively visualize the results from the newly implemented log categorization and analysis processes, facilitating an intuitive and actionable display of data for operational monitoring and decision-making.

Grafana has been used to display the categorized logs using dynamic visual components such as bar charts, pie charts, and tables. These visualisations show the distribution of log categories over time, highlighting the frequency and trends of various log types, including errors and warnings. This allows system administrators and support personnel to quickly identify and focus on the most critical issues that require attention. Figure 3 shows an example of a dashboard that we created to demonstrate these capabilities.

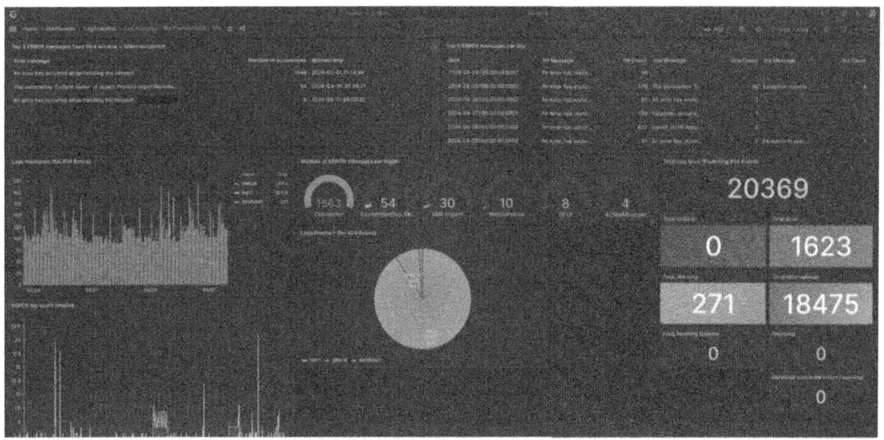

Fig. 3. A Dashboard leveraging the capabilities offered by the new setup

In addition, Grafana's real-time monitoring capabilities can now leveraged to offer up-to-the-minute insights into the application's health. The dashboards can be configured to receive live data feeds from Elasticsearch, ensuring that the displayed information is always up-to-date, which is critical for enabling real-time monitoring and rapid response to emerging issues. Furthermore, Grafana can now be set up to send alerts based on user-specified triggers identified through the log analysis. For example, if the frequency of a particular error category exceeds a predefined threshold, Grafana can trigger an alert to notify the relevant teams. These alerts can be customised to match the severity and nature of the issues, ensuring appropriate prioritisation and response.

CAPE Service Point. In this project, we also modified the CSP Mendix model. In the new scenario, the workflow is simplified by reducing the dependency on multiple processes and storage within CSP. Leverage the categorization capabilities of Elasticsearch instead. These changes resulted in the development of a new microflow that handles the interaction with Elasticsearch and subsequently retrieves the data for the generation of health checks. This single streamlined microflow replaces the entire log collection, aggregation, and log storage logic within CSP. The microflow directly queries Elasticsearch instead of calling the Mendix API for logs. The response from Elasticsearch includes logs that are already categorized and ranked based on frequency and severity. These categorised and ranked logs are used to automatically compile improved health check reports. These reports are more accurate, timely, and comprehensive than the current implementation.

4.4 Horus Dashboard

In addition to the improvements to the observability infrastructure, we also created an overview page to monitor application health as a dashboard, which we called Horus. This dashboard is made up of two layers of information, namely basic panels and advanced panels. The general overview displays the basic panels and provides information related to four aspects of application health. These panels provide the most high-level information on the status of the application selected in the dashboard. As shown in Fig. 4.

This overview shows the status of all the tickets, alerts and log metrics related to the two selected applications. For each of these panels, we present the most high-level information, such as the number of open Priority 1 tickets or critical alerts. Additionally, for each piece of information, we include a trend that shows the difference between the currently selected time window (seven days in the example) and the same window before that. Furthermore, based on these trends different traffic lights indicate the severity of the trend accordingly with the colours green, orange, or red. The severity thresholds can be personalised for each end user, providing users with an easy and clear overview of the current IT landscape health status. If the user wants to know more details about one of the panels, they can click on them, and the advanced panels are opened.

Figure 5 shows that these panels include more detailed information on each category of information. For tickets and alerts, this consists of graphs showing the distribution of the count presented in the basic overview. Furthermore, a time series chart shows how tickets and alerts progress over time. Both of these

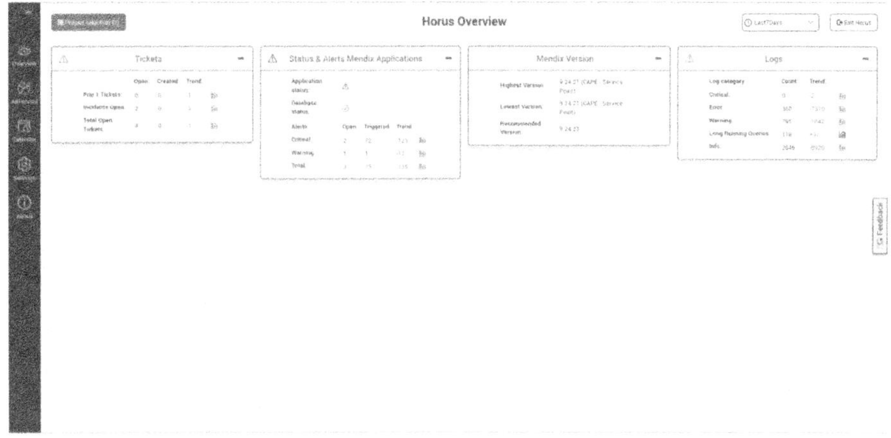

Fig. 4. The basic overview panels of Horus

charts were implemented using the Plotly JavaScript Open Source Graphing Library [25], which also means that they are interactive, so clicking them opens overview pages for the selected data point.

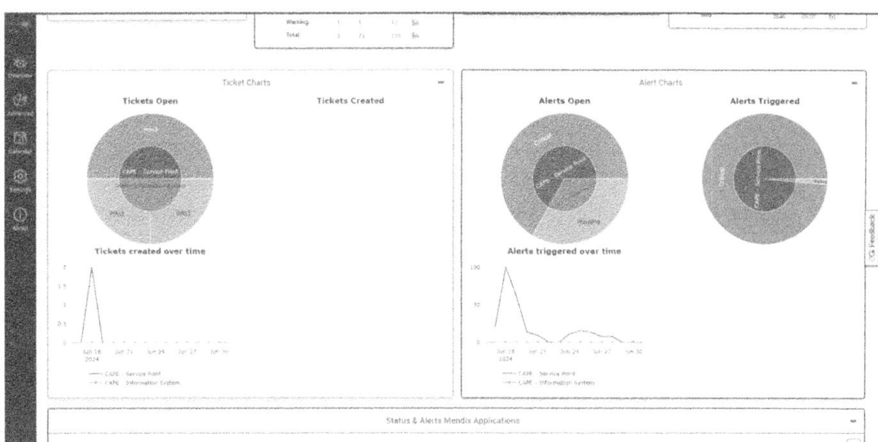

Fig. 5. The advanced panels for tickets and alerts of Horus

For example, if a user clicks on a certain alert level of an application, it opens an overview of those alerts for that specific application in the time window, so that users do not have to manually look for the tickets or alerts when needed.

Next to this, the user can click on the status & alerts and the logs basic overview panel to open the two advanced panels shown in Fig. 6. This provides an overview of the status of each component of the selected applications. Furthermore, the logs advanced panel shows a Grafana embedded panel, implemented with IFrame, which is a log histogram that displays the distribution of different error severities over time. The screenshots in Fig. 6 should give some insights into the functionality offered by Horus.

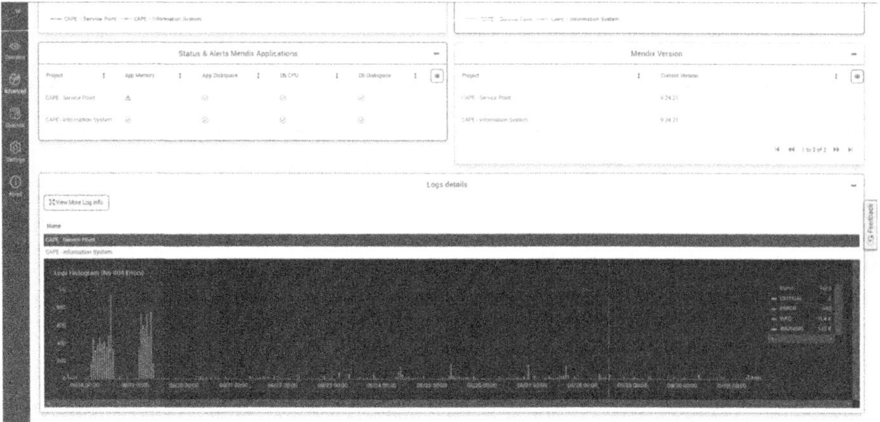

Fig. 6. The advanced panels for health status and logs of Horus

4.5 Solution Implementation Plan

The implementation plan for any IT system, particularly business-critical solutions like the one we proposed, involves careful consideration of various deployment strategies to ensure effectiveness and minimize disruption to ongoing operations. Before deciding on an implementation strategy, we evaluated each strategy based on specific organizational needs, risk assessments, and the critical nature of the systems involved. The following are common strategies were considered for implementing the proposed solution:

- *Big Bang Rollout* [19,24]*:* This strategy consists of a complete and simultaneous transition from the old system to the new system across the entire organisation at a specific point in time. While this can be the fastest method to implement, it is also the riskiest, as it leaves little room for error and adjustment.
- *Phased Rollout* [19,24]*:* This strategy consists of implementing the new system in stages over a specific period. In each phase, the solution is rolled out to a different segment of the end users. This can be done based on application, team, customer or even department. This strategy reduces the risk because it allows lessons learned in earlier phases to be applied to later ones.
- *Parallel Adoption* [19]*:* In this strategy, both the old and new systems run simultaneously for a significant period of time. This strategy is less risky

because it allows users to transition gradually and ensures that the organisation can revert to the old system if significant issues arise in the new system. In this strategy, it is critical to ensure backwards compatibility.

- *Pilot Implementation* [24]*:* This consists of rolling out the new system to a small controlled group within the organisation before a full-scale implementation. This strategy can help uncover potential issues with the new system while limiting the impact on the broader organization.

For the deployment of our solution, we recommend a combination of the aforementioned strategies. This consists of creating a pilot implementation after which a phased rollout will begin, the exact segmentation of the phases can be determined at a later point, however, for this plan the choice is made to do this per application. Following the phased rollout, a transition period in which a parallel adoption takes place. During this period, both the old and new ways should run in parallel, ensuring that business-critical processes are not hindered and end users experience a smooth transition. Figure 7 shows that the implementation process iterates between rolling out the solution for new phases and running parallel. After successfully upgrading all the applications the process transitions to the last step namely the Full Rollout. In this step, all the transitions are double-checked to ensure they are set up properly before the old indices and field names are removed from Elastic.

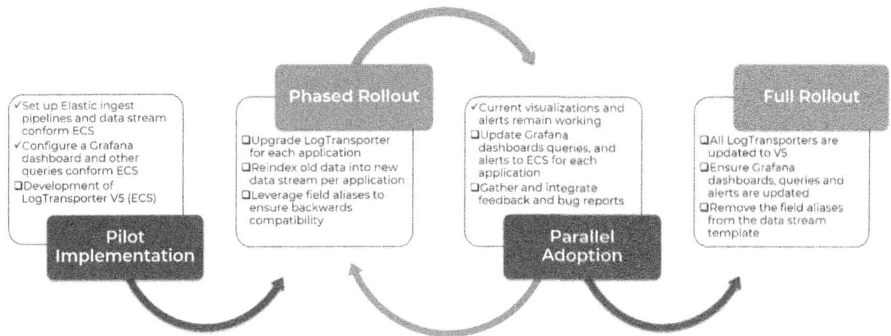

Fig. 7. A visualisation of the solution implementation plan

4.6 Achievements

Overall, this project at CAPE Groep has culminated in an enhancement of CSP and CAPE Groep's observability infrastructure, through integration of advanced Elasticsearch functionalities and use of Grafana and the custom Horus dashboard for visualisation. The primary objective of the project was to automate or enhance one of the processes within CSP. After initial investigation, interviews, and research the decision was made to focus on addressing the inefficiencies in

CSP's existing log management and health check processes. By leveraging Elasticsearch's machine learning features for log categorization and anomaly detection, along with its powerful text categorisation and aggregation functions, we significantly automated and streamlined CSP's approach to log analysis. Hereby satisfying RQ1 and RQ2. Furthermore, automated processes have significantly reduced the time and support required to manage logs and generate reports. This has not only reduced errors-prone manual labour previously required, but also increased the accuracy and timeliness of the health check reports provided to customers, satisfying RQ3.

Improved Health Check Reports. By leveraging Elasticsearch's categorization capabilities, CSP can improve the way health checks are conducted. Currently, health checks are generated through a resource-intensive process that combines log entries, which often requires manual intervention. This method is not only inefficient but also prone to errors, affecting the reliability and validity of the reports provided to customers. With the proposed solution, logs are automatically categorized and analyzed using Elasticsearch's machine learning capabilities or search categorization functionality, which can detect anomalies and categorize text in real-time. This process not only speeds up data processing but also increases the accuracy of health checks by ensuring that all data is considered and appropriately categorized. We compared the old and new implementation and as is shown in Fig. 8, multiple types of errors were previously not identified and shown in the report. This can be verified by comparing Fig. 8 to Fig. 1, which displays the results of the old implementation for the same application. A satisfied consultant pointed out that "In the past, almost all reports were missing data or contained inaccurate information, I can already tell this is greatly improved". Overall, by eliminating the need for nightly log collection and aggregation within CSP, we significantly reduce the computational load on its servers. Furthermore, as the logs are processed and categorized at real-time by Elasticsearch, the health check reports generated are more current and reflect better the actual system status. The streamlined CSP microflow allows for a more efficient process flow, reducing the steps involved in generating reports and thereby decreasing the potential for errors and reducing the overall CSP complexity. All of this combined results in a more efficient, accurate, scalable, and reliable observability infrastructure.

Improved Service Quality. The shift to an automated, Elasticsearch-powered setup for log analysis and health checks directly translated to improved service quality for CSP's customers. Automated categorisation and anomaly detection provide CSP with the ability to quickly identify and address issues before they impact service delivery. Furthermore, the enhanced data analysis capabilities ensure that health reports are both accurate and timely, fostering trust and reliability among clients. Next to this, the further development of the Horus dashboard has improved the visualization landscape at CSP, further satisfying RQ3. Customized dashboards now provide more and improved dynamic and

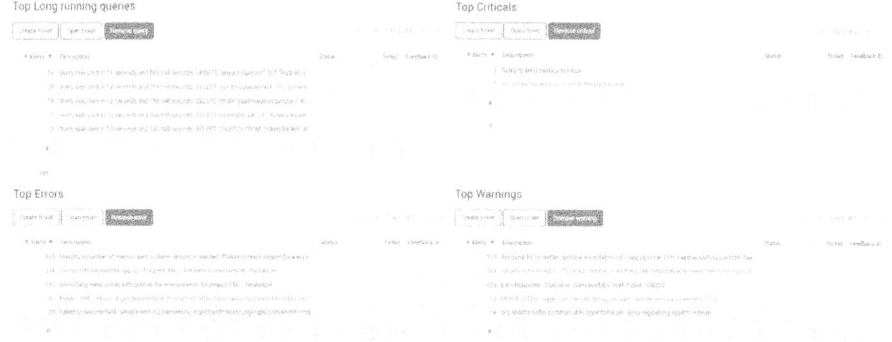

Fig. 8. The log data reported by leveraging the proposed solution

real-time insights into the application's health, allowing for rapid response to emerging issues. This enhancement has not only improved internal operational efficiency but has also boosted the quality of service CSP provides to its clients, enhancing customer satisfaction and trust.

More generally, the architectural redesign using Elasticsearch as the backbone for CAPE Groep's observability infrastructure presents a robust solution that reduces architectural complexity, decreases resource consumption, and significantly improves reliability and accuracy of operational health checks. This strategic overhaul not only streamlines internal processes but also enhances quality of service delivered to customers. By effectively leveraging modern technologies, such as Elasticsearch and Grafana, CSP has not only addressed some of its immediate operational challenges but also laid a foundation for continuous improvement and innovation. As CSP continues to grow and evolve, the flexibility and scalability provided by these enhancements are expected to play a crucial role in its ability to meet future challenges and capitalize on new opportunities.

5 Reflection

5.1 Limitations

Given that the project was mainly conducted by a student during an internship of only 14 weeks, there is a potential for sub-optimal solutions and missed opportunities. Many of the technologies and concepts explored during this project were new for the student, and given the fairly limited time frame concessions had to be made in terms of time spent researching possible solutions. This could have resulted in a sub-optimal solution design, however, given the produced benefits and usage of industry-wide adopted technologies this should be fairly limited. Furthermore, the initial implementation prioritised functionality over performance optimization. As a result, some processes can possibly be made more efficient. Finally, given that the research focused on the practical implications of the solution, a systematic or methodological evaluation of the benefits is not preferred. However, the results have been validated with qualitative feedback from management and consultants involved with the process.

5.2 Future Directions

While the project has achieved substantial improvements, there are several areas where future work could further enhance CAPE Groep's and CSP's capabilities. First of all, integrating non-Mendix applications and other additional data sources. The current setup is tested for Mendix applications, but there are many other types of applications within CAPE Groep's IT portfolio. Expanding the types and sources of data integrated into the Elasticsearch framework could provide more comprehensive insights across other operational areas. Furthermore, the current setup lays the foundation for enhanced security features by integrating access logs into Elasticsearch. Integrating advanced security analytics into the observability infrastructure could help in better detecting and mitigating potential security threats. Next to this, performance benchmarking and optimization efforts can be made to ensure that the system remains responsive and scalable as data volumes grow. Finally, there is the opportunity for advanced predictive analytics. More complex machine learning models could predict potential system failures before they occur, further enhancing proactive monitoring.

6 Evidence

The case report was authored through a combination of primary practitioner involvement, stakeholder interviews, literature review, and practical implementation. The main author was a practitioner involved in the project as an intern. One of the co-authors is directly associated with CAPE Groep and provided firsthand insights and guidance on report writing. Interviews and regular feedback sessions with key stakeholders, such as the Support team lead and CSP product owner, were conducted to gather requirements and validate findings. A review of relevant academic literature and technical documentation from Elastic and Grafana informed the project's methodologies and solutions. Practical implementation and testing within CAPE Groep's infrastructure were employed to ensure the feasibility and effectiveness of the proposed solutions. This comprehensive approach, combining direct practitioner input, research, and iterative development, ensured the accuracy and relevance of the project and its report.

7 Conclusion

To conclude, the project to enhance CSP's log analysis capabilities was a significant step forward to improve the system's functionality and user experience. While several challenges were faced and some limitations were identified, the integration of Elasticsearch's Machine Learning capabilities and Grafana's visualization tools, along with the Horus dashboard, streamlined operations, reduced manual intervention and provided comprehensive real-time insights into application health. The improved log categorization supported CAPE Groep's analysis of common issues, enhancing the accuracy of health check reports. Enhanced automated anomaly detection and customisable alerts ensured proactive issue identification, improving system reliability. The Horus dashboard offered dynamic insights into recurring log entries and operational anomalies, optimizing IT operations. This strategic overhaul reduced architectural complexity, decreased resource consumption, and significantly enhanced operational health checks, ultimately boosting service quality and customer satisfaction. Seamlessly integrating with CSP and CAPE Groep's infrastructure, the proposal provides a solid solution with a foundation for future improvements. By addressing the identified omissions and continuing to refine the solution, CAPE Groep can further enhance CSP, delivering even greater value to its users and customers.

References

1. Ali, S., Boufaied, C., Bianculli, D., Branco, P., Briand, L.C., Aschbacher, N.: An empirical study on log-based anomaly detection using machine learning. ArXiv abs/2307.16714 (2023). https://api.semanticscholar.org/CorpusID:260334470
2. Bertero, C., Roy, M., Sauvanaud, C., Tredan, G.: Experience report: log mining using natural language processing and application to anomaly detection. In: 2017 IEEE 28th International Symposium on Software Reliability Engineering (ISSRE), pp. 351–360 (2017). https://doi.org/10.1109/ISSRE.2017.43
3. Białecki, A., Muir, R., Ingersoll, G.: Apache Lucene 4 (2012)
4. Cândido, J., Aniche, M., van Deursen, A.: Log-based software monitoring: a systematic mapping study. PeerJ Comput. Sci. **7**, e489 (2021). https://doi.org/10.7717/peerj-cs.489
5. CAPE Groep: Mendix Marketplace - LogTransporter (2024). https://marketplace.mendix.com/link/component/218262
6. Courcy, D.: Elastic 7.16: Streamlined data integrations drive results that matter (2021). https://www.elastic.co/blog/whats-new-elastic-7-16-0
7. Du, S., Cao, J.: Behavioral anomaly detection approach based on log monitoring. In: 2015 International Conference on Behavioral, Economic and Socio-cultural Computing (BESC), pp. 188–194 (2015). https://doi.org/10.1109/BESC.2015.7365981
8. Elastic: Anomaly detection job types. https://www.elastic.co/guide/en/machine-learning/current/ml-anomaly-detection-job-types.html
9. Elastic: Categorize text aggregation. https://www.elastic.co/guide/en/elasticsearch/reference/current/search-aggregations-bucket-categorize-text-aggregation.html
10. Elastic: Elastic Common Schema. https://www.elastic.co/elasticsearch/common-schema
11. Folmer, E., Verhoosel, J.: State of the art on semantic is standardization, interoperability & quality. J. Biomech. (2011)
12. Gormley, C., Tong, Z.: Elasticsearch the Definitive Guide: A Distributed Real-Time Search and Analytics Engine. O'Reilly Media, 1 edn. (2015)

13. Grafana Labs: About Grafana. https://grafana.com/docs/grafana/latest/introduction/
14. He, P., Zhu, J., Zheng, Z., Lyu, M.R.: Drain: an online log parsing approach with fixed depth tree. In: 2017 IEEE International Conference on Web Services (ICWS), pp. 33–40 (2017). https://doi.org/10.1109/ICWS.2017.13
15. Kozhukh, D.: An easy look at Grafana architecture (2024). https://www.kozhuhds.com/blog/an-easy-look-at-grafana-architecture/
16. Kumar, G., Basri, S., Imam, A.A., Khowaja, S.A., Capretz, L.F., Balogun, A.O.: Data harmonization for heterogeneous datasets: a systematic literature review. Appl. Sci. **11**(17), 8275 (2021). https://doi.org/10.3390/app11178275
17. Layer, L., et al.: Automatic log analysis with NLP for the CMS workflow handling. In: EPJ Web of Conferences, vol. 245, p. 03006 (2020). https://doi.org/10.1051/epjconf/202024503006
18. Le, V., Zhang, H.: Log-based anomaly detection without log parsing. In: 2021 36th IEEE/ACM International Conference on Automated Software Engineering (ASE), pp. 492–504 (2021). https://doi.org/10.1109/ASE51524.2021.9678773
19. Madkan, P.: Empirical study of ERP implementation strategies-filling gaps between the success and failure of ERP implementation process. Int. J. Inf. Comput. Technol. **4**(6), 633–642 (2014)
20. Mendix: Deploy API (2024). https://docs.mendix.com/apidocs-mxsdk/apidocs/deploy-api/
21. Meng, W., et al.: A semantic-aware representation framework for online log analysis, pp. 1–7 (2020). https://doi.org/10.1109/ICCCN49398.2020.9209707
22. Mikolov, T., Sutskever, I., Chen, K., Corrado, G.S., Dean, J.: Distributed representations of words and phrases and their compositionality. In: Advances in Neural Information Processing Systems, vol. 26 (2013)
23. Mitra, M., Sy, D.: The rise of elastic stack (2016). https://doi.org/10.13140/RG.2.2.17596.03203
24. Münch, J., Armbrust, O., Kowalczyk, M., Soto, M.: Prescriptive Process Models. In: Münch, J., Armbrust, O., Kowalczyk, M., Soto, M. (eds.) Software Process Definition and Management, pp. 19–77. Springer, Heidelberg (2012). https://doi.org/10.1007/978-3-642-24291-5_2
25. Plotly: Plotly JavaScript Open Source Graphing Library. https://plotly.com/javascript/
26. Srivastava, D.: An introduction to data visualization tools and techniques in various domains. Int. J. Comput. Trends Technol. **71**, 125–130 (2023). https://doi.org/10.14445/22312803/IJCTT-V71I4P116 https://doi.org/10.14445/22312803/IJCTT-V71I4P116
27. Trent, B.: Categorize your logs with Elasticsearch categorize_text aggregation (2022). https://www.elastic.co/blog/categorize-your-logs-with-the-new-elasticsearch-categorize-text-search-aggregation
28. Wang, J., et al.: LogEvent2vec: LogEvent-to-vector based anomaly detection for large-scale logs in internet of things. Sens. (Switz.) **20**(9) (2020). https://doi.org/10.3390/s20092451
29. Wang, J., Zhao, C., He, S., Gu, Y., Alfarraj, O., Abugabah, A.: LogUAD: log unsupervised anomaly detection based on word2Vec. Comput. Syst. Sci. Eng. **41**(3), 1207–1222 (2022). https://doi.org/10.32604/csse.2022.022365
30. Wei, Y., Li, M., Xu, B.: Research on Establish an Efficient Log Analysis System with Kafka and Elastic Search. J. Softw. Eng. Appl. **10**(11), 843–853 (2017). https://doi.org/10.4236/jsea.2017.1011047

31. Yu, B., et al.: Deep learning or classical machine learning? An empirical study on log-based anomaly detection. In: Proceedings of the IEEE/ACM 46th International Conference on Software Engineering, ICSE 2024, Association for Computing Machinery, New York (2024). https://doi.org/10.1145/3597503.3623308
32. Zamfir, V.A., Carabas, M., Carabas, C., Tapus, N.: Systems monitoring and big data analysis using the elastic search system. In: Proceedings - 2019 22nd International Conference on Control Systems and Computer Science, CSCS 2019, pp. 188–193. Institute of Electrical and Electronics Engineers Inc. (2019). https://doi.org/10.1109/CSCS.2019.00039
33. Zhao, K., Xia, M.: Forming interoperability through interorganizational systems standards. J. Manag. Inf. Syst. **30**(4), 269–298 (2014). https://doi.org/10.2753/MIS0742-1222300410
34. Zhou, J., Qian, Y., Zou, Q., Liu, P., Xiang, J.: DeepSyslog: deep anomaly detection on syslog using sentence embedding and metadata. IEEE Trans. Inf. Forensics Secur. (2022). https://doi.org/10.1109/TIFS.2022.3201379

Joint CBI–EDOC Tools and Demos Track

A Web-Based Modelling Tool for Object-Centric Business Processes

Lisa Arnold(✉), Marius Breitmayer, and Manfred Reichert

Institute of Databases and Information Systems, Ulm University, James-Franck-Ring 1, 89081 Ulm, Germany
{lisa.arnold,marius.breitmayer,manfred.reichert}@uni-ulm.de

Abstract. Business processes have the potential to enhance efficiency, flexibility, productivity and revenue by, for example, automating. They can automate routine procedures thereby reducing costs of a process. In recent years, a plethora of frameworks have been developed that facilitate the modelling of activity-centric business processes. Nevertheless, there is a paucity of frameworks that concentrate on object-centric or data-driven business processes. Furthermore, the majority of commercially available business process tools provide local applications and only a limited number leveraging the benefits of a web-based environment. This demonstration paper presents the implementation of a web-based modelling environment that implements the object-centric business process management approach: *PHILharmonicFlows*. The implementation is a redesigned and enhanced web-based edition of the original, locally developed prototype. Moreover, the web-based framework incorporates additional features, including sophisticated verification algorithms, measurement metrics for the monitoring component, a more user-friendly graphical user interface (GUI), and functions that enable the modelling of a business process in greater detail than the original prototype, by setting constraints.

Keywords: Business process modelling tool · object-centric BPM · web-based · business process management · graphical user interface

1 Introduction

The advent of web-based technologies eliminated the need for different versions for an individual version for every operating system, removed installation hurdles, outsourced computing power, and required administrators to maintain the framework without inconveniencing end users. Business process modelling tools, such as the workflow management system *Camunda*, have recently taken advantage of these benefits as well [1]. Nevertheless, most of the workflow management systems focus on traditional activity-centric approaches, concentrating on the execution order of their activities. In addition to these traditional approaches, a new paradigm of object-centric business process management has emerged in

M. Kaczmarek-Heß et al. (Eds.): EDOC 2024 Workshops, LNBIP 537, pp. 267–275, 2025.
https://doi.org/10.1007/978-3-031-79059-1_16

recent years, exemplified by the framework *PHILharmonicFlows*, which focuses on business objects and their business data as they exist in real processes [2]. In the object-centric process management paradigm, a business process is described in terms of interacting business objects that correspond to real-world entities. These business objects and their relations are manifested in the *Relational Process Structure* (RPS) [3]. This includes a hierarchical structure derived from the cardinalities specified for object relations. In addition, business attributes can be defined for each business object. The RPS, with its business objects and object attributes, defines the holistic data model of an object-centric business process. At runtime, any number of object instances (restricted by their cardinalities) can be created by the business objects. The runtime behaviour of these business objects is defined in terms of object lifecycles [4]. In contrast to activity-centric processes, object-centric business processes typically exhibit greater flexibility, as the objects within the processes can be processed largely independent of one another [2].

In [5], the implementation of modelling objects with their relations and their lifecycle processes for object-centric business processes is presented. This implementation is constructed as a locally installed software tool utilising a distributed microservice-based software architecture (original framework for short). The web-based framework[1] presented in this paper constitutes a reimplementation of the original framework, which has been extended to include expressions for coordination process constraints [6], easy setting permissions, and sophisticated verification. Furthermore, it incorporates measurement metrics (e.g. weights for *Kalman* filter [7]) for monitoring predictions. The latter minimises complexity for the modeller, thereby facilitating the creation of correct business processes without the necessity for extensive knowledge of the sophisticated object-oriented process paradigm.

In [8], the original framework is extended by a runtime engine which automatically generates user sheets based on the structure of its lifecycle processes. The lifecycle contains states that are linked to each other. Each state can contain any number of steps (except the end state), which represent the input fields in the form sheets. Furthermore, the aforementioned steps are based on the business attributes that have been defined in the business objects within the data model.

The remainder of this paper is structured as follows. Section 2 provides insight into the core functionality offered by the web-based, object-centric business process framework, as well as an explanation of the functionality extensions in comparison to the original framework. Section 3 presents the development of the monitoring tool, including a description of its technical architecture, with an overview of the components, frameworks and libraries employed. Section 4 concludes the paper.

---

[1] A screencast is available on ResearchGate: https://www.researchgate.net/publication/382713623_A_Screencast_for_PHILharmonicFlows_A_web-based_Modelling_Tool_for_object-centric_Business_Processes.

2 Object-Centric Business Processes

The object-centric business process modelling tool is comprised of four distinct components: the data model (RPS and business data), their respective lifecycles, the coordination process(es) and the associated permissions.

Data Model: The data model comprises two key elements: the *Relational Process Structure* (RPS) and the business attributes. Figure 1 depicts a screenshot of the *Data Model* module. The RPS establishes the hierarchy and the relations between the business objects, as well as the cardinalities thereof. The web-based tool has been enhanced to incorporate more a sophisticated approach towards the cardinalities. The original framework only permits one-to-many relations, whereas the web-based tool permits many-to-many relations. Furthermore, it is crucial to emphasise that the placeholders m and n can be constrained by fixed values, both above and below (e.g. *3..5 : 2..n*).

In addition, each business object is characterised by a number of business attributes describing the data associated with that business object. These attributes are defined by a specified data type (i.e. *String*, *Number*, *Boolean*, *Date*, *File*, or *Relation*) and serves as the foundation for the input fields of the auto-generated form fields. Furthermore, the attribute types *String*, *Number*, and *Date* permit the definition of these attributes as list attributes enabling the provision of multiple values within a single attribute. Moreover, the web-based framework is capable of restricting the input of an attribute resulting in a drop-down menu at runtime. If invalid entries are made (e.g. minimum is greater than maximum restriction) corresponding error messages are generated to inform users at runtime. The implementation of a testing procedure for valid input (i.e. semantic and syntactic correctness) serves to prevent the occurrence of deadlocks at runtime. Such deadlocks may be created by invalid attributes and arise with the automatically generated user forms. In the original framework, no mechanism was in place for verifying the attributes.

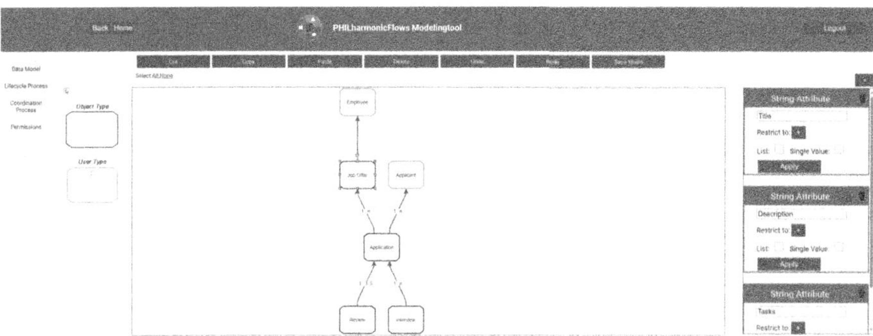

Fig. 1. Data Model of a recruitment business process example with its RPS and business attributes.

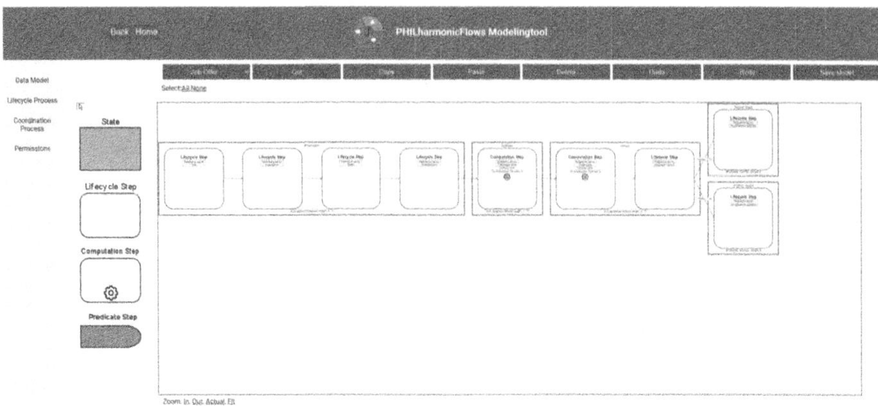

Fig. 2. Lifecycle process of the Business Object *Job Offer*.

Lifecycle Processes: The runtime behaviour of each business object is specified by a lifecycle process. Figure 2 depicts a screenshot of the *Lifecycle* module within the *PHILharmonicFlows* framework. The runtime engine [8] automatically generates user sheets for user interactions based on the pre-defined lifecycle structure. A lifecycle state represents one form sheet during the execution of the business process. A runtime, each lifecycle is initiated in one specific start state and subsequently progresses through a series of intermediate states, ultimately terminating in an empty end state, which is characterised by the absence of any steps. Each state can be further refined by a number of steps that refer to a business attribute. At runtime, each step results in a form field. Lifecycles support three types of steps: the *basic step*, which creates an input field based on business attributes; the *computation step*, which sets a specific value (e.g. a date or random number); and the *predicate step*, which models a decision based on defined expressions (e.g. 'amount < 500').

In comparison to the original framework, the incorporation of a sophisticated verification process and the automated determination of the *Kalman* weight for progress calculation has resulted in an extension of the lifecycles. In the event of erroneous modelling of lifecycles, an error message is returned to the end user. Furthermore, the verification algorithm utilises a 'prevent and highlight' technique. The prevent logic is employed to block transitions to previous states, thereby avoiding the formation of cycles or loops. In order to facilitate comprehension for the modeller, prohibited states are indicated by a red highlight. Conversely, permissible states are indicated by a green highlight. This technique prevents of lengthy error-finding processes, particularly in the case of large process models. In the case that a multitude of start states exists and a modeller clicks on the error message, all start states are indicated by a red highlight. Moreover, the *Kalman* weight for the monitoring tool has been incorporated. The *Kalman* weight is a value between 1 and 5 that is automatically determined based on the number and type of steps within a state. The *Kalman* filter is capable of predicting the progress of a single lifecycle instance based on the aforementioned *Kalman* weights, thereby eliminating the necessity for an event log. In addition, the *Kalman* weight can be set by a modeller manually when the estimated effort is greater or less than the automatically determined one in order to achieve better results in determining progress [7].

Coordination Processes: A *coordination process* controls the interactions between the lifecycles of multiple objects and defines the sequence of states between multiple lifecycle states. Thereby, a coordination step refers to a state of a lifecycle process. In general, a coordination process is defined from the perspective of one business object, i.e. the lifecycle of one object is extended with lifecycle states of other objects to represent their correlations and interactions. More specifically, a coordination process can be viewed as a graph where vertices represent the coordination steps and edges represent the coordination transitions. The coordination process graph is a directed, acyclic, and connected graph excluding backward transitions and loops. Otherwise, cyclic dependencies and thus deadlocks are possible. Therefore, the acyclicity of coordination processes is not a limitation of expressiveness, but a necessity for correctness [6]. In contrast to the original framework, the web-based version is extended by a sophisticated verification algorithm to identify, for example, cycles that span multiple coordination processes and are therefore difficult for a modeller to detect. Figure 3 depicts a screenshot of the *Coordination Process* module within the *PHILharmonicFlows* framework. The verification algorithm employed an active mechanism to prevent erroneous modelling of the coordination process, whereby any attempted modifications are blocked and invalid targets (i.e. coordination transitions and previous ports or coordination steps) are highlighted in red. In addition, a passive mechanism was utilised to examine the coordination process in nine distinct error cases, returning error messages to the modeller if modelling mistakes are introduced. Furthermore, the web-based framework is augmented with the capacity to impose constraints for each coordination transition. These constraints can be leveraged to facilitate the execution of a business

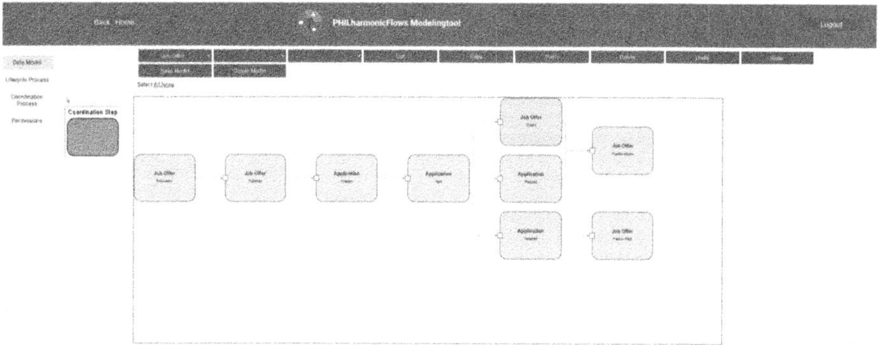

Fig. 3. Coordination process of the Business Objects *Job Offer* and *Application*.

process in a more targeted and precise manner. To illustrate, in the case of a research conference review process, a paper will be deemed appropriate for acceptance when at least 50% of the three to five assessors have determined that the paper meets the requisite standards for acceptance. The web-based *PHILharmonicFlows* framework allows the modeller to define constraints of this nature.

Permissions: In the original framework, permissions are only listed in a table on the *Permissions* tab and cannot be modified there. To illustrate, the permissions for business attributes are established in an additional tab within the data model, while the permissions for lifecycle states are configured in a drop-down menu on the button for each state. When initially defining permissions in the original framework, many modellers encounter difficulties in locating the appropriate setting for the permissions. Consequently, the configuration of permissions can now be carried out directly on the *Permissions* module as depicted in Fig. 4. In detail, permissions can be defined for each business object depending on the individual users or user groups (i.e. user type). Furthermore, the ability to assign execution rights to each user for each state in the lifecycle (i.e. the activation of the 'Next' button on the form sheets at runtime) has been incorporated. In addition, the rights to read, write, or none can be specified for each user with respect to each business attribute.

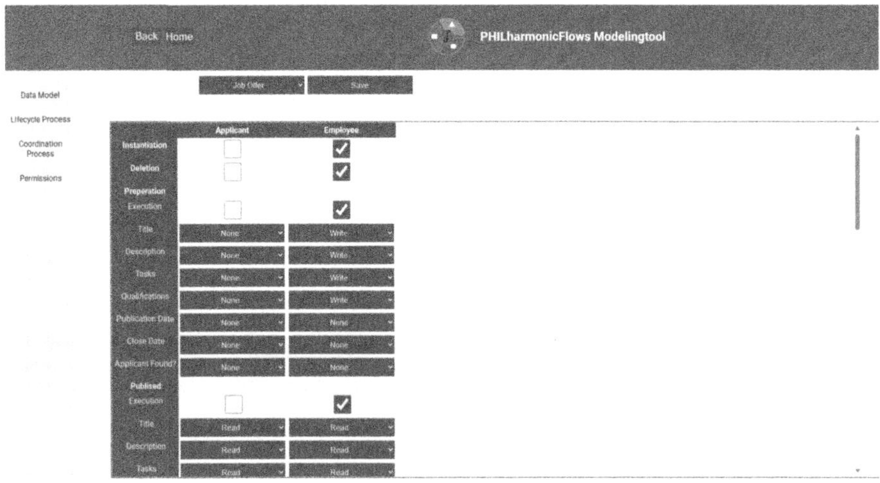

Fig. 4. Permissions of the Business Object *Job Offer*.

3 Structure of the Modelling Tool

The web-based implementation of *PHILharmonicFlows* was developed primarily in *TypeScript*. The **front end** of the application has been constructed using the

NextJS framework. The framework employs the *React* library for the component-based development of reusable front end elements. The graphs are created and manipulated using an extension of the *mxGraph* JavaScript library, namely *ts-mxGraph*. This extension extends the mx-Graph library with types, thereby making it TypeScript compatible. mxGraph is a client-side library for creating and modelling diagrams and graphs that works on all common browsers without any additional add-ons. The front end of the web-based *PHILharmonicFlows* framework constitutes by a set of pages, components, and assets. A page may contain one or more *React* elements, which in turn may contain other elements, components, or simple *HTML* elements. The pages delineate the content that will be rendered in the user's browser while they interact with the application. Components contain reusable code, which may be employed in a variety of contexts. For instance, the editor component is utilized in the data model editor, the lifecycle process editor, and the coordination process editor. Assets contain the styling of the application in *Cascading Style Sheets* (CSS) files. The front end is in communication with the controllers of the back end and the editor services, receiving data that is necessary for its rendering or sending data from the front end to the database.

The application's **back end** is based on the *Node.js* framework *NestJs*, which is designed for the development of scalable server-side applications. Upon deployment of the application in a Docker container, a *NestJs* web server is initiated, facilitating the transfer of requisite data to the front end. The back end is constituted by modules, controllers and editors. The controllers represent the primary conduit for communication between the front end and the back end. The transfer of data is accomplished by transmitting a request from the front end to a designated route, which is made available by a controller. The controller will then transfer the request and its associated data to a service. This service then manipulates the request data, if necessary, and executes a database call, and a response is transmitted to the request's originator. If data is previously retrieved from the database, the front end may engage in direct communication with the editor or parser services.

The data of *PHILharmonicFlows* is managed using the *MongoDB* database management system (i.e. *NoSQL* := Not only SQL), a non-relational database that employs the use of documents structured in a JSON-like format. Regardless, it is possible to utilise logical references between disparate stored documents, thereby representing the relations between them. Furthermore, it offers a multitude of query and aggregation functions, which result in enhanced performance compared to relational databases. Furthermore, *MongoDB* enables straightforward vertical and horizontal scaling due to its non-relational architecture [9,10]. The front end is responsible for communicating with the MongoDB database in order to retrieve the necessary data and present it to the user in an appropriate format. As soon as the user makes any modifications to the modelled process, these changes are sent to the back end, where they are then reflected in the database.

The *PHILharmonicFlows* application, including of both its front end and back end components, as well as the database is executed within a dedicated **docker** container to ensure portability and scalability. Each container is configured to expose a port, thereby facilitating external access. This ensures that the user is able to interact with the application by sending requests to a designated controller endpoint. Typically, user requests are initiated through the graphical user interface (GUI), which is defined by the front end.

4 Summary and Outlook

This paper presents the redesigned and enhanced web-based framework of the object-centric business process *PHILharmonicFlows*, originally developed at the local level. The web-based framework eliminates the challenges associated with the installation and management of the application, as well as offering the outsourcing of computing resources. Moreover, the web-based framework incorporates additional features, including sophisticated verification algorithms, measurement metrics for the monitoring component as well as the setting of permissions in a user-friendly manner, and the possibility of defining expressions for coordination process constraints. The web-based *PHILharmonicFlows* is currently still under development. Further work focuses on enhancing the user-friendliness and user interface of the lifecycle processes. This involves the configuration of the states and steps, which is a highly intricate matter. In addition, further work is focused on the validation of expressions defined in the coordination process constraints, the implementation of an export and import function, and the development of additional measurement metrics for the predictions generated by the monitoring tool.

Acknowledgment. This work is part of the ProcMape project, funded by the KMU Innovative Program of the Federal Ministry of Education and Research, Germany (F.No. 01IS23045B).

References

1. Ruecker, B.: Practical Process Automation. O'Reilly Media, Inc. (2021)
2. Künzle, V., Reichert, M.: PHILharmonicFlows: towards a framework for object-aware process management. J. Softw. Maint. Evol. Res. Pract. **23**, 205–244 (2011)
3. Steinau, S., Andrews, K., Reichert, M. The relational process structure. In: CAiSE 2018, pp. 53–67. Springer (2018)
4. Steinau, S., Andrews, K., Reichert, M.: Executing lifecycle processes in object-aware process management. In: SIMPDA 2018, pp. 25–44. Springer (2017)
5. Steinau, S., Andrews, K., Reichert, M.: A modeling tool for PHILharmonicFlows objects and lifecycle processes. In: BPMD 2017 (2017)
6. Steinau, S., Andrews, K., Reichert, M.: Coordinating large distributed relational process structures. Softw. Syst. Model. **20**(5), 1403–1435 (2021). https://doi.org/10.1007/s10270-020-00835-0

7. Arnold, L., Breitmayer, M., Reichert, M.: A one-dimensional Kalman filter for real-time progress prediction in object lifecycle processes. In: EDOCW, pp. 176–185. IEEE (2021)
8. Andrews, K., Steinau, S., Reichert, M.: A tool for supporting ad-hoc changes to object-aware processes. In: EDOCW, pp. 220–223. IEEE (2018)
9. Nayak, A., Poriya, A., Poojary, D.: Type of NoSQL databases and its comparison with relational databases. Int. J. Appl. Inf. Syst. 16–19 (2013)
10. Sahib, S.G.G.: A review of non relational databases their types advantages and disadvantages. Int. J. Eng. Technol. (2013)

UML-MX©: Boosting Power of Object-Oriented Modeling and Enriching User Experience

Ulrich Frank(✉) and Pierre Maier

University of Duisburg-Essen, Essen, Germany
ulrich.frank@uni-due.de, pierre.maier@uni-due.de

Abstract. Despite their considerable dissemination, existing UML modeling tools suffer from significant limitations that stand in the way of their profitable use in practice as well as in teaching. This paper presents a new UML modeling tool, called UML-MX©, that overcomes these limitations. It is based on a language architecture that not only enables the integration of class and object diagrams, but also the execution of objects in the diagram editor. Thus, it promotes a more inspiring learning experience. At the same time, it goes beyond the limitations of traditional approaches to model-driven software development by enabling a common representation of models and programs.

Keywords: multi-level language architecture · teaching UML · executable models

1 Introduction

Despite justified criticism of various weaknesses, UML is widely used in practice. Object-oriented modeling with UML is also an integral part of many curricula, both in computer science and business informatics. In this paper, we present a UML object-model editor that promises substantial advantages over existing UML modeling tools. It is worth noting that the development of a UML tool was not actually on our research agenda. For more than ten years, our research was mainly focused on the development and use of domain-specific languages in general and multi-level language architectures in particular. This work led to the development of a multi-level modeling and execution environment, the XModeler^ML© [3] (for more details see www.le4mm.org), [9], which is based on the foundational language engineering environment XModeler© [7]. UML played no role in this context, since the aim of our research was to overcome the limitations of languages like UML. Nevertheless, we still had to deal with UML as part of our teaching program – mainly in a modeling course at Bachelor level.

Against this background, and in view of the large number of existing UML tools, it may seem absurd to develop yet another UML modeling tool. However, there are two main reasons why we decided to do so. On the one hand, we had to

M. Kaczmarek-Heß et al. (Eds.): EDOC 2024 Workshops, LNBIP 537, pp. 276–286, 2025.
https://doi.org/10.1007/978-3-031-79059-1_17

realize that despite the obvious advantages associated with multi-level language architectures, software developers and modelers are often reluctant to adopt multi-level modeling. The effort to learn and appreciate multi-level modeling is perceived as rather high, not to say as daunting. In addition, there is no standard yet, which is a threat to the protection of respective investments. Against this background, it became evident that providing convincing incentives for using multi-level modeling is essential for its adoption. On the other hand, our experience with teaching object-oriented modeling reveals that students often struggle with learning how to design a proper object model, a fact that led to the question how students' modeling skills could be effectively improved. One possible answer to this question was to provide them with a modeling environment that enriches their learning experience by providing a more natural access to objects and classes.

At first, the emphasis of our work was mainly on lowering the entry barriers to multi-level modeling for modelers and software developers. Based on the assumption that UML is still used by many, we came to the conclusion that providing modelers with a UML object-model editor that offers clear advantages over traditional UML tools might work as an effective incentive. Once modelers got used to these advantages, it might be easier to draw their attention to further multi-level features and eventually to multi-level modeling in general. From a managerial perspective this approach makes sense, too. At first, stick to the standard, then gradually extend it to a more versatile and powerful tool. The idea was, in other words, to introduce multi-level modeling through the backdoor [3].

In parallel we worked on improving a course on object-oriented modeling in a Bachelor's program and a Master's course on advanced modeling and DSML design. In both cases, we were not satisfied with the students' achievements. Even though students represent a different target group than professional users, it became obvious that a UML editor that is based on a multi-level language architecture would also help with improving teaching and learning of object-oriented modeling. In addition, it would be suited to pave would be suited to pave the way for teaching the development and application of DSMLs and, eventually, of multi-level models.

The UML-MX© ("Modeling and Execution") tool presented in this paper serves both purposes. In the following we will describe benefits of using a multi-level tool like the XModeler^{ML} for creating and using UML class diagrams and then define requirements for a dedicated UML object model editor based on the XModeler^{ML} (Sect. 2). Against this background, we present the design and implementation of UML-MX© (Sect. 3) as well as a preliminary evaluation (Sect. 4).

2 Prospects and Requirements

Given the limited resources we had for developing UML-MX©, it was essential that the XModeler^{ML} already provides substantial benefits for developing UML-like object models. However, its additional features, such as an arbitrary number of classification levels, deferred instantiation of properties, and the fact that every class is an object is likely to be perceived as confusing, both by experienced professionals and students. Therefore, UML-MX© should allow to benefit from specific advantages of a multi-level language architecture without placing the burden on users to learn specific multi-level concepts.

2.1 Existing Benefits

A multi-level language architecture offers some clear attractive advantages for creating and using object models. In the industrial application of conceptual modeling, model-driven software development is often regarded as a particularly efficient way to produce code of high quality [10]. In the ideal case, code is widely, if not entirely, generated from models. However, a serious problem stands in the way of this appealing vision. Model and code are represented separately, with the result that sooner or later they will no longer be synchronised. As a consequence, the investments in the models gradually lose their value. That may lead to the question why there is need for generating code, and, as a consequence, for two separate representations anyway. In fact, there is no compelling reason for this. Rather, this circumstance is due to the limitations of common object-oriented programming languages. Classes, which are conceptually located at M1, are actually represented by objects at M0 in the model editor. Objects at M0 do not allow for further instantiation. Therefore, generating code is the only option to enable the instantiation and execution of models. UML even provides two languages for creating class and object diagrams, without offering a proper integration of the two.

By contrast, a multi-level language architecture does not only allow for an arbitrary number of classification levels, it also stipulates that every class is an object, that is, has state and is executable. Hence, classes that are conceptually located at M1 can be implemented at M1. In other words: model and code share the same representation. This is at least the case for executable multi-level languages like the FMML^X which was developed by our team [3]. As a consequence, modelers are relieved from the burden of synchronizing code and model. At the same time testing a model is supported by checking its instances in the same editor. In addition, there are two further goodies provided by the XModeler^{ML} already. Constraints are immediately effective after their specification. They are specified with XOCL, an extended, executable version of OCL [7]. Delegation is not just a pattern like in UML but a language concept with execution semantics [6].

Students are likely to benefit from the integration of class and object diagrams, too. First, there are various studies, which indicate that beginners often struggle with the abstraction required to appreciate the concept of a class. It is easier for them to think of particular objects at first. Therefore, a tool that allows to look not only at classes and objects simultaneously, but also to see the effect that changing a class has on its instances immediately should help students with developing a proper understanding of the fundamental dichotomy of types and instances.

Also, the common representation of object models and their instantiations helps with illustrating problems originating in misleading abstraction. This is, the case, e.g., for circles or for the inappropriate use of specialization. While corresponding object models may look fine at first glance, looking at corresponding instances will often immediately reveal the problem.

2.2 Specific Requirements

Making use of the features already provided by the XModeler^{ML} would suffice to realise a significant advance over existing UML modeling tools. This applies in particular to the ability to edit class and object diagrams together as well as the executability of objects and constraints. Therefore, the development of UML-MX© was mainly aimed at avoiding the confusion caused by multi-level concepts. To provide for a systematic development of the tool, we conducted a requirements analysis. The following requirements are grouped into three categories. General requirements are marked with "G", those that are marked with an "S" are specifically focused on teaching and learning issues, while "P" marks requirements that may concern professional developers.

As the scope of this paper is limited and the didactically motivated extensions of UML-MX© will be described in more detail in another publication, we will limit ourselves here to a small selection of corresponding requirements.

Requirement G1: Abstract syntax, semantics and concrete syntax should widely correspond to the UML. *Rationale*: Professionals should be familiar with the UML and students are supposed to learn it.

Requirement G2: Specific multi-level concepts and corresponding GUI elements should be effectively hidden from users. *Rationale*: Multi-level concepts could distract from UML, and might be perceived as confusing.

Requirement P3: The tool should allow for adding new language concepts. *Rationale*: To increase productivity and quality in modeling projects it can be helpful to add specific language concepts to the UML that are immediately effective after their specification – even while working on a model. The UML addresses this need with stereotypes. UML tools hardly allow for defining a precise semantics of stereotypes.

Requirement G3: An advanced UML editor should offer optional concepts suited to overcome specific shortcomings of the UML. These extensions should be monotonic, that is, they should not prevent from using UML in a "regular" way. *Rationale*: Respective extensions would facilitate a more efficient and consistent use of UML.

Requirement S1: A UML editor used for educational purposes should offer modeling exercises to students. *Rationale*: Including modeling exercises helps students to apply their knowledge and self-assess their skills.

Requirement S2: A UML editor should give instructive feedback on modeling errors. *Rationale:* Offering detailed and instructive feedback on errors helps students understand their mistakes and thus improve their modeling skills. Instead of causing frustration, mistakes should be perceived as promoting learning progress.

Requirement S3: A seamless transition from UML to DSML development and full-scale multi-level modeling should be supported. *Rationale*: Enabling a seamless transition to DSMLs and multi-level modeling ensures that students can build upon foundational modeling knowledge to address more specific and complex modeling needs step-by-step.

Most of these requirements are widely satisfied already by inherent features of the XModeler^{ML} already, which will be shown in the next section.

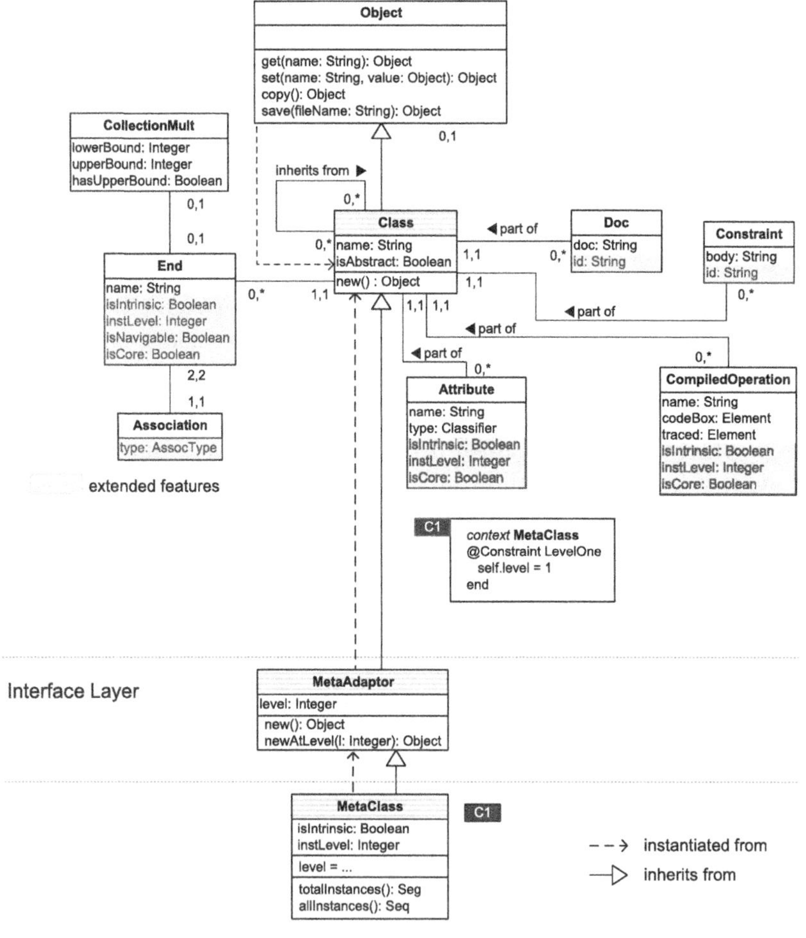

Fig. 1. Foundational Meta Model of UML-MX©.

3 Design and Implementation

At the core of the proposed tool is a language architecture that is enabled by a specific meta model.

3.1 Meta Model

The XModeler^{ML} is based on a reflexive meta model called XCore ([7], pp. 40), which is extended by specific multi-level features resulting in the multi-level language FMML^{X} (see Fig. 1).

It allows for creating multiple classification levels. It also makes sure that every class is an object, since `Class` inherits from `Object`. Objects can execute operations that are defined with the class (instance of `Class`), the objects are instantiated from. Regular FMML^{X} classes can be instantiated at any level from the class `MetaClass`.

The meta model allows to modify existing language features and add new ones with full execution semantics (req. P1).

3.2 Adaptation of GUI and Concrete Syntax

UML-MX© differs from the regular XModeler^{ML} in three ways. First, multi-level language features irrelevant for modeling UML classes and objects have been faded out for the user (Req. G2). Different from the XModeler^{ML}, every class created with UML-MX© is always at M1. As a consequence, the instantiation level of all class properties such as attributes, operations and associations is zero.

Second, the concrete syntax of UML was widely adopted (Req. G1). As shown in Fig. 2, the graphical notation corresponds to UML, with the exception of added features such as delegation and constraints.

Third, a *guided-modeling mode* has been implemented that serves as the basis for self-guided training exercises (Req. S1).

UML-MX© and XModeler^{ML} represent two versions of the same system. To allow for a smooth transition from UML to multi-level languages (Req. S3), additional GUI elements can be gradually unlocked, eventually resulting in a fully-featured multi-level modeling tool.

In order to overcome certain limitations of UML, UML-MX© implements an extended version of UML, called UML++. Note that these extensions are monotonic, that is, they do not exclude "regular" use of UML:

- Objects and classes may be modeled within the same diagram.
- An object created with UML++ is always instantiated from its actual, previously defined class.
- The specification of operations is not restricted to their signature but may also contain a body, which can be accessed by double-clicking on the signature.
- Representations of UML++ objects include a compartment for the return values of their operations.

- Each attribute in UML++ is specified either by a given data type or class (such as `Date`) or by a user-defined class.
- In UML++, the representation of a class contains an additional compartment that includes identifiers of its constraints.
- Violations to constraints are shown in UML++ objects. This includes violations of custom constraints (XOCL expressions) or implicit constraints such as association multiplicity.
- In contrast to the UML, UML++ provides native support for delegation relationships as a means to overcome pitfalls of specialization (see Req. G3).

We have specified ten learning units that each contain an exemplary illustration and a set of modeling exercises. Modeling exercises are opened in the guided-modeling mode, which assists students in developing a model step-by-step.

3.3 Demonstration

Figure 2 serves to demonstrate the use of the UML-MX© environment. The tool itself, as well as screencasts that demonstrate the guided tool introduction, can be accessed via www.LE4MM.org/uml-mx/. In contrast to prevalent UML class-diagram editors, the palette is dynamically extended by every class that is created within a diagram. Users can click a class on the palette and then click on the modeling canvas to create an instance of this class. By selecting `Class` from the palette, users can create a new class. The same principle applies to associations, links, delegations, and notes.

The specification of attributes can refer to standard data types (like `String`), predefined classes (like `Date`), user-defined classes, or user-defined enumerations. Slot values are accepted only if they conform to the specification of the corresponding attribute.

In UML-MX©, the context of a constraint is added automatically, users must only specify the XOCL expression. Users can furthermore specify custom fail messages that are shown in an object if the constraint is being violated (see object `Modeling` in Fig. 2). For a detailed illustration of how to specify and evaluate constraints see the screencast at www.LE4MM.org/uml-mx/.

Operations contain a body written in XOCL. Operations may or may not be shown in objects. In Fig. 2, for example, the operation `getCourses(): Set(Course)` is not displayed in student objects. Two modes to add/modify operations are available for students: a standard mode and an expert mode. In standard mode, users can only adjust the signature of the operation. The body can only be modified in the expert mode.

Furthermore, users can manage a model's complexity with views and diagrams. Views are divisions of a diagram based on layout alone. A diagram is a visual representation of a model that can be manipulated in the editor (Fig. 2 shows one UML++ diagram). Users can create multiple diagrams for a model, allowing for a separation of class and object diagrams if desired.

4 Evaluation

Most of the requirements listed in Subsect. 2 have been fully implemented, which follows from the description of the implementation in Subsect. 3. Others, especially those that aim at additional support for students such as requirements S1 or S3 are subject of ongoing work. The step-by-step transition is currently supported only to a limited extend: by switching didactic mode from true to false in the file `users.properties`, one can move from UML-MX© to the XModeler^{ML} or, in other words, from UML++ to a multi-level language that enables the specification and execution of DSMLs.

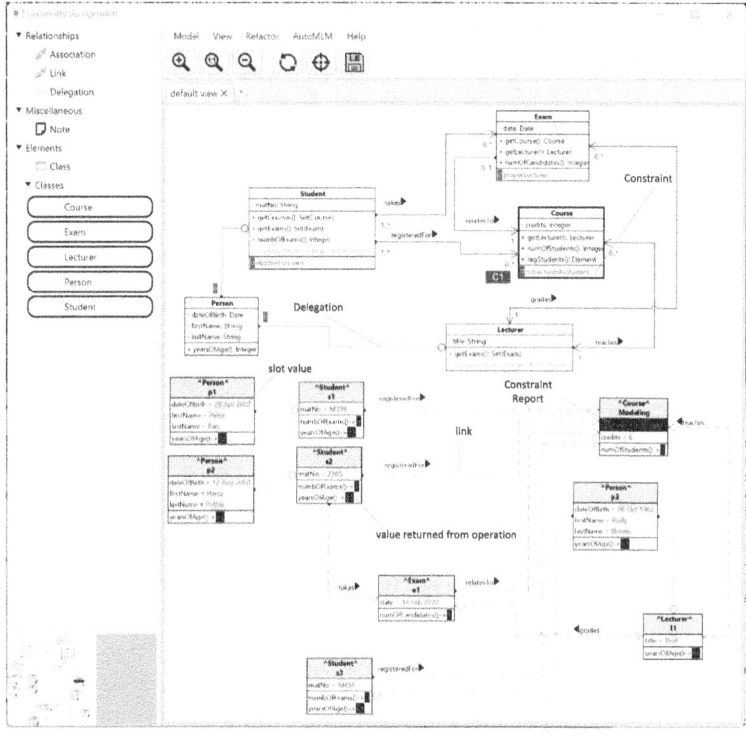

Fig. 2. Screenshot of Diagram Editor within UML-MX©.

4.1 Preliminary Results from Using the Tool

Object-oriented modeling with UML class diagrams has been taught by our group for over twenty years. In recent years, we used MEMO4ADO, an enterprise-modeling tool developed on the basis of the meta-modeling platform ADOxx, as a modeling tool throughout the course [13]. It includes an editor for common UML class diagrams. Last semester, we used the XModeler^{ML} for teaching object-oriented modeling. It still featured multi-level modeling concepts and lacked UML notation. Students could use either MEMO4ADO or XModeler^{ML}. Subsequently, they were asked to complete a survey on their experience with using the tool as part of the assignment.

Overall, we received mixed feedback from these first exploratory experiments with students. On the one side, many noted that the tool was confusing especially with respect to the offered multi-level concepts. On the other side, the instantiation of models at run-time appeared to support students effectively in their learning process. For one, creation of object diagrams seemed to be intuitive to many students. Without any explicit prompt, students created objects already in the first in-class assignment. Students noted that the creation of object diagrams provided valuable feedback on the correctness of the corresponding class diagram. For example, modeling object diagrams clarified whether the multiplicity of an association was suited for linking objects.

4.2 Related Work

Teaching object-oriented modeling is linked to the overarching goal of developing abstraction skills [8]. Some researchers propose to focus more on modeling objects than classes alone as a means to make students better understand the various dependencies between classes and objects (e.g., [1] and [2]). As noted by [12], UML modeling tools fail to adequately support modeling object and classes since class and object diagrams are not well integrated. We conducted a preliminary survey on current tool support for UML class and object diagrams. While some consistency checks are often provided (e.g., class name in object corresponds to the name of a class), they cannot imitate an executable run-time environment. To the best of our knowledge, no self-standing modeling tool allows for the specification and execution of operations within diagrams or validates constraints on the object level.

5 Conclusions and Future Work

In retrospect, UML-MX© is the result of an unusual, yet fortunate coincidence of technology push and demand pull forces. As a side effect, so to speak, our many years of research on multi-level language architectures have resulted in the opportunity to realise a modeling tool that makes a clear difference to conventional tools and promises considerable advantages, both in teaching and in practical application. To the best of our knowledge, no other UML editor is available that would allow for a common representation of class and object diagrams or would even enable the execution of models without the need for code generation. Preliminary results from using a predecessor of UML-MX© in modeling courses indicate that the additional features implemented especially to support students are suited to add further value. We also assume that using UML-MX©

is suited to serve as a door opener for appreciating higher levels of abstraction as they are provided by multi-level language and model editors such as the XModeler^{ML}. The smooth transition from the UML-MX© environment to the XModeler^{ML} makes it all the easier to get started with multi-level modeling. Our future research is aimed at adding other UML diagram types such as use case diagrams and add further support for students and teachers. We also plan on conducting more sophisticated experiments with UML-MX© in the future.

References

1. Andrianoff, S.K., Levine, D.B.: Role playing in an object-oriented world. In: Gersting, J., Walker, H.M. (eds.) SIGCSE 2002: Proceedings of the 33rd SIGCSE Technical Symposium on Computer Science Education, pp. 121–125 (2002)
2. Brinda, T.: Student experiments in object-oriented modeling. In: Cassel, L., Reis, R.A. (eds.) Informatics Curricula and Teaching Methods: IFIP TC3/WG3.2 Conference on Informatics Curricula, Teaching Methods and Best Practice (ICTEM 2002), pp. 13–20. Springer, Heidelberg (2003)
3. Frank, U.: Multi-level modeling: cornerstones of a rationale. Softw. Syst. Model. **21**, 451–480 (2022)
4. Frank, U.: Multilevel modeling. Toward a new paradigm of conceptual modeling and information systems design. Bus. Inf. Syst. Eng. **6**(6), 319–337 (2014)
5. Frank, U., Clark, T.: Multi-level design of process-oriented enterprise information systems. Enterp. Modell. Inf. Syst. Archit. (EMISAJ) **17**, 1–50 (2022). https://doi.org/10.18417/EMISA.17.10
6. Clark, T., Frank, U., Gulden, J., Töpel, D.: An extended concept of delegation and its implementation within a modelling and programming language architecture. Enterp. Modell. Inf. Syst. Archit. (EMISAJ) **21** (2024)
7. Clark, T., Sammut, P., Willans, J.: Applied Metamodelling: A Foundation for Language Driven Development, 2nd edn. Ceteva (2008)
8. Engels, G., Hausmann, J.H., Lohmann, M., Sauer, S.: Teaching UML is teaching software engineering is teaching abstraction. In: Bruel, J.-M. (ed.) Satellite Events at the MoDELS 2005 Conference: MoDELS 2005 International Workshop OCLWS, MoDeVA, MARTES, AOM, MTiP, WiSME, MODAUI, Nfc, MDD, WUsCaM, Montego Bay, Jamaica, 2–7 October 2005, Revised Selected Papers, pp. 306–319. Springer, Heidelberg (2006)
9. Frank, U., Clark, T.: Language engineering for multi-level modeling (LE4MM): a long-term project to promote the integrated development of languages, models and code. In: Font, J., Arcega, L., et al. (eds): Proceedings of the Research Projects Exhibition at the 35th International Conference on Advanced Information Systems Engineering (CAiSE 2023), pp. 97–104. CEUR, 3413 (2010)
10. France, R.B., Rumpe, B.: Model-driven development of complex software: a research roadmap. In: Briand, L.C., Wolf, A.L. (eds.): Workshop on the Future of Software Engineering (FOSE 2007). International Conference on Software Engineering (ISCE 2007), pp. 37–54. IEEE CS Press (2007)
11. Atkinson, C., Kühne, T.: The essence of multilevel metamodeling. In: Gogolla, M., Kobryn, C. (eds.) UML 2001 - The Unified Modeling Language. Modeling Languages, Concepts, and Tools. 4th International Conference, Toronto, Canada, 1–5 October 2001. LNCS, vol. 2185, pp. 19–33. Springer, Heidelberg (2016)

12. Moisan, S., Rigault, J.-P.: Teaching object-oriented modeling and uml to various audiences. In: Ghosh, S. (ed.) Models in Software Engineering: Workshops and Symposia at MODELS 2009, Denver, CO, USA, 4–9, October 2009. Reports and Revised Selected Papers, pp. 40–54. Springer, Heidelberg (2010)
13. Bock, A., Frank, U., Kaczmarek-Heß, M.: MEMO4ADO: a comprehensive environment for multi-perspective enterprise modeling. In: Modellierung 2022 Satellite Events, pp. 245–255 (2022)

The Simplified Platform, Cases 2024

Mark A. T. Mulder(✉) and Rick Mulder

TEEC2, Hoevelaken, The Netherlands
markmulder@teec2.nl

Abstract. The Simplified platform is the web-based approach to modelling and meta-modelling. This platform started from the experience with a previous research tool for modelling Design and Engineering Methodology for Organisations (DEMO) and has increased the available notations to OntoUML and ArchiMate. The cloud-based platform's extension ability makes it suitable for research and business applications. The platform's configurable notations, flexible user interface, and real-time transformation, verification, and visualisations make it adaptable and understandable for every stakeholder. This update paper will list the current state of the simplified platform.

Keywords: Modelling · Meta-modelling · Collaboration · Enterprise Engineering

1 Introduction

The history of the Simplified modelling platform started with the research project towards the PhD 'Enabling the automatic verification and exchange DEMO models' [5]. The DEMO [1,3] method is a core method (based on a theoretically founded methodology) within the discipline of Enterprise Engineering (EE) [2]. We have described the history in detail in our previous paper [6].

The lack of good tooling for demo modelling prompted us to start the development of a new tool. We created a cloud-based modelling platform which supports collaborative design, multiple notations, API and white label UI integration that would allow customers to apply their own corporate design language to the UI and multiple languages, all while applying state-of-the-art development methods.

The platform consists of total of six layers, divided in two servers: application server (involving the layers interface, message, process, cache, and persistence), and database server (database layer). The interface layer consists of two interfaces for accessing the platform. Further information on the architecture was published earlier [7]. The modelling part of the back-end is designed to store the model and the metamodel of a notation or methodology. The architecture uses dynamic metamodels that restrict the models on run-time. The notation architecture structure is visualised in Fig. 1. Developers and Users use different terminologie, causing you to look at the same thing from two different perspectives as seen in Fig. 1. Whereas the user defines a model, the developer only sees

M. Kaczmarek-Heß et al. (Eds.): EDOC 2024 Workshops, LNBIP 537, pp. 287–297, 2025.
https://doi.org/10.1007/978-3-031-79059-1_18

the metamodel being instantiated. The platform is now available under licence on https://simplified.engineering/.

This paper describes six relevant cases we did in the past year. These cases will be reported in the STARR format. Finally, we conclude with a summary of this platform's current state of affairs.

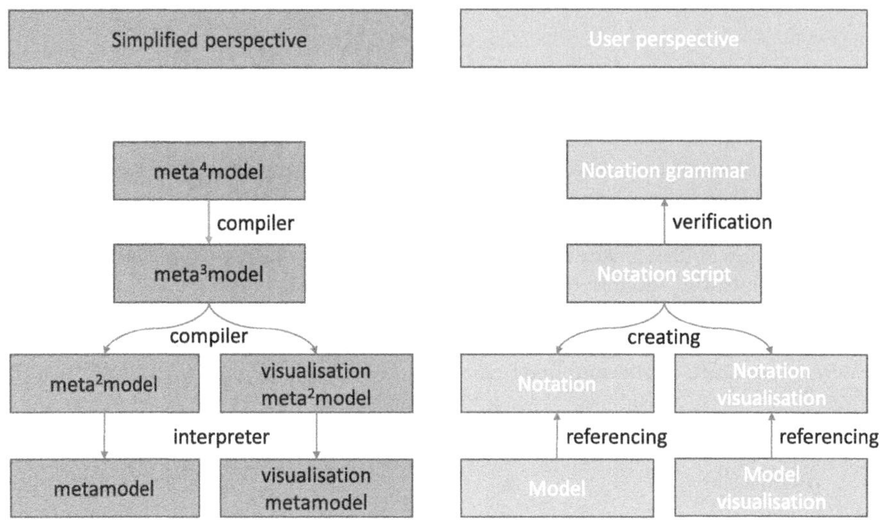

Fig. 1. Notations from different perspectives.

2 Cases

In this section, we will discuss several cases we encountered in the last year. We will use the STARR reporting for these cases.

2.1 Governmental

The first case contents is still confidential but we can give some generic remarks.

Situation. Our customer needed a research project to get an answer on the integration of Simplified Modelling Platform (SMP) within their own environment. Their desire to switch to SMP was caused by the inability of their current tools to solve their pain points.

Task. We have developed a server extension that is able to convert a model, complying to a custom notation, into a JSON format, and push this JSON to a Git environment. The process involves two steps: First, the model is created in within a simplified repository and model environment. Subsequently, while the server extension is running, the user brings up the context menu for the diagram and chooses the method to convert to JSON and publish to a gitlab environment. In the background a message is sent that lets the server know that the user wants to run a function in an extension execute a task. The server forwards this request to the extension along with any possible parameters needed for this operation. The server extension then receives this request and executes the function, requesting additional information from the server. The extension then creates the JSON and commits this to the Git server. The Git server can then start the CI/CD process upon receiving a new JSON being uploaded to the GitLab.

Approach. We have used an iterative approach to create the right environment to customise the notation and create the server extension step by step to meet the demands.

We started by analysing their problems step by step, translating them into tool solutions. With the tool solutions we modelled their problems, until we encountered the next problem, restarting this process of analysing.

Result. The custom notation and the server extension have been created, and the integration between the SMP and Git environment has been established with a server extension under the control of the customer. Figure 2 shows the architecture of notations and models used to export the model information and generate the data and trigger to start the Ci/CD process in Git.

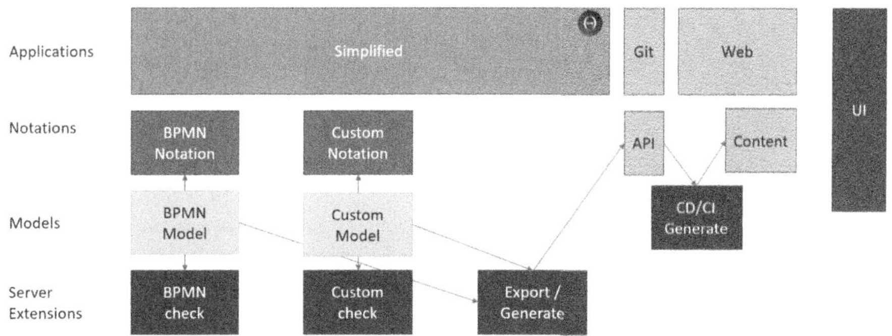

Fig. 2. Architecture and Process for the Governmental Case

Reflection. While the process is ongoing, we have learned about creating custom notation in a modelling environment, just like in the Problem-Solution Chain (PSC) case. The integration with multiple Git environments has brought good opportunities to store models in a vendor-independent location.

2.2 Problem-Solution Chains (PSCs)

For the previous case and this case, that is to be published later in detail, we created a new way of creating a notation.

Situation. A colleague researcher approached us to model a research problem executed by a master student. No other existing tools could quickly and easily create a custom notation. The core idea behind PSCs is that basic but solid 'problem-solution thinking' is key in the early stages of problem-solving, including business-IT alignment efforts linking business needs and IT functionalities. The use of PSCs mainly aims to support steps 2–4 in the six-step approach of [4].

Task. We needed to create a domain notation and a domain model that represented the research topic PSC.

Approach. During interactive sessions we created the notation that complied with the research topic.

Result. The new method allows for creating a model that represents a notation using a custom notation specification. By choosing the 'elevate model', shown in the architectural view in Fig. 3, a function that will convert a modelled notation, as shown in Fig. 4, into a useable notation on the platform, one can realise, within the same environment, a new notation that is active right away. This allows for easy adjusting and designing new notations in research projects.

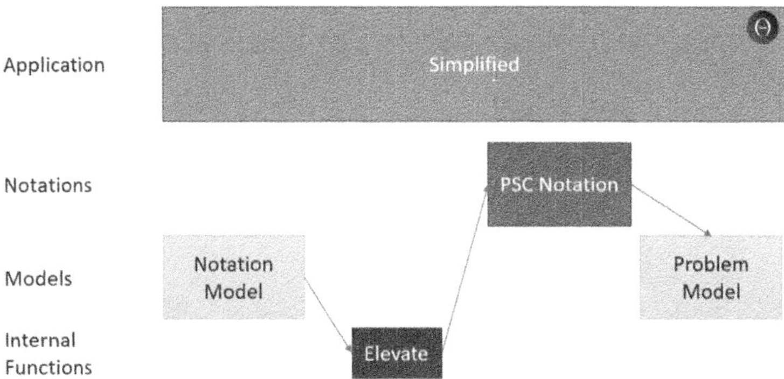

Fig. 3. Architecture and Process for the PSC Case

Reflection. During the interactive session, we found that creating the notation as a script did not meet the stakeholders' needs. Therefore, we added the creation of the notation as a model. This will be published later this year.

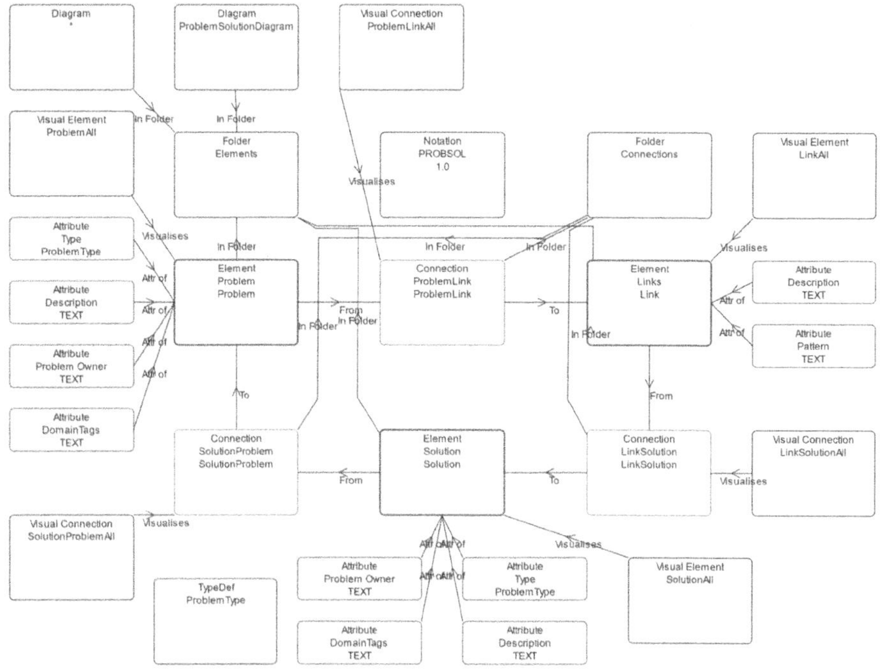

Fig. 4. Part of PSC Meta Model in SMP

2.3 Staging Generation with Transformations Between JSON DEMO IG

In this case we created a server extension that supports model transformation allowing for the creation of a data warehouse staging and reporting environment within the InformationGrid platform.

Situation. For a customer, we created the storage of information in the IG environment. This information acts as a data hub and a data warehouse from where the datamarts are populated.

Task. The process starts with the import of a one-level deep JSON structure that is converted to a DEMO Entity Type (ET) that is usually found on the fact diagram. This ET is converted from the source model in DEMO notation to the target model in InformationGrid (IG) notation components in simplified, mirroring the structure in IG itself. This is automatically generated and converted to several components in the low-code platform, using an API to create the components. This pipeline allows changes to the source model to be forwarded to the platform in an automated process.

Approach. After doing this process manually several times, we decided to automate the transformation. Using the existing examples, we deduced the format and created the transformation algorithm.

Result. The generation of the staging area results in a reduction of programming from two to three hours to five minutes and a reduction of error to almost zero. This is shown in the hours we have spent creating solutions for the customer before and after creating the generation. Figure 5 shows the steps and the components used for this functionality of creating the staging from a JSON input.

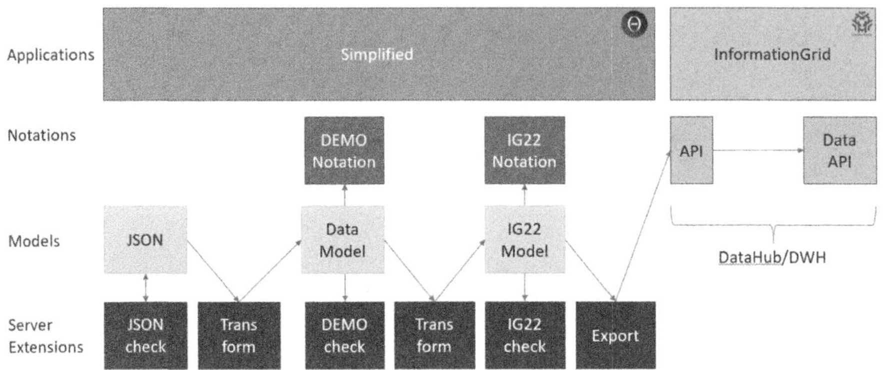

Fig. 5. Architecture and Process for the Staging Case

Reflection. The generation of this staging area was a good step towards the complete generation of DEMO entities to the IG environment project that is running now. The generation has had a single update since its first inception to optimise the performance of the IG system by using the build-in indexes.

2.4 VISI Generation to IG

VISI is an ISO-standard[1] for a workflow notation and execution used in the construction branch[2]. Executing a workflow in the IG environment[3] is possible and can be generated.

Situation. At the start of this project there were 3 suppliers of software that could process VISI messages of the VISI framework. Target of this process is to be able to run a domain driven design model to generate the operational part of the software on a low/no-code platform.

Task. The project consists of the transformation of the VISI model to the generic format of the SMP. Thereafter the transformation of the VISI notation to the InformationGrid 2022 (IG22) notation will create an potential executable model of the VISI framework. The upload of the IG22 model to IG creates an callable

[1] https://github.com/nl-digigo/visi/tree/master/VISI%201.6/Documentation.
[2] https://www.digigo.nu/standaarden/visi/.
[3] https://nl-digigo.github.io/visi/visi1.6.

API that can receive and produce messages. The server extension on SMP will complete the communication between IG and the SOAP interface. A special UI interfaces between the users and the information in IG.

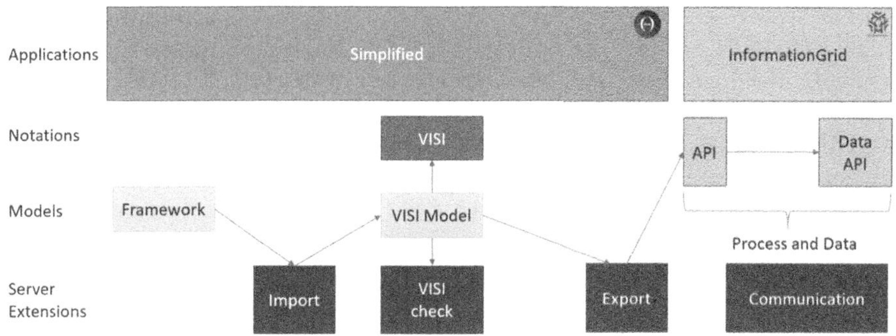

Fig. 6. Architecture and Process for the VISI Case

Approach. We are iterating over all parts of the modelling and transformations needed to make a complete executable form of the model. The project is very dynamic as the VISI standard also evolves during the project.

Result. The current state of this case is that the model has been transformed from the exchange XML to the IG model and needs the right preconditions to be able to execute the messages within the IG platform. Figure 6 shows the import of the VISI framework (the stored model) and the processing of that model to the execution environment. The communication extension allows for messaging between different implementations of the standard.

Reflection. This project took longer than expected because of the changing preconditions, changing standards and developments in the target platform. We hope this project will be finished by the end of 2024.

2.5 Business Process Model and Notation (BPMN) Transformation to System Dynamics (SD)

The fifth case is the guidance of the creation of a BPMN-SD transformation server extension [8]. This was the first time an external party had created a simplified server extension.

Situation. We wish to transform a BPMN model to SD. This is a research project for a master student. The mapping between BPMN and SD was expected to exist, and would be able to be programmed. Challenges lie in finding the exact mapping, which will not be one to one.

Task. The main objective of the project was to create a server extension that was able to transform a BPMN model in Simplified into a SD model in simplified. This was a masters project and the duration was a little over a year.

Approach. As a start we provide a template for the server extension. This contains the neccessary parts for connectivity, communication, and a library of callable methods in order to retrieve data from Simplified. Close contact was kept with the master student through the use of discord. In order to better support the transformation, we created a new tranformation method from the ground up. The transformation was designed so that it can transform an abitrary number of elements in a tree structure to another arbitrary number of elements in another tree structure. This allowed for the freedom to do a 1-many or many-many mapping as needed, in addition to 1-1 mappings.

Result. The result is a server extension that transforms BPMN models to SD models. We have created a generic transformations for Chain to Chain transformation and enhanced the notation uploading and visualisation. Figure 7 shows a simple architecture with a single serverextension performing the transformation.

Reflection. During this exercise we upgraded the documentation on notation scripts because it was unclear how to use them. We also created a new way of uploading notations allowing for deletion of old, and creation of new attributes with the relink option to keep models valid while updating the notation due to research insights. Next, we added metamodeller UI changes, such as last script uploaded, and error messages handling to provide feedback, and predefined variables and a easy way to add variables to test your shape. Furthermore, we allowed the use of variables in for example rectangles. A big step was the addition of the transformation of a tree of elements into a tree of different elements was created,

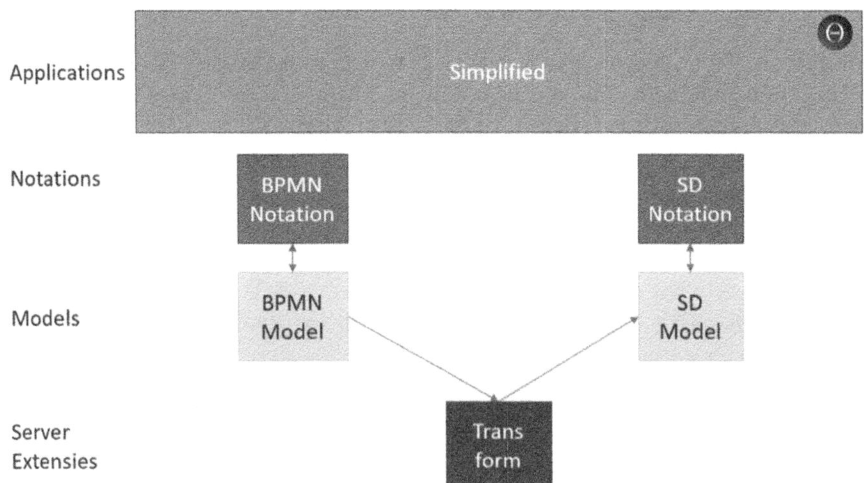

Fig. 7. Architecture and Process for the BPMN Case

called chain to chain. Finally, we learned that it was very beneficial (or required) to have basic programming knowledge in the way of setting up programs, splitting functions instead of writing big functions, and creating sections based on actions you want to accomplish.

2.6 Glossary Listing

Glossary was requested due to a wish to have the terminology in one way for the modeller and a different way for stakeholders.

Situation. A customer needed a glossary list for definitions in the company. This glossary would be used to define the information of parts of the model, as well as information that did not directly relate to any model in the SMP.

Task. We needed a way to create, edit and view all definitions within a glossary. To make this happen, we have created a notation, 'glossary', with the element 'glossary item', which can hold definitions. A separate functionality can later transform these definitions in linkable HTML formatted texts. We split the functional UI into two parts, a creator for terminology and a display, where you can also edit them. The creator can create a single item in the appropriate location in the model. The display will list all items of the same type in a default dynamic table. We created this dynamic table to edit specific types as well.

Approach. We have started with a basic design that can do all fundamental functionality. In the validation of the functionality with a focus group we have noted extra functionality that will be implemented in the next iteration.

Result. While the project was intended to create a glossary list, the generic build of SMP allowed us to reuse this functional UI to create model elements without visuals or diagrams. Figure 8 shows a partial view of the viewer interface and Fig. 9 shows the interface to add new glossary items without a visualisation on a diagram.

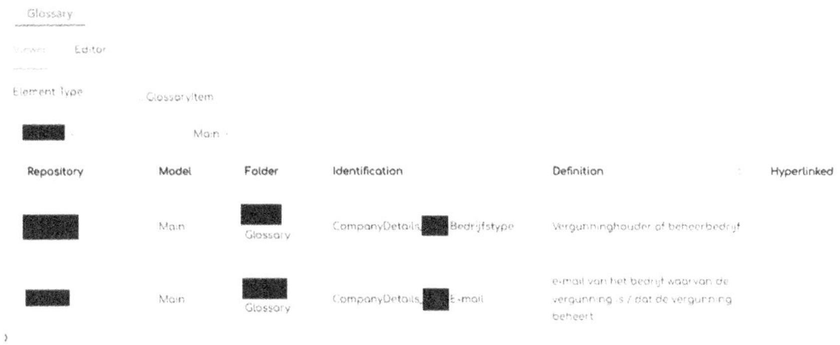

Fig. 8. Architecture and Process for the BPMN Case

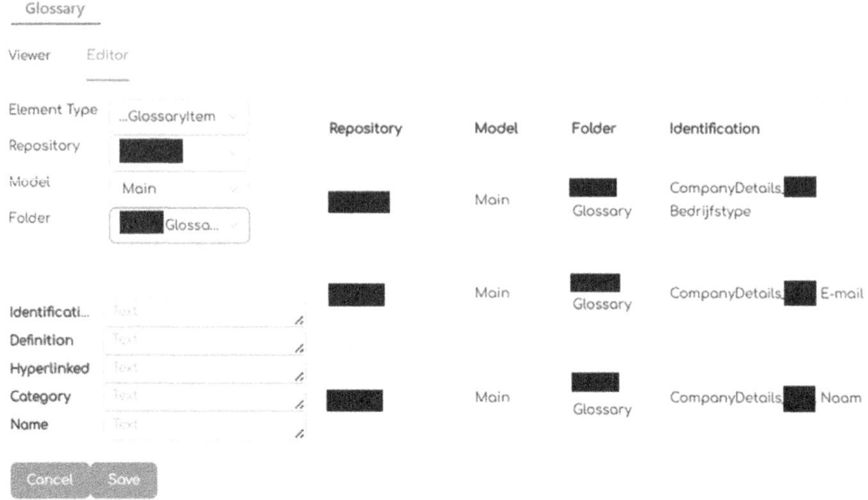

Fig. 9. Architecture and Process for the BPMN Case

Reflection. We have added a group of stakeholders to the platform using a UI that represents the business thinking in lists. Definitions can be added to the glossary without knowing how to model. The list can also be queried (through simple filters for now), which will allow for more complex queries in the model environment.

3 Conclusion

The Simplified Modelling Platform (SMP) development solves more and more limitations that we experienced during the modelling of organisation and information. The platform supports the collaborative design and multiple notations expressed in multiple languages. It now also supports exporting modelled information to Git systems like gitlab and github, giving you control over your created data. On the notation side we have created an intuitive way to visually model notations, removing the barrier to creating your own notations. We have extended our staging generation capabilities to InformationGrid in multiple ways, taking away many repetitive steps and making the process much less error prone. Lastly, we have developed a generic transformation syntax for tree to tree transformations, enabling transformations between several notations. Feature extensions are done in a modular fashion, allowing for future feature development without disruption. Additional research is needed to extend modelling's features, and a broader investigation of the limitations and gaps of other modelling tools has yet to be conducted.

We encountered a lot of supported projects that reveal the need of changes to modelling and modelling tools. We are positive that we can support these research and commercial needs for modelling.

Finally, many features that come with specific modelling methodologies will be added.

References

1. Dietz, J.L.G.: Enterprise Ontology – Theory and Methodology (2006)
2. Dietz, J.L.G., et al.: The discipline of enterprise engineering (2013)
3. Dietz, J.L.G., Mulder, H.B.F.: Enterprise ontology: a human-centric approach to understanding the essence of organisation (2020)
4. Luftman, J., Brier, T.: Achieving and sustaining business-it alignment. Calif. Manage. Rev. **42** (1999). https://doi.org/10.2307/41166021
5. Mulder, M.A.T.: Enabling the automatic verification and exchange demo models (2022)
6. Mulder, M.A.T., Mulder, R., Bodnar, F., van Kessel, M., Vicente, J.G., et al.: The simplified platform, an overview (2022)
7. Mulder, M.A.T., Proper, H.A., Bodnar, F., Mulder, R.: Simplified enterprise modelling platform architecture. In: Clark, T., Zschaler, S., Barn, B., Sandkuhl, K. (eds.) PoEM (Forum), volume Proceedings of the Forum at Practice of Enterprise Modeling 2022 (PoEM-Forum 2022), pp. 16–30, London, United Kingdom. CEUR (2022)
8. Ruci, E.: Transforming business process models into system dynamics models – developing a transformation tool. Master's thesis, Technische Universität Wien, Vienna, Austria (2024). https://doi.org/10.34726/hss.2024.112680

CBI Mini Dagstuhl Seminars

Fundamentals of Conceptual Modeling
A "Mini-Dagstuhl Seminar at CBI 2024"

Heinrich C. Mayr[1](✉) and Bernhard Thalheim[2]

[1] Alpen-Adria-Universität Klagenfurt, 9020 Klagenfurt am Wörthersee, Austria
heinrich.mayr@aau.at
[2] Christian Albrechts University Kiel, 24118 Kiel, Germany
bernhard.thalheim@email.uni-kiel.de

Keywords: Model · Conceptual Model · Metamodel · Abstraction · Meaning · Standardization · Model Serialization · Triptych Paradigm

1 Preliminary Remarks

The field of conceptual modeling (CM) has a huge base of foundational work on which research and development build. Recently, researchers have been exploring in particular the state [19,47,52,67,75], the foundations [28,31,51,84]), focal points and corresponding research communities [23,43,49,55,70] of the discipline. Nevertheless, there are still a number of open fundamental questions that need to be clarified from a scientific point of view, but which are also important for the use of conceptual modeling in practice, e.g.:

- How should the meaning of models be specified?
- What are the elements of a theory of abstraction for modeling?
- How can we manage complexity in the use of models?
- What are the means for quality-aware modeling?
- What does it take to be able to rely on models?
- How to interleave Modeling and Development?

To discuss approaches and answers to questions of this kind, we organized a "Mini-Dagstuhl" seminar on the occasion of the CBI 2024 in Vienna and asked the participants to submit a position paper. These contributions (11 in total) are reproduced below,

They were presented at the seminar and discussed in depth. It became clear that there is still a need for clarification in many respects, both in terms of terminology, methodology and formal principles. As a result of this first meeting, it can be stated that the need for a comprehensive model theory together with a modeling methodology for the application of modeling in practice is generally recognized. I.e., we need a kind of "Konstruktionslehre"[1] as a methodology of model construction. The term "*modelology*" [77], for example, might be used as a umbrella term here, which, however, is not yet common knowledge.

[1] the German term for theory and methodology of constructing in the technical sciences.

M. Kaczmarek-Heß et al. (Eds.): EDOC 2024 Workshops, LNBIP 537, pp. 301–324, 2025.
https://doi.org/10.1007/978-3-031-79059-1_19

Due to the brevity of the position papers, we have refrained from briefly describing their content here. Instead, in addition to the questions listed above, we include some aspects needing further research as can be derived from these papers, and which will be the subject of further joint work:

- meta-meta model standardization,
- interoperability, model serialization,
- learn from/transfer principles of mathematical models,
- delimitation of the terms conceptual, physical, logical etc. models,
- comprehensive typification of models (along characteristics).

We thank all contributors and look forward to a fruitful collaboration. The contributors in alphabetic order:

- Colin Atkinson, Universität Mannheim, Germany, *Sect.* 7
- Dominik Bork, TU Wien, Austria, *Sect.* 10
- Victoria Döller, University of Vienna, Austria, *Sect.* 9
- Vadim Ermolayev, Ukrainian Catholic University, Lviv, Ukraine, *Sect.* 11
- Tomas Jonsson, Genicore AB, Gothenburg, Sweden, *Sect.* 5
- Roland Kaschek, Germany, *Sect.* 8
- Roman Lukyanenko, University of Virginia, Charlottesville, US, *Sect.* 6
- Judith Michael, RWTH Aachen, Germany, *Sect.* 3
- Rebecca Morgan, University of South Australia, Adelaide, *Sect.* 2
- Henderik A. Proper, TU Wien, Vienna, Austria, *Sect.* 4

2 When is a Model a Conceptual One?

by **Rebecca Morgan**
University of South Australia, Adelaide, rebecca.morgan@unisa.edu.au

As with art, many of us know it when we see it, but it is not always clear when a model is not a conceptual model. It appears that conceptual models are accepted as residing in a higher abstraction level than, say, data or logical models but there does not appear to be clear agreement about what that abstraction level actually is or even what constitutes a conceptual model. Is it a framework for communicating system design or an abstract psychological representation of tasks or behaviour? A quick Google search reveals that there appear to be as many different definitions as there are potential applications, but in my opinion, there is a chance of a generally accepted, unambiguous and (mostly) comprehensive definition of terms in the field of conceptual modelling. Although there are many definitions and viewpoints, I am of the belief that there is a common thread in all the definitions of 'conceptual model':

A conceptual model is an abstract representation of a given domain which is expressed using a controlled vocabulary and has a defined purpose/s. A conceptual model consists of a set of entities, properties and relationships which can be mapped to real-life entities (physical or otherwise), their meaning or semantics and logical constructs which determine behaviour and support reasoning. However, this definition is incomplete.

For example, is an executable model a conceptual model? Where is the differentiation between model and reality if the model itself is capable of producing or changing real-world entities? Using the model-driven perspective, conceptual models are generally accepted to be software and platform independent. Ordinarily, one applies model transformations to a conceptual model to obtain platform-independent and subsequently platform-specific model for code generation. The term 'conceptual model' seems to be synonymous with 'conceptual data model' for many practitioners, who then distinguish between conceptual, logical and physical data models. However, there are many applications in which these distinctions are not clear. There is not always a clear distinction between model interpretation and direct execution and code generation, for example.

Perhaps we should be using a 'bottom-up' approach to developing our theory of conceptual modelling, identifying the problems faced by practitioners and end-users as a first step towards a more unified theory and methodology. General acceptance can be obtained if the definitions are perceived to be sufficiently useful and accurate. Practitioners in the field of conceptual modelling may not concern themselves with strict theory, however, a sound methodology based on solid theoretical principles with appropriate tool support would be appreciated by many. ER diagrams and UML are ubiquitous and already widely accepted since they solve real-world problems and are communicable to non-experts. Ambiguity can be resolved through appropriate articulation of the concepts via ontological theory or the like. Comprehensiveness is arguably more difficult to achieve, given that a conceptual model may theoretically represent any real-life domain and for many different purposes. However, comprehensiveness should be achievable if we pay attention to the 5W's.

I believe that the biggest barriers on the way to a general theory and methodology of conceptual modelling lie in the subjective design choices which are made over the lifespan of the model and the difficulties in translating the abstract representation to the concrete implementation. Since the act of modelling is an art as well as a science, there is a great deal of variation in design decisions, processes and outputs. Developing a model of modelling processes and workflows will help, through restricting the available choices and reducing complexity. However, developing a unified methodology for turning the abstract representation into concrete implementation will be a very complex problem to solve.

3 Conceptual Modeling Foundations, MDE and Digital Twin Engineering

by **Judith Michael**
RWTH Aachen University, Aachen, Germany, michael@se-rwth.de

We aim to understand and handle the complexity of large software-intensive systems using software and systems modeling methods. Digital twins of such complex systems enable analyzing the past and present of a system, optimizing the running system, and predicting the future by using different models about and data of the twinned system [35]. Digital twin engineering and operation combines different model types [20,22], e.g., for describing the physical asset [54], for generating the digital twin [5], for describing the runtime state and processes [8,16], or linking the digital twin with other systems [44,71]. This requires different disciplines to work together and understand the modeling methods representing different perspectives and the kinds of abstractions they make. This observation is underpinned by a study about conceptual modeling, business process modeling, and model-driven engineering communities [55]: About half of the community members agreed that they are closely connected and a large majority would like to be even more connected. However, this requires a better understanding of the modeling research approaches among them. To better ground our modeling research, it would be helpful to find answers to the following questions:

- How do conceptual models fit into different classifications of model types?
- What is the relationship between a conceptual model and models used in Model-Driven Engineering (MDE)?
- How can conceptual models contribute to digital twin engineering?
- How can conceptual modeling foundations contribute to the Model-Based Software Engineering Body of Knowledge?

In the following, we discuss these questions and give some first hints on where to start a community discussion.

Types of Models. Mayr and Thalheim [51] propose eight characteristics and their features for describing conceptual models. To improve the understanding between different communities, a comparison of the different types of models and their characteristics would help. According to the Model-Based Software Engineering Body of Knowledge [18], conceptual models are information models. Considering the argumentation of Mayr and Thalheim [51], they can be more than pure information models as they are enhanced by concepts from a concept space. Looking into the literature, there exist different model classifications, e.g., Boyes and Watson [15] differentiate between data models and physical entity models with several subtypes, Michael et al. [54] (based on Novak et al. [60]) show a classification of models in hydraulic engineering, e.g., conceptual, empirical, analytical, numerical, computational models. There exists a categorization based on time properties and focus of the models: *structure*, *behavior*, *function*. Other commonly used classifications differentiate between models used for *generation* or code synthesis, and *interpreted* models, e.g., models@runtime [8]. In addition, there are other terms for types of models we are using in software engineering, e.g., domain models, requirements engineering models, simulation models, and system models. It would be interesting to investigate which characteristics they share (e.g., by providing a table) and which characteristics differentiate them. In addition, we would need a Venn Diagram describing where they overlap (similar to the one used in [21] describing the relationship between low-code and MDE).

Conceptual Models and Model-Driven Engineering. In MDE, we often use the term *system models* to describe a set of models we use in a generation process, e.g., different types of UML models, OCL models, SysML, and GUI models in a textual representation. In Fig. 1, we show a first approach for describing the overlap between system models and conceptual models. Here, the evolution of models over time is interesting. When (1) creating a conceptual model (Fig. 1), what is needed to (2) evolve to be a conceptual and a system model, and what happens to this model type when, e.g., the notion space is not defined any more (3). What characteristics do a conceptual model need to be (I) a conceptual and a system model from its creation on, e.g., a clearly defined notion space? And if (A) a model is created as a system model, what does it need to identify additionally (B) as a conceptual model and in which cases could these additions be helpful?

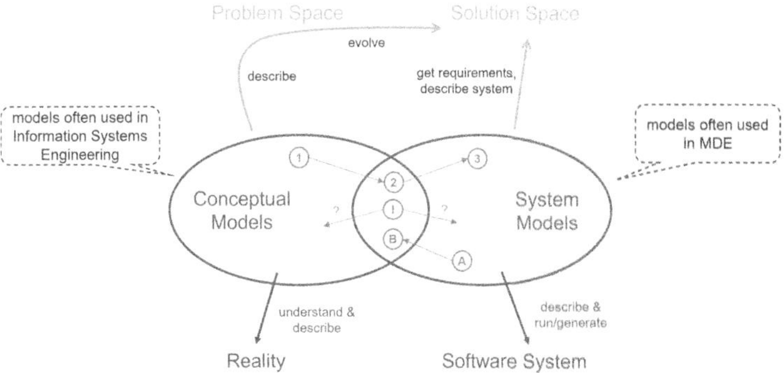

Fig. 1. Relationship between conceptual models and system models used for MDE

In addition, the question occurs if conceptual models are per-se usable or not usable for MDE. And if they have to be abstract and grounded in the problem space or have to be on a higher (conceptual) level so that they are not usable for MDE per definition.

Conceptual Models in Digital Twin Engineering. For digital twin engineering, it is becoming increasingly relevant to combine models from different application domains, with different levels of detail and characteristics, into a common system to better understand twinned objects, socio-technical systems [9], systems-of-systems [57], and ecosystems [56]. Digital twins use heterogeneous models, i.e. descriptive, prescriptive and prescriptive models [22], and their evolving data.

Up until now, the role of conceptual models in digital twin engineering has not been investigated well. There exist first works on using conceptual models for design thinking processes for digital twin engineering [78], or on the role of ontologies in digital twins [40]. A better foundation would contribute to a better understanding of what conceptual models can be used. Defining a notion space[2] is not only helpful but essential for any engineered digital twin, as this clarifies the used concepts and supports the understanding of different user groups. Thus, a better understanding of the influences of certain characteristics of conceptual models on the different participating users and application domains in every digital twin engineering process would be helpful.

Contributing to the Software Engineering Body of Knowledge. For a better integration of modeling theory for complex systems, we need to integrate the developed foundations of conceptual modeling in existing Body of Knowledge (BoK) collections, e.g., the Model-Based Software Engineering Body of Knowledge [18]. Here, it would be good to check the BoK and identify if additions from the conceptual modeling perspective would make sense. A Dagstuhl-like setting would be the right place to do so.

Conclusion. As identified in [55], collaborations between different modeling communities would be beneficial for various research topics. When looking at ideas and new visions of conceptual modeling [50] or recent discussions on abstractions engineering [7], we have to ask ourselves what the right place for conceptual modeling is. Coming from information system engineering and databases its methods seem to fit well in other research areas, however, its usage should not be just a relabeling of terms. We need to systematically specify in which development phase which kinds of systems with which representation paradigms and languages for which purpose conceptual models can be created for whom and what their usage characteristics are.

Acknowledgment. The research reported on in section was funded by the Deutsche Forschungsgemeinschaft (DFG, German Research Foundation) – Model-Based DevOps – 505496753. Website: https://mbdo.github.io.

4 Conceptual Modeling as an Essential Cognitive Skill

by **Hend***erik* **A. Proper**
TU Wien, Vienna, Austria, henderik.proper@tuwien.ac.at

This position statement centers on two complementary points. First, we argue that *conceptual modeling* should not be 'framed' into a 'database design only' narrative, and should be acknowledged as being a much broader discipline aimed at revealing, capturing, and studying the conceptual structures of (existing, or envisaged) domains in general. Second, we argue that more work is needed to understand the way in which we (as humans) create conceptual models, while also developing more insights on how to learn (and continuously develop) conceptual modeling skills.

[2] Please note that the term *notion space* is used on purpose. It should not be mixed up with the term ontology. An ontology represents only one way to realize it. There are also other encyclopedic grounding options.

We [66] take the perspective that humanity has long since used models to understand, redesign, communicate about, and shape, the world around us, including many different social, economic, biological, physical, and digital aspects. These models may take different shapes and forms, such as sketches, precise drawings, textual specifications, or tangible forms, all aiming to 'mimic' key properties of some original; i.e. the *domain* of the model. As such, these models are *domain models*, which we [65,66] understand to be: *a social artifact that is understood, and acknowledged, by a collective human agent to represent an abstraction of some domain for a particular cognitive purpose.*

In the context of information systems engineering, and database design in particular, an important role is played by *conceptual models*; which we [65,66] regard as a specific class of domain models. In the information systems engineering context, a conceptual model is typically used to capture the essential structures of some domain of interest (the *universe of discourse*), while avoiding the inclusion of implementation/storage details [37]. The field of information systems engineering, indeed, provides a fruitful application area for conceptual modeling. At the same time, however, we suggest to avoid a 'framing' of what a conceptual model is to this application area only, and follow a more generalized understanding of the notion of *conceptual model* and its potential role. More specifically, based on [28,64], we currently understand a *conceptual model* to be: *a domain model where the purpose of the model is dominated by the ambition to remain as-true-as-possible to the conceptualization of the domain by the collective agent, while there is an explicit mapping from the elements in the model to the latter domain conceptualization.*

We would argue that the ambition of a conceptual model, as implied by the latter definition, to remain *as-true-as-possible to the conceptualization of the domain* is not only of value in the context of information systems engineering, but other contexts as well. A conceptual model provides an explicit – human understandable – representation of a theory about the entities and their ties that are assumed to exist in a given *domain of interest*. In line with this, we observe that in many different endeavors in which we (as humans) aim to understand the workings of some domain and/or aim to express, or study, design alternatives, we actually do so in terms of (purpose and situation specific) conceptual models. This includes many examples across science and engineering at large.

Given the general, and often critical, potential role of conceptual models, we argue that it is also important to learn the skill to create conceptual models. In line with this, we argue there to be a need for more research regarding both the cognitive processes involved [80] in the creation of conceptual models, as well as strategies to teach conceptual modeling. One interesting avenue is the role of explicit verbalization if 'fact' instances as advocated by the so-called fact-based modeling approaches [33,36]. An example would be *The person with name 'Erik Proper' works for the University with name 'TU Wien'*.

As posited in [36], the use of such verbalizations leads to (1) models that are based of evidence (in terms of the example facts) taken from the domain of interest, (2) the models are a direct reflection of the communication about the domain of interest, (3) the models embed/use the language as used by the domain experts, enabling validation by these experts. At the same time these posited benefits are not (yet) validated in terms of empirical evidence in terms of experiments and/or observations from practice. Even more, the way in which such verbalizations may benefit the actual task – and learning – of (conceptual) modeling deserves more investigation.

Finally, one interesting avenue of potentially relevant research regarding the latter, is work done regarding the potential benefits of 'think aloud' protocols in support of cognitive processes [10,34,59] (including modeling processes). Here we would argue that verbalizing examples/facts from the domain to be modeled, especially when embedded in a process of verbal ('aloud') clarification and exploration, has a strong link to such 'think aloud' protocols.

5 Phenomenological Conceptual Modelling

by **Tomas Jonsson**
Genicore AB, Gothenburg, Sweden, tomas@genicore.se

Phenomenological conceptual modelling is intended to guide modeling of concepts into meaningful structures for information systems, communicating with human actors. It is guided by Husserlian phenomenology and further evolved with abstractions of type, properties and state. **Introduction.** A conceptual model is a structure of concepts, which are in themselves mental items. The model may be internal or external. Externalised conceptual structure is a communicable conceptual model. The structure of the model may be influenced by or adhere to certain meta structures, such as language grammar and ontology.

A model should be a meaningful, useful instrument for some purpose in human activity, such as information systems design. The information system is regarded as a communicating actor, exchanging data with a human actor. Compatibility between actors mental model would make such communication efficient.

In order to create structures of concepts and data which will be easily understood by human actors, knowledge of how human mind structures concepts in a natural way is of essence.

The purpose of phenomenological conceptual modeling is to create conceptual structures which are close to natural (non academic) mental conceptual structures. As such, the language (rules) for a phenomenological conceptual model intend to mimic (part of) the conceptual meta structure of mind.

Phenomenological conceptual model philosophy can be briefly described, paraphrasing Wittgenstein [81] and inspired by [83] as:

- 1. The world is everything that is the case.
- 1.1 The world is the totality of factual objects, not of things.
- 1.2 For a factual object to be considered to exist, it has properties and/or relations with state of affairs (formal ontology), which can be referred to in language (logic), which can be experienced in acts of consciousness (phenomenology) and which can be judged based on knowledge (epistemology).

In [38] basic language related aspects for phenomenological modeling are described.

Concepts Related to Object. Firstly, objects belong to different regions of reality-perception. Categories put forward in [39] argue for the following categories, thing, location, actor, event, agreement and value. Further, parts of objects are properties, relations to other objects and state of properties and relations.

To be considered to exist, objects have in themselves a non explicit identity. However, an object can also have one or more identity signatures which are patterns of features distinguishing one object from another.

Abstractions. Object type abstraction represent a set of objects and possibly a set of object types. The type contain the set of properties and relations which are common for all objects in the set.

Along with object type abstraction follows abstractions of properties, relations and values. The value domain for an abstracted property contains the set of values of the abstracted properties.

Categories: An object type is in itself a category of objects and further categories can be expressed by defining object state or set of states, i.e. abstract state.

Time abstractions such as duration, phases and phase chains (life cycle) are also part of object and type definitions.

Model Abstraction, Perspectives and Messages. As phenomenological modeling in itself, aspires to define an internal structure of concepts, to be communicated with an external human actor, it does not define communication as such. Communication is an exchange of messages, containing concepts and state. Thus pure phenomenological modelling must be accompanied with a message model (interface) language, to define messages based on the phenomenological model. Each message or set of messages can be seen as a perspective (abstraction) of the model, meaningful and useful to a human actor

6 Theory of Conceptual Modeling Complexity Reduction

by **Roman Lukyanenko**
University of Virginia, Charlottesville, United States

William James famously described the world as "blooming and buzzing confusion". Indeed, any object can be described in a myriad of different ways owing both to its complex nature (some believe there are no simple, structureless objects [17]) and virtually unlimited ways to conceptualize it [68]. A key function of conceptual modeling is to reduce complexity of the problem and solution domains [77]. By reducing complexity, conceptual models permit effective communication, problem-solving and design in the world of limitless possibilities.

Despite this important function, little is understood about how conceptual modeling achieves complexity reduction [48, 77]. There is no systematic way to measure complexity reduction and guide the efforts to improve this critical function in conceptual modeling languages and methods.

We propose a theory of conceptual modeling complexity reduction. It assumes a spatiotemporal infinity of objects undergoing constant change. The aim of modeling is capturing only those aspects of reality necessary for a specific purpose. We define six levels of complexity, each progressively simplifying representation, and matching different representational goals.

At the highest, Level 6, we model a holistic view, integrating both internal and external object dynamics to consider the interactions between an object's components and other objects within a complex environment. Moving to Level 5, the focus narrows by treating other objects as atomic, but preserving the focal object (or domain of objects) internal dynamics and emergent behaviors. At Level 4, the model abandons internal dynamics, leaving the object's components and properties. Level 3 removes the object's internal complexity and considers the atomic object and basic external dynamics. At Level 2, the model is simplified by removing the external dynamics, and only considering other objects in terms of ill-defined environment, or the context for the focal object. Finally, at Level 1, the sole object is modeled in its most basic form-as atomic, unchanging, and isolated, characterized by its intrinsic properties.

The theory provides a basis for analyzing, evaluating and shaping complexity potential of conceptual modeling languages and methods. For example, a language that can effectively model at Level 6 has a high degree of expressive power, but also, if used to the fullest, will not yield large complexity reduction. Conversely, a language (or its subset) limited to Level 1 offers maximal reduction by only modeling simple, isolated objects with minimal context. By systematically applying the levels, it becomes possible to assess the strengths and limitations of conceptual modeling languages in handling different degrees of complexity, and refine these languages to match the evolving modeling needs. Future work is needed on formalization of the complexity theory and on evaluating its applicability across different modeling contexts.

7 Reconciling Ontological and Linguistic Classification in Conceptual Modeling

by **Colin Atkinson**

University of Mannheim, colin.atkinson@uni-mannheim.de

Conceptual modeling plays a crucial role in abstracting real-world phenomena into meaningful representations. One of the ongoing challenges is reconciling ontological and linguistic classification, especially in domains requiring deep characterisation [3]. I believe that the future of conceptual modeling lies in harmonizing these two forms of classification to build more robust, adaptable models that minimize accidental complexity [4]. Ontological classification refers to categorizing real-world entities based on their intrinsic properties and relationships [29]. It aims for universal, stable categories that accurately represent reality [24]. Ontologies help ensure that models are semantically consistent and structurally sound. Linguistic classification, on the other hand, concerns the labels and terms used to describe entities. These classifications are rooted in human language and often vary across domains [73]. Unlike ontological categories, linguistic classifications are more fluid, reflecting the ongoing evolution in languages and engineering approaches [79].

The tension between these two forms of classification can create challenges in conceptual modeling. For example, while ontological categories remain stable, linguistic classifications often shift across domains, leading to ambiguity and misalignment in models [32]. This divergence poses risks to the semantic coherence of deep models, which depend on precise definitions across different layers of abstraction [58].

The key to addressing this issue is integrating ontological stability with linguistic flexibility [2]. By formalizing the relationship between linguistic terms and ontological categories, we can build models that adapt to changing linguistic contexts while maintaining ontological rigor. Multi-level models provide a natural platform for this, as they deal with abstraction and classification across different, orthogonal dimensions [1]. Embedding semantic links between fluid linguistic categories and stable ontological entities will allow for more dynamic and accurate models.

In addition, advancements in artificial intelligence and natural language processing can support this reconciliation. AI can help monitor and adapt to linguistic shifts while ensuring that underlying ontological frameworks remain intact, enabling models to better handle the complexity of real-world systems. In conclusion, the future of conceptual modeling lies in fully reconciling ontological and linguistic classification. By integrating multi-level modeling techniques with evolving linguistic and AI tools, we can create more adaptable, semantically rich models that effectively address complex real-world phenomena.

8 A Calculation View at Conceptual Models

by **Roland Kaschek**
Germany, rolandkaschek@gmail.com

Models. The rhetorical devices analogy [69], metaphor [46] and model enable transferring knowledge from one item to another. Amongst these, metaphor and model has become important to informatics. In the tradition of Stachowiak [74], one says, that an an agent A uses an item M as model for item O if A under specified circumstances and at a specified point in time investigates M to derive a searched for information about O. This typically applies if M is not identical to O. Note, that M needs not to be an artifact and may predate, postdate or has come into existence at the same time as O has. Quality aspects of items used as models are of interest if and when models are being used in practice. Given an agent, any usage circumstances and time of use, any item may be a model for any other item. However, considering quality aspects for the model, it might turn out to be a rather poor model.

If one takes for granted the utterance ascribed to Socrates "I know, that I do not know", then one, would consider human knowledge as principally limited and thus subject to permanent change, a point also implied by [25]. In particular, one would not claim to know how the world really is in which one lives. Therefore, one would require a model for any attempt to obtain knowledge about the world. This also follows from the world being that vast, that it cannot be used in full for obtaining knowledge about a part of it. Software has been turned into a business. Every software producer who wants to survive the competition must produce efficiently, effective software and be able to deploy and maintain their software as well as replace any legacy software.

Software production nowadays often is organized by iterating the activities requirements elicitation, design, implementation, test, deployment and maintenance. During elicitation the functionality to be implemented is figured out, as is the intended way of using it and the quality of service to be provided. Design immediately follows requirements elicitation and immediately is followed by implementation. Design thus figures out a way to implement the desired functionality, I. e. provides the mathematics to be implemented later in the software process.

Conceptual Models. A conceptual model is a model, that relates to or consists of concepts. We are going to discard the mere relating to concepts and say, that a conceptual model is a notional model. However, notion here is not understood as actual content of some individuals brain. It rather is supposed to mean a standardized language representation of such content. Conceptual models tend to conform to a publicly available specification language, proposed by leading systems analysts. It may abuse Mathematical language and may use signs and concepts that are believed easier to grasp than mathematical concepts. Examples may be publicly available that illustrate the use of that language at important cases. Well known analysts, may be watching over the appropriate use of that language. Physical models, have been used e.g. in Medicine, Biology, Mathematics or Economy. In particular their use in Medicine is indispensable.

A quantity [72] is a notion for which an additive rule is known, attaching to it a non negative number, called amount of that quantity. A quantity's amount may be regarded as either constant or variable and is said to measure that quantity. A quantity may be measured from different angels and thus may have several amounts or even classes of amounts. In Informatics the amounts may be considered as code for more semantically meaningful signs and be replaced by these. Standard Mathematical operations may be used to define quantities from quantities. We are going to call a quantity a known or an unknown, respectively, if its measure is known or unknown. A Mathematical or calculation model is a collection of quantities some of which are connected to others by functions, relationships, equations, formula or algorithms. The purpose of the Mathematical model is to specify calculations for obtaining the amounts of its unknowns. The conceptual model (possibly among others) specifies calculations to be carried out and thus is regarded a Mathematical model.

To solve a Mathematical problem one writes down the knowns and the unknowns and then plunders the Mathematical Universe for quantities, relationships amongst quantities and formula or algorithms in such way that the amounts of the unknowns can be approximated or calculated. Informatics operates the same way as Mathematics does, but rather exploits the Informatics Universe, which is a super set of the Mathematics Universe.

In Mathematics, traditionally, the creator of a model evaluates it themselves. In Informatics, however, a machine is going to do so. Therefore, usually an algorithm exists that translates the conceptual model (via a logical model) into the physical model, that can be evaluated by the available hardware. In Mathematics the model user often needs to have a relatively deep and comprehensive understanding of the model. This often is not true in Informatics. Rather, often proficiency in using the hardware, some critical software and an overall understanding of the universe of discourse suffices.

Calculation is a form of drawing inferences. To the extent the unknowns have been measured a Mathematical model can be used to draw new inferences about that part of the world, the model user, by the model, would refer to. Clearly, any such reference is based on a judgment [41] on part of the model user or some authority they trust, about adequacy of substituting worldly items, or what they consider as such, by model quantities. A Mathematical model that is referred to an alleged part of the world, can be used to teach individuals about that alleged part of the world and can be increased beyond what would be needed to measure the unknowns in the model. Obviously, some of the well known quality aspects of items apply to conceptual models. However, in this paper, they are not being focused at.

9 Meta-concepts Revisited: Looking for a Common Meta^{2}Model that Meets the Needs of the State of the Art in Conceptual Modeling

by **Victoria Döller**

Research Group Knowledge Engineering, Faculty of Computer Science, University of Vienna, Austria, victoria.doeller@univie.ac.at

In conceptual modeling metamodels are used to specify the vocabulary and grammar of a modeling method. A metamodel provides an exact definition of what can be expressed with the language and what not. This precision is for a good reason, as the intended language is supposed to create meaningful, valuable model artifacts. Nonetheless, method engineers themselves often use tacit assumptions and implicit understanding of what can be defined in a metamodel and how to specify [12]. This might be acceptable when building rudimental modeling languages intending to express items and arrows in between (potentially enriched with a nice notation). However, minimalistic meta-concepts of object types and relation types are insufficient to meet the needs of realizing semantically correct, conducive, processable models with sophisticated modeling methods, and practices on this level are inadequate for conceptual modeling as a mature scientific discipline.

In contrast to, e.g., the existence of several approaches for bases of ontologies, so-called foundational ontologies like the Unified Foundational Ontology (UFO) [30], conceptual modeling research is not equipped with an exhaustive model of the concepts on meta^2-level, i.e., a meta^{2}model, not even with a commonly applied, exhaustive listing of these concepts. The Meta-Object Facility (MOF) [61] provides standardized meta-concepts for use in the OMG specifications. Due to its tedious evolution, MOF reacts rather slowly to new trends, requirements, and concepts.

Only a few contributions investigate metalanguages and meta-concepts theoretically, e.g., [51], and have rather a small echo in conceptual modeling practices. From an empirical perspective, a survey analyzing established metamodeling platforms according to the available meta-concepts was conducted over ten years ago [42]. This indifference to a comprehensive and reliable metalanguage is curious as the choice of a meta^{2}model is a crucial gatekeeper for any further realization and implementation of a modeling method. Furthermore, in isolated cases, various trends in conceptual modeling research argue for the need for additional sophisticated meta-concepts (at least implicitly).

One example of a needed refurbishing of the initially mentioned plain meta-concepts is the required upvaluation of relation types. Relations carry a lot of information in our models and should be treated as first-rate elements. The role of relations has been investigated from different perspectives, e.g., the consideration of the reification of relations from mere arrows to substantive artifacts [27] or the differentiation of semantically different types of relations, e.g., part-whole proportions, specializations, or intension/extension relations [51]. These different types of relations immediately also address the central interests of the subfield of multi-level modeling (MLM) [26]. A few meta-concepts that must be considered in a comprehensive meta^{2}model to be capable of addressing the requests claimed by MLM are the *powertype pattern* [63] or the *clabject* [2].

A meta-concept that is rather uncommon in conceptual modeling but might be worth discussing is a concept to capture constructs in the model that are not instantiated by the modeler but a composition of other elements. Their existence emerges purely out of the coexistence of these other elements. Examples for this are probability trees as connected components of single events or traps as a subset of places in Petri Nets that expose a specific behavior. This idea is akin to the concept of *derived type* in information bases as introduced in [62, Chap. 8]. Neither *tree* nor *trap* are a concept in the metamodel because metamodels only know directly instantiable types (prescribed by the meta-concepts of the meta^{2}model). Still, they are first-class concepts in the domain carrying their own properties. To be able to "talk" about these concepts, i.e., make statements about them in the modeling method, which is especially important in the light of model operationalization, we have to include them in our alphabet.

In addition to that, it is also appropriate to think about a universal means to link elements of different metamodels (on a conceptional level, not an implementational one) to allow for an interleaving of modeling languages and open up the seclusion of methods. This is currently only attempted by a few domain-specific, bilateral transformation approaches. Tackling this issue on the meta^2-level would give a general instrument to method interoperability.

So, the concluding questions appear to be: What are the meta-concepts in conceptual modeling that address the current research needs? Can we arrange them in a comprehensive meta^{2}model, i.e., can we tackle conceptual modeling with conceptual modeling? And finally, to avoid the same deficiency as mentioned in the beginning, is this meta^{2}model capable of expressing itself?

10 Standardization in Conceptual Modeling: A Means to Unleash Creativity and Foster Maturity

by **Dominik Bork**

Business Informatics Group, TU Wien, Austria, dominik.bork@tuwien.ac.at

Conceptual Modeling Research

Conceptual modeling research has traditionally been characterized by a plethora of definitions, frameworks, theories, techniques, and tools. Exemplary stated here are prevalent discussions about 'What is (not) a conceptual model?' and 'What is conceptual modeling'? However, the discussion does not stop here. In fact, one can see a rich set of different, often even controversial, definitions and flavors of, e.g., multi-level modeling, multi-view modeling, multi-paradigm modeling, and ontology-driven conceptual modeling, amongst many more. Even most of the core concepts like 'model', 'modeling method', and 'metamodel' are not generally defined and widely accepted.

While in research, it is generally accepted and common sense, to introduce definitions of concepts and phenomena, it becomes problematic when these definitions relate to things that are already defined but to which no relationship is explicitly stated. As a consequence, the research landscape becomes diluted and fundamental concepts need to be explicitly defined in the introduction of scientific papers. This also establishes high entry barriers for early career researchers starting in the modeling domain.

It is often claimed, that standardization limits or even prohibits creativity and progress. Compare, for example, the recent discussion of mobile phone vendors to object against a common charging technology within the European Union. In contrast, the motion this paper puts forward is, that standardization in conceptual modeling is crucial for fostering creativity and maturity. By establishing common frameworks, languages, terminology, and theories, standardization can provide a stable foundation upon which innovation can be fostered. Such standardization also enables a maturation that the conceptual modeling community can greatly benefit from.

What and Why to Standardize? Clearly, standardization should not start with the aim of realizing a commonly agreed-upon theoretical foundation or a shared terminology. Instead, we propose that standardization should start bottomup by looking at the formats in which we specify, (de-)serialize, and interact with modeling languages and their conforming models. The following is a non-conclusive list of aspects we believe standardization is both feasible and fruitful. The list shall exemplify current pitfalls, sketch means to mitigate these, and shed light on the positive outcomes of such standardization.

Model Serialization Format: The format in which conceptual models are serialized differs from tool vendor to tool vendor and often even for one tool vendor with respect to different modeling languages. It is hugely unfortunate, that models of one modeling language are serialized in multiple formats in different tools. This is a huge barrier to establishing interoperability as the demand for model transformations increases unnecessarily [11].

Modeling Language Definition: As reported in [12], a huge diversity in modeling language specification techniques exist. These techniques have differences in their expressiveness and in their comprehensibility. This hampers the comprehension of new languages being proposed in the community, and it increases frustration for both authors and reviewers of conceptual modeling contributions. A standardized and formalized means to specify modeling languages would be a great asset.

Modeling Tool Development: A recent development in software engineering is interesting and can have a huge impact on the conceptual modeling community: the Language Server Protocol (LSP) [13]. LSP separates the language smarts and heavy lifting like Abstract Syntax Tree (AST) generation and parsing to a language server while the user interaction is focused on a language client. The server and client communicate via standardized LSP messages. The LSP standardization resulted in many creative developments in the IDE market and has made VS Code the currently most used IDE for software developers. Transposing this idea to conceptual modeling will have a huge impact on the conceptual modeling community, primarily in elevating the development of modern and flexible modeling tools, cf. [14,53].

Conclusion. Standardization in conceptual modeling is a double-edged sword. While it provides numerous benefits, including fostering creativity and promoting maturity, lowering entry barriers, and enabling reuse and interoperability, it also presents challenges related to the identification of the point after which further standardization stifles innovation, the standardization process itself (whom to involve, how to reach consensus, etc.). A balanced approach, one that encourages both the establishment of shared foundations and the exploration of new methodologies and tools, will be crucial for the continued growth and impact of the conceptual modeling discipline.

11 Toward Compact Formal Discourse Models for Neuro-Symbolic AI

by **Vadim Ermolayev**
Ukrainian Catholic University, Lviv, Ukraine, ermolayev@ucu.edu.ua

The challenge of building an AI system for performing intellectual tasks at a level comparable to human brain has long been a motivator for researchers in several communities. Contributions, developing and putting solution fragments together, have been witnessed in the last decades. However, we are still far away from solving the puzzle. The analysis of the evolution of relevant intellectual thought points out different ways of attacking the challenge. These are oppositely directed along the axis of abstraction, hence there is a chance that they meet at a solution state. However, several impedance mismatches hamper the top-downs fusing with bottom-ups synergistically. Furthermore, the problem has several facets of complexity, which makes it multi-dimensional. The facets are multi-linguality/modality, cultural, organizational, community silos, scalability, or expressive power, to mention a few. To keep the discussion focused, it is further constrained to the intertwining of textual data, ontologies and knowledge graphs, conceptual models, and large language models (LLMs).

Perhaps, Guarino et al. [29] were the first to outline the way to develop adequate formal representations of the perceived real world, such as ontologies. Notably, conceptualization, as an intertwining of extensional and intensional relational structures, was one of the cornerstones in their approach. The role of a conceptualization, as a model, is to bridge the interpretations of a domain of discourse, on one hand, and the required commitment of the language chosen to specify the knowledge about this domain, on the other hand. A similar bridging role has been discussed by Mayr and Thalheim [51]. It looks straightforward that the interpretations of a real or possible world(s) are acquired from the corresponding discourses around the domain. For example, the discourses for scholarly domains are formed by respective publications. The intertwining of explicit and implicit relational structures recalls a double helix in Genetics. The difference is that, in modelling and developing descriptive domain theories, the top-down helix (interpretations) and bottom-up helix (facts) grow towards each other and, hopefully, meet in the middle of the abstraction hierarchy to be bridged using conceptualizations and language commitments. Following this allusion, it would be nice to deliberate about what might be a knowledge gene, chromosome, DNA, or genome. Further, recalling that a human genome is composed of just 23 pairs of chromosomes, it might be useful to extract knowledge chromosomes for a discourse. These knowledge representation modules will further allow to devise a compact core schema of a domain ontology to enable proper and explainable reasoning over the facts in the corresponding discourse. Empowering generative AI models with such a core ontology would be a step toward Neuro-Symbolic AI solutions of demanded quality.

One possible way, applicable to textual data and facts that are dissolved in these data, is knowledge extraction from texts. It is known (c.f. [82]) that the initial step in the corresponding workflow is terminology extraction. Hence, extracting a minimal but representative set of terms for a domain could be regarded as a good initial approximation for the mentioned core ontology. One of the available approaches for this step is Terminology Saturation Analysis (TSA) [45]. It allows extracting compact terminologies which are proven representative regarding the majority opinion or mainstream in the discourse. After building an ontology using this core terminology, it could be populated with the facts relating corresponding documents that carry relevant terms. The resulting Discourse Knowledge Graph (DKG) might be regarded as a knowledge genome of the domain in focus. At the top level of the abstraction hierarchy, foundational ontologies, like e.g. UFO [6] could help frame out the development of the core domain ontology. The tools like OntoUML [6] could effectively be used for validating and refining conceptualizations with a human in the loop. It could be noted that discourse document collections, extracted core terminologies and ontologies, and DKGs could be used to fine-tune LLMs for respective domains. The approach discussed here is domain neutral.

12 Models in Modelology (Modellkunde): The Art, Practice, Engineering, and Science of Models and Modelling

by **Bernhard Thalheim**
Christian-Albrechts University, Kiel, bernhard.thalheim@email.uni-kiel.de

Models Everywhere, At Any Time, For Everyone
Models are used in many ways in science and technology as well as in all phases of daily life up to ceremonies, presentations, stencils or a guide.

That's why models are universal tools of every human activity, since every object and idea *can become a model* and models are also usually much simpler as well as focused on concrete use. That's why we need the new discipline modelology.

Our Thesis: Every object and every idea can be used as a model *in an application scenario*, if it becomes useful in the scenario as an instrument in a function.

Through this use and function, an object or idea becomes a model, at least for a certain or long time for the respective model user in its context and environment.

Behind the thesis: Models are works of art of thinking and deed. They come in the most diverse forms: small ingenious, ever-present, medium-sized or even elaborate ones of imposing size and full of hidden secrets. Quiet ones, animated by a flash of inspiration. Groundbreaking and revolutionary. Methodically overwhelmingly sophisticated ones that stand on the shoulders of giants. Simple ones that are so well put together that everyone likes them and understands them and cannot refuse them.

Therefore: Modelology is a new Discipline

Modelology [77] is study of models and modelling as well as model usage as an overarching art and craft for all areas of life, science and technology. It means colloquially the totality of human knowledge and abilities over the handling of all their life cases by skilled craftsmanship with models.

The study of models and modelling as well as model usage [76] takes into account the heterogeneity of the many different scenarios, functions and forms of use, capabilities of the users, and fundamentals through a systematics of modelling and model usage.

This means that, among other things, questions to be answered include:

- When does something become a model? What is its journey?
- What are the (essential) characteristics of a model?
- What quality is really expected from a model?
- To what extent can a model be trusted?
- Which characteristics exclude being a model?
- To what extent is a model suitable or appropriate in a given application and when not?
- What potential and what performance can be expected from a model?
- Etc.

The Notion of Model-Being

Definition 1 [Generic notion of model]. [76] *A model is a well-formed, adequate, and dependable instrument that represents 'something' (called origin as a source, archetype, starting point) and that functions in scenarios of use.*

Its criteria of well-formedness, adequacy, and dependability must be commonly accepted by its *community of practice* within some *context* and correspond to the *functions* that a model fulfills in *utilisation scenarios*.

As an instrument or more specifically an artifact a model comes with its *background*, e.g. paradigms, assumptions, postulates, language, thought community, etc. The background its often given only in an implicit form. The background is often implicit and hidden.

A well-formed instrument is *adequate* for a collection of origins if it is *analogous* to the origins to be represented according to some analogy criterion, it is more *focused* (e.g. simpler, truncated, more abstract or reduced) than the origins being modelled, and it sufficiently satisfies its *purpose*. Well-formedness enables an instrument to be *justified* by an empirical corroboration according to its objectives, by rational coherence and conformity explicitly stated through conformity formulas or statements, by falsifiability or validation, and by stability and plasticity within a collection of origins. The instrument is *sufficient* by its *quality* characterisation for internal quality, external quality and quality in use or through quality characteristics such as correctness, generality, usefulness, comprehensibility, parsimony, robustness, novelty etc. Sufficiency is typically combined with some assurance evaluation (tolerance, modality, confidence, and restrictions). A well-formed instrument is called *dependable* if it is sufficient and is justified for some of the justification properties and some of the sufficiency characteristics.

We notice that all properties are parametric and can be refined in dependence of their envisioned function in scenarios of use. Configuration is one typical refinement in modelling. For instance, conceptual models in database structure modelling use a Triptych pattern [76](paper 44 in collection 3) that bridges meaning of concepts and expression of concepts. Configuration can be based on a characterisation of the nature of the model, on an embedment into the application landscape and their scenarios, on strategic matrices for achieving modelling objectives with implicit background knowledge and prowess, and on tactical supporters and enablers for attaining objectives.

References

1. Atkinson, C., Gutheil, M., Kennel, B.: A flexible infrastructure for multilevel language engineering. IEEE Trans. Softw. Eng. **35**(6), 742–755 (2009)
2. Atkinson, C., Kühne, T.: The essence of multilevel metamodeling. In: International Conference on the Unified Modeling Language, pp. 19–33. Springer (2001)
3. Atkinson, C., Kuhne, T.: Model-driven development: a metamodeling foundation. IEEE Softw. **20**(5), 36–41 (2003)
4. Atkinson, C., Kühne, T.: Reducing accidental complexity in domain models. Softw. Syst. Model. **7**, 345–359 (2008)
5. Bano, D., Michael, J., Rumpe, B., Varga, S., Weske, M.: Process-aware digital twin cockpit synthesis from event logs. J. Comput. Lang. (COLA) **70** (2022). https://doi.org/10.1016/j.cola.2022.101121
6. Barcelos, P.P.F., et al.: A FAIR model catalog for ontology-driven conceptual modeling research. In: Conceptual Modeling - 41st International Conference, ER 2022. LNCS, vol. 13607, pp. 3–17. Springer (2022)
7. Bencomo, N., et al.: Abstraction engineering (2024). https://arxiv.org/abs/2408.14074
8. Bencomo, N., Götz, S., Song, H.: Models@run.time: a guided tour of the state of the art and research challenges. Softw. Syst. Model. **18**(5), 3049–3082 (2019). https://doi.org/10.1007/s10270-018-00712-x
9. Bonetti, F., Bucchiarone, A., Michael, J., Cicchetti, A., Marconi, A., Rumpe, B.: Digital twins of socio-technical ecosystems to drive societal change. In: International Conference on Model Driven Engineering Languages and Systems Companion (MODELS-C). ACM/IEEE (2024). https://doi.org/10.1145/3652620.3686248
10. Boren, T., Ramey, J.: Thinking aloud: reconciling theory and practice. IEEE Trans. Prof. Commun. **43**(3), 261–278 (2000)
11. Bork, D., Anagnostou, K., Wimmer, M.: Interoperable metamodeling platforms: the case of bridging ADOxx and EMF. In: 34th International Conference on Advanced Information Systems Engineering, pp. 479–497. Springer (2001)
12. Bork, D., Karagiannis, D., Pittl, B.: A survey of modeling language specification techniques. Inf. Syst. **87**, 101425 (2020)
13. Bork, D., Langer, P.: Language server protocol: an introduction to the protocol, its use, and adoption for web modeling tools. Enterp. Model. Inf. Syst. Archit. Int. J. Concept. Model. **18**(9), 1–16 (2023)

14. Bork, D., Langer, P., Ortmayr, T.: A vision for flexible GLSP-based web modeling tools. In: The Practice of Enterprise Modeling - 16th IFIP Working Conference, PoEM 2023. LNBIP, vol. 497, pp. 109–124. Springer (2023)
15. Boyes, H., Watson, T.: Digital twins: an analysis framework and open issues. Comput. Ind. **143**, 103763 (2022)
16. Brockhoff, T., et al.: Process prediction with digital twins. In: International Conference on Model Driven Engineering Languages and Systems Companion (MODELS-C), pp. 182–187. ACM/IEEE (2021)
17. Bunge, M.A.: Philosophy of Science: Volume 2, From Explanation to Justification. Routledge, New York (2017)
18. Burgueño, L., et al.: Contents for a model-based software engineering body of knowledge. Softw. Syst. Model. **18**(6), 3193–3205 (2019)
19. Castellanos, A., Samuel, B., Recker, J., Jabbari, M., Lukyanenko, R.: Conceptual modeling research: revisiting and updating wand and weber's 2002 research agenda. AIS SIGSAND, pp. 1–12 (2018)
20. Combemale, B., et al.: Model-based DevOps: foundations and challenges. In: International Conference on Model Driven Engineering Languages and Systems Companion (MODELS-C), pp. 429–433. ACM/IEEE (2023)
21. Di Ruscio, D., Kolovos, D., de Lara, J., Pierantonio, A., Tisi, M., Wimmer, M.: Low-code development and model-driven engineering: two sides of the same coin? Softw. Syst. Model. **21**(2), 437–446 (2022). https://doi.org/10.1007/s10270-021-00970-2
22. Eramo, R., Bordeleau, F., Combemale, B., van Den Brand, M., Wimmer, M., Wortmann, A.: Conceptualizing digital twins. IEEE Softw. **39**(2), 39–46 (2022). https://doi.org/10.1109/MS.2021.3130755
23. Eriksson, O., Johannesson, P., Bergholtz, M.: The case for classes and instances - a response to representing instances: the case for reengineering conceptual modelling grammars. Eur. J. Inf. Syst. **28**(6), 681–693 (2019)
24. Falkenberg, E.D., et al.: Frisco: a framework of information system concepts: the Frisco report (web edition). In: International Federation for Information Processing (IFIP) (1998)
25. Fleck, L.: Entstehung und Entwicklung einer wissenschaftlichen Tatsache; Einführung in die Lehre vom Denkstil und Denkkollektiv, vol. 312. Suhrkamp Taschenbuch Wissenschaft, neuauflage 1980 edn. (1935)
26. Frank, U.: Multilevel modeling: toward a new paradigm of conceptual modeling and information systems design. Bus. Inf. Syst. Eng. **6**, 319–337 (2014)
27. Guarino, N., Guizzardi, G.: We need to discuss the relationship: revisiting relationships as modeling constructs. In: Zdravkovic, J., Kirikova, M., Johannesson, P. (eds.) Advanced Information Systems Engineering, pp. 279–294. Springer (2015)
28. Guarino, N., Guizzardi, G., Mylopoulos, J.: On the philosophical foundations of conceptual models. Inf. Model. Knowl. Bases **XXXI**, 1–15 (2019)
29. Guarino, N., Oberle, D., Staab, S.: What is an ontology? In: Handbook on Ontologies, pp. 1–17. Springer, Heidelberg (2009)
30. Guizzardi, G., Botti Benevides, A., Fonseca, C.M., Porello, D., Almeida, J.P.A., Prince Sales, T.: UFO: unified foundational ontology. Appl. Ontol. **17**(1), 167–210 (2022)
31. Guizzardi, G., Wagner, G., Almeida, J.P.A., Guizzardi, R.: Towards ontological foundations for conceptual modeling: the unified foundational ontology (UFO) story. Appl. Ontol. **10**, 259–271 (2015)
32. Halpin, T.: Object-role modeling (ORM/NIAM). In: Handbook on Architectures of Information Systems, pp. 81–103. Springer (2006)

33. Halpin, T.A., Morgan, T.: Information Modeling and Relational Databases. Data Management Systems, 2nd edn. Morgan Kaufmann (2008)
34. Heerkens, H., Heijden, B.V.D.: On a tool for analysing cognitive processes using exploratory think-aloud experiments. Int. J. Hum. Resour. Dev. Manag. **5**(3), 240–283 (2005)
35. Heithoff, M., Hellwig, A., Michael, J., Rumpe, B.: Digital twins for sustainable software systems. In: GREENS 2023, pp. 19–23. IEEE (2023)
36. Hoppenbrouwers, S.J.B.A., Proper, H.A., Nijssen, M.: Towards key principles of fact based thinking. In: On the Move to Meaningful Internet Systems: OTM 2018 Workshops. LNCS, vol. 11231, pp. 77–86. Springer (2018)
37. ISO/IEC JTC 1/SC 32 Techn. Committee on Data management and interchange: Information processing systems – Concepts and terminology for the conceptual schema and the information base. Technical report. ISO/TR 9007:1987, ISO (1987)
38. Jonsson, T.: Conceptual data systems architecture principles for information systems. Front. Comput. Sci. **4**, 1008296 (2023)
39. Jonsson, T., Enquist, H.: Phenomenological framework for model enabled enterprise information systems. In: New Trends in Databases and Information Systems, vol. 1064, pp. 176–187. Springer, Cham (2019)
40. Karabulut, E., Pileggi, S.F., Groth, P., Degeler, V.: Ontologies in digital twins: a systematic literature review. Futur. Gener. Comput. Syst. **153**, 442–456 (2024). https://doi.org/10.1016/j.future.2023.12.013
41. Kaschek, R.: Konzeptionelle Modellierung. Habilitation thesis, Alpen-Adria-Universität Klagenfurt (2003)
42. Kern, H., Hummel, A., Kühne, S.: Towards a comparative analysis of meta-metamodels. In: Proceedings of the Compilation of the co-located Workshops on DSM 2011, TMC 2011, AGERE! 2011, AOOPES 2011, NEAT 2011, & VMIL 2011, pp. 7–12. ACM (2011)
43. Khatri, V., Samuel, B.M.: Analytics for managerial work. Commun. ACM **62**(4), 100 (2019)
44. Kirchhof, J.C., Michael, J., Rumpe, B., Varga, S., Wortmann, A.: Model-driven digital twin construction: synthesizing the integration of cyber-physical systems with their information systems. In: Proceedings of the 23rd ACM/IEEE International Conference on Model Driven Engineering Languages and Systems, pp. 90–101. ACM (2020)
45. Kosa, V., Ermolayev, V.: Terminology Saturation - Detection, Measurement and Use. Springer (2022)
46. Lakoff, G., Johnson, M.: Metaphors we Live By. University of Chicago Press (1980)
47. Lima, H.C., Laender, A.H., Moro, M.M., de Oliveira, J.P.: An analysis of the collaboration network of the international conference on conceptual modeling at the age of 40. Data Knowl. Eng. **130** (2020)
48. Lukyanenko, R., Storey, V.C., Pastor, O.: System: a core conceptual modeling construct for capturing complexity. DKE **141**, 1–29 (2022)
49. Lukyanenko, R., Castellanos, A., Parsons, J., Tremblay, M.C., Storey, V.C.: Using conceptual modeling research to support machine learning. In: Information Systems Engineering in Responsible Information Systems (CAiSE Forum 2019), pp. 70–81 (2019)
50. Lukyanenko, R., Samuel, B., Storey, V., Sturm, A.: Conceptual modeling systems: a vision for the future of conceptual modeling. In: ER Forum and PhD Symposium 2022, vol. 3211. CEUR-WS (2022)
51. Mayr, H.C., Thalheim, B.: The triptych of conceptual modeling. Softw. Syst. Model. **20**(1), 7–24 (2021)

52. Mayr, H.C., Thalheim, B.: Conceptual modeling: a still unfinished saga. about prejudices, aberrations, solutions and challenges. Informing Possible Future Worlds, pp. 103–122 (2024)
53. Metin, H., Bork, D.: On developing and operating GLSP-based web modeling tools: lessons learned from BIGUML. In: 26th ACM/IEEE International Conference on Model Driven Engineering Languages and Systems, MODELS 2023, pp. 129–139. IEEE (2023)
54. Michael, J., et al.: Integrating models of civil structures in digital twins: state-of-the-Art and challenges. J. Infrastruct. Intell. Resilience (2024)
55. Michael, J., Bork, D., Wimmer, M., Mayr, H.C.: Quo Vadis modeling? Findings of a community survey, an ad-hoc bibliometric analysis, and expert interviews on data, process, and software modeling. J. Softw. Syst. Model. (SoSyM) **23**(1), 7–28 (2024)
56. Michael, J., David, I., Bork, D.: Digital twin evolution for sustainable smart ecosystems. In: International Conference on Model Driven Engineering Languages and Systems Companion (MODELS-C). ACM (2024)
57. Michael, J., Pfeiffer, J., Rumpe, B., Wortmann, A.: Integration challenges for digital twin systems-of-systems. In: 10th IEEE/ACM International Workshop on Software Engineering for Systems-of-Systems and Software Ecosystems. IEEE (2022)
58. Mylopoulos, J., Borgida, A., Jarke, M., Koubarakis, M.: Telos: representing knowledge about information systems. ACM Trans. Inf. Syst. (TOIS) **8**(4), 325–362 (1990)
59. Noushad, B., Van Gerven, P.W.M., Bruin, A.: Twelve tips for applying the think-aloud method to capture cognitive processes. Med. Teach. **46**, 1–6 (2023)
60. Novak, P., Guinot, V., Jeffrey, A., Reeve, D.E.: Hydraulic Modelling - An Introduction: Principles, Methods, and Applications, 1st edn. Spon Press, London (2010)
61. Object Management Group (OMG): Meta Object Facility (MOF) Core Specification Version 2.5.1 (2019)
62. Olivé, A.: Conceptual Modeling of Information Systems. Springer, Heidelberg (2007)
63. Partridge, C., de Cesare, S., Mitchell, A., Odell, J.: Formalization of the classification pattern: survey of classification modeling in information systems engineering. Softw. Syst. Model. **17**(1), 167–203 (2018)
64. Proper, H.A., Guizzardi, G.: On domain modelling and requisite variety. In: Grabis, J., Bork, D. (eds.) PoEM 2020. LNBIP, vol. 400, pp. 186–196. Springer, Cham (2020). https://doi.org/10.1007/978-3-030-63479-7_13
65. Proper, H.A., Guizzardi, G.: On domain conceptualization. In: Aveiro, D., Guizzardi, G., Pergl, R., Proper, H.A. (eds.) EEWC 2020. LNBIP, vol. 411, pp. 49–69. Springer, Cham (2021). https://doi.org/10.1007/978-3-030-74196-9_4
66. Proper, H.A., Guizzardi, G.: On views, diagrams, programs, animations, and other models. In: Informing Possible Future Worlds - Essays in Honour of Ulrich Frank, chap. 5, pp. 123–138. Logos Verlag, Berlin, Germany (2024)
67. Recker, J., Lukyanenko, R., Jabbari, M., Samuel, B.M., Castellano, A.: From representation to mediation: a new agenda for conceptual modeling research in a digital world. MIS Q. **45**(1), 269–300 (2020)
68. Rosch, E.: Classification of real-world objects: origins and representations in cognition. In: Thinking: Readings in Cognitive Science, pp. 212–222. Cambridge University Press (1977)
69. Safra, J., et al. (eds.) J.A.C.: Analogy. Encyclopedia Britannica (2013)
70. Sandkuhl, K., et al.: Analytics for managerial work. Bus. Inf. Syst. Eng. **60**, 69–80 (2018)

71. Shekhovtsov, V.A., Ranasinghe, S., Mayr, H.C., Michael, J.: Domain specific models as system links. In: Advances in Conceptual Modeling Workshops (ER 2018), pp. 330–340. Springer (2018)
72. Smirnow, W.: Lehrbuch der höheren Mathematik, Teil 1. Europa Lehrmittel, Haan-Gruiten (2017)
73. Sowa, J.F.: Knowledge Representation: Logical, Philosophical, and Computation Foundations. Brooks/Cole (2000)
74. Stachowiak, H.: Allgemeine Modelltheorie. Springer (1973)
75. Storey, V.C., Lukyanenko, R., Castellanos, A.: Conceptual modeling: topics, themes, and technology trends. ACM Comput. Surv. **55** (2023)
76. Thalheim, B.: Models, to model, and modelling. Collections of papers. https://www.researchgate.net (search keyphrase "Towards a theory of models, especially conceptual models and modelling"), also academia.edu (2009–2021)
77. Thalheim, B.: Modelology - the new science, life and practice discipline. In: Information Modelling and Knowledge Bases XXXV. Frontiers in Artificial Intelligence and Applications, vol. 380, pp. 1–19. IOS Press (2023)
78. Voelz, A., Muck, C., Amlashi, D.M., Karagiannis, D.: Bridging haptic design thinking and cyber-physical environments through digital twins using conceptual modeling. In: 22nd International Conference on Perspectives in Business Informatics Research (BIR 2023), pp. 195–208 (2023)
79. Wand, Y., Weber, R.: On the deep structure of information systems. Inf. Syst. J. **5**(3), 203–223 (1995)
80. Wilmont, I., Hengeveld, S., Barendsen, E., Hoppenbrouwers, S.J.B.A.: Cognitive mechanisms of conceptual modelling – How do people do it? In: Conceptual Modeling – 32th International Conference, ER 2013. LNCS, vol. 8217, pp. 74–87. Springer (2013)
81. Wittgenstein, L.: Tractatus Logico-Philosophicus. International Library of Psychology, Philosophy and Scientific Method. Translated by Ramsey and Ogden (1922)
82. Wong, W., Liu, W., Bennamoun, M.: Ontology learning from text: a look back and into the future. ACM Comput. Surv. **44**(4), 20:1–20:36 (2012)
83. Woodruff Smith, D.: "Pure" logic, ontology, and phenomenology. Revue internationale de philosophie **224**(2003/2 (n° 224)), 21–44 (2003)
84. Yu, E.: Social modelling and i*. conceptual modeling: foundations and applications. In: Conceptual Modeling: Foundations and Applications: Essays in Honor of John Mylopoulos, pp. 99–121 (2009)

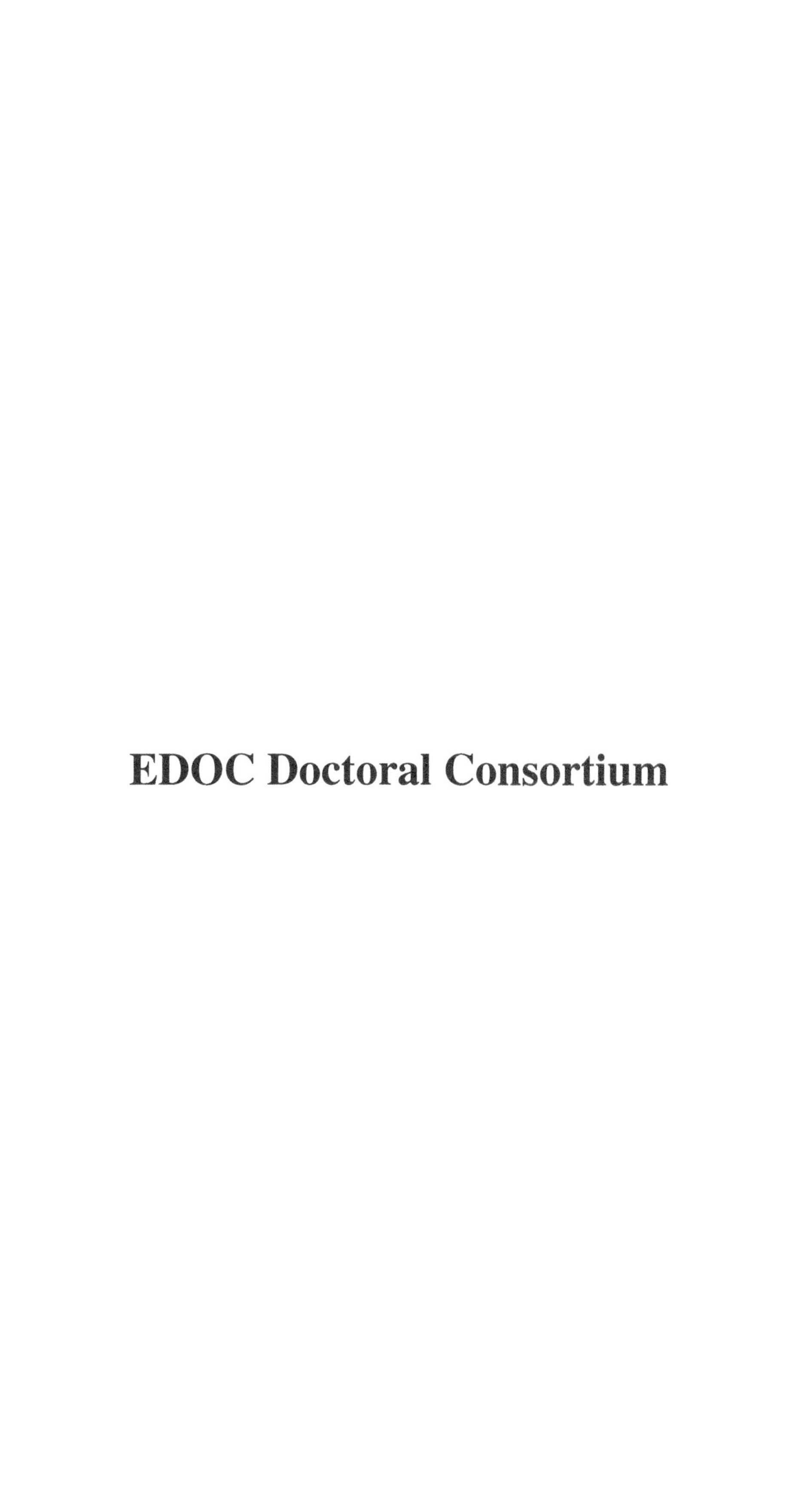

EDOC Doctoral Consortium

Towards Resilient Construction Logistics with Digital Twins

Fatemeh Massah(✉)

Pervasive Systems, University of Twente Enschede, Enschede, The Netherlands
f.massah@utwente.nl

Abstract. Efficient logistics management is key for maintaining project timelines, controlling budgets, and enhancing productivity and promoting sustainability within the construction industry. However, challenges such as delays in material delivery, equipment malfunctions, and labor shortages require effective management strategies to prevent significant disruptions. This research explores the application of digital twin (DT) technology to optimize construction planning and execution through real-time monitoring, simulation, and analysis. By leveraging advanced sensing and communication technologies, this study aims to develop and validate DT models specifically tailored for construction logistics. The anticipated outcomes include improved decision-making, enhanced collaboration, and increased efficiency, which are expected to result in reduced costs and shortened timelines. The findings have the potential to strengthen the competitiveness and operational efficiency of the construction industry.

Keywords: Digital Twin · Construction Logistics · Resilience · Data-Driven Insights

1 Introduction

The construction sector must accelerate the adoption of digital technologies to address sector-specific challenges and retain its competitive edge. Despite the long-term benefits, adoption has been slow, largely due to significant upfront investments required [1]. A key technological trend influencing various sectors, including construction, is digitization, which affects individuals, communities, and nations alike [15]. However, the construction sector faces unique technical barriers, notably the complexity of deploying digital solutions across geographically dispersed project sites [11]. Promising technologies such as Building Information Modeling (BIM) offer potential [29], yet their global update has been sluggish. This hesitation stems from perceived risks and the complexities associated with developing and integrating technologies into industry practices [1,12].

In recent decades, the built environment has witnessed strides toward greater efficiency and sustainability. Innovative project management methods, enhanced by IT advancements, are now addressing the demands of real estate owners for

M. Kaczmarek-Heß et al. (Eds.): EDOC 2024 Workshops, LNBIP 537, pp. 327–334, 2025.
https://doi.org/10.1007/978-3-031-79059-1_20

timely, high-quality projects that comply with stringent environmental regulations [7]. While industries such as automotive, manufacturing, and services have leveraged IT to enhance their competitiveness, the construction industry has struggled to keep pace, lagging behind various other sectors [2]. However, the construction industry has also seen notable advancements, such as the increased adoption of BIM and Digital Twin (DT) technologies, which enhance project visualization, coordination, and management [16]. These technologies are driving improvements in project efficiency and sustainability, demonstrating the industry's capacity for innovation.

Despite advancements, the construction industry faces persistent challenging, including low productivity, poor reputation, unpredictability, fragmentation, and insufficient R&D investment [28]. Addressing these challenges requires ongoing efforts, such as advancing technologies and improving practices to maximize digital transformation benefits.

Since its emergence in the early 21st century, DT technology has gained momentum and is now on a path to becoming a widely accepted and implemented innovation [14]. DTs create virtual models of physical assets or processes, enabling the simulation of real-world behaviors, performance analysis, and optimization for improved business outcomes [17]. The maturation of technologies, including affordable data storage, powerful processing capabilities, and reliable high-speed networks, has been instrumental in this progress [4].

For DT technology to achieve broad acceptance within the construction industry, it must directly address the sector's most pressing challenges [28]. The technology offers potential benefits, including improved project planning, increased operational efficiency, improved risk management, and cost savings [3,6]. As a result, both industry and academia are increasingly focused on integrating DT concepts, with major companies adopting them in their products and researchers exploring their technological and business implications.

This research focuses on optimizing construction logistics, a key area often hampered by delays in material deliveries, equipment malfunctions, and labor shortages. This paper is structured as follows. Section 2 provides a problem statement and a brief overview of prior research in this domain. Section 3 outlines the anticipated project's methodology, discussing the study's design and anticipated results. Finally, Sect. 4 concludes the paper by summarizing key findings and proposing future research directions.

2 Problem Statement and Related Work

2.1 Problem Statement

Construction logistics processes are frequently disrupted by factors such as adverse weather conditions, raw material shortages, extended waiting times, and system failures [9,19]. These disruptions can complicate decision-making. Despite its economic significance, the construction sector has been slow to adopt modern data-driven methodologies for process optimization. In contrast, other industries have demonstrated increased efficiency through the implementation of such techniques.

Given the role of construction within broader supply chains, inefficiencies and disruptions can propagate, negatively impacting overall productivity across multiple sectors. One barrier to achieve operational insights may be the absence of robust data management systems. Construction logistics likely generate various data that may need to be collected, referenced, and synchronized for decision-making. The research explores the potential of DTs to possibly enhance decision-making in construction logistics through real-time data integration.(see Fig. 1). DTs can be data-driven, model-driven, or a hybrid of both [6], and their application promises improvements in logistics management, operational efficiency, and project sustainability.

This research addresses the following **Research Question:** How can the implementation of DT technology in construction logistics enhance real-time, data-driven decision-making and improve overall efficiency in the construction industry? This research is further broken down into these subquestions: a) How can identifying inefficiencies in construction logistics motivate the adoption of DT technology for real-time decision-making? b) What are the key objectives for implementing DT technology in construction supply chains, based on existing literature? c) How should an initial architecture for DTs in construction supply chains be designed? d) How can simulations of DT technology assess potential impacts in an illustrative scenario within an enterprise architecture framework?

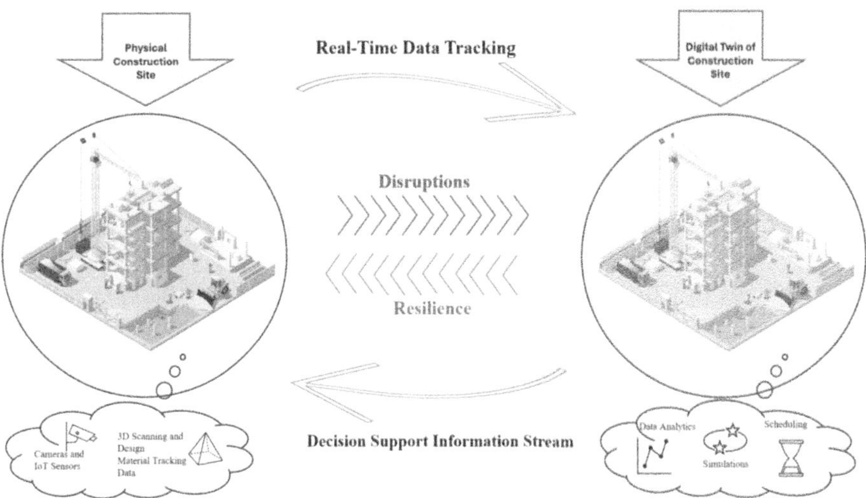

Fig. 1. Informal conceptual framework for the digital twin in an construction site

The research investigates the application of data, particularly from DT models, across multiple domains within the construction industry. By examining how such data can improve construction logistics networks, the study addresses gaps in the adoption and integration of data-driven strategies. A key focus is on the potential of DTs to sustain operational efficiency while simultaneously promoting sustainability and resilience in construction processes. Figure 1 illustrates the proposed conceptual framework for the DT implementation on construction sites. In this framework, real-time data is collected from the physical site and processed through the DT using simulation and analysis. This processed data is converted into actionable insights, enabling decision-makers to optimize operations, especially in managing disruptions.

2.2 Related Work

Construction Industry Logistics and Disruptions. The construction industry faces persistent challenges such as fragmentation, waste, low productivity, cost overruns, and disputes [27]. These issues underscores the need for integrated systems to improve logistics and overall project outcomes [10,26,30]. Work of [31] further highlight the vulnerabilities introduced by fragmented teams and unpredictable site conditions. Solutions such as BIM, supply chain integration, and improved logistics are increasingly recognized as strategies to boost efficiency and resilience.

Data-Driven Insights for Construction Logistics. Effective data acquisition and exchange is a prerequisite for improving performance in construction projects [8]. However, despite the industry's large volumes of data, a gap remains in understanding the impact of Big Data and digital technologies throughout the entire project lifecycle [25]. Current research focuses mainly on specific technologies but lack an analysis of their organizational and technological implications across project phases. While data integration has been explored, the influence of Big Data on end-to-end project execution remains under-researched. Our work addresses this by evaluating the role of data-driven DT technologies in improving construction logistics and project outcomes.

Digital Twin in Construction Industry. Digital transformation in construction has been uneven, with areas like architecture and project management seeing more digitization than others, such as supplier management [18]. As the industry grapples with rising costs and challenging sustainability practices, digital strategies, including DTs, are gaining traction [13]. DTs have the potential to enhance monitoring, secure data management, and optimization across the design, construction, and operational phases of built assets [5]. However, the integration of Big Data technologies with DTs remains limited, hampering the realization of their full potential [23,24]. For example, recent studies highlight the potential of DTs but note challenges in data scalability and integration [20,21]. Our research aims to bridge these gaps by exploring the practical applications of DTs in construction supply chains to enhance real-time logistics and decision-making.

3 Methodology

This research investigates the impact of data-driven insights and DTs on the efficiency of construction logistics networks, utilizing various research approaches.

3.1 Research Design

To meet this study's objectives, we will describe the functionality and goals of a DT tailored to construction logistics, collect data from real-world case studies, and develop an initial DT design, which is iteratively refined for accuracy and reliability.

We adopt the Design Science Research Methodology (DSRM) as outlined by [22], chosen for its structured, theory-driven integration and its iterative refinement process. The artifacts developed through DSRM are key to addressing the specific challenges and objectives of this study. Figure 2 illustrates the anticipated research process.

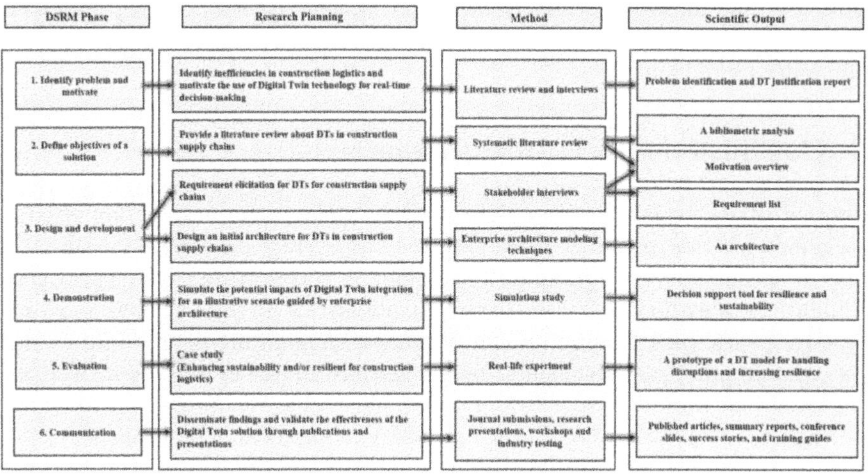

Fig. 2. An overview of the research methodology

The DT design incorporates synchronized data to form a virtual representation of the logistics network, providing real-time insights and predictive analytics. This model simulates potential disruptions and optimizes resource allocation using advanced data processing and predictive algorithms.

This doctoral research aims to demonstrate the role of DT technology in advancing construction logistics management by addressing key objectives and providing actionable solutions.

3.2 Expected Results

The construction sector depends on efficient logistics for timely project delivery, and decision-makers increasingly require real-time, data-driven insights for performance optimization. This need is amplified by recent advances in digital technologies such as Internet of highlights the urgency for more effective logistics management strategies. Recent advancements in digital technologies like Internet of Things (IoT), cloud computing, and predictive analytics, which have transformed logistics by enabling real-time monitoring and management across supply chains.

DTs enhance the resilience and sustainability of construction logistics by simulating disruption scenarios and facilitating robust contingency planning, enabling swift recovery from unforeseen events. This proactive approach minimizes downtime, maintains project continuity, and optimize resource usage, contributing to reduced waste and lower carbon emissions.

In this study, DTs will provide real-time, actionable insights related to proactive decision-making in construction logistics. By monitoring inventory, equipment, and transportation, DTs will anticipate bottlenecks, optimize resource allocation, and improve both efficiency and cost-effectiveness. Furthermore, DTs will strengthen resilience through rapid disruption recovery and promote sustainability by reducing waste.

4 Conclusion and Future Research

In recent years, the integration of advanced technologies in construction logistics has gained traction, enabling decision-makers to leverage data-driven insights for process optimization. A promising technology in this domain is the use of DTs. While the application of DT in construction logistics presents numerous potential advantages, their adoption remains limited, highlighting the need for further research and practical implementation. This study addresses this gap by utilizing real-time data from case studies to develop and refine DT models for construction logistics. Through monitoring inventory, equipment, and transportation, DTs are expected to alleviate bottlenecks, optimize resource allocation, enhance allocation, and contribute to greater resiliency and sustainability.

Future research could focus on integrating advanced analytics and machine learning into DT models to enhance predictive capabilities and explore standardized frameworks for broader industry adoption. Additionally, investigating the role of DT models in reducing the environmental impact of construction logistics-such as emissions tracking and resource optimization-holds promise. Further studies may also evaluate DT's contribution to improving network resilience, assess economic implications, and implement real-world pilot projects.

Acknowledgment. This work has received funding from the ECOLOGIC project (funded by the Dutch Ministry of Infrastructure and Water Management and TKI Dinalog; case no. 31192090). The author would also like to thank Rob Bemthuis and Martijn Koot for sharing their insights.

References

1. Agarwal, R., Chandrasekaran, S., Sridhar, M.: Imagining construction's digital future. McKinsey & Company **24**(06) (2016)
2. Arayici, Y., Coates, P., et al.: A system engineering perspective to knowledge transfer: a case study approach of BIM adoption. Virtual Reality-Hum. Comput. Interact. **2006**, 179–206 (2012)
3. Bar-Cohen, A., Matin, K., Jankowski, N., Sharar, D.: Two-phase thermal ground planes: technology development and parametric results. J. Electron. Packag. **137**(1), 010801 (2015)
4. Barykin, S.Y., Kapustina, I.V., Kirillova, T.V., Yadykin, V.K., Konnikov, Y.A.: Economics of digital ecosystems. J. Open Innov. Technol. Market Complex. **6**(4), 124 (2020)
5. Boje, C., Guerriero, A., Kubicki, S., Rezgui, Y.: Towards a semantic construction digital twin: directions for future research. Autom. Constr. **114**, 103179 (2020)
6. Boschert, S., Rosen, R.: Digital twin-the simulation aspect. Mechatronic futures: challenges and solutions for mechatronic systems and their designers, pp. 59–74 (2016)
7. Chathuranga, S., Jayasinghe, S., Antucheviciene, J., Wickramarachchi, R., Udayanga, N., Weerakkody, W.S.: Practices driving the adoption of agile project management methodologies in the design stage of building construction projects. Buildings **13**(4), 1079 (2023)
8. Dawood, N., Akinsola, A., Hobbs, B.: Development of automated communication of system for managing site information using internet technology. Autom. Constr. **11**(5), 557–572 (2002)
9. Ekanayake, E., Shen, G.Q., Kumaraswamy, M.M., Owusu, E.K.: Identifying supply chain vulnerabilities in industrialized construction: an overview. Int. J. Constr. Manag. **22**(8), 1464–1477 (2022)
10. Formoso, C.T., Soibelman, L., De Cesare, C., Isatto, E.L.: Material waste in building industry: main causes and prevention. J. Constr. Eng. Manag. **128**(4), 316–325 (2002)
11. George, A.S.: 5G-enabled digital transformation: mapping the landscape of possibilities and problems (2024)
12. Ghaffarianhoseini, A., et al.: Building Information Modelling (BIM) uptake: clear benefits, understanding its implementation, risks and challenges. Renew. Sustain. Energy Rev. **75**, 1046–1053 (2017)
13. Greif, T., Stein, N., Flath, C.M.: Peeking into the void: digital twins for construction site logistics. Comput. Ind. **121**, 103264 (2020)
14. Hu, W., Zhang, T., Deng, X., Liu, Z., Tan, J.: Digital twin: a state-of-the-art review of its enabling technologies, applications and challenges. J. Intell. Manuf. Spec. Equipment **2**(1), 1–34 (2021)
15. Leviäkangas, P., Paik, S.M., Moon, S.: Keeping up with the pace of digitization: the case of the Australian construction industry. Technol. Soc. **50**, 33–43 (2017)
16. Makarov, D., Vahdatikhaki, F., Miller, S., Mowlaei, S., Dorée, A.: Usability assessment of compaction operator support systems using virtual prototyping. Autom. Constr. **129**, 103784 (2021)
17. Marmolejo-Saucedo, J.A.: Design and development of digital twins: a case study in supply chains. Mob. Netw. Appl. **25**(6), 2141–2160 (2020)
18. Musarat, M.A., Sadiq, A., Alaloul, W.S., Abdul Wahab, M.M.: A systematic review on enhancement in quality of life through digitalization in the construction industry. Sustainability **15**(1), 202 (2022)

19. Nesarnobari, S., Shahzad, W., Jelodar, M.B., Sutrisna, M.: Investigation of the effects of supply chain disruptions on offsite construction projects. In: International Conference on Engineering, Project, and Production Management, pp. 161–172. Springer (2024)
20. Opoku, D.G.J., Perera, S., Osei-Kyei, R., Rashidi, M.: Digital twin application in the construction industry: a literature review. J. Build. Eng. **40**, 102726 (2021)
21. Opoku, D., Perera, S., Osei-Kyei, R., Rashidi, M., Famakinwa, T., Bamdad, K.: Drivers for digital twin adoption in the construction industry: a systematic literature review (2022)
22. Peffers, K., Tuunanen, T., Rothenberger, M.A., Chatterjee, S.: A design science research methodology for information systems research. J. Manag. Inf. Syst. **24**(3), 45–77 (2007)
23. Rathore, M.M., Shah, S.A., Shukla, D., Bentafat, E., Bakiras, S.: The role of AI, machine learning, and big data in digital twinning: a systematic literature review, challenges, and opportunities. IEEE Access **9**, 32030–32052 (2021)
24. Samuelson, O., Stehn, L.: Digital transformation in construction-a review. J. Inf. Technol. Constr. **28**, 385–404 (2023)
25. Sarkar, B.D., Shankar, R.: Understanding the barriers of port logistics for effective operation in the Industry 4.0 era: data-driven decision making. Int. J. Inf. Manag. Data Insights **1**(2), 100031 (2021)
26. Sepanosian, T., Küpers, X., Joza, P., Massah, F., Bemthuis, R.: An IoT-based architecture for real-time emission monitoring at construction sites. In: 2024 IEEE 26th International Conference on Business Informatics (CBI), pp. 139–148 (2024)
27. Shen, W., Hao, Q., Mak, H., Neelamkavil, J., Xie, H., Dickinson, J., Thomas, R., Pardasani, A., Xue, H.: Systems integration and collaboration in architecture, engineering, construction, and facilities management: a review. Adv. Eng. Inform. **24**(2), 196–207 (2010)
28. Siebert, M.: Applying a Systems Thinking Approach to the Construction Industry. Taylor & Francis (2023)
29. Vitente, L.S., Ong, A.K.S., German, J.D.: Assessment of adoption and acceptance of building information modeling for building construction among industries in Qatar. Buildings **14**(5), 1433 (2024)
30. Xue, X., Li, X., Shen, Q., Wang, Y.: An agent-based framework for supply chain coordination in construction. Autom. Constr. **14**(3), 413–430 (2005)
31. Zainal Abidin, N.A., Ingirige, B.: The dynamics of vulnerabilities and capabilities in improving resilience within Malaysian construction supply chain. Constr. Innov. **18**(4), 412–432 (2018)

iRESEARCH – 2nd International Workshop on Empirical Methodologies for Research in Enterprise Architecture and Service-oriented Computing

Report from the iRESEARCH 2024 Workshop Chairs

In the past decades, the EDOC conference and its co-located workshops have presented many research initiatives in which Enterprise Architecture (EA) and Service-Oriented Computing (SOC) scholars carried out empirical studies with practitioners and for practitioners in industry. The various industry-university collaborations represented at EDOC have opened up a conversation about evaluating frameworks, approaches, and tools and comparing their resilience, sustainability, usefulness, and effectiveness in specific practical contexts. In particular, service-oriented approaches and EA approaches are increasingly often applied in the context of new areas, such as artificial intelligence-enabled enterprise computing, the Internet of Things, digital ecosystems, digital twins, and green and cloud computing, among others. The EDOC community's heightened interest in empirical evaluation has led to the accumulation and publishing of empirical evidence through design science research, exploratory and confirmatory case studies, interview-based studies, focus groups, and surveys. The purpose of the second International Workshop on Empirical Methodologies for Research in Enterprise Architecture and Service-Oriented Computing (iRESEARCH) at EDOC 2024 was to initiate a conversation on the interfaces of the EA/SOC and Empirical Research Methodologies (ERM) disciplines.

The goals of the workshop were:

- to open up an interdisciplinary debate on the steadily moving frontiers in empirical methodologies in support of EA and SOC research projects and
- to expand the network of researchers designing and conducting empirical studies in EA and in the sub-fields of SOC, which in turn will lead to cross-fertilization between these two fields and ERM.

The targeted outcomes of this workshop included the identification of open research problems and possible solutions to these problems, regarding (1) evaluation and comparison of EA and service-oriented methods, processes, and tools in context; (2) emerging research methods; (3) new and unexpected forms of collaboration with industrial partners in empirical research projects; and (4) evaluation of transferability of empirical results to practice.

In 2024, the iRESEARCH workshop program featured a tutorial and an empirical study illustrating two contexts of industry-relevant research carried out with practitioners on board. The tutorial was on how to apply the Design Science Research paradigm in PhD research projects that focus on Data Analytics. Multiple Design Science Research methodologies were presented and the suitability of each one was illustrated in a specific Data Analytics research context. Examples from the practice of the presenter were used to illustrate the points. The follow-up questions-and-answers session leveraged the knowledge of the attendees and their experience to come up with a list of open issues which could be discussed further in the next edition of the workshop, hopefully in 2025. After the tutorial, attendees enjoyed a presentation on the industrial application of design science in the context of data mesh architectures. We hope you enjoyed the workshop and the review of the workshop proceedings.

Acknowledgments We would like to thank the Program Committee members for their dedication to rigorous and timely peer review, which allowed us to highlight the very best research from the empirical EDOC community. We also thank the authors who considered iRESEARCH as the destination of their empirical papers. Finally, we would like to express our appreciation for the timely response and assistance that we received from the Organizing Committee and the staff of the EDOC 2024 conference and, in particular, to the EDOC 2024 General Chairs, Henderik A. Proper and Miguel Mira da Silva.

October 2024

Maya Daneva
Faiza A. Bukhsh

Organization

Workshop Chairs

Maya Daneva	University of Twente, The Netherlands
Faiza A. Bukhsh	University of Twente, The Netherlands

Programme Committee

Jelena Zdravkovic	Stockholm University, Sweden
Saïd Assar	IMT Business School, France
Pnina Soffer	University of Haifa, Israel
Hajo Reijers	Utrecht University, The Netherlands
Jeewanie Jayasinghe Arachchige	University of Twente, The Netherlands
Oscar Pastor	Universidad Politécnica de Valencia, Spain
Hans Weigand	Tilburg University, The Netherlands
Selmin Nurcan	Université de Paris 1 Panthéon-Sorbonne, France
Dimka Karastoyanova	University of Groningen, The Netherlands
Claudia Negri Ribalta	University of Luxembourg, Luxembourg
Sybren de Kinderen	Eindhoven University of Technology, The Netherlands
Marite Kirikova	Riga Technical University, Latvia
Yves Wautelet	Katholieke Universiteit Leuven, Belgium
Patrizio De Alencar Silva	Universidade Federal de Pernambuco, Brazil

Towards a Data Mesh Reference Architecture

Daniel van der Werf, João Moreira(✉), and Jean Paul Sebastian Piest

University of Twente, Enschede, The Netherlands
{j.luizrebelomoreira,j.p.s.piest}@utwente.nl

Abstract. The increasing complexity and volume of organizational data have led to the emergence of the Data Mesh paradigm, a data architecture with a federated governance aimed at addressing the limitations of traditional monolithic data systems that has overlapping principles with the microservices architectural style. Although related work exists, the majority of architectural approaches regarding Data Mesh are conceptual, technology-centric or vendor specific. This paper introduces a Data Mesh Reference Architecture (RA) using the ArchiMate enterprise architecture modeling language, designed to assist organizations in implementing (or migrating towards) data mesh solutions. The RA comprises three main components: domain architecture, self-serve data platform architecture, and federated governance, which reflect the main Data Mesh principles. Through a systematic literature review, four data mesh archetypes (Pure, Semi-Pure, Hybrid, and Distributed) were identified, along with challenges, limitations, and motivational factors for adoption. A questionnaire-based validation among experts confirmed the RA's utility, quality, and variability. However, practical validation was not conducted within this study. The study contributes to both literature and practice by offering a structured approach and a set of reference models for designing data mesh architectures. Future research can contribute to practical validation, assessment of RA-driven design efficiency, and extending the RA with domain-driven solution architectures.

Keywords: Data Mesh · Reference Architecture · Data Architecture · Data Mesh Archetype · ArchiMate

1 Introduction

In recent years, the rising interest in data-driven decision-making has led organizations to invest heavily in data storage and processing solutions. Initially, data platforms evolved from simple data warehouses to more complex two-tier architectures combining data lakes and data warehouses (lakehouses). However, these systems face limitations, including difficulties regarding the processing semi-structured data, high costs, and complexity in managing data pipelines. As businesses generate increasing amounts of data, centralized monolithic data

M. Kaczmarek-Heß et al. (Eds.): EDOC 2024 Workshops, LNBIP 537, pp. 339–353, 2025.
https://doi.org/10.1007/978-3-031-79059-1_21

architectures, managed by central data teams, have become bottlenecks, struggling to scale, leading to inefficiencies in data cleaning, preparation, and access. These architectures also suffer from low domain-specific knowledge, lack of ownership, siloed structures, and long lead times for accessing data, making them less responsive to modern business needs [1–4].

The Data Mesh paradigm - introduced by Zhamak Dehghani in an article in 2019[1] and further detailed in her book [5] - represents a shift from centralized, monolithic data architectures to a decentralized, domain-driven approach with federated governance. It focuses on four core principles: treating data as a product, domain-oriented decentralized data ownership, self-serve data platforms, and federated computational governance. By decentralizing data management, Data Mesh addresses the bottlenecks and inefficiencies of traditional centralized systems, enabling better scalability, ownership, and faster data access. Data products, managed within their respective domains, enhance collaboration and data quality, while the self-serve platform supports efficiency. However, implementing Data Mesh requires significant organizational changes and strong governance to avoid siloing and ensure consistency [1,6–8].

This paper presents a Reference Architecture (RA) for Data Mesh. The RA is based on a Systematic Literature Review (SLR) and modelled using ArchiMate. The main research question that is discussed in this paper is stated as follows "... ?".

This paper is structured as follows. Section 2 describes selected related work that formed the theoretical foundation for the RA, including the main concepts of this study, with emphasis on Data Mesh and Enterprise Architecture. Section 3 presents the SLR that serves the purpose of answering the earlier introduced MRQ and derived Knowledge Questions (KQs). Section 4 presents the Data Mesh RA. Section 5 describes how the architecture was validated. Section 6 discusses the results of the research in relation to related work. Section 7 concludes this paper and outlines future work.

2 Background

This section covers foundational theoretical knowledge on key concepts, including Data Mesh, EA, and RAs.

2.1 Data Mesh

Data mesh is a decentralized, domain-oriented approach to managing enterprise data architecture, aiming to address challenges faced by large, data-driven organizations [9]. It draws inspiration from the microservice architecture used in software engineering, which responded to the inefficiencies of monolithic systems. Similar to how microservices decentralize application development, data mesh decentralizes data ownership and management across various domains,

[1] https://martinfowler.com/articles/data-monolith-to-mesh.html.

making it scalable and adaptable. Each domain in a data mesh operates like an independent unit responsible for its data products, fostering accountability and collaboration across the organization to meet dynamic business requirements [10].

The four core principles of data mesh, as outlined by Dehghani[2], are: treating data as a product, domain-oriented decentralized ownership, self-serve data infrastructure, and federated computational governance. Treating data as a product means data must be accessible, self-explanatory, secure, and valuable to the business. Data products should be designed with key attributes, ensuring they are discoverable, trustworthy, and interoperable, among others. To implement a data mesh, organizations must undergo cultural and organizational changes, with teams becoming responsible for their data as a product to serve others [6,11]. Domain-oriented decentralized data ownership assigns responsibility to specific business units or teams to manage and publish data products [12]. Domains are aligned with business functions, allowing them to independently produce data in line with organizational objectives [6,7]. The self-serve platform enables these domains to create and maintain their data products using shared infrastructure like computational resources, storage, and security, all managed by a central support team. The federated computational governance ensures that while domains operate independently, they follow enforceable protocols and policies for data standards, security, and communication, maintaining overall cohesion [3,4,13].

Implementing data mesh brings both benefits and challenges. It promotes scalability, adaptability, and cost efficiency, yet it requires significant organizational restructuring and cultural shifts [1,14]. Teams need to develop new capabilities to manage their data independently, while effective governance, discoverability, and data security remain critical. Additionally, replicating efforts across domains can lead to inefficiencies if not managed properly [15,16]. Despite these challenges, data mesh is a versatile methodology that can be applied not only within organizations but also across industries to enhance collaboration and secure data sharing [2].

2.2 Enterprise Architecture

EA provides a comprehensive view of an organization's IT infrastructure, applications, and data architecture, aligning IT strategy with business goals [17]. By offering a layered structure, EA helps organizations model their current state and develop a blueprint for transitioning to future states. This holistic approach enhances decision-making, improves change management, and supports the alignment between business processes and IT. EA's layered approach, as defined by the TOGAF standard, includes business, data, application, and technology architectures, each providing distinct insights to help guide an organization's growth and transformation, especially when adopting decentralized architectures like data mesh.

[2] https://martinfowler.com/articles/data-mesh-principles.html.

While EA offers several benefits such as strategic alignment, risk management, and process optimization, maintaining it poses challenges. Complex organizational structures and fragmented information hinder the effectiveness of EA [18]. Additionally, lack of alignment between EA practices and business goals can lead to siloed operations and poor transparency. Despite these issues, EA remains valuable for facilitating technological integration, supporting decision-making, and ensuring that IT infrastructure aligns with organizational objectives. Standards like ArchiMate further support EA by providing a modeling language to visualize business layers, aiding communication and collaboration across teams [19].

RAs serve as templates or blueprints to streamline the creation of solution architectures. RAs offer a standard set of vocabulary, best practices, and architectural principles that accelerate the design process and ensure consistency across projects. They assist in technology evaluation and enable organizations to make informed decisions aligned with their strategic goals. By encapsulating industry standards and best practices, RAs support architects in designing efficient and effective architectures, contributing to the overall success of enterprise architecture initiatives [20].

3 Systematic Literature Review

This section addresses the following knowledge questions through a systematic literature review (SLR) by following a well-known SLR method [21]:

KQ 1. What are the key components constituting a data mesh and what are the limitations?

KQ 1-a: What different kinds of data mesh archetypes exists?
KQ 1-b: What are common components of a data mesh?
KQ 1-c: What are the limitations of data mesh?

KQ 2. Which factors determine if data mesh is a valid approach for an organization?

KQ 2-a: What are the main indicators to consider the switch to a data mesh?
KQ 2-b: What is the impact of data mesh on the existing architecture?
KQ 2-c: Which other data methodologies are there?

KQ 3. Are there existing data mesh reference architectures?

KQ 3-a: What are characteristics of data reference architectures?
KQ 3-b: What parts of other data reference architectures can be re-used?

KQ 4. How to develop a reference architecture?

KQ 4-a: What are the goals and requirements of a reference architecture?
KQ 4-b: Which method can be used to design and develop the reference architecture?

KQ 5. How can a reference architecture be validated? Literature for this question will be gathered from the studies examined for KQ 3 and KQ 4

3.1 Planning, Search and Selection

In the planning phase of this SLR, Scopus, IEEE, and Google Scholar were chosen, with Scopus and IEEE providing peer-reviewed sources and Google Scholar supplementing with a broader range of results, including non-peer-reviewed materials. The search for "Data Mesh" yielded 83 results from IEEE, 111 from Scopus, and 3800 from Google Scholar. Some grey literature, such as foundational works on data mesh, was also included to ensure comprehensive coverage [1]. Search queries were carefully constructed to avoid irrelevant results, focusing specifically on "Data Mesh" and "Reference Architecture".

Inclusion and exclusion criteria were applied to manage the number of articles and maintain focus on relevant, high-quality studies. Peer-reviewed, English, and well-written articles with detailed metadata were prioritized, while incomplete, duplicate, or irrelevant articles were excluded. Only the first 20 search results, sorted by relevance, were evaluated for manageability. After applying these criteria, the remaining articles were reviewed for their abstracts and conclusions, resulting in 61 articles being selected for further analysis. The complete report documenting the systematic literature review can be found in [22].

3.2 Data Mesh Archetypes and Components

This subsection explores the main archetypes of data meshes, their components, and the limitations they present [8].

Data mesh architectures, though flexible, typically consist of key components necessary for effective implementation. These include domains, a self-serve data platform, and a federated governance layer [23]. However, data meshes are not a one-size-fits-all solution, and their structure can vary significantly between organizations. Various topologies have been identified in existing literature, ranging from a fine-grained, fully decentralized mesh to more managed, centralized forms. Importantly, a data mesh's specific archetype depends on an organization's requirements, and no single archetype solves all organizational data challenges [14].

The first archetype, a fine-grained fully federated mesh, represents the most theoretical and decentralized form of a data mesh, where each domain operates independently, handling its own data and communication. While offering high flexibility and domain specialization, this approach poses challenges, such as capability duplication, high costs, and complexity. The fully governed mesh, another variation, introduces a central data distribution layer to tackle some of these issues. In this model, domains retain autonomy, but data distribution is controlled through a central layer, improving compliance at the cost of flexibility. The hybrid federated mesh offers a middle ground, combining both centralized and decentralized elements, thus simplifying management but adding some overhead [23].

A variety of other archetypes also exist, such as the value-chain aligned and coarse-grained meshes, which are suitable for organizations with different operational models, such as those involved in complex supply chains or those that have expanded through mergers and acquisitions. These archetypes introduce varying degrees of centralization and domain responsibility, accommodating larger or more complex business structures. While each archetype has advantages, such as improved governance or simplified implementation, they all come with their own limitations. These include potential bottlenecks in data flow, difficulty adding new domains, and the potential for siloed data [8,23].

In terms of components, a data mesh typically consists of domains, a self-serve data platform, and federated governance. These components are further divided into elements such as data products, data catalogs, and security protocols [24]. The self-serve platform provides tools for data storage, processing, and analytics, while the governance layer ensures compliance and standardization across domains [25]. Security is a key concern, requiring robust mechanisms for access control and data integrity. Finally, monitoring tools track the use of data products and enforce compliance, making visibility and governance an integral part of the architecture. This modular approach ensures that data meshes remain adaptable to an organization's specific needs [7,8,26].

3.3 Data Mesh Implementation and Migration

The implementation of or migration to a data mesh architecture requires careful consideration of various motivating factors and prerequisites specific to each organization. Data mesh is most beneficial for companies looking to reduce bottlenecks, improve collaboration, enhance data ownership, and increase scalability. The primary motivations include a need for a scalable and agile architecture, addressing data silos, and leveraging domain knowledge more effectively [4]. Prerequisites for transitioning include high data literacy, technical expertise, and a clear understanding of domain boundaries. Companies with a low demand for real-time, high-volume data or insufficient resources may not find data mesh suitable [14].

Transitioning to a data mesh involves significant organizational and architectural changes. The shift from a monolithic to a distributed architecture decentralizes data ownership, requiring new governance models, continuous monitoring, and updated roles and responsibilities. It also demands investments in infrastructure and tools to enable a self-serve data platform. While this transition increases management complexity, it offers long-term benefits like improved scalability, resource allocation, and the ability to leverage data as a strategic asset. However, it requires ongoing effort to ensure compliance with governance standards and efficient coordination across domains [27].

Finally, a data mesh is not always the best fit, and other data methodologies like data warehouses, data lakes, data lakehouses, and data fabrics offer alternative solutions. These centralized architectures provide varying degrees of scalability, real-time processing, and management complexity. Each has its own strengths and limitations, and organizations must evaluate their specific needs, capabilities, and goals to determine whether a data mesh or one of these alternatives is the best fit for their data strategy [24,28].

3.4 Data Mesh Challenges and Limitations

The challenges and limitations of implementing a data mesh approach arise from both organizational and technical layers, as it requires changes in how a company operates and manages data. Organizationally, companies must align business and technology needs, which includes a company-wide cultural shift in handling data. Change management becomes a major challenge as it involves overcoming resistance, fostering a common understanding of data mesh principles, and training employees to adapt to new responsibilities [11]. A significant limitation is the need for increased data literacy and technical expertise, which can be a bottleneck for organizations lacking these resources. Additionally, the complexity of data management increases, posing challenges in security, privacy, and governance [7,14].

On the technical side, a data mesh impacts the existing data architecture, with challenges around integrating the right systems and engines, ensuring interoperability, and managing network strain [29]. Effort duplication, where different domains repeat the same work, and the risk of data duplication are concerns that arise from the federated nature of a data mesh. Establishing high-quality data products, setting clear standards, and maintaining data consistency across domains are further challenges. Additionally, handling changes in data, updating metadata across federated systems, and managing the deletion of data products create technical complexities that need to be addressed [1].

To mitigate these challenges, several strategies are proposed [30,31]. For organizational issues, careful planning, people management, and training programs are recommended to address resistance and the need for technical expertise. Implementing strong governance, setting clear roles and responsibilities, and standardizing communication are crucial for managing data complexity and ensuring compliance. Security and privacy concerns can be tackled through standardized security measures, data encryption, and automated compliance checks. On the technical side, leveraging metadata, establishing standards to reduce data duplication, and implementing monitoring systems for data changes and product consistency are key solutions [14,30,31].

In summary, data mesh implementations face both organizational and technical hurdles, including the need for data literacy, governance challenges, cost concerns, and maintaining data quality. However, with careful planning, governance structures, and the right technical strategies, many of these challenges can be mitigated. Solutions include targeted training, improved infrastructure planning, and the use of standardized tools and processes to streamline operations and ensure effective data management.

3.5 Reference Architectures

In the study of existing data mesh reference architectures, one architecture by Goedegebuure et al. (2023) was identified [1]. To address this gap, we explored related data reference architectures across various industries and methodologies, examining 19 in total. These architectures vary in their design styles, with many opting for free-form modelling without using formal languages. Most validate their designs by mapping them to existing solution architectures. Despite the differences, common themes emerge, such as a lack of detailed domain modelling in some cases, particularly in data mesh-related architectures, which limits their direct applicability.

We focus on developing a new reference architecture by drawing on components from existing models and leveraging established methodologies for designing reference architectures. Two primary design approaches were highlighted: Angelov et al.'s (2012) framework [32], which provides a structured approach to analyzing and designing reference architectures, and Galster and Avgeriou's (2011) empirical method for grounding reference architectures through data collection, construction, and evaluation [33]. The latter was chosen for this study due to its focus on validation, aligning with the research's design methodology. The validation approach of the reference architecture includes expert opinions, inspired by previous studies that employed surveys and case studies to ensure the architecture's relevance, scalability, and applicability.

4 Reference Architecture for Data Mesh Design

This section describes the design of the data mesh reference architecture (RA) according to the 6 step method proposed by Galster and Avgeriou [33].

4.1 Development Approach

This RA development method was chosen because it includes a validation process that aligns with the engineering cycle and integrates aspects of Angelov et al.'s (2012) framework [32]. The six steps are: (1) decide on the type of RA; (2) select the design strategy; (3) empirical collection of data; (4) construction of the RA; (5) enable the RA with variability; and (6) evaluate the RA to check its validity.

The usage context for the RA is classified as "industry-cross-cutting", and we incorporated the answers for the 3 key questions of the method (why, where, and when questions). The envisioned RA is created to facilitate architects on designing data mesh solution architectures, to be used in multiple organizations, and is a "classical reference architecture" as the technologies necessary to create solution architectures are readily available. Therefore, the RA is classified as type 3: "classical facilitation reference architecture for multiple organizations".

For the design strategy, it was decided to build the RA from scratch, as the only existing data mesh RA did not fully cover the scope of this study. The design is practice-driven, drawing on insights from the literature review, and grounded in empirical data collected to ensure the RA addresses relevant components and requirements. The RA was constructed using the ArchiMate modeling language due to its clarity and extensibility, besides being a standard language for representing enterprise architectures.

Another deliberate design choice is to include a component only once in the architecture even if multiple instances of this component are present in a solution architecture. For example, a Domain Team can be responsible for multiple business processes or applications but only one business process was modelled to keep the models clear and readable.

4.2 Domain-Driven Data as a Product

The Domain-Driven Data as a Product model, illustrated in Fig. 1, outlines the key processes carried out within a domain in a data mesh, as well as the main components supporting these processes. At the top of the architecture is the Domain Team, which is responsible for executing these processes. Firstly, they oversee a business process that generates operational data, which is then stored in a designated data storage system. Secondly, the Domain Team manages the creation, distribution, retention, and decommissioning of data products. This process consists of these steps: the data product is first created based on the operational data, then it is accompanied by a data contract and made compliant with federated governance policies before being published in the data product catalog for use by other domains. After distribution, the Domain Team must ensure proper retention by monitoring, updating, and eventually discontinuing the data product once it reaches the end of its lifecycle. Lastly, the Domain Team is responsible for performing data analytics.

The Domain Team leverages the capabilities of the Self-Serve Data Platform to establish the necessary infrastructure and make data products available to other domains participating in the data mesh, facilitated through the Data Product Catalog. The Federated Governance layer acts as an overarching governance structure, setting standards for communication, data product documentation, and other policies to ensure a secure and interoperable data mesh.

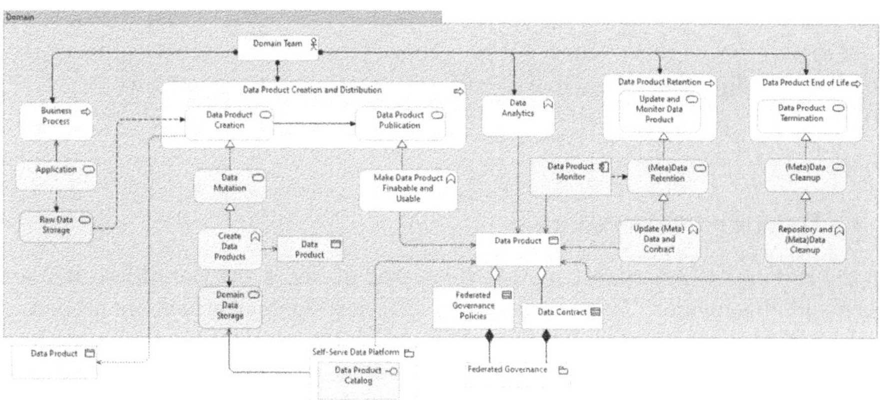

Fig. 1. ArchiMate model addressing domain-driven data as a product

4.3 Self-serve Data Platform

The Self-Serve Data Platform model, illustrated in Fig. 2, entails a capability model that is composed of a collection of capabilities that are provided to the domains participating in the data mesh and is managed by the Self-Serve Platform Team. The capabilities provided by the Self-Serve Platform are not hosted on the platform itself, rather the Domains still have to implement these technologies in their own environments. The Data Storage capability can be realized by the traditional data warehouse and lake technology services, while the Data Store Engine capability is realized by database management system (DBMS) and Access Control capability is realized by an Authentication Engine service. Query Engine can be realized through an application interface, while a Data Visualization application can realize the capabilities of data visualization and monitoring. Lastly, the ETL pipeline capability is realized by an ETL solution that is assigned to an application process.

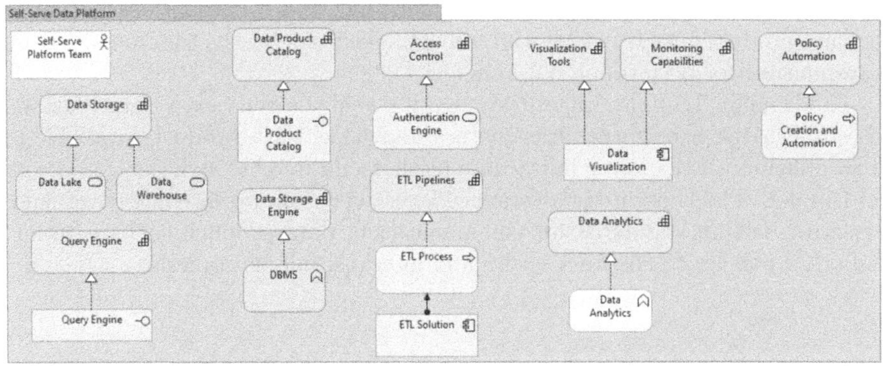

Fig. 2. ArchiMate model addressing self-serve data platform

4.4 Federated Governance

In the Federated Governance model, illustrated in Fig. 3, the Data Mesh RA key principles are covered. These principles realize certain goals which are needed to make a data mesh function. For example, one goal is to create Secure Data Mesh since security is crucial. This goal is realized by principles on access policies, compliance, privacy and exchange policies in place that define standards and requirements to achieve a secure data mesh. Additionally, interoperability is a key principle to address the concept of Data Product, especially when these data products are exchanged among different domains, ensuring both technical and semantic interoperability. Lastly, a documentation policy is needed to ensure traceability and usability of data products.

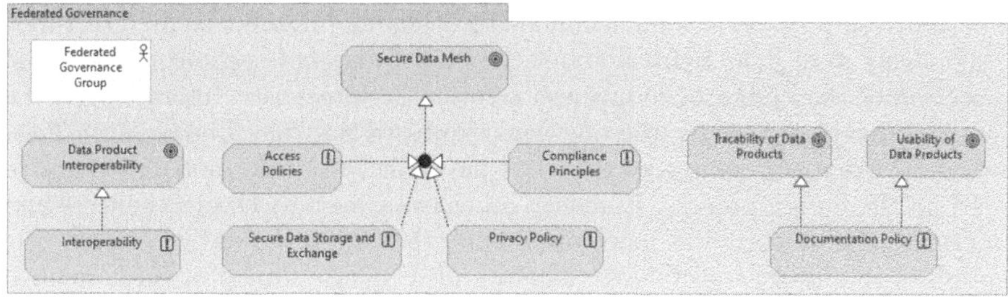

Fig. 3. ArchiMate model addressing federated governance

5 Validation

We used the validation methodology by Galster and Avgeriou (2011) [33], and we were inspired the Design Science Research methodology [34] to validate the proposed Data Mesh RA. Expert opinion was chosen as validation method because it provides valuable insights, especially in assessing aspects like perceived usefulness, quality, and variability of the RA. The decision to gather feedback from experts with varying roles and knowledge levels aligns with the study's aim to improve data mesh architectures by providing strategic design guidance.

The questionnaire itself was divided into sections, starting with an introduction to gather participants' roles and their familiarity with concepts like *Data Mesh*, *Enterprise Architecture* (EA), and *ArchiMate*. Subsequent sections assessed the perceived usefulness, quality, and variability of the RA through Likert scale questions, with participants discussing the three RA models, i.e., the Domain, Self-Serve Data Platform, and Federated Governance. Each section concluded with optional open-ended questions to allow participants to provide additional feedback and suggestions for improvement, ensuring that the evaluation was comprehensive and addressed the critical aspects necessary for refining the RA.

The questionnaire was distributed within one of the biggest consultancy companies in data solution services, and to the wider data mesh community, resulting in responses from 32 participants across a range of professional roles, including Enterprise Architects, Data Architects, and Consultants. Most participants had at least some familiarity with the *Data Mesh* and *EA* concepts, with over 75% possessing theoretical or hands-on experience with *Data Mesh*. The study successfully collected diverse profiles and relevant feedback, particularly from data consultants and tech consultants, ensuring that the validation results were well-rounded and informative for improving the RA. The complete report describing the details of this research can be found here [22].

6 Discussion

The results of the validation through the questionnaire reveal a generally positive reception towards the data mesh RA, particularly in terms of its relevance to data-driven projects and its likelihood of being used in solution architectures. Respondents were more neutral about the model's ease of use and its potential to accelerate the design of data mesh solution architectures. Interestingly, the Data Architects, especially the one who expressed a strong bias against RAs, were more skeptical, giving lower scores particularly on the model's ability to speed up the design process. However, other roles, such as Data Engineers and Enterprise Architects, were more optimistic, showing a generally positive perception of the model's usefulness. The overall response leaned towards neutral but slightly skewed to the positive side, reflecting mixed opinions across different roles.

In the quality and variability sections, a similar pattern emerged, with a tendency towards neutral or positive responses. While the Data Architects and CIO remained more critical of the model's quality, other respondents, including the Professional Trainer, expressed a more favorable view. The Data Architects raised concerns about the level of detail, but removing the responses of one outlier (particularly the biased Data Architect) improved the overall perception of the quality of the model. In terms of variability, respondents were largely positive, especially regarding the model's adaptability across multiple use cases and industries. The feedback suggests that, while there is some skepticism, especially among more experienced roles like Data Architects, the data mesh RA is generally viewed as useful and adaptable by the majority of participants.

In the additional feedback section of the questionnaire, respondents offered valuable insights into the models, highlighting both strengths and areas for improvement. For the usefulness section, many respondents appreciated the role of the models in facilitating communication and early-stage exploration of solutions. However, multiple participants, including Data Architects and Enterprise Architects, suggested that the model requires constant evolution to stay relevant as use cases change. A recurring theme was the need for clearer guidance, such as step-by-step processes or better explanation of model components, as the current version was seen as difficult to understand. Respondents also recommended better representation of different stakeholders and actors, as well as improvements in data visualization and monitoring capabilities.

In the quality and variability sections, respondents echoed similar concerns about the need for model evolution and the lack of guidance. While the quality of the model received mixed reviews, with a median score of 3.1 out of 5, variability scored the highest at 3.9, indicating the model's potential for use across various industries and contexts. Suggestions for improvement included adding principles related to data quality and ownership in the Federated Governance Architecture, rethinking the term ETL to reflect broader data processes, and ensuring clearer interaction between domains, which requires higher semantic interoperability. Overall, while the feedback was mostly positive, it underscored that the model is a good starting point but requires further refinement to enhance its usability, adaptability, and relevance in different use cases.

7 Conclusion

The main contributions of this research include the resulting analysis of the systematic literature review, and the development of a Data Mesh RA using the ArchiMate enterprise architecture modeling language. This RA provides a structured blueprint for solution architects to design data mesh solutions, detailing core elements like domain-driven data as a product, self-serve platforms, and federated governance. Additionally, the study proposed four data mesh archetypes, helping organizations tailor their data mesh structures based on maturity and capabilities. We also extended the literature on data mesh by analyzing its components, challenges, and comparing it with alternative data architectures like data warehouses, lakehouses, and data fabrics.

Key lessons learned from this study highlight that the data mesh approach requires a high level of technical expertise, organizational readiness, and strong governance mechanisms to manage complexity and ensure compliance with the four data mesh principles. We identified key motivational factors and prerequisites for transitioning to a data mesh architecture, emphasizing that proper planning and cultural readiness are crucial for success. The validation process, though only based on expert opinion, revealed that the proposed RA shows good variability, usability, and quality, making it adaptable across different industries and use cases. However, real-world testing remains necessary to fully confirm its practical effectiveness. One of the core limitations of this research is that the validation relied solely on expert feedback, which may introduce bias. Additionally, potential gaps in the literature review and the use of a single group of respondents with varying expertise could impact the completeness of the findings.

Future research is recommended to validate the RA through case studies across different industries and to refine the RA models by addressing feedback from users. In addition, it is necessary more precise guidelines on migrating a complex IT landscape to a data mash architecture, measuring the potential costs and return of investment. Furthermore, ontologies play an important role to address semantic interoperability in data meshes, especially among domains that have overlapping, and sometimes conflicting, terminology. Therefore, we believe that the adoption of the Findable, Accessible, Interoperable and Reusable (FAIR) data principles can improve the adoption of data meshes. Finally, the data mesh approach seems compatible with the International Data Spaces (IDS) reference architecture, and future work is required to investigate their relations.

References

1. Goedegebuure, A., et al.: Data mesh: a systematic gray literature review. ACM Comput. Surv. (2024)
2. Podlesny, N.J., Kayem, A.V.D.M., Meinel, C.: CoK: a survey of privacy challenges in relation to data meshes. In: Strauss, C., Cuzzocrea, A., Kotsis, G., Tjoa, A.M., Khalil, I. (eds.) DEXA 2022. LNCS, vol. 13426, pp. 85–102. Springer, Cham (2022)
3. Falconi, M., Plebani, P.: Adopting data mesh principles to boost data sharing for clinical trials. In: 2023 IEEE International Conference on Digital Health (ICDH), pp. 298–306 (2023)

4. Pakrashi, A., Wallace, D., Namee, B.M., Greene, D., Guéret, C.: Cowmesh: a data-mesh architecture to unify dairy industry data for prediction and monitoring. Front. Artif. Intell. **6** (2023)
5. Dehghani, Z., Fowler, M.: Data Mesh: Delivering Data-driven Value at Scale. O'Reilly Media (2022)
6. Driessen, S., van den Heuvel, W.-J., Monsieur, G.: ProMoTe: a data product model template for data meshes. In: Almeida, J.P.A., Borbinha, J., Guizzardi, G., Link, S., Zdravkovic, J. (eds.) ER 2023. LNCS, vol. 14320, pp. 125–142. Springer, Cham (2023). https://doi.org/10.1007/978-3-031-47262-6_7
7. Machado, I.A., Costa, C., Santos, M.Y.: Data mesh: concepts and principles of a paradigm shift in data architectures. Procedia Comput. Sci. **196**, 263–271 (2022). International Conference on ENTERprise Information Systems / ProjMAN - International Conference on Project MANagement / HCist - International Conference on Health and Social Care Information Systems and Technologies 2021
8. Pongpech, W.A.: A distributed data mesh paradigm for an event-based smart communities monitoring product. Procedia Comput. Sci. **220**, 584–591 (2023). The 14th International Conference on Ambient Systems, Networks and Technologies Networks (ANT) and The 6th International Conference on Emerging Data and Industry 4.0 (EDI40)
9. Ashraf, A., Hassan, A., Mahdi, H.: Key lessons from microservices for data mesh adoption. In: 2023 International Mobile, Intelligent, and Ubiquitous Computing Conference (MIUCC), pp. 1–8 (2023)
10. Jonkman, C.: Organisational maturity assessment during the paradigm shift from monoliths to data mesh - design science research in developing a data mesh maturity assessment model. Master's thesis, TU Delft (2023). https://repository.tudelft.nl/record/uuid:294d7df5-511c-4149-9507-21be6379375d
11. Vestues, K., Hanssen, G.K., Mikalsen, M., Buan, T.A., Conboy, K.: Agile data management in NAV: a case study. In: Stray, V., Stol, K.-J., Paasivaara, M., Kruchten, P. (eds.) XP 2022, pp. 220–235. Springer, Cham (2022). https://doi.org/10.1007/978-3-031-08169-9_14
12. Hooshmand, Y., Resch, J., Wischnewski, P., Patil, P.: From a monolithic PLM landscape to a federated domain and data mesh. Proc. Des. Soc. **2**, 713–722 (2022)
13. Hendriks, K.W.: Data governance structures in data mesh architectures (2023)
14. Bode, J., Kühl, N., Kreuzberger, D., Holtmann, C.: Toward avoiding the data mess: industry insights from data mesh implementations. IEEE Access **12**, 95402–95416 (2024)
15. Sedlak, B., et al.: Towards serverless data exchange within federations. In: Aiello, M., Barzen, J., Dustdar, S., Leymann, F. (eds.) SummerSOC 2023. CCIS, vol. 1847, pp. 144–153. Springer, Cham (2023). https://doi.org/10.1007/978-3-031-45728-9_9
16. Vestues, K., Hanssen, G.K., Mikalsen, M., Buan, T.A., Conboy, K.: Agile data management in NAV: a case study (2022)
17. Hermawan, R.A., Sumitra, I.D.: Designing enterprise architecture using togaf architecture development method. In: IOP Conference Series: Materials Science and Engineering, vol. 662, no. 4, p. 042021 (2019)
18. dela Cruz, N., Tobin, M., Schenz, G., Barden, D.: Enterprise data architecture: development scenarios using ORM. In: Meersman, R., Dillon, T., Herrero, P. (eds.) OTM 2011. LNCS, vol. 7046, pp. 278–287. Springer, Heidelberg (2011). https://doi.org/10.1007/978-3-642-25126-9_39
19. Sanyoto, A.E.A., Saputra, M.C.: Archimate's strengths and weaknesses as EA modeling language: a systematic mapping study. In: 2023 Eighth International Conference on Informatics and Computing (ICIC), pp. 1–6 (2023)

20. Sang, G.M., Xu, L., de Vrieze, P.: Simplifying big data analytics systems with a reference architecture. In: Camarinha-Matos, L.M., Afsarmanesh, H., Fornasiero, R. (eds.) PRO-VE 2017. IAICT, vol. 506, pp. 242–249. Springer, Cham (2017). https://doi.org/10.1007/978-3-319-65151-4_23
21. Carrera-Rivera, A., Ochoa, W., Larrinaga, F., Lasa, G.: How-to conduct a systematic literature review: a quick guide for computer science research. Methods X **9** (2022)
22. van der Werf, D.: Towards a data mesh: reference architecture. Master's thesis, University of Twente (2024)
23. Strengholt, P.: Data Management at Scale: Modern Data Architecture with Data Mesh and Data Fabric. O'Reilly Media (2023)
24. Dibouliya, A., Jotwani, D.V.: Review on data mesh architecture and its impact. J. Harbin Eng. Univ. (2023)
25. Butte, V.K., Butte, S.: Enterprise data strategy: a decentralized data mesh approach. In: 2022 International Conference on Data Analytics for Business and Industry (ICDABI), pp. 62–66 (2022)
26. Kancharla, J.R., Kumar, S.M.: Breaking down data silos: data mesh to achieve effective aggregation in data localization. In: 2023 International Conference on Computer, Electronics & Electrical Engineering & their Applications (IC2E3), pp. 1–5 (2023)
27. Dončević, J., Fertalj, K., Brcic, M., Kovač, M.: Mask-mediator-wrapper architecture as a data mesh driver. IEEE Trans. Softw. Eng. **50**(4), 900–910 (2024)
28. Dahdal, S., Poltronieri, F., Tortonesi, M., Stefanelli, C., Suri, N.: A data mesh approach for enabling data-centric applications at the tactical edge. In: 2023 International Conference on Military Communications and Information Systems (ICMCIS), pp. 1–9 (2023)
29. McEachen, N., Lewis, J.: Enabling knowledge sharing by managing dependencies and interoperability between interlinked spatial knowledge graphs. Int. Arch. Photogrammetry Remote Sens. Spatial Inf. Sci. **XLVIII-4/W7-2023**, 117–124 (2023)
30. Krystek, M., Morzy, M., Mazurek, C., Pukacki, J.: Introducing data mesh paradigm for smart city platforms design. In: Proceedings of the Annual Hawaii International Conference on System Sciences, vol. 2023-January, pp. 6885–6892 (2023)
31. Kraska, T., et al.: Check out the big brain on brad: simplifying cloud data processing with learned automated data meshes. Proc. VLDB Endow. **16**(11), 3293–3301 (2023)
32. Angelov, S., Grefen, P., Greefhorst, D.: A framework for analysis and design of software reference architectures. Inf. Softw. Technol. **54**(4), 417–431 (2012)
33. Galster, M., Avgeriou, P.: Empirically-grounded reference architectures: a proposal. In: Proceedings of the Joint ACM SIGSOFT Conference – QoSA and ACM SIGSOFT Symposium – ISARCS on Quality of Software Architectures – QoSA and Architecting Critical Systems – ISARCS, QoSA-ISARCS 2011, pp. 153–158. Association for Computing Machinery, New York (2011)
34. Wieringa, R.J.: What is Design Science?, pp. 3–11. Springer, Heidelberg (2014)

MIDas4CS – 2nd Workshop on the Modelling and Implementation of Digital Twins for Complex Systems

Report from the MIDas4CS 2024 Workshop Chairs

The concept of Digital Twin (DT) is becoming increasingly popular since it was introduced in the scope of Smart Industry (Industry 4.0). A DT is a digital representation of a physical twin that is a real-world entity, system, or event. It mirrors a distinctive object, process, building, or human, regardless of whether that thing is tangible or non-tangible in the real world. DTs provide potential benefits such as real-time remote monitoring and control; greater efficiency and safety; predictive maintenance and scheduling; scenario and risk assessment; better intra- and inter-team synergy and collaboration; more efficient and informed decision support systems; personalisation of products and services; and better documentation and communication.

The ultimate purpose of DTs is to improve decision-making for solving real-world problems, by using the digital model to create the information necessary and subsequently applying the decisions in the real world. Nowadays, DTs are not limited to industrial applications but are spreading to other areas as well, such as, for example, in the healthcare domain, in personalised medicine and clinical trials for drug development.

This workshop series focuses on getting a better understanding of the techniques that can be used to model and implement DTs and their applications in different domains. We aim to attract researchers and industry practitioners to discuss formal definitions of DTs as well as to describe applications of DTs in different domains. Contributions on tooling for DTs are also welcome.

The second edition of MIDas4CS was organised in conjunction with EDOC 2024 within the 2024 edition of the Business Informatics Week. This workshop attracted 4 international submissions, and each of them was by at least two members of the Programme Committee. From these submissions, 2 submissions were accepted as full papers for presentation at the workshop. An additional paper, originally submitted to the EDOC 2024 main track, was redirected to this workshop due to its focus on the DT topic. An additional presentation on the DT topic was delivered by a student participating in the Doctoral Consortium. The papers were presented during the first day of the conference in two sessions of one and a half hours each.

T. Itäpelto presented a novel Reference Architecture for designing or extending a Critical Infrastructure (CI) enhancing cybersecurity with DTs. The authors claim that existing testing methodologies prove inadequate and may compromise the CI's operational continuity, therefore they propose to shift testing activities to a DT connected to the CI. The authors demonstrate the feasibility of this reference architecture, focusing on what-if testing using DT-enabled attack simulations.

C. Canal presented ongoing work that aims at the realisation of a DT System for human crowd motion prediction centred on the Artax framework, which stores people's movements as traces through time. They described the current state of the framework and explained how they aim to apply it to anticipate dangerous situations caused by crowds and to warn people.

I. Compagnucci presented a conceptual architecture focusing on the concept of Digital Process Twin (DPT). A DPT enables what-if analysis to virtually predict process performance after the implementation changes, allowing for optimisation before real-world application. The authors claim that there is currently a lack of frameworks for implementing DPT, and propose AdaptiveTwin, which is a framework that implements a conceptual architecture using a multi-modelling approach, combining domain data and process modelling along with a data-driven process simulation technique.

F. Massah presented (paper included in the Doctoral Consortium section of the proceedings) ongoing research that explores the application of DTs in the construction industry to optimise construction planning and execution through real-time monitoring, simulation, and analysis.

The workshop sessions were chaired by F. Fornari and J. L. Moreira. During the workshop, an open discussion on the adoption of DTs among participants took place with the aim to exchange practices and insights, and foster possible future research collaborations.

We hope that the reader will find the selection of papers insightful and useful to keep track of the latest advances related to DTs.

Acknowledgments. We thank the authors for their contributions, and the members of the Programme Committee for their invaluable contribution by thoroughly reviewing the submissions. We also wish to thank the organisers of EDOC 2024 and the Business Informatics Week 2024 for their support of the organisation of this workshop.

October 2024

Pedro Valderas
Fabrizio Fornari
Luís Ferreira Pires
Marten van Sinderen
João Luiz Rebelo Moreira

Organization

Workshop Chairs

Pedro Valderas	Universitat Politècnica de València, Spain
Fabrizio Fornari	University of Camerino, Italy
Luís Ferreira Pires	University of Twente, The Netherlands
Marten van Sinderen	University of Twente, The Netherlands
João Moreira	University of Twente, The Netherlands

Programme Committee

Abel Armas Cervantes	University of Melbourne, Australia
Barbara Re	University of Camerino, Italy
Estefanía Serral	KU Leuven, Belgium
Victoria Torres Bosch	Universitat Politècnica de València, Spain
Erik Proper	Technical University of Vienna, Austria
Tony Clark	Aston University, UK
Francis Bordeleau	École de Technologie Supérieure, Canada
Philipp Zech	University of Innsbruck, Austria
Ruth Breu	University of Innsbruck, Austria
Vinay Kulkarni	TCS Research, India

Towards a Digital Twin System for Human Crowd Motion Prediction

Ignacio Alba(✉), Javier Troya, and Carlos Canal

Universidad de Málaga ITIS Software, Málaga, Spain
{nachoalav,jtroya,carloscanal}@uma.es

Abstract. In many local festivals and in events such as pop concerts or sporting events, crowds might generate dangerous situations like the case of panic stampedes. How to anticipate these situations is challenging. Despite there are simulation models of people motion, it is very difficult to predict real people behavior. In this paper, we advocate the application of digital twins to monitor and analyze real people motion. We implement the *Artax* framework, which stores people movements as traces through time. We describe the current state of our framework and explain how we aim to apply it for anticipating dangerous situations caused by crowds and warning people.

Keywords: Digital Twin · Smart Cities · Human Motion

1 Introduction

In many countries and cities, tourism is one of the pillars of economy. In touristic cities open to the ocean or with a passable river, big cruise ships almost daily dock in their ports and thousands of tourists disembark and fill the city in peak season. If all the tourists decide to visit the same touristic points at the same time, they will likely produce crowds. There are also events in which crowds are always generated, such as pop concerts, sporting events and demonstrations. Even when celebrating the local festival in some cities crowds will for sure take place. We can think for instance of Sanfermines (Pamplona, Spain), Oktoberfest (Munich, Germany) or Carnival (Rio de Janerio, Brazil). Finally, there are also overpopulated cities where crowds are generated daily, such as Tokio (Japan), New Delhi (India), Shanghai (China) or Mexico City (Mexico).

Crowds might cause serious dangerous situations [23], especially in a panic stampede [4]. Therefore, there is the need to find solutions that try to avoid these situations. Smart Cities aim to use technology for providing useful services to their citizens and to solve urban problems [2], however, not much has been done in the context of avoiding problems caused by people crowds.

There are approaches that try to simulate people dynamics by modeling their behavior. For instance, the authors in [22] apply a multi-group microscopic model to generate real-time trajectories for all people moving in a virtual defined environment. The work in [3] combines modern game development technologies

M. Kaczmarek-Heß et al. (Eds.): EDOC 2024 Workshops, LNBIP 537, pp. 359–372, 2025.
https://doi.org/10.1007/978-3-031-79059-1_22

with traditional agent-based modeling methods for simulating people flow at an airport, and there are other approaches that try to focus on the behavior in individuals within crowds [13]. However, all these works are about simulation, and they do not consider real people moving in a real environment.

A Digital Twin (DT) is a comprehensive digital representation of a system, employing models and data for representing its properties, conditions, and actions [24]. DTs are continuously updated with real-time information about their physical counterparts [14], facilitating two-way feedback between their digital model and the physical entities represented in it, allowing real-time monitoring, adopting adaptation policies, and enhancing decision-making processes. The use of DTs in Smart Cities, conforming the so-called Urban Digital Twins or Digital Twin City, has already been proposed [5,16]. The problem, again, is that current works do not focus on human crowds.

This paper presents ongoing work around a framework, named *Artax*, with the ultimate goal of addressing dangerous situations caused by crowds. We define an architecture that considers real people movements gathered by tracking the positions of their smartphones. Our framework is able to gather together the position of many people through time by storing them in traces. Since an experiment with real people might take a considerable amount of time and resources, our framework implements a simulated scenario integrating state-of-the-art tools, and it is prepared to replace the simulated data with real data. Regarding the simulation part, our framework allows to configure different parameters so that people motion is simulated for our purposes.

The rest of this paper is structured as follows. After this introduction, in Sect. 2 we motivate our work. Then, Sect. 3 describes different aspects of our framework, while Sect. 4 gives some details of its implementation. After this, a couple of validating scenarios are described in Sect. 5, and conclusions and future work are summarized in Sect. 6.

2 Motivation and Background

Smart cities apply Information Technologies to solve specific urban problems, such as the identification of traffic patterns to improve urban mobility, or improving the accessibility of city resources and utilities in order to provide better services to their citizens. Digital Twins are being proved as a promising approach for the development of smart cities (see for instance [24] for a review of the literature). A Digital Twin City [5] —also known as Urban Digital Twin (UDT)— models specific city aspects as an effective way to make a city smart. Similarly to other digital twins, UDTs facilitate two-way feedback between the model and the physical entities represented in it, enabling real-time monitoring for cities, proposing adaptation policies, and enhancing decision-making processes.

Just to mention a few initiatives within the research field of UDTs, Ruiz et al. proposed BODIT [21], a UDT of the public transportation system in the city of Badalona (Spain). They use a traffic simulator and a genetic algorithm to reproduce the city's traffic and adapt to different situations. Bus schedules are used to predict and detect a lack of punctuality at bus stops, enabling informed decision-making as a response to unusual situations such as accidents. Another interesting related work is that of Lehtola et al. [12] studied the impact of digital twins in smart cities. In their work, the authors emphasize the necessity of taking humans into consideration to ensure successful implementation in order to improve decision-making, which is a concern that we also share.

Indeed, the interest in the social aspects of smart cities is growing fast. For this reason, citizens must be considered as first-class entities of the UDT, since they are the fundamental key to this ecosystem. However, the role of people has often been neglected: smart city applications typically focus on collecting and analyzing data coming from all kinds of sensors, including some related to human activities, but without really integrating individual users into the loop, just considering them collectively, i.e., as a crowd, not as distinct individuals.

In previous works, we presented the concepts of *Human Microservices* [11], and *Digital Avatars* (DAs) [18,19]. These models allow to incorporate individuals into UDT models. This way, we can achieve better planning of city infrastructures, adapting them to the context of the people who use them. Both initiatives derive from the People as a Service (PeaaS) [6] paradigm, which provides a conceptual model for application development focused on the smartphone as an interface to its owner.

In particular, the purpose of a DA is to serve as a digital representation of a person, facilitating their participation in collaborative and social computing systems. Thus, DAs are smartphone-based virtual representations of their users which act as virtual assistants in their interaction with the environment. The purpose of DAs is to exploit citizens' personal information, habits, and preferences for benefiting from better services, while the users keep full control of their data, including storage location and access control [17].

However, one of the problems of incorporating humans into UDT proposals is how to obtain a good dataset coming from a significant number of individuals. While there is a huge amount of open data available for any kind of UDT purposes, data sources coming from groups or real users are scarce[1], and people are reluctant to install apps in their smartphones and share their information even for research purposes. This is where synthetic data comes into the picture. As it will be shown in this paper, in our approach we employ The ONE tool [10] for generating individual path trajectories that although synthetic are realistic enough as input for Machine Learning techniques. Despite The ONE is in origin a tool for opportunistic network simulation [7,8], it has also been successfully used for simulating human path trajectories (see [1,9] as examples).

3 Designing the Artax Framework

In this section we explain how the Artax framework has been designed and modelled. We also present the main elements of its architecture.

[1] One of the rare publicly available examples can be found in https://www.kaggle.com/datasets/chetanism/foursquare-nyc-and-tokyo-checkin-dataset/data.

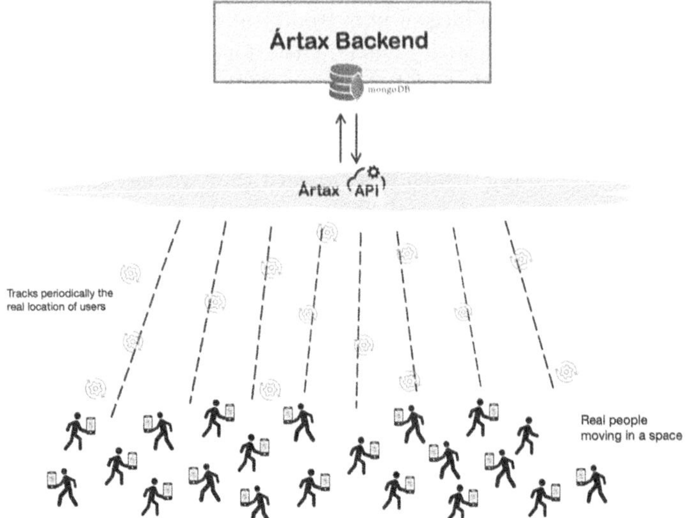

Fig. 1. High-level representation of the Artax framework, collecting traces of movements from its users.

3.1 Overview

The Artax framework collects information about people's movements through their smartphones (Fig. 1), which constitutes a digital twin of people motion. Each user's device tracks the movements of its owner, building a trace consisting of a sequence of GPS positions and timestamps. This information is periodically sent to the backend through a REST API, where it is stored. How well the system works (how precise and accurate its predictions will be) depends largely on the quantity and quality of the available information about its users. However, before storing it, data is anonymized, and it can also be conveniently obfuscated so that the actual position of any user at a given time cannot be precisely determined.

Figure 1 portraits a real-life scenario where people are moving throughout a given open space. The system gets the location of each user from the GPS sensors of their smartphone, through a mobile application which constitutes the frontend of the system, as can be seen in the figure. The data collected is periodically sent to the backend where it is used to build and update a dataset of people's flow over the area, which can be used for inferring crowd movement patterns and detecting risk situations.

However, this scenario points out one of the main challenges of our approach: the problem of obtaining enough data for training the system. How to address this problem is described in the next section.

3.2 Dataset of People Motion

In order to achieve a digital twin of people motion, we require traces of movements for a large number of users over a given area. With that, predictions of future paths and detection of risks can be inferred by the digital twin. Two alternatives can be considered.

One option consists in having a large amount of people willing to collaborate with our project, where each person installs the Artax mobile app in their smartphone, and gives it permissions to access their location while they spend a certain amount of time moving from one place to another in the area, and possibly producing crowd situations in particular zones. In terms of realism, the collected information would be notably valuable regarding how real people move and how different crowd situations occur. However, this option is hard to achieve in practice as it is difficult to recruit enough people to carry out the required experiments.

An alternative would consist in using a public dataset of people's movements. Some of these datasets exist, but there are also significant drawbacks in them. The main shortcoming is to find a dataset that adjusts to our needs. A good number of the datasets that can be found on the Internet are private, while others would simply not serve our purpose (the traces correspond to a small number of individuals, to people moving through a small enclosed space such as an office, or the movements refer to vehicles, instead of pedestrians, or people travelling from a country to another, to name a few).

As both options have their advantages and shortcomings, we decided to build a synthetic dataset specifically tailored for our needs. This way we can have enough data to train the system and we can precisely define the movement and crowd scenarios that interest us. For this purpose, we set up a simulation environment which is presented in the next section.

3.3 Simulating Users and Their Smartphones

The architecture of the Artax framework in Fig. 1 has been extended for overcoming the lack of available data exposed in the previous section. The Artax simulation environment allows the creation of a dataset of people's paths in a realistic way. For that, we start with the generation of traces of movements of a number of simulated or synthetic users sharing a common space with The ONE tool [10], and we feed each of these traces into virtual smartphones in turn simulated with the Perses tool [15]. The virtual smartphones have installed the same Artax app used in the real-life scenario, and they are run in the Amazon AWS cloud platform, where they behave and communicate with the Artax backend exactly as real devices would do. The Artax architecture extended with simulation capabilities is shown in Fig. 2, where the right part depicts the simulation environment, showing the analogy between both real-life and simulated scenarios. In the following we describe the main elements of the simulation environments: The ONE and Perses.

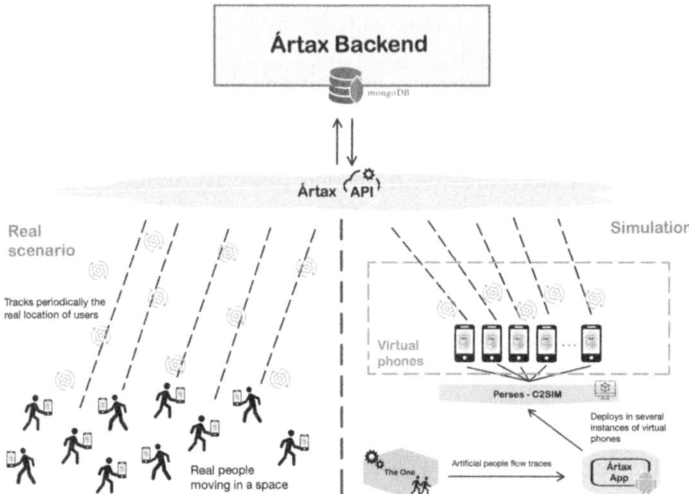

Fig. 2. Artax architecture considering the scenario with real users (on the left) and the simulation environment that reproduces it (on the right).

The ONE. The ONE (Opportunistic Network Environment) is a simulation tool originally developed for the research and evaluation of DTN (Delay Tolerant Network) routing protocols, modelling message routing and handling between nodes representing interconnected mobile devices such as smartphones. The tool is publicly available[2] and it provides information about the simulated scenarios, including all kind of measurements of performance and reports and visualization of the message routing and mobility of the devices, and it is commonly used for experimenting with opportunistic networks.

However, we are not interested in measuring and evaluating message routing, but in mobility. Thus, we use the tool for defining and simulating scenarios in which a certain number of nodes (representing people and their smartphones) move through a given area, specified by a map which describes their feasible paths. The result of the simulation is a sequence of snapshots with the location of all the nodes at each time step, from which we reconstruct each node's path, representing the trace followed by one of the simulated individuals. The number of nodes, the space and paths where they move, and their patterns of movement are some of the parameterized elements on the scenario. It is also possible to define groups of nodes each presenting different behaviors. In order to achieve our desired behavior, we needed to slightly modify The ONE's source code. In particular, we made the positions (coordinates) publicly available and logged them during the simulation while the scenario is being executed.

Once the defined scenario is simulated and the traces of movements are generated, the results are fed into the *Artax* app. This is when Perses comes into picture.

[2] https://akeranen.github.io/the-one.

Perses. Perses [15] is a virtualization framework for building scenarios involving virtual mobile devices of different characteristics. The virtual devices are run in the Amazon AWS platform. The tool is specifically designed for evaluating the behavior and performance of complex distributed mobile applications. Similar to The ONE in terms of flexibility, Perses scenarios can also be configured, indicating aspects as the simulation time, the number and type of the virtualized devices, and some of their specific features. The Perses virtualization tool is also publicly available[3].

For simulating a particular scenario we deploy a number of instances of virtual mobile devices, each endowed with the same Artax app already described for the real-life scenario, and the path followed by a given individual, as resulting from The ONE. Then, the virtualization framework starts execution, with the virtual smartphones behaving as in a real-life situation, and communicating with the Artax API for periodically sending their location to the backend.

Once we have described the Artax architecture, the experimental setup, and its main elements, we delve into the technical aspects of the Artax backend in the next section.

4 Implementation

In this section we discuss the technical aspects of the elements described in the previous section.

4.1 Artax Android App

This is the mobile application that tracks the people's locations and sends them to the backend. The main idea behind this app is to have a virtual profile for each user that stores useful data. It keeps some information such as persons' names and surnames, and other data like their age or whether they have any disability, which might be useful information when dealing with dangerous situations caused by crowds (cf. Sect. 4.3).

As we explained in the previous section and exemplified in Fig. 2, our application considers both a real-life and a simulated scenarios. For this reason, the app presents two slightly different execution flows depending on the context where it is running, where the major difference is on the data processed and the resources used. Indeed, the app deploys into virtual smartphones when simulating, so it is better to free the software from some elements that may cause errors due to the limitations/restrictions of the platform, or simply just to be cautious. For example, one of the limitations that presents the virtualized smartphones is the lack of GPS access. Before digging into the specific differences of both execution modes, we detail some technical aspects of the app.

Artax has been developed in *Java* using *Android Studio*. The user interfaces, which in Android are layouts, consist in XML files where some components that

[3] https://github.com/perses-org/perses.

Android offers are used. It also presents multi-language support for English and Spanish depending on the operating system's settings. The app's main components are described in the following.

- A **client** that communicates with the *Artax* API. This client builds the requests to be made, enqueues them and gets the corresponding API response.
- A **local database** to store the user's information. The app installs a **SQLite** local database the first time that it is executed on the smartphone, with the data being recovered on successive executions by querying the database. To begin with, we have defined a **User Contract** where the *User* table structure is defined. The most important aspect of this element is the **helper** that we introduced in order to interact and operate over the database. This helper obtains the local database and allows the execution of SQL statements to query or manipulate the table.
  This is not present on the simulation scenario in order to free resources in the simulated smartphones. In addition, it does not make sense to install a local database and store data on those devices since these smartphones are shut down when the simulation is over.
- A Java **class** that models the user so it can be treated as an object.
- The app makes use of Google's **location services** to be able to track the device location while it is moving. For this to be correctly functional, a **Location Listener** has been included which listens to any event related to the device location update or the activation/deactivation of the provider. This is managed by the **Location Manager**, which requests location updates from the listener and indicates the provider that determines the position—this provider is the GPS. This is all encapsulated by a **Location Service**.
  An important aspect to consider is that, to be able to use the location services, first the user has to give the necessary permissions. For this purpose, we introduce a **Permission Manager** that manages which permissions are granted on our application, and can request them. In our case, the most useful permissions are the *COARSE LOCATION* and the *FINE LOCATION* permissions. Basically, the difference them lies in the accuracy in which the position will be determined. The apps gives users the option of choosing whatever choice they prefer.
  Needless to say, the simulated smpartphones do not make use of any GPS service.
- A **Location Monitor** that periodically interacts with the **location service** described above to get the current location of the device. Once the monitor gets the location, it generates the current timestamp and sends this data to the **API client** to forward it to the *backend*. It also updates the view to display on screen the latest tracked location and logs the motion trace into an external text file.
  The periodic task has been implemented using a *single thread executor service* which receives an Android **handler** that runs the task on said thread. The virtualized smartphones use a **Simulation Location Monitor** that imple-

ments the periodic task in the same way but does not intercede with any location service.

After summarizing the main components, we describe the execution flow in the two different modes. In the ***real-life functioning***, when users open the app for the first time (the local database is created, as we mentioned above), they are redirected to a form where they introduce their name, surname, birth date and whether they are affected by any disability. Next, the data is stored on the local database and sent to the API, then the user is redirected to the main activity of the application. If users' data have already been stored on any previous execution, when they open the app they are on the main activity. This is determined by querying the local database and checking whether there is any result. The interface of this main activity simply displays the information on the screen. Users can swap what is being shown alternating between the user data and the current location info. When the main activity executes and the user has been queried, then location permissions are asked to be granted by the user and, when said permissions are given, the location service and monitoring activate.

Regarding the ***simulation*** mode, when the simulation starts, the activity that contains the form executes but, since there is no interaction with the user, the data is randomly generated. The generated birth date lies within a period of time from 70 years ago to the present day, and to determine if the "user" is affected by any disability real statistics about disabled population in Spain are taken into account. This data is also sent to the API, but now it is not stored on any local database, since this is not even created. A User object is created with this information and passed onto the main activity. Unlike the other scenario, no permissions are asked to be granted. Instead, the simulation monitor just activates and the task begins to execute periodically.

4.2 Artax REST API

This software follows an architecture based on microservices to foster reliability and flexibility, so this REST API integrates the *frontend* of the system, which is the Android app, with the *backend*. There are two services: one for the users and another for the locations. Both services present basic CRUD functions.

Regarding the database (cf. Fig. 2), the data is stored within a *Mongo DB* database that is hosted in a *Mongo DB Atlas* cluster.

The REST API has been implemented using the *Node.js* framework *Express*. We have also used the *mongoose* ODM (Object Document Mapping - analog to an ORM but for non-relational databases) to connect the API to the database and define simple schemas to carry out *Mongo DB*'s data validation. The API REST has been deployed on the *Vercel* cloud platform, so it is publicly available via *https*.

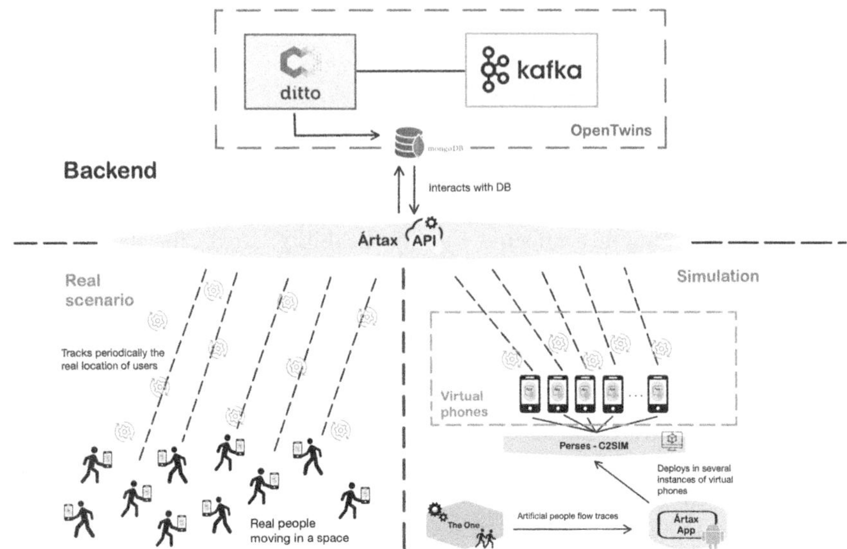

Fig. 3. Artax's full architecture.

4.3 Artax Backend

The Artax backend represents the part of the digital twin that offers the services of forecasting dangerous situations due to crowds and alerting the users. We are relying on the *OpenTwins*[4] framework [20] for materializing this backend, whose structure is displayed in Fig. 3.

OpenTwins is an open-source framework, developed at University of Malaga, specifically designed for the development of digital twins. This platform allows the creation and management of digital twins, and it facilitates the orchestration of the different services that intertwine with each other. These services are all open-source and are integrated within the same framework. *OpenTwins* presents a variety of components used to offer different services: from basic digital twin functionality to 3D visualization of the system, IoT data streams, or machine learning aspects. Out of the components offered, Artax uses *Eclipse Ditto* and *Kafka ML*. *Ditto* is one of the most extended solutions for digital twin implementation, whereas *Kafka ML* is the main component in *OpenTwins* that is responsible for providing machine learning features to the system.

In order to make predictions and forecast dangerous situations, we need to train a machine learning (ML) model. We do this on an external platform, namely *Jupyter Notebook*. Kafka receives the ML model once that it has been already defined and trained, and connects it to Ditto.

4 https://github.com/ertis-research/opentwins.

5 Experimentation

The current state of our Artax framework allows to define scenarios of people motion. So far, we have defined two scenarios that will be used for validating the forecasting functionality once it is finished. Right now, we are analyzing how people movements are performed in these simulations, so that they can be effectively used to simulate real people.

The first scenario consists of 400 nodes moving freely throughout the streets of a predefined urban area. This would represent an ordinary motion situation, meaning that large crowds might take place or not, as the nodes are moving randomly. A graphical visualization of this scenario is displayed in Fig. 4, where we can see the map with streets through which people, represented by their ID, are moving.

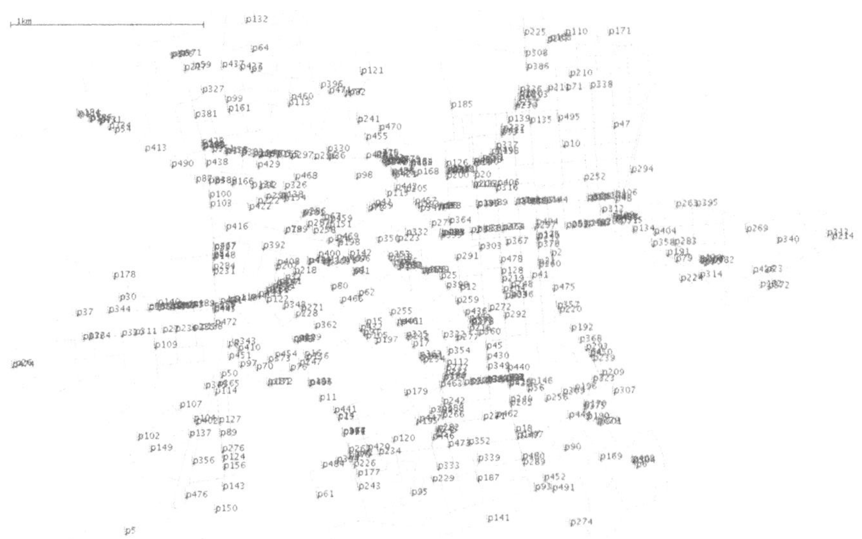

Fig. 4. Screenshot of the execution of the general test scenario.

The second scenario consists of 200 nodes moving in an extremely reduced space. Its main goal is to generate crowds. The nodes move along a triangle-shaped map, whose feasible paths are the edges of the figure—it is actually a rather simple scenario. This scenario can be seen in Fig. 5, where we can see that crowds are already taking place.

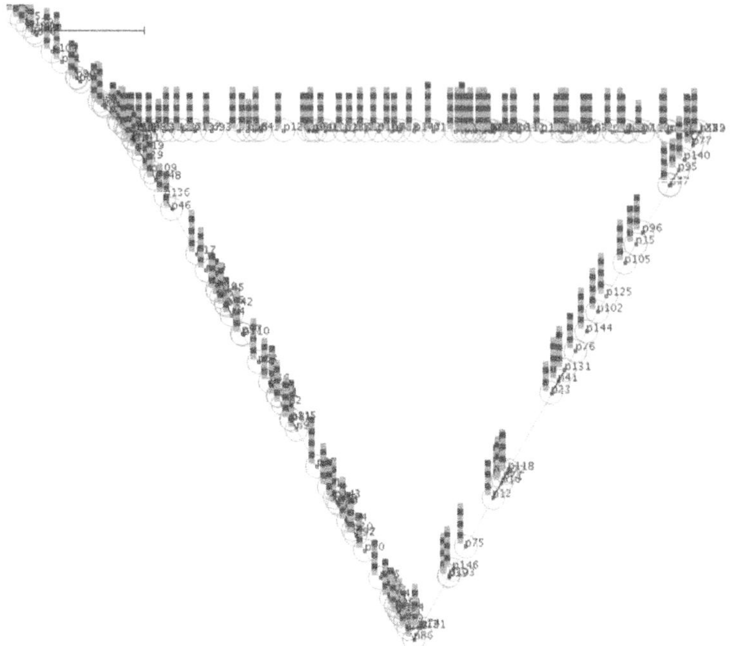

Fig. 5. Screenshot of the execution of the crowded test scenario.

6 Conclusions

This paper has presented the ongoing work centered on the *Artax* framework, which is built as a Urban Digital Twin that focuses on people motion. We have described the architecture and implementation of this framework, whose ultimate goal is to monitor people motion and detect potentially dangerous situations before they take place, so that people can be warned. The interface with which people interact with our framework is their own smartphones. We have described an architecture that considers both real people being tracked through their smartphones and a simulated environment where artificial nodes represent people movements.

As future work, we want to keep working on the backed part of our framework. In particular, we aim to focus on the machine learning component that will predict dangerous situations caused by crowds, and we will develop an alerting system to notify users when they might be in danger and to give them recommendations on how to act (such as taking an alternative path).

Finally, although challenging to put into practice, we would like to perform experiments with real people moving in a real space. For this, we might think of some reward to give to the people who will be participating in the experiments. Their task is actually simple: they would simply need to install our Artax app in their smartphones and walk in an open space following some movement patterns that we will dictate.

Acknowledgments. This work has been partially funded by the Spanish Ministry of Science, Innovation, and Universities (projects PID2021-125527NB-I00, TED2021-130666B-I00, and TED2021-130523B-I00).

References

1. Azabal, M.J., Berrocal, J., Soares, V.N.G.J., García-Alonso, J., Galán-Jiménez, J.: A self-sustainable opportunistic solution for emergency detection in ageing people living in rural areas. Wirel. Networks **29**(5), 2353–2370 (2023). https://doi.org/10.1007/S11276-023-03294-9
2. Batty, M., Axhausen, K., Giannotti, F., et al.: Smart cities of the future. Eur. Phys. J. Spec. Top. **214**, 481–518 (2012). https://doi.org/10.1140/epjst/e2012-01703-3
3. Bein Fahlander, L., Mossberg, M.: Simulating people flow at an airport: case study: Arlanda airport (2020)
4. Bunde, A., Kropp, J., Schellnhuber, H.J., Helbing, D., Farkas, I.J., Vicsek, T.: Crowd disasters and simulation of panic situations. In: The Science of Disasters: Climate Disruptions, Heart Attacks, and Market Crashes, pp. 330–350 (2002)
5. Deng, T., Zhang, K., Shen, Z.J.M.: A systematic review of a digital twin city: a new pattern of urban governance toward smart cities. MSC J. **6**(2), 125–134 (2021)
6. Guillén, J., Miranda, J., Berrocal, J., García-Alonso, J., Murillo, J.M., Canal, C.: People as a service: a mobile-centric model for providing collective sociological profiles. IEEE Softw. **31**(2), 48–53 (2014). https://doi.org/10.1109/MS.2013.140
7. Herrera, J.L., Chen, H.Y., Berrocal, J., Murillo, J.M., Julien, C.: Context-aware privacy-preserving access control for mobile computing. Pervasive Mob. Comput. **87**, 101725 (2022). https://doi.org/10.1016/j.pmcj.2022.101725. https://www.sciencedirect.com/science/article/pii/S1574119222001389
8. Jesús-Azabal, M., Herrera, J.L., Laso, S., Galán-Jiménez, J.: Oppnets and rural areas: an opportunistic solution for remote communications. Wirel. Commun. Mob. Comput. **2021**(1), 8883501 (2021). https://doi.org/10.1155/2021/8883501. https://onlinelibrary.wiley.com/doi/abs/10.1155/2021/8883501
9. Keränen, A., Kärkkäinen, T., Ott, J.: Simulating mobility and DTNs with the ONE (invited paper). J. Commun. **5**(2), 92–105 (2010). https://doi.org/10.4304/JCM.5.2.92-105
10. Keränen, A., Ott, J., Kärkkäinen, T.: The ONE simulator for DTN protocol evaluation. In: SIMUTools '09: Proceedings of the 2nd International Conference on Simulation Tools and Techniques. ICST, New York, NY, USA (2009)
11. Laso, S., Berrocal, J., García-Alonso, J., Canal, C., Manuel Murillo, J.: Human microservices: a framework for turning humans into service providers. Software Pract. Exp. **51**(9), 1910–1935 (2021)
12. Lehtola, V.V., et al.: Digital twin of a city: review of technology serving city needs. Int. J. Appl. Earth Obs. Geoinf. **114**, 102915 (2022)
13. Lemercier, S., et al.: Realistic following behaviors for crowd simulation. In: Computer Graphics Forum, vol. 31, pp. 489–498. Wiley Online Library (2012)
14. Madni, A.M., Madni, C.C., Lucero, S.D.: Leveraging digital twin technology in model-based systems engineering. Systems **7**(1), 7 (2019)

15. Mangas, S.L., Olmeda, J.J.B., Fernández, P., Cortés, A.R., Rodríguez, J.M.M.: Perses: a framework for the continuous evaluation of the QoS of distributed mobile applications. In: Pervasive and Mobile Computing (2022)
16. Moreno, N., Toro-Gálvez, L., Troya-Castilla, J., Canal-Velasco, J.C., et al.: Modeling urban digital twins over the cloud-to-thing continuum. In: Mess Workshop @ STAF 2023 (2023)
17. Pérez-Vereda, A., Cabañero, L., Moreno, N., Hervás, R., Canal, C.: Distributed crowdsensing based on mobile personal data stores. In: Bravo, J., Urzáiz, G. (eds.) Proceedings of the 15th International Conference on Ubiquitous Computing & Ambient Intelligence (UCAmI 2023) - Volume 3, Riviera Maya, Mexico, 28-29 November, 2023. Lecture Notes in Networks and Systems, vol. 841, pp. 3–15. Springer, Cham (2023). https://doi.org/10.1007/978-3-031-48590-9_1
18. Pérez-Vereda, A., Hervás, R., Canal, C.: Digital avatars: a programming framework for personalized human interactions through virtual profiles. Pervasive Mob. Comput. **87**, 101718 (2022). https://doi.org/10.1016/J.PMCJ.2022.101718
19. Pérez-Vereda, A., Murillo, J.M., Canal, C.: Dynamically programmable virtual profiles as a service. In: 2019 IEEE SmartWorld/SCALCOM/UIC/ATC/CBDCom/IOP/SCI, pp. 1789–1794 (2019)
20. Robles, J., Martín, C., Díaz, M.: OpenTwins: an open-source framework for the development of next-gen compositional digital twins. In: Computers in Industry (2023)
21. Ruiz, P., Seredynski, M., Torné, Á., Dorronsoro, B.: A digital twin for bus operation in public urban transportation systems. In: Big Data Intelligence and Computing, pp. 40–52 (2023)
22. Saeed, R.A., Recupero, D.R., Remagnino, P.: Simulating people dynamics. In: 2021 17th International Conference on Intelligent Environments (IE), pp. 1–8 (2021). https://doi.org/10.1109/IE51775.2021.9486478
23. Soomaroo, L., Murray, V.: Disasters at mass gatherings: lessons from history. PLoS Curr. **4** (2012)
24. Wang, H., Chen, X., Jia, F., Cheng, X.: Digital twin-supported smart city: status, challenges and future research directions. Expert Syst. Appl. **217**, 119531 (2023). https://doi.org/10.1016/j.eswa.2023.119531. https://www.sciencedirect.com/science/article/pii/S0957417423000325

A Digital Process Twin Conceptual Architecture for What-If Process Analysis

Ivan Compagnucci[1(✉)], Barbara Re[2], Estefanía Serral Asensio[3], and Monique Snoeck[3]

[1] Gran Sasso Science Institute, L'Aquila, Italy
ivan.compagnucci@gssi.it
[2] Computer Science Division, University of Camerino, Camerino, Italy
barbara.re@unicam.it
[3] Faculty of Economics and Business, KU Leuven, Leuven, Belgium
{estefania.asensio,monique.snoeck}@kuleuven.be

Abstract. Business processes require continuous changes or interventions to remain efficient and competitive over time. However, implementing these changes-such as reordering or adding new tasks- can negatively affect the overall process performance. A longstanding problem in Business Process Management is that of forecasting *ex-ante* the values that process performance measures will assume after implementing changes. To achieve this, the concept of Digital Process Twins, which extends the well-established Digital Twin paradigm, paves the way for new interesting opportunities. Digital Process Twins enable enhanced *what-if* analysis by virtually predicting process performance under various changes, thus allowing for informed decision-making before actuating process changes in the real world. However, despite recognition as one of the new key enablers of modern process re-engineerization, a comprehensive approach to implementing Digital Process Twins is still lacking. This paper proposes a novel conceptual architecture for deploying Digital Process Twins to address this gap. Additionally, we introduce DOLLY, a framework that implements such conceptual architecture using a multi-modeling approach combining domain data and process modeling along with a data-driven process simulation technique.

Keywords: Business Process · Digital Process Twin · Internet of Things

1 Introduction

Nowadays, organizations constantly strive to enhance and sustain the efficiency and performance of their operational processes [16]. This necessity is fueled by several factors, including the increasing competitiveness of the global market, environmental shifts, variations in resource availability, emergent business opportunities, and the advent of new technologies [15]. A notable example of these advancements is the emerging field of IoT-Enhanced Business Processes

M. Kaczmarek-Heß et al. (Eds.): EDOC 2024 Workshops, LNBIP 537, pp. 373–388, 2025.
https://doi.org/10.1007/978-3-031-79059-1_23

[8,9,32], where IoT devices are increasingly being integrated into processes to optimize further and automate business operations. However, for a long time, a problem in the field of Business Process Management is that of *what-if process analysis*: predicting the values that one or more process performance measures will assume after a given business process changes or interventions [4,15,18].

A similar problem has been addressed in mechanical and industrial engineering using the Digital Twin paradigm. Digital Twins are virtual replicas of real-world systems synchronized at specific levels of detail. They accurately predict the performance and behavior of their physical counterparts over time, offering valuable insights for optimization and decision-making [19]. Initially adopted in the manufacturing sector to virtually replicate, simulate, and predict the performance of physical machines, the concept of Digital Twin is starting to be applied to organizational processes, providing a new approach to re-engineering modern business processes [15,18]. Gartner estimates that by 2026, 25% of global enterprises will move towards creating Digital Twins for their business processes [21].

In light of this, the integration of Business Process Management practices with the Digital Twin paradigm is being seen as a promising solution for helping organizations manage process changes while maintaining resilience and control over their operations [4,15,18]. Just as traditional Digital Twins replicate and predict the performance of physical assets, Digital Process Twins offer analogous capabilities for business processes. Implementing changes in business processes typically involves significant time, resources and risk of failure, leading to high expenses [16]. This integration facilitates *what-if* process analysis, allowing organizations to simulate potential changes and predict their impact on process performance *ex-ante* in a virtual, safe, and risk-free environment [15,18,24]. However, despite being recently recognized as a key enabler for digital transformation in organizational processes [4,15,24], there is currently no detailed framework for fully exploiting the opportunities that a Digital Process Twin can provide [18].

The contributions of this work are twofold. First, we propose a novel conceptual architecture for implementing Digital Process Twins. The proposed architecture employs heterogeneous digital models and Business Process Management techniques to replicate the *as-is* process and reason about the performance of a *to-be* process after virtually implementing process changes. Secondly, we present Dolly, a framework that implements the proposed Digital Process Twin's conceptual architecture. Dollyuses a multi-modeling approach that combines an IoT domain model with the MERODE methodology and BPMN, enabling the simulation and prediction of process changes' impact on performance before real-world implementation.

The rest of the paper is organized as follows. Section 2 presents background knowledge. Section 3 presents a conceptual architecture for implementing Digital Process Twins. Section 4 introduces the Dollyframework supporting the Digital Process Twin conceptual architecture in practice. Section 5 reports on the

DOLLYevaluation. Finally, Sect. 6 discusses related works, and Sect. 7 summarizes and concludes the paper.

2 Background

This section overviews the most relevant aspects of deploying the Digital Process Twin. First, we introduce MERODE, a model-driven method used to support the design of digital models for Digital Process Twin. Additionally, we discuss the Business Process Simulation technique, which is fundamental for conducting "what-if" analyses and estimating business process performance.

2.1 The MERODE Methodology

Adopting a Model-Driven Engineering approach in developing Digital Twins is fundamental to fully leverage their potential [19,23]. A noteworthy approach within this domain is the MERODE methodology [30]. MERODE uses object-oriented domain modeling to develop enterprise information systems, structuring the design and implementation of intra-organizational enterprise information systems into three distinct layers: the Domain layer, the Information System Services layer, and the Business Process layer [30].

The Domain layer defines *business objects*, including their attributes and relationships. A business object represents a real-world entity relevant to a business process, such as data, documents, people, events, or other elements participating in a business process [16]. Examples of business objects could include *Container* and *Shipment*, which can be instantiated to link a container with a specific shipment. Additionally, a *Sensor* equipped on each container constantly monitors and tracks data in real-time, providing comprehensive information about the shipment's status and conditions. The domain layer enables code generation from a conceptual model named "MERODE Domain Model", facilitating the transition to a functional prototype of the information system [29,30]. The MERODE Domain Model consists of three views: a *Class Diagram*, an *Object Event Table*, and a set of *Finite State Machines*. The class diagram defines business objects and their relationships, while the object event table maps event types triggered by business objects. When an event fires, it triggers the execution of methods on business objects used to create, modify, or end business object instances. Finite state machines specify the life cycles of business objects, depicting object behavior triggered by events. A MERODE Domain model can be modeled using the MERLIN Modeling Tool[1], providing model consistency and correctness assessment features.

The Information System Services layer acts as a bridge between business objects and business processes. Input services update the business objects by modifying their attributes or state, while output services provide access to data.

The Business Process layer sits above the Information System Services layer. Its purpose is to facilitate interactions between processes and the Domain layer

[1] https://www.merlin-academic.com/.

via Information System Services, ensuring the update and exchange of information with business objects.

2.2 Data-Driven Business Process Simulation

Traditional Business Process Simulations allow business experts to estimate the performance of business processes under varying conditions and constraints [1]. To run a simulation, a Simulation Model is required. This model digitally replicates real-world processes, including detailed mappings of process flows, activities, decision points, and resources. In addition, it necessitates a set of Simulation Parameters that represent quantitative variables such as activity processing times and costs used to ensure that the Simulation Model accurately reflects real-world conditions [1,27]. However, the manual creation and fine-tuning of Business Simulation Models is an error-prone task, involving a complex set of models and parameters defined and assessed manually by business experts. This approach often leads to inaccurate models and requires significant time to identify the optimal scenario for desired performance outcomes [6,14].

Data-driven process simulation offers a solution by leveraging real data to discover accurate and enhanced simulation-ready models [6,14]. Unlike traditional process simulations, which rely on manually gathered and interpreted information, data-driven simulations utilize historical and real-time data from event logs. Mining techniques based on past event logs of the process [6,22] are employed to ensure that simulation-ready models and parameters are reasonable and aligned with reality [1]. Historical data provide retrospective insights through process mining techniques, while real-time data enable continuous updates to the simulation model, ensuring it accurately reflects the current state of the process during the simulation [14].

Once the simulation model is configured, it is ready to be simulated, and results can be interpreted. To this end, Key Performance Indicators (KPIs) are crucial for evaluating the performance and effectiveness of business processes. KPIs are values for measuring the effectiveness in achieving specific goals of a business process [1]. They include metrics such as cycle time distribution, waiting time distribution, cost distribution, and resource utilization, providing benchmarks for evaluating overall process performance. By assessing the KPIs, the *what-if* questions mentioned above can be answered, and different process redesigns can be compared.

3 Conceptualizing Digital Twins

Implementing a Digital Twin infrastructure is a non-trivial task [19,25]. Despite the emergence of various implementations from both research and practical applications [17,25], no single solution can be considered a silver bullet for implementing a full-fledged Digital Twin [19]. A Digital Twin environment typically includes a collection of interconnected models and data that replicate a real-world system [19]. It provides services, including design, development, analysis, simulation, and optimization, enabling a thorough understanding and enhancement of the replicated system's performance [17,19].

3.1 A Conceptual Architecture for Digital Twin

In [17], the authors explored various characterizations of the core elements of Digital Twins. This effort was directed at providing a clearer understanding of the foundational components of Digital Twins. They proposed a generic and conceptual architecture for facilitating the systematic engineering of new domain-independent Digital Twin applications. According to [17], a Digital Twin adheres to a three-component architecture described as a three-element tuple:

$$A_{DT} = \langle Actual\ System, Models, Data \rangle$$

where the *Actual System* represent a real-world system or object; *Models* provide digital representations of the Actual System; and *Data* represents current and historical data of the Actual System, crucial for instantiating digital models. The three main components of the architecture are described in the follows.

- The **Actual System** refers to the real-world system that the Digital Twin aims to replicate. It involves collecting, storing, calculating, and inferring data specific to the system. These activities are essential for the Digital Twin to capture relevant aspects, features, and relationships of the Actual System within its operational contexts and environments.
- The **Data** component is about storing and representing current and historical data from the Actual System. Data and information are important to accurately provides information to models and reflect the actual system in the digital space of the Digital Twin environment, enabling accurate and fair analysis.
- The **Models** establish digital representations of the Actual System considering different perspectives. As stated by [17], it includes three types of models: *descriptive*, *predictive*, and *prescriptive*. *Descriptive models* capture and organize data to accurately replicate the Actual System. *Predictive models* support decision-making using aggregated data and insights from descriptive models to anticipate future system behavior and conduct "what-if" analyses. Finally, *Prescriptive models* incorporate insights from "what-if" analyses into adaptive actions aimed at optimizing the Actual System.

3.2 A Conceptual Architecture for Digital Process Twin

Digital Process Twins have recently been acknowledged as crucial enablers for digital transformation within organizational processes [4,15,18]. However, there is still a lack of comprehensive implementations to effectively leverage the Digital Process Twins paradigm. In the following, we propose a conceptual architectural approach tailored for the engineering and deployment of Digital Process Twins, drawing upon the conceptualization outlined in the previous Subsection. Figure 1 depicts a visual representation of the proposed conceptual architecture.

The **Actual System** here refers to a business process, which consists of actions, events, and decisions that lead to creating a service or product [16]. Typically, business processes encompass various perspectives, which the authors in [26] categorize into six distinct perspectives described in the following.

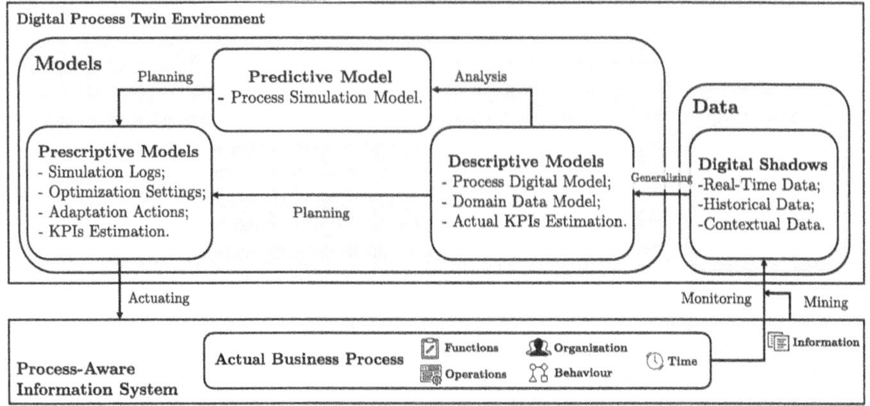

Fig. 1. The Conceptual Architecture for Digital Process Twin.

- **Function Perspective:** atomic activities representing specific business tasks within the process.
- **Behavior Perspective:** dynamic behavior including control flow, activity order, and constraints.
- **Information Perspective:** data used/generated in the process, organized via domain models (class diagrams, finite state machines).
- **Organization Perspective:** roles of participants and organizational units, ensuring proper task assignment.
- **Operation Perspective:** implementation details and integration with application services, supporting business functions.
- **Time Perspective:** temporal constraints like deadlines and durations, ensuring timely execution.

Process-Aware Information Systems integrate and manage these business processes by incorporating the aforementioned perspectives, facilitating control, monitoring, and analysis [26]. The information generated by these systems provide valuable information and data on various aspects of the process. These systems generate valuable information, including historical data stored in event logs and real-time data on ongoing process instances, which offer essential information for creating a digital process replica.

The **Data** component entails collecting and storing process-relevant data directly from the process and the Process-Aware Information System. Data are organized through *Digital Shadows*, which are abstracted and aggregated data structures that provide a one-way data flow from the Actual System to its digital representation [3,24]. Information is transmitted to the Digital Shadow to establish a synchronous linkage between the Actual System and its corresponding Digital Process Twin. Data is fundamental for two reasons: first, it instantiates digital models that accurately replicate the Actual System; second, by populating these models, it enables detailed analyses that provide insights and drive improvements in the Actual System. The data flow, represented in Fig. 1 by the "Monitoring/Mining" arrow, illustrates two methods of data collection: real-time monitoring of ongoing business process instances and historical data extraction using Process Mining techniques [2]. Real-time data includes information about the current status of the process (i.e., resource usage, active tasks, actual process KPIs). Historical data, including event logs of past process executions, organizational documents outlining procedures, and additional contextual data, provides valuable information for Process Mining analyses [2].

Considering the **Model** component, *descriptive models* aim to create a digital replica of the process [17]. Therefore, the first step is defining a model able to properly represent the actual business process embedding the six typical perspectives of business processes described below. Ensuring the quality of the process model is crucial, because it enables precise monitoring, analysis, and optimization of business processes, leading to improved efficiency, predictive maintenance, and informed decision-making [16,34]. In this context, Business Process Model and Notation (BPMN) stands out as the most common and effective standard for designing a business process model for organizations [10,11]. A BPMN diagram details the sequence of activities, control rules, and interactions between process participants, providing a clear and comprehensive representation of the entire process. It represents specific *behaviors*, *functions*, *operations*, *organizational* and *time* perspectives of the process. The model of the process is obtained by adopting process mining discovery algorithms [2], which analyze event logs from the Process-Aware Information System to ensure the model is accurate and reflects reality. In parallel, the domain data model manages the *information* perspective, organizing and structuring data relevant to the process. This includes class diagrams and finite state machines that define the relationships and states of business objects, ensuring data integrity and supporting the retrieval of process-related information.

To conduct *what-if* analyses, a *predictive model* representing the digital replica of the actual business process is employed. However, to implement and test new process changes, business experts must manually adjust the process structure (i.e., reordering tasks and adding new resources). For this reason, the digital replica should be modified by (i) manually implementing the necessary changes to the process model; (ii) discovering optimal *Simulation Parameters* using existing mining approaches on historical data [6,22]; (iii) leveraging real-time data from a Domain Model [26]. This enables the creation of a data-driven process simulation model, allowing for the virtual implementation of changes and the estimation of the new process's performance through simulation. Finally, simulation insights can be translated into the form of *Prescriptive Models*. They consist of estimating KPIs and analyzing event logs to reason about the impact of changes made to the process. These insights are translated into actions, evaluated by business experts, and, if beneficial, implemented in the actual business process. To complete the feedback loop between the Digital Twin and the Actual System, the "Actuating" arrow involves implementing and executing actions on the Actual System based on prescriptive models. This approach helps reduce costs, save time, and provide a risk-free environment for virtual testing.

4 DOLLY: A Framework for Implementing Digital Process Twins

This section introduces DOLLY, a framework based on the Digital Process Twin conceptual architecture proposed in Subsect. 3.2 It adopts a multi-modeling approach, integrating domain data models formalized with the MERODE methodology, the standard BPMN language for process modeling, and data-driven simulation techniques for what-if process analysis. Figure 2 provides an overview of DOLLY, highlighting its three key components: the Actual System, Data, and Models.

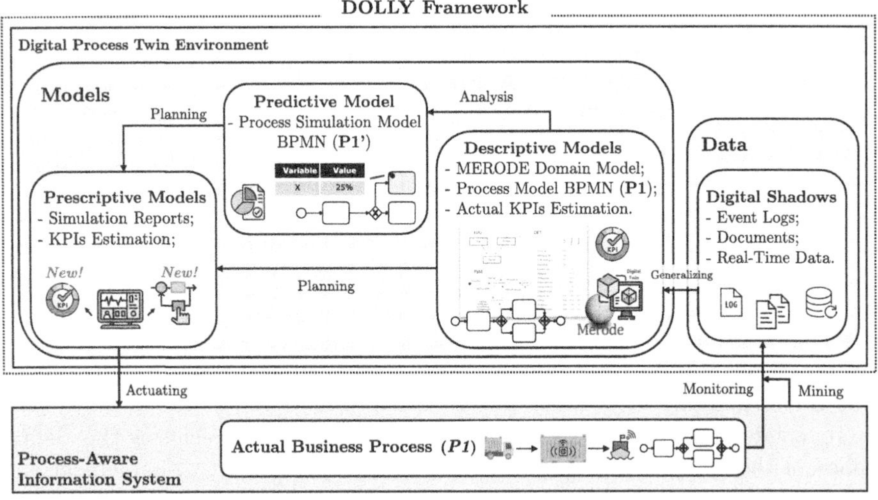

Fig. 2. DOLLY: Framework Overview.

To create a digital copy of the **Actual Process** *(P1)*, DOLLYallows to leverage data from the Process-Aware Information System that implements the actual business process. The **Data** extracted includes real-time information from ongoing process instances via an embedded Camunda Engine, as well as historical data obtained by uploading an event log representing previous process executions. The event log is used to discover the structure of the actual BPMN process model *(P1)* through Process Mining techniques [2]. On the other hand, Real-time data are used to instantiate the MERODE Domain Model. In [31], the authors demonstrate how MERODE bridges the gap between data and process modeling by linking these two domains formally. It allows to handling of domain process data by continuously monitoring business objects' status, relationships, actions, and actual process KPIs. This enables real-time management of their data, providing current status information within the process. Moreover, MERODE supports formal verification, reusability, and flexibility [30], creating descriptive models that accurately reflect business processes from multiple perspectives.

Then, to evaluate the impact of potential process changes, a new BPMN model (*P1'*) is derived by modifying the digital counterpart *P1* of the actual process. Unlike *P1*, the *P1'* model necessitate additional features. First, it includes manual changes applied by business experts, implementing the desired changes to the process. Additionally, to effectively run simulations, *P1'* requires defining simulation parameters. These parameters are discovered using SimuBridge [22], which allows mining techniques to be performed on historical process data, ensuring that simulations are based on real information. Furthermore, *P1'* integrates real-time data from the MERODE Domain Model, aligning domain data with the current state of the ongoing process instance. This real-time data is essential for maintaining the accuracy and relevance of the simulations. By simulating *P1'*, which acts as a *predictive model*, it is possible to conduct "what-if" analysis within the Digital Process Twin, allowing for the evaluation of potential changes and providing valuable insights into their impact before real-world implementation. To run simulations on BPMN models, DOLLYembedded BIMP UI, a business process simulator. This integration allows users to simulate business processes effectively, leveraging a user-friendly interface to visualize, analyze, and download simulation results.

Business experts then evaluate the impact of the changes on process performance by carefully analyzing the simulation results. If the performance improves or remains unchanged, the changes suggested by the prescriptive models can be considered for implementation. If performance does not improve, *P1'* is revised and tested again. This iterative approach enables continuous process adjustments based on real-time data, simulation feedback, and desired process changes.

5 Framework Evaluation

This section presents a real-world implementation of DOLLYin a smart harbor scenario. The objective is to evaluate the framework's capabilities. A smart harbor represents a technologically advanced port that leverages innovative technologies and data-driven solutions to enhance operational efficiency [28]. This scenario focuses on an IoT-enabled business process that represents modern processes designed for automation through IoT integration. While smart harbors encompass various processes, we will focus on container dispatching.

5.1 The Container Dispatch Business Process

Context. The process starts with the arrival of a cargo container at the harbor and ends when it is loaded onto a cargo ship, indicating that it's ready for shipment. The containers involved in dispatching are equipped with IoT devices (i.e., RFID sensors) to track their status during the dispatching. When containers reach the harbor, their information (i.e., IoT data and shipping documents) is recorded in the system and transmitted to the Storage Area. Then, it is relocated to the Control Area for quality inspection. Quality control is conducted by cross-referencing the container's arrival data with the information gathered during manual quality inspection. If the container fails the quality test, a manual inspection is conducted to address potential quality issues, and the container is then returned to the Storage Area. Once quality problems are resolved, the container is moved to the Shipping Area and loaded onto the cargo ship.

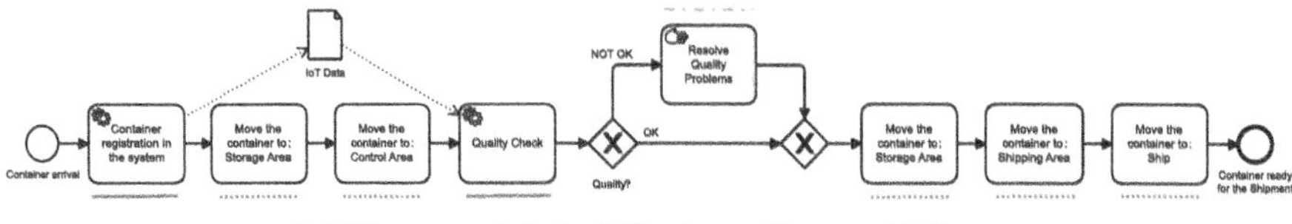

(a) Discovered Actual Business Process (*P1*).

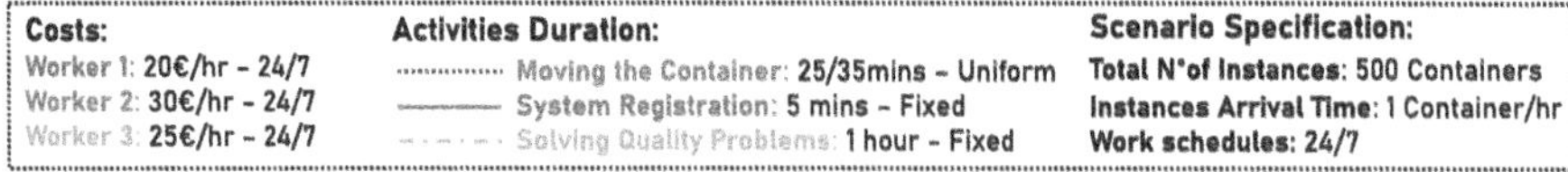

(b) Mined Simulation Parameters.

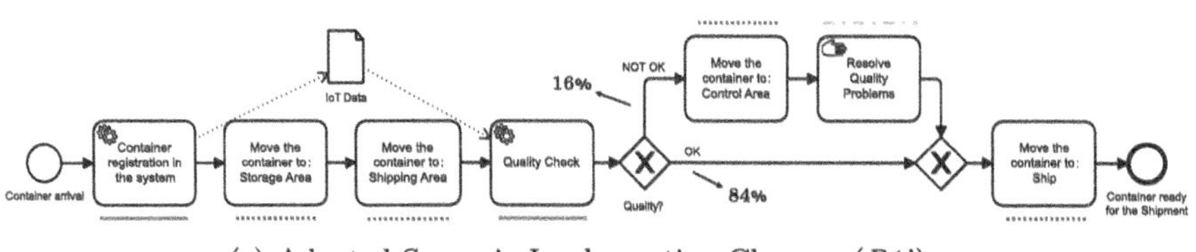

(c) Adapted Scenario Implementing Changes (*P1'*).

Fig. 3. Simulation Parameters and Models of the Container Dispatch Process.

Process Data. The event logs were generated considering two primary data sources: (i) logs from the smart harbor system, which contains the sequences of activities performed for each process instance and trace attributes, and (ii) IoT sensor data, which tracks the arrival and quality of the containers considering temperature and humidity. The process event logs were generated using CDLG [20], a tool specifically designed to create synthetic event logs integrating concept drifts and noise, such as missing event data. Event logs are based on patterns and data observed in real-life operations from the Tuscan Port Community System[2].

[2] https://tpcs.tpcs.eu/.

The event log comprises 7 activities, 3 resources, 33,910 events related to 5000 cases, and 67 execution paths (process variants).

5.2 Use Case Instantiation

Actual Business Process. As a first step, we employed the inductive miner process mining algorithm to discover the actual business process *P1* from the event log, applying a threshold to mitigate noise. The process structure has been slightly adapted to better align with real-world operations. Figure 3a depicts the process model discovered (*P1*). Automated tasks are designated as service tasks, while the manual task of resolving quality problems is identified as a manual task. Additionally, a data object has been incorporated to represent IoT data utilized during container registration and quality check activities. The initial container registration in the system involves capturing this IoT data, which is crucial for subsequent quality assessments. Analysis of the structure of the event log and the derived process is provided through a python notebook[3].

MERODE Domain Model. In [12], we utilized a MERODE Domain Model to develop a Digital Twin for manufacturing applications. Building on this, we have implemented the domain model within DOLLYto generate *Prescriptive Models* for implementing Digital Process Twins.

After discovering the actual process, the MERODE Domain Model is instantiated and mapped to the business objects participating. For example, creating instances of the *Device* class allows real-time retrieval of data, status, and actions from physical devices. These digital models, formed by class diagrams, finite state machines and object event tables, are dynamically synchronized with business objects at the business process level, capturing real-time and historical data. Each business object is "tracked" by these models, and every action it performs is updated both in the process and in the domain model instances. This ensures that both real-time and past data produced by business objects can be retrieved for analysis. A representation of the MERODE Domain Model is shown in Fig. 4. Further details on the specification and instantiation of the MERODE IoT Domain Model are available online[4].

Data-Driven Process Simulation. At this stage, we assumed the involvement of business experts to introduce changes to the actual process. For this use case, we address the question: *How can we modify the process to reduce total costs and cycle time while maintaining the same operational efficiency?* Using *bpmn.io*, a BPMN modeler embedded in DOLLY, changes were manually applied to the digital process replica (*P1*), resulting in an adapted version, *P1'*. This adaptation aimed to simplify the workflow, reduce costs, and shorten the process cycle time. In *P1'*, the container is moved to the Control Area only if it fails the quality check, eliminating unnecessary movements. Figure 3c depicts the adapted version of the process *P1'*.

[3] https://dub.sh/BPDiscovery-ipynb.

[4] https://github.com/IvanComp/Dolly/blob/main/README.md.

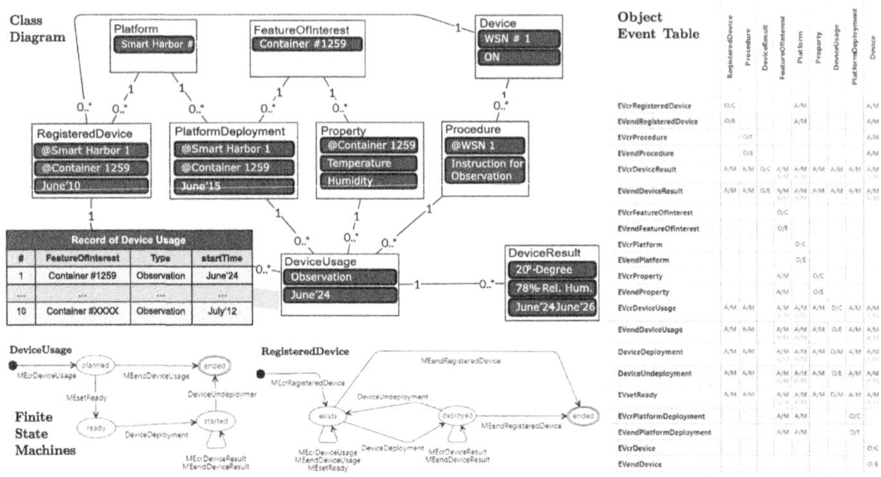

Fig. 4. MERODE Domain Model Instantiation.

The event log was then used to discover the optimal simulation parameters for the process simulation model *P1'* using SimuBridge [22]. SimuBridge integrates components such as control flow, activity duration, and resource utilization by analyzing a *.xes* event log file. It leverages the Simod mining algorithm [7], which enhances accuracy to derive models and simulation parameters from event logs. The simulation parameters mined are as follows: Worker 1 handles container system registration and quality checks, earning €20 per hour; Worker 2 manages container movements, earning €30 per hour; Worker 3 performs manual quality inspections, earning €25 per hour. Figure 3b shows these parameters, with each task differentiated by shapes and colors based on the resource associated. For all workers, a 24/7 working timetable was considered. Activities have varying durations: the container quality check takes 1 h while recording and checking container data in the system takes 5 min. To better reflect reality, container movements follow a uniform time distribution, varying between 25 and 35 min. Containers have an 84% chance of passing the quality test, as required by the XOR gateway for outgoing sequence flows (84% OK, 16% NOT OK). Additionally, a fixed distribution time is assigned to each instance's arrival.

Finally, we simulated *P1'* using BIMP UI, a scalable and fast BPMN simulator and compared the KPIs derived from *P1* and *P1'*. As motivated by the Digital Process Twin architecture, we employed a hybrid approach integrating mined optimal simulation parameters, real-time data from the MERODE Domain Model, and manual changes to the actual process *P1*. This method continuously updates and reflects the process model, resulting in a data-driven simulation model *P1'*.

Results Evaluation. Table 1 presents the KPIs for *P1* and *P1'*. The KPIs are categorized into cycle time distribution, cost distribution, and resource utiliza-

Table 1. KPIs of the Simulation for *P1* and *P1'*.

Legend: ↓ *Reduction*, ↑ *Increase*. — **Hrs:** Hours, **Wks:** Weekends.

KPIs	Original Scenario *(P1)*				Adapted Scenario *(P1')*			
	Min.	Max.	Avg.	Total	Min.	Max.	Avg.	Total
Cycle Time Distr.	3.7 Hrs	15.6 Hrs	11.7 Hrs	12.6 Wks	1.5 Hrs ↓	9.2 Hrs ↓	5 Hrs ↓	12.4 Wks ↓
Cost Distr.	€ 68.20	€ 110.40	€ 80.10	€ 40,054.20	€ 40.40 ↓	€ 93.70 ↓	€ 53.50↓	€ 26,767.50 ↓
	Worker 1	Worker 2	Worker 3	Total	Worker 1	Worker 2	Worker 3	Total
Resource Utiliz.	58.75%	2.00%	3.44%	64.19%	37.54% ↓	1.98% ↓	3.92% ↑	43.44% ↓

tion. In terms of cycle time distribution, *P1'* shows significant improvements with reduced minimum, maximum, and average cycle times, indicating a more efficient process. Regarding cost distribution, *P1'* showed cost savings, with lower minimum, maximum, and average costs, and a significantly reduced total cost, indicating better time efficiency and cost-effectiveness. In resource utilization, *P1'* shows mixed results. Workers 1 and 2 have significantly improved utilization, while Worker 3's workload increases. A graphical comparison between the KPIs values of *P1* and *P1'* is shown in Fig. 5 and available online[5]. The *P1* and *P1'* versions of the simulation models, the SimuBridge project file and the simulation results are available online.[6]. The DOLLYsource code and instructions for running are available online[7].

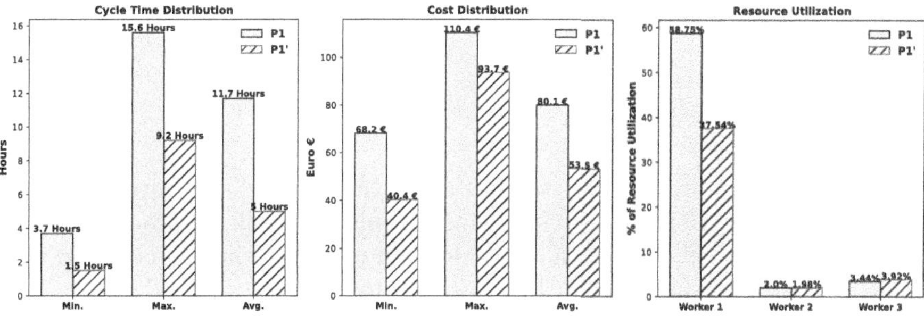

Fig. 5. Comparison of the KPIs for *P1* and *P1'*.

6 Related Work

The concept of Digital Twin has been extensively explored across various domains and purposes [19,23]. Significant research has focused on implementing Digital Twins in industrial sectors, particularly in replicating and simulating machines and devices used in manufacturing processes [3,23,25].

[5] https://bit.ly/Dolly_AnalisysResults_ipynb.

[6] https://zenodo.org/records/12671621.

[7] https://github.com/IvanComp/Dolly.

Despite the growing interest, only a limited number of research works focus on implementing Digital Process Twins. For instance, [33] proposes a micro-service architecture to integrate physical IoT entities into IoT-Enhanced Business Processes. This approach uses a model-driven development method that combines BPMN models and Digital Twins Definition Language models via Java microservices, allowing IoT virtual replicas to be integrated into real-world processes. However, it lacks capabilities for continuous optimization and adaptation of IoT-Enhanced Business Processes. Similarly, PROWIN [13] is a framework designed for monitoring and executing IoT-Enhanced Business Processes in a multi-robot scenario. It uses the Gazebo Simulator for 3D visualization of the operating scenario and the process's evolution, offering a detailed view of the system's execution. Nonetheless, it does not address the specifics of the software infrastructure needed for maintaining runtime synchronization with the real world. In [5], authors present a framework for managing IoT-Enhanced Business Processes. This solution extends the BPMN standard and integrates models for analysis, featuring a model-to-text transformation engine, an interaction broker for IoT infrastructure, a simulation engine, and a business process engine. However, it lacks detailed real-time communication with physical counterparts.

This work advances the state of the art by proposing a novel conceptual architecture for deploying Digital Process Twins. It outlines a procedure for creating, managing, and simulating digital replicas of business processes to assess potential changes before real-world implementation. Additionally, we introduce Dolly, a prototype framework that allows to implementation of the proposed Digital Process Twin conceptual architecture.

7 Conclusion

In this paper, we moved a first step in introducing a novel conceptual architecture for deploying Digital Process Twins to enhance resilient process changes and support informed decision-making through predictive insights derived from data-driven process simulations. The architecture integrates heterogeneous digital models (e.g., descriptive, predictive, and prescriptive) to design, synchronize, and simulate a high-fidelity digital replica of business processes, leveraging data extracted from real-time business object monitoring and process mining analysis.

The conceptual architecture promotes a feedback loop mechanism that utilizes data-driven process simulation on the process replica to continuously assess the potential impacts of desired process changes. If process performance improves or remains stable, these changes are considered to be actuated by business experts in the real-world process. Moreover, conducting tests on digital replicas enables secure, risk-free evaluation of changes, thereby reducing deployment costs and accelerating process updates. The approach was evaluated using Dolly, an early-prototype framework implementing the proposed Digital Process Twins architecture in the context of a container dispatching process, revealing significant improvements.

In future research, we aim to improve further Dolly, currently in its prototype stage, focusing on performance in high data volume environments, such as typical IoT settings. We also plan to test DOLLYin more complex and larger-scale scenarios for more accurate and realistic evaluation.

References

1. van der Aalst, W.M.P.: Business process simulation survival guide. In: BPM, Introduction, Methods, and Information Systems, pp. 337–370. Handbooks on Information Systems, Springer (2015)
2. van der Aalst, W.M.P., Carmona, J. (eds.): Process Mining Handbook, Lecture Notes in Business Information Processing, vol. 448. Springer (2022)
3. Becker, F., et al.: A Conceptual Model for Digital Shadows in Industry and Its Application. In: Conceptual Modeling, pp. 271–281. Springer (2021)
4. Beerepoot, I., et al.: The biggest business process management problems to solve before we die. Comput. Ind. **146**, 103837 (2023)
5. Bocciarelli, P., D'Ambrogio, A., Panetti, T.: A model based framework for IoT-aware business process management. Future Internet **15**(2) (2023)
6. Camargo, M., Dumas, M., González-Rojas, O.: Automated discovery of business process simulation models from event logs. Dec. Sup. Syst. **134**, 113284 (2020)
7. Camargo, M., Dumas, M., Rojas, O.G.: Simod: a tool for automated discovery of business process simulation models. In: BPM Demo. CEUR Workshop Proceedings, vol. 2420, pp. 139–143. CEUR-WS.org (2019)
8. Compagnucci, I., Corradini, F., Fornari, F., Polini, A., Re, B., Tiezzi, F.: Modelling notations for IoT-aware business processes: a systematic literature review. In: BPM Workshops. LNBIP, vol. 397, pp. 108–121. Springer (2020)
9. Compagnucci, I., Corradini, F., Fornari, F., Polini, A., Re, B., Tiezzi, F.: A systematic literature review on IoT-aware business process modeling views, requirements and notations. Softw. Syst. Model. **14**(1), 1–36 (2022)
10. Compagnucci, I., Corradini, F., Fornari, F., Re, B.: Trends on the usage of BPMN 2.0 from publicly available repositories. In: Perspectives in Business Informatics Research. LNBIP, vol. 430, pp. 84–99. Springer (2021)
11. Compagnucci, I., Corradini, F., Fornari, F., Re, B.: A study on the usage of the BPMN notation for designing process collaboration, choreography, and conversation models. Bus. Inf. Syst. Eng. **66**, 43–66 (2024)
12. Compagnucci, I., Snoeck, M., Asensio, E.S.: Supporting digital twins systems integrating the MERODE approach. In: 2023 ACM/IEEE International Conference on Model Driven Engineering Languages and Systems Companion (MODELS-C), pp. 449–458 (2023)
13. Corradini, F., Pettinari, S., Re, B., Rossi, L., Tiezzi, F.: Executable digital process twins: towards the enhancement of process-driven systems. Big Data Cogn. Comput. **7**(3) (2023)
14. Depaire, B., Martin, N.: Data-driven process simulation. In: Sakr, S., Zomaya, A.Y. (eds.) Encyclopedia of Big Data Technologies. Springer (2019)
15. Dumas, M.: Constructing digital twins for accurate and reliable what-if business process analysis. In: Conference on Business Process Management. CEUR Workshop Proceedings, vol. 2938, pp. 23–27 (2021)
16. Dumas, M., La Rosa, M., Mendling, J., Reijers, H.A.: Fundamentals of Business Process Management. Springer (2018)
17. Eramo, R., Bordeleau, F., Combemale, B., van den Brand, M., Wimmer, M., Wortmann, A.: Conceptualizing digital twins. IEEE Softw. **39**(2), 39–46 (2022)

18. Fornari, F., et al.: Digital Twins of Business Processes: A Research Manifesto. arXiv (2024). https://arxiv.org/abs/
19. Grieves, M.W.: Digital Twins: Past, Present, and Future, pp. 97–121. Springer (2023)
20. Grimm, J., Kraus, A., van der Aa, H.: CDLG: a tool for the generation of event logs with concept drifts. In: BPM Demo. CEUR Workshop Proceedings, vol. 3216, pp. 92–96. CEUR-WS.org (2022)
21. Kerremans, M., Sugden, D., Duffy, N.: Magic quadrant for process mining platforms. Gartner, Inc. (2024). https://www.gartner.com/doc/reprints?id=1-2HEH7GJM&ct=240426&st=sb. Accessed 8 July
22. Leon, B., Klessascheck, F., Nepeina, S., Warmuth, C., Kampik, T., Pufahl, L.: Simubridge: discovery and management of process simulation scenarios. In: BPM Demo. CEUR Workshop Proceedings, vol. 3469, pp. 77–81. CEUR-WS.org (2023)
23. Liu, M., Fang, S., Dong, H., Xu, C.: Review of digital twin about concepts, technologies, and industrial applications. Manuf. Syst. **58**, 346–361 (2021)
24. Rabe, M., Kilic, E.: Framing the digital business process twin: from a holistic maturity model to a specific and substantial use case in the automotive industry. In: BPM Workshops, pp. 353–364. Springer (2024)
25. Rasheed, A., San, O., Kvamsdal, T.: Digital twin: values, challenges and enablers from a modeling perspective. IEEE Access **8**(1), 21980–22012 (2020)
26. Reichert, M., Weber, B.: Enabling Flexibility in Process-Aware Information Systems - Challenges, Methods, Technologies. Springer (2012)
27. Rosenthal, K., Ternes, B., Strecker, S.: Business process simulation on procedural graphical process models. Bus. Inf. Syst. Eng. **63**(5), 569–602 (2021)
28. Saragiotis, P.: Business process management in the port sector: a literature review. Marit. Bus. Rev. **4** (2019)
29. Snoeck, M., Dedene, G.: Existence dependency: the key to semantic integrity between structural and behavioral aspects of object types. IEEE Trans. Software Eng. **24**(4), 233–251 (1998)
30. Snoeck, M.: Enterprise Information Systems Engineering - The MERODE Approach. The Enterprise Engineering Series. Springer (2014)
31. Snoeck, M., Verbruggen, C., De Smedt, J., De Weerdt, J.: Supporting data-aware processes with MERODE. Softw. Syst. Model. (2023)
32. Torres, V., Serral, E., Valderas, P., Pelechano, V., Grefen, P.: Modeling of IoT devices in business processes: a systematic mapping study. In: Business Informatics, pp. 221–230. IEEE (2020)
33. Valderas, P.: Supporting the implementation of digital twins for IoT-enhanced BPs. In: Information Science and the Connected World. LNBIP, vol. 476, pp. 222–238. Springer (2023)
34. Vemuri, P., Poelmans, S., Compagnucci, I., Snoeck, M.: Using formative assessment and feedback to train novice modelers in business process modeling. In: ACM/IEEE International Conference on Model Driven Engineering Languages and Systems Companion (MODELS-C), pp. 130–137 (2023)

Reference Architecture of Cybersecurity Digital Twin

Taru Itäpelto[1(✉)], Mohammed Elhajj[1], Marten van Sinderen[1], and Maria Iacob[2]

[1] Semantics Cybersecurity and Services (EEMCS-SCS), University of Twente, PO BOX 217, 7500 AE Enschede, The Netherlands
{t.m.itapelto,m.elhajj,m.j.vansideren}@utwente.nl
[2] Section Industrial Engineering and Business Information Systems (BMS-HBE-IEBIS), University of Twente, PO BOX 217, 7500 AE Enschede, The Netherlands
m.e.iacob@utwente.nl
https://www.utwente.nl/en/eemcs/scs/ , https://www.utwente.nl/en/bms/iebis/

Abstract. The transformation of previously isolated Critical Infrastructures (CIs) into intricate Systems-of-Systems has rendered them vulnerable to various threats. CIs are characterized by long life cycles and high availability requirements, which pose significant challenges in maintaining cybersecurity throughout their operational life cycle. Existing testing methodologies prove inadequate and may compromise the CI's operational continuity. This paper proposes to shift testing activities to a Digital Twin (DT) connected to the CI. The DT provides a digital counterpart of the real system, enabling cost-effective testing without compromising operational integrity. For this approach, we present an enterprise architecture called the cybersecurity DT reference architecture. Through a camera surveillance system use case, we demonstrate the feasibility of this reference architecture, focusing on what-if testing using DT-enabled attack simulations. We show how to enhance decision-making when evaluating system configurations and how to deploy optimized configurations to the real system.

Keywords: Digital Twin · Critical Infrastructure · cybersecurity · Enterprise Architecture · DT

1 Introduction

In recent years, concerns regarding the cybersecurity of Critical Infrastructures (CIs) have emerged as a focal point of research and societal attention. Key sectors such as energy, water, communication, and transportation systems form the backbone of modern societies, playing a pivotal role in sustaining economic activities and ensuring the health and safety of citizens [1,15].

M. Kaczmarek-Heß et al. (Eds.): EDOC 2024 Workshops, LNBIP 537, pp. 389–404, 2025.
https://doi.org/10.1007/978-3-031-79059-1_24

Historically, CIs were characterized by physical and digital isolation [15]. However, by introducing increased connectivity and integrating advanced functionalities, such as Internet of Things (IoT) and cloud-based solutions, CIs have ushered in a new era. IoT applications facilitate remote monitoring and control, along with intelligent analysis of big data using Artificial Intelligence/Machine Learning (AI/ML). Nevertheless, these advantages are accompanied by drawbacks, including new security threats [10,15]. Ensuring CIs' security throughout its Life Cycle (LC) requires continuous testing. Albeit, existing testing methods for CIs prove inadequate and may compromise operational continuity [15].

The Digital Twin (DT), a virtual replica of a Real System (RS), is regarded as a promising solution for enhancing the cybersecurity of a CI throughout its LC [6,7] if the challenges it introduces, such as DT's cybersecurity, are properly addressed [6]. Even though definitions of DT vary in the literature [3,9], we adopt the one from [9]. This definition distinguishes three main components of the DT concept: the actual system of interest, called the Real System (RS); the virtual counterpart that maintains a digital copy of the RS, called the DT; and the bi-directional communication, known as twinning, that synchronizes the RS and DT.

This paper addresses these cybersecurity challenges by proposing to shift testing activities to a DT connected to the CI, focusing on enhancing both the CI's and the DT's cybersecurity. We present an Enterprise Architecture for this approach, which can function as a reference architecture (RA) for cybersecurity Digital Twins in CI domains. With the Surveillance System (SS) use case, we exemplify how the RA can support three DT-enabled smart security services: what-if testing, decision support, and optimization. DT-enabled smart services, which can be dynamically added, removed, or modified, are motivated by evolving security concerns throughout the CI's LC. SSs, widely used in CIs such as nuclear power plants, can accidentally serve as entry points for attackers due to IoT vulnerabilities, underscoring the necessity for robust security throughout their LC. For instance, unauthorized access to nuclear power plant management systems could have severe consequences. DT-enabled what-if testing allows for efficient and effective virtual testing of various configurations and responses without disrupting CI operations. This supports informed decision-making and optimization through a feedback loop between DT and RS. Our example system is relevant to CIs and illustrates how our RA can be applied to a real-world CI component, an IoT-enabled SS integrated into a nuclear power plant. To our knowledge, this is the first time a generalised RA has been introduced to enhance the security of CIs using DT.

The rest of the paper is organized as follows: We present the rationale behind the proposed RA and other background information in Sect. 2 and related work in Sect. 3. Following these, we propose the DT-CI system's RA in Sect. 4, illustrate its overview in Sect. 4.1, and detailed layered perspectives of the RS in Sect. 4.2 and the DT in Sect. 4.3. Furthermore, we integrate the example use case-specific changes to these detailed models. Additionally, we introduce the architecture of the SS-specific DT-enabled smart services, i.e. what-if testing, decision-making support, and optimization in Sect. 4.4. Subsequently, we address the limitations of our approach, along with potential future research avenues in Sect. 5. Finally, we summarize our paper in Sect. 6.

2 Background

CIs are essential to society's functioning, economy, and security [1,15]. These systems are often cyber-physical systems (CPS), which consist of critical physical parts controlled and monitored by cyber parts and a network connecting these two parts [14]. Examples of physical part assets are IoT sensors, actuators, and embedded systems. However, cyber part components, such as management applications, could also be considered critical assets needing protection. The digitization of previously isolated CIs has resulted in them forming complex System-of-Systems with various (inter)dependencies with other systems and CIs. For simplicity, with the term *RS*, we refer to CI as an IoT-empowered CPS and System-of-Systems in the rest of the paper. We also consider that DT is used to monitor, analyze, and improve the security of such a system's critical assets, including the IT systems used to manage the physical part.

Ensuring the CI's cybersecurity throughout its life cycle (LC) necessitates continuous security testing and maintaining appropriate security measures. On the other hand, the unique characteristics of CIs impose specific demands on testing procedures. Firstly, the testing process must not disrupt the operation of CIs. Secondly, CIs have a long life cycle (lasting 30–40 years [4]), so it is essential to maintain and test the cybersecurity measures considering evolving threats, requirements, systems, and operating contexts throughout the entire life cycle of the CI [3,15].

However, with current security testing methods, it is difficult to test these complex System-of-Systems and mitigate all possible current threats; it might even be unobtainable [2]. One example of such a method is pen and paper testing, which is not an adequate tool for testing even the current systems [15]. On the other hand, penetration testing might endanger the availability of the RS [15]. Using traditional, isolated testbeds is not viable since keeping these up-to-date is difficult and costly. Furthermore, testbeds often have different settings and functionalities, which makes them different from the RS, and test results are possibly inaccurate [15].

One potential suggested solution to address these challenges is DT, an evolving mirror of RS empowering a thorough understanding of the changing RS, its dependencies, and operating context [6]. It is essential to remain attentive concerning emerging threats from evolving operating conditions and the complex network of systems and dependencies. On the other hand, our proposed DT-CI integration facilitates the selection and deployment of effective and efficient countermeasures. Effective countermeasures address all relevant threats, while efficient ones have the least redundancy and minimal impact on the CI's operation.

Because of the pivotal role of CIs, it is important to get a grip on the proper alignment between stakeholders' concerns and goals on the one hand and the technical design and implementation of the CI on the other. Enterprise Architecture [11] is a proper conceptual tool for this. An Enterprise Architecture provides an integrated view of an enterprise system in an enterprise context, which helps to identify and maintain the mentioned alignment during the LC of the system. A widely accepted framework and modelling language for Enterprise Architecture is ArchiMate[1]. ArchiMate also provides useful structures and patterns, like security overlay [13], which we utilize to model the security requirements of the proposed architecture of DT-enhanced CI discussed in Sect. 4.5.

3 Related Work

To the best of our knowledge, only a few studies have been conducted integrating DT and Enterprise Architecture to improve a system's cybersecurity. Sellitto and Masi et al. [12,17] introduce a cybersecurity perspective, an extension viewpoint integrated into the existing architecture of a RS. This viewpoint was employed to identify the necessary countermeasures for elevating the modelled RS's security level to a predetermined standard. In their initial study [17], they proposed utilizing Enterprise Architecture models, while their subsequent work [12] allowed the incorporation of any architecture models. By iterating the process of attack simulation and incorporating feedback into architecture models, they successfully devised a RS architecture with a cost-effective set of countermeasures capable of mitigating the specified security threats to an acceptable degree.

Masi et al. [12] referred to their solution as a Digital Shadow due to its ability to run simulations and modify architecture models, but lacking automatic data exchange between the Operational Remote System (ORS) and its DT. In contrast, we consider a DT-enhanced approach, incorporating bidirectional, real-time twinning between the operational RS and its DT. The DT utilizes real-time data collected from the RS to realise its services. The feedback loop in the other direction enables DT to deploy the chosen countermeasures to RS to optimize it and improve its cybersecurity.

4 Proposed Solution

This section will present our proposed RA for a DT-CI system and exemplify its application to a nuclear power plant's SS and three DT-enabled smart security services.

We start with the assumption that DT's fidelity is sufficient, i.e., that DT accurately represents the RS and its behaviour, and that continuous monitoring and testing of the DT are conducted to maintain this accuracy.

Within the scope of this RA, we made some modelling choices, such as integrating the general reference and the specific application example architectures, modelling each component only once, modelling only publish-subscribe paradigm-based communication, and omitting separate, additional sensors and

[1] https://www.opengroup.org/archimate-forum/archimate-overview.

actuators possibly deployed to RS to enable DT-based specific smart services. These choices allow us to simplify our models and avoid redundancy.

In all of our models, we have used the darkness of the colours to distinguish elements belonging only to the general reference (darkest green), both the general reference and the example SS (lighter green/blue/yellow), or only to the example SS (lightest green/blue/yellow) architectures. For example, in *On-site* tier of *RS* in Fig. 2, the lighest colour components (e.g. *Camers(s)*) belong only to the SS, the darkest green colour components (e.g. *Actuators*) only to the general reference and others (e.g. *Log(s)*) to both architectures.

The following models[2] will be discussed in detail in subsequent sections: Overview of the DT-CI system's RA in Sect. 4.1, *RS* model in Sect. 4.2, *DT* model in Sect. 4.3, *Smart Services* model in Sect. 4.4, and Security model in Sect. 4.5.

4.1 Overview of the Reference Architecture (RA)

In this section, we will provide an overview of our proposed DT-CI system's RA, comprising three core components: the *RS*, *DT*, and the use case specific *Smart Services* as illustrated in Fig. 1. The overview architecture encompasses three ArchiMate layers: the business layer with yellow, the application with blue, and the technology layer with green elements.

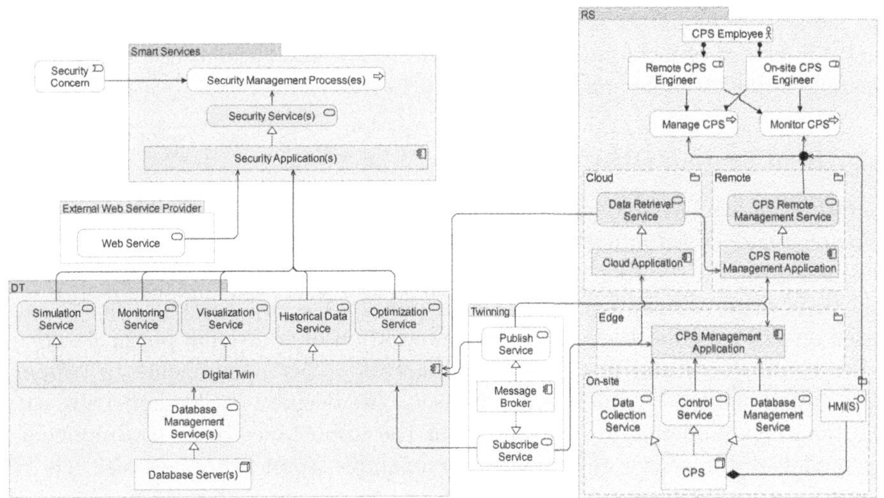

Fig. 1. Total view of the proposed solution (Color figure online)

[2] High-resolution images of the models available in: https://gitlab.utwente.nl/itapelto/whattwin.

The *RS* embraces the *On-site*, *Edge*, *Cloud* and *Remote* tiers. It can be monitored and controlled on-site or remotely by *On-site/Remote CPS Engineers*. We discuss the detailed model of this cloud-edge-based *RS* in Sect. 4.2.

The *DT* has *Simulation*, *Monitoring*, *Visualization*, *Historical Data* and *Optimization* services, which the example use case specific *Smart Services*, i.e. *Security Application(s)* build on top of DT's services and offering *Security Services* to *Security Management Process(es)*. We will elaborate on the *DT* in Sect. 4.3 and the example use case specific *Smart services* in Sect. 4.4.

One of the key functionalities of the proposed DT-CI system is the bidirectional communication between *DT* and *RS*, i.e. *Twinning*. The twins' ability to publish and subscribe messages to/from the other twin facilitates seamless mapping and synchronization between digital and physical realms. For clarity, we chose this widely used communication paradigm in IoT and cloud-based applications. This choice does not affect the modelling of RA but should be replaced with the DT-CI-specific communication architecture when applying our RA to a specific RS. *DT* subscribes to data messages published by *RS* and *RS* subscribes to control/optimization messages published by *DT*.

Following the introduction of the high-level architecture model, we will provide in-depth, layered insights into the two main components of the DT-CI system and the example use case specific smart security services in the subsequent Sects. 4.2–4.4. Additionally, since DT increases the attack surface [6], paying attention to the fundamental communication-related security features is essential when applying our DT-CI system's RA in a practical system. To simplify our models, we elaborate security functionalities in a separate security model in Sect. 4.5 instead of including them in this overview and the detailed *DT*, *RS* and example application use case specific *Smart services* models.

4.2 Real System (RS)

As discussed, we have modelled the *RS* as an IoT and cloud-based system, with *On-site*, *Edge*, *Cloud* and *Remote* tiers illustrated in Fig. 2. We emphasize that depending on the specific RS and desired DT-enabled smart security services and their requirements, collecting the required data and applying the changes based on *DT*'s feedback might require integration of additional physical and/or cyber components and instrumenting the RSs' cyber components to support these functionalities. As mentioned in Sect. 4, we decided not to model any such additional components. Still, to highlight the importance of such components, we modelled one sensor relevant to our example application use case, i.e. SS camera's *Angle Sensor(s)*.

To exemplify the application of our RA to a specific CI, we have illustrated *Nuclear Power Plant*'s SS-specific architecture components with light colours (yellow/blue/green/grey) in Fig. 2. Even when a SS is integrated as a security measure, its components must be secured throughout their LC [7,16]. Although the SS might be secure against current threats, ongoing updates, additions, or removals of physical, cyber, or hybrid components could introduce new vulnerabilities exploitable by unknown threats.

As a model of a CPS, the *RS*'s *On-site* component consists of physical and cyber (application) layers. In the physical layer (depicted in green in Fig. 2), each *Actuator*, *Sensor* and *Embedded System* provide a low-level *Data Collection Software* to retrieve/collect their data and logs, and *Control Software* to control them. *Sensor(s)* monitor the *Physical Device(s) and Machine(s)* and their operational context, while *Actuator(s)* facilitate actions on these. *Embedded systems* serve as integrated platforms for managing all these components.

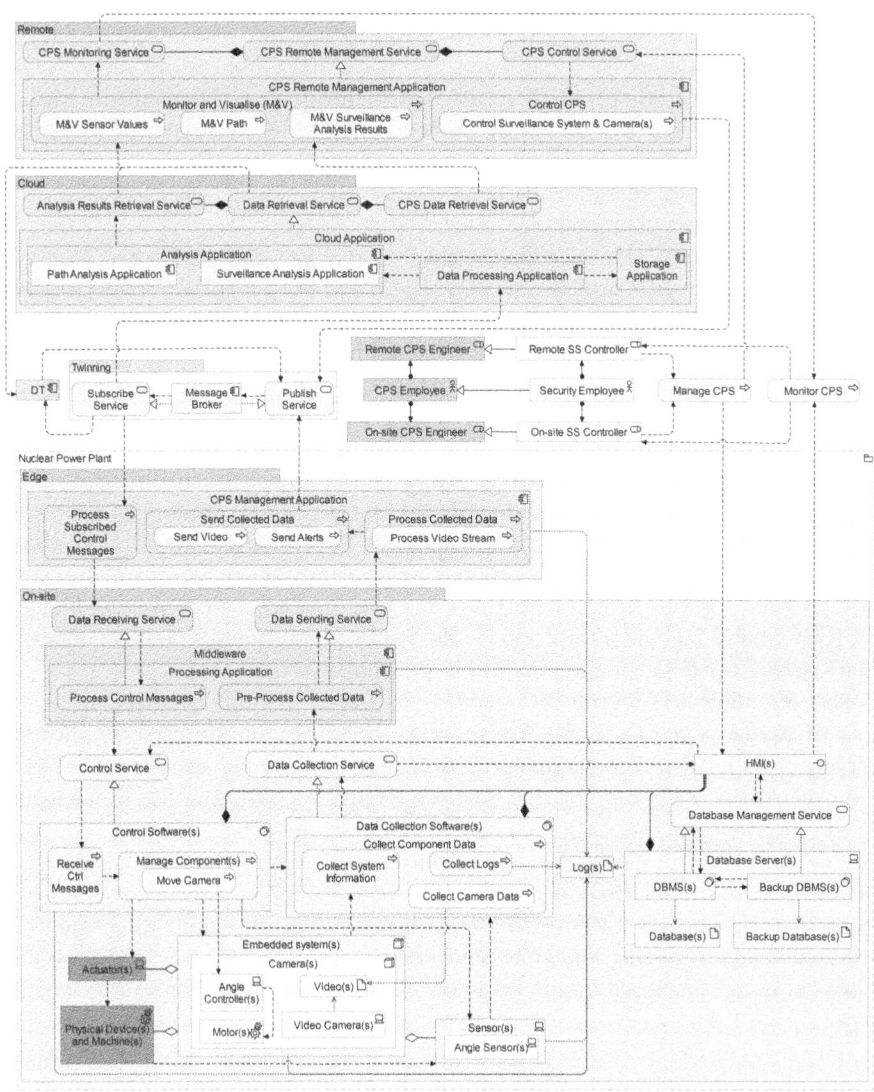

Fig. 2. Layered View of the Real System (Color figure online)

The control options could include a possibility to *Manage Component(s)*, i.e. to re-configure, re-calibrate, update the component or install new software to them. Collected data could include *Logs* from all *RS* components and *System information*, such as file system, system inventory and general system information acquired, for example, by periodically executing system commands.

Within the realm of data management, *Databases* accessible through *Database Management Service(s)* realized by database management systems, i.e. *DBMS(s)* play a crucial role. They store collected data, encompassing a wide range of information such as sensor readings, system details, and behavioural patterns. These databases are not only repositories but also essential for *RS* recovery. *Backup databases* are utilized to retrieve data and restore the *RS* with recovered data. As SS-specific components (lightest green elements in Fig. 2), we have modelled the *Camera(s)* as embedded systems consisting of *Motor(s)*, their *Angle Controller(s)* and *Video Camera(s)* capable to shooting surveillance *Video(s)* and storing them locally, e.g. to a memory card. Each *Camera*'s *Control Software* allows changing the camera angle (*Move Camera*) via *Motor(s)*. *Data Collection Software* can collect (*Collect Camera Data*) the stored *Video(s)* and store to the on-site database using *Database Management Service*. An *Angle Sensor(s)* responsible for monitoring the surveillance camera's angle were integrated as evidence of the RA supporting additional components required to implement DT-enabled smart services. *DT* or *Data Collection Software* could be instrumented to collect its data to detect attacks targeting SS.

The components illustrated with the darkest green colour in Fig. 2 represent components commonly used in *CPS*s but which are not used in the SS.

The nature of the collected data is highly adaptable and tailored to the specific needs of the *RS* and its distinct use cases. This data includes details about sensor readings, system states, components details, topology, hardware and software specifics, processes, configurations, network flows, control commands, logs, etc. It could also include information collected by possible additional DT-enabled smart service-specific components integrated into the *RS*.

Our RA allows *CPS Employee* playing the role of *Remote/On-site CPS Engineer* to *Manage/Monitor CPS*, its the *On-site* infrastructure directly through *HMI(s)* or using *RS*'s internal communication channels. For simplicity, we have also utilized the *Twinning* for this purpose. When applying the RA to a specific *RS*, its internal communication channels should be specified.

The *Middleware* application acts as a central control hub to manage the collected *RS* data and *Process Control Messages* from *CPS Management Application*. It is responsible for *Pre-Process Collect Data* process, including functionalities such as formatting and timestamping the collected *On-site* real-time and historical data before sending it into the *CPS Management Application* on the *Edge*.

The *Process Collected Data* process of *CPS Management Application* at the *Edge* is in charge of processing data before the *Send Collected Data* process sends it to the *Cloud* and *DT*. Some examples of processing functionalities could include data filtering, analyzing, aggregating, and transformation. We opted for edge-enhanced data processing to reduce network and computation load on the *DT* and *Cloud* as proposed by [5]. Specific data, like detailed *RS* state and behaviour information, is exclusively targeted for the *DT*'s high-fidelity simulations. Albeit real-time data could directly reach the *CPS Remote Management Application*, we introduced a *Cloud* intermediary. This *Cloud* stores, processes, and analyzes the data before the *CPS Remote Management Application* accesses it. Although this approach might introduce some delay due to the additional layer, it avoids redundant services in the *CPS Remote Management Application.* In time-sensitive scenarios, direct end-to-end communication channels between the *Middleware* (or even *Data Collection Software*) and the *CPS Remote Management* applications could be an alternative solution, considering the impact of each layer on data transfer throughput. The SS-specific components in the *Edge* consist of *Process Video Stream* and *Send Video/Alerts* processes. The former is capable of quick, less resource-demanding but coarser anomaly detection than the *Cloud*, and the latter sends video and possible alerts of detected anomalies to the *Cloud.*

The *Cloud* is a versatile data management and analysis platform. Its *Data Processing Application* filters, cleans, transforms, and aggregates the subscribed data before *Storage Application* stores it in cloud storage and *Analysis Application* analyzes it. Additionally, the Cloud's *Analysis Application* employs advanced techniques, such as ML/AI, and Big Data, spatial, temporal, and statistical analysis methods to analyze the received data. In our example use case, the intruder's physical path could be analyzed by *Path Analysis Application*, and *Surveillance Analysis Application* could detect potential anomalies, such as intrusions. In essence, the *Cloud* stores data and provides sophisticated analytical capabilities, making it a powerful tool for processing real-time and historical data.

The final tier, *Remote* in our *RS* model includes the *CPS Remote Management Application*, empowering engineers to *Monitor and Visualize (M&V)* and *Control CPS* remotely. Leveraging data processed, stored, analyzed, and served by the *Cloud*, this application enhances the detection of significant events, such as alarms, through visualization. Examples of SS's monitored and visualized data and analysis results include *Surveillance Analysis Results*, *Sensor Values*, and intruder's physical *Path.* The *Remote SS Controller* and *On-site SS Controllers*, the general reference architecture *Remote CPS Engineer* and *On-site CPS Engineer* roles' specializations, may utilize the *Control Surveillance System & Camera(s)* process through the *CPS Control Service* to manage the SS or to move cameras, i.e. change the camera angles.

4.3 Digital Twin (DT)

Figure 3 illustrates the *DT*'s architectural structure, encompassing both application and technology layers. Applying this part of the RA to the example SS does not introduce any changes.

For *DT* to function effectively, it necessitates data and models to create a high-fidelity simulation environment and support the functionalities outlined in the model. The DT as a virtual replica of RS consists of various models of RS, its behaviour, and context. Moreover, DT functionalities might necessitate creating and maintaining other models, like ML/AI and attack models used by *Predict*, *Simulate* and *Analyze* processes.

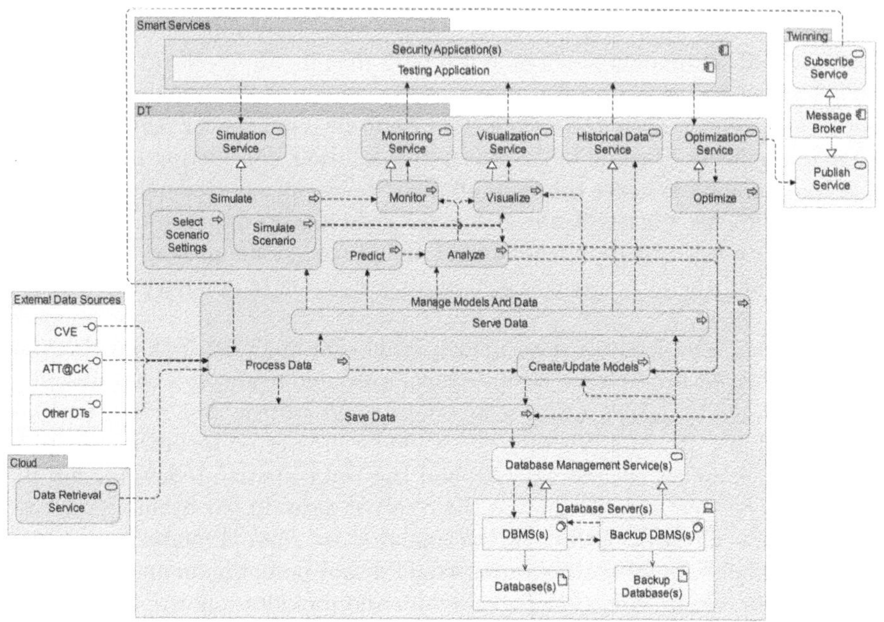

Fig. 3. Layered view for DT

The necessary data can be generated by the various *RS* tiers, *Smart Services* or *External Data Sources*. We discussed the highly adaptable *RS* data in Sect. 4.2 obtained through *Twinning* or retrieved from *Cloud*. External data sources may include databases like Mitre ATT@CK[3] that offer attack tactics and techniques and Mitre CVE[4] providing information on common vulnerabilities. Furthermore, DT might incorporate information from other DTs within (inter)connected and (inter)dependent systems, enriching its data pool.

In our example, the third data source, SS-specific *Testing Application* (see Sect. 4.4) as an example *Smart Service*, includes data related to test scenarios, such as simulation and scenario options and deployed optimizations.

DT provides five services to other applications, like to *Smart Services*: *Simulate*, *Monitor*, *Visualize*, *Optimize*, and *Historical Data Service*. These services are enabled by the corresponding and underlying *Analyze*, *Predict*, and *Manage models and data* processes.

[3] https://attack.mitre.org/resources/working-with-attack/.
[4] https://cve.mitre.org/.

The *Manage Models And Data* process involves various sub-processes, including *Process, Save* and *Serve Data*, and *Create/Update Models.* Initially, received data, *DT* models, and analysis results are processed, stored, and managed in databases in a similar way as in *RS*'s *Cloud* and *On-site.* This data can be accessed by the *Create/Update Models* and *Serve Data* processes. The *Create/Update Models* process may create or update system or attack models or knowledge graphs and train or retrain ML/AI Models using both real-time and historical data obtained from *Process Data* process and *Database Server(s).* Used data could include results from *Analyze* process, and knowledge graphs can be used to visualize system state and security-related knowledge.

As discussed in Sect. 4, we assume that the *Create/Update Models* process maintains and updates the required *DT*'s models throughout *RS*'s LC to ensure fidelity.

The *Serve Data* process delivers diverse information to *DT*'s other processes. The served data includes attack, ML/AI, system state and behaviour models, knowledge graphs, real-time and historical system and analysis results data.

The *DT*'s *Analyze* process examines real-time and historical data using various methods and creates knowledge graphs representing knowledge models. Besides, this process incorporates predictions from the *Predict* process, which utilizes ML/AI models and real-time data to predict future system states, behaviours, or threats. The analysis results could be used by the *Monitor*, *Visualize*, and *Create/Update Models* processes. Monitoring and visualizing knowledge graphs and possible safety and security rule violations facilitate testing engineers' reasoning on the *RS* and support knowledge-based decision-making [8]. Also, such results could be used to update models and knowledge graphs.

The *Simulate* process allows virtual exploration and experimentation of the *RS* and its behaviour under different scenarios through *Select Scenario Settings* process. *Simulate Scenario* process uses various *RS* models, including system state, system behaviour and attack models, along with replicated real-time and historical *RS* data. Consecutive attack simulations allow for comparing the effectiveness and efficiency of different countermeasures against the tested attacks utilizing the historical system data and analysis results. The outcomes of these simulations are analyzed, monitored, and visualized to allow tracking of simulation, system states, behaviour, and security metrics.

DT also enables optimizing *RS* through its *Optimize* process, which implements the requested modifications to the *RS* and to the corresponding *DT* models to maintain their fidelity using *Create/Update Models* process. These optimizations can involve adjustments to *RS*'s components and their arrangements, configurations, safety protocols, security rules, or other relevant parameters.

After introducing our detailed DT model, we proceed to the example nuclear power plant's SS-specific *Smart Services* model, a model of a *Testing Application* enabling what-if testing, decision-making support and optimization of the *RS*.

4.4 Smart Services Example: Testing Application

To ensure the security of our example application use case - a nuclear power plant's SS throughout its LC - we illustrate a *Testing Application* as a *Smart Services* triggered by *Security Concerns* and built on top of DT's services in Fig. 4.

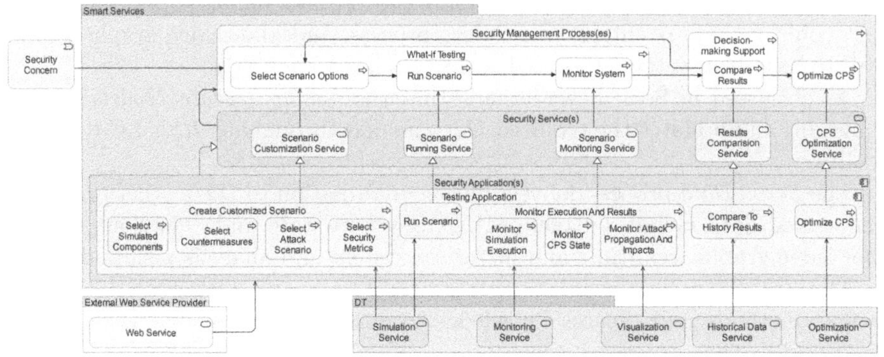

Fig. 4. Testing Application Model

Testing application allows the testing engineers to perform DT-enabled simulations, i.e., *What-if Testing* of various configurations, test scenarios, and countermeasures, such as existing or planned countermeasures against possibly evolving or new threats, to gain insights into their efficiency, effectiveness, and impact. DT can also visualize these simulations and insights along with historical data, facilitating comparisons (*Compare Results*) and gaining *Decision-making Support* regarding required and the most efficient and effective actions/options, which then can be deployed to the *RS* using *DT*'s *Optimization Service.*

The initial phase of *What-if Testing* facilitated by *Testing Application* involves configuring the simulation scenario through *Create Customized Scenario* process comprising processes such as *Select Simulated Components*, tested *Countermeasures*, *Attack Scenario* parameters, and pertinent *Security Metrics.* Given the complexity of System-of-Systems, one, several, or all *RS*'s components can be simulated. The *Select Attack Scenario* consists of attacker properties definition, which could include defining the attacker's goals, target vulnerabilities, and attack methods, such as attack tactics, techniques and procedures. The final step of *Create Customized Scenario* is to *Select Security Metrics* from the *DT*'s predefined set, validated by CPS security experts. This step-by-step approach ensures a thorough and organized simulation process, enabling detailed testing of various System-of-Systems scenarios and variables. Customizable parameters and metrics are crucial for a comprehensive security evaluation.

After initialization, the *Run Scenario* process initiates the simulation execution. It allows security engineers to *Monitor Execution And Results*, including

Monitoring Simulation Execution/CPS State/Attack Propagation And Impacts. Visualization of the monitored information, such as CPS or attack parameter values and security metrics, is a crucial functionality enabled by DT, aiding in detecting alerts and extracting key insights from extensive data. The *Compare to History Results* process facilitates *Decision-making Support* by allowing to *Compare Results* of current and historical simulations, helping determine the most effective and efficient set of countermeasures. Finally, testing engineers can decide to start another simulation with other options or *Optimize CPS* by optimizing its configurations or updating safety&security rules or countermeasures.

We have represented the *Testing Application* as an externally provided *Web Service*. If it is self-hosted, this component requires more detailed modelling.

As outlined in this section, the example application use case model completes our detailed examination of the RA components. The upcoming model will explore security mechanisms encompassing the entire RA.

4.5 Security Overlay

The security goals, controls, and principles outlined in our security model illustrated in Fig. 5 should be implemented across the entire RA, including all its components and layers.

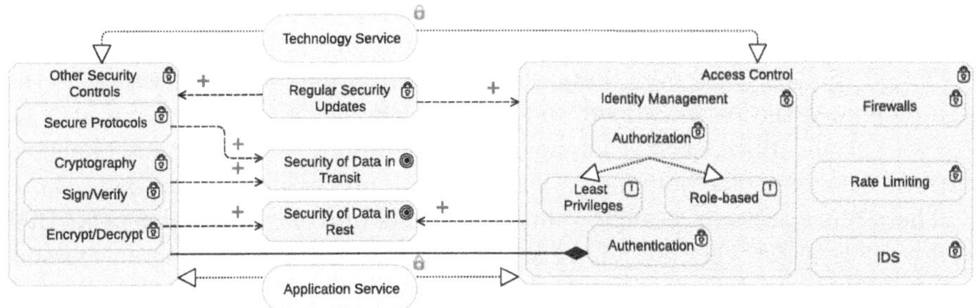

Fig. 5. Security view

While DT can enhance the cybersecurity of mirrored systems, it also expands attack surface [6]. Unauthorized access to DT's data could provide valuable insights to attackers on targeting the RS without detection, using techniques like zero-day attacks or Advanced Persistent Threats (APTs). This includes gaining access to confidential information, details about the RS's most vulnerable components, countermeasures, and valuable assets [6]. Exploiting access to the DT, attackers could control or manipulate the RS, causing disruption or malfunction to RS's operation [15].

Ensuring *Security of Data in Rest* entails *Encrypt*ing all the stored data to ensure privacy and confidentiality, while *Security of Data in Transit* can be protected using *Secure Protocols* and cryptographic algorithms to *Encrypt* and/or digitally *Sign* all communications between different layers to ensure integrity. Furthermore, services accessible through networks should be guarded using *Firewalls*, *Rate Limiting* techniques, and Intrusion Detection Systems (*IDS*). All incoming messages must undergo *Authentication*, and subsequent actions should adhere to proper *Authorization*, following principles such as *Least Privileges* and *Role-based Access Control*. To maintain security throughout the extended LC of CIs, performing *Regular Security Updates* is essential across all RA components.

5 Discussion

Although the suggested approach is a generalization, we believe that it could be extended and adapted to match any RS aiming to integrate DT-enabled services. We have simplified the RA to offer a broad overview of the system. It may be necessary to introduce additional abstraction levels or break down models into smaller, more specific sub-models. For instance, details such as data collection methods, periods and processing, DT functionalities, detailed analysis methods, required fidelity and granularity, security requirements, data synchronization, and other relevant factors should be further specified to align with the specific use case and its expected outcomes or requirements.

Ensuring synchronization is important, especially in CIs, which include multiple heterogeneous systems, each possibly equipped with its DTs. These diverse DTs may depend on each other's services, requiring synchronization of data collected from various systems and sources to generate accurate simulation and prediction models. Moreover, data should undergo maximal processing at the edge to reduce the network load and enhance the DT's processing speed. The use case specifications, such as latency, fidelity, granularity, inputs, and expected outputs, determine the boundaries for edge data processing capabilities.

These blueprints can provide valuable insights into the essential aspects that need consideration when designing a new system. When extending an existing system with DT-enhanced services, RA can be employed to develop migration and implementation plans for transitioning from the existing system to the target system.

The proposed RA is designed with modularity in mind, enabling the changing/reusing of individual components without disrupting the entire system. However, when modifying the physical system, corresponding adjustments in its DT are imperative. The DT-enabled *Smart Services* stand out as the most adaptable module for modification, as shown with what-if testing scenario.

While one might argue that our RA modelling should have initially centered around the essential smart services of security monitoring and attack detection, our ongoing systematic literature review highlighted a notable gap: existing research [2,3,15] has extensively explored these aspects. Additionally, our review identified relevant studies on 'what-if testing' discussed in Sect. 2. Unlike our approach, these works [12,17] focus on identifying a set of countermeasures based on architectural models to achieve an acceptable risk level instead of integrating real-time data from the RS.

6 Conclusions

Securing CIs has grown increasingly complex due to the evolving nature of these systems [15]. Contemporary CIs have transformed into complex System-of-Systems, seamlessly integrating the IoT with numerous interconnections and dependencies [10,15]. These changes have notably expanded the potential attack points within these systems, effectively enlarging their attack surface [15].

Given their essential role and the potential for significant economic and societal repercussions in the event of a successful attack [1], CIs have become prime targets for malicious actors, including those with substantial resources and capabilities at the governmental level. However, testing these systems has become increasingly challenging due to the high costs and complexity of building and sustaining high-fidelity test environments [15]. Additionally, traditional penetration testing methods pose a risk to the operation and availability of these systems.

This paper proposed a novel RA for designing a new cybersecurity DT-enhanced CI and extending an existing CI with a DT. Our proposed RA is novel in considering CI as an IoT and cloud-based complex System-of-Systems and modelling DT-enabled what-if testing, decision-support, and optimization security use cases. Moreover, we have exemplified how these proposed architecture models could be applied to a real-world use case, namely a camera surveillance system commonly used in various systems, like in a nuclear power plant. We illustrated how DT's services could support three smart security services to improve SS's security: what-if testing, decision-making support, and optimization. The main idea behind the what-if testing was to identify and decide on effective and efficient countermeasures to mitigate existing or emerging risks during the LC of RS. By incorporating the outcomes back into the architectural model, i.e. optimizing the RS, we make necessary modifications to maintain an acceptable risk level and promptly act on emerging threats. This approach showcased the effectiveness of utilizing a DT, enabling tasks like vulnerability assessment and security testing without disrupting the operational system.

In the future, we plan to extend our RA to cover other smart security services, such as security monitoring and attack detection and we intend to apply the RA to an operational CI for testing and development purposes.

References

1. CISA Cybersecurity & Infrastructure Security Agency: Critical infrastructure sectors. https://www.cisa.gov/critical-infrastructure-sectors. Accessed 08 Aug 2024
2. De Benedictis, A., Esposito, C., Somma, A.: Toward the adoption of secure cyber digital twins to enhance cyber-physical systems security. In: Vallecillo, A., Visser, J., Pérez-Castillo, R. (eds.) Quality of Information and Communications Technology, pp. 307–321. Springer, Cham (2022)
3. Dietz, M., Hageman, L., von Hornung, C., Pernul, G.: Employing digital twins for security-by-design system testing. In: Proceedings of the 2022 ACM Workshop on Secure and Trustworthy Cyber-Physical Systems, pp. 97–106. Sat-CPS 2022. Association for Computing Machinery, New York (2022)

4. Hallmans, D., Sandström, K., Larsson, S., Nolte, T.: Challenges in providing sustainable analytic of system of systems with long life time. In: 2021 16th International Conference of System of Systems Engineering (SoSE), pp. 69–74 (2021). https://doi.org/10.1109/SOSE52739.2021.9497465
5. Han, Q., Zhang, J., Ding, H., Sun, J., Zhang, H., Yuan, D.: Cloud-edge collaborative-based digital twin system for hardware limited IIoT scenario. In: 2023 IEEE Smart World Congress (SWC), pp. 1–8 (2023). https://doi.org/10.1109/SWC57546.2023.10448579
6. Holmes, D., Papathanasaki, M., Maglaras, L., Ferrag, M.A., Nepal, S., Janicke, H.: Digital twins and cyber security - solution or challenge? In: 2021 6th South-East Europe Design Automation, Computer Engineering, Computer Networks and Social Media Conference (SEEDA-CECNSM), pp. 1–8 (2021). https://doi.org/10.1109/SEEDA-CECNSM53056.2021.9566277
7. Itäpelto, T.: Digital twin enhanced critical infrastructure life cycle security. In: 2023 IEEE Smart World Congress (SWC), pp. 1–3 (2023). https://doi.org/10.1109/SWC57546.2023.10448804
8. Jia, Y., Gu, Z., Li, A., Han, W.: Introduction to the MDATA model. In: Jia, Y., Gu, Z., Li, A. (eds.) MDATA: A New Knowledge Representation Model: Theory, Methods and Applications, pp. 1–18. Springer, Cham (2021). https://doi.org/10.1007/978-3-030-71590-8_1
9. Kritzinger, W., Karner, M., Traar, G., Henjes, J., Sihn, W.: Digital twin in manufacturing: a categorical literature review and classification. IFAC-PapersOnLine **51**(11), 1016–1022 (2018). https://doi.org/10.1016/j.ifacol.2018.08.474
10. Lampropoulos, G., Siakas, K.: Enhancing and securing cyber-physical systems and industry 4.0 through digital twins: a critical review. J. Softw. Evol. Process **35**(7), e2494 (2023). https://doi.org/10.1002/smr.2494
11. Lankhorst, M.: Introduction to Enterprise Architecture, pp. 1–11. Springer, Heidelberg (2009). https://doi.org/10.1007/978-3-642-01310-2_1
12. Masi, M., Sellitto, G.P., Aranha, H., Pavleska, T.: Securing critical infrastructures with a cybersecurity digital twin. Softw. Syst. Model. **22**(2), 689-707 (2023). https://doi.org/10.1007/s10270-022-01075-0
13. Mayer, N., Feltus, C.: Evaluation of the risk and security overlay of archimate to model information system security risks. In: 2017 IEEE 21st International Enterprise Distributed Object Computing Workshop (EDOCW), pp. 106–116 (2017). https://doi.org/10.1109/EDOCW.2017.30
14. Noor, M.M., Selamat, A., Husain, N.A., Krejcar, O.: Security and safety in cyber-physical system (CPS): an inclusive threat model. J. Adv. Res. Appl. Sci. Eng. Technol. **40**(2), 176–202 (2024). https://doi.org/10.37934/araset.40.2.176202
15. Patzer, F., Meshram, A., Birnstill, P., Haas, C., Beyerer, J.: Towards computer-aided security life cycle management for critical industrial control systems. In: Luiijf, E., Žutautaitė, I., Hämmerli, B.M. (eds.) Critical Information Infrastructures Security, pp. 45–56. Springer, Cham (2019)
16. Pawlicka, A., Puchalski, D., Pawlicki, M., Kozik, R., Choraś, M.: How to secure the IoT-based surveillance systems in an elegant way. In: 2023 IEEE International Conference on Cyber Security and Resilience (CSR), pp. 636–640 (2023). https://doi.org/10.1109/CSR57506.2023.10224938
17. Sellitto, G.P., Masi, M., Pavleska, T., Aranha, H.: A cyber security digital twin for critical infrastructure protection: the intelligent transport system use case. In: Serral, E., Stirna, J., Ralyté, J., Grabis, J. (eds.) The Practice of Enterprise Modeling, pp. 230–244. Lecture Notes in Business Information Processing. Springer, Cham (2021). https://doi.org/10.1007/978-3-030-91279-6_16

Author Index

M. Kaczmarek-Heß et al. (Eds.): EDOC 2024 Workshops, LNBIP 537, pp. 405–406, 2025.
https://doi.org/10.1007/978-3-031-79059-1

The manufacturer's authorised representative in the EU is Springer Nature Customer Service Centre GmbH, Europaplatz 3, 69115 Heidelberg, Germany. If you have any concerns regarding our products, please contact ProductSafety@springernature.com

Printed and bound by CPI Group (UK) Ltd, Croydon, CR0 4YY
27/04/2026
02097562-0009